The Secrets of Buddhist Meditation

CLASSICS IN EAST ASIAN BUDDHISM

The Secrets of Buddhist Meditation

Visionary Meditation Texts from Early Medieval China

ERIC M. GREENE

A KURODA INSTITUTE BOOK
University of Hawaiʻi Press
Honolulu

Printed in the United States of America

26 25 24 23 22 21 6 5 4 3 2 1

Library of Congress Cataloging-in-Publication Data

Names: Greene, Eric M., author.
Title: The secrets of Buddhist meditation : visionary meditation texts from early medieval China / Eric M. Greene.
Other titles: Chan mi yao fa jing. English. | Classics in East Asian Buddhism.
Description: Honolulu : University of Hawai'i Press, 2021. | Series: Classics in East Asian Buddhism | Chiefly translations of Chan mi yao fa jing (Chan essentials) and Zhi chan bing mi yao fa (Methods for curing). | Includes bibliographical references and index.
Identifiers: LCCN 2020025389 | ISBN 9780824884444 (hardcover) | ISBN 9780824886868 (adobe pdf) | ISBN 9780824886844 (epub) | ISBN 9780824886851 (kindle edition)
Subjects: LCSH: Meditation—Buddhism.
Classification: LCC BQ5612 .G74 2021 | DDC 294.3/44350951—dc23
LC record available at https://lccn.loc.gov/2020025389

The Kuroda Institute for the Study of Buddhism is a nonprofit, educational corporation founded in 1976. One of its primary objectives is to promote scholarship on the historical, philosophical, and cultural ramifications of Buddhism. In association with the University of Hawai'i Press, the Institute also publishes Studies in East Asian Buddhism. To complement these scholarly studies, the Institute also makes available in the present series reliable translations of some of the major classics of East Asian Buddhism.

University of Hawai'i Press books are printed on acid-free paper and meet the guidelines for permanence and durability of the Council on Library Resources.

Kuroda Institute
Classics in East Asian Buddhism

The Record of Tung-Shan
William F. Powell

Tracing Back the Radiance: Chinul's Korean Way of Zen
Robert E. Buswell Jr.

The Great Calming and Contemplation: A Study and Annotated Translation of the First Chapter of Chih-i's Mo-ho chih-kuan
Neal Donner and Daniel Stevenson

Inquiry into the Origin of Humanity: An Annotated Translation of Tsung-mi's Yüan jen lun *with a Modern Commentary*
Peter N. Gregory

Zen in Medieval Vietnam: A Study and Translation of the Thiền Uyển Tập Anh
Cuong Tu Nguyen

Hōnen's Senchakushū: *Passages on the Selection of the Nembutsu in the Original Vow*
Senchakushū English Translation Project

The Origins of Buddhist Monastic Codes in China: An Annotated Translation and Study of the Changyuan qinggui
Yifa

The Scriptures of Wŏn Buddhism: A Translation of Wŏnbulgyo kyojŏn *with Introduction*
Bongkil Chung

Personal Salvation and Filial Piety: Two Precious Scroll Narratives of Guanyin and Her Acolytes
Wilt L. Idema

Signs from the Unseen Realm: Buddhist Miracle Tales from Early Medieval China
Robert Ford Campany

The Secrets of Buddhist Meditation: Visionary Meditation Texts from Early Medieval China
Eric M. Greene

For my parents

Contents

Preface

This book is a study and translation of two fifth-century Chinese Buddhist apocryphal sutras—texts written in the form of Indian Buddhist sutras translated into Chinese but in actuality composed or substantially compiled in China—whose central topic is Buddhist meditation, the seated, contemplative practice that in East Asia has most commonly been known as *chan* 禪 ("zen" in its Japanese pronunciation).

The wider historical context of these two texts, and others like them, I have discussed in detail in a companion volume called *Chan Before Chan: Meditation, Repentance, and Visionary Experience in Chinese Buddhism* (cited as *Chan Before Chan* in the notes). There I take up the rise of *chan*, in the early fifth century of the common era, as a widely practiced discipline in Chinese Buddhism; the growing prestige accorded to "meditation masters" (*chanshi* 禪師) during this time; the development in China of a widespread culture of the kind of visionary meditation described in the contemplative literature of this era; and the way that seated meditation came to be, throughout the fifth, sixth, and seventh centuries, constitutively integrated into a broader cultic program in which "repentance" (*chanhui* 懺悔) was the guiding form and the destruction of sin the overarching goal. In *Chan Before Chan,* I also discuss the relationship and contrast between these earlier forms of Chinese *chan* and the approaches to it characteristic of the so-called Chan School, which arose during the late seventh century and whose distinctive teachings concerning meditation and Buddhism more broadly would prove so enduring in East Asia and, especially in various modernist incarnations of Japanese Zen, around the world today.

In contrast to *Chan Before Chan*'s wider historical and cultural tableau of Buddhist meditation in early medieval China, the present volume focuses on the content and textual histories of the two apocryphal sutras known as the *Chan Essentials* and *Methods for Curing.* It seeks to make these texts available to modern readers as artifacts of an approach to Buddhist meditation that, even though heretofore little studied or understood among scholars, was in fact the mainstream one for considerable periods of Chinese Buddhist history. Accordingly, Part I of this book provides a study of the structure and important themes of these two texts, as well as an analysis of their historical formation as "apocryphal" Chinese Buddhist scriptures, a process we are able to observe in their case at an unusual level of detail. Complete, annotated English translations are given in Part II.

As a project, the translation of an ancient Buddhist scripture whose main topic is meditation would have required little justification during much of the twentieth century. Today, the value of such an undertaking may be less clear. At least among scholars of religion, annotated translations or editions of primary texts as a product, and "canonical" scriptures and "elite" Buddhist topics such as meditation as a subject, have both lost much of their former cachet. This change in status reflects more broadly the reorientation of the humanities, over the past several generations of scholarship, away from an older, curatorial model in which the scholar's main task was to preserve and transmit a "canon" whose value to the present was assumed. Although this is not the place for an extended analysis of such changing fashions, given that it can no longer be assumed out of hand it does seem appropriate to begin this book with at least a few general comments about what I take to be the value of the work of translation that occupies a large share of it.

Indeed, the lowered esteem often now accorded to lengthy translations of ancient texts, as a useful professional enterprise for a scholar of religion, arguably rests on a dubious distinction between translation as a purely "descriptive" task and the superiority of "analysis." In calling this distinction dubious, my point is not merely that properly translating a premodern religious text requires real intellectual labor, though that is also true (Haberman and Nattier 1996). It is, rather, that the production of adequately annotated translations of new, previously unstudied documents—in the present case, texts about Buddhist meditation rather different in character from those familiar to modern scholars—influences the trajectory of a given field, over the long run, in a manner distinct from, *and not exactly replicable by*, other forms of scholarly production.

Consider, for example, the persistent specter in contemporary Buddhist Studies of a tendency to view the purest form of Buddhism as its "original" variety and to see this as best reflected in the scriptures of the Pāli canon, the only complete such collection surviving in an Indian language. For several decades now scholars have repeatedly pointed out that this approach to Buddhism should be rejected. From a purely historical point of view, while of undeniably ancient pedigree, the Pāli canon is, we now recognize, a selective collection. Many of the most important developments in our understanding of even ancient Indian Buddhism have occurred as scholars have expanded the scope of their sources to include archeological remains as well as other canonical Buddhist literatures such as those preserved in Sanskrit or in Chinese and Tibetan translation. More broadly, even if the Pāli canon gave us direct access to "original" Buddhism (which it does not), to take *that* as the standard—for defining what real Buddhism is, or what parts of it are most worthy of our attention—is a methodology that most now find inescapably tinged with an "Orientalist" logic that privileges the dusty tomes of our libraries above the lives of most actual Buddhists past or present.

However—and this is my point—privileging the Pāli canon as a source for the study of Buddhism is not a free-floating ideology that modern scholars just happen to have subscribed to until recently. Buddhologists of the nineteenth and early twentieth centuries did more than merely argue for the centrality of the Pāli canon for our understanding of Buddhism; they made this argument concrete by editing that canon and then translating it nearly completely into English and other European languages. In scope, these early editions and translations remain unsurpassed in many areas of inquiry. The Pāli *vinaya*, for example, is still the only Indian Buddhist monastic code to be fully edited and translated into a Western language.[1]

In this way, a particular terrain for inquiry was *sedimented*. The massive translation projects of the earliest generations of modern Buddhologists produced not just the texts themselves, and not just conclusions about them, but a space wherein future scholarship on Indian Buddhism could proceed more easily and where it therefore often did.[2] This has occurred for other geographical traditions of Buddhism as well: in East Asia, where even fewer large collections of primary sources have been adequately translated, the sedimented influence of those "classics" that have been is even greater.

Translation thus creates a feedback loop, from which definitive escape requires more than merely new arguments drawn from personal forays into heretofore unexplored archives. Such arguments are, of course, also necessary. But in addition, the sedimented terrain itself must be reshaped with new deposits. These deposits not only form the ground for whatever historical or interpretive revisioning those who present them think they should occasion, but also then become available to be used by others, later, in unanticipated ways. It is this capacity to serve as the foundation for future, as-yet-unimaginable forms of inquiry that ensures that translations and studies of rich primary texts often have longer shelf lives than all but the most accomplished works of purely second-order analysis. This is so, not least, for pedagogical reasons. To the extent that we are committed to imparting to students not just the facts of what we think Buddhism is but also the humanistic skills of reading and interpreting, what they learn will always have a nontrivial relationship with the sources available in reliable English translation. (And this is true even when the "reading" we ask of students goes beyond literary texts, as it often now does.) Although a number of classroom-oriented introductions to Buddhism have appeared in recent years with selections of primary texts shaped by contemporary academic understanding

1. A few sizeable portions of other *vinayas* have more recently been edited and translated into Western languages (Hu-von Hinüber 1994; Heirman 2002; Karashima 2012).

2. On these issues in the case of premodern Indian religion more broadly, see Nemec 2009.

of what Buddhism is (Lewis 2014; Lopez 1995 and 2015), a far more limited set of options is available when one's focus narrows to the topic of Buddhist meditation. Here the terrain is dominated by established classics—the *Smṛtyupasthāna* sutras, the *Visuddhimagga*, and, in East Asia, the Platform Sutra and the writings of Dōgen and Hakuin (see, e.g., Shaw 2006). Without denying the importance of these sources, their selection as the sole canonical representatives of traditional Buddhist meditation literature is historically inaccurate. It is also ideologically suspect, since what is most readily available in English is usually the texts that have been identified as normative in the traditions of Buddhist meditation enjoying the greatest appeal in the modern West (*vipassanā* and Zen, for example). Reliance on these texts alone will tend to produce a perspective conforming to the presuppositions of those traditions in particular. If the ghosts of Orientalist scholarship on Buddhism have lingered past their welcome, it is in part because that scholarship did not just make assertions about Buddhism but further allied those claims to the production of a large corpus of edited and translated texts in which they often find confirmation. To exorcise these ghosts, we must therefore do more than simply explain how they have gotten it wrong; we must actually change the "canon" of Buddhism as it is accessible to students, nonspecialists, and those working in disparate geographical, linguistic, and temporal subfields of Buddhist Studies itself.

The fifth-century Chinese texts I introduce and translate in this volume have never been seen by any modern scholar as part of the canon from which we should form our understanding of the character and history of Buddhist meditation. In presenting them here, my aim is not only to argue that they should be, but also to make it possible for them to be so treated by others in the future—to whatever ends may be relevant to their own pursuits. To that extent, this book is a small step in the reshaping of the terrain bequeathed to us by earlier generations of Buddhist Studies scholarship, a terrain whose presence we cannot and should not simply wish away—for it too is the "real" Buddhism—but within which we must work, adding new vistas to disclose things previously unseen and to lend new perspective to what we already knew was there.

Acknowledgments

This book owes its existence to the help of many people. My thanks go firstly to Robert Sharf and Funayama Tōru 船山徹. Their long tutelage was essential to this project and others besides. Ochiai Toshinori 落合俊典 introduced me to the world of "old Buddhist manuscripts" (古寫經) and helped me gain access to material that has greatly enriched this book. The sources I study in this book first came to my attention through the work of Yamabe Nobuyoshi 山部能宜, who in his writings and in person has helped me a great deal. Daniel Stuart read a preliminary draft of the translations in Part II and provided much useful feedback. Michael Radich also read the manuscript just before publication and gave many helpful comments and suggestions. The anonymous reviewers commissioned by the Kuroda series editorial board also have my gratitude for their exacting reviews, which have improved the final version of the book greatly and spared me from many mistakes. I also wish to thank the Kuroda series general editor, Robert E. Buswell Jr., and Stephanie Chun and Stuart Kiang of the University of Hawai'i Press for their assistance and enthusiasm.

A long list of other people helped in ways large and small as I researched and wrote this book. First, a special thanks to all my colleagues in the Department of Religious Studies at Yale, who have provided an exceptionally supportive atmosphere over the past several years. At the risk of leaving someone out, I also want to thank Alexander von Rospatt, Robert Ashmore, Jacob Dalton, Mark Csikszentmihalyi, T. Griffith Foulk, Patricia Berger, Sally Goldman, Jens-Uwe Hartmann, Giulio Agostini, Natasha Heller, Bruce Williams, Mugitani Kunio 麦谷邦夫, Kinugawa Kenji 衣川賢次, Kogachi Ryūichi 古勝隆一, Iyanaga Nobumi 彌永信美, Lilla Russell-Smith, Rupert Gethin, Rita Langer, Lothar Ledderose, Claudia Wenzel, Jinhua Chen, Costantino Moretti, Stefan Baums, Robert Kritzer, Antonello Palumbo, Peirce Salguero, Jan Nattier, Bryan Lowe, James Benn, Zhang Xiaoyan 張小艷, Chen Ruifeng 陳瑞峰, Ikeda Masanori 池田将則, Phyllis Granoff, Koichi Shinohara, and the dearly missed Stefano Zacchetti.

My translation of section 1.5 of the *Methods for Curing* was originally published in *Buddhism and Medicine: An Anthology of Pre-Modern Sources*, edited by C. Pierce Salguero (Columbia University Press, 2017). It is reprinted here with permission, with minor variations in style and annotation.

Funding supporting various stages of the research leading to this book has come from the Group in Buddhist Studies (Berkeley), the Center for East Asian Studies (Berkeley), the Fulbright-Hays program, the International College of Postgraduate Buddhist Studies (Tokyo), and the Morse Fellowship (Yale). The publication of the book has also been assisted by the Frederick W. Hilles Publication Fund of Yale University. I want to thank all these organizations for their generous support.

Conventions and Abbreviations

All translations appearing in this book are my own unless otherwise noted.

Citations of the Chinese dynastic histories are from the 1963–1964 *Zhong hua shu ju* editions and are given by fascicle (卷) followed by page number. "Song dynasty" refers to the Liu Song 劉宋 dynasty (420–479) unless otherwise noted. All dates are CE unless otherwise noted.

Transcriptions of Chinese are given in Pinyin. The titles of Chinese texts are transcribed following the American Library Association–Library of Congress guidelines, which call for a space between each character (e.g., *lao shi* 老師) except for toponyms (Beijing 北京) and proper names (Zhiyi 智顗); additionally, I join the syllables of known transcriptions from Indic languages (*pusa* 菩薩). Outside a bibliographic context, I join Pinyin syllables as appropriate (*zuochan* 坐禪, *zhiguan* 止觀, and so forth). The character 祕 is always transcribed in its informal modern Mandarin pronunciation *mi*, not its formal pronunciation *bi*. This character appears in the forms 祕 and 秘 interchangeably in my sources, and I have regularized it, in all cases, to 祕 to avoid undue confusion or ambiguity.

I use the word "Indic" to denote the original language(s) from which Chinese Buddhist texts were translated; I give Indic words in their Sanskrit form unless otherwise noted.

Conventions specific to the translations in Part II, as well as abbreviations for and information pertaining to the different editions of the *Chan Essentials* and *Methods for Curing*, are discussed in the introduction to Part II.

Abbreviations

BQNZ *Biqiuni zhuan* 比丘尼傳
CMY *Chan mi yao fa jing* 禪祕要法經
CSZJJ *Chu san zang ji ji* 出三藏記集
DMDL *Damoduoluo chan jing* 達摩多羅禪經
DZDL *Da zhi du lun* 大智度論
GFSMH *Guan fo sanmei hai jing* 觀佛三昧海經

GSZ	*Gao seng zhuan* 高僧傳
HMJ	*Hong ming ji* 弘明集
LH	Late Han Chinese (following Schuessler 2009)
MC	Middle Chinese (following Schuessler 2009)
P.	Pāli
Skt.	Sanskrit
T	*Taishō shinshū daizōkyō* 大正新修大藏經. Passages are cited by text number, followed by volume, page, register (a, b, or c), and line number(s).
WMCJ	*Wu men chan jing yao yong fa* 五門禪經要用法
YQJYY	*Yi qie jing yin yi* 一切經音義
Z	*Shinsan dai Nihon zoku zōkyō* 新纂大日本續藏經. Passages are cited by text number, followed by volume, page, register (a, b, or c), and line number(s).
ZCB	*Zhi chan bing mi yao fa* 治禪病祕要法

The Secrets of Buddhist Meditation

PART I

Introduction to the *Chan Essentials* and *Methods for Curing*

CHAPTER 1

Meditation and Meditation Literature in Early Medieval Chinese Buddhism

Sometime in the middle of the fifth century, possibly in the year 455 at a nunnery near what is now the city of Nanjing, something happened seemingly for the first time in the history of Buddhism: precise instructions for how to assume the seated posture of Buddhist meditation (*dhyāna*; *chan* 禪) were written down. These instructions begin as follows:

> In a quiet place, spread out a sitting cloth, sit cross-legged, arrange your robes, straighten your body, and sit upright. Uncover your right shoulder and place your left hand on top of your right hand. Close your eyes and press your tongue against the palate.[1]

These same directives, nearly identically worded, were incorporated into many later Buddhist meditation manuals in East Asia. Eventually included in the famous meditation primer of the thirteenth-century Japanese Zen master Dōgen, they are to this day ritually recited in Japanese Zen temples and even some American Zen communities (Bielefeldt 1988).

This book is a study and translation of the text in which these instructions first appear—the *Scripture on the Secret Essential Methods of Chan* (*Chan mi yao fa jing* 禪祕要法經)—along with what was originally a kind of appendix to it, the *Secret Methods for Curing Chan Sickness* (*Zhi chan bing mi yao fa* 治禪病祕要法). Both are "apocryphal" scriptures—texts taking the form of translations of Indian Buddhist sutras that were in fact new compositions

1. *Chan Essentials* 1.1.1. Previous scholars have noted that within extant Buddhist literature, Chinese or otherwise, these appear to be the oldest instructions for the meditation posture more detailed than simply to sit with legs crossed (Ōtani 1970, 209, and Otokawa 1995).

written or at least assembled in nontrivial fashion in China.[2] These texts are among the very earliest substantial Chinese compositions dedicated to this topic. They thus stand at, or close to, the font of all later East Asian traditions of Buddhist meditation. Their significance as historical sources, however, extends beyond a strictly East Asian setting. In the broader history of Buddhism, these texts are notable as the earliest written sources anywhere to record certain kinds of information about meditation, such as the details of proper meditation posture as mentioned above, that hitherto had been the preserve of oral tradition and personal initiation. To this extent they indeed provide, as their titles claim, the "secrets" of Buddhist meditation.

From the available evidence, seated meditation became a regular feature of Chinese Buddhist monastic life only beginning in the early fifth century.[3] There had been, before this time, a long history of Chinese interest in this distinctive and normatively central Buddhist activity—the practice by which, as the story goes, the Buddha reached his final liberation after abandoning the fruitless bodily mortifications favored by his religious rivals. By the late second century of the common era, the first translators of Indian Buddhist literature into Chinese had already coined the word *chan*, the Chinese phonetic rendering of the Indic word *dhyāna*, that would become the central term for Buddhist meditation in the East Asian Buddhist lexicon. From that early era, there survived a significant number of texts pertaining to *chan* that were studied and discussed by later generations of Chinese Buddhists. Nevertheless, for over two hundred years that interest in Buddhist meditation and meditative attainment remained largely theoretical, unsustained by any living traditions of practice. The annals of Chinese Buddhist hagiography, for example, record not a single meditation teacher, let alone practitioner of meditation, among the many Indian or Central Asian Buddhist monks who came to China bringing Buddhist texts, teachings, objects, ritual knowledge, and the example of their own presence between the mid-100s and the turn of the fifth century. Whether this silence reflects the total absence of any organized traditions of meditation practice among Chinese Buddhists of this era, or merely their failure to rise to a noticeable level of importance, things changed rather suddenly in the early 400s with the arrival, in the old capital city of Chang'an, of the Gandhāran monk Buddhabhadra, seem-

2. During the fifth century, when these texts were composed, China was not a unified entity, either politically or ethnically, or, at the level of spoken language, linguistically. My references to "China" and "Chinese Buddhism" here and throughout should therefore be taken heuristically, as a way of pointing to the wider Buddhist culture that, whatever its many local particularities, was at the same time united by its shared use of, and potential access to, literary Chinese as a common written language and a "canon" of Buddhist texts available in it (one that was, of course, not everywhere or at all times the same).

3. This paragraph summarizes the first chapter of *Chan Before Chan* (Greene 2021).

ingly the first person in Chinese history to bear the title *chanshi* 禪師, a "master of meditation."[4]

The early fifth century was a particularly fertile time in nearly all areas of Chinese Buddhist thought and practice. In the span of only a few decades numerous prolific translation teams produced graceful Chinese versions of dozens of new and often enormous Indian Buddhist scriptures and commentaries, as well as several complete monastic codes, a genre of canonical Buddhist literature largely unavailable in China before this time. This new literature—tens of thousands of pages worth, were it ever to be completely translated into English—inspired centuries of scholastic reflection, cultic practice, and developments in monastic organization. While we should certainly avoid the philological fallacy equating the history of Chinese Buddhism with the history of its texts, still, the fact that the Buddhist translations of the early fifth century largely displaced those that had come before without themselves being displaced by the literary productions of subsequent eras, is an indication that, during this same era, other, less visible traditions were also forged that would remain bedrocks of Chinese and East Asian Buddhism for centuries to come and even to the present day.

The arrival of *chan* master Buddhabhadra heralded one of these developments—what we might call a "*chan* boom," lasting for much of Song (420–479) dynasty in south China.[5] A large number of Indian masters gained fame during this era primarily as teachers of meditation, a seemingly new pathway to patronage for foreign Buddhists in China, and many Chinese Buddhist monks and nuns, including some who frequented emperors and occupied the highest echelons of the clerical establishment, were or claimed to be their students and gained similar renown.

Though its textual production did not aspire to match that of the great translation workshops of the day, the *chan* boom of the fifth century did create a substantial literature devoted to the topic, works that came to be categorized as a distinct canonical genre—the so-called *chanjing* 禪經, or "*chan* scriptures."[6] Many of these texts, as well as certain examples from earlier centuries retrospectively classified as such, are Chinese translations of various kinds of post-canonical Indian Buddhist meditation manuals.[7] Because almost none of this literature is extant in the original Indic languages, scholars have long valued these Chinese translations as sources

---

4. Buddhabhadra's name is variously transcribed in medieval texts, most frequently as *Fotuobatuo* 佛陀跋陀 or *Fodabatuo* 佛大跋陀. His name was also sometimes translated as Juexian 覺賢.

5. Buddhabhadra was supposedly invited to China by a Chinese monk who had met him while studying meditation in India (*GSZ*, T.2059:50.334c19–21; 339b). Like the wave of Asian teachers of Buddhist meditation that appeared in the United States and Europe beginning in the 1950s and 60s, the *chan* boom of fifth-century China may have been as much a product of demand as of supply.

6. I discuss the category of the *chan* scriptures in more detail in *Chan Before Chan*, chap. 1.

7. For a survey of the surviving fifth-century *chan* scriptures, see Yamabe 1999c, 72–114.

for the study of the Buddhist meditation traditions that flourished during the early centuries of the common era in northwest India, where almost all the famous foreign *chan* masters of fifth-century China supposedly trained.[8]

But also appearing at this time were certain other *chan* scriptures that masqueraded as direct translations of pre-existing Indian texts but were of Chinese origin. The most prominent examples of these are the *Chan Essentials* and *Methods for Curing*, both translated in Part II of this book. Unlike many such Chinese Buddhist "apocrypha," which attest most readily to distinctly *Chinese* responses to or interpretations of Indian ideas, these two texts are valuable as sources for both Chinese and Indian Buddhism. As Yamabe Nobuyoshi has convincingly demonstrated, we have just enough textual evidence from Central Asia—in the form of the fragmentary Sanskrit text of uncertain date known to scholars as the "Yogalehrbuch" (meditation manual)[9]—to be certain that the broad contours of the approach to Buddhist meditation advocated by the *Chan Essentials* and *Methods for Curing*, in which elaborate and unusual visionary experiences play a prominent role, were not simply Chinese inventions (Yamabe 1999b). These texts therefore serve, to some degree, as windows onto the Indian traditions of Buddhist meditation that were taught by the Indian and Central Asian *chan* masters who plied their trade in fifth-century China, practices largely invisible in the more doctrinally oriented treatises that are otherwise our only sources of information about this topic during the middle period of Indian Buddhism (ca. 200 BCE–400 CE).

Yet, even while containing information relevant to our understanding of Indian Buddhism, the *Chan Essentials* and *Methods for Curing* demonstrably reached their final form only after a long process of development as Chinese texts. They were, it seems, end products of a process encompassing the recording, compiling, editing, and expansion of the teachings of the foreign *chan* masters active in China during the early fifth century. As we will see in Chapter 4, separate moments within this process can even be identified by comparing a few sections of the *Chan Essentials* to their counterparts in an earlier and simpler Chinese meditation manual on whose basis the later text was clearly composed. In this way, what the *Chan Essentials* and *Methods for Curing* show us are concrete instances in which Indian traditions of Buddhist meditation were actively taken up in China and deemed sufficiently important—and distinct enough from what was already so

8. On the "meditation practitioners" (*yogācāras*) of northwest India during this era, see Demiéville 1954; Nishi 1975, 123–374; Deleanu 1993; Kodama, Nakayama, and Naomi 1992 and 1993; Odani 1996; Yamabe, Fujitani, and Harada 2002; Abe 2011; and Stuart 2015, 1:225–242. These so-called *yogācāras* were probably not an organized group (see Silk 2000). Their relationship to the Yogācāra philosophical school is also a topic of debate.

9. Schlingloff 1964; Hartmann and Röllicke 2006. "Yogalehrbuch," the German title Schlingloff gave to his edition of this originally nameless document, is now conventionally used by scholars as a proper name for the text. An English translation is currently in progress.

available—that it was necessary or desirable to craft them into the literary form of a canonical sutra, thereby investing them with what proved to be a long-lasting prestige and authority.

For several hundred years following their composition, the *Chan Essentials* and *Methods for Curing* were arguably the key canonical reference points for the nature and practice of seated Buddhist meditation in China. The earliest known source to cite these texts, a sixth-century Chinese monastic code, reveals well the status they had by then attained. Citing scriptural passages to exhort monks and nuns in the "three trainings" of monastic discipline, meditation, and wisdom (a standard canonical categorization of the path to salvation), it uses the *Chan Essentials* alone, which it calls simply the "*chan* scripture," to set forth the importance of training in meditation:

> The *chan* scripture says: If one is able to cultivate the contemplation of the white bones and see even a single one of the three hundred and sixty bones, and if later one does not commit any evil deeds, then after death one will go straight to Tuṣita heaven. How much more so one who successfully [sees] his entire skeleton![10]

The *Chan Essentials* and *Methods for Curing* did not pervade the lives of medieval Chinese Buddhists in the manner of a famous scripture such as the *Lotus Sutra*, which for centuries and down to the present has occasioned ever proliferating learned exegesis, popular devotion, and artistic elaboration. Meditation was, after all, always an elite discipline that only a few Buddhists engaged in extensively. For those who did, however, these texts were among the most authoritative canonical sources. Citations of them appear in a range of sixth- and seventh-century Buddhist writings and encyclopedias. In the voluminous meditation treatises of Zhiyi 智顗 (538–597), which became standard reference works on *chan* for much of the later East Asian Buddhist tradition, these two texts are the only fifth-century *chan* scriptures directly cited at length.[11] Even in the early eighth century—when the Bodhidharma lineage (that is, the nascent Chan School) had begun to reshape perceptions of the true character of *chan*—the *Chan Essentials*, in an excerpted form, was still important enough to be carved onto the walls of a cave at the Grove of the Reclining Buddha (Wofoyuan 臥佛院) in Sichuan, along with other famous scriptures (Greene 2018).

10. 禪經云：若能修白骨觀，三百六十節中但得一節，於後不作諸惡，是人命終直生兜率天，何況全身得也。(Tsukamoto 1975, 295). This paraphrases *Chan Essentials* 4.32.4, though the line "and if later one does not commit any evil deeds" has seemingly been added. Rebirth in the heaven of Maitreya is also mentioned at *Chan Essentials* 1.14.8, 1.18.20.1, and 4.32.12. On this monastic code, known only from a single, now-lost Dunhuang manuscript, see Appendix 1, no. 1.

11. On Zhiyi's debt to these texts, see *Chan Before Chan*, chap. 3. On the citations of the *Chan Essentials* and *Methods for Curing* preserved in medieval Chinese sources, see Appendix 1.

Visionary Meditation

Compared with canonical presentations of *dhyāna* in the early Buddhist sutras, or classical Indian treatises on the "path" to liberation such as the *Visuddhimagga, Yogācārabhūmi, Bhāvanākramas*, or even Chinese equivalents such as Zhiyi's *Mohe zhi guan*, the *Chan Essentials* and *Methods for Curing* may at first appear rather unusual. The predominant approach of classical Buddhist meditation literature is to discuss the goals and fruits of meditation, and the majority of its practices and methods, in largely discursive, doctrinal, and psychological terms even though the particular techniques covered may well be concrete and embodied (involving moral discipline, posture, the breath, and so forth). In these texts, meditation, whatever else it may have been in practice, is presented as a path whose successive stages are distinguished above all by the qualities of mind the meditator acquires or develops, the psychological defilements (*kleśa*) abandoned or weakened, and the specific doctrinal truths whose realization brings the meditator—who at the higher levels of progress often appears in such literature as essentially a free-floating consciousness—gradually nearer to liberation.

In the *Chan Essentials* and *Methods for Curing*, on the other hand, the meditator's journey is not psychological but *visionary*. Although these texts do make reference to a vaguely defined classical model of named stages—one seemingly of Sarvāstivāda inspiration, ranging from initial meditative attainment up through the highest goal of liberation from rebirth, the state of the arhat—what is placed within the containers of these named stages is something rather different from what can be found in the equivalent sections of classical meditation treatises. Take this example from the second section of the *Chan Essentials*: the meditator, having concentrated his mind upon his own skull as a means of contemplating bodily impurity (an eminently traditional method of Buddhist meditation),

> sees a great bright light shining from the crown of his skull. It looks like a flame the size of a spear in length and thickness. It emerges from the crown of the skull and then reverses itself so that it points downward and reenters through the crown of the skull. Passing through the crown of the skull, it enters his neck bone. Emerging from his neck bone, it enters his chest bone. Emerging from his chest bone, it enters his navel. Emerging from his navel, it enters his coccyx. After entering his coccyx, it disappears. With its disappearance, there immediately appears a spontaneously arising great cloud of light. It is adorned with jewels and pure jewel-flowers more exquisite than all other material forms. Within the cloud is a buddha named Śākyamuni, replete in radiance, endowed with the thirty-two major and eighty minor marks, each one radiating a thousand lights. These lights are extremely bright, blazing forth like a hundred thousand million suns. This buddha preaches the teaching of the four truths. His light dazzling, he

> stands before the practitioner and lays his hand upon his head. (*Chan Essentials* 2.20.9–10)

Successful meditation, as depicted here, is primarily an elaborate visionary journey. And this is not something the *Chan Essentials* and *Methods for Curing* merely state abstractly, but something they embody by devoting the majority of their space to descriptions such as this.[12]

Whatever else it might mean to claim that progress in meditation will take the form of visions such as those described above, it is an understanding of such progress practically the polar opposite of what would later become the orthodox perspective of the Chinese Chan School, which treated concrete meditative visions, by virtue of their very concreteness, as *not* signs of attainment at all.[13] For this reason, for those familiar with the history of Buddhism in East Asia, it may seem that the *Chan Essentials* and *Methods for Curing* promote practices and aspirations more typical of "Pure Land" or "Esoteric" (Tantric) Buddhism rather than *chan* or "meditation" per se. Past scholars, on the few occasions they have confronted these texts, have indeed often resorted to convoluted explanations concerning their relationship to these other traditions, whose supposed distinctions have so often structured modern understandings of East Asian Buddhism. Michel Strickmann, for example, when citing a procedure from the *Methods for Curing* for repelling demons that disturb meditators, suggests that this text shows us

> in what consisted... the nightmare of the meditator even before Tantrism embellished the field of visions. There is an important difference between these two contexts: Tantric ritual intentionally creates visions, while Buddhist meditation traditionally seeks to exclude them. Thus when everything went according to plan, these two procedures would have seemed altogether distinct.[14]

Yet by focusing only on this one section of the text, where demonic visions are discussed and treated as signs of meditation gone wrong, Strickmann failed to note that this is not the only or even typical way that the *Methods for Curing* discusses meditative visionary experience. For the purpose of understanding the concrete goals of religious practice that were valued, even at the level of elite, scriptural literature, it is anachronistic to see much distinction between the categories *chan*, Pure Land, and Tantra during the

12. The emphasis on visionary experience in the *Chan Essentials* and *Methods for Curing* is broadly in keeping with a rising interest in concrete visions in several areas of Indian religion during the first centuries of the common era (Beyer 1977). On visionary meditative experience in these texts, see also *Chan Before Chan*, chap. 2.

13. As I argue elsewhere (*Chan Before Chan*, chap. 5), the approach to meditation promulgated in the texts of the early Chan School was often structured as a rejection of the kind of meditation discussed in the *Chan Essentials* and *Methods for Curing*.

14. Strickmann 1996, 321–322.

fifth and sixth centuries. In China—and, we must presume, in the Indian and Central Asian traditions to which the many foreign *chan* masters then active in China were heir—seated meditation was a discipline that produced, and whose fruits were thereby confirmed by, elaborate visions of various kinds. And accordingly, mastery of Buddhist meditation was associated with visionary accomplishment in many circles of society, and this view is reflected in other literary genres, including monastic hagiography and popular miracle tales, as well as in a few pieces of relevant material culture that have survived.[15]

The Historiography of Buddhist Meditation in China

Modern scholars have rarely seen the fifth-century *chan* scriptures produced in China, even those that were incontrovertibly read, used, and valued by later Chinese Buddhists, as significant sources for understanding the history of Buddhist meditation in China and East Asia. Some of the blame for this neglect can be attributed to the influence of the long-held, though by now no longer widely believed, narrative according to which it was only after the reunification of the Chinese realm in 589 under the Sui dynasty, after four centuries of fragmentation, that Chinese Buddhism truly came into its own. Only then, it is supposed, did Chinese Buddhism reach the stage of "independent growth" (Wright 1959) seen in the development of the distinctly Chinese schools of Tiantai, Chan, Huayan, or Pure Land, moving in this way beyond an earlier era characterized (paradoxically) as excessively *and* insufficiently faithful to India—that is, as bearing "the mark either of rapt imitation of Indian forms or of flawed and often incomplete understanding of that foreign religion."[16]

More recently, the scholarly models informing this "master narrative" of Chinese Buddhist history have become less persuasive, and the impulse to evaluate Chinese Buddhism in terms of fidelity to Indian precedents has itself come to seem like a misguided intellectual project.[17] Scholarly attention has, accordingly, increasingly turned to precisely what was once dismissed as the imperfect understandings of a still immature Chinese Buddhism, perhaps above all to those sources where the dividing lines between Bud-

15. See *Chan Before Chan*, chap. 2.

16. Gimello 1976, 1. I here cite the opening passage of Gimello's PhD dissertation not to single him out, let alone to criticize this monumental and regrettably never published work, but simply because it concisely and eloquently expresses what was for a long time the usual way of thinking about the early history of Chinese Buddhism.

17. "Master narrative" is Sharf's (2002a) term for this long-standing story, which he urges we should move past. Western scholars of Chinese Buddhism have in recent decades been particularly keen to see beyond the model that takes the Tang "schools" as the pinnacle of mature Chinese Buddhism. This model owes much to the concerns of modern Japanese historians of Chinese Buddhism, whose perspective has often been shaped by the status of the Tang schools as the source to which many sects of Japanese Buddhism trace themselves.

dhism, Daoism, and other Chinese religious or intellectual systems become murky or evaporate entirely and which, in this respect, prefigure the form that Chinese "popular" religion was to assume in subsequent eras.[18] For such research, the countless blatantly (it seems to us) "apocryphal" Chinese Buddhist scriptures that survive from the roughly two-hundred-year period from 400 to 600, the first epoch for which we have such material in abundance, have provided much fertile terrain (Overmyer 1990; Strickmann 2002; Mollier 2008). So too has the vast and still comparatively understudied world of medieval Daoism, whose sources also begin to survive in large numbers from this period, and which, precisely as "flawed" interpretations of it, have been argued by some to reveal the true extent of Buddhism's influence in China (Zürcher 1982; Chappell 2005; Bokenkamp 2007).

But while scholars have in these ways rehabilitated what previously were dismissed as immature and partial Chinese readings of Indian Buddhism, they have, conversely, paid less attention to those parts of pre-Tang Buddhism once seen as merely the "rapt imitation of Indian forms." (We might of course ask why "rapt imitation," were this an accurate characterization, would not be interesting—as if continuity were a natural state of affairs requiring no work or agency and thus not in need of explanation or appreciation.) It is in this category that the fifth-century *chan* scriptures have generally been placed, as excessively "Indian" and therefore not historically relevant to *Chinese* Buddhism. This reading is implicitly informed by the sectarian model of Chinese Buddhist history in that it takes truly Chinese forms of Buddhist meditation to have begun with, and simultaneously to have reached their highest forms in, early Chan and Tiantai—the two later "schools" that discuss the theory and practice of meditation most systematically. Chinese writings on Buddhist meditation that came before Chan or Tiantai, such as the *chan* scriptures, are then conveniently categorized, if only implicitly, as the "rapt imitation of Indian forms," as showing us nothing more than the traditional forms of Indian meditation that Chinese Buddhists would eventually and inexorably move beyond.[19] More perniciously, scholars have then often defined the distinctiveness of Chan or Tiantai, relative to each other, by ascribing the other to an inferior stage of development. Thus the "sudden" approach to meditation of the early Chan School is often contrasted with Zhiyi's understanding of the path, which is seen as Indian in its architecture

18. Zürcher 1982 remains an influential, programmatic outline of this approach, at the time a quite new way of thinking about early Chinese Buddhism, which to a great extent continues to define the state of the field (Teiser 2007, xxiv).

19. Particularly influential in setting these parameters was Nukariya Kaiten's 忽滑谷快天 (1925) magisterial *History of Zen Thought* (*Zengaku shisōshi* 禪學思想史), whose introductory sections remain the most comprehensive study of meditation (*chan*) before the rise of the Chan School as it can be gleaned from canonical Chinese Buddhist texts. In all these sources Nukariya sees but partial or incomplete versions of the "pure Chan" (*junzen* 純禪) inaugurated by Bodhidharma. Sasaki 1978 (first published in 1936) was a similar project undertaken from the Tiantai perspective.

owing to its "gradualist" perspective (Bielefeldt 1988, 78–106; McRae 1992) or its "hair-splitting analysis of meditative practices" (Faure 1986, 119). Scholars of Tiantai, of course, have tended to take the contrary view, deriding Chan, with its supposedly exclusive focus on concentrative meditation (*dhyāna* in the strict sense), as merely an "Indian" or "Hīnayāna" approach (Sekiguchi 1969, 123–142).[20]

Whether they see Chan or Tiantai as its true flowering, scholars have thus often imagined that the practice of Buddhist meditation in China, having somehow taken hold at an unspecified date, remained for a long time in a quasi "Indian" or "Hīnayāna" stasis—and that we know what *this* means is usually simply assumed—until eventually revolutionized by either Zhiyi, Bodhidharma, or both.[21] The fifth-century *chan* scriptures, if they appear at all in these narratives, are merely the prelude to greater things, examples of a culturally (Indian) and religiously (Hīnayāna) conservative and unoriginal approach to Buddhist meditation that was destined to be transcended by mature Chinese Buddhism.

Shorn of a certain triumphalism, this narrative might still form the basis of an accurate history were it true that Chinese Buddhists have always been expressly dissatisfied with Hīnayāna approaches to meditation and resolutely Mahāyāna in their orientation. Yet as contemporary scholarship has shown, "Mahāyāna" is a considerably more complicated and contested notion than most textbook accounts would have it (Harrison 2018). Its value as a second-order term for neutrally differentiating different approaches to Buddhism is problematic to say the least. The question of how the doxographical categories Mahāyāna and Hīnayāna were understood and used by medieval Chinese Buddhists themselves, as regards meditation or anything else, is not a topic that can be fully unraveled here.[22] For the purposes of situating them historically, it suffices to note that the *Chan Essentials* and *Methods for Curing* promised their readers rewards that almost all Chinese Buddhists throughout the fifth and sixth centuries considered marvelous and wonderful things—benefits such as rebirth in the heaven of the future buddha Maitreya, concrete meditative visions of various kinds, and, at the highest levels, the four stages of sainthood (from stream-enterer to arhat).[23]

---

20. In much of this historiography there is a noticeable conflation of the categories "Hīnayāna," "India," and "concentration" (*śamatha* rather than *vipaśyanā*).

21. Western scholars usually split the difference between the Chan-Tiantai rivalries of Japanese scholarship to conclude that *both* Chan and Tiantai, in their own ways, represent the apogee of truly "Mahāyāna" approaches to meditation in China (Dumoulin 1994, 1:63–83; Donner 1977; W. Lai 1983, 65–71; Sørensen 2012, 58).

22. Some early Chan School authors did, in the eighth century, disparage texts such as the *Chan Essentials* and *Methods for Curing* as purveying merely a "Hīnayāna" approach (see *Chan Before Chan*, chap. 5). Such classifications are, of course, polemical, and, more to the point, even *as* polemics are not relevant to the fifth- and sixth-century context.

23. To judge from the epigraphic record, for example, rebirth in the heaven of Maitreya or on earth when Maitreya has become a buddha, a key benefit promised by the *Chan Essentials*, was a common postmortem aspiration among all classes of Buddhists in China for much of

In short, the *Chan Essentials* and *Methods for Curing* were actively composed or assembled in China, were looked to by later Chinese authors as among if not the most authoritative canonical explanations of *chan*, and describe the fruits of seated meditation in a way that aligns closely with how the ideal of meditative mastery was depicted in hagiographical and other sources. For these reasons, they are among our best windows onto the mainstream understanding of Buddhist meditation that prevailed in China during the fifth, sixth, and even seventh centuries.

The *Chan* Scriptures and the Contemplation Scriptures

In the passage from the *Chan Essentials* cited above, it is stated that when the successful meditator has focused his mind intently on his own skull and experienced a vision of glowing light radiating from his body, he will eventually encounter the Buddha:

> Within the cloud is a buddha named Śākyamuni, replete in radiance, endowed with the thirty-two major and eighty minor marks... This buddha preaches the teaching of the four truths. His light dazzling, he stands before the practitioner and lays his hand upon his head. (*Chan Essentials* 2.20.10)

This moment is but one of many in the *Chan Essentials* and *Methods for Curing* in which advanced meditative attainment is described as an encounter with a tangible, concrete form of the Buddha (or buddhas).[24] It is not surprising, therefore, to find that these two texts have often caught the attention of scholars whose primary interest is the development of so-called Pure Land Buddhism, usually described as an approach to Buddhist soteriology that emphasizes not meditation per se, seen as an inner, psychologically grounded technique of mental cultivation, but devotion to an external deity with whom real contact is desired and in whose presence one wishes to be reborn.

But from this perspective too, the *Chan Essentials* and *Methods for Curing* have usually been accorded lesser status as mere prologues to something

the fifth and sixth centuries (Hou 1998, 196–204). In *Chan Before Chan*, chaps. 2 and 3, I discuss the congruence between the distinctly "visionary" approach to meditation in the *Chan Essentials* and *Methods for Curing* and early Chinese hagiographic depictions of meditative mastery. Even though almost all Chinese Buddhists identified as followers of the Mahāyāna, during this era the so-called Hīnayāna fruits of the four stages of sainthood were nevertheless clearly held to be praiseworthy and valuable achievements (Campany 2012, 33; Funayama 2019, 66–68; *BQNZ*, T.2063:50.939c4; *GSZ*, T.2059:50.342a26–b1; *Guan dingjing*, T.1331:21.530b17–18). The widespread Chinese cult of famous Indian arhats (Joo 2007) similarly shows that such states of sanctity were probably always seen in China as having considerable worth. On the categories of Buddhist sainthood that were applied to living and recently deceased Chinese Buddhists in this era, see Funayama 2005.

24. For more examples of the way these texts depict the encounter with the Buddha, see "The Bodies of the Buddha" in chap. 3.

better—in this case, the *Amitāyus Contemplation Scripture* (*Guan Wuliangshou fo jing*).[25] This text was without question one of the most important scriptures of medieval Chinese Buddhism. This fact, coupled with its centrality for the Japanese Pure Land sects that see it as providing scriptural proof of their central doctrine—that merely intoning the name of the Buddha Amitāyus (Amtitābha) assures rebirth in his Pure Land—has made it the focus of a good deal of modern scholarly research. The relevance of the *Chan Essentials* and *Methods for Curing* for understanding its history first became apparent in the wake of one of the great discoveries of early twentieth-century Japanese Buddhology, namely, that the *Amitāyus Contemplation Scripture* is itself an apocryphal Chinese scripture rather than a translation of an Indian text, as had always been believed, and that it was composed, or at the least compiled from originally separate parts, sometime in the early fifth century in China. This discovery was abetted by the realization that the *Amitāyus Contemplation Scripture* is closely connected—philologically, thematically, bibliographically, and hence seemingly historically—to a larger and previously unrecognized corpus of fifth-century Chinese Buddhist scriptures, the so-called Contemplation Scriptures, each dedicated to the cult of a specific Buddhist deity or deities whose worship lies in the "contemplation" (*guan* 觀) of their physical forms. Connections were also drawn to the *Chan Essentials* and *Methods for Curing*, which, while slightly further afield thematically, have an equally close linguistic and historical relationship.[26]

The discovery of the Chinese origins of the *Amitāyus Contemplation Scripture*, coupled with the existence of a previously unrecognized category of similar texts, did not, however, prompt scholars to see in these connections a newly apparent historical context that could be freshly approached unconstrained by later doxographies, which never treated the Contemplation Scriptures as a group. Instead, this other material has for the most part been taken up with the primary aim of explaining the background and origins

25. The so-called Contemplation Scriptures (see next note) frequently circulated under the titles X觀經, rather than 觀X經, as they appear today. This can be seen both from early citations of the texts by other writers (Greene 2016c, 294n15) and also in some early catalogs, such as the fragments of the fifth-century *Zhong jing bie lu* 眾經別錄 (Pelliot no. 3747), which titles the Contemplation Scripture devoted to the bodhisattvas Medicine King 藥王 and Medicine Lord 藥上 as *Yaowang Yaoshang pusa guan jing* 藥王藥上菩薩觀經 (Fang 1997, 1:17), not *Guan Yaowang Yaoshang pusa jing*, as this text (T.1161) is transmitted today. With these references in mind, and to emphasize their existence as a cohesive group, I translate the titles of the Contemplation Scriptures as X *Contemplation Scripture*, rather than *Scripture on the Contemplation of* X.

26. Mochizuki 1946, 283–298, was the first to identify the Contemplation Scriptures as a distinct group. A voluminous literature on their origins has followed, focused on the *Amitāyus Contemplation Scripture*. Important works in this long tradition of scholarship include Tsukinowa 1971, 43–176; Kasugai 1953; Fujita 1970, 116–136; 2007, 163–232; Sueki 1986; Yamada 1976; Pas 1977; Silk 1997; Kagawa 1999; and Yamabe 1999c. On the connection between the Contemplation Scriptures and the *Chan Essentials* and *Methods for Curing*, see Tsukinowa 1971, 102–110; Yamabe 1999b and 1999c.

of a still presumptively unique *Amitāyus Contemplation Scripture.*[27] Under this approach, scholars have treated the other Contemplation Scriptures, along with the *Chan Essentials* and *Methods for Curing*, as sources indicative of the context out of which the *Amitāyus Contemplation Scripture* emerged but then transcended. In short, while the large body of modern scholarship dedicated to the early history of Pure Land Buddhism in China has often mentioned the *Chan Essentials* and *Methods for Curing* in passing, these texts have generally been characterized as transitional representatives of the putatively Hīnayāna meditation practices of Indian and Central Asian Buddhism that, in turn, were superseded by the distinctly Pure Land (and Mahāyāna) approach of the *Amitāyus Contemplation Scripture.*[28]

As a normative theology justifying a special status for the *Amitāyus Contemplation Scripture*—which in the Japanese Pure Land understanding authorizes a distinctly *non*-meditative practice of intoning the Buddha's name that obviates the need for difficult-to-attain states of trance (*dhyāna* or *samādhi*)—this view is as acceptable as any. But as a matter of history, it is misleading to suggest that Chinese Buddhists themselves treated the *Chan Essentials* and *Methods for Curing* as mere stepping-stones to something else. Indeed, more broadly, as other scholars have established, medieval Chinese Buddhists did not set up, in either theory or practice, a categorical opposition between the salvific "other power" of an external deity (Pure Land) and the "self-power" of meditation (*chan*). For example, many of the figures later promoted to the status of Pure Land patriarchs, such as Shandao 善導 (613–681), were known, to their contemporaries, as *chan* masters, that is, as masters of meditation (Sharf 2002b, 302). Medieval Chinese Buddhists, in the fifth century as well, understood these domains to be intimately connected. In fact, all the fifth-century translators whose names were eventually linked to the transmission and translation of the Contemplation Scriptures, including the *Amitāyus Contemplation Scripture*, were either known as *chan* masters or also credited with the translation of *chan* scriptures.

Still, it is the case that the Contemplation Scriptures are stylistically and rhetorically very different from the fifth-century *chan* scriptures in general and the *Chan Essentials* and *Methods for Curing* in particular. Though they similarly emphasize the activities of "contemplation" (*guan*) or "imagination" (*xiang* 想)—concepts that play an important role in the *chan* scriptures, as we will see—the Contemplation Scriptures almost never claim to teach *chan.*[29]

---

27. Yamabe 1999c and Mai 2009 are two notable exceptions that take up the Contemplation Scriptures as a whole, without privileging the *Amitāyus Contemplation Scripture.*

28. See for example Tōdō 1960; Myōjin 1993; Ōminami 1975; Nōnin 1993; Irisawa 1999.

29. The *Ocean-Samādhi Contemplation Scripture* (*Guan fo sanmei hai jing; GFSMH*), which differs from the other Contemplation Scriptures in important ways (it is, for example, ten times the length of the others), is an occasional exception (*GFSMH*, T.643:15.647c8; 692c7–8; 695a17; 695b2; 695b22–23). On the meaning and usage in these sources of key terms of meditative activity such as *guan* and *xiang*, see "Meditation in the *Chan Essentials* and *Methods for Curing*" in chap. 2.

This divergence correlates with a relatively clear contrast in *genre:* the Contemplation Scriptures all resemble typical Mahāyāna sutras and feature familiar Mahāyāna deities, protagonists, and soteriological fruits, while the only *chan* scriptures written as sutras, the *Chan Essentials* and *Methods for Curing*, are modeled on the scriptural style of the Āgama / Nikāyas, largely feature the "historical" Buddha and his chief disciples, and for the most part take arhatship as the highest goal.[30]

From the perspective of the scriptural classification schemes (*panjiao* 判教) later employed in Chinese Buddhism, we might be tempted to take this divergence as evidence of a normative hierarchy between the superior Mahāyāna practices of the Contemplation Scriptures and the inferior Hīnayāna practices of the *chan* scriptures. But there is no evidence to suggest that this is a view fifth-century Chinese Buddhists would have subscribed to. We would do better to see this contrast in genre as an index of two slightly different audiences. Some hagiographies of famous fifth-century *chan* masters imply as much. According to the *Biographies of Eminent Monks*, compiled in the early sixth century, it was the *chan* master Kālayaśas who translated two of the Contemplation Scriptures in the 420s:

> Initially Kālayaśas lived at the Daolin monastery on Mount Zhong, where the monk Baozhi studied *chan* practices with him. The monk Senghan asked him to translate the *Medicine King Contemplation Scripture* and the *Amitāyus Contemplation Scripture*. . . . As secret techniques for overturning karmic obstructions and a universal cause of rebirth in the pure land, these two texts were chanted and appreciated throughout the land of Song.[31]

As both a teacher of *chan* and a transmitter of certain Contemplation Scriptures, Kālayaśas's activities are indeed distinguished, but not as superior and inferior—they are two different aspects of his teachings, directed at differently inclined disciples: Senghan, a famous scholar and exegete, and Baozhi, a *chan* master and miracle worker.[32] A similar pattern appears in the biography of the *chan* master Dharmamitra (d. 442), the supposed translator of the *Samantabhadra Contemplation Scripture* (*Guan Puxian pusa xing fa jing*). According to this biography, Dharmamitra was, above all, a ritual

30. The *Methods for Curing* occasionally mentions deities and attainments more typical of Mahāyāna literature (*Methods for Curing* 1.12.3–4, 1.14.16–17, 1.15.4, 2.11). What I describe here as the contrast between the Mahāyāna and Āgama / Nikāya scriptural idioms is, of course, only a loose and heuristic one. There do exist texts universally accepted as Mahāyāna in character, such as many of those in the *Prajñāpāramitā* corpus, that lack most of the features I here associate with a Mahāyāna scriptural idiom.

31. 初止鐘山道林精舍，沙門寶誌崇其禪法。沙門僧含請譯藥王藥上觀及無量壽觀...以此二經是轉障之祕術，淨土之洪因，故沈吟嗟味，流通宋國。(*GSZ*, T.2059:50.343c16–21). Kālayaśas is called a "*chan* master" at *Meisōden shō*, Z.1523:77.348c3 and *BQNZ*, T.2063:50.940b26–27; 945c21–22. In the *Gao seng zhuan*, he is grouped among the "translators," but this is true of all foreign monks in this collection.

32. *GSZ*, T.2059:50.370b14–c2 and 394a15–395b1.

master specializing in the then-popular Samantabhadra abstinence ceremonies (普賢齋)—rituals seemingly linked, in reality or in the mind of the biographer, to the *Samantabhadra Contemplation Scripture*—with clients including Empress Yuán 袁 (d. 441) and her family.[33] But Dharmamitra is also depicted as a teacher of *chan* to a few monkish disciples, the founder of numerous "*chan* halls," and the translator of several *chan* scriptures, one of which catalogers would eventually equate with the *Chan Essentials*.[34]

In historical memory, the Contemplation Scriptures and the *chan* scriptures were thus equally the legacy of the famous foreign *chan* masters of the early fifth century. The Contemplation Scriptures were the more accessible part. They could bring some of the benefits commonly associated with *chan* even to those who could not or did not master *chan* itself, which even in the wake of the *chan* boom of the early 400s was still undoubtedly thought of as an elite discipline whose depths very few could hope to fathom. It is in light of such differentiation that we should read the passages in certain Contemplation Scriptures that actively distance their teachings from activities that, in the fifth century, would have been associated with *chan*. One passage, for example, notes that neither the contemplation of impurity nor meditation on the breath are necessary.[35] Another claims that its teachings allow one to gain miraculous visions of the deities in question *without* entering a state of trance (*ding* 定).[36] And yet another notes in passing that the future buddha Maitreya, a figure often linked to the mastery of *chan* (Demiéville 1954), "neither cultivated *chan* nor severed the defilements" in his most recent birth.[37] These claims would not have been taken by fifth-century readers as rejecting the world of *chan* as we find it in texts such as the *Chan Essentials* and *Methods for Curing*. Instead, they would have been seen as opening a side door to allow access to its fruits—and in this, they show us the extent to which such aspirations were seen, during this era of Chinese Buddhism, as among the highest and most worthy of religious goals.

In sum, the *Chan Essentials* and *Methods for Curing* deserve more than the mere adjunct status to which historians of Chinese Buddhism have relegated them. Far from being incomplete forms of something yet to come, they show us what was, for several centuries in early medieval China, the mainstream understanding of Buddhist meditation and its promised results. It is to the details of this understanding that we now turn.

33. *GSZ*, T.2059:50.343a2–4 (emending 哀 to 袁). On Empress Yuan, see *Song shu*, 41.1283–1286. On the popularity of these Samantabhadra rituals during the fifth and sixth centuries, see Stevenson 1987, 200–214.

34. For more details on the texts traditionally associated with Dharmamitra, see chap. 4.

35. *GFSMH*, T.643:15.682b26–c3.

36. *Guan Puxian pusa xing fa jing*, T.277:9.389c21–24.

37. 不修禪定不斷煩惱。(*Guan Mile pusa shang sheng doushuai tian jing*, T.452:14.418c6–8).

CHAPTER 2

Buddhist Meditation according to the *Chan Essentials* and *Methods for Curing*

The *Chan Essentials* and *Methods for Curing*, whether we consider them individually, as they come to us in the received Chinese Buddhist canons, or together as a single collection, as they likely circulated in the fifth century (see chap. 4), are difficult texts to summarize. Unlike typical Buddhist path treatises or even short meditation manuals, neither of these texts aims to present an overarching, coherent system of meditation. This makes for challenging reading, and the loose formal structures of the two texts offer only a modicum of assistance. On a quick perusal, baroque visions parade in endless succession before the reader's eye, together with instructions pertaining to classic Buddhist techniques of meditation, such as meditation on the breath and the contemplation of impurity, mixed with warnings about what happens when things go wrong, methods to counteract the resulting mishaps, and the occasional narrative interlude.

Though the lack of clear structure or theoretical explanation in these texts may itself be an important clue to how they were supposed to be read and used, at the same time it is possible to discern within them a few basic patterns and presuppositions concerning the way meditation was thought to be practiced, how it was supposed to progress, and the differing results it might entail. The goal of this chapter is to reconstruct these patterns in order to grasp the logic of the texts themselves—and accordingly, to be able to read them without the feeling of being completely at sea. Understanding their inherent logic will also allow us to draw some conclusions about what purpose these texts, as texts, were intended to serve.

Outline and Structure of the *Chan Essentials* and *Methods for Curing*

Before discussing how the *Chan Essentials* and *Methods for Curing* depict the practice and fruits of meditation, it will be helpful to first consider their overall style, form, and organizational schemes.

Scriptural Idiom

Both the *Chan Essentials* and *Methods for Curing* are collections of multiple short, nominally independent sutras. Their literary model was clearly the scriptures of the Indian Buddhist Āgama / Nikāya collections, usually considered the earliest form of Buddhist literature. Both texts imitate this model in their cast of characters (the monk disciples of the Buddha with nary a bodhisattva to be seen), the down-to-earth settings, and the formulas of entrustment that conclude each sutra.[1] Within the known corpus of Chinese Buddhist scriptural literature, the arrangement of these texts as *collections* of multiple short sutras, whose beginnings and endings do not align with the scroll divisions, is not found outside the translations of the Āgamas.[2] This mimicry of the Āgama style is, moreover, seemingly unique among Chinese Buddhist apocryphal sutras, for which Mahāyāna literature provided the more usual models.

As mentioned in Chapter 1, modern scholars have tended to see the *Chan Essentials* and *Methods for Curing* as exemplars of a "Lesser Vehicle" or Hīnayāna approach to meditation that Chinese Buddhists quickly sought to move beyond. It is easy to construe the scriptural idiom of the two texts as confirmation of such an assessment. Yet here one might remember that since An Shigao's early translations of meditation texts in the second century, the topic of *chan* had almost always been presented in Chinese Buddhist literature within a mainstream—that is, not specifically Mahāyāna—Buddhist doctrinal and literary context, one whose soteriological goals, such as arhatship, were not seen as lesser achievements. Indeed turning the tables, the very fact that fifth-century Chinese Buddhists wanting to present an authoritative account of *chan* would adopt the scriptural idiom and doctrinal context of the Āgamas suggests that these containers had, at that time, a positive value as the proper and expected form for canonical teachings associated with Buddhist meditation.

Narrative Frames

The four sutras of the *Chan Essentials* and the two making up the *Methods for Curing* are each framed by an introductory narrative with a roughly similar plot: a monk (or, in one case, two monks) wishing to practice meditation (*chan*) is beset by certain difficulties that are resolved by the Buddha's instructions. Interestingly, most of the protagonists are explicitly described

1. A few exceptions to this faithful imitation of the Āgama style, in the form of brief mentions of bodhisattvas or the bodhisattva path, occur in the *Methods for Curing* (1.6.3, 1.9.3, 1.12.3, 1.14.16–17, 1.15.4, 2.10).

2. The opening lines of the received versions of the *Methods for Curing* even claim that the text was part of a Saṃyuktāgama (*Za ahan* 雜阿含). If this attribution is original to the text—it was clearly present no later than the sixth century (see Appendix 1, no. 3)—it would show that the attempt to imitate the Āgama scriptural idiom was a conscious choice of the authors or compilers.

as students of the Buddha's major disciples, and the Buddha usually intervenes only after his disciples have failed or realized their own inadequacy as teachers. Thus, for example, Panthaka, protagonist of the third sutra of the *Chan Essentials*, is a student of Kātyāyana, but that great arhat has been unable to lead him to awakening (*Chan Essentials* 3.0.1). In the fourth sutra, Mahākāśyapa judges that his personal disciple, a certain Agnidatta, will never become an arhat, but the Buddha eventually provides a special method enabling this to happen (4.0.2). Fifth-century Chinese authors sometimes described the Indian *chan* scriptures that had been translated into Chinese as part of a special set of teachings about meditation that were only written down long after the Buddha's death, by later masters who had been heir to an oral transmission.[3] It is tempting to see the narratives of the *Chan Essentials* and *Methods for Curing* as in some way one-upping that origin tale, promising the "secret" (as their full titles proudly claim) teachings of meditation delivered directly by the Buddha himself over and against what was transmitted through the generations by his great disciples and then written down in more traditional *chan* scriptures.

The protagonists of the narratives of the *Chan Essentials* and *Methods for Curing* are also alike in usually being known but decidedly minor figures from Indian Buddhist lore who here feature in stories that, though novel in their major elements, have at least a vague trace of connection to the traditional tales about them.[4] Like their careful imitation of the Āgama scriptural form, this too suggests that the *Chan Essentials* and *Methods for Curing* were put together by relatively learned authors or compilers who actively attempted to ensure that these texts would be accepted as genuine by an audience sophisticated enough to be suspicious of patently fabricated characters or scenarios. At the same time, however, we can see with the benefit of hindsight that these hypothetical authors did not have a flawless grasp of their source materials. The name of the protagonist of the first sutra, Kauṣṭhilananda, appears to have resulted from an error—inadvertently taking as a single person the two famous arhats, Kauṣṭhila and Nanda, whose names are listed sequentially in a passage in the *Lotus Sutra*. However, even an error of this sort is revealing. It would seem that our authors took the trouble to scour a well-known Buddhist sutra for what they thought was an obscure yet authentic Indian Buddhist personage, one whose historicity could stand up to scrutiny and lend authenticity to their text. And, indeed, the Indian origins of the *Chan Essentials* and *Methods for Curing* were, as far as we can tell, never questioned by later Chinese Buddhists.

But though the narratives of each sutra have been crafted with care,

3. *CSZJJ*, T.2145:55.65c11–19

4. See Appendix 4. In this respect the narratives resemble the frame story of the *Amitāyus Contemplation Scripture*, which also adapts, to novel ends, a known story from Buddhist literature (the imprisonment of King Bimbisāra) and takes for its protagonist a usually minor figure therein (Queen Vaidehī).

they sit lightly atop the material they frame. In the first sutra of the *Chan Essentials*, the narrative of Kauṣṭhilananda, who is instructed in meditation by the Buddha, occupies only a short introductory section. After Kauṣṭhilananda follows these instructions and becomes an arhat (1.0.1–1.1.8), the Buddha continues to preach what is clearly the continuation of these methods, but now to his generic interlocutor Ānanda, with no further mention of Kauṣṭhilananda or indeed any further narrative at all. The remaining sutras of the *Chan Essentials* and those of the *Methods for Curing* are similar in this regard. The narratives, it is safe to conclude, were at some point joined, relatively hastily, to an originally independent set of meditation instructions.[5] The presence of at least one serious problem of coherence—Nandi, introduced as an arhat at the beginning of the second sutra, later succeeds in becoming an arhat (*Chan Essentials* 2.19.3.1–3)—suggests that the texts did not receive a careful final editing.

The Five Gates of Meditation

In the case of the *Chan Essentials*, the sutra narratives also appear intended to help structure a diversity of possible meditation methods in keeping with the idea, common in Indian Buddhist literature, that the methods and objects of meditation should be suited to different meditators according to their temperament.[6] Most of the Indian *chan* scriptures translated into Chinese in the early fifth century deploy this idea, commonly through a fivefold division of meditation topics aligned with five different temperaments.[7] The clearest example of this arrangement occurs in the *Meditation Scripture* (*Zuo chan sanmei jing*), translated by Kumārajīva in the early fifth century:

1. Bodily impurity (*bujing* 不淨; *aśubhā*), for those afflicted by lust
2. Love (*cixin* 慈心; *maitrī*), for those afflicted by hatred
3. Conditionality (*yinyuan* 因緣; *pratītyasamutpāda*), for those afflicted by ignorance
4. The breath (*nian xi* 念息; *ānāpāna*), for those afflicted by speculative thinking
5. The Buddha (*nianfo* 念佛; *buddhānusmṛti*), for those with "equally distributed" defilements or grave sins[8]

---

5. Scholars have similarly argued that the *Amitāyus Contemplation Scripture* was created by joining a narrative frame to a set of once independent meditation instructions (Yamada 1976).

6. Such ideas appear already in the Nikāya / Āgamas (see, e.g., *Aṅguttara-nikāya*, 4.353) and are a mainstay of later meditation treatises such as the *Visuddhimagga* (Ñāṇamoli 1976, 102–111).

7. Ōminami 1977, 80–81; Sakurabe 1980; Odani 1995, 69. Notable examples include the *Yogācārabhūmi* of Saṅgharakṣa (*Xiu xing dao di jing*, T.606:15.191c17–192b14) and, among extant Indic language sources, the *Śrāvakabhūmi* (Deleanu 2012, 13–14).

8. *ZCSM*, T.614:15.271a1–277b9. For more information on the *Meditation Scripture*, see *Chan Before Chan*, chap. 2.

This list became standard among medieval Chinese exegetes, who called it the "five gates of *chan*" (五門禪).[9]

The sutra narratives of the *Chan Essentials* make at least some effort to frame the ensuing instructions as part of such a system by linking each protagonist to a principal defilement and an appropriate meditation object.[10] In the fourth sutra, Agnidatta's difficulties are explained as having resulted from his being a murderer in a previous life, for which the Buddha duly prescribes the meditative cultivation of love, the usual method for those plagued by hatred (4.0.4.2). In the second sutra, when Nandi requests a method to treat meditators with grave sins (2.0.1), the Buddha explains the technique of "bringing to mind the Buddha" (2.19.1.1), just what the *Meditation Scripture* also prescribes for this condition. The second half of Nandi's sutra, perhaps alluding to the canonical stories about a monk of this name who violated his celibacy, prescribes the normal method for curing lust, namely, the "contemplation of impurity" (2.20.6; 2.20.11–18). This addition to the second sutra brings the number of methods, across the four sutras, up to five.

Thus whoever compiled the *Chan Essentials* knew, and wanted readers to know that they knew, the standard forms and structures for discussing the practice of meditation in post-canonical Indian Buddhist literature. At the same time, there are some noticeable gaps in the execution. In the second half of the second sutra, even though the treatment for lust is something that looks like the contemplation of impurity, when it comes time to formally *name* this meditation method it is also called "breath contemplation" (2.20.1; 2.20.19). Similarly the third sutra links the protagonist Panthaka to the defilement of ignorance (3.0.3), seeming thereby to allude to the traditional Indian Buddhist stories about this figure. Yet nothing in the practice the Buddha then teaches to Panthaka aligns with meditation on *pratītyasamutpāda*, the method normally associated with ignorance. The compilers of the *Chan Essentials* thus seem inspired but not entirely constrained by the usual typologies found in the formal Indian and Chinese meditation literature of this era. It remains uncertain, however, if the departures from the standard schemes occurred because of gaps in knowledge of such typologies, a certain creativity, a hasty execution, or simply a less than complete interest in formal classifications.

The Path to Liberation

One additional reason the framing narratives of the *Chan Essentials* do not provide a fully coherent system for aligning different meditation methods

9. The *Meditation Scripture*'s fivefold list of primary meditation topics differs from the fivefold lists in extant Indian sources, which do not include *buddhānusmṛti* and where the fifth method is, rather, "analysis of the primary elements" (*dhātu-prabheda*), often said to treat the defilement of "pride" (*Śrāvakabhūmi*, 2:52).

10. For more on the characters who appear in these narratives, see Appendix 4.

with differently disposed practitioners is that these narratives sit atop a clearly different structure, stretching across all four sutras, consisting of a linear path of meditative progress beginning from initial meditative attainment up through arhatship. Such linear models of the "path" (*mārga*) are, of course, common if not universal in Indian Buddhist texts on meditation.

The *Chan Essentials* makes this linear course of progress explicit by assigning names and numbers, at the conclusion of each subsection, to each stage of progress.[11] Taken collectively, these names and their ordering suggest a clear pattern that is, again, informed by known Indian doctrines yet also curiously idiosyncratic.

In the first sutra, the first sixteen numbered stages constitute subtypes of the contemplation of bodily impurity; they conclude with the attainment of "bodily mindfulness" (1.17.7) as the seventeenth stage, and the "gate of impurity" (1.18.20.3), as the eighteenth, seeming to provide a collective title for the entire first sutra. In the second sutra, after the "*samādhi* of the contemplation of the Buddha" (2.19.3.4), the attainment of the "breath-counting contemplation" (2.20.19) leads to, in the third sutra, the stages of "heat" (3.21.11.1), "summit" (3.22.3), and "accessory to the stage called summit" (3.23.3) and eventually to the attainments of "stream-enterer" (3.26.16), "candidacy for once-returner" (3.27.5), "once-returner" (3.29.5), and finally "non-returner" (3.30.7). Although the explicit numbering system ceases here, the fourth sutra is clearly intended as the conclusion to the ordered sequence of the first three sutras since it is framed as a method allowing the monk Agnidatta, already a non-returner, to reach the final attainment of arhatship (4.31.30).

Taken as a whole, this sequence is obviously modeled, loosely, on the path to liberation as described in many Sarvāstivāda-Vaibhāṣika treatises. According to such sources, the path begins with either the contemplation of impurity or breath meditation and goes on to the attainment of the bases of mindfulness (*smṛtyupasthāna*), followed by the four "aids to penetration" (*nirvedhabhāgīya-kuśalamūla;* 四善根位)—heat (*ūṣmagata*), summit (*mūrdhan*), acceptance (*kṣānti*), and "highest worldly *dharmas*" (*laukikāgra-dharma*)—and finally the four fruits of the stream-enterer, once-returner, non-returner, and arhat.[12] But again, although this model has inspired the author(s), things do not line up systematically. The *Chan Essentials* thus alludes to the idea, found in Sarvāstivāda-Vaibhāṣika treatises, that prior to each of the four

11. The numbers are usually assigned after the Buddha entrusts the preceding teachings to Ānanda, but occasionally before the entrustment (1.15.1.4) or when there is no entrustment scene (1.16.2).

12. This model was not necessarily limited to the Sarvāstivāda-Vaibhāṣikas. For a basic overview of this model, drawing from the *Abhidharmakośa*, see Gethin 1998, 194–198. The inclusion of the "*samādhi* of the contemplation of the Buddha" has no counterpart in the usual Sarvāstivāda-Vaibhāṣika scheme. On the four aids to penetration as described in Vaibhāṣika sources, see Buswell 1997 and Hurvitz 1977. Structurally, the aids to penetration serve as intermediaries between the mundane (*laukika*) and transcendent (*lokottara*) attainments.

fruits there is a preliminary stage of the "candidate" (*pratipannaka*) for that fruit (making for eight total levels), but it inexplicably lists such a stage only for the once-returner (3.27.5). Similarly baffling is the failure to mention the third and fourth of the aids to penetration, namely, "acceptance" and "highest worldly *dharmas*."[13]

The authors or compilers of both the *Chan Essentials* and *Methods for Curing* thus had a great deal of nontrivial knowledge about the stages of the path to liberation. They were also familiar with technical details from the elaborate Sarvāstivāda-Vaibhāṣika analyses of the moment of awakening. The *Methods for Curing*, for example, explains that one becomes an arhat in the "thirty-fourth mental moment" (1.14.14), a reference to the idea that the moment of awakening is divisible into the sixteen mental moments of the "path of seeing" (*darśana-mārga*) and the eighteen mental moments of the "path of meditation (*bhāvanā-mārga*). Both the *Chan Essentials* (3.30.4) and *Methods for Curing* (1.14.14) also allude to a different, equally complex Sarvāstivāda-Vaibhāṣika theory concerning the eighteen mental moments of the "immediately successive path" (*ānantarya-mārga*) and the "path of liberation" (*vimukti-mārga*), the steps by which a meditator becomes liberated from any given sphere of existence.[14]

But in the end, these scholastic theories, like the names of the stages of the path, are mentioned only in passing. They are not elements of a system that the authors were interested in theorizing or developing, but only the formal titles of doctrinal categories with which the texts seek to align the elaborate meditative visions and experiences that constituted, as I discuss below, the primary topic of concern.

Methods for Curing

Compared with the *Chan Essentials*, the structure of the *Methods for Curing* is much simpler because it is transparently not a linear path but a collection of discrete methods for "curing" problems that may arise in meditation. As in the *Chan Essentials*, each of the two sutras of the *Methods for Curing* begins with a brief narrative that frames the ensuing text as the Buddha's teachings delivered in response to problems that arose for specific meditators on a certain occasion. These problems are clearly divided between techniques for curing meditation-induced "sicknesses" (病), in the first sutra, and methods for dispelling the various "demons" (鬼魅) that may harass meditators, in the second.

The methods for curing meditation-induced sickness are collectively introduced by a story of a group of monks who have been driven insane

13. The third *nirvedhabhāgīya*, acceptance (*kṣānti*), often marks a transition away from the mundane (*laukika*) path, on which one remains subject to backsliding (Buswell 1997, 590). The *Chan Essentials* could thus perhaps intend to assimilate the third and fourth *nirvedhabhāgīyas* with the attainments of the four fruits.

14. See the notes to the relevant sections of the translations.

when a loud noise disturbs them while they are immersed in the "contemplation of the wind element" (風大觀).[15] The Buddha provides a technique for curing (*zhi* 治) this condition by imagining one's body encased in a soundproof dome (1.2.4) and the channels of one's heart being filled with milk (1.3.3–4). Subsequent sections present similar maladies induced by meditation or to which meditators are particularly susceptible. A meditator who gives rise to lust, for example, may suffer physical harm or be driven insane when the "channels" (*mai* 脈) connected to his penis, stimulated by lustful thoughts, become disturbed and negatively influence other parts of his body (1.7.1–8). Another section provides a long ritual for "healing" violations of the precepts, necessary because such violations lead to frightening visions that provoke madness or aberrant behavior (1.9.2). Some of the sicknesses discussed are more patently psychological than physical, such as that of excessive love for music (1.11).

The second and much shorter sutra of the *Methods for Curing* provides only two methods. The first is a technique for repelling a succubus-like demon named "Buti" who causes nocturnal emissions (2.5). This evidently well-known method was often cited in later Chinese meditation texts.[16] A second section (2.9) gives a method for invoking the protection of the two bodhisattvas Medicine King and Medicine Lord so as to fend off the demons who attack meditators and cause "aching joints, itchy palms, pain on the soles of the feet," and other similar discomforts such as numbness in the legs (a sensation that will be immediately familiar to anyone who has sat in the Buddhist meditation posture for long periods of time). Despite introducing them merely as devices for treating such problems, most sections of the *Methods for Curing* ascribe to the techniques the power to simultaneously effectuate soteriological progress or even to lead directly to arhatship or other advanced attainments, as I discuss below.

Although the *Methods for Curing* sits outside the ordered path of the *Chan Essentials*, the two texts complement each other: the *Chan Essentials* sketches a linear path of progress toward liberation while the *Methods for Curing* focuses on remedies for general problems that beset meditators on that path. The two texts, as I discuss in Chapter 4, probably circulated as a single collection at the outset, the *Methods for Curing* appearing as a kind of appendix taking up certain issues mentioned in the *Chan Essentials* but not discussed there in depth. For example, the *Chan Essentials* alludes often but only in passing to the possibility of meditatively induced physical maladies, a topic discussed at length throughout the *Methods for Curing*. Similarly the *Chan Essentials* frequently says that meditators, upon encountering certain visions, will need to perform a ritual of repentance (*chanhui* 懺悔), but it provides

15. Meditation on the "wind element" figures prominently in the *Chan Essentials:* the "trance of the wind element" (風大定) is mentioned throughout the third sutra, and at 4.0.5 is implied to be the normal method for becoming an arhat.

16. See Appendix 1, no. 3, i–j.

only the barest outline of what this should entail, whereas the *Methods for Curing* devotes an entire section to the details of just such a rite (1.9). Knowledge of, or access to, the various remedies provided by the *Methods for Curing* thus seems to have been assumed for those following the linear course of practice prescribed in the *Chan Essentials.*

Meditation in the *Chan Essentials* and *Methods for Curing*

Let us now step back and consider what these texts have to say about what meditation is, how it takes place, and how it progresses; and then, given this basic understanding, what kind of information these texts seem to have been designed to convey and to what ends they might have been put.

Basic Sequence

Heuristically, it will be helpful to begin by considering the overall movement that I call the "basic sequence" and will divide, for the sake of analysis, into six elements or stages. What these represent is not a fixed sequence of steps or practices—the details we actually find vary considerably throughout the texts—but six aspects of meditation that the texts bring up on a recurring basis within the context of many of the different levels of practice and attainment they present:

1. An account of an initial technique directing the meditator to apply the mind in a particular way—often, but not always, a visually oriented exercise of "meditative imagination" (*xiang* 想).
2. A description of the initial result of the preceding practice, usually the experience of a concrete vision.
3. An account of a problematic situation, one that manifests directly through the previous vision or else is explained as the meaning of the occurrence of that vision.
4. Directives for rectifying the problem, usually by a different method of meditation that counteracts the problem or the performance of a ritual of repentance and purification.
5. A description of the result of the new practice, again usually a vision.
6. The formal naming of this result as a particular stage of attainment.

These six elements and the movement of a meditator through them can be observed throughout the *Chan Essentials* and *Methods for Curing*. The opening sections of the *Chan Essentials* provide a convenient place to consider them.

Contemplation of Impurity

The meditation technique with which the *Chan Essentials* begins—and therefore its first step along the path to awakening—is the form of the classic Buddhist contemplation of impurity (*aśubha-bhāvanā; bujing guan* 不淨觀) that Chinese sources typically call the "white bone contemplation" (*baigu guan* 白骨觀). The white bone contemplation is described, in one form or another, in most of the fifth-century Chinese *chan* scriptures.[17] The *Chan Essentials* clearly sees it as a central element of seated meditation: it recurs throughout the text, is often presupposed as the ground of other practices (see, e.g., 3.21.2), and is named at the conclusion of the fourth sutra as a possible title for the *Chan Essentials* as a whole (4.32.1; 4.32.4). Though the term "white bone contemplation" has no known Indic equivalent, what Chinese texts denote by this word is a well-known form of the contemplation of impurity that, by a certain point in time, was the primary form of this practice in post-canonical Sarvāstivāda-Vaibhāṣika literature.

Early Buddhist literature describes two main ways of meditating on bodily impurity: analysis of (1) one's own body as comprised of thirty-two or thirty-six impurities (*aśuci*) such as hair, blood, bones, and the organs, or (2) the foul (*aśubha*) nature of external bodies through the contemplation of a decaying corpse. In the early Buddhist sutras, both methods are discussed under the rubric "mindfulness of the body" (*kāyagatānusmṛti*). Sarvāstivāda-Vaibhāṣika treatises and pre-fifth-century Chinese translations of Indian meditation treatises, meanwhile, describe them as the "internal" and "external" forms of the impurity meditation, respectively.[18]

In the descriptions of these practices found in early Sarvāstivāda or Sarvāstivāda-inspired treatises such as the *Mahāvibhāṣā* or the *Śrāvakabhūmi*, the external impurity meditation requires an actual corpse or a painting or sculpture of a corpse. The meditator first contemplates it, grasps its image (*nimitta*), and then imagines his or her own body in a similar condition (Kritzer 2017). Later literature, however, describes a purely imaginative exercise, without the need for an external corpse of any kind.[19] Following these instructions, a meditator simply imagines his own body transforming into a skeleton and then focuses his mind upon it. It is this version of the meditation

17. On the "white bone contemplation" in Indian and Chinese sources, see Abe 2014. Although "white bone" (白骨) can just mean "skeleton," in the *Chan Essentials* the color of the skeleton one sees is relevant and not always white (see, e.g., 1.7.2). For this reason, I translate *baigu guan* as "white bone contemplation" rather than "skeleton contemplation." The earliest Chinese source to describe the procedure later called by this name is Kumārajīva's *Meditation Scripture* (*ZCSM*, T.614:15.272a). It is also mentioned in the *Da zhi du lun*, also translated by Kumārajīva, which, however, does not present it as the general form of the impurity contemplation (as does the *Meditation Scripture*), but only as the "purity liberation," the third of the eight *vimokṣas* (*DZDL*, T.1509:25.215b18–22). The term "white bone contemplation" itself is first attested, as far as I can determine, in the *Da banniepan jing* (T.374:12.516c14)—in one of the unparalleled sections not known in other versions of this text—translated into Chinese probably in the 420s (J. Chen 2004).

18. Dhammajoti 2009b, 248–263; Dessein 2014; Kritzer 2017. Theravāda sources, in contrast, classify only the corpse meditation as the *aśubha-bhāvanā*, putting the meditation on internal body parts within "mindfulness of the body" (Ñāṇamoli, 1976, 173–190; 235–259).

19. Greene 2013, 273–276. The canonical *smṛtyupasthāna* texts themselves can be read as implying a purely imaginative exercise (Ñāṇamoli and Bodhi 1995, 1192n150). Actual instances of meditative corpse viewing are, however, also clearly mentioned in very early Indian Buddhist sources (Norman 1969, 42).

on impurity that is described in the *Abhidharmakośa-bhāṣya*, where it is the introductory method of meditation par excellence:

> The practitioner who wishes to meditate on impurity first fixes his mind on some part of his own body, such as his big toe or his forehead, or wherever else is pleasing to him. Then, purifying the bones by progressive imagination (*adhimokṣa*) of the rotting away of the flesh, he sees only the skeleton. In order to extend his imagination, he next imagines (*adhimucyate*) a second skeleton in exactly the same way until, by progressively taking in the monastery, park, and countryside, he imagines the earth encircled by the ocean as full of skeletons. Then, in order to gather in his mind, he gathers in until he imagines just his own skeleton.[20]

This form of the contemplation of impurity is what Chinese Buddhist sources call the "white bone contemplation" and for which the *Chan Essentials* was, by a long measure, the most elaborate account in any text from any era.

In the first section of the first sutra of the *Chan Essentials*, the Buddha prescribes to Kauṣṭhilananda a version of this practice:

> Fix[21] your thoughts on the tip of your left big toe. Carefully contemplate one segment of the toe. Imagine it swelling. Carefully contemplate it until it is very clear. Then imagine the swelling bursting open. When you see the first segment [of bone beneath], make it extremely white and pure, as if glowing with white light. Seeing these things, next contemplate the entire toe bone. Make the flesh strip away until you see the toe bone. Make it extremely clear, as if glowing with white light. (1.1.1)[22]

Next, the meditator must continue to imagine (*xiang* 想) the flesh stripping away from each successive bodily segment until he sees (*jian* 見) the white bones beneath, proceeding first up the legs, then to the ribs, chest, and finally arms (1.1.2–3). Then the meditator must focus on his head, contemplating (*guan* 觀) first its different layers of skin and then, proceeding inward, the brain and its "channels" (*mai* 脈). He must then contemplate

---

20. *aśubhāṃ bhāvayitukāma ādito yogācāraḥ / svāṅgāvayave cittaṃ nibadhnāti pādāṅguṣṭhe lalāṭe yatra vāsyābhiratiḥ / sa tatra māṃsa-kleda-pātādhimokṣa-krameṇāsthiviśodhayan sakalām asthisaṃkalāṃ paśyati / tathaiva ca punar dvitīyām adhimucyate yāvad vihārārāma-kṣetra-krameṇa samudraparyantām pṛthivīm asthisaṃkalāṃ pūrṇām adhimucyate 'dhimokṣābhivardhanārtham / punaś ca saṃkṣipan yāvad ekām eva svām asthisaṃkalām adhimucyate citta-saṃkṣepārtham* (*Abhidharmakośabhāṣyam*, 338.5–10). Translation by Gethin 2006, 98, with some modifications and following the emendations to the Sanskrit suggested by Silk 2000, 289.

21. The verb *xi* 繫, which I generally translate as "to fix," is used throughout the *Chan Essentials* to mean focusing the mind on an object. Its literal meaning, "to tie," is close to that of the verb *ni*+√*bandh* that is used in the *Abhidharmakośa-bhāṣya* passage cited above.

22. 先當繫念著左脚大指上，諦觀指半節。作泡起想。諦觀極使明了。然後作泡潰想。見指半節，極令白淨，如有白光。見此事已，次觀一節。令肉劈去，見指一節，極令明了，如有白光。(*CMY*, T.613:15.243b27–c2).

his throat and then his internal organs, concluding with the so-called receptacle of undigested food (*āmāśaya; shengzang* 生藏), wherein he sees the many worms that aid in digestion (1.1.5). The meditator must then imagine that all his internal organs liquefy and flow into his stomach, whence he vomits them up into a heaping mass on the ground. Evacuating himself of all fleshy bits, only his skeleton then remains (1.1.7). After a brief narrative interlude, in which Kauṣṭhilananda follows this method and becomes an arhat (1.1.9–10), the Buddha continues his instructions, now directing them to a generic meditator who must repeat the "white bone contemplation," beginning this time from the forehead (1.2.1.1), until he sees skeletons filling the entire world (1.2.1.3). He must then repeat it again for other forms of the corpse, imagining himself as a broken, crumbling skeleton (1.2.2.1), a corpse whose flesh "darkens and oozes like fatty meat scorched by the rays of the sun" (1.3.1), a bloated corpse (1.4.1), a corpse like a sack of skin (1.5.1), an inflated sack of skin (1.6.1), a fresh corpse (1.8.2), detached bones (1.10.3), and so forth. These assorted ways of viewing the body as a corpse clearly take inspiration from, but do not exactly reproduce any known version of, the common classification of the contemplation of impurity into subtypes based on the stage of decay of the corpse viewed by the meditator.[23]

Contemplation, Imagination, and Confirmatory Visions

Because later Chinese Buddhist sources often used them indiscriminately, the various verbs of mental activity prescribed in the *Chan Essentials* and *Methods for Curing* may at first glance seem only vaguely differentiated from one another: verbs such as "contemplate" (*guan*), "imagine" (*xiang*), "see" (*jian*), or "bring to mind" (*nian*). However, these words, at least as *verbs*, are in fact used with precision.[24] To "contemplate" (*guan*) is almost always to direct the attention to something that is presumed to *already* exist or to have previously been seen in a vision. The verb "imagine" (*xiang*)—which I sometimes translate as "meditatively imagine" or "meditative imagination" in order to bring out its particular valence within this body of literature—refers to the meditator's use of the mind to newly *create* a mental object or vision that was not already there. "To see" (*jian*), finally, refers to the meditator's sudden perception or apprehension of something *new*, in the progress of the visionary narrative, that has come into being or been revealed in some way. These usages are relatively strict. The active manipulation of the object of the meditator's attention or vision—for example, its transformation, under the direction of the meditator's mind, into something else—is almost never

23. Indian sources usually name nine or ten stages of bodily decay (Dhammajoti 2009b, 258–263; Dessein 2014, 134).

24. As *nouns*, the words are not always distinguished; either can refer to the entirety of a previously described meditation practice (see *Chan Essentials* 1.1.2, n. 16).

called "contemplation" (*guan*).[25] In some cases, the verb "contemplate" designates the initial focus of the mind on the object while an additional verb then describes the active manipulation of it, such as in the passage above where the meditator must "contemplate the toe bone *and make* the flesh strip away" (觀一節令肉劈去) or, elsewhere, "contemplate [his] body *and make it into* a skeleton" (自觀身作一白骨人; *Chan Essentials* 1.2.2.1). Most often, however, a different verb appears in such cases—*xiang*, "to imagine," a word that throughout the *Chan Essentials* and *Methods for Curing* describes the active manipulation of visionary objects or the creation of new ones.[26]

The "creation" of visionary objects denoted by the verb *xiang* does not, however, refer only to *phenomenological* creation. The mere act of coming to mentally "see" something is not itself to "imagine." When the meditator, in the opening scenes of the first sutra of the *Chan Essentials*, focuses his attention on, and eventually comes to see, his brain, lungs, liver, spleen, or the millions of worms in his gut, this is all "contemplating," not "imagining" (*Chan Essentials* 1.1.5). In contrast, when he envisions the flesh of his toe swelling and then bursting open (1.1.1), this is imagining, not contemplating.

These contrasts align closely with the Sarvāstivāda-Vaibhāṣika distinction between the two kinds of "mental application" (*manaskāra*): (1) mental application with regard to what is real (*tattva-manaskāra*) and (2) mental application based on *adhimukti* (*adhimukti-manaskāra*).[27] The contrast here is between the mind taking as its object something real—*dharma*s, truths such as impermanence, or one's own skeleton or internal organs—and its counterfactual, imaginative perception of things through the power of "conviction" (*adhimukti*), such as when a meditator sees the flesh of his body rotting away.[28]

Some version of this contrast seems to inform the clear distinction in

---

25. Though *guan* is used in the texts primarily in reference to visual objects, it occasionally introduces discursive meditation topics: "He contemplates *that* his body is empty and free of any distinguishing marks" (*Chan Essentials* 3.26.15). As I suggest below, the *Chan Essentials* and *Methods for Curing* use *guan* to mean meditatively directing the mind toward an ontologically real object. This reading fits with the cases where *guan* is followed by a discursive object because, to take the cited passage, it is in fact true, in Buddhist reckoning, that the body is empty. "Contemplating" this is therefore attending to something that is *real*. In both texts, the more usual verb for meditative consideration of Buddhist doctrinal truths in a discursive vein is *siwei* 思惟, which I translate as "reflect" (see *Chan Essentials* 1.2.2.2, n. 56).

26. *Xiang* also occasionally introduces "thoughts" of a discursive nature (*Chan Essentials* 2.19.2.3; 3.27.4). But, in contrast with the topics that are the object of *guan* (see previous note), the object of *xiang* is never a statement of Buddhist doctrinal truth. Hence *guan* and *xiang* are being carefully distinguished at this level as well.

27. Dhammajoti 2009a, 219–222. Cf. *Śrāvakabhūmi*, 3.136 (*bhūta-manaskāra* rather than *tattva-manaskāra*).

28. *Apidamo shun zheng li lun* (*Nyāyānusāra*), T.1562:29.672a16–b8. On the various senses of "adhimukti / adhimokṣa" see Sakurabe 1975, 34–39; Dhammajoti 2009b, 272–273. As a verb, *adhi+√muc* can point to more than a mere subjective mental state, namely, to a willful act that "changes something by magic into something else" (Edgerton 1953, 2:14, "adhimucyate"; see also Cone 2001, 93, "adhimuccati").

the *Chan Essentials* between "contemplating" (*guan*), which is directing the mind toward something that already exists, and "imagining" (*xiang*), which is generating, by the power of the mind alone, a new object of perception that does not actually exist in the world.[29] (Note that the expression *guanxiang* 觀想, a common word in later Chinese Buddhist literature for the mental activity of meditation, never occurs in either the *Chan Essentials* and *Methods for Curing* or any of the Contemplation Scriptures.) The contrast between *guan* and *xiang* is therefore based not on their mere phenomenology as different mental states but on the putative ontology of their objects, making it difficult to translate them using neutral, "etic" psychological terminology. (*Guan*, for example, could be described as the kind of mental activity that produces *clairvoyance*, something for which we do not have, suffice it to say, a ready English equivalent.)

Because its object is *unreal* and thus arguably merely a delusion, there was debate in Indian Buddhist literature concerning the soteriological value of meditative practice making use of "mental application based on *adhimukti*," some schools arguing that this could not, in itself, lead to liberation.[30] We may see traces of this discomfort in certain parts of the *Chan Essentials* and *Methods for Curing* where certain visions are dismissed as mere "false imagination" (*wangxiang* 妄想).[31] Still, on the whole "meditative imagination," as we may call it, is the key activity within the program these texts prescribe.

Whatever the Indian traditions these texts took inspiration from, casting imagination as a potent form of action was also in keeping with broader intellectual trends in fourth- and fifth-century China. Imaginative visionary journeys were already a long-established part of Chinese religious culture (Schipper 1995; Robinet 1993), and imagination, as a special faculty deployed by the poet, painter, or landscape aficionado, was a much discussed belletristic ideal. Some scholars have suggested that its appeal among the Chinese literati of this era owes something to Buddhist inspiration (Tian 2005), and while this may be true to some extent, fifth-century

29. The *Chan Essentials* may have drawn this terminological specificity from Indian Buddhist meditation literature. Note, for example, how in the brief passage from the *Abhidharmakośa-bhāṣya* cited above, it is always the verb *adhimucyate*—which I translated as "imagine" and which is here functionally equivalent to *xiang* in the *Chan Essentials*—that describes the meditator's perception of the flesh rotting away from his body, but *paśyati* (to see) that describes his perception of the bones, which unlike the rotting flesh really do exist as such. Though *xiang* in the *Chan Essentials* parallels *adhimucyate* in the *Abhidharmakośa-bhāṣya* passage, in Chinese translations of Indian Buddhist texts *xiang* often translates *saṃjñā* (conception), a word also used in the context of meditation (Vetter 2000, 26). Indeed, the frequent combination of *xiang* in the *Chan Essentials* and *Methods for Curing* with verbs such as *qi* 起 (give rise to), *sheng* 生 (produce), or *zuo* 作 (make) are clearly calques on the usual Buddhist-Hybrid Sanskrit construction of X-*saṃjñā ut+√pad* (Edgerton 1953, 2:552), "form a mental conception X." These calques had, by the fifth century, become naturalized within the language of Chinese Buddhist literature.

30. Cox 1988, 51; Dhammajoti 2009b, 281–286; Eltschinger 2009, 193.

31. *Chan Essentials* 1.2.2.4, 1.14.5, 1.15.2.4, 1.18.7, 4.31.14.

Chinese Buddhist meditation literature itself, at least at the level of terminology, suggests a contrary direction of influence. For it is only in the examples of this literature that were composed in China rather than translated directly from Indic originals—namely, the *Chan Essentials*, the *Methods for Curing*, and above all the Contemplation Scriptures, especially the *Amitāyus Contemplation Scripture*—that the key form of meditative action is so consistently called "imagination" (*xiang*).[32]

Although contemplation and imagination are the key meditative *techniques* proposed in the *Chan Essentials* and *Methods for Curing*, of equal or even greater importance is the concept of "seeing" (*jian* 見), a verb used in these texts, and in ordinary Chinese grammar as well, to indicate not just the attempt to perceive something but the completed act of perceiving it (Geaney 2002, 41). Most of the meditative practices in the *Chan Essentials* and *Methods for Curing* thus lead to some final act of *seeing*, the second step in the basic sequence I outlined above.

The "seeing" that a given meditative technique produces is more than the perfect seeing of things only imagined earlier, however. In other words, meditation in the *Chan Essentials* and *Methods for Curing* is not just a matter of *visualizing*—gradually refining one's visual imagination until finally seeing with perception-like clarity—some already specified object or scene.[33] What the meditator ultimately comes to "see" are things—often said to arise suddenly or without effort or intentionality—that could never have been anticipated based only on the prescribed meditative techniques. Thus while in the white bone contemplation detailed in the introductory instructions in the *Chan Essentials* the meditator is first directed to imagine the flesh of his body gradually rotting away until seeing a complete, pure white skeleton, this is not the end, for then:

> Four *yakṣa*-demons suddenly spring out of the ground, their eyes flaming and their tongues like poisonous snakes. Each *yakṣa* has six heads and each head is different—one like a mountain, the others like the heads of a cat, a tiger, a wolf, a dog, and a rat. Their hands are like those of an ape. The tips of each of their ten fingers are poisonous snakes.... Their horrid appearance is truly frightful. These four *yakṣa*s then stand in a line before the practitioner, each bearing on its back the nine kinds of corpses. (1.1.7)

32. Notably, the "A format" sections of the *Five Gates*, which contain an earlier form of material that would eventually get rewritten as the *Chan Essentials* (see chap. 4), barely mention imagination (*xiang*) even when describing concrete visions. The parallel passages in *Chan Essentials*, meanwhile, use this word frequently. This might imply that the re-description of Buddhist visionary meditation practice in terms of imagination (*xiang*) was something that occurred primarily in sources written or compiled by Chinese authors, rather than those directly translated from Indic-language sources.

33. On the concept of "visualization," a word coined by European experimental psychologists in the late nineteenth century, see Greene 2016c.

By way of closure to this section of the sutra, the Buddha then declares to Ānanda that this sight is "the initial confirmatory vision (*jingjie* 境界) of the meditation on impurity" (1.1.8).

This word *jingjie* was used in medieval Chinese Buddhist literature to translate several distinct albeit related Indic technical terms, including *viṣaya, jñeya,* and *ālambana.* All these words, in the context of meditation, can denote what we might call the meditator's "cognitive object"—that thing or idea toward which the meditator directs the mind, and of which the meditator eventually gains perfect cognition. In the context of fifth-century Chinese Buddhist meditation literature, however, we must usually construe *jingjie* not simply as any cognitive or meditative object but as the cognitive object (most often a concrete visionary object) that is *normatively* associated with a given level of attainment, and hence whose appearance as an object of experience serves to confirm that attainment. These events (which some classical Indian Buddhist meditation treatises also describe, albeit in a generally simpler form) I term "confirmatory visions" or, when outside their usual visionary modality, "confirmatory experiences."[34]

The raison d'être of the *Chan Essentials* and *Methods for Curing* is the description of these confirmatory visions and—especially in the *Chan Essentials*—the arrangement of them in an ordered, hierarchical, and canonical or canonically inspired set of named stages. In contrast to more commonplace meditation treatises, the *Chan Essentials* names these stages not in order to discursively explicate their natures as discrete psychological states, nor to explain the concrete techniques of meditation that produce them, but to identify the normative levels of Buddhist soteriological attainment for which the visions in question, whose description claims the lion's share of the text's attention, are the evidence.

These texts, in other words, do not answer the question *what truth or doctrine is realized at each stage of the path,* but rather *what stage of the path has one attained when this experience occurs?* If, as Sven Bretfeld's (2015) cogent argument has it, traditional path treatises such as the *Visuddhimagga* use the timeless story of a meditator ascending the path to awakening to frame the vast edifice of Buddhist systematic thought, the *Chan Essentials* and *Methods for Curing* can be said to do something quite different. They use the formal stages of the Buddhist path as a frame that gives canonically significant meaning to a kaleidoscopic array of elaborate visions. And we might even further say that inasmuch as these visions are sometimes said to be but a small fraction of what will be seen by those who reach a given stage, readers are invited, among other things, to imagine that their own idiosyncratic meditative visions, or those of others, might also turn out to be true signs of sanctity of some kind.[35]

---

34. For a more detailed discussion of "confirmatory visions" in the *Chan Essentials, Methods for Curing,* and other fifth-century Chinese *chan* scriptures, see *Chan Before Chan,* chap. 2.

35. The *Chan Essentials* states on several occasions that it contains only a small sample of the visions that successful meditators will obtain (1.12.7, 1.18.20.3, 3.24.4, 3.27.5, and 3.30.6).

Treating Meditation Gone Awry

Although most of the individual sections of the *Chan Essentials* and *Methods for Curing* depict the ideal meditator as eventually obtaining concrete visions that confirm a particular, named achievement, the route is not necessarily a linear one. It is not simply that a given practice either produces the desired confirmatory vision or not. Often, in the third and fourth steps of the basic sequence, the meditator must first respond in some way to earlier visions or experiences, not all of which are good or pleasant. These earlier visions are, in this way, presented as signs indicating the necessity of the prescribed responses.

These responses, and the situations that prompt them, take several different forms. One recurring pattern occurs under the name "inverse contemplation" (*yiguan* 易觀) or "inverse meditation" (*yixiang* 易想).[36] The second section of the *Chan Essentials* gives the first instance of this. After the meditator repeats the first exercises and again comes to see the heaping mass of his disgorged internal organs (1.2.1.1), he must perform an inverse contemplation to prevent excessive disgust from arising, which might lead to suicide.[37] The inverse contemplation is here accomplished by imagining white light glowing from within one's bones. By meditating in this way and coming to see the white light, the meditator—or, rather, the successful meditator—then has a vision of the aforementioned heap of impurities being consumed by the *yakṣas* (1.2.1.2). Although this sequence is short, its logic is similar to what occurs in situations where more elaborate confirmatory visions are involved: the sign that a given practice has been successful—in this case, the meditation on white light to eliminate excessive loathing—is not merely the full accomplishment of the method as it was prescribed, but the subsequent appearance of a vision whose content was not itself prefigured within the instructions.

---

36. *Chan Essentials* 1.2.1.1, 1.3.3, 1.4.4–6, 1.12.5, 1.14.1, 3.27.2. These expressions occur often enough to suggest they are technical terms. The source of the idea of the "inverse contemplation" is unclear. If derived from Indian Buddhist literature in Chinese translation or otherwise, one candidate would be *vivarta*, "turning away," the fifth of the six stages of breath meditation (*ānāpānasmṛti*) that are much discussed in the *chan* scriptures (Deleanu 1992). According to these accounts, at the stage of *vivarta* the meditator ceases considering the "particular characteristics" (*svalakṣaṇa*) of breath itself and instead discerns its "general characteristics" (*sāmānyalakṣaṇa*)—impermanence, non-self and so forth (Matsuda 1989, 19)—thereby beginning the process of abandoning the defilements. In Kumārajīva's *Meditation Scripture*, the word *vivarta* was translated as *zhuanguan* 轉觀, meaning either the "shifting contemplation" or the "shifting of 'contemplation,'" contemplation (*guan*) being the fourth stage of breath meditation (*ZCSM*, T.614:15.275b7–11). As I discuss below, the "inverse contemplation," in the *Chan Essentials*, often involves meditating on the emptiness of previously discerned objects. There might, therefore, be some connection between *zhuanguan* in Kumārajīva's text and the word *yiguan* ("inverse contemplation") in the *Chan Essentials*.

37. This echoes the famous canonical tale of the monks driven to suicide by their meditations on bodily impurity; see Wiltshire 1983 and Anālayo 2014. For another example, see *Chan Essentials* 1.4.3.

The inverse contemplation itself operates in several different modes. In its first and second occurrence (1.3.3), it is a kind of "purity" meditation that counteracts the loathing generated by the contemplation of impurity.[38] But in its next instance, it is a meditation on the emptiness of both impurity and purity (1.4.4–5). It thus embodies in miniature the basic character of the path of meditation in the *Chan Essentials*, in which each successive practice effectuates progress but also leads to a problematic condition—signaled by concrete visions, states of bodily or mental disruption, or emotions such as fear—whose countering, by some further practice, leads to the next and higher level. This idea is also foundational to the *Methods for Curing*, whose methods cure specific meditatively induced problems, but then usually also lead to formal progress along the path.[39]

Although they are not explicitly categorized as such, we can identify four distinct treatments prescribed by the *Chan Essentials* and *Methods for Curing* in such situations. First, the meditator, in some cases, must respond to the problematic situation by giving attention to a directly opposing idea or image, usually by way of an extended flight of meditative imagination (*xiang*). It is this that occurs when, as described above, the meditator counteracts excessive loathing by imagining something pure. But there are many other examples, not all of which are explicitly identified as an inverse contemplation. Some occur in the *Chan Essentials* (1.14.1, 1.16.1), but many more feature in the *Methods for Curing*, which dispenses, to take but a few examples, methods for eliminating disturbing noises—by imagining one's eardrums coated in ghee (1.2.3); curing meditatively induced madness—by imagining the channels of one's heart irrigated with divine milk (1.3.3); taming the excessive bodily heat generated in the fire *samādhi*—by imagining one's body bathed in light (1.4.1); and curing lust-induced madness—by imagining smearing one's eyes with impure sexual fluids (1.7.1–7).

Second, when the problematic state is a physical malady, it often can be treated by special foods or medicines.[40] (I discuss these ideas in more detail below.) Third, some meditative visions are said to be signs of past sins indicating the need for a ritual of repentance (*chanhui*) whose success in purifying the sin will be revealed by a new and different vision.[41] As mentioned above, the *Chan Essentials* provides only generic information about the required rituals of repentance—that one must create a pure ritual space,

38. In this instance, the "inverse contemplation" may have originally had some connection to the so-called purity liberation (*śubha-vimokṣa*), third of the eight liberation (*vimokṣa*) meditations. According to some Sarvāstivāda-Vaibhāṣika sources, the "purity liberation" is a meditation on pure or beautiful forms that counteracts or opposes the first two liberations, which are discussed as versions of the contemplation of impurity (Dhammajoti 2009b, 267–268, 276–281).

39. See "Somatic Soteriology" in chap. 3.

40. *Chan Essentials* 1.13.3, 1.14.2, 1.16.1, 1.17.3, 1.18.13, 3.24.2.

41. *Chan Essentials* 1.1.7, 1.2.1.5, 1.13.3, 1.14.6, 1.17.3, 1.18.8, 1.18.14, 1.18.16, 2.19.1.9, 2.19.1.10, 2.19.2.4, 2.20.7, 2.20.8, 3.23.1. See also chap. 3.

venerate the buddhas at the six daily intervals, and so forth—while the *Methods for Curing* has an entire subsection describing one such ritual in detail (1.9).

Fourth—and only here do we get to methods typically thought of as Buddhist "meditation"—in many cases the fear, loathing, or bodily illness generated by an earlier exercise is to be countered by reflecting on the emptiness or mind-produced nature of the previously experienced vision, the meditator's own person, or all things. The instructions for these exercises draw for the most part on mainstream Buddhist doctrines and use well-known canonical pericopes and categories of analysis such as the five *skandhas* and twelve links of dependent origination (*pratītyasamutpāda*).[42]

That progress along the path of meditation ultimately requires all four of these treatments together may well be the central argument of both the *Chan Essentials* and *Methods for Curing*. The thirteenth section of the *Chan Essentials* provides a particularly clear illustration of how these different modalities of practice were imagined as working together. Having first carried out the white bone contemplation, the meditator now turns his gaze downward and sees through the earth to the bottom of the universe, where a horde of demons spews fire that fills the world (1.13.1). At this point, the meditator "becomes extremely alarmed and afraid.... He is perpetually afflicted by pain in his heart and his skull feels as if it is about to burst" (1.13.2). Entering trance again, he sees "ten giant millipedes... with twelve hundred feet resembling poisonous dragons" (1.13.3). This vision is explained as a sign that the meditator must carry out a ritual of repentance and consume medicine made from butter. Then he must perform an inverse contemplation that directly vanquishes the vision of the mass of fire:

> He should imagine the various mountains as ice or frost that is melted by the fire, which, when it blazes high, merely steams his body warm [and does not burn it]. He further imagines a dragon and makes it spew forth rocks that smother the fire. He must then imagine the rocks broken into dust. The dragon further spews forth wind, which gathers up all the tiny particles of dust and piles them up until they form a mountain, upon which innumerable trees and thorny brambles then grow spontaneously. Then, pure water of five colors flows through the brambles. These waters collect at the summit of the mountain, frozen still like a mass of ice. (1.14.1)

The practitioner then contemplates his own skeleton again and sees millions of skeletons of all different kinds—yellow, green, or purple, smeared with pus, blood, or dirt, or "like infected sores, leaking noxious, multicolored pus"—filling the universe (1.14.3). Yet again the meditator feels great fear and has a further vision of demons coming to attack him (1.14.4). This then necessitates a meditation on emptiness:

42. See, e.g., *Chan Essentials* 1.14.6, 2.20.15, 2.20.17, 4.31.18.

> He must then extend his right hand and tap the skeletons with his finger, thinking: "These skeletons come from false imagination and appear only because of incorrect discrimination. My own body is also thus. It arises from the four elements and is but an [empty] village where the six sense gates cohabitate." (1.14.5)

Here, as throughout, even though the meditator contemplates the empty, mind-produced nature of the visionary objects, this does not lead to their total elimination. Rather, this act of meditation produces another, different vision that confirms that emptiness has been successfully contemplated.[43] Thus, when the meditator has touched his finger to the visionary skeletons and contemplated their emptiness:

> The white skeletons shatter into dust, forming a pile on the ground like a snow-covered mountain. As for the other skeletons of various colors, they are suddenly eaten up by a giant snake. On top of the mound of white snow there is a white-jade person, his body straight and imposing, thirty-six *yojana*s tall, with a neck as red as fire and white light glowing in his eyes. The various white waters and crystal pillars all suddenly enter the crown of the white-jade man's head. The many dragons, demons, vipers, snakes, monkeys, lions, and cats all run in fright. Fearing the great fire, they scurry up and down the tree. The ninety-nine snakes... all gather atop the tree. The poisonous dragon twists and turns, coiling around the tree. The practitioner further sees a black elephant standing beneath the tree. (1.14.5)

Then the meditator must go even further, contemplating not just the emptiness of the skeletons but the emptiness of even the earth-element of which they are composed.[44] This leads to yet more visions that signal the meditator's further progress toward awakening.

Strategies of Objectification

Because the *Chan Essentials* and *Methods for Curing* do not aim to expound an architectonic doctrinal edifice, it would be dangerous to claim that any

43. *Chan Essentials* 1.15.2.5, 1.17.5, 1.18.4, 1.18.7–8, 1.18.11–12, 1.18.16, 2.19.1.12–2.19.2.2, 2.20.17–18, 3.26.15, 4.31.2–3, 4.31.14, 4.31.21–27, and *Methods for Curing* 1.4.2.

44. Despite its non-Mahāyāna doctrinal framework, the *Chan Essentials* explicitly endorses the emptiness of *dharmas* (see 1.18.15, where "the emptiness of all *dharmas*" is added to the standard four marks of suffering, emptiness, impermanence, and non-self). In the East Asian Buddhist exegetical tradition, that *dharmas* too are "empty" is usually taken as a defining characteristic of Mahāyāna philosophy. In fact, the emptiness of *dharmas* was endorsed by at least some otherwise entirely non-Mahāyāna Indian schools (Harrison 1982, 225–227). Of particular note for an assessment of the intellectual background of the *Chan Essentials* and *Methods for Curing* is the comment in the *Mahāvibhāṣā* that in the "stages of the contemplation [methods] of the *yogācāras*" (瑜伽師修觀位) meditators realize the "non-self of all dharmas" (一切法非我; *Apidamo da piposha lun*, T.1545:27.45a23).

single key makes sense of their "system" of meditation. We can, however, point to at least one guiding logic that encapsulates the main difference between how they depict progress along the path of meditation and how such progress usually appears in classic path treatises and better-known Buddhist meditation manuals. I will call this the logic of *objectification*: in these texts, stages of meditative progress more typically defined in terms of the psychological attributes of the meditator's inner mind—attributes such as the absence or presence of specific mental defilements or virtues and the discernment of Buddhist truths—are discussed as things whose presence is communicated, not only to the meditator but to readers of these texts as well, primarily by the occurrence of visions that are "objective" in that they are differentiated from each other by their content, by the concrete objects and events that occur within them.

The logic here is akin to that which Freud attributes to the dream. In an oft-quoted passage, he puts it this way:

> The direction taken by the displacement [that occurs during dreams] usually results in a colorless and abstract expression in the dream-thought being exchanged for a pictorial and concrete one. The advantage, and accordingly the purpose, of such a change jumps to the eyes. *A thing that is pictorial is, from the point of view of a dream, a thing that is capable of being represented.*... A dream-thought is unusable so long as it is expressed in an abstract form; but when once it has been transformed into pictorial language, *contrasts and identifications of the kind which the dream-work requires, and which it creates if they are not already present, can be established.* (Freud 2010, 354, emphasis mine)

For Freud, the distinctly *pictorial* quality of the dream makes it possible for abstract ideas or feelings, otherwise hidden in the subconscious of his patients, to be represented—and thereby to become available objectively (that is, as *objects*) and hence publicly, for interpretive work. In a similar manner the *Chan Essentials* and *Methods for Curing* claim that meditative visions make something within the meditator's mind that is hidden even to himself—the particular psychic transformations constitutive of the meditative attainments he may or may not have reached—communicatively available as a series of concrete images. These images are now accessible, though not necessarily immediately understandable, to the meditator. They are also potentially accessible to anyone else who might have the skill and knowledge to interpret them correctly, because as concrete images they can now be reliably described to others.

Hence for both Freud and our fifth-century Chinese Buddhist meditation texts, what is ultimately at stake in the *textual* elaboration of visionary experiences is the authority of someone other than the visionary.[45] To claim

45. Obeyesekere thus moves too quickly, I think, when he suggests that we should see

that awakening and other states of meditative attainment are signaled by dreamlike visions concretizes what might otherwise be an irredeemably individual experience. It makes such attainments a matter of truly personal experience—*you* must really see this vision, it is claimed—while at the same time objectifying, and hence making public, the interpretive authority concerning the significance of those experiences. Sources from fifth- and sixth-century China often imply that the ability to accurately judge the import of the meditative experiences of others was a key attribute of the true *chan* master.[46] To this extent, the *Chan Essentials* and *Methods for Curing* present themselves not so much as manuals of instruction for those wishing to practice meditation, but as authoritative texts containing the knowledge needed to judge the meditative experiences of others.

Visionary Dramas

Within the accounts of meditative attainment in the *Chan Essentials* and *Methods for Curing*, we can point to two distinct modalities of objectification. First is the lengthy presentation of concrete visionary scenes, something that occupies most of the space within the texts as a whole. What any given scene or element of these scenes is supposed to mean—why these visions in particular are the sign of the attainment in question—is often impossible to say. In a set of visions from early in the *Chan Essentials*, for instance, the meditator sees a row of skeletons each raising their right hand, then both hands, then extending their ten fingers (1.2.1.3–4). The accumulation of small, precise details certainly gives the impression that something significant is happening here. But all we can say for certain is what is then declared explicitly—that this is the vision that occurs upon reaching the named attainment.

In a few cases, the content of the vision seems to be something like a concrete instantiation of what formal doctrine says will occur at the given level of attainment. In mild form, this becomes a kind of dramatization of the abstract truths the meditator supposedly realizes at the moment in question. At the climax of the first sutra, the meditator must contemplate emptiness, following a typical script for the discursive analysis of his person as merely an agglomeration of parts animated by the chain of dependent

---

in the dreamlike visionary experience the "original" form of the Buddha's awakening, one only later reformulated into the "rational" categories of Buddhist doctrine (2012, 19–74). Because he believes that formulations of the Buddha's awakening in terms of visionary experience were the raw material out of which later doctrinal explanations were crafted, Obeyesekere does not ask what purposes the framing of Buddhist awakening or meditative attainment (or any other religious achievements) in distinctly visionary terms might have served. At the least, texts such as the *Chan Essentials* and *Methods for Curing* show that the historical relationship between textual elaborations of Buddhist meditative experience and attainment as a distinctly visionary phenomenon, and abstract, impersonal, or doctrinal formulations thereof, is more complex than Obeyesekere assumes.

46. See *Chan Before Chan*, chap. 2.

origination (1.18.4). The vision that confirms his eventual realization of emptiness takes this form:

> He suddenly sees . . . his body becoming as completely transparent as beryl. Just as a person carrying a beryl parasol can look up at the sky and see everything clearly, at this moment, because the practitioner has contemplated emptiness and learned the teaching of non-self with respect to both himself and others, he sees his two legs as tubes of beryl, and looking down he sees [through them] all kinds of marvelous things. (1.18.4)

The meditator's cognitive grasp of emptiness is here seemingly objectified as a vision of his body becoming literally empty and transparent. In another passage, having contemplated emptiness, "he sees his body as the trunk of a plantain tree, without anything solid inside. Or else he sees his heart-organ as foam on the water. He hears sounds from outside as echoes" (1.15.2.5). The images of a (pithless) plantain tree, foam, and an echo are all standard canonical metaphors for the foundational Buddhist idea that all things are ultimately empty and insubstantial. Here, however, these images are not metaphors but concrete objects of experience. These are the experiences that occur, it is claimed, to a meditator who grasps emptiness. They are thus the objective signs of his having truly reached this understanding.[47]

The longest and most involved example of this kind is the narrative—spreading across multiple sections of the *Chan Essentials* with a clear beginning, middle, and end—concerning an enormous tree first seen growing from a pool of water in a set of visions eventually said to be associated with the "ninety-eight defilements" (1.12.7–8). Later, when contemplating emptiness, the meditator has a further vision in which a host of wild beasts and demons take refuge in the tree, beneath which a black elephant appears (1.14.5). The elephant attacks the creatures, and the tree begins to shake (1.14.7). Four elephants, and then eight, appear and wrap their trunks around the tree and try to uproot it but cannot (1.17.2). Eventually, the elephants again battle the demons and a lion joins the fray to aid them (1.17.4). Adamantine mountains then emerge from the ground and protect the tree (1.18.2); after a further meditation on emptiness, the elephants destroy the adamantine mountains and resume their assault (1.18.12). When the elephants themselves are then killed by a demon, from the bottom of the universe appear "five adamantine (*vajra*) wheels" and "five adamantine beings" who hack the tree and burn away its branches, leaving behind only the "heartwood" (1.18.17–18). This event is clearly supposed to be a momentous one, as the text declares that arhatship is now inevitable (1.18.19), though formally this stage is classified only as the full attainment of the contempla-

47. For similar examples, see *Chan Essentials* 1.3.3, 1.16.1, 3.24.1, and *Methods for Curing* 1.4.2. That the meditator is said to *hear* the echoes makes clear that these images are not purely metaphorical.

tion of impurity. (Mainstream Buddhist doctrine normally holds that certainty of arhatship occurs only at the stage of stream-entry). Visions associated with the tree resume in the fourth sutra (4.31.11). As one of the final visions, just before the meditator becomes an arhat, a "mighty warrior" appears and uproots the tree, which is then burned into dust by a fire generated from the "four bright jewel-like fruits in the practitioner's heart" (4.31.27).[48]

It is fairly obvious that the destruction of the tree, slowly unfolding across this long visionary narrative, is the instantiation of the destruction of the meditator's defilements (*kleśa*), which some Sarvāstivāda-Vaibhāṣika sources indeed analogize to a tree that the path to liberation uproots.[49] The black elephants presumably have something to do with the *dhyāna*s: four and then eight in number, perhaps incarnating the four *dhyāna*s and four formless *samāpatti*s, they shake but do not destroy the tree, a task left for the "adamantine" beings or the "great warrior," just as, according to some doctrinal sources, *dhyāna* "shakes" the mountain of the defilements, which is destroyed only by the adamantine *samādhi* (*vajropamasamādhi*).[50] The narrative of the tree is the most involved example where the visions lend themselves to being read as the transmutation, into concrete images, of the mental transformations that formal doctrine associates with a given stage of meditative attainment. But on a smaller scale, other such examples are scattered throughout both the *Chan Essentials* and the *Methods for Curing*.

Yet more interesting than our ability to occasionally read the visions in such terms is that the *Chan Essentials* and *Methods for Curing* themselves do *not* do this. Their purpose as texts was not, it seems, to provide such explanations but merely to indicate the correlations between the visions and the attainments they are claimed to signal.[51] What the *Chan Essentials* tells us about the attainment of the first stage of sainthood (stream-entry)—and

---

48. Some seemingly unrelated visions of a tree also occur in the third sutra (3.26.11–12).

49. *Apidamo da piposha lun*, T.1545:27.238b7; *Apitan piposha lun*, T.1546:28.184a4. The *Abhidharmakośa-bhāṣya* compares the defilements to a tree because they continue to give rise to evil karma just as a tree produces flowers and fruits each year (*Abhidharmakośabhāṣyam*, 150–151; La Vallée Poussin 1988, 2:437–438). In *Chan Essentials* 4.31.28, just after the tree has been destroyed, the meditator reflects that the "seeds and branches of the ninety-eight defilements fill the triple world." The defilements are also discussed using tree imagery in some of the Contemplation Scriptures (*GFSMH*, T.643:15.682b28; *Guan Puxian pusa xing fa jing*, T.277:9.392c8–12). More broadly, vegetation imagery is a common Buddhist simile for the continuity of karma (Collins 1982, 218–24).

50. *DZDL*, T.1509:25.218b4–8. On the "adamantine *samādhi*," see *Methods for Curing* 1.14.14, n. 196. An equation between the elephants and the *dhyāna*s is, however, troubled by *Chan Essentials* 4.31.27, where there are only *six* elephants. I am unaware of traditional similes comparing the *dhyāna*s to elephants. In one of the Contemplation Scriptures, the power of *nianfo* (念佛) is likened to a black elephant who recovers a stolen jewel by tearing down the tree in which the thief hides (*GFSMH*, T.643:15.695c5–19).

51. The one exception is *Methods for Curing* 1.9.6. Importantly, however, this passage does not simply explain the symbolic meaning of certain visionary images but gives an account of the words through which the meditation master should convey this information to a student who has already experienced them, in the context of a ritual of repentance.

this is relevant historically because it shows us what information about becoming a stream-enterer was deemed to be important by those who wrote and used these texts—is primarily that at this moment the meditator

> sees his body suddenly become very large and shine brightly, as impressive as a mountain made of the seven treasures.... [The light of] lotus flowers flows into his heart. It fills his *maṇi*-jewel heart ten times....A light suddenly appears above his head like a golden cloud or a jeweled canopy, or like silver. It enters his body through the crown of the head and shields the light of his *maṇi*-jewel heart. (3.26.15)

It might well be possible to construe the details of this scene as somehow instantiating specific things that Buddhist doctrine says occur when one becomes a stream-enterer. But knowing this information is apparently not necessary in order to determine who is a stream-enterer and who is not. The answer to this question, the *Chan Essentials* asserts, is simply the one who sees *this.*[52]

Meta-preaching

The second modality of objectification in the *Chan Essentials* and *Methods for Curing* is via the trope that I will call *meta-preaching*—the sign of certain meditative attainments is presented as a visionary experience in which the Buddha, buddhas, or other deities *preach* to the meditator the discursive content of key Buddhist doctrines or truths. Though the logic of these scenes is not made explicit, the idea seems to be that hearing this content is an experience equivalent to the realization of the truths in question, which is what frequently characterizes advanced meditative attainment in more typical Buddhist meditation literature. These events occur throughout the two texts, particularly when the meditator is on the cusp of a momentous attainment. In one of the final episodes of the first sutra, as the meditator gets close to attaining the contemplation of impurity, he has a vision of the seven buddhas of the past, headed by Śākyamuni, who preach for him the four noble truths and explain the principles of suffering, emptiness, impermanence, non-self, and the emptiness of all dharmas (1.18.15–19). Similar encounters with buddhas who preach standard doctrines occur throughout the *Chan Essentials* and *Methods for Curing*, with the preaching scene either the primary event or one element of a more complex vision.[53]

Because these texts are themselves framed as sutras preached by the Buddha, the scenes of meta-preaching lead to some problems of voicing. In

52. The passage cited here adds a caveat: one who is truly a stream-enterer will also not further violate any of the five precepts. (That stream-enterers are incapable of such violations is a standard doctrinal claim.) This, however, is the only passage in the *Chan Essentials* that links the validity of a given attainment to external behavior.

53. *Chan Essentials* 2.19.2.3, 2.20.10, 2.20.15, 3.30.4; *Methods for Curing* 1.4.2, 1.5.16, 1.6.5, 1.8.2, 1.13.4, 1.14.12, 1.14.17, 2.11.

Chan Essentials 4.31.15, the meditator has a vision in which Śākyamuni Buddha appears and preaches not a list of doctrines, as the visionary buddhas usually do, but instructions for the "contemplation of the wind element." These instructions are then described in a long series of passages (4.31.15–28) stylistically indistinguishable from the meditation instructions elsewhere in the *Chan Essentials*. Here, in other words, it is unclear if we have instructions for the contemplation of the wind element delivered by the (historical) Buddha of the outer-frame narrative of the sutra, or the content of preaching whose delivery to the meditator in a vision constitutes a sign of attainment.[54] Whether these ambiguities are intentional or not is unclear. In any event, it is more commonly the case that scenes of meta-preaching do not describe the content of the preaching in full but merely state in list form the topics that the visionary buddhas in question will explain.

That hearing the Dharma directly from a buddha is an enormously powerful experience is, of course, an old and pervasive idea in Buddhism. In the early scriptures, it is in fact at such moments, rather than while meditating alone in the forest, that the Buddha's disciples are most commonly depicted as reaching awakening (Masefield 1987). Early Mahāyāna sources similarly emphasize using meditation to make contact with buddhas presently dwelling in other world systems so as to hear their teachings (Harrison 2003). Thus at least part of what has motivated the trope of meta-preaching in the *Chan Essentials* and *Methods for Curing* is presumably that this is how meditation was thought to ultimately work—it leads, eventually, to some kind of real contact with buddhas or other Buddhist deities who through their preaching instantly transport the meditator into enlightenment.

But whatever background may inform this understanding of what happens during meditation, as we consider what other functions these ideas may have served in the social settings where this kind of meditation literature was written and circulated, we should also note how these scenes of meta-preaching provide an additional way of objectifying meditative attainment. By asserting that what occurs at moments of advanced meditative attainment is a vision of the Buddha preaching the content of the doctrines whose inner realization is elsewhere held up as the substance of such attainments—the four noble truths, dependent origination, and so on—this inner realization becomes objectified. That is to say, its occurrence for a given person is made into an event that is describable in words, easily communicated to others and thereby laid claim to, and reliably differentiated from alternatives: namely, a vision of the Buddha or buddhas preaching the discursive content of just those very doctrines.

54. *Methods for Curing* 1.8.2 is similar in this regard.

CHAPTER 3

Ritual Repentance, Buddha Bodies, and Somatic Soteriology

The previous chapters give a basic overview of the historical significance of the *Chan Essentials* and *Methods for Curing* and consider in broad terms their approach to the practice of Buddhist meditation. In this chapter I explore in greater detail three of the most distinctive ideas about Buddhist meditation found in these texts: (1) the notion that progress along the meditative path includes, as an integral component, the performance of rituals of repentance; (2) the claim that meditation leads to tangible encounters with some form of the Buddha or buddhas; and (3) the principle of what I call "somatic soteriology," the idea that the path to Buddhist awakening implicates the transformation of not just the mind but also the body.

Although these ideas all appear in some forms of later Buddhist meditation literature, in both India and China, their place in the history of Buddhism as a whole has remained unclear because they are not discussed at length in the systematic, pre-Tantric Indian treatises such as the *Visuddhimagga* or *Yogācārabhūmi* that have typically informed our sense of "traditional" approaches to Buddhist meditation. (The idea that one might use meditation to contact the buddhas or other deities is, however, well attested in some strains of early Mahāyāna literature.) Among other things, the *Chan Essentials* and *Methods for Curing* show us that by the late fourth century, if not earlier, all three of these ideas were already part of a widespread and long-lasting culture of Indian Buddhist meditation, one not restricted to a specifically Mahāyāna orientation, and that these traditions were brought to China in the fifth century, in one form or another, by the many Indian *chan* masters who helped establish the first enduring traditions of Buddhist meditation in East Asia. For these reasons, the accounts of these ideas in the *Chan Essentials* and *Methods for Curing* comprise a crucial link in our understanding of their evolution across both South and East Asia.

Repentance and the Ritual Independence of Meditation

One striking feature of the *Chan Essentials* and *Methods for Curing*, when compared with early canonical accounts of Buddhist meditation or middle-period Indian treatises on this subject, is that they depict the path of meditation as being punctuated by a great deal of activity that might at first appear to be distinct from meditation itself and which we might heuristically call "ritual-devotional" in nature. Within the two texts, this activity is generally characterized as "repentance" (*chanhui* 懺悔), a term that in Chinese Buddhism denotes various kinds of ritual acts, of varying degrees of complexity, carried out either individually or communally and making use of a range of objects of worship and devotion. In broadest terms, the stated aim of a Chinese Buddhist ritual of repentance was the elimination or attenuation of sin (*zui* 罪), meaning transgression of Buddhist precepts that one has voluntarily assumed, such as the monastic or lay precepts, or bad karma more generally, accumulated in this life or lifetimes past. In early medieval China, repentance was one of the most common modalities of Buddhist ritual writ large.[1]

That seated Buddhist meditation would, in practice, occur within a wider, more complex ritual and devotional setting is not in itself surprising. The question, however, is the relationship between that context and meditation itself. Many distinctly modernist forms of Buddhism see meditation as something easily and ideally detachable from such contexts, as something that can and should be taken up without these external practices that are, by way of this framing, dismissed as mere cultural trappings (McMahan 2008). This understanding aligns to some extent with the interpretations of early Western scholars who took Buddhist doctrine to imply that meditation, as the inner transformation of the mind, is a higher practice, superior to and hence normatively different from the mere accrual of good karma accomplished by typical Buddhist cultic activity or appeals to the help of powers and deities lying outside oneself.[2]

As more recent scholarship argues, however, to insist that meditation (mind) is inherently opposed to ritual (body / action) is a "Protestant" reading of Buddhism that does not accurately reflect how the activity we usually call meditation was and is carried out in Buddhist societies (Swearer 1995, 208). Yet it is important to recognize that the misreading proffered by early Western scholars and many modernist Buddhists has not been pulled out of a hat:

---

1. The role of repentance in medieval Chinese Buddhism is discussed in Kuo 1994; Williams 2002; Hong 2014; and *Chan Before Chan*, chap. 4.

2. See, for example, Heiler 1922 and Smart 1958. Even quite recent scholarship continues to distinguish the inner, psychologically grounded and technique-based cultivation of "meditation," as understood in Buddhism or with Buddhism as a key example, from "devotion," which aims for an outward contact with external agents or objects, supposedly most prevalent in or characteristic of Western religions (Eifring 2016, 5).

classical Buddhist treatises do indeed typically present seated meditation as something that ideally transcends everything outside itself, including any (other) ritual activities. For example, when the model Buddhist practitioner depicted in the *Visuddhimagga* sits down to meditate, nothing more is needed. Like the Buddha, after his abandonment of fasting and bodily mortification in favor of meditation (*dhyāna*), the meditator of the *Visuddhimagga* is depicted continuing along an entirely inward path as an increasingly refined consciousness trending ever upward toward awakening.

Yet, even though they present the higher reaches of the path in this way, treatises such as the *Visuddhimagga* do acknowledge that meditation depends on a loosely defined ritual context inasmuch as they say that success in meditation is only possible for those who have first perfected *discipline*.[3] This is an ancient idea within Buddhism, enshrined in the canonical formula of the so-called three trainings consisting of discipline (*śīla*), meditation (*dhyāna*), and wisdom (*prajñā*), with the three elements conceived as an ordered set of virtues, the latter depending on the former.

Claiming that meditation is dependent on discipline places it within a ritual context in at least two respects. First, because it means that before practicing meditation one must receive the Buddhist discipline (the precepts), that is to say, one must first become a monk, nun, or lay follower through a ritual of ordination or initiation. Second, because if after initiation one transgresses the precepts, one's purity must be reestablished through the appropriate ritual means. Both of these points are mentioned, albeit usually briefly, in Indian meditation treatises composed prior to the fifth century. For example the so-called *Meditation Scripture* (*Zuo chan sanmei jing*), translated into Chinese by Kumārajīva in the early 400s, makes clear, in its opening passages, that potential meditators must first ritually purify themselves of any transgressions of the *vinaya*, though this short notice is the only discussion of these ideas in this text.[4] Thus, while classical Buddhist meditation treatises typically do acknowledge that meditators must also engage in external rituals, they assign those rituals an entirely *preliminary* role. Formally, they are no more than vehicles for establishing the purity necessary to begin or succeed in meditation, and this model informs later Buddhist literature on meditation from a variety of traditions (Crosby 2005).

What distinguishes the *Chan Essentials* and *Methods for Curing* from traditional schemes is that they explicitly make external ritual far more than a preliminary purification.[5] In the *Chan Essentials*, the ordered sequence of meditative attainments leading to liberation includes many different moments when the practitioner must cease meditation and carry out a ritual of repentance (*chanhui*). Moreover, these rituals are inherently linked to the meditator's progress because it is the content of previously attained medita-

---

3. For a more thorough treatment of these issues, see *Chan Before Chan*, chaps. 3 and 4.
4. *ZCSM*, T.614:15.270c28–271a5.
5. In this paragraph I summarize *Chan Before Chan*, chap. 3.

tive visions that signals the need for them, and their success or failure is similarly communicated by subsequent visions. By the time the *Chan Essentials* and *Methods for Curing* were composed, in the early fifth century, seated meditation probably had in *practice* long been joined to a wider ritual program in this kind of comprehensive manner. But these texts remain notable in the extant history of Buddhist literature as the earliest examples of formal meditation treatises that present the core part of the path to liberation as not just an inner meditative journey but something necessarily punctuated by external rituals.

Because we do not possess a complete archive of medieval Buddhist literature, we can wonder if the *Chan Essentials* and *Methods for Curing* were in fact as unprecedented, in these respects, as they appear to us now. Though this is certainly possible, we can still gain some appreciation of their novelty by comparing them to an immediate ancestor, a fifth-century Chinese text transmitted under the title *Essential Procedures from the Chan Scriptures in Five Gates* (*Wu men chan jing yao yong fa*).

As I discuss in greater detail in Chapter 4, the textual formation of the *Chan Essentials* took place when previously existing but schematic Chinese meditation manuals similar in form and content to the *Five Gates* were expanded, elaborated, and written out in the form of a Buddhist sutra. We do not know if the *Five Gates* was itself the translation of an Indic-language meditation manual, as its classification in later catalogs suggests, or if it was also a purely Chinese composition. Whatever the case, since the *Chan Essentials* was based on it, the *Five Gates* is at least one step closer to the Indian Buddhist literary tradition. It is therefore noticeable that even in those passages where the *Chan Essentials* directly parallels the *Five Gates*, the latter omits any mention of repentance. Setting parallel sections of the two texts side by side, we see that one of the ways the *Chan Essentials* expands on the material in the *Five Gates* is by explaining when certain meditative visions, usually described without comment in the *Five Gates*, indicate that a meditator must carry out a ritual of repentance. This can be seen in the parallel passages in table 1, which, within the larger scheme of the *Chan Essentials*, occur just before the meditator attains stream-entry, the first level of sainthood. As the two passages make clear, one thing the *Chan Essentials* adds to the instructions in the *Five Gates* is an explicit reading of the significance of certain meditative visions, interpreting them either as a sign of progress ("not far from attaining the path") or—and this is crucial—as requiring a ritual of repentance. In other words, what is described in the *Five Gates* as a linear, internal path of seated meditation and visionary experience is now supplemented by a parallel track of rituals of repentance that will apparently be required *throughout* the meditator's journey.

In portraying seated meditation as one element of a wider endeavor, the *Chan Essentials* and *Methods for Curing* are among our earliest traces of the kind of elaborate meditative-ritual programs that in Chinese Buddhism would eventually be codified by Zhiyi, in the late sixth century (Stevenson

Table 1. Comparison of parallel passages in *Chan Essentials* and *Five Gates*

Chan Essentials 3.23.1[a]	*Five Gates*[b]
[The practitioner] must be further instructed to fix his thoughts and contemplate the white bones. He must make the scattered bones collect in one place, in a pile like wind-blown snow, white like a snow-covered mountain. <u>If he sees this, [it means] he will be able to easily attain the path.</u>	Next instruct [the practitioner] to focus his mind and after causing the bones to become white and pure make them scatter and float to the ground. On the ground they are like snow.
However, if he has violated the precepts, either in this life or a past life, the pile of bones will appear like ash or dirt instead, or he will see various strange creatures on the surface of the pile. <u>In that case he must again repent by confessing his transgressions to a wise person.</u>	Or they may be like rotting earth. Above them there may be white light, or various strange creatures.
<u>After repenting,</u> he will see an intense white light surrounding the pile of bones and reaching up into the formless realms. Whether in trance or not, he will feel constant ease and happiness.	Instruct [the practitioner] to continue contemplating. If he says: "I continue to see [the bones] like this, and within my body I feel happiness," then [the master] must say...

[a] 復當更教繫念觀諸白骨。令諸散骨，如風吹雪，聚在一處，自然成積，白如雪山。若見此事，得道不難。若有先身犯戒者，今身犯戒者，見散骨積，猶如灰土，或於其上，見諸黑[>異]物。復當懺悔，向於智者，自說己過。既懺悔已，見骨積上，有大白光，乃至無色界。出定入定，恒得安樂。 (*CMY*, T.613:15.259c25–260a3). See *Chan Essentials* 3.23.1 for text-critical notes.

[b] 次教注意，令骨白淨已，分散飄落。在地如雪。在地或如爛土。其上或有白光種種異物。教更觀之。若言續見如是，身中快樂，當語... (*WMCJ*, T.619:15.328a6–8).

1986). In South Asia too, different versions of such programs eventually became fundamental to both Tantric Buddhism and even many traditions of Theravāda Buddhist meditation (Crosby 2013). Given the eventual prevalence of such systems, in a wide variety of Buddhist settings, it would not be out of place to surmise that the practice of Buddhist meditation, on the ground, has always been integrated in this way into a diverse ritual and cultic milieu. At the least, there is certainly no reason to see this as a *Chinese* innovation even though the *Chan Essentials* and *Methods for Curing* were largely composed in China. Just as with the details of meditation posture, for which these texts are the earliest written sources, their historical novelty may lie primarily in their preservation of certain kinds of information about the practice and theory of meditation that in earlier eras had simply never been committed to an authoritative written form.

The Bodies of the Buddha

The *Chan Essentials*, and to a lesser extent the *Methods for Curing*, present an unusual set of ideas about the different forms in which a meditator will encounter the Buddha. The vocabulary used here is not perfectly consistent, nor is there an exact precedent or source for this account of the different bodies of the Buddha and the manner in which they can be met. But the basic idea is easy enough to state: that even though the Buddha is gone from this world, and even though there are no other buddhas presently living in distant worlds (as typical Mahāyāna understanding would have it), one can nevertheless make tangible contact with Śākyamuni, the historical Buddha of our era, as well as with the other six buddhas of the past known from mainstream Buddhist literature. Contact with these various buddhas is, moreover, a central part of the path of meditation and instrumental in the attainment of its fruits.

Below, I first summarize the various scenarios in which these ideas appear, primarily from the *Chan Essentials*, and then consider their possible sources and their significance in the context of fifth-century Chinese Buddhism.

Modalities of Encountering the Buddha(s)

Within what it calls the eighteenth contemplation, the final stage of the contemplation of impurity, the *Chan Essentials* provides the first of several descriptions of the meditator's encounter with the buddhas.[6] Having contemplated emptiness and gained a vision of the black elephants and the tree of the defilements, the meditator must now repent and again focus his mind on his own body, whereupon he will see countless buddhas filling the universe (1.18.9). "Gleaming and resplendent," these buddhas are described as "buddha images" (*foxiang* 佛像) or "transformation buddhas" (*huafo* 化佛).[7] Upon seeing them, the meditator also sees his own body as pure, "a tall and stately mountain made of the seven precious substances." These visions are then criticized as ultimately unreal. The meditator must reflect that just as it is a delusion to see his own body as pure, since it is in truth impure, so too any pure buddha images are but mind-generated illusions (1.18.10–11). They are neither the Buddha's flesh-and-blood "body of birth" (*shengshen* 生身) nor his more abstract "Dharma body" (*fashen* 法身). Meditating thus on the

6. A brief earlier encounter is also mentioned in 1.11.2–3.

7. In translated Chinese Buddhist texts, *huafo* often renders *nirmāṇa-buddha*, a magical apparition, identical to his own body, created by the Buddha. The idea of a *nirmāṇa-buddha* should be distinguished from the Buddha's *nirmāṇa-kāya* or "transformation body," a concept that in the more developed, "three body" systems characterizes any historical, flesh-and-blood buddha as a mere "transformation" (*nirmāṇa*) of the formless Dharma body.

illusory nature of any pure internal or external body, the practitioner then experiences further visions of the black elephants (1.18.12), contemplates emptiness, and is thrust into a state of near madness (1.18.13), following which he must again repent.

Within this ritual of repentance—and here we enter the culminating section of the entire first sutra—the meditator

> ...will suddenly see the Tathāgata's [the Buddha's] true emanation (如來真影),[8] who touches his head and commends him: "O Dharma child, well done, well done! Today you have properly contemplated the buddhas' teaching of emptiness."

The meditator then sees the emanations (*ying* 影) of the five hundred great arhats and the six other buddhas of the past. When the Buddha's emanation touches the meditator's head again, he suddenly sees the "material bodies" (*seshen* 色身) of the seven buddhas as well as the many transformation buddhas they then emit (1.18.15). The meditator again reflects that the buddhas have, in truth, only *two* bodies: a material body (seemingly equivalent to the "body of birth" mentioned earlier), which the meditator has seen, and a five-part Dharma body, which he has not yet seen (1.18.16). The meditator then considers the buddhas' material bodies to be illusions, dreams, and echoes, and he contemplates their emptiness. This causes the disappearance of the transformation buddhas, but *not* of the emanations of the seven buddhas and great arhats, who now preach further teachings, hearing which the practitioner becomes destined for arhatship (1.18.19).

The second sutra of the *Chan Essentials* presents a similar sequence of visionary encounters with the Buddha, though it uses slightly different terminology. The context now is explicitly the meditation method of *nianfo*, "bringing to mind the Buddha," which the practitioner must carry out by first imagining an image (像) of the Buddha, described in rich but idiosyncratic iconographic detail (2.19.1.3–7).[9] Following the same pattern used in the first sutra with the imagined skeletons, the meditator expands his field of vision and sees multiple copies of the imagined buddha image filling the universe (2.19.1.8), as well as similar images in different postures (walking and lying down). All these images then emit a host of transformation buddhas (2.19.1.10–11).

Just as in the first sutra, the meditator must next negate the ultimate reality of these ever-multiplying images by conceiving of them as mind-

8. I discuss the term "emanation" (*ying*) in greater detail in "The Emanations of the Buddha" below.

9. The unusual descriptions here are clearly based on artistic representations of the Buddha, rather than the classical scheme of the Buddha's primary and secondary marks. Very similar descriptions occur in the *Ocean-Samādhi Contemplation Scripture* (Yamabe 1999c, 216–262).

produced. Then, in a pointed endorsement of the single-buddha-at-a-time cosmology of mainstream Buddhism:

> [The meditator] must then think: "In the past there was a buddha named Śākyamuni, who instructed sentient beings his entire life. After forty-nine years in this world, he disappeared into final nirvana like a fire going out when the fuel is spent, extinguished without remainder. Today I use my mind to imagine, and by imagining I see many images. *In arriving these images do not arrive from somewhere, and in going do not go anywhere.* I see them falsely, by way of imagination." With this thought, the images gradually disappear, leaving only a single image sitting with legs crossed atop a lotus flower. (2.19.1.12)

Although the meditator is again urged to reject as unreal any mind-generated visions of the Buddha (I will return below to the import of the specific language used here) and to consider that the Buddha is well and truly gone from this world, this does not prevent some kind of true contact with the Buddha. For just as in the first sutra, a real and efficacious counterpart to the merely imagined transformation buddhas or buddha images then appears. Contemplating that even the single image he beholds is itself merely manifested by the power of the Buddha, the meditator resolves to contemplate what is now called the "true Buddha" (*zhenfo* 真佛; 2.19.2.2).[10]

> He then immediately sees the [true] body of the Buddha, which is as marvelous as pure beryl encasing adamant.... Holding a pitcher of water in his hands, the Buddha stands in the air... [and] pours it on the practitioner's head. It fills the interior of his body, and he sees the eighty families of worms gradually shrivel up wherever the water flows within his body.... Those whose sinful karma has been removed will now hear the Buddha preach the Dharma.... Having been taught these things, because he has seen the Buddha and heard the marvelous Dharma the practitioner's mind will be liberated and he will soon become an arhat as surely as water follows its course. (2.19.2.2–3)

Finally, the fourth sutra of the *Chan Essentials* again presents a similar sequence of events.[11] Here the meditator begins by contemplating the Buddha (*guanfo* 觀佛). This leads initially to a vision of millions of buddhas (4.31.1), but this vision is dismissed on the grounds that ultimately speaking the Buddha is not a "material image" (*sexiang* 色像) but rather the Dharma

10. Here, the "true" Buddha is contrasted with a single "image" (*xiang* 像) that is dismissed as "merely an emanation." This terminology differs from the first sutra, where the "emanation" was synonymous with the "true" Buddha.

11. Other examples of an encounter with a buddha that is *not* negated as empty or merely mind produced occur later in the second sutra, as well as in the third sutra (2.20.10, 2.20.15, 3.26.2, and 3.29.3). Only one of these later examples uses the term "true buddha" (3.26.2).

body, here described as the buddha-qualities of the ten powers, four fearlessnesses, eighteen unique qualities, great compassion, and great love (4.31.2).[12] Despite this apparent rejection of seeing the Buddha as a concrete material thing, as in the first sutra the meditator transcends his initial vision only to arrive at a subsequent, truer yet still concrete one:

> He suddenly feels a great happiness. He sees his body as a mass of lotus flowers filling the universe in all directions. He sees seated buddhas sitting atop lotus flowers, preaching the profound teachings of emptiness, non-self, non-wishing, and non-doing, and the entrances to the fourteen stages of sainthood. (4.31.3)

This vision of a *multiplicity* of buddhas is, however, still not the ultimate goal. Again, the meditator must consider that beyond the buddhas' material bodies is the Dharma body (4.31.13–14). Moreover, with Śākyamuni Buddha having long since passed into nirvana, it can only be by "false imagination" (*wangxiang* 妄想) that one sees the Buddha as a material image (4.31.14). Once again, however, this meditation on the mind-made nature of the visions eliminates only their multiplicity. What remains, when the practitioner has done it successfully, is a single buddha who now addresses the meditator as "Dharma child" (as the so-called true emanation did in the first sutra), preaches a teaching that leads him onward (4.31.15), and later explains the three "gates to deliverance" (*vimokṣa-mukha*), hearing which the meditator becomes an arhat (4.31.29–30).

Across the sections of the *Chan Essentials* in which the meditator encounters the Buddha or buddhas in various ways, we can discern a basic pattern despite the inconsistency of the terminology. As a first step, by engaging in various meditation techniques, only some of which are focused specifically on the Buddha or his physical form, the meditator eventually obtains a vision of what are variously termed transformation buddhas (*huafo*), buddha images (*foxiang*), or, in 1.11.2, a "sixteen-foot" (丈六) buddha.[13] These visions are then all *negated:* the meditator considers them to have been merely *imagined*, and they disappear. In the first sutra (1.18.15) and fourth sutra (4.31.3), this leads to a further concrete vision of what is called either the "material body" (*seshen*) of the Buddha (or buddhas) or the "body of birth" (*shengshen*)—that is, the flesh-and-blood form in which the Buddha appeared on earth. However, this vision, even though seemingly superior to the visions of a multiplicity of transformation buddhas, must also be transcended, and to this end the meditator then contemplates the emptiness of any material image of the Buddha whatsoever, on the grounds that the Buddha's true nature is, rather, the Dharma body. But yet again, successfully contemplating these

12. These qualities are formally identified as the "Dharma body" in 4.31.14.

13. These labels all point to something similar in appearance to a statue or painting of the Buddha. On the "sixteen-foot" Buddha, see 1.11.2, n. 102.

things leads not to the negation of all concrete visions but to a more exalted one, a final and more substantial encounter with what the first sutra calls the Buddha's "emanation" or "true emanation" and what the later passages call the "true buddha" (*zhenfo*). The emanation or true Buddha appears to the meditator but also interacts with him: he preaches, touches the meditator's head, or consecrates him with pure water, immediately producing a momentous attainment such as arhatship or the certainty thereof. These encounters are all presented as tangible: the true Buddha the meditator meets is not an abstract principle or an indescribable absolute, but an embodied, resplendent form. These same ideas appear, in abbreviated form, in the *Methods for Curing*, which also discusses the process of making contact with the emanations of the seven buddhas of the past, whose preaching propels the meditator into awakening (1.14.10–11).

Theories of the Buddha's Embodiments: India and China

From the above summary we can see that the *Chan Essentials* and *Methods for Curing* have a broadly shared understanding of the various ways that successful meditators will or should encounter the buddhas. It is unclear, however, to what extent we should see this understanding as belonging to an integral theory of buddha bodies. In part, the problem is one of genre: these texts do not aim to expound a scholastic system but rather to label the experiences obtained during the course of an ideal meditator's progress using concepts, such as those of the "emanation" or "true buddha," whose significance to readers is already assumed.

Moreover, even if we were satisfied that we understood the meaning of those labels and their interrelations, it still would be unclear what the resulting system could be compared to. Indeed, the fourth and fifth centuries, in both Indian and Chinese Buddhism, was a time of enormous doctrinal foment concerning the different possible embodiments of the buddhas and, accordingly, the manner in which living beings in the present might hope to encounter them. Sources from this era proposed a profusion of new theories, each with different, though often overlapping terminology (Radich 2010 and 2011; Funayama 1995, 94–101), and none of these systems aligns precisely with what later would become the standard "three body" theory laid out in textbook accounts of the Mahāyāna. Nor have the nuances of this doctrinal history yet been fully charted by modern scholarship.[14]

We can, however, make two pertinent observations about how the *Chan Essentials* and *Methods for Curing* handle these questions. First, if a technical model of buddha bodies inspired them, directly or indirectly, it must have been one akin to the Sarvāstivāda-Vaibhāṣika theory according to which the Buddha has two bodies, a flesh-and-blood "body of birth" (*shengshen* 生身; **saṃbhavakāya*) and a "Dharma body" conceived as the corpus of qualities that define a buddha's gnosis or liberation, of which there were several

14. Some sense of the complexity of these questions can be gleaned from Radich 2007.

interrelated typologies (Radich 2010, 127–142). As Radich observes, the only known Indian Buddhist sources that use the term "body of birth" as part of such a theory are the *Mahāvibhāṣā* and the *Da zhi du lun*. The appearance of this term in the *Chan Essentials* in this meaning (1.18.10) is therefore noteworthy, as is the fact that the *Chan Essentials*, in the fourth sutra, similarly defines the Dharma body as the corpus of buddha-qualities (the eighteen unique qualities and / or the five pure *skandhas*) rather than the corpus of the Buddha's teaching (the meaning of the term in the early Buddhist scriptures) or the formless, indescribable absolute truth (its usual meaning in the three-body buddhologies of later Mahāyāna).[15] As with its enumeration of the stages on the path to liberation, discussed in Chapter 2, we see here again that the doctrinal background of the *Chan Essentials* and *Methods for Curing*, to the extent that one can be made out, is at least loosely Sarvāstivāda-Vaibhāṣika in orientation.

Second, it is possible to discern, in the *Chan Essentials* in particular, an active opposition to other ideas about the nature of the Buddha that we know were important in China at this time. Notable in this regard are the two passages, in the first and second sutras, that instruct the meditator to dismiss the reality of the transformation buddhas encountered during meditation on the ground that, being mind produced, they "do not come [to me], nor do I go [to them]."[16] This kind of language, in reference to a vision of the Buddha or buddhas, unmistakably recalls the best known early Mahāyāna text giving instructions for meditation on the Buddha's physical form: the *Pratyutpanna-samādhi* (*Banzhou sanmei jing* 般舟三昧經), which in early medieval China was the foundational scriptural warrant for the cult to the buddha Amitāyus / Amitābha.[17] However, the *Pratyutpanna-samādhi* uses the Perfection-of-Wisdom style language of "not coming and not going" primarily to explain how, even without one physically traveling to other world systems, meditation *does* produce true contact with the many buddhas presently living there (Harrison 1990, 40–42). It would seem, then, as if the *Chan Essentials* is refuting, on two grounds, precisely what the *Pratyutpanna-samādhi* proposes. First, the *Chan Essentials* forcefully denies the reality of any presently existing buddhas at all (2.19.1.12), pushing back in this way against a key claim of early Mahāyāna literature more broadly. And second, it uses the language of "not coming and not going" at cross-purposes—that

15. *Chan Essentials* 4.31.14. Other passages in the fourth sutra (4.31.1, 4.31.3) imply something similar but do not explicitly use the term "Dharma body."

16. 諸佛不來我亦不去 (1.18.10; *CMY*, T.613:15.253b17); 來無所從去無所至 (2.19.1.12; *CMY*, T.613:15.256a17). This same language, which can be found in a great many Chinese translations of Indian Mahāyāna texts, is deployed in reference to other kinds of visionary objects throughout the *Chan Essentials* (*CMY*, T.613:15.246b13; 246c23; 247a21; 247a24; 251a1).

17. Its full title is the *Pratyutpanna-buddha-saṃmukhāvasthita-samādhi-sūtra* ("The *Samādhi* of Direct Encounter with the Buddhas of the Present"). This sutra was first translated into Chinese in the late second century; see Harrison 1990, 207–272, for a description of its many Chinese translations and their problems of attribution.

is, not to argue that mind-produced encounters with other buddhas are as real as anything else (as the *Pratyutpanna-samādhi* has it), but to say that such things, as mere hallucinations, must be transcended in favor of the "true emanations" of Śākyamuni and the other buddhas of the past. It is these *past* buddhas who in the *Chan Essentials* are somehow accessible in exalted, tangible, and non-imagined form, and who, through their preaching, propel the meditator toward liberation.

Two aspects of the situation in fifth-century China help explain why some Buddhists might have proposed, or been inclined to accept, this understanding of the nature and significance of meditative contact with the buddhas. First, throughout the fifth century, in south China at least, some teachers actively denied the existence of buddhas other than Śākyamuni. Early sixth-century sources claim that these views were first promoted during the Yuanjia (424–453) era by a monk named Zhu Fadu 竺法度, who taught the "Hīnayāna" path and denied the validity of the Mahāyāna teachings (Boucher 2014). Arguing that "the buddhas of the ten directions do not exist," Zhu Fadu supposedly instructed his followers to worship only Śākyamuni and prohibited the reading of Mahāyāna scriptures.[18] Zhu Fadu's teachings were followed by at least some prominent nuns in the southern capital during his lifetime. That early sixth-century historians felt it necessary to criticize these traditions suggests they were still somewhat popular at that time.[19]

Second, the emphasis in the *Chan Essentials* and *Methods for Curing* on making real contact with the buddhas, and on distinguishing this from merely imagined encounters (described in language reminiscent of the *Pratyutpanna-samādhi*), may remind us of a famous moment in the early fifth-century epistolary exchange between Kumārajīva and Huiyuan 慧遠 (334–416).[20] This exchange began when the latter, after reading Kumārajīva's *Da zhi du lun*—the first translation into Chinese of an Indian Buddhist treatise (as opposed to a sutra) that systematically argues for Mahāyāna doctrines versus their Hīnayāna counterparts—posed a series of questions to Kumārajīva about these new teachings, many of them concerning the text's novel (to Huiyuan) treatment of the Dharma body of the Buddha as an instantiation of the Mahāyāna notion of ultimate emptiness.

While seemingly technical, Huiyuan's questions here were not purely theoretical. As discussions of the nature of the bodies of the Buddha invariably do, they bore on the practical matter of how, when, and in what forms ritualists or meditators might hope to make contact with the Buddha (Sharf 2002a, 116). Huiyuan had been deeply influenced by the Sarvāstivāda-Vaibhāṣika scholastic treatises translated in great numbers in the 380s under

18. *CSZJJ*, T.2145:55.41a1–2

19. The link posited between Zhu Fadu's teachings and nuns' communities in particular is especially intriguing in light of the records suggesting that the *Chan Essentials* and *Methods for Curing* were first written down at a nunnery; see "Record of Production" in chap. 4.

20. For a survey of this exchange, see Ōchō 1958–1979, 2:229–306; Zürcher 1972, 227–229; Wagner 1971; and especially Tu 2006, 137–182.

the supervision of his own teacher Dao'an 道安 (Palumbo 2013, 9–35), and he had reservations about the tendency of some Mahāyāna sources to assert that *all* tangible representations of the Buddha are necessarily "empty." Although Huiyuan was devoted to the *Pratyutpanna-samādhi* and the ritual worship of Amitāyus it promotes (Zürcher 1972, 219–221), he was apparently unsatisfied with the way it likens all meditative encounters with the buddhas to dreams:

> If the Buddha [encountered by a practitioner] is the same as something seen in a dream, then it belongs to one's own imagination (*xiang*). [According to the *Pratyutpanna-samādhi,*] when imagination is concentrated, trance (*ding*) is obtained and one sees the Buddha. [And as the *Pratyutpanna-samādhi* says] one sees the Buddha without him coming from outside and without one going to him.... [Yet] if the Buddha does not come [from outside,] how can there be liberation? Where would that liberation come from? *When speaking of a true stimulus that causes a response from outside, one should not use a dream as an analogy.*[21]

Scholars have often taken this and other questions he addressed to Kumārajīva as revealing Huiyuan's flawed grasp of Buddhism owing to his failure to think outside the categories of Chinese thought, or at the least, his commitment to a naïve Hīnayāna realism that could not grasp the Mahāyāna doctrine that all things, even buddhas, are empty (Robinson 1967, 109; Tian 2005, 74–75). Huiyuan, in this reading, is the eager but confused student trying but ultimately failing to grasp the subtleties of a Madhyamaka philosophy assumed to be consistent and unproblematic. And yet, as Tu Yanqiu has argued persuasively, this reading misrepresents Huiyuan's tone, which is not at all supplicating, and fails to give credit to his astute and careful questions, which contrast with Kumārajīva's often rambling and unsystematic replies. Huiyuan's questions, Tu suggests, are best read not as requests for instruction but as *challenges* issued by someone secure in his rank as a senior Chinese Buddhist monk and confident in his understanding, based on decades of study of mainstream doctrinal treatises (Tu 2006, 146).

Read more charitably, Huiyuan's question to Kumārajīva amounts to this: if the buddhas seen in meditation are mind produced and hence dreamlike, what distinguishes delusion from awakening? What difference would there then be between the dreams of an ordinary person and an encounter with the buddhas that is true inasmuch as it really does lead to liberation? What Huiyuan's question exposes is a tension inherent in a good deal of

21. 若佛同夢中之所見，則是我想之所矚。想相專則成定，定則見佛。所見之佛，不自外來，我亦不往 . . . 佛不來而云何有解。解其安從乎。若真感外應，則不得以夢為喻。 (Kimura 1960, 35; *Jiumoluoshi fa shi da yi*, T.1856:45.134b4–13). For a translation of Huiyuan's entire question and Kumārajīva's response, and an analysis of the issues at stake, see Jones 2008.

Mahāyāna philosophy—one that is inevitable when the semantic denial of an absolute distinction between delusion (us) and awakening (the buddhas) bumps up against the pragmatic effect of this assertion as a claim concerning how one might go from delusion to awakening by understanding this very truth. Such a tension plays out in various ways in later Indian, Chinese, and Tibetan Buddhist thought, but here it suffices to note that Huiyuan's doubts about the coherence of likening true encounters with the buddhas to mind-made dreams are not naïve, are not solely the result of his hopelessly Chinese perspective, and are not confusions for which Kumārajīva himself necessarily had a clear answer.[22]

To return to the *Chan Essentials* and *Methods for Curing*, the way these texts depict meditative contact with the buddhas shows that in the years following Huiyuan's death—often portrayed as a new era in which Kumārajīva's translations finally permitted a correct understanding of Mahāyāna emptiness—Chinese Buddhists did not cease longing for true but still concrete encounters with the buddhas as distinct from dreams, fantasies, or painted images.[23] Huiyuan would no doubt have nodded approvingly when the *Chan Essentials* sharply distinguishes between "imagined" (*xiang*) buddhas and the true emanations whose appearance is both the sign and cause of soteriological attainment. That the *Chan Essentials* presents these encounters in pointed opposition to dreamlike ones described in language reminiscent of the *Pratyutpanna-samādhi* may even suggest that we have here a kind of

22. Importantly, to judge from the Indian Buddhist literature he translated, Kumārajīva had no knowledge of the mind-only metaphysics of the only-then-emerging Yogācāra school, which might have allowed a more robust defense of Mahāyāna emptiness against an Abhidharmika-like skeptic such as Huiyuan and a more systematic explanation of the incipient form of mind-only ideas seen in the *Pratyutpanna-samādhi*.

23. An explanation of such encounters was the centerpiece of the theories invented by Chinese Buddhist scholiasts of this era concerning what they called the "two kinds of Dharma body" (二種法身). These theories, not fully prefigured in Indian sources, are discussed in the fragments that survive from the writings of key southern-dynasties Chinese exegetes (Funayama 1995, 94–101). These commentators typically made an initial division between the Buddha's "Dharma body" and his "sixteen-foot" (丈六) body, the latter denoting both the living Buddha (in the past) but also icons or statues of the Buddha (in the present)—in short, the tangible forms of the Buddha accessible even to ordinary beings. Some authors stopped here, saying that the "Dharma body" and the "sixteen-foot" body are ultimately nondual. But more commonly, the "Dharma body" was divided into a "true" (真) aspect, fundamentally quiescent and empty, and a "response" (應) aspect, which pervades space and time but is tangible and can appear in response to the prayers of living beings. Importantly, this concept of the "response" body did *not* aim to explain the "historical" Buddha, as would the *nirmāṇa-kāya* of the later three-body systems. The response body, conceptualized through the "stimulus and response" (*ganying* 感應) metaphysics of post-Han Chinese thought, was, rather, the form of the Buddha that appeared *in the present* through miracles, ritual, or meditative means. The *Chan Essentials*, however, may also be attempting to one-up these theories. For while most of the authors in question accepted that the "response" buddha is part of the "Dharma body," they reserved the epithet "true" for its unmoving (i.e., nonresponsive and hence imperceptible) aspect. The *Chan Essentials*, in contrast, explicitly calls the tangible buddha potentially encountered in meditation the "true buddha."

echo of Huiyuan's own doubts about that text—doubts, it would seem, that continued to percolate among southern Chinese Buddhists of the fifth century.

The Emanations of the Buddhas

When considering how the *Chan Essentials* and *Methods for Curing* may have fit into the intellectual landscape of early fifth-century Chinese Buddhism, we must take special note of the concept of the "emanation" (*ying*). In the first sutra of the *Chan Essentials*, and in a number of places in the *Methods for Curing*, this word denotes the true, real form of the Buddha that the meditator eventually encounters after various illusory forms have been experienced but dismissed as empty or otherwise unreal. This terminology is notable because the concept of the "Buddha's emanation" (*foying* 佛影) was widely discussed during this era, above all in connection with a famous pilgrimage site in the mountains around Nagarahāra (modern Jalalabad, Afghanistan), known in China as the "cave of the Buddha's emanation."[24] According to the legends first made known in China through early fifth-century texts such as the *Da zhi du lun* and the accounts of Chinese pilgrims who visited the cave, the Buddha, while he was alive, once cast his "emanation" into the walls of the cave, where it remained visible to later visitors. The emanation supposedly resisted copying and artists who tried could never capture it adequately. It was thus viewable only by those who visited the cave, where it appeared when seen from a distance but became invisible when examined up close.[25] In early fifth-century China, interest in this cave and the Buddha's "emanation" it contained was so great that Huiyuan built, in the hills around his temple, a replica of the cave and hung there a painted image of the emanation, whose appearance and iconography he determined in consultation with the foreign *chan* master Buddhabhadra, who had personally seen the original cave.[26]

Several famous poems and inscriptions for this painting, by Huiyuan

24. *Foying ku* 佛影窟. *Foying* is often translated as "Buddha's shadow." However, "shadow" is a misleading rendering of *ying*, which more broadly denotes anything cast by a body, be it darkness *or* light. In the case of the Buddha, it is the latter that is more relevant. Taken thus, the word *ying* is similar in meaning to the (etymologically related and sometimes interchangeable) word *jing* 景, the "iridescent emanation" by which the gods can illuminate the interior of a Daoist adept's body (Kaltenmark 1969).

25. The biography of Xuanzang, who visited it in the seventh century, reports rather that the image became visible in response to prayers and devotions (*Da tang da cien si san zang fa shi zhuan*, T.2053:50.229c26–230a12).

26. Zürcher 1972, 224–225; Rhie 2002, 113–137; E. Wang 2014. The *Ocean-Samādhi Contemplation Scripture* provides a detailed account of the founding legend of the cultic site in Gandhāra and a method for the "contemplation of the Buddha's emanation" (觀佛影; *GFSMH*, T.643:15.681b15–c1). This, however, is described as a meditation on the moment in the Buddha's life when he cast his emanation into the cave wall. In the *Chan Essentials* and *Methods for Curing*, in contrast, the emanation is separated from a specific narrative context and presented as a form of the Buddha one might encounter anywhere.

and others in his circle, have survived. Huiyuan's poem, although susceptible to a number of interpretations, can be read as an account not of the physical painting to which it was joined, but of the emanation itself—that is, the miraculous form in which the buddhas "respond" (*ying* 應) and become visible to a sufficiently devoted practitioner. This idea is made particularly clear in the following lines:

> When the stimulus [of the practitioner] is profound there is a response;
> when the striking is sincere, [the bell-like sage] reverberates in echo.[27]
> The sound thus bequeathed lingers in the grotto;
> salvific awakening is profoundly experienced.
> If you manage to contact it,
> your merit will be unprecedented.[28]

In his prose introduction to the poem, Huiyuan also discusses the emanation as the still-accessible counterpart to the Buddha's bodily form (*xing* 形), long since gone from the world. Not recognizing the reality of the emanation, skeptics in Huiyuan's own day, he writes, have wrongly given up hope of ever meeting the Buddha in person:

> The Buddha sometimes hides all traces of himself, thereby exalting what is fundamental [i.e., formlessness]; sometimes he manifests as a living being, thereby giving himself a fixed bodily shape. Sometimes he arises singly and of his own accord, in a realm we cannot access [in India in the past], sometimes he exists in dependence [on that earlier form], in the space of what exists [in the here and now].[29] The one that arises singly and of his own accord is the form; that which is dependent on it is the emanation [i.e., the form's "shadow"]. Now as for this profound encounter [with the emanation], is it dependent [on something else, and hence secondary,]

27. Here Huiyuan invokes the trope, common in the "dark learning" (*xuanxue*) idiom of this era, that the sage (*shengren* 聖人) is like a bell, by nature silent and unmoving, that still responds unfailingly when "struck" by circumstances or the inquiries of others (Ashmore 2010, 146–148).

28. 感徹乃應，扣誠發響。留音停岫，津悟冥賞。撫之有會，功弗由曩。(*GSZ*, T.2059:50.358b19–21; *Guang hong ming ji*, T.2103:52.198.a21–22); cf. E. Wang 2014, 417, whose translation I differ from in some respects.

29. "Arising singly... in a realm we cannot access" might also mean the unlocalized realm of the absolute Dharma body. But given how Huiyuan then links this realm to the Buddha's "form," and contrasts the "emanation" as something that depends on that form, at least part of what must be meant here is the living Buddha of history. Huiyuan can also be read as intentionally conflating the idea of the absolute Dharma body with the living Buddha of India's past. The idea of "dependence," especially the contrast between "having dependence" (*youdai* 有待) and "being without dependence" (*wudai* 無待), derives from the Zhuangzi. Huiyuan here raises the contrast between these two states only to then reject the making of such distinctions, a move characteristic of the Guo Xiang commentary to the Zhuangzi that provided so much of the vocabulary for fourth- and fifth-century Chinese intellectual discourse (Ziporyn 2003, 20).

> or not? As I see it, this would be like trying to make a distinction where there is no distinction. Indeed, the Dharma body is originally nondual, so who could draw lines between the form and the emanation? Yet those in the present day who hear about Buddhism all merely revere the Buddha's body of long ago, not realizing the divine response here and now. They but vainly know that the perfect teaching is without all form as they then try to delimit its perceptible traces by the activities [of the Buddha while alive in the past]. What a profound error![30]

For Huiyuan, then, although the Buddha's physical form is gone, he remains accessible as an emanation, a "divine response" in the present.

Given the appearance of "true emanation" as a technical term in the *Chan Essentials*, it is interesting that this rare expression also appears in some hagiographic accounts of the visionary encounters of those in Huiyuan's circle on Mount Lu.[31] As a way of referring to a concrete encounter with the Buddha ontologically and soteriologically superior to dream or fantasy, this concept evidently had a measure of social life in south China around the time when the *Chan Essentials* was put into final form.

As Erik Zürcher observed long ago, we know that obtaining a concrete encounter with a tangible, visionary form of the Buddha was an aspiration of many of those who frequented Huiyuan's community. Zürcher, however, sharply distinguished between this interest in a "concrete object of worship, perceptible by the senses," which he associated with "rudimentary, popularized techniques connected with the cult of Amitābha and the commemoration of the Buddha," and Huiyuan's interest in meditation (*dhyāna*), the "laborious procedures of mental concentration and trance of the Hīnayānistic type" that he assumed were unsuitable for or unappealing to the many lay followers in Huiyuan's community (Zürcher 1972, 222). In this analysis we see the same forced distinctions between "meditation" and "devotion," or *chan* and Pure Land, that have often guided the search, in this epoch of Chinese Buddhist history, for the germs of the traditions that in later centuries were sometimes (though not always) more clearly distinguished. If

30. 如來或晦先跡以崇基，或顯生塗而定體。或獨發於莫尋之境，或相待於既有之場。獨發類乎形，相待類乎影。推夫冥寄為有待耶，為無待耶。自我而觀，則有間於無間矣。求之法身原無二統，形影之分孰際之哉。而今之聞道者，咸摹聖體於曠代之外，不悟靈應之在茲。徒知圓化之非形，而動止方其跡。豈不誣哉。 (Gu*ang hong ming ji*, T.2103:52.197c24–198a7)

31. *Lushan ji*, T.2095:51.1039c11, describing the visions obtained, through the practice of *nianfo*, by Liu Yimin 劉移民, one of Huiyuan's best known aristocratic followers. The *Lushan ji* was compiled by Chen Shunyu 陳舜俞 (d. 1076) and is hence rather late for our purposes. The story of Liu Yimin's vision, however, is also told in two fifth-century sources: a letter from Huiyuan to Liu Yimin preserved in the *Guang hong ming ji* 廣弘明集, and an anecdote about Liu Yimin in Liu Yiqing's 劉義慶 (403–444) *Xuan yan ji* 宣驗記 (Ji Z. 2007, 288–293). These accounts do not use the term "true emanation." Still, given that interest in the Buddha's "emanation" seems to have been primarily a fifth-century phenomenon, I am inclined to believe that the *Lushan ji* does preserve an early version of Liu Yimin's story.

the *Chan Essentials* and *Methods for Curing* show us anything, it is that in the early fifth century, even while there were distinctions between different classes of Buddhists and the practices deemed accessible to them, encounters with a tangible Buddha and other concrete visionary experiences were not only valued and sought by everyone; they were themselves precisely what was presented in authoritative canonical literature as the proper fruits of the "laborious procedures of mental concentration and trance of the Hīnayānistic type."

Medicine, Healing, and Somatic Soteriology

The *Chan Essentials* and *Methods for Curing*, despite adhering to a largely mainstream doctrinal framework, both understand the path of meditation as necessarily implicating the transformation of a meditator's body, not just the mind or consciousness. Moreover, the manner in which they treat the body's role in meditation differs markedly from the views on this subject seen in early canonical Buddhist texts or the major middle-period Indian meditation treatises.

Let us start with a point that even a casual reader of these texts will not fail to notice—that meditation is deemed likely to produce a range of distinctly bodily disturbances. For example, after emerging from a vision in which flames engulf his scattered bones, the practitioner will not only feel great terror, but "his body will be hot and sweaty" (*Chan Essentials* 1.2.2.3). After a later vision, "when he emerges from trance, his body feels exhausted, as if he had been traveling in the desert during the summer with no water" (1.4.3), or, after yet further visions, he finds himself "perpetually afflicted by pain in his heart and his skull feels as if it is about to burst" (1.13.2). That meditation might provoke physical maladies—that it is a high-risk, high-reward activity—is also a central theme of the *Methods for Curing*. In that text, the possibilities are described in even greater detail, often using the technical language of Chinese medicine. Thus, if a meditator

> employs his mind with too much tension, is too rough with his breathing, or sleeps in too Spartan conditions, he will, owing to external winds, become afflicted by cold. As a result, his stomach tube and spleen and kidney channels will become agitated, and wind will stir within his tendons. A reverse *qi* (*niqi* 逆氣) will stagnate in his chest. All his joints will leak water, which will accumulate in his chest. His blood will roil, his *qi* will erupt, his head will ache, his back will swell, and all his tendons will seize up. (1.6.1)

Here the *Methods for Curing* provides some of the earliest known examples of a theme with a long afterlife in Chinese religious culture—the idea that the very same methods of mental and bodily cultivation that lead to perfection, transcendence, and power can also go horribly wrong, resulting in illness, death, or enslavement to demons.[32]

Both the *Chan Essentials* and *Methods for Curing* often link the distressing physical symptoms that meditation can produce to the specific objects meditated upon. Meditating on *emptiness* can make the body dangerously weak (*Chan Essentials* 1.16.1). Contemplating one's own body as "a sack of skin filled with air" can similarly lead to physical exhaustion (3.24.1). The *Methods for Curing*, as usual, presents such ideas in greater detail: meditating on the fire element can inadvertently heat the body's "fire channels" (*huomai* 火脈), leading to headaches, bloodshot eyes, and difficulty hearing (1.13.1). So too, a meditator who enters the "*samādhi* of the water element" may, as a result, "feel no desire to eat or drink and suffer from a burning sensation in the stomach region. His water channels become increasingly agitated, and he suffers from continual diarrhea" (1.12.1). Taking the fire and water elements of the body as objects of meditation may, it seems, accidently disturb the bodily channels linked to those elements, leading to an associated illness (as stipulated by Buddhist humoral theory, discussed below).

We need not assume Cartesian dualism to say that in the *Chan Essentials* and *Methods for Curing*, these problems are presented as decidedly on the physical side of the mind-body spectrum. Thus, for example, the cure for them often involves consuming foods, medicines, and, in one notable case, meat (*Chan Essentials* 1.14.2). In the *Chan Essentials*, those made weak by meditating on emptiness are advised to consume butter (1.16.1; 3.24.2), and in other circumstances, to "seek good medicines with which to restore the body" (1.17.3) or to "beg for fine food and restorative medicines so as to heal the body, enabling one to sit comfortably" (1.18.13). The *Methods for Curing*, while largely focusing on purely meditative techniques for healing, also prescribes what it calls "worldly medicines" (1.6.2; 1.12.3) such as milk, honey, and the *harītakī* (myrobolan plum) fruit (1.2.2).

That a Buddhist text would discuss methods for bodily healing or promise good health as a fruit of religious practice is not in itself surprising (Zysk 1991; Salguero 2017). Moreover, even the earliest Indian Buddhist texts acknowledge that meditation has a somatic component to the extent that cultivating *dhyāna* requires placing the body into particular postures, employs different parts or aspects of the body (such as the breath) as the focus of attention, and is said to lead to embodied powers, such as the ability to fly, and the production of a "mind-made body," or, occasionally, physical well-being (Anālayo 2015).[33] But at the same time, most systematic accounts of the path of meditation in early Buddhism depict manipulation of the

32. A later technical term for this condition—*zouhuo rumo* 走火入魔 or "qigong psychosis" as it is sometimes loosely translated—can in modern Mandarin denote, among other conditions, Internet or video game addiction. These ideas, in a more traditional form, are a staple of modern *wuxia* 武俠 (kung-fu) fiction and film, among many other places.

33. On the "mind-made body" (P. *manomayakāya*), see Radich 2007, 227–284.

body as a largely preliminary technique, just as they do external ritual procedures in general. So too, they classify any bodily effects of meditation as secondary in value. In these sources, the distinctive work of meditation remains largely a *mental* training by which one confronts, and then overcomes, negative conditions that are psychological or cognitive in nature and resist obvious localization within the meditator's somatic existence.[34]

The relatively greater importance that the *Chan Essentials* and *Methods for Curing* assign to the body does not necessarily mean that the authors of these texts were themselves instituting an entirely new approach to Buddhist meditation. The distinctly psychological slant of early Buddhist discussions of meditation had indeed been strategic and polemical at least in part. Together with other doctrines—that karma is generated only by intentional action, for example—it differentiated Buddhist discipline from that of rival groups such as the Jains, for whom the defilements that bind us to rebirth are physical impurities, can be generated by even nonintentional action, and must be "shaken off" through painful asceticism (Bronkhorst 1986). In other words, the urge to make the higher stages of Buddhist meditation an exclusively mental rather than physical affair may not have always had the same urgency outside formal doctrine and other contexts where the differences between Buddhism and its rivals needed to be highlighted. Once again, from an historical point of view, the somatic orientation of the *Chan Essentials* and *Methods for Curing*, in which the hindrances to Buddhist meditation are conceptualized in bodily terms, may well seem novel only because this was one of the first times that these ideas were recorded and formalized in scripture, making them fit to be copied and preserved to the present.

From a *long durée* perspective, the way the *Chan Essentials* and *Methods for Curing* hint at a distinctly somatic element to the path to liberation foreshadows the systematic development of such ideas within Tantra, in both its Buddhist and non-Buddhist varieties. We find in them, however, only a few vague traces of any specific pre-histories to those later developments, such as a passage in the *Chan Essentials* that alludes to five power centers in the body—the crown of the head, the throat, the chest, the navel, and the coccyx (2.20.9)—that remain unnamed but whose locations align with maps of bodily focal points (*cakra*) that become important in many forms of Indian Tantra.[35] In relation to these power centers, we might further point to *Methods for Curing* 1.7.4, an important passage (discussed below) that adumbrates a

34. One can, to be sure, occasionally find examples and language within even early canonical materials pointing to an embodied aspect to the meditative path, such as the repeating pericope describing true realization as occurring when one has "touched [the truth] with the body" (P. *kāyena phusitvā;* La Vallée Poussin 1937; Radich 2007, 256–266). My point is simply that, arguably for polemical reasons as I discuss below, these ways of formulating the nature of meditation remain unsystematized in early sources and occupy but a minuscule percentage of path treatises such as the *Visuddhimagga.*

35. White 2003, 224–225. The earliest examples White notes for these ideas are eighth-century yogic texts. The *Chan Essentials* precedes this by several centuries.

connection, through the bodily channels, between the (male) sexual organs (the lowest *cakra*) and the crown of the head (the highest), a circuit that is the subject of much discussion in both Daoist and Tantric methods of physiological cultivation. I leave it to others to chart further connections, if any exist, to the various "subtle body" processes of later Indian religions. Here I simply observe that the *Chan Essentials* and *Methods for Curing*, while composed in China and hence only imperfect reflections of conditions in fourth- or fifth-century India, suggest that even at this time at least some Indian Buddhist traditions had come to conceive of the path from ordinary being to liberated saint as something involving all aspects of one's person.

Medical Theories and Terminology: Chinese, Indian, and Both

Either as a cause or consequence of their ideas about the somatic elements of the path to liberation, the composers of the *Chan Essentials* and *Methods for Curing* were clearly interested in linking Buddhist meditation to a self-consciously medical domain. Several procedures for treating meditatively induced illness in the *Methods for Curing* thus involve, at least in part, the imaginative performance of recognizable medical procedures. These include trepanation (1.5.5), enemas (1.5.11), and acupuncture (1.5.10).[36] The discussion of acupuncture—described unambiguously and in terms evocative of Chinese medical knowledge ("balancing the various *qi*" and "strengthening the large intestine and kidney channels")—is another sign that this text is not simply the Chinese translation of an Indic source. Similar in this regard are the instructions, in a different exercise, to meditate on the breath not while seated but while lying on one's back, the normal posture in pre-Buddhist Chinese breath-circulation methods but one that Indian Buddhist texts never, to my knowledge, prescribe for the formal practice of meditation.[37]

This section of the *Methods for Curing* is particularly rich in language evocative of Chinese medicine. The subsection is introduced as a way to heal "blockage" (*ye* 噎), a technical name for a condition that early Chinese medical texts describe as involving difficulty in digestion.[38] Blockage, the *Methods for Curing* tells us, occurs when agitation in the "stomach tube" (*weiguan* 胃管) and spleen and kidney channels produces a reverse *qi* (*niqi* 逆氣) that stagnates in the chest. These terms, all exceedingly rare or otherwise unattested

36. Trepanation (the surgical opening of the skull) is mentioned in early Indian medical texts, is discussed in Buddhist legends of the famous healer Jīvaka, and is attested in India archeologically by skeletons showing traces of it (Zysk 1993, 67–68).

37. *Methods for Curing* 1.6.2. For examples of early Chinese (Daoist or other) breath circulation methods that specify this posture, see Maspero 1971, 501, 510, 513, 515. There are examples from Indian Buddhist literature of adepts entering states of meditation while lying down (such as, famously, the Buddha at the time of his death), though always on the side not the back. In any event, to formally prescribe a reclining posture for meditation would be highly anomalous for an Indian Buddhist source.

38. *Zhong yi da ci dian*, 1688

in extant Chinese Buddhist literature, are part of the technical vocabulary of Chinese medicine and are used here in a way suggesting either real knowledge of that domain or a studied attempt to imitate it.[39] Even so, we cannot necessarily conclude that these parts of the *Methods for Curing* were composed de novo by a Chinese author. Translators of Indian Buddhist texts often took pains to render Indian medical terminology in ways that would permit correct identification of the object in question given standard Chinese medical theories.[40] This kind of translation practice may account for some of the medical vocabulary in the *Chan Essentials* and *Methods for Curing*, such as the "lung-point" (*feishu* 肺腧) which these texts present merely as one item within the often unusual lists of internal organs to be contemplated during the meditation on bodily impurity, but which Chinese medical texts describe as the acupuncture and moxibustion point associated with the lungs, located on the chest at the level of the space between the third and fourth vertebrae.[41] Since neither the *Chan Essentials* nor *Methods for Curing* engages substantively with any distinctive medical implications of the "lung-point," we might wonder if this word was primarily intended merely to denote the location of an otherwise unclear Indic anatomical term, perhaps one of the proto-*cakra*s, of which these texts seem aware as mentioned above.[42]

In any event, the composers or compilers of the *Chan Essentials* and *Methods for Curing* evidently wished to mark their competence in the register of Chinese medicine. They also wanted to do the same for that of Indian medicine, which medieval Chinese audiences usually took to be Buddhist regardless of origin. In *Methods for Curing* 1.4, to take one example, those meditating on the four

39. On "reverse *qi*," see *Zhong yi da ci dian*, 1163. One of the few Chinese Buddhist texts to mention this term is the *Ocean-Samādhi Contemplation Scripture* (*GFSMH*, T.643:15.670c17–18). The term "stomach tube" is first attested in a third-century biography of the physician Huatuo 華佗 (*San guo zhi*, 29.800). Later medical literature describes it as something whose stimulation by acupuncture will cure cold illnesses (*Zhong yi da ci dian*, 1080). The stomach tube appears prominently in key early Daoist physiological meditation texts, notably the (outer) *Huang ting nei jing jing* 黃庭內景經 and the *Laozi zhong jing* 老子中經 (*Yun ji qi qian*, 311, 433, 442, 447). Apart from the *Chan Essentials* and *Methods for Curing* (1.12.3), the only canonical Chinese Buddhist text to use the word "stomach tube" is the *Ocean-Samādhi Contemplation Scripture*, where it is also linked to "cold illnesses that impede digestion" (*GFSMH*, T.643:15.652b15–17).

40. Some fifth-century translators, for example, rendered the technical concept of a phlegm (*śleṣman* or *kapha*) illness as "lung illness" (肺病), probably because Chinese medicine associates the lungs with *yin* 陰 (cold) illnesses and phlegm was linked to cold in Indian medical understanding (Salguero 2010, 123–129). Phlegm was eventually translated as *tan* 痰, and this concept later entered the Chinese medical lexicon (Endō et al. 1993).

41. *Chan Essentials* 1.1.4; *Methods for Curing* 1.5.4 and 1.7.4. On the "lung-point" of Chinese medicine, see *Zhong yi da ci dian*, 949, citing *Ling shu* 靈樞 52. Dunhuang manuscripts Stein nos. 6168 and 6262 both provide diagrams showing the location of the lung-point along the front side of the body (Lo 2005, 237).

42. Speculatively, we might wonder if it points to the throat (*kaṇṭha*) *cakra*. In the *Chan Essentials* and *Methods for Curing*, the lung-point is listed immediately after the "throat" (咽喉 or 喉嚨), as it is in the *Ocean-Samādhi Contemplation Scripture*, the only other Chinese Buddhist text to use the word (*GFSMH*, T.15:643.652b17).

elements (*sida* 四大; *mahābhūta*) are instructed to prevent those elements from becoming imbalanced within the body, the main cause of sickness according to Buddhist medical theories, by aligning one's practice with the seasons, meditating on fire in the spring and earth in the autumn. Although to adjust one's meditation in accord with the seasons dovetails with the principles of Chinese medicine, where such correlations are common, identifiably Indian theories govern the alignment in this case. "Spring" (春), it turns out, was the typical Chinese translation of the name of the Indian hot season (*grīṣma*), a time when (cold) phlegm illnesses predominate, according to Indian medical theories; warming the body by meditating on fire would thus counteract the illnesses characteristic of this season.[43]

Although the *Methods for Curing* makes use of Indian medical theories, this fact alone does not inform us of the identity—cultural, linguistic, or geographical—of the author(s) of these sections or the source(s) from which they drew, since the relevant information was, by the early fifth century, fully available in existing Chinese translations of Indian Buddhist texts. But we do find a compelling case for a truly transcultural and multilinguistic origin to the text (or the material out of which it was assembled) at *Methods for Curing* 1.12. Here we read that diarrhea—"down-going" (*xia* 下) in the Chinese—must be cured first by an elaborate exercise of meditative imagination in which the practitioner envisions the drying out of the oceans of the world (1.12.2), and then by summoning the god Yuduoluojia 欝多羅伽, a name unattested elsewhere but one that corresponds phonetically to "Uttaraga."[44] The god Upward-Goer (*uttara-ga*) thus has the power to cure the "down-going" of diarrhea. The Indic name of the patron saint of incontinent yogis has evidently been chosen in light of the specifically *Chinese* word for this condition.[45]

The conjunction here of at least some direct knowledge of things Indian with a similar level of knowledge of the Chinese side allows us to glimpse, however indirectly, the social milieu in which this text was produced. And as did the *Chan Essentials*' liberal use of technical doctrines concerning the

43. Though I am unable to account for the prescription to meditate on "earth" during the autumn, the connection between spring and cold illness aligns with how these matters are treated in Dharmakṣema's early fifth-century translation of the *Suvarṇabhāsottama-sūtra*, a key Buddhist text in which Indian (Āyurvedic) medical theories are discussed and a primary source for Buddhist medical ideas in East Asia (Salguero 2017). In the *Suvarṇabhāsottama-sūtra*, four Indian seasons—hot (*grīṣma*), rains (*varṣa*), autumn (*śārada*), and cold (*hemanta*)—are correlated with excesses in the humors (*doṣa*) of, respectively, phlegm (*kapha*), wind (*vāta*), bile (*pitta*), and their combination (*saṃnipāta*) as the fourth (Nobel 1937, 178–179). Dharmakṣema translates the Chinese names of these seasons as spring (春), summer (夏), autumn (秋), and winter (冬), respectively (*Jin guang ming jing*, T.663:16.351c29–352a1; so too *Fo yi jing*, T.793:17.737a28–29; cf. *San fa du lun*, T.1506:25.26a23–26, which mentions only three seasons). Thus the hot (*grīṣma*) season of spring (春) is a time of excessive phlegm, the humor associated with cold (Salguero 2010, 128; Unschuld 1985, 142).

44. The god is first introduced as Yuduojia 欝多伽, then later as Yuduoluojia. The transcription *yu-duo-luo* 欝多羅, in fifth-century sources, renders *uttara* (upper) in, among other contexts, the common word *uttara-saṅgha* 欝多羅僧 (the "upper" monks' robe).

45. A similar example occurs at *Methods for Curing* 1.6.4, where a medicine named *abaddha* (unbound) cures the medical condition of "blockage" (*ye* 噎).

stages of the path to liberation, it also shows us that even though the *Methods for Curing* was composed in China, it was intended for a relatively discerning and sophisticated audience, one that would not have been satisfied with the kind of blatantly apocryphal Buddhist sutras, full of patently fake Indian names and other obvious (to us) signs of Chinese authorship, that appeared in great numbers in the fifth and sixth centuries.

Dhyāna, Materiality, and Buddhist Medicine

The *Chan Essentials* and *Methods for Curing* both suggest that meditation might disrupt the body and hence cause illness. No systematic explanation is provided as to why this would be. But it is an intuitively plausible idea given: (1) the theoretical bases of so-called Buddhist medicine, which are presupposed and elaborated on within these texts, and (2) the usual Buddhist understanding that meditation—*dhyāna*—in some manner joins a meditator to the heavenly realms of purified materiality.

Indian Buddhist authors were fully cognizant of the pan-Indian, "Āyurvedic" theory that bodily illness results from disturbances in the three *doṣa*s (faults) of wind, bile, and phlegm. But they in addition proposed their own theory of corporeal health based on the four primary elements of earth, water, wind, and fire that in Buddhist doctrine are the fundamental constituents of the material world. In this twist on Indian humoral theory, illness is caused by imbalances in these four elements within the body, with some sources going so far as to posit 101 modes of disruption for each element, yielding 404 possible illnesses in total.[46]

The *Methods for Curing* and *Chan Essentials* presuppose this Buddhist theory of disease. It is, accordingly, imbalance—literally, "coarseness" (*cuse* 麁澁)[47]—in the four elements that necessitates the "enveloping butter" contemplation prescribed in *Methods for Curing* 1.5.[48] So too the *Chan Essentials* says that medicinal foods work by "harmonizing the four elements" (1.14.8) or by "regulating the *qi* of the four elements" (4.32.13.2), and it is notable that the four elements are here referred to as four kinds of *qi* (pneuma), the energy-substance whose disharmony and regulation is similarly implicated in the cause and cure of disease according to traditional Chinese medicine.[49]

46. Demiéville 1937, 227; Unschuld 1985, 141–142; Fukunaga 1980, 56–57. The four-element disease theory had a certain amount of influence in medieval Chinese medical thinking (see Salguero 2010, 63n103 for references).

47. Perhaps from Skt. *karkaśa*, meaning hard, coarse, or rough (Salguero 2014, 72).

48. The "enveloping butter" meditation is best known among scholars of East Asian Buddhism from the writings of the eighteenth-century Japanese Zen master Hakuin, who claims to have used it to cure his "Zen sickness" (Waddell 2001, 113).

49. That the four elements are species of *qi* is implied elsewhere in the *Chan Essentials* (1.15.2.1, 4.31.22) and the *Methods for Curing* (1.9.6). See also *GFSMH*, T.643:15.646c16–17. In *Methods for Curing* 1.9.6, however, "earth *qi*" (地氣) seems to mean not the earth element alone but a container that includes all four elements; here, the word should probably be taken in a more resolutely Chinese meaning in which the opposition between "earthly *qi*" and "heavenly *qi*" marks the distinction between body / materiality and mind / spirit.

The *Methods for Curing* further acknowledges a more elaborate physiological system of 404 bodily "channels" (*mai* 脈), a number recalling the Buddhist idea of 404 illnesses, also mentioned in this text (1.12.5). I know of no earlier references, in Chinese or Indian sources, to a system of 404 bodily channels, nor of any later ones in China that do not derive from the *Methods for Curing.* Again we may note in passing the potential resonances here with ideas common in pre- and non-Buddhist Chinese thought (the "vessel" systems of Chinese medicine and Daoist cultivation practices) as well as in later Indian Tantric systems (the *nāḍī* channels). In the *Methods for Curing,* the 404 channels or vessels and their connection to the heart are introduced at the beginning of the first sutra, where it is stated that their disturbance, by harsh sounds, will lead meditators to madness (1.2.1). In later passages, curing occurs when divine beings pour medicines into these channels (1.3.2–3, 1.5.6) or when they are pacified by other means (1.5.10). The precise arrangement of the 404 channels is only hinted at—they connect to the bones and the brain (1.5.3) and also the sexual organs (1.7.1–5).[50]

Given these ideas about the causes of illness, one may wonder why meditation was regarded as capable of provoking it. The crucial notion here is one shared by all Buddhist traditions: that the distinctive states of consciousness that define meditative attainment—the formal stages of *dhyāna*—also characterize the denizens of the so-called heavens of pure or refined materiality (*rūpa-dhātu*). This means, firstly, that the attainment of *dhyāna* leads to rebirth in those heavens. A number of Indian Buddhist sources that were translated into Chinese by the mid-fifth century, including some of the early *chan* scriptures, go further to discuss the idea that meditative attainment puts one into *physical* contact with heavenly realms even while alive. In greater or lesser detail, these sources explain that, upon obtaining *dhyāna,* physical matter from the heavens of refined materiality will infuse the meditator's body. This, it is said, accounts for the connection between *dhyāna* and the attainment of magical power—one can fly, for example, when one's body becomes permeated by the lighter atoms of the *rūpa-dhātu.*[51]

---

50. Zhiyi's writings (late sixth century) contain a detailed account of the physiology of the 404 channels as part of a method of meditation he claims was taught by many northern *chan* masters (Tada 1976; Aoki 1989; H. Wang 2001, 187–245). It is worth citing here as the only other independent description of these channels: "The heart channel is the chief of the body's channels. From it branch forth the [four] channels of the four elements, each of which [divides into] ten. Within each of these are yet further nine more channels, yielding a total of four hundred [which when added to the four channels of the four elements makes 404 (?)], which stretch from head to toe. Within these 404 channels flow the currents of wind, *qi,* and blood. Within the blood of these channels there are many tiny worms, which live within the channels." 身內諸脈，心脈為主。復從心脈內，生四大之脈。一大各十脈。十脈之內，一一復各九脈，合成四百脈，從頭至足。四百四脈，內悉有風氣血流相注。此脈血之內，亦有諸細微之蟲，依脈而住。 (*Shi chan boluomi ci di fa men,* T.1916:46.530b27–c2). See also Guanding's *Qing Guanyin jing shu,* T.1800:39.976b11–17, which follows Zhiyi closely.

51. *Chan fa yao jie,* T.616:15.295a27–297c12; *DZDL,* T.1509:25.98a7–8; 240b29; 264c20–25; 306a19; 699a20; *Za apitan xin lun,* T.1552:28.920c19.

These ideas were known to learned Chinese Buddhists of the fifth and sixth centuries. Zhiyi, writing in the late sixth century, explains that it is the infusion of matter from the *rūpa-dhātu* into the meditator's body that produces the unusual physical sensations (what he calls the "contacts," *chu* 觸) attendant upon the initial attainment of *dhyāna*.[52] Zhiyi takes pains to distinguish such occurrences from what he says are the very similar sensations of meditatively induced illness, a topic on which he wrote a great deal, drawing extensively from the *Methods for Curing*. Before Zhiyi, some of the Indian *chan* scriptures translated into Chinese in the early fifth century also hint at the close connection between these possibilities. The *Chan Scripture of Dharmatrāta* (*Damoduoluo chan jing*), translated by Buddhabhadra in the early 400s, notes that "the coarse four elements are extinguished and the supple four elements arise" upon attaining *dhyāna* (presumably the first *dhyāna*, though this is not explicit).[53] It is unclear if the arising of the "supple four elements" here means the penetration of pure heavenly matter into the meditator's body. But, regardless, regression in meditation occurs, according to this text, when "the coarse four elements stir within the body."[54] It is this precise term—"coarse four elements," otherwise unattested in Chinese Buddhist literature—that is seen as the source of meditatively induced sickness in the *Methods for Curing*.

From passages like these, a rough theory readily emerges as to why meditation can produce physical illness, as the *Chan Essentials* and *Methods for Curing* both repeatedly claim. Precisely because it transforms the physical matter of the body when successful, meditation, either by its nature or when carried out less than optimally, can also bring about imbalances in one's bodily makeup and hence illness.

Any attempt to provide a more systematic account of how all this was thought to work is, however, thwarted by the practical rather than theoretical concerns of the *Chan Essentials* and *Methods for Curing*. As a rule, these texts are oriented toward supplying concrete solutions to specific problems, not explicating why these solutions work or what exactly caused the difficulties. It is in this very insistence on providing practical information that we can see even more clearly one of their key contentions—that the power of meditation is a double-edged sword, capable of elevating one to higher spheres of mind *and* matter, but also, for precisely this reason, dangerous.

Somatic Soteriology and the Physiology of Desire

Besides implying that meditators risk incurring physical illness, the *Chan Essentials* and *Methods for Curing* occasionally hint that the path to Buddhist

52. *Shi chanboluomi cidi famen*, T.1916:46.510b8–12

53. 麁澁四大滅，隨順四大生。(*DMDL*, T.618:15.320b24–25; see also 317a6–7; 322b1–2; 322b14). Yamabe (2016, 14) has discussed a refrain from the *Śrāvakabhūmi* that might be related to this statement.

54. 麁澁四大種，還從身內起。(*DMDL*, T.618:15.302c13–14)

liberation itself has a nonnegotiable connection to the purification and healing of the body. This notion of "somatic soteriology," as we might call it, eventually became a staple of Indian Tantra, Buddhist and otherwise, but the examples we find in these two texts are notable as some of the earliest known claims to this effect in Buddhist literature.

To begin with, bodily purification is a recurring theme in the "confirmatory visions" that denote meditative progress. The "true Buddha" who appears in *Chan Essentials* 2.19.2.2 pours pure water onto the meditator's head, filling his body and destroying the eighty families of worms, meditation on which was part of the contemplations of bodily impurity discussed in previous sections of the text. This form of "consecration" (*guan* 灌), as it is here called, occurs repeatedly in the visions and is another example of a trope better known from Tantric literature. Elsewhere, after the meditator has imagined his body filled with pus and other impurities, he has a vision of these impurities being burned away by fire, leaving him blissful and relaxed (*Chan Essentials* 3.23.2). These visions are rarely given any explicit interpretation. But on one occasion we find something close, when a visionary buddha delivers to the meditator the following instructions:

> In a former life, owing to lust, hatred, and confusion, you committed many evil deeds. The obstruction of ignorance has caused you to receive a mortal body for lifetime upon lifetime. You must now contemplate [all the impure things] within your body shriveling up and being burned into oblivion by the external fires. (*Chan Essentials* 2.20.11)

Bodily impurity is here correlated with lack of spiritual progress, because rebirth in bodily form at all owes to the mental defilements of past lifetimes, and by extension the elimination of bodily impurity, if only in visionary form, aligns with the meditator's forward movement along the path.[55]

In the *Methods for Curing*, these ideas become more explicit when techniques initially prescribed for curing meditatively induced physical maladies ultimately prove to be methods that lead to awakening and liberation. This basic sequence informs many of the text's subsections, including the framing narrative of the first sutra where the Buddha assigns various monks a method for "softening and curing the internal wind element" that first heals their ailment but then leads them to arhatship (1.3.5). Section 1.4 presents a four-part sequence initially introduced as a means of curing imbalances in the four elements provoked by meditation, which then leads to progressively more advanced soteriological attainments, culminating in an encounter with the seven buddhas of the past (1.4.1–4). Similarly, the "enveloping butter contemplation" of section 1.5 is initially prescribed for meditators beset by the seemingly physical malady of excessive gas (caused, again, by imbalance

55. The *Ocean-Samādhi Contemplation Scripture* contains a somewhat similar passage equating the bodily worms and the *kleśas* (*GFSMH*, T.643:15.664c2–4).

in the four elements), but concludes with a visionary consecration by Lord Brahmā that "tames the ninety-eight defilements" (1.5.16–17). A meditator assailed by cold winds that lead to "blockage"—described in a highly medicalized idiom—is treated by a long sequence of techniques by which he eventually becomes either an arhat or firmly established on the bodhisattva path (1.6.5). The method prescribed for curing diarrhea ultimately "eliminates the ocean of karmic obstructions," thereby placing the meditator near to awakening (1.12.5). So too, in the second sutra, the method for dispelling the demons who give meditators "aching joints, itchy palms . . . blurry vision, or a numb bottom" (2.9) in the end leads to the practitioner's becoming a stream-enterer (2.11).

If Buddhist liberation can be a side effect, as it were, of methods whose more immediate aim is bodily healing (just as bodily illness can be the side effect of meditation improperly performed), this may result because the *Chan Essentials* and *Methods for Curing* describe at least some of the mental defilements of classical Buddhist doctrine as operating by way of definite physiological mechanisms. The most interesting example of this occurs in *Methods for Curing* 1.7, where the "method for curing practitioners injured by lust" (治行者貪婬患法) is introduced as follows: if someone immersed in "trance" (定) perceives a desirable sensory object, "wind will stir the four hundred four channels connecting his eyes and sexual organs," leading to a disturbance in the meditator's "heart wind" and subsequent madness.

Here the determining influence of the *mind* in governing one's response to sensory contact—usually the emphasis in a Buddhist analysis—is absent, as if deliberately excluded. In spite (or because) of suppressing unwholesome states of mind, trance apparently makes a meditator strangely vulnerable to lust-provoking sights through an initially physiological reaction that eventually rebounds on the mind / heart and produces madness. The instructions for treating this problem, which include an unusually graphic meditation on the impurity of sexual intercourse, describe in detail the anatomical structures that make this possible. First, the meditator, here presumed to be a man whose lust has been provoked by the sight of a woman, must contemplate the female sexual organs and the production of female sexual / reproductive fluid (menstrual blood) that is, we are told, in truth the excreta of worms that live in the body (*Methods for Curing* 1.7.3).[56] The production of male sexual fluid must also then be contemplated. This provides an occasion for an outline of the physiology of male lust:

> In a man's body, because of sins from past lives, the four hundred four channels spread from the eyes throughout the four limbs, reaching then

56. Note that the meditator "contemplates" (*guan* 觀), rather than "imagines" (*xiang* 想) these things, presumably because, as objects and processes within the human body, they are all real things. On this contrast in usage between *guan* and *xiang*, see "Contemplation, Imagination, and Confirmatory Visions" in chap. 2.

> to the entrails and finally to the place below the receptacle of raw food and above the receptacle of digested food [where the worms who produce the male sexual fluid live].... [The channels] extend to the "hidden organ" [of the penis]....Going upward, the channels connect to the heart and then all the way to the crown of the head.
>
> When a man's eye encounters a visible form, wind stirs his heart. The four hundred four channels fall sway to the wind, moving without cease. The eighty thousand families of worms open their mouths in unison. A pus-like substance flows from their eyes and through the channels until it reaches the top of the worms' heads.[57] These worms [comprising the sexual fluid] shake wildly, lose control, and charge toward the woman's sexual organs....
>
> [Thus is it that male and female reproductive fluids are] created through the perfume-like conditioning of the ninety-eight defilements, the eighty thousand families of worms, and the movements of the earth, water, fire, and wind elements. (1.7.4–5)

Here the workings of lust are imagined as a series of largely physiological interactions, the "movements of the earth, water, fire, and wind elements." Sin from past lives endows male bodies with the anatomy of the 404 channels that link the eyes and the sexual organs in such a way that particular sights set off a chain reaction leading to the production of the sexual fluid and then ejaculation. (The production of the corresponding female reproductive fluid, menstrual blood, results merely from drinking water; see 1.7.3.)

It is of particular interest that at the conclusion to this sketch of the male body consumed by lust there is a passing mention of the influence on this process of the "defilements" (*shi* 使; *kleśa*), the negative psychological tendencies whose purification is the goal of Buddhist meditation and the cause of ultimate liberation, according to formal Buddhist doctrine. Yet nothing specific is said here about the nature of this influence. As a whole, this passage leaves the impression that the defilements are closely connected if not identical to the "movements of the earth, water, fire, and wind elements" that comprise the main drama, and such a connection is indeed hinted at in similar passages in the *Chan Essentials.* The twelfth section of that text—containing the meditator's first vision of the "tree of the defilements" whose uprooting is correlated with his subsequent attainment of arhatship—is eventually given two names: the "contemplation of the earth, fire, wind, and water elements" and the "confirmatory vision of the ninety-eight defilements" (1.12.8). Another passage, after saying that the defilement of ignorance is the root cause of suffering (an entirely orthodox Buddhist claim), goes on to ground the existence and persistence of ignorance in the four primary elements:

57. This presumably refers to the "tendon-like worms" (筋色蟲) that, in the full passage, latch on to the womb.

> From where does ignorance come? How does it grow and develop such that it fills the triple world? Contemplating ignorance, [I see that] it grows depending upon the earth element, moves relying on the wind element, gets its solidity from the earth element, is nurtured by the fire element, and is given multifariousness by the water element. (*Chan Essentials* 4.31.8)

The next passage takes this reasoning a step further: not just ignorance, but all the elements of the chain of causation (*pratītyasamutpāda*) normally classified as defiled mental activity as opposed to the fixed inheritance of past karma or the next-life fruits of present karma—namely, volition, attachment, clinging, and coming into being—are themselves generated by, or linked in some fundamental way to, the four material elements (4.31.9).

In these examples we see the outlines of a theory, not yet systematic, that makes spiritual defilement and bodily illness, seen as grounded in the four material elements, versions of the same thing, or, at the least, susceptible to an endless series of mutual interrelationship even within a single body and a single lifetime.[58] This version of somatic soteriology is unquestionably different from those that would eventually become the mainstays of Buddhist and other forms of Tantra, and whether future research can shed more light on connections between them remains to be seen. What can be said for now is simply that these ideas, like many that eventually became central to the practice and ideology of Buddhist Tantra, apparently have deeper roots than has often been suspected, within Buddhism if not elsewhere.[59] Here, just as with the issues of ritual repentance and meditative contact with the buddhas discussed earlier in this chapter, we do best to take the *Chan Essentials* and *Methods for Curing* as artifacts of a moment in the history of Buddhism when, owing perhaps to the unprecedented influx of Indian *chan* masters in the early fifth century, certain kinds of ideas associated with Buddhist meditation practice that had previously not been committed to scriptural form were, in China, written down and given explicitly canonical status and authority as the secrets of Buddhist meditation.

58. Such ideas must also be part of the explanation for why the *Chan Essentials* assigns such outsized importance to the meditations on the four primary elements (the third sutra in particular seems to correlate them with the achievement of the four fruits of salvation.

59. On the presectarian roots of many Tantric ideas and practices in India, see Davidson 2017. Iyanaga Nobumi (2019) has also recently shown that fifth-century Chinese Buddhist sources preserve evidence of the oracular, child-possession (*āveśa*) rituals that have usually been seen as distinctive to later Tantra.

CHAPTER 4

Textual Histories and the Making of Chinese Meditation Scriptures

In the previous chapters, when introducing the structure, content, and major themes of the *Chan Essentials* and *Methods for Curing*, I took as given the status of these texts as apocryphal Chinese Buddhist scriptures. In this chapter I will put this assertion on firmer ground and also take up the related question of the history of these documents in China and the mode and manner of their production. The conclusion of this chapter can be stated easily enough in advance: although informed by various Indian traditions, the *Chan Essentials* and *Methods for Curing* were nevertheless composed by authors and redactors working in China in the fifth century, where the texts originally circulated together as a part of a single collection.

In an attempt to make their textual histories as comprehensible as possible, I have relegated a certain amount of raw documentary evidence to the appendices. Even so, the task of charting these matters remains complex and necessarily technical. As a result, this chapter is primarily intended for readers interested in the bibliographic history of Chinese Buddhism and the formation of apocryphal Chinese Buddhist literature, which we can observe in the case of the *Chan Essentials* and *Methods for Curing* at an unusual level of detail. Others may wish to skip the following pages and may do so with assurance that the previous three chapters are sufficient preparation to begin reading the translations themselves.

Composition and Translation

Although I say that the *Chan Essentials* and *Methods for Curing* were composed in China rather than merely translated from Indian sources, this is a shorthand. My intention in saying it is not to depict the precise manner of these texts' creation, which was quite complicated as we will see, but to convey the methodological point that they are products of fifth-century Chinese Buddhism and may be used as sources for its history. When surveying the transmitted canons of Chinese Buddhism, scholars have traditionally treated those texts written by Chinese Buddhists as categorically different from the many Chinese translations of Indian Buddhist texts. Sorting out which texts belong in which of these categories has long been a fundamental task for historians of Indian Buddhism, to ensure that texts composed in China but made to look like the translations of Indian scriptures are not accidentally taken as sources for the study of Indian Buddhism, and also for scholars of Chinese Buddhism, who are often most interested in precisely those sources because they provide evidence for the uptake of Buddhism in China and the way it was made to speak to specifically Chinese concerns. The notion that the received corpus of Chinese Buddhist scriptures can be neatly divided into these two classes parallels the concerns of medieval Chinese Buddhist bibliographers, to whom modern scholars are necessarily indebted, who always viewed a text's status as a "translation" from an Indic original as the singular mark of its canonicity (Tokuno 1990).

However, as has been increasingly recognized, many medieval Chinese Buddhist texts do not fall into only one of these two categories.[1] A strict classification as either translation or composition, and hence as either Indian or Chinese, is impossible in the case of Buddhist commentaries composed in China and in Chinese but on the basis of lectures delivered by an Indian teacher, or of pastiches of previously translated Chinese texts woven together in a new form. Such texts, examples of which have been shown to survive from the very earliest days of Chinese Buddhism (Zacchetti 2004), have often been neglected by modern scholars precisely because they do not fit neatly into either domain. With a genesis too uncertain to be taken seriously by historians of Indian Buddhism, they also tend to be too "Indian" in their concerns and simultaneously too bereft of blatant adaptations of distinctly Chinese cultural forms to be seen as relevant to the history of Chinese Buddhism itself.

It is into this liminal category that the *Chan Essentials* and *Methods for Curing* must ultimately be placed. Owing to my own interest in the history of Chinese Buddhism, my primary concern is to establish their value as sources for that history, and this entails showing, at the outset, that Chinese Buddhists—meaning individuals whose access to the Buddhist tradition was mediated by Chinese-language sources and whose expected conversation partners were the same—were instrumental in their creation. But we must also acknowledge that these texts did not spring into existence from the mere imagination of a solitary forger. Nor did they emerge from a cultural environment that was purely "Chinese" in any simplistic sense. The origins of the *Chan Essentials* and *Methods for Curing* lie simultaneously in pre-existing Chinese texts that may themselves have derived more directly from

1. Funayama 2002, 2006, and 2007; Yamabe 1999c; Silk 1997 and 2008; Shinohara 2015; Radich 2018. For a survey of the category of apocryphal Chinese Buddhist scriptures, see Funayama 2015.

Indic-language sources, in traditions of practice and knowledge that were not Chinese inventions but were inherited from teachings propagated by the many foreign *chan* masters active in fifth-century China, and, finally, in the manner in which all of these strands came together in the hands of the Chinese Buddhists who sought to ground those texts and traditions in the authoritative form of a Buddhist sutra.

From One Text to Two

The *Chan Essentials* and *Methods for Curing* come down to us, in the printed Chinese Buddhist canons and extant medieval manuscripts and inscriptions, as two distinct texts attributed to two different translators. Yet evidence suggests they originally circulated together as a single collection, a format that would fit with their existing structures harmoniously since both are collections of multiple, narratively independent sutras.

Between their appearance in the fifth century and the first printed editions of the Buddhist canon in the tenth century (in which their form was fixed), the material now contained in the *Chan Essentials* and *Methods for Curing* circulated under several different titles and formats (see Appendix 3). Variation of this kind was not uncommon for medieval Chinese Buddhist texts. For the *Chan Essentials* and *Methods for Curing*, however, more substantial issues exist. When we examine citations preserved in sixth- and seventh-century sources, for example, we find that the title "Chan Essentials" often names passages now contained in the *Methods for Curing*, and vice versa (see Appendix 1). This was not a simple matter of two admittedly similar titles having been occasionally interchanged. Some recensions contained, as part of a single document, material from both texts (Appendix 3).

By the mid-700s, bibliographers had put this evidently confusing situation into some order. The title "Methods for Curing" was thereafter reserved for a one-scroll text claimed to have been translated in the mid-fifth century by the layman Juqu Jingsheng 沮渠京聲.[2] The title "Chan Essentials," meanwhile, was linked to a three-scroll text deemed to be Kumārajīva's translation. These are the arrangements and attributions that appear, with only minor variations, in the printed canons of the tenth century and beyond, from which the received editions of the texts derive.[3]

These received forms of the *Chan Essentials* and *Methods for Curing* certainly yield, for each text, a coherent whole. But the medieval bibliographic evidence points to a close, intertwining relationship between the two texts during their early transmission and circulation. Our earliest surviving

2. The earliest sources name him as "Juqu marquis of Anyang" 沮渠安陽侯 (*CSZJJ*, T.2145:55.13a14; 66a26; 106b23; *GSZ*, T.2059:50.337a4). His given name, Jingsheng 京聲, is first mentioned in the *Zhong jing mu lu* of 594 (T.2146:55.144b23).

3. The most significant divergence is that in the Tang catalogs the *Methods for Curing* is always listed as one scroll, while in the printed canons it is always two scrolls.

records for these texts are the biographies of translators that Sengyou 僧祐 (445–518) included in his *Chu san zang ji ji*. These biographies, completed during the Qi 齊 dynasty (479–502),[4] mention only a single relevant document: a text in *five* scrolls with the long title *Scripture on the Secrets of Chan and the Healing of Illness* (*Chan yao mi mi zhi bing jing* 禪要祕密治病經).[5] This text, which I will argue is likely to have contained the totality of the *Chan Essentials* and *Methods for Curing*, is mentioned in the *Chu san zang ji ji* biography of Juqu Jingsheng, to whom the *Methods for Curing* alone would later be attributed. At the same time, the biographies of the two translators who would later be linked to the *Chan Essentials*—Kumārajīva and Dharmamitra—list many texts, including texts on meditation, but none with a similar title.[6]

When we follow the references to the so-called *Scripture on the Secrets of Chan and the Healing of Illness* in later sources, we observe two things occurring in tandem: the text going by this name shrinks in size and eventually disappears at the same time that new *chan* texts begin to appear whose titles include the distinctive word "secret." These new texts eventually stabilize as the *Chan Essentials* and *Methods for Curing*.

These changes are first visible in sources dating to the early Liang 梁 dynasty (502–557). The catalog section of Sengyou's *Chu san zang ji ji*, which postdates the biographies and was edited up until around the year 515,[7] still mentions a *Scripture on the Secrets of Chan and the Healing of Illness* but gives its size as *two*, not five scrolls (see table 2). Meanwhile the Indian *chan* master Dharmamitra—founder of the Dinglin temple where Sengyou himself resided—is linked in this catalog to a new text, the *Chan mi yao* 禪祕要, in three (or five) scrolls, that is unmentioned in his earlier biography.[8] This

4. On the dating of the *Chu san zang ji ji* biographies and catalog, see Naitō 1958 and Palumbo 2003, 197.

5. *CSZJJ*, T.2145:55.106c3 (S, Q, and Y here, but not elsewhere, read 禪要祕密治禪病經). Here and below, in addition to the Taishō edition of the *Chu san zang ji ji* I have consulted the versions in K[1], J, Q, and a manuscript version from Nanatsudera, provided to me by Prof. Ochiai Toshinori. (For a key to the abbreviations used for the different printed editions of the Chinese Buddhist canon, see the introduction to the translations in this volume).

6. *CSZJJ*, T.2145:55.101b27; 105a21–22. None of the titles of the texts attributed to these figures contain the distinctive word "secret" (*mi* 祕). Dharmamitra's biography says explicitly he translated only *three* texts, all of which are listed. As discussed below, the catalog section of the *Chu san zang ji ji*, completed later than the biographies, attributes to Dharmamitra a fourth text that later catalogers saw as equivalent to the *Chan Essentials*.

7. For this dating, see n. 4 above. Sengyou assembled the catalog using the library of the Dinglin 定林 temple, where he lived, as well as the Liang imperial library.

8. Modern scholars usually assume that this *Chan mi yao* is the *Chan Essentials* (Sakaino 1935, 862–863; Tōdō 1960, 404), even if they concede that, as an apocryphal text, Dharmamitra was not its true translator (Yamabe 1999c, 107). But given how confusing the references to texts with this or a similar name later become (see Appendix 3), precisely what *Chan mi yao* points to in this instance is, I think, an open question. On Dharmamitra's founding of the Dinglin temple, see *CSZJJ*, T.2145:55.205a28–b4; *GSZ*, T.2059:50.343a11–17. Juqu Jingsheng also supposedly spent time at the Dinglin temple (*CSZJJ*, T.2059:55.106c13–14; *GSZ*, T.2059:50.337a20–21).

Table 2. Texts and translators as recorded in sixth-century sources

Source	*Text title*	*Translator*	*Length (scrolls)*
Chu san zang ji ji (biographies; before 503)	*Chan yao mi mi zhi bing jing* 禪要祕密治病經	Juqu Jingsheng	5
Chu san zang ji ji (catalog; up to 515)	1. *Chan mi yao* 禪祕要	Dharmamitra	3 (or 5)
	2. *Chan yao mi mi zhi bing jing* 禪要祕密治病經	Juqu Jingsheng	2
	3. *Chan mi yao jing* 禪祕要經	Juqu Jingsheng (excerpt from no. 2)	1
	4. *Zhi chan gui mei bu an jing* 治禪鬼魅不安經[a]	Juqu Jingsheng (excerpt from no. 2)	1
Ming seng zhuan (completed in 514)	*Chan mi yao* 禪祕要	Dharmamitra	3
Gao seng zhuan (ca. 520–530)[b]	*Chan jing chan fa yao* 禪經禪法要[c]	Dharmamitra	Unstated
	Chan mi yao zhi bing jing 禪祕要治病經	Juqu Jingsheng	5

[a] This title is very close to the one assigned to the second sutra of the received *Methods for Curing* (T.620:15.341a23–24).

[b] On the dating of the *Gao seng zhuan*, see Ji Y. 2009, 33–35.

[c] The name *Chan jing chan fa yao* 禪經禪法要 here is problematic. It may be an error for the title mentioned in Dharmamitra's *Chu san zang ji ji* biography, there called *Zhu jing chan fa yao* 諸經禪法要, which must point to a single text since the total number of texts in this list is specified. It is also possible that the biography, following the *Chu san zang ji ji* catalog, wishes to assign Dharmamitra two chan texts, a *Chan jing* and a *Chan fa yao*. Some editions of Dharmamitra's biography read *Chan jing fa yao* 禪經法要 (*Zhong hua da zang jing*, 61.276c14).

text, moreover, is given the suspiciously exact translation date of Yuanjia 18 (441–442).[9] The fragments of Dharmamitra's biography from the *Ming seng zhuan* 明僧傳, completed in 514 give this same information.[10] Adding to the confusion—and here we can only sympathize with the medieval bibliographers—the *Chu san zang ji ji* catalog further reports that the same title, *Chan mi yao*, was also used for one of two independently circulating

9. *CSZJJ*, T.2145:55.12c1. The catalog attributes four texts to Dharmamitra, but only this one has an exact date.

10. *Meisōden shō*, Z.1523:77.355b10. On the dating of the *Ming seng zhuan*, see Ji Y. 2009, 199.

extracts from Juqu Jingsheng's *Scripture on the Secrets of Chan and the Healing of Illness*.[11] By the early sixth century, then, Juqu Jingsheng's long *chan* text was already sometimes divided into shorter texts bearing different titles.

The text called *Scripture on the Secrets of Chan and the Healing of Illness*, attributed to Juqu Jingsheng in these sixth-century sources, vanishes from later records. Catalogs from the Sui-Tang era (581–907), when describing texts personally seen by their authors, attribute to Juqu Jingsheng a text in one scroll bearing the rather different title *Zhi chan bing mi yao fa* 治禪病祕要法.[12] Based on its identical name, as well as its length in sheets of paper (information the catalogs sometimes record), this must be equivalent to the received text of the *Methods for Curing*.

Modern scholars have usually assumed that the *Scripture on the Secrets of Chan and the Healing of Illness* mentioned in early sixth-century sources is the same text as the received *Methods for Curing*. This identification has seemed plausible for two reasons. First, because the texts seem to be similar in size: the received *Methods for Curing* is in two scrolls, the same as the *Chu san zang ji ji* catalog description of the *Scripture on the Secrets of Chan and the Healing of Illness*. And second, because the colophon to the *Scripture on the Secrets of Chan and the Healing of Illness*, included elsewhere in the *Chu san zang ji ji*, is the same colophon found at the end of the transmitted versions of the *Methods for Curing*.

This colophon, however, may be of less evidentiary value than one might think. In Sengyou's *Chu san zang ji ji*, the colophon is named the "postproduction note" (出經後記) to the *Scripture on the Secrets of Chan and the Healing of Illness* (*CSZJJ*, T.2145:55.66a24). As Sengyou encountered it, however, this colophon would have been appended directly to the end of the text in question, without an independent title of its own.[13] Internally, the colophon specifies neither the name nor the size of the text to which it was attached. Strictly speaking, then, the colophon demonstrates only that the *last* segment of the received *Methods for Curing* is the same as the final segment of the *Scripture on the Secrets of Chan and the Healing of Illness* seen by Sengyou, who presumably copied the colophon from there and gave it a title based on the name of that text.

The apparent congruence in size (two scrolls) between the received *Methods for Curing* and the *Scripture on the Secrets of Chan and the Healing of*

11. *CSZJJ*, T.2145:55.30c7–8

12. For the Sui-Tang catalog data, see Appendix 3, table 8. Although this new title contains many of the same characters as the old one, it invokes the distinctive idea of healing "meditation illness" (*chan bing* 禪病), a word that does not occur in earlier titles of the text or even within the *Methods for Curing* itself. This word, and something close to the new title, is first attested in one of Zhiyi's citations of the *Methods for Curing* (Appendix 1, 3a).

13. This is how the colophon appears in most received versions of the *Methods for Curing* (K^1, J, P, S, Y, Q, and Kg), immediately after the text but before the final listing of the title "Methods for Curing." Only in K, and following this the Taishō edition, is the colophon given its own title of "postface" (後序).

Illness as described in catalogs is also deceptive. Indeed, our very earliest source—the *Chu san zang ji ji* biography of Juqu Jingsheng—describes the *Scripture on the Secrets of Chan and the Healing of Illness* as *five* scrolls in length, not two. Medieval Chinese texts did, it is true, often change their formatting. The five-scroll text listed in Juqu Jingsheng's biography could have been rearranged into the two-scroll text listed in the later *Chu san zang ji ji* catalog. Yet even if this were so, we can be certain that the extant *Methods for Curing* (two scrolls) was never a five-scroll text because its scrolls are already unusually short. Each is only half the length of the scrolls of the *Chan Essentials*, for example. Dividing the extant *Methods for Curing* into five parts would yield scrolls of roughly six Tang-era sheets of paper each, an impossibly short length.[14]

For this reason, the five-scroll *Scripture on the Secrets of Chan and the Healing of Illness* listed in Juqu Jingsheng's earliest biography must have contained more material than the extant *Methods for Curing*, which before the printed editions of the tenth century always circulated in a one-scroll format befitting its size of approximately 30 Tang-era sheets of paper.[15] The original *Scripture on the Secrets of Chan and the Healing of Illness* evidently lost at least some material, and possibly a great deal of it, between the late fifth and late sixth centuries. By the late sixth century, the original text bearing this name was gone, with only the newly titled and much shorter *Methods for Curing* remaining.

While we cannot track this process exactly, as mentioned above we can observe that a number of new and differently titled texts pertaining to the "secrets" of meditation appeared as the *Scripture on the Secrets of Chan and the Healing of Illness* grew smaller (see table 3). By no later than the early 500s there had appeared the *Chan mi yao* (Secrets of Meditation), attributed to the translator Dharmamitra, and a *Chan mi yao jing* (Scripture on the Secrets of Meditation), acknowledged as an excerpt of Juqu Jingsheng's original text. By the late sixth century, catalogs mention yet another text, the *Chan mi yao fa* attributed to Kumārajīva, probably the direct ancestor of the received *Chan Essentials*.

If we add this data to the linguistic and other similarities between the *Chan Essentials* and *Methods for Curing* that have long been noted by scholars,

14. Scrolls of long Buddhist texts were usually between 20 and 30 sheets (紙) each (Fujieda 1999, 178). The two scrolls of the extant *Methods for Curing* are already on the short side of this, equivalent to roughly 15 sheets in Tang-dynasty sizes. There are, moreover, no internal divisions of the text that would justify a five-part arrangement.

15. Transmitted Sui and Tang catalogs always record the *Methods for Curing* as one scroll (see Appendix 3, table 8). Japanese manuscript versions of the *Methods for Curing* stemming from Tang lineages are also all in a single scroll (*Nihon genson hasshu issaikyō mokuroku*, 236). Copying records from the eighth-century Japanese imperial scriptoria similarly describe the text as one scroll, of 30–35 sheets when that information is given (*Dai Nihon komonjo*, 2.707; 8.222; 10.324 [corrected to one in the margin]; 12.154; 12.447; 12.503; 12.538; 18.354; 20.352; 20.511; 20.549; 21.565; 23.132; 24.443).

Table 3. Texts on the "secrets" of *chan*, ca. 500–600

Before 500 (*Chu san zang ji ji* biographies)	Early 500s (*Chu san zang ji ji* catalog and other Liang-era sources)	ca. 600 (*Sui* and early Tang catalogs)
Chan yao mi mi zhi bing jing 禪要祕密治病經 (*Scripture on the Secrets of Chan and the Healing of Illness*). 5 scrolls. Juqu Jingsheng.	*Chan mi yao* 禪祕要. 3 or 5 scrolls. Dharmamitra.	*Chan mi yao [jing]* 禪祕要[經]. 3 / 4 / 5 scrolls. Dharmamitra.
	Chan yao mi mi zhi bing jing 禪要祕密治病經. 2 scrolls. Juqu Jingsheng.	*Chan mi yao fa* 禪祕要法. 3 scrolls. Kumārajīva.
	Chan mi yao jing 禪祕要經. 1 scroll. (Excerpted from Juqu Jingsheng's *Chan yao mi mi zhi bing jing*.)	*Zhi chan bing mi yao* 治禪病祕要. 1 scroll. Juqu Jingsheng.

we are led to the conclusion that what is described in the late fifth century as Juqu Jingsheng's five-scroll *Scripture on the Secrets of Chan and the Healing of Illness* contained the totality of what is now two separate texts, the *Chan Essentials* and *Methods for Curing*.[16] In fact, these two titles arguably align with the two halves of the original title of Juqu Jingsheng's text: *Chan mi yao [fa jing]* 禪祕要[法經] (Chan Essentials) with *Chan yao mi mi* 禪要祕密 (Secrets of Chan), and *Zhi chan bing mi yao fa* 治禪病祕要法 (Methods for Curing) with *Zhi bing jing* 治病經 (Scripture on Healing Illness).[17]

Because the *Chan Essentials* portion of this hypothesized collection provides a complete path to arhatship, it is not hard to see how it could have come to stand on its own. Still, a single text with content equivalent to the *Chan Essentials* followed immediately by the *Methods for Curing* would also be coherent. Both texts are already compilations of multiple sutras, each framed in a similar way by the story of a meditator who experiences a hindrance for which the Buddha's ensuing instructions provide a solution. There is also a clear thematic continuity between the end of the *Chan Essentials* and the

16. It is unclear how this collection would have been divided. Possibly one sutra per scroll, with the final and very short sutra of the *Methods for Curing* added to the fifth scroll. But this would have made for scrolls of uneven length (the first sutra of the *Chan Essentials* is nearly twice the length of the second, for example). Alternatively, we know that four-scroll recensions of the *Chan Essentials* existed, with divisions not at sutra boundaries. *Tempyō Chan Essentials 1* apparently represents the first scroll of such an arrangement (see Appendix 3). Together with a one-scroll *Methods for Curing*, this would yield five scrolls of roughly equal size.

17. This is even clearer if we use the title of Juqu Jingsheng's five-scroll text given in his *Gao seng zhuan* biography, namely, *Chan mi yao zhi bing jing* 禪祕要治病經 (*GSZ*, T.2059:50.337a11–12). The first half of this title precisely matches the name of the three-scroll text attributed to Dharmamitra in the *Chu san zang ji ji* catalog. The *Methods for Curing* also sometimes circulated under the shorter name *Zhi chan bing jing* 治禪病經 (Appendix 3, table 9), which is closer than the received title to the second half of the original title of Juqu Jingsheng's text.

beginning of the *Methods for Curing*. The last sutra of the former features the story of Agnidatta, who is unable to reach arhatship because, having suffered madness in a past life owing to a disturbance in the wind element, he would now go mad if he were to enter the "wind element" meditation (*Chan Essentials* 4.0.1–5). In the *Methods for Curing*, the frame story of the first sutra dovetails nicely with this: the Buddha provides a method to cure practitioners who have gone mad while immersed in meditation on the wind element (1.1.2). Read back to back, the *Chan Essentials* and *Methods for Curing* combine to form a coherent collection that charts the path of meditation leading up to arhatship (attained in the fourth sutra of the *Chan Essentials*) and then provides, as an appendix, methods for alleviating meditatively induced illness and thwarting demonic attacks.

Some measure of external confirmation that the *Chan Essentials* and *Methods for Curing* once appeared together as a single document in this format actually turns up in a somewhat unexpected place—the late sixth-century meditation treatises of Zhiyi, who we know was familiar with both texts.[18] The core sections of these treatises mirror the structure of the hypothetical *Scripture on the Secrets of Chan and the Healing of Illness* as I have described it, namely, an exposition of the complete path of meditation followed by, in this order, techniques for curing the sicknesses and then demonic interference that plague meditators.[19] Why Zhiyi would have arranged his meditation texts in this way, which is quite different from the linear format typically found in Indian path treatises, has never been explained by modern scholars. We may now hypothesize, however, that Zhiyi was simply following the format of what would have at the time been the most authoritative canonical source of information about the practice of meditation—the *Chan Essentials* and *Methods for Curing*, a then-single compendium that claimed, in its opening pages, to contain the first teachings on Buddhist meditation ever delivered in our world (*Chan Essentials* 1.1.10).

From Meditation Manuals to Meditation Scriptures

Hundreds of apocryphal Buddhist scriptures were created in China between the second and tenth centuries (Cao 2011). Some were eventually included in the printed canons while others were lost or excluded, surviving only in manuscript caches such as the Dunhuang documents. Though from surveying the extant examples we can learn a great deal about the content of such apocryphal literature, we almost never know anything precise about how

18. Zhiyi's meditation treatises often cite both texts under a variety of names and inherit from them in other ways as well. On his citations, see Appendix 1; and on his debt to their content, see *Chan Before Chan*, chap. 3.

19. This is the order of the core part of the *Shi chan boluomi ci di fa men*, on the "internal expedients" (內方便). The *Xiao zhi guan* also uses this order as its general structure, with a final section on "realizing the fruit" (證果) placed as a conclusion, though it inverts the ordering of "illness" and "demonic attack" (Sekiguchi 1969, 26).

such texts came into existence. Some may well have had "authors" in something close to the modern sense. But many others were likely the result of efforts that lie somewhere between the activities we think of as "composition" and "translation." For them, we must envision a more complicated process in which pre-existing Buddhist texts and translations were borrowed, copied, extracted, reshaped, and edited, possibly over many years with many hands at work.

These usually invisible details are not incidental—they implicate the evidentiary value of these sources. An apocryphal Chinese Buddhist text that does nothing more than gather together individual stories that had each been translated from an Indian source must be read differently—in terms of the evidence it provides for the activities and interests of Buddhists in China—than one in which passages, personages, or themes from Indian Buddhist literature have been appropriated but then put to entirely new ends. This is one reason scholars who read apocryphal Chinese Buddhist literature tend to direct their attention to moments when ideas, characters, or topoi of clearly non-Indian origin appear: when Confucius appears in a Buddhist sutra (Ishibashi 1991), for example, a precise textual history is unnecessary to be certain that here is a trace of how Buddhist ideas were being taken up in a Chinese cultural setting.

The *Chan Essentials* and *Methods for Curing* lack this kind of blatantly apocryphal content for the most part. Nevertheless, we can assess to a certain degree the level of active intervention required to create them, relative to Indian Buddhist sources in Chinese translation, because another surviving fifth-century meditation manual—the so-called *Five Gates* (*Wu men chan jing yao yong fa*)—preserves some of the raw materials, already written in Chinese but not yet crafted into the literary form of a sutra, that went into a sizeable portion of the *Chan Essentials*.

The relationship between these texts allows us to draw three conclusions. First, it provides definitive proof, above and beyond other forms of internal evidence (see Appendix 2), that this part of the *Chan Essentials* was created in China rather than directly translated from an Indic source. (Moreover, given its overall uniformity of style and content, we may safely apply this conclusion to the remainder of the *Chan Essentials* and to the *Methods for Curing* as well.) Second, it demonstrates the *minimum* level of editorial or authorial intervention lying between any Indic sources in Chinese translation and the final versions. Third, it provides the basis for a more general hypothesis about the production of these texts (and perhaps the closely related Contemplation Scriptures as well)—namely, that they were created when individuals for whom literary Chinese was the scriptural language of choice took meditation manuals already written in Chinese (manuals that were either the translations of Indic originals or records of the oral teachings of one or more of the fifth-century Indian *chan* masters then in China), elaborated and expanded them, and finally gave them the imprimatur of the sutra form.

The *Five Gates*

The *Five Gates* is a short and enigmatic meditation manual that by the turn of the sixth century at the latest was held to be a translation made by Dharmamitra (d. 442), one of the most famous foreign *chan* masters of the early Song dynasty.[20] Like many other fifth-century *chan* scriptures, the *Five Gates* is framed not as a sutra but as a compilation of meditation teachings assembled by past Indian masters, in this case, the patriarch Buddhamitra 佛陀蜜多.[21] Though Dharmamitra's true role in the production of the *Five Gates* is not certain, nothing excludes the possibility that this text is, or was directly derived from, the translation of one or more Indic sources.

Structurally, the *Five Gates* is less a complete, coherent work with a beginning, middle, and end than a loosely organized assemblage of notes on diverse topics associated with the practice of meditation.[22] Stylistically, it clearly contains two distinct strata. One set of passages—which I call the "B format" sections—present a number of named meditation practices in a relatively straightforward manner. Here we find short explanations of the "white bone contemplation method" (白骨觀法) the "*samādhi* of the contemplation of the buddha" (觀佛三昧), the "method for contemplating the buddhas of the ten directions" (觀十方諸佛法), and the "contemplation method of the four immeasurable minds" (四無量觀法) among others.[23] These portions of the *Five Gates* share a similar expository style and furthermore reappear, nearly verbatim and together with other similar methods, in a different text called the *Concise Essentials of Meditation* (*Si wei lüe yao fa*), as well as in the *Contemplation Scripture of the Buddha* known only from the Dunhuang manuscripts.[24] Although these three overlapping texts may well draw from a common, now-lost source, the *Five Gates* appears to preserve

20. *CSZJJ*, T.2145:55.12c2. Dharmamitra's biography in the *Ming seng zhuan* refers to a *Wu men chan jing* 五門禪經 (*Meisōden shō*, Z.1523:77.355b10), presumably the same text. Dharmamitra's biography from the *Chu san zang ji ji* lists, as his only *chan*-related text, an "Essential Methods of Chan [from] Various Scriptures" (諸經禪法要; *CSZJJ*, T.2145:55.12c2). This title probably points to the *Five Gates* as well; the name suggests a collection of methods drawn from various sources, which fits the content of the *Five Gates* as we have it.

21. Buddhamitra's name appears on extant copies of the *Five Gates*; we can be certain he was connected to the *Five Gates* by no later than the early sixth century (*Fan fan yu*, T.2130:54.1000c10). He is named as an Indian patriarch in other fifth-century sources (*Fu fa zang yin yuan zhuan*, T.2058:50.314a4–5; Demiéville 1954, 360n3).

22. For an outline of the *Five Gates*, see Yamabe 2010 and Demiéville 1954, 360–363.

23. *WMCJ*, T.619:15.326c25–327a7; 327a8–c1; 327c2–16; 332a22–b21.

24. I discuss this text below. An edition based on Stein no. 2585, the most complete manuscript, is included in the Taishō (T.2914). As for the *Concise Essentials*, it is attributed to An Shigao in the *Chu san zang ji ji* (T.2145:55.6a16), but its vocabulary clearly implies a post-Kumārajīva dating (Sakaino 1935, 462). It is notable for its "method for contemplating the Buddha of Immeasurable Life" (觀無量壽佛法; *Si wei lüe yao fa*, T.617:15.299c19), recalling the *Amitāyus Contemplation Scripture*, as well as a "Lotus-*samādhi* contemplation method" (法華三昧觀法; ibid., 300b24–c14), the earliest reference to the "Lotus-*samādhi*" which would later be so important for Zhiyi and others (Lai W. 2001). The *Concise Essentials* has been translated into English by Mukhopadhyaya 1950 and Willemen 2012.

the least developed form of the material.[25] This is made particularly clear by a passage featuring a well-known canonical pericope on the impurity of the body: reproduced in its traditional form in the *Five Gates*, the corresponding *Concise Essentials* version interrupts the canonical formula, at an awkward location, with a long digression.[26]

That the *Five Gates* is in general a fragmentary record of material that later Chinese-authored or compiled meditation manuals sometimes expanded or adapted is directly relevant for our assessment of the other layer of this text, which I call the "A-format" sections. These sections are clearly distinguished from the B-format sections by their literary form as a *dialog* between a meditation master, who assigns various topics of meditation, and a meditation practitioner, who reports to the master his experiences, usually visions. These remarkable passages bear an unmistakable, if historically difficult to account for resemblance to meditation treatises of the *borān kammaṭṭhāna* (Tantric Theravāda) traditions of Southeast Asia, first attested only centuries later.[27]

The initial A-format passages typically provide the meditation teacher's direct speech, a description of the practitioner's visions, an account of the process whereby he then reports the visions to the master, and the further instructions the master gives in response:

> The master further instructs him: "From now on put aside the previous two contemplations and fix your mind to your navel." After receiving the master's instructions, [the practitioner] single-mindedly contemplates his

25. Yamabe (2010) has proposed that the "chaotic" arrangement of the *Five Gates* when compared with the *Concise Essentials* implies that the *Five Gates* borrowed these sections from the *Concise Essentials*. The *Five Gates* is, clearly, a composite text. But we need not assume that the more orderly text was the source of the more chaotic one; if anything, the reverse is more likely, all things being equal.

26. *WMCJ*, T.619:15.332c7–25 and *Si wei lüe yao fa*, T.617:15.298b18–c18. Giving a version of the famous refrain that one should enumerate the impurities of the body as a farmer would identify different grains in a storehouse (see, e.g., *Zhong ahan jing*, T.26:1.583b4–17), the *Five Gates* closely follows the pericope, saying that one should first inspect the 36 impurities in one's own body in this way, then contemplate the bodies of others similarly. The *Concise Essentials*, after describing the meditator's contemplation of his own body, digresses for several lines before then returning to the closing words of the original pericope, that "one's own body is like this, and so too the bodies of others" (內身如此外身不異; T.617:15.298b29–c12). It is unlikely that a later editor would have removed from the *Concise Essentials* passage precisely those lines that restore the pericope to its original form. Here, at least, it must be the *Concise Essentials* that has expanded on a source resembling the *Five Gates*.

27. Bizot 1992 is particularly similar in form and style. On the *borān kammaṭṭhāna* traditions, see Crosby 2000 and 2013; Bernon 2000. Though other Indian meditation treatises sometimes provide examples of the speech by which the teacher should instruct a disciple (see, e.g., *Śrāvakabhūmi*, 3.118), the *Five Gates* is unusual—and this is what it shares with the *borān kammaṭṭhāna* literature—in including the words uttered by the meditator reporting his experiences. A thoroughgoing comparison between these two bodies of literature, separated in time by over a millennium, would undoubtedly be illuminating.

> navel.... He sees something within his navel, like a heron's egg, pure white in color.
>
> He goes and tells the master [what he has experienced]. The master says: "Look further at this place." [The practitioner] does as the master instructs. Contemplating it, [he sees] a lotus flower, with a beryl stem.[28]... The practitioner then feels happy and relaxed. He sees his own body to be as pure as a jewel.
>
> He then tells the master what he has seen. The master says: "Good!"... The master then instructs him: "Further contemplate within your navel." He contemplates as instructed and sees that on the crown of his head is a five-colored light. Having seen this, he tells the master.[29]

This passage merely describes the visions the meditator obtains and states that they are told to the master. Later in the A-format sections, the *Five Gates* also renders the first-person speech through which the meditator might report his visions:

> Instruct [the practitioner] to contemplate his body. If he says: "I see my body to be entirely pure, like a ball of light," then instruct him to contemplate the buddhas [and mentally] perform obeisance and make offerings to them one after another. If he says: "I see an array of innumerable buddhas and I scatter flowers in offerings to all of these buddhas, one after the other, in their entirety," then this is the twenty-fourth thing. Instruct him to contemplate the flowers that have been offered. If he says: "I see the flowers falling beside the buddhas and transforming into flower canopies...[30]

Note here the repeating words "I see" (我見), which, in this passage and throughout the A-format sections, introduce the meditator's speech concerning his visions, a pattern that will prove an important clue as we consider the relationship between the *Five Gates* and the *Chan Essentials*.

The *Five Gates* and the *Chan Essentials*

The parallels between the *Five Gates* and the *Chan Essentials* were first observed by Yamabe Nobuyoshi, who realized that the entirety of the third sutra of the *Chan Essentials* could be aligned with a long section of the *Five*

28. Here a long vision is described in detail.

29. 師復更教言，汝從今捨前二觀，係心在齊。即受師教，一心觀齊...見齊有物，猶如鴈卵，其色鮮白。即往白師。師言，汝更視在[>此]處。如師所教。觀已，有蓮花，琉璃為莖...行人爾時身體柔軟輕悅。自見己身明淨如雜寶色。即以所見白師。師言，大善...師教言，更觀齊中。即如教觀，見頂有五色光焰。見已白師。(*WMCJ*, T.619:15.326a14–28).

30. 教自觀身。若言，我自見身，悉明淨，喻如聚光。教令觀佛，次第作禮供養。若言，我見無量諸佛行列，我持眾花次第灑散，供養諸佛悉令周遍。是二十四事。教令觀此所供養花。若言，我見花墮者，在於佛邊便成花帳...(*WMCJ*, 329c24–29).

Gates (all in what I have called the A-format).[31] The relationship between the two texts, or their debt to a common source, is beyond question: the same topics and visionary imagery appear in precisely the same order, although their treatment in the *Five Gates* is always shorter and more schematic. Yet the *Five Gates* is not merely a condensed version of the *Chan Essentials*.[32] Setting the two texts side by side, we can see that the *Chan Essentials*, written as a sutra, must have been based on either the *Five Gates* itself or another Chinese text similar to it in form. Here, in short, we get a small glimpse of how a schematic meditation manual written in Chinese was transformed into a fully developed apocryphal sutra.

The parallels between the *Five Gates* and the *Chan Essentials* begin after the narrative introduction to the third sutra as the Buddha delivers meditation instructions to the protagonist Panthaka (see table 4). The master-disciple dialog format of the *Five Gates* becomes more explicit as the section progresses, while the level of correspondence between the texts remains fairly constant. A similar sequence of practices and visions is presented in each text, always lengthier and more elaborate in the *Chan Essentials*.[33] Parallel in content, the two texts share specific and often unusual words and phrases, suggesting that the two documents are related as Chinese texts, not merely as different translations of similar underlying Indic-language content.

Whatever intermediary texts may once have existed, the *Chan Essentials* was evidently composed with reference to an anterior source that closely resembled the dialog format of the *Five Gates*. Several reasons compel this conclusion rather than the reverse. First, the *Five Gates* not only fails to include anything resembling the narrative sections of the *Chan Essentials*, but it often presents material from both before and after important narrative interludes (e.g., Panthaka's becoming an arhat) as a single, integrated sequence (see table 5). This is revealing because if the *Five Gates* had been based on the *Chan Essentials*, summarizing it while excluding the narratives, we would still expect those narrative breaks to have helped the compiler divide his summary into sections of even the most minimal kind, which did not happen.

Second, comparing the texts to each other also makes evident an occasional problem of voicing in the *Chan Essentials*. In the first parallel passage in table 4, the Buddha's first-person instructions to Panthaka are phrased as simple imperative verbs telling Panthaka what to do: "you should now carefully contemplate," and so forth. Yet slightly further along (table 5), the

31. *WMCJ*, T.619:15.327c18–329a10. See Yamabe 1999c, 92; Yamabe 2010, 1050.

32. This is the hypothesis favored by Yamabe (see previous note).

33. The two texts often frame the material differently as well. In table 4, the *Five Gates* presents the contrast between a vision of few versus many skeletons not as a progressive sequence, as does the *Chan Essentials*, but as two different visions, each with a different meaning. Other passages in the *Five Gates* make similar interpretations. For further details, see *Chan Before Chan*, chap. 2.

Table 4. *Chan Essentials* versus *Five Gates* (1)

Chan Essentials 3.21.2–3 (*CMY,* T.613:15.258c28–259a12)	*Five Gates* (T.619:15.327c18–21)
The Buddha said to Panthaka: Without shifting your mind to anything else, you should now carefully contemplate the bone in the large toe (大指) of your [right] foot. Make a swelling gradually appear on top of the bone. Then cause it to swell up (膖脹) further.	First instruct [the practitioner] to concentrate his mind and contemplate the top of the large toe of his right foot. [The practitioner] sees it swelling. 先教注意觀右脚大指上。見洪脹。
Next use your mind (以意) to make the swelling gradually bigger until it is the size of a bean. Next use your mind (以意) to make the swelling rot away and the flesh split open with yellow pus flowing out. Within the yellow pus blood flows profusely. When the flesh has entirely rotted away from that single bone, you will see only (肌膚爛盡唯見) the bone of the right toe, white like *ke*-jade or snow.	Using his mind, he should peel [the skin?] away and make a yellow liquid flow out, as if pus and blood were emerging. When the skin and flesh have rotted away, [the practitioner] sees only the white bones. 以意發抓却之。令黃汁流如膿血出。肌肉爛盡已，唯見白骨。
When you see this one bone in this manner, gradually expand from the right foot until half the body swells up and rots away.... Seeing half the body in this way, now see the entire body swell up and rot away while discharging horrible pus and an outflow of blood...	When these things have all been seen, [the practitioner] should be further taught the bone contemplation. 盡見，應廣教骨觀。
Having contemplated [and] then seen one [such bloated corpse and skeleton], now see two. Seeing two, go on to see three...four...until you see the entire world (一天下) full of them.	If he sees the entire world [filled with skeletons], he should be instructed in the great vehicle. If he [only] sees them nearby, he should be instructed in the small vehicle. 若見滿一天下者，宜教大乘。若見近者，宜教小乘。

Buddha's direct speech to Panthaka now includes, before the actual meditation instructions, the verb "instruct" (*jiao* 教). Either the Buddha is saying "I instruct you," unlike earlier in this section, or he is suggesting that Panthaka be instructed by someone else, which makes little sense given the context. But while this language feels out of place here, when it continues in later passages in the *Chan Essentials*, it begins to fit. After Panthaka becomes an arhat, the Buddha no longer delivers his teachings directly to a prospective meditator, but to Ānanda, to whom they are presented as the

Table 5. *Chan Essentials* versus *Five Gates* (2)

Chan Essentials 3.21.8 and 3.21.10 (*CMY*, T.613:15.259a26–b27)	*Five Gates* (T.619:15.327c27–328a1)
[You, Panthaka,] must be instructed to contemplate the white bones again (復教更觀白骨). If you see other things, under no circumstances should you follow after them. Merely make the mind clear, so that you see your white skeleton, [white] as a snow-covered mountain.	Instruct [the practitioner] to continue contemplating the white bones. 教熟[>續][b]觀白骨。
If you see other things (若見餘物), rouse your mind and eliminate them with this thought: "The Buddha has instructed me to contemplate the bones. Why do these other meditative visions appear? I must now single-mindedly contemplate the bones." [*narrative sequence in which Panthaka becomes an arhat, the Buddha now continues preaching to Ānanda*]	If he sees other things, [the master] should say to the one before him [the practitioner]: "This too is good.[c] But for now, put this aside and only contemplate the white bones." 若見餘物，當語前人[d]，此亦好耳，置是事，但觀白骨。
Next, [the practitioner] should contemplate his body and see the white bones, white like *ke*-jade or snow. The skeletons then reenter his body, and the glowing light of the white bones entirely disappears. Seeing this, the practitioner suddenly feels joyous and serene in mind. When he emerges from trance, the crown of his head feels warm . . . Continuing [his meditation], he further perceives his body becoming warm (續復自見身體溫暖), and he feels joyful and happy. His countenance appears serene. He needs but little sleep, and his body is free of all pain or trouble. Having attained this stage of "heat" (得此暖法),[a] he constantly feels warmth in his belly, and he is perpetually joyful.	If [the practitioner] contemplates the white bones for a long time and says: "I feel a warmth within my body," then instruct him to continue contemplating. [If] having perceived the feeling of warmth he feels peaceful and happy, this is the stage of "heat." 若久觀白骨云：我身中覺煖，教令續觀。見煖覺已，安隱和悅者，此是煖法。

[a] See "The Path to Liberation" in chap. 2.

[b] Emendation tentative, based on the similar use of 續 below and the full context of the passage.

[c] Similar usage occurs elsewhere in the *Five Gates* (326a1; 328c7, c11, c17; 329a1).

[d] The line is awkward. Perhaps emend 當語前[>行]人. Or more dramatically: 當語前[>師]<師>人[>言] ("[The practitioner] must tell the master. The master says. . . ."), based on the repeating pattern 白師師言 (326a1, a10, a17, a26, a28, b9, b22, c3; 328b20).

method Ānanda should use to instruct future practitioners (3.21.9.3 and passim).

Yet if this language of "instructing" sits unevenly in the narrative of the *Chan Essentials*, it is entirely natural in *all* the parallel passages in the *Five Gates*. This same style is even found in the many A-format passages of the *Five Gates* that have no parallel in the *Chan Essentials*.[34] Once again we are led to surmise that the entire third sutra of the *Chan Essentials* was adapted from a source constructed like the *Five Gates*—namely, as a set of directives for how a meditation teacher should instruct a student. As these passages were adapted to the narrative demands of the *Chan Essentials*, sometimes only a minimal change of voicing was required (such as when the Buddha preaches to Ānanda). But occasionally, notably when the Buddha gives direct instruction to Panthaka, more substantial editing was needed, and this editing was not completely successful.

This hypothesis is confirmed in a later passage where the voicing of a master-disciple dialog intrudes conspicuously into the narrative of the *Chan Essentials* (see table 6). In these passages, while the parallels in content and phrasing are much as they are elsewhere, what stands out for special notice is the final paragraph in the *Chan Essentials*, in which the Buddha's preaching to Ānanda is introduced by the words "I see" (我見). For the Buddha to say that *he* sees this vision makes no sense at all, as this vision, given the context, can only be what the meditator sees. Yet this wording is entirely unproblematic in the *Five Gates*, which renders, both here and throughout its A-format sections, the meditator's first-person speech as he reports his visions to the master, speech always beginning with these same words "I see." This formula occurs over seventy times in the *Five Gates*, including in many passages that have no parallel in the *Chan Essentials*.[35] Why these words were retained in this one passage of the *Chan Essentials* is not clear. It may simply have been careless editing, which this text shows in other cases as well.[36] Whatever the reasons, its presence implies that it must be the *Chan Essentials* that was created on the basis of the *Five Gates* (or a source similar to it in form and content), not the opposite.

Still, many questions about this process remain unanswered. Did a single individual simply rewrite the *Five Gates* or a similar manual or manuals into

34. The stylistic uniformity among the A-format sections of the *Five Gates*, those parallel to the *Chan Essentials* as well as those not, is another argument against Yamabe's theory that the *Five Gates* passages that parallel the *Chan Essentials* are not part of the "original" text of the *Five Gates* (Yamabe 1999c, 92; Yamabe 2010).

35. Apart from the clear-cut case shown in table 6, in a few additional passages in the *Chan Essentials* pronoun usage more fitting for a master-disciple dialog intrudes into the Buddha's preaching; see *Chan Essentials* 2.20.8, n. 361; 3.21.5, n. 400; and 3.29.5, n. 489.

36. In addition to a major narrative contradiction in the story of Nandi in the second sutra (see *Chan Essentials* 2.0.1, n. 282), minor problems include 3.21.11, which seems to restate the content of 3.21.10, only framing it more explicitly as the Buddha's preaching, and 1.1.2, where the editors have seemingly forgotten to begin with "the Buddha said."

Table 6. *Chan Essentials* versus *Five Gates* (3)

Chan Essentials 3.24.1–3.26.1 (T.613:15.260a8–b13)	*Five Gates* (T.619:15.328a10–16)
Next the practitioner must again be instructed to fix his thoughts, steady his mind, and then contemplate his own body as a bundle of brush (自觀己身猶如草束)... he must be instructed to again contemplate his body gathered back together like a bundle of dry brush (如乾草束).	Next instruct [the practitioner] to contemplate his body as a bundle of brush, or an empty burlap sack. 次教觀身如草束，或如空葦囊。
He now sees his body as firm and strong... when he contemplates his body, it again resembles an empty sack (空囊). A flame appears inside and burns it up entirely (有火從內燒此身盡). When his body has been completely consumed, he will constantly see the light of this fire whenever he enters trance... entirely incinerated, he suddenly knows that he has no self (無我)...	If he says: "I see my body as a bundle of dry brush, or an empty burlap sack. A fire arises and burns it up entirely, and then there is no self," 若言：我見自身如乾草束，或如空葦囊，有火燒盡，乃無有我。
He must again be instructed to fix his thoughts and reflect. Fixing his thoughts on the tip of his nose, he again contemplates (更觀) the fire [and reflects]: "From where does it arise (從何處起)?" In contemplating the fire, he contemplates that his own body is entirely without self. When he sees there is no self, the fire spontaneously goes out... [*narrative interlude*]	then instruct him to again contemplate, [saying]: "When you see [the fire] arise, from where does it arise? When it passes away, from where does it pass away? Contemplate this." 教令更觀：汝意[>見][a]起時從何處起，滅時從何處滅。觀之。
The Buddha said to Ānanda: I see (我見) that when the fire goes out, it goes out beginning at the tip of the nose (火滅時，先從鼻滅) and then goes out all at once in the rest of the body. Internally, the heart-fire and the eighty-eight defilements are all extinguished as well, and [the practitioner's] body feels pure, cool, balanced, and harmonized within (身中清涼調和得所). [He] deeply realizes and sees with perfect clarity that there definitely is no self (深自覺悟，了了分明，決定無我). Whether in trance or not, he always knows that within the body there is no self.	The one contemplating must say: "I see that the perception of fire, when it arises, arises from my mind, and when it goes out, it goes out [beginning at] my nose. When [the fire on] the nose goes out, the body is harmonized and peaceful within. I do not perceive there to be a self, and this is perfectly clear." 觀者要言：我見卒[>火][b]覺起時從意起，滅時鼻頭滅，鼻頭滅時，身中和靜。不覺有我，了了分明。

[a]Emendation tentative. We might instead construe 汝意 (your mind) as the subject of the verb "arise," but based on the ensuing dialog of the subject here is clearly the fire.

[b]The curious expression "seeing the perception of fire" (見火覺), in addition to fitting with the *Chan Essentials* parallel, is identical in form to the expression "seeing the perception of heat" (見煖覺) that occurs earlier in the *Five Gates* (*WMCJ*, T.619:15.327c29).

the *Chan Essentials?* Or did the manuals evolve more gradually? While the full details of the process lie beyond our grasp, there is another source that sheds some light on the kind of textual development that meditation manuals such as the *Five Gates* may have routinely undergone as they were copied and circulated, paving the way for the eventual emergence of an apocryphal sutra such as the *Chan Essentials.*

This source is Stein Dunhuang manuscript no. 2585, bearing the nondescript title *Contemplation Scripture of the Buddha* (*Fo shuo guan jing* 佛說觀經), which, as mentioned above, is one of two presumably fifth-century sources containing a nearly exact copy of several sections of the *Five Gates.*[37] The major parallels between Stein no. 2585 and the *Five Gates* lie in the B-format sections of the latter. But there are also a few counterparts to the A-format sections (though not to any that also are paralleled in the *Chan Essentials*).[38]

What is noticeable about Stein no. 2585 in relation to the *Five Gates* is that in reformulating the shared passages it removes certain words and phrases, underlined in the left column of table 7. This is a reduction in detail, not an expansion as occurs with the *Chan Essentials.* Yet it is striking that what Stein no. 2585 removes is most (though not all) of the words pertaining to the *mechanics of the master-disciple interaction.*

Compared with the *Five Gates,* Stein no. 2585 has undergone something akin to what linguists call *entextualization*—the process of taking a sample of speech and making it replicable, as a "text," by modifying those parts whose meaning depends on the immediate situation of the utterance, features such as spatial deictics (*here* or *there*) that necessarily change meaning in a new context.[39] The *Five Gates,* of course, is already a text in this sense; it is not, and probably never was, the raw transcript of an actual master-disciple dialog. Still, Stein no. 2585 can be considered a more entextualized version of the *Five Gates* because it suppresses the lexical markers of its imagined context—personal pronouns and direct references to the speakers and their bodily movements before each act of speaking—and thereby becomes a document that even while retaining the same content is no longer tied to a dialog format, thus approximating more closely the literary style of the abstract, universal, and context-free teachings on meditation delivered by the Buddha in the *Chan Essentials.*

37. Fragments of the *Contemplation Scripture of the Buddha* (which despite its name is not framed as a sutra) also survive on Dunhuang manuscripts Pelliot no. 3835 (no. 3) and Дх no. 15 from the St. Petersburg collection (*E cang Dunhuang wen xian,* 6:19–20), where they have been incorporated into a Tantric ritual manual. It is probably from a version such as this that the same instructions found their way into the Mongolian meditation manual studied by Aleksei Pozdenyev in the late nineteenth century (see Yamabe 2010).

38. For a table showing what is shared between the texts, see Yamabe 2010, 1054. The second source that shares content with the *Five Gates,* the *Concise Essentials,* only has parallels to the B-format sections.

39. On entextualization, see Silverstein and Urban 1996.

Table 7. *Five Gates* and Stein manuscript no. 2585

Five Gates (T.619)	Stein no. 2585 (T.2914)
[The practitioner] should then get up from his seat, kneel before the master and say: "Concentrating my mind in my cell, it is just as if I am seeing the Buddha." 即從座起，跪白師言，我房中係念，見佛無異。(325c22)	Then say to the master: "Concentrating my mind, it is just as if I am seeing the Buddha." 即白師云，係念見佛無異。(1460a14–15)
When [he has seen the previously described vision] in this way, he should go and tell this to the master. The master then says... 如是已，即往白師。師言... (326a9–10)	When [he has seen the previously described vision] in this way, the master says... 如是已，如[>即]師云... (1460a29)
The master must further instruct [him], saying: "From now on you should put aside the previous two contemplations. Concentrate your mind on your navel." Having received the master's instructions, [the practitioner] single-mindedly contemplates his navel. 師復更教言，汝從今捨前二觀，係心在齊。即受師教，一心觀齊。(326a14)	Further have [the practitioner] put aside the previous two contemplations and concentrate [his] mind on his navel. [He] then single-mindedly contemplates his navel. 復令捨前二觀，係心在臍。即一心觀臍。(1460b3)
The master instructs, saying: "Further contemplate within your navel." [The practitioner] contemplates as instructed. He sees a five-colored glowing flame appear atop his head. Having seen this, he tells the master. The master says: "Further contemplate the five auspicious signs within these five flames." Having contemplated as instructed, [the practitioner] sees a single buddha appear. 師教言，更觀齊中。即如教觀，見頂有五色光焰。見已白師。師言，更觀五光有五瑞相。如教觀已，見有一佛。(326a27–29)	Again, have him further contemplate his navel, and he will see five auspicious signs appear atop his head. Having contemplated this, he will see a single buddha appear. 復令有[>更]觀臍中即見頂有五瑞相。觀已見有一佛。(1460b14–15)

The Origins of Chinese Meditation Scriptures

Although only the third section of the *Chan Essentials* has a parallel in the *Five Gates*, given its uniformity of style and the persistently weak integration between its narrative frames and the meditation instructions preached by the Buddha, we can safely conclude that the entirety of the *Chan Essentials* and the *Methods for Curing*, to which it was originally joined, had a similar origin. The *Five Gates*, for its part, shows little sign of being a complete text.[40]

40. Apart from its lack of a clear beginning, middle, or end, the *Five Gates* sometimes states explicitly that it is but a summary of a larger body of lore (*WMCJ*, T.619:15.330a20; 331a6–7; 332a12; 326c12).

It is, we may presume, a small remnant of an originally much larger body of schematic meditation manuals that circulated in fifth-century China either as translations of Indic texts or as transcriptions of the oral teachings of the foreign *chan* masters active in south China at that time. To judge from the *Five Gates,* these manuals described the topics of meditation that practitioners must learn, the sequence of practices to be done together, and the kinds of visions that these practices could or should produce. Such manuals must have circulated in various forms. We know they were copied and occasionally modified in the process, as attested by Stein no. 2585, and some of them, it seems, were eventually rewritten as sutras.

This process may also explain the creation of the Contemplation Scriptures, whose stylistic, linguistic, thematic, and historical connections to the *Chan Essentials* and *Methods for Curing* scholars have long noted. As we saw in Chapter 1, the question of the origins of the Contemplation Scriptures, and of the *Amitāyus Contemplation Scripture* in particular, has been a subject of intensive scholarly investigation for nearly a century. Most modern scholars now accept that these texts cannot be described as mere translations of purely Indic sources or, conversely, as simple Chinese forgeries. Instead, they are best seen as complex works based on Indian or Central Asian traditions but compiled and edited within the cultural sphere of Chinese Buddhism.[41]

Yet these conclusions, as far as they go, merely restate the facts—namely, that these texts, though informed by authentically Indian narratives and traditions of practice, did not exist as such outside China. Apart from the observation, based on internal evidence, that the narrative frame of the *Amitāyus Contemplation Scripture* had a separate origin from that of the meditation instructions to which it was later joined (Yamada 1976), no concrete hypothesis has yet been formulated as to the precise mechanisms whereby the Contemplation Scriptures were formed. Even the most sophisticated analyses of their origins have in the end reached only the (vaguely apologetic) conclusion that these texts, despite their Chinese "form," have a "core" that is Indian and hence must have been composed by those with some (unspecified) means of direct access to Indian or Central Asian Buddhist traditions not otherwise available in China.[42]

The relationship between the *Five Gates* and the *Chan Essentials* provides the possibility of a more robust historical assessment of these issues. In the *Five Gates* we have a surviving example of a pre-existing meditation manual,

41. For an overview of these arguments, see Fujita 1970, 116–136; 2007, 163–232. Textual (Fujita 1990, 163) and art-historical (Yamabe 1999a) evidence has suggested to some that the Silk Roads region of Turfan—historically a meeting point of Chinese and Indian spheres of cultural influence—may be where the final Chinese versions of the texts were compiled. (I discuss this theory in *Chan Before Chan,* chap. 2, n. 126.)

42. See, e.g., Sueki 1992, 65–66. Yamabe makes similar arguments about the other Contemplation Scriptures, considering them all to be what he calls "hybrid apocrypha" (Yamabe 1999c).

already in Chinese, out of which a meditation sutra, the *Chan Essentials*, was eventually crafted. This shows us the *minimum* level of textual evolution that took place entirely based on source materials already written in Chinese. Whatever the status of the *Five Gates* itself, as a direct translation of an Indic source or something else, the *Chan Essentials* was demonstrably the final product of a substantial editorial process carried out by individuals working in the Chinese language, one far more complex than merely tacking a sutra narrative onto a relatively complete Indian or Central Asian meditation manual.

The extent of this work is an index of the degree to which the worked-on material had a social life in China. Even though the *Chan Essentials* and *Methods for Curing* (and similarly, the Contemplation Scriptures) lack the blatantly Chinese cultural elements that scholars usually consider reliable signs of active intervention by Chinese authors, we may nevertheless feel confident that in reading them we are attending to something that mattered to fifth-century Chinese Buddhists. These texts are not the mere "dead weight" of Indian scriptures translated into Chinese but then forgotten or ignored (Zürcher 1995, 173), but traces of the birth of an enduring part of Chinese Buddhism itself.

The Making of a Scripture

If we believe that the bulk of the *Chan Essentials* and *Methods for Curing* was crafted on the basis of earlier Chinese meditation manuals more or less similar to the A-format sections of the *Five Gates*, what can be said about when, how, and why that crafting took place and the manner in which the final product was presented and promulgated? Even though these questions can be answered only in part, they are worth considering, however briefly, by way of conclusion.

Scriptural Form

As we have already seen, creating these texts involved the transformation of meditation instructions that previously circulated in other forms into the literary genre of a Buddhist sutra. That this would be the favored form was not necessarily self-evident. Indeed, the fifth-century *chan* scriptures that were in fact translated from Indian originals were not, in respect of their genre, sutras. Those who first transmitted and used these texts in China knew this and did not find them less authoritative for it. Huiyuan's preface to the meditation text translated by Buddhabhadra, for example, describes the *chan* scriptures as a class of texts compiled long after the Buddha had died but within which were preserved secret oral teachings not included in the original canon.[43] This origin story, which Huiyuan presumably learned from Buddhabhadra, is clearly an effort to ascribe canonical authority to a

43. *CSZJJ*, T.2145:55.65c11–12

body of patently post-canonical literature. But the existence of this story shows us that when the *chan* scriptures were first introduced to China, in the early fifth century, their status as something other than sutras in the traditional sense was not only accepted but argued to be a mark of prestige, a privilege accessible only to the initiated.

Thus the creation of the *Chan Essentials* and *Methods for Curing* was arguably motivated by concerns somewhat different from those informing the composition of other apocryphal scriptures. In typical such texts, the central problematic was usually the desire to use the literary form of a sutra to present ideas, practices, doctrines, or myths that were in fact derived from Chinese thought and Chinese concerns as nonetheless "Indian"—in other words, as authentically Buddhist. In contrast, what is most Chinese about the *Chan Essentials* and *Methods for Curing* is not their content but the form they took as sutras. At least some Chinese Buddhists in the early fifth century, having been introduced to new traditions of Buddhist meditation under the influence of foreign *chan* masters, evidently felt the need to ground their practices in a textual form possessing greater authority than the unimpressive and schematic meditation manuals, such as the *Five Gates*, that were probably never intended for widespread circulation. And this had its desired effect. Framed as sutras, the *Chan Essentials* and *Methods for Curing* ultimately enjoyed far more prestige than any of the other fifth-century *chan* scriptures and became the only such texts regularly cited in later Chinese writings about meditation (see Appendix 1).

We might say, then, that the composition of the *Chan Essentials* and *Methods for Curing* speaks to a convert's zeal—to a concern on the part of fifth-century Chinese Buddhists for establishing the orthodoxy of their teachings that was *greater* than what was demanded by the Indian traditions they had inherited. The *Chan Essentials* epitomizes this zeal when it claims not only to have been preached by the Buddha, but to record his very first discourse on the subject of meditation. This claim appears in the narrative portions of the first sutra, after Kauṣṭhilananda, whom none of the Buddha's five hundred awakened disciples had been able to successfully instruct, is taught by the Buddha how to meditate and quickly becomes an arhat (1.0.5 and 1.1.8). The significance of this event is then summarized:

> It was on that occasion that the World-honored One, because of this haughty monk Kauṣṭhilananda, *instituted for the first time the rules concerning mental concentration*, saying to the fourfold assembly: "From now on, monks, nuns, and laymen or laywomen who strive for the unconditioned path [of nirvana] must fix their thoughts and focus their minds on a single spot." (1.1.10)

This passage unmistakably echoes the form and conventions of the *vinaya*, where each monastic rule is explained as having been instituted by the

Buddha in response to a specific incident.[44] This, the *Chan Essentials* states, was the occasion, brought about by Kauṣṭhilananda, when the Buddha first ordered his disciples to meditate. The *Chan Essentials* here lays claim to something more than a generic canonical sanction. It purports to contain not simply a direct record of the Buddha's teachings on meditation, but the very origin of all ensuing traditions of Buddhist meditation practice. This same trope reoccurs in the third sutra, claimed to be the Buddha's first teaching of the "white bone contemplation" (3.21.9). And lest one think that the Buddha's first teaching on meditation contains only introductory methods, the reader is also assured, now borrowing a trope familiar from Mahāyāna literature, that the *Chan Essentials* provides both the original teachings on meditation *and* those that, being so profound, most people will fail to understand and later generations will forget or disparage (4.32.15–16).

Record of Production

We have seen, then, some of the considerations that may have motivated the authors of the *Chan Essentials* and *Methods for Curing* to craft their texts in the form they did. Going further, we can also discern something of how these two texts were initially presented to the public from the short document that Sengyou includes in his *Chu san zang ji ji* as the colophon to the *Scripture on the Secrets of Chan and the Healing of Illness* (the original title for the entirety of the *Chan Essentials* and the *Methods for Curing*). As we are about to see, much care was taken to ensure that the authenticity of these texts could be validated even to a scrupulous, well-informed critic.

This colophon records the circumstances in which text was first produced, at a nunnery in south China in the year 455. As the colophon is short, I give it here in full:

> Juqu [Jingsheng], marquis of Anyang and younger paternal cousin of [Juqu Mengsun 沮渠蒙遜] the king of Hexi, studied with the Indian Mahāyāna monk Buddhasena at the Vajra hermitage of the Gomatī temple in Khotan. [Buddhasena] was extraordinarily gifted, unrivaled throughout many lands. He could recite half a million verses [of scripture] and was also knowledgeable concerning methods of *chan*. He had mastered both Buddhist and secular writings and there was no text of any kind in which he was not proficient. Thus was he known in the world as a lion among men. Juqu personally received the transmission [of this text] from him and could recite it from memory without mistake. On the eighth day of the ninth month of the second year of the Xiaojian era of the Song dynasty (455), he began to transcribe this scripture at the Bamboo Grove monastery. He

44. The specific vocabulary used here concerning the "institution" (制) of a rule finds a particularly close parallel in the *Pi'naiye* (see, e.g., T.1464:24.874b6–8), one of the earliest extensive *vinaya* collections translated into Chinese, in the late fourth century.

> finished on the twenty-fifth day of that month. The nun Huijun was the sponsor.[45]

This colophon is not likely an accurate account of the origins of the *Chan Essentials* and *Methods for Curing*. Nor can we say if there is any truth to the story of the travels to Khotan of "Juqu, marquis of Anyang," a shadowy figure remembered as the translator of a small number of Buddhist scriptures and here claimed to be a member of the royal family of the ill-fated Northern Liang 北涼 (397–439) kingdom.[46] What we can say, however, is that the colophon is likely an authentic record of an early, if not the first, production of a written Chinese copy of these texts.

In thinking about that production, let us note that the colophon does not claim to be a record of the text's *translation*. It tells us merely the time, place (a prominent nunnery near the Chinese capital),[47] and method (by Juqu Jingsheng, under the patronage of a famous nun known for her practice of meditation)[48] of its initial transcription (*shuchu* 書出).[49] The focus lies exclusively on the question of when it was first written down, and how and from whom Juqu Jingsheng had memorized a text that seems to have always

45. 河西王從弟大沮渠安陽侯，於于闐國衢摩帝大寺<金剛阿練若住處>，從天竺比丘大乘沙門佛陀斯那。其人天才特拔，諸國獨步，誦半億偈，兼明禪法，內外綜博，無籍不練。故世人咸曰人中師子。沮渠親面稟受，憶誦無滯，以宋孝建二年九月八日，<於竹園精舍>書出此經。至其月二十五日訖。尼慧濬為檀越。 (*CSZJJ*, T.2145:55.66a25–b2). The words "at the Vajra hermitage" are supplied from the version at the end of received copies of the *Methods for Curing* itself.

46. We are presumably meant to infer that Juqu settled in south China after the fall of the Northern Liang (which ruled modern Gansu province) to the Northern Wei in 439, when the surviving Liang rulers fled west to Turfan, where they held power until 460 (Yu 2006, 255–259). The Song court, in south China, enjoyed a close relationship with the Liang rulers, with whom they were united in opposition to the Northern Wei. (A document from the Astana graveyard in Turfan, dated to 477, records the presence there of envoys from the Song court; see Hansen 2017, 155). Early secular histories about the Northern Liang do not mention Juqu Jingsheng; his biography in the Ming dynasty reconstruction of the early sixth-century *Shi liu guo chun qiu* 十六國春秋 appears to derive entirely from the *Chu san zang ji ji* biography.

47. According to the *Jiankang shi lu* 建康實錄 (p. 429), the Zhuyuan temple was one *li* northwest of the capital city of Jiankang (modern Nanjing) and was built in Yuanjia 11 / 12 (434–early 435). Huijun is said to have been its founding abbess (*BQNZ*, T.2063:50.940c19–941a7).

48. Huijun's biography describes her as having "without exception entered all the deep states of *chan* and the secret contemplations" (深禪祕觀無不必入; *BQNZ*, T.2063:50.940c19–941a7). "Secret contemplation" is a very unusual term; it may be intended to invoke the *Chan Essentials* and *Methods for Curing*, the only known Chinese Buddhist texts from this era that speak of "secret" methods of meditation.

49. *Chu* 出, literally "produce," often implies "translate" (J. Chen 2005), but could mean both translation and composition, depending on the context (see, e.g., *Kaiyuan shi jiao lu*, T.2154:55.676b28–c4). The precise term used in the colophon—*shuchu* 書出, "produce by copying"—is rare. In later catalogs, it emphatically means the *copying out* of a previously memorized Indic-language text prior to it being translated into Chinese (*Li dai san bao ji*, T.2034:49.77b14–16). Thus it seems to mean "transcribe," which fits the context of the colophon.

been in Chinese. Indeed, the colophon conspicuously fails to provide the kind of information usually found in records of the translations of medieval Chinese Buddhist texts, a process that, when it is described in any detail, always involved multiple people carrying out distinct roles.[50] As a falsified record of a translation, this colophon is an obvious failure, and this suggests it was not intended as one.[51]

Indeed, later Chinese bibliographic sources clearly did not take the colophon as documenting an act of translation. Juqu Jingsheng's biography in the *Chu san zang ji ji*, which draws from the colophon, says that he translated this text after returning from Khotan but *before* arriving in south China.[52] In this version, the events at the Bamboo Grove monastery clearly involve an already translated text: Huijun asks Juqu Jingsheng to *copy down* (*chuanxie* 傳寫) the text, and here the meaning is unambiguous. Moreover, she asks him to do this after first overhearing him reciting it, implying that it was already in Chinese, since Huijun could, apparently, recognize it for what it was.[53] Having so thoroughly mastered it, Juqu Jingsheng then "put brush to paper without any trouble and in seventeen days produced five scrolls."[54]

Though the colophon did not seek to document a translation, which was the primary criterion of textual authenticity for Buddhist bibliographers but not necessarily for the wider Chinese public (Campany 1993), the information it did include was nonetheless carefully chosen with an eye to certifying the authenticity of the text by other means. The name of the Indian guru in Khotan from whom Juqu Jingsheng supposedly learned the text—"Buddhasena"—would have been known in south China in the first half of the fifth century, at least in elite Buddhist circles, as the name of the teacher of Buddhabhadra, who was himself the first *chan* master in China and the translator of the *Chan Scripture of Dharmatrāta*, a text attributed in part to this same Buddhasena.[55] Juqu Jingsheng's travels are also described in a manner both plausible and precise: named are not only the city of Khotan, where other Chinese Buddhist pilgrims of this era are said to have acquired

50. For a summary of these procedures, see Zürcher 1972, 31.

51. That the colophon does not describe an act of translation was noted by Tsukinowa (1971, 104).

52. *CSZJJ*, T.2145:55.106c2–5 (see also *GSZ*, T.2059:50.337a11–14). A further detail is here added: that what Juqu Jingsheng learned in Khotan from Buddhasena was based on an "Indic text" (胡本).

53. Juqu Jingsheng's biography in the *Gao seng zhuan*, appended to the biography of Dharmakṣema (Tanwuchen 曇無讖), removes this scene, perhaps realizing that it is odd to imagine him reciting a text in Chinese translation that he memorized in its putatively original, Indic form (*GSZ*, T.2059:50.337a18–20).

54. 臨筆無滯，旬有七日出為五卷。(*CSZJJ*, T.2145:55.106c10–13)

55. Buddhasena's name was transcribed in several different forms (*GSZ*, T.2059:50.337a9; *Li dai san bao ji*, T.2034:49.84c15; *CSZJJ*, T.2145:55.66a26; 106b29). On the records pertaining to him, see Lin 1949, 341–351.

new texts, but also a specific monastery, the Gomatī temple, also well known in south China at this time.[56]

These details do more than lend the story in the colophon an air of plausibility. They conform to a well-known standard for scriptural authenticity put forth in the *Mahāparinirvāṇa-sūtra*. There the Buddha declares, as he is dying, that after his death an (orally memorized) sutra is to be accepted as genuine if the person who presents it testifies to have learned it either from the Buddha, from a community of learned monks, or from a single learned monk.[57] Interestingly, in Faxian's early fifth-century Chinese translation of this text, a further detail is added: the person presenting a new sutra must declare that "I personally [learned it] from a learned monk of such-and-such a temple [or of] such-such a hermitage... [and I] properly understood its meaning and learned to recite it flawlessly."[58] The colophon obligingly conforms to the spirit and even the specific wording of this passage. It too gives the name of the temple where Buddhasena resided, praises him as learned, says that Juqu Jingsheng learned to recite the text perfectly, and even gives the name of the "hermitage" (阿練若住處) within the larger temple where Buddhasena supposedly resided.

The colophon, in short, is carefully constructed. Aligning the information it provides with well-known facts concerning people and places, it has followed to the letter a canonical checklist for the authentication of new and previously unknown sutras. None of this, of course, provides certainty about the true life and times of the mysterious Juqu Jingsheng. With his claims of royal ancestry (unverified in any independent sources) and discipleship

56. The Jumadi 衢摩帝 (Skt. *Gomatī) temple is mentioned by Faxian as the largest in Khotan (*Gao seng Faxian zhuan*, T.2085:51.857b8–9). He specifically calls it a Mahāyāna temple, aligning with the colophon's unusual characterization of Buddhasena as a "Mahāyāna" monk. The temple was linked to the origins of Buddhism in Khotan, and paintings depicting its founding survive from the ruins (Forte 2020, 48–55). On Buddhism in Khotan, see Skjærvø 2012 and Kumamoto 2012. The *Scripture of the Wise and Foolish* (*Xian yu jing*) is the best documented case of a Buddhist text claimed to have been acquired in Khotan by Chinese pilgrims during the fifth century (Mair 1993). By the seventh century, there were temples run by Chinese Buddhist monks in Khotan (Kuwayama 1992, 47, 193), and Chinese Buddhist texts, of uncertain date, have been found in the ruins of the city (Kumamoto 2012, 145). Sizeable Chinese presence in Khotan probably dates only from the seventh-century Tang military expansion into Central Asia. But it is not impossible that a fifth-century pilgrim could have obtained in Khotan a new *Chinese* Buddhist text. We have the example of a Dunhuang manuscript of a Chinese *dhāraṇī* text that claims it was translated into Chinese in Khotan (Makita and Fukui 1984, 131–151), and a colophon surviving only in an eighth-century source speaks of a text translated into Chinese, in Khotan, in the fourth century (*Kaiyuan shi jiao lu*, T.2154:55.617a18–19). Finally, it has now been established that some of the oldest Khotanese-language Buddhist texts, long thought to have been translated exclusively from Sanskrit sources, were translated from Chinese versions (Loukota 2019). This suggests that Chinese Buddhist texts were physically present in Khotan from quite early on.

57. *Dīgha-nikāya*, 2.127; Waldschmidt 1950–1951, 238–246.

58. 我親從某僧伽藍某阿練若住處，有一上座比丘...善解其義，受持讀誦，極自通利。 (*Da banniepan jing*, T.7:1.196a1–10). The traditional attribution of this translation to Faxian (though not its early fifth-century date) has recently been contested by Michael Radich (2018).

under famous but distant Indian teachers, we can easily imagine him, among the southern Chinese Buddhist clergy of his day, as a kind of Romanov pretender. Regardless, what the colophon does allow us to see with some clarity is the attention to detail that went into this early account of the origins of the Chinese text of the *Chan Essentials* and *Method for Curing*. And from this we may infer that these texts were first produced, vouched for, and disseminated among Chinese Buddhists assumed to be of a certain level of literacy and sophistication.

Conclusions

In this chapter I have sought to ground the study of the *Chan Essentials* and *Methods for Curing* in a careful consideration of their textual histories and the cultural environment in which they were produced and circulated. As I have maintained, the *Chan Essentials* and *Methods for Curing* began their lives together, as a single document composed of multiple, narratively independent sutras in the style of the Āgama scriptures. Late fifth-century sources suggest that this collection was originally named *Scripture on the Secrets of Chan and the Healing of Illness* and that it was claimed to have been brought to south China, but not translated per se, in the mid-fifth century by Juqu Jingsheng, putatively of Northern Liang royal descent, who had memorized its contents while studying in Khotan with a famous Indian meditation master. However, rather than the direct transmission of a long-lost Indian sutra, the *Chan Essentials* and *Methods for Curing* were in fact put together from earlier and more rudimentary (from a literary standpoint) Chinese meditation manuals, of which only the fragmentary example of the *Five Gates* survives. These earlier manuals, which differed substantially from the more systematic Indian meditation treatises that were translated into Chinese in the fifth century, emphasized the unusual visions that mark progress in meditation. The earlier history of these manuals, as either the records of oral teachings or the Chinese translation of similarly schematic Indian manuals, cannot be determined. But we can be confident that they were the products, directly or at some level of remove, of the traditions of meditation that were introduced to Chinese Buddhists by the many foreign *chan* masters, such as Buddhabhadra and Dharmamitra, who gained fame and patronage in south China during the early fifth century.

Similar in background to the more famous Contemplation Scriptures, which were linked to some of these same meditation teachers and which emerged in a similar milieu, the *Chan Essentials* and *Methods for Curing* are "apocryphal" scriptures in that their content reflects the activities, interests, and concerns of Buddhists in China in the fifth century. But they are not *blatantly* apocryphal in the sense of being permeated by distinctly Chinese rather than Indian Buddhist ideas. They were created by and addressed to an elite audience interested in new scriptures only to the extent they accorded, in form and content, with demonstrably Indian Buddhist precedents.

It is for this very reason that these texts give us a rare window onto not only the traditions of Buddhist meditation that took shape in the fifth century in China, when *chan* was taken up by appreciable numbers of Chinese Buddhists for the first time, but also those that preceded it, in India and Central Asia, for which we have little other direct evidence.

PART II

Translations

Introduction to the Translations

Primary Sources

My translations of the *Chan Essentials* and *Methods for Curing* take the Chinese Buddhist Electronic Text Association's digital editions (of 2008, 2014, and 2016) of the Taishō editions (T) as the base texts. I have also used the following editions:

K[1] The first carving of the Koryŏ canon. *Gaoli da zang jing chu ke ben ji kan*, 33:363–483 (*Chan Essentials*) and 32:291–332 (*Methods for Curing*).

K The second carving of the Koryŏ canon. *Gaoli da zang jing*, 20:945–985 (*Chan Essentials*) and 20:712–726 (*Methods for Curing*). Theoretically, these are equivalent to the base texts of the Taishō edition, but in practice there are errors in the Taishō relative to K, on the order of one per page.[1]

J The Zhaocheng 趙城 edition (the Jin 金 canon) of the *Methods for Curing* only (*Zhong hua da zang jing*, 34:325–344).

P The Kaiyuan 開元 temple edition (both texts), held in the library of the Japanese Imperial Household Agency. These editions were collated by the Taishō editors under the designation "palace" (宫).[2] I have consulted the originals through the microfilm copy held in the library of the International Research Institute for Advanced Buddhology at Soka University.[3]

S and Y The Sixi 思溪 and Puning 普寧 editions (both texts), as

1. It is customary to say that the base text of the Taishō edition is K. However, the Taishō editors did not, in fact, directly consult a copy of K but rather used the modern *Dai Nihon kōtei shukusatsu daizōkyō* 大日本校訂縮刷大蔵経 (published 1880–1885, often called the Tokyo edition), itself based on the copy of K held at the Zōjōji 増上寺 temple. Errors in the Taishō relative to K often result from errors in the Tokyo edition.

2. The palace edition as collated by the Taishō editors includes some texts from the Kaiyuan temple canon (carved between 1112 and 1176, sometimes called the Chongning 崇寧 canon) and others from the Dongchan 東禪 temple canon (carved between 1080 and 1112, sometimes called the Pilu 毗盧 canon). Collectively these two are sometimes called the Fuzhou 福州 editions of the canon (Li and He 2003, 161–222).

3. I wish to thank Jan Nattier and the late John McRae for helping me access these microfilms when I visited Soka University in 2010.

represented by the Taishō apparatus under the abbreviations "Song" (宋) and "Yuan" (元), respectively.[4] These editions I have been able to access only through the Taishō apparatus. Misprints in the Taishō therefore typically show, in my notes, as agreement in all available versions except these.

Q The Qisha 磧砂 editions of the *Chan Essential* (no. 802) and *Methods for Curing* (no. 775), consulted through the forty-volume *Xin wen feng* 新文豐 photolithographic reprint (*Song ban Qisha da zang jing*).

Sgz The five-scroll Tempyō-era manuscript from the Shōsōin 正倉院, entitled *Chan mi yao jing* 禪祕要經, which includes material covering scrolls 1, 2, and half of scroll 3 of the *Chan Essentials.* Readings from this manuscript were collated by the Taishō editors, but I have been able to make use of the published photographs of the original manuscript (*Kunaichō shōsōin jimusho shozō shōgozō kyōkan*, nos. 268–272). This manuscript is mostly complete, excepting some loss at the beginning of scroll 1. The peculiarities of the Shōsōin manuscripts, as well as the titles I use to refer to its individual sections, are discussed in Appendix 3.

Kg The Kongō-ji 金剛寺 manuscripts of the *Chan Essentials* and *Methods for Curing.*[5] These complete manuscripts date to the Heian or Kamakura periods.

This is not the place for an extended discussion of the history of the Chinese Buddhist canon and the relationship between its versions (see Wu and Chia 2016). But I will briefly mention here that these editions of the *Chan Essentials* and *Methods for Curing* fall into three broad families: (1) editions in the lineage of the tenth-century Kaibao 開寶 canon, the first printed edition of the Chinese Buddhist canon (K^1, K, J); (2) editions in the Southern (江南) lineage (P, S, Y, Q); and (3) lineages based on manuscripts brought to Japan in the 700s from the Chinese capitals (Sgz, Kg). Agreement in editions across two or more of these three families is thus significant, though certainly not determinative, since even our very earliest copies (Sgz and the excerpts in W, discussed below) date to several hundred years after the original composition of the texts.

Other Sources

In addition to the above sources, I have had access to two Japanese manuscripts of the *Chan Essentials* from Nanatsudera 七寺.[6] These appear to be in

4. These collation notes were also not newly made by the Taishō editors but were, like the base text itself, taken from the Tokyo edition, whose editors had drawn from the printings of these editions held in the Zōjōji temple.

5. Access to the Kongō-ji texts was made possible by visits to the International College of Postgraduate Buddhist Studies in Tokyo. I thank Prof. Ochiai Toshinori 落合俊典 for his assistance.

6. Copies of these were generously provided by Prof. Ochiai Toshinori.

a direct lineage from the Shōsōin manuscript (Sgz) or something very close to it, with many subsequent copying errors. I have for this reason not included them in my collation notes. Though I have examined them, I also do not refer to any of the Ming- and Qing-dynasty printed editions of *Chan Essentials* and *Methods for Curing*, which are of little additional text-critical value.

The Dunhuang and Turfan manuscripts contain only the tiniest fragments of either the *Chan Essentials* or *Methods for Curing*. Three fragments of the *Chan Essentials*, seemingly from a single original manuscript, are found in the St. Petersburg collection (Дx18543, Дx18545, and Дx18591).[7] A handful of small fragments, of both the *Chan Essentials* and *Methods for Curing*, have been found among the still not fully cataloged Turfan documents collected by the Ōtani expedition, now housed in the Lüshun 旅順 museum.[8] These fragments are all of less than a few dozen characters.

Various citations of both texts are preserved in other medieval sources, attesting to their popularity down through the eighth century (see Appendix 1). I occasionally refer to these citations in the notes. Two are of special interest and merit their own abbreviations:

W Excerpts from each of the four sutras of the *Chan Essentials*, carved in cave 59 of the Wofoyuan 臥佛院 in Anyue 安岳 county, Sichuan, and dated by colophon to the year 735. Because I elsewhere examine in some detail what is revealed by the choice of passages, in the translation I mark the excerpts in underlined text.[9]

Jt Selective excerpts from the second sutra of the *Chan Essentials*, in Fazhao's 法照 (fl. ca. 750) *Jing tu wu hui nian fo song jing guan xing yi* 淨土五會念佛誦經觀行儀 (Pelliot no. 2066).[10]

I have, finally, consulted two modern Japanese *kakikudashi*-style renderings of the *Chan Essentials* (Satō 1931, 179–266) and *Methods for Curing* (Shiozaki 2006, 336–376). These are not true translations, but they have occasionally been helpful for parsing the oftentimes convoluted grammar of the texts. I have not noted the many cases where I have disagreed with their interpretations.

---

7. I would like to thank Chen Ruifeng for alerting me to Tai 2007, which identifies these fragments.

8. Liu Guangtang 2006, 14–15; Guo and Wang 2007, 69. According to Ikeda Masanori 池田将則, who has seen photographs of these fragments, the calligraphy, format, and paper quality suggest a Tang-dynasty dating (personal communication, November 2009).

9. For a transcription of the carving, see Bemmann and Sun 2018, 345–348.

10. An edition is provided as T.2827 (the relevant passages are 1255a4–27). I have also consulted the photographs available online through the Bibliothèque Nationale de France (http://gallica.bnf.fr/).

Text-Critical Notation

When emending or following a variant relative to the Taishō edition base text, I note this as follows:

水[>永, S, Q]: reading 水 as 永, based on S and Q.
<佛, Kg>說: insert 佛 before 說, based on Kg.
佛{法}: remove 法, based on my own emendation.

In a few cases I have relocated short phrases 16–18 characters forward or backward. During the manuscript era, Buddhist sutras were normally copied in a fixed format of 16–18 characters per column. Knowing this number, it is sometimes possible to spot cases where, in the course of early transmission, one or more characters appear to have been wrongly copied from the preceding to following column or vice versa. (This occurred relatively easily because when manuscripts were checked for errors, characters or phrases the original copyist had accidently skipped were often added back, in smaller characters, in the space between columns; when recopying the corrected manuscript, an error could then be made by associating the inserted text with the wrong column.) We can even see this error directly in two examples, one from the *Chan Essentials* preserved in only some editions (4.32.3), and one found in all editions of the *Methods for Curing* (1.14.18). Relocating entire phrases, without a textual witness, is certainly a drastic emendation; I resort to it only on a few select occasions.

When following textual variants or making emendations, I give a short excerpt of the Chinese in the notes. Those wishing to examine my choices more closely will, I assume, have the readily available Taishō text at hand. It has not been my intention to provide a complete critical edition of the Chinese text. Accordingly, I have noted variant readings only when I follow them or when they provide a plausible alternative with a noteworthy difference in meaning.

Numbering and Divisions

The *Chan Essentials* comprises four individual sutras, each with its own opening narrative. An internal numbering system of thirty "contemplations" spans the first three sutras. To respect but not be constrained by the two internal ordering systems, I have divided the text into sections and subsections (1.1.1, 1.1.2, 1.2.1, etc.) as follows: the first number denotes the sutra (four in total), the second number the thirty-contemplation numbering system, and the third number (and in some cases fourth or fifth numbers) my own further subdivisions. Because the thirty numbered contemplations span the sutra boundaries, my own numbering reflects this. Section 1.18 at the end of the first sutra is thus followed by section 2.19 at the start of the second sutra. The narrative introductions to each sutra, being presented outside the numbered contemplations, I mark as "0." The introduction to the second sutra is thus numbered as 2.0.1, 2.0.2, etc., followed immediately by 2.19.1, the first section of the nineteenth contemplation. The internal numbering stops after the third sutra. I label the first half of the fourth sutra, framed as a final method of meditation, as subsections of 4.31. The second half of the fourth sutra, which amounts to an extended conclusion, I label as 4.32.

For the *Methods for Curing*, I use a similar system based on the two sutras into which the text is divided. The first sutra has clearly marked internal divisions with differently titled "methods." I follow these to make the first level of subdivision. I have then broken each section into my own further divisions for ease of reading. In both texts, to help orient the reader, I have added my own brief titles to the sections and subsections. Some parts of the *Methods for Curing* have their own titles, which I have used in those cases.

Translation Conventions

In general, I have aimed for a translation that is both readable to the uninitiated and close enough to the Chinese text to make it possible for those who wish to consult the original to easily see what I have done. I have tried to avoid the Sinological crutch of endless square brackets denoting what is implied but not literally given, at least when this occurs in a manner unremarkable enough to be just normal Chinese prose. I have exercised restraint as concerns extensive discussion of alternative possible interpretations to the more obscure passages, though a few such discussions can be found in the notes. Even when not wishing to indicate changes I have made to the Taishō base texts, I occasionally include short excerpts from the original Chinese, either in-line (for individual terms) or in the notes (for longer phrases), in cases where I deem that specialists will find this information particularly welcome. I have translated the texts integrally, except for a few elisions of long repetitions, marked with ellipses. Passages that appear in the original texts as interlinear notes, written or printed in half-column-width characters, are rendered in a small font in the translation.

Following the relatively standard practice of scholars of Chinese Buddhism, I usually translate into English Buddhist technical terms that have full semantic weight as Chinese words and give in Sanskrit transliteration terms that in the Chinese too were originally transcriptions from an Indic language. For more obscure Indic technical terminology transcribed phonetically in the Chinese, on first instance I give the word in an English translation followed by the Sanskrit form in parentheses. For the classes of demonic creatures that populate some of the visions, rendered in Chinese phonetic transcription, I give the Sanskrit form of the name followed by, at the first instance in any given section, "demon" ("*rākṣasa*-demon," and so forth). I make a few more general exceptions to these practices. Because their literal renderings produce awkward English, some Buddhist technical terms that appear in the Chinese as semantic translations I give in their Sanskrit form, including *tathāgata* (*rulai* 如來), *skandha* (*yin* 陰), and *dharma*[s] (*fa* 法). Conversely, I translate as "monk," "nun," "layman," and "laywoman" the standard Chinese transcriptions of the titles *bhikṣu, bhikṣuṇī, upāsaka,* and *upāsikā,* and I similarly render the Chinese transcriptions of the first three stages of traditional Buddhist sainthood—*xutuohuan* 須陀洹 (*śrotāpanna*), *situohan* 斯陀含 (*sakṛdāgāmin*), and *a'nahan* 阿那含 (*anāgāmin*)—with the standard English translations "stream-enterer," "once-returner," and "non-returner." I retain "arhat" for the fourth stage (*luohan* 羅漢). The words *piliuli* 毘琉璃 and *liuli* 琉璃, transcriptions of Skt. *vaiḍūrya,* I translate as "beryl," which derives ultimately from this same word.

I always translate *yi* 億 as "million," taking it not as a specific quantity but in its generic meaning of "a very large number." (In Chinese Buddhist literature it often translates words such as Skt. *koṭi* that also have this sense.) Three different Chinese transcriptions of *stūpa* I translate as "sanctuary" (*shuaipo* 兜婆, *toupo* 偷婆, *ta* 塔). In all cases in these texts, this word points to some kind of cultic space. The word *chuang* 幢, which appears often as an element of various meditative visions, was used in Chinese Buddhist writings to translate *dhvaja,* which means both a flag or pennant (as *chuang* originally meant in Chinese) but also flag *staff,* and hence "pillar" (a common usage later, primarily in the word *jingchuang* 經幢 or "sutra pillar," a kind of stone pillar on which scriptures were carved). In the *Chan Essentials* and *Methods for Curing,* "pillar" often seems more appropriate, and I have translated accordingly. The word *jin'gang* 金剛, the Chinese Buddhist neologism that was used to render Skt. *vajra* (a hard, indestructible material), I always translate as "adamant" or "adamantine"; the meaning, in most cases, should be taken as "made of adamant," not merely "hard as adamant."

Literary Chinese is generally written without third-person pronouns. In translating these texts, readability has often required a singular pronoun in reference to the assumed "practitioner" or "meditator" they address. I have consistently used the masculine. This introduces a degree of specificity not inherent in the original. Still, there are many reasons to think the implied audience of these texts is male: the protagonists of the sutras are all monks, and female bodies are the implied objects of sexual desire (*Chan Essentials* 1.15.1.4, 1.18.3, and 1.18.7, but see *Methods for Curing* 1.7.7). *Methods for Curing* 1.14.3, in which the meditator experiences a vision of hordes of demons emerging from a giant blood-stained female sexual organ, is surely right out of the nightmares of a would-be celibate monk. An entire section is also devoted to the problems that arise from nocturnal emissions (*Methods for Curing* 2.5). Still, despite these assumptions (shared by most traditional Buddhist meditation literature), the compiler(s) of these texts did also claim that their methods would be useful for everyone: nuns and laywomen are thus specifically included among the intended audience (*Chan Essentials* 2.20.6, 4.32.6–7, 4.32.10–11; *Methods for Curing* 1.9.1, 1.10.1), as well as among the possible speakers of certain ritual pronouncements (*Methods for Curing* 1.9.8). Moreover, it even seems likely, as discussed in Chapter 4, that these texts were first written down, if not actually composed, at a nunnery at the request of an eminent female meditation master.

When the context clearly specifies only one buddha, I treat the word as a proper noun (the Buddha), but when demanded by context, I switch to "a buddha" or "buddhas." The need for these gymnastics is dictated by English grammar, not the conceptual world of the texts themselves. Readers should understand that the distinction between "a buddha" and "the Buddha" was not necessarily salient in medieval China.

Because most passages in both texts are framed as the Buddha's direct speech, I have refrained from placing all such text within quotation marks. The beginning and ends of direct speech are, in any event, often not marked explicitly. Other instances of direct speech, either within the outer frame narratives or within the interior stories, are marked as such as needed.

Scripture on the Secret Essential Methods of Chan

(*Chan Essentials*)

Chan mi yao fa jing 禪祕要法經

(T.613:15.242c22–269c22)

[1] [Kauṣṭhilananda]

[1.0] [Introduction]

[1.0.1] [Kauṣṭhilananda Is Unable to Understand]

Thus have I heard. Once, the Buddha was dwelling in the city of Rājagṛha, in the Kalandaka-bird bamboo garden together with a great assembly of one thousand two hundred fifty monks and five hundred eminent voice-hearers (*śrāvaka*), including Śāriputra, the great Maudgalyāyana, Mahākāśyapa, and Mahākātyāyana.

On this occasion, a clever and learned[1] monk from Rājagṛha named Mahākauṣṭhilananda[2] [243a] came before the Buddha, paid reverence to him, and circled him seven times. The World-honored One, then in deep trance, remained silent. Kauṣṭhilananda,[3] seeing the Buddha was in trance, went to Śāriputra, bowed to his feet, and said: "Venerable Śāriputra, please preach for me in full the essential meaning of the teachings." At that, Śāriputra told him the four noble truths and explained their meaning. He did this once and then again, as many as seven[4] times, but Kauṣṭhilananda's confusions remained unresolved. So, in a similar manner, he bowed to the feet of each of the five hundred voice-hearers and asked to hear the essentials of the teachings. Again, each of the voice-hearers expounded for him, seven times, the teaching of the four noble truths. But Kauṣṭhilananda's confusions remained unresolved, so he returned to the Buddha and paid him reverence.

1. As becomes clear below, this refers to his secular, non-Buddhist learning.
2. On this name, and its problems, see Appendix 4.
3. From this point on, the prefix *mohe* 摩訶 (*mahā* 'great') is dropped.
4. 六[>七, K[1], K, P, Q, Kg]. The Taishō is presumably a misprint; Sgz is missing here.

[1.0.2] [Kauṣṭhilananda Is Ashamed]

When the World-honored One emerged from trance, he saw Kauṣṭhilananda with his head bowed at his feet. With tears raining down his face, Kauṣṭhilananda beseeched the World-honored One: "Please turn for me the wheel of the true Dharma!" At this, the World-honored One too explained, seven times, the teaching of the four noble truths. Just as before, Kauṣṭhilananda was unable to understand. But five hundred young gods, hearing the Buddha's preaching, immediately attained the pure Dharma eye. Making offerings of heavenly flowers to the Buddha, they said: "World-honored One, we rapidly attained benefit today, thanks to the monk Kauṣṭhilananda. We have seen the teaching as it really is and have become stream-enterers."

When Kauṣṭhilananda heard what these gods said, he was deeply ashamed. Whimpering pitifully, he threw his body to the ground without speaking, like a great mountain collapsing.[5] Placing all four limbs on the ground before the Buddha, he repented his transgressions.

[1.0.3] [Ānanda Inquires about Kauṣṭhilananda's Past]

Then Ānanda arose from his seat and arranged his robes. Uncovering his right shoulder, he made reverence to the Buddha, circled him three times, and kneeling before him with his palms together said: "World-honored One, why has this monk Kauṣṭhilananda been born so learned, with mastery of the four Vedas, the Vaiśeṣika[6] scriptures, astronomy, and all the technical arts? Further, what sin did he commit such that [even with this learning] only the Buddha's teaching has he been unable to taste, despite being a monk for many years? You, the World-honored Tathāgata, have personally preached the Dharma for him, yet like one deaf from birth he neither hears nor understands. The great generals of the Buddha's teaching have one after the other turned the wheel of the Dharma. All five hundred have preached the Dharma for him, yet still it is no use. Please, O honored one among the gods, explain this for me. Tell me about this monk's past deeds."

After Ānanda had made this inquiry, the Buddha smiled and a five-colored light emerged from his mouth, circled him seven times, and then reentered his head through the top. He said to Ānanda: "Listen carefully, listen carefully, and ponder it well. I will now explain this matter for you." Ānanda said to the Buddha [243b]: "May it be so, World-honored One, for I do earnestly desire to hear."

---

5. Or: the collapsing of Mount Tai (太山). On this expression and its appearance in Chinese Buddhist literature, see Tanaka 1997.

6. *Weishiji* 違世羈. This transcription of *vaiśeṣika* (a school of Indian philosophy) is unattested elsewhere. Fifth-century Chinese Buddhist texts regularly give the somewhat similar *wei-shi-shi* 衛世師 (*Cheng shi lun*, T.1646:32.261b15; *Da banniepan jing*, T.374:12.487a27). The final *ji* 羈 (MC *kje*) might render –*ka* but could also be a graphic error for *shi* 師.

[1.0.4] [Kauṣṭhilananda's Past Lives]

The Buddha said to Ānanda: "Incalculable eons in the past, this monk Kauṣṭhilananda [lived during the era of] a World-honored Buddha named Lamplighter (Dīpaṅkara), a Thus-come One, Worthy of Offerings, Of Right and Universal Knowledge, Perfect in Conduct and Wisdom, Well-gone, Knower of the World, Unsurpassed One, Tamer of Men, Teacher of Gods and Humans, Buddha, World-honored One.[7] During that buddha's ministry there was a wise and learned monk named Ārjavananda,[8] who because of his great learning became haughty and heedless (放逸) and failed to cultivate the four bases of mindfulness (四念處). When he reached the end of his bodily life, he fell into a dark and gloomy hell. Emerging from hell, he was reborn among the dragons and the elephants.[9] For five hundred lifetimes he was reborn as a dragon king, and for five hundred lifetimes as an elephant king. Finishing these lifetimes in the animal realm, he was then reborn in the heavens owing to the power of having upheld the precepts while a monk. When his life in the heavens ended, he was reborn as a human being. Because in a previous life he chanted the Buddhist scriptures, he has now been able to meet a buddha. But because he was heedless and failed to cultivate the four bases of mindfulness, in his present life he has been unable to awaken."

[1.0.5] [The Buddha Teaches Kauṣṭhilananda]

When Kauṣṭhilananda heard what the Buddha said, he immediately got up from his seat, put his palms together, knelt with both knees on the ground, and said: "World-honored One, may you, O honored one among the gods, please teach me how to fix my mind."[10]

The Buddha then said to Kauṣṭhilananda: "Listen carefully, listen carefully, and ponder it well. Today you have wasted no time in asking the Tathāgata for the ambrosia of the true teaching that destroys the rapacious, distracted mind, for the medicine of all buddhas of the three times that cures afflictions and blocks all forms of heedlessness, and to reveal the true eightfold path for all humans and gods. You must now contemplate carefully. Do not allow your mind to become distracted."

---

7. This is a standard list of epithets of a buddha.

8. 阿純難陀. This curious name is elsewhere attested only as the Chinese transcription of the title of one of the bodhisattva stages (C. Chen 2004, 41).

9. *Long* 龍 (dragon) and *xiang* 象 (elephant) are here treated as different animals. This may be a trace of the text's Chinese authorship, as *longxiang* usually translates a single Indic word, Skt. *hasti-nāga* 'elephant' (Ogiwara 1979, 319, 1553; *Kōsetsu Bukkyōgo daijiten*, 142; Funayama 2013, 218).

10. The verb "to fix" (繫), literally "to tie," is used throughout the *Chan Essentials* and *Methods for Curing* to denote the preliminary meditative act of concentrating or attaching the mind to some chosen object. For more details on the terminology of meditation in the texts, see chap. 2, pp. 27–32.

When the Buddha had spoken these words, fifty foolish old[11] monks from the assembly also said to Ānanda: "The World-honored One is now going to teach the method for removing heedlessness. We too wish to take this opportunity to learn about this matter. Please, venerable sir, speak to the Buddha about this on our behalf." Once they had said this, the Buddha said to these monks: "Not only for you, but for all heedless people in the future will I now teach this method for concentrating the mind to the monk Kauṣṭhilananda here in the bamboo garden of the Kalandaka birds."

[1.1] [First Contemplation: The Impurity of the Body]

[1.1.1] [The Bone of the Big Toe]

The Buddha said to Kauṣṭhilananda: "Hear my words and do not forget them. From today forward, you must cultivate the monkish practice [of meditation] as follows. In a quiet place, spread out a sitting cloth, sit cross-legged, arrange your robes, straighten your body, and sit upright. Uncover your right shoulder and place your left hand on top of your right hand. Close your eyes and press your tongue against the palate. Calm your mind and make it still. Do not allow it to wander.

"First, fix your thoughts on the tip of your left big toe. Carefully contemplate (觀) one segment of the toe. Imagine (想) it swelling. Carefully contemplate it until it is very clear. Then imagine the swelling bursting open. When you see the first segment [of bone beneath], make it extremely white and pure, as if glowing with white light. Seeing these things, [243c] next contemplate the entire toe bone. Make the flesh strip away until you see the toe bone. Make it extremely clear, as if glowing with white light."

The Buddha said to Kauṣṭhilananda: "This is called the method for fixing one's thoughts." When Kauṣṭhilananda heard the Buddha's words, he joyfully undertook to carry them out.[12]

[1.1.2] [The Five Toe Bones]

[The Buddha continued]:[13] Having contemplated one toe bone, next contemplate two toe bones. Contemplating two bones, next contemplate three. Contemplating three bones, allow the mind to gradually expand.[14] You must

11. *Moheluo* 摩訶羅 (*mahallaka*). Usually understood to mean either "old" or "foolish" (*Fan fan yu*, T.2130:54.9995c23), this word is frequently used as a term of abuse for foolish old monks in the *vinaya* (the Chinese word almost never appears outside translations of Indic *vinaya* literature). This particular transcription seems to appear most frequently in the early fifth-century translation of the *Mahāsāṅghika-vinaya* (T.1425).

12. 歡喜奉行. This stock phrase is typically part of the closing formula for Buddhist sutras (Bingenheimer 2011, 51–56) and is repeated throughout the *Chan Essentials*. Its repeated use within the *body* of a single sutra is highly unusual, and may be another indication of Chinese authorship.

13. Some text is missing here or the editors have forgotten to frame the ensuing passage as the Buddha's speech.

14. The unusual expression "[allow] the mind to gradually expand" (心漸廣大), describing the expansion or multiplication of the object of contemplation, also occurs in two of the

contemplate five bones until you see the five toe bones glowing as if with white light, the white bones clearly apparent. Fix your mind in this manner, carefully contemplating the five toe bones without allowing it to wander. If the mind wanders, seize it firmly and bring it back,[15] and again bring to mind the first segment [of the big toe].

When this meditation is complete,[16] your entire body will feel warm and there will be a sensation of heat in your belly.[17] Once you have attained this meditation it is known as "dwelling with mind well-fixed" (繫心住).

[1.1.3] [The Remaining Bones]

After the mind is settled, next imagine the flesh on the top of the foot splitting wide open[18] so that you see the upper foot bone. Make it extremely clear so that you see the upper foot bone to be white like snow or white *ke*-jade.[19]

When this meditation is complete, next contemplate the ankles,[20] and make the flesh split open so that you see the ankle bone, making it brilliantly white. Next contemplate the calf bone and make the flesh fall off so that you see the calf bone, brilliantly white. Next contemplate the knee bone and make it brilliantly white and clear too. Next contemplate the pelvis bone and make it extremely white too. Next contemplate the ribs. Imagine the flesh spliting open from between each rib and falling off, so that you see only the ribs, white like snow or *ke*-jade. Continue until you see the spine, making it extremely clear. Next contemplate the bones of the shoulder. Imagine the flesh of the shoulder as if cut with a knife from the shoulder to

---

Contemplation Scriptures (*GFSMH*, T.643:15.691a22–23; *Guan Yaowang Yaoshang er pusa jing*, T.1161:20.662c15).

15. 攝令使還. This expression and the similar "seize [the mind] and return it [to the object]" (攝之令還) are found throughout the meditation texts translated by Kumārajīva (*ZCSM*, T.614:15.272b7–8; *Chan fa yao jie*, T.616:15.296b5; *DZDL*, T.1509:25.215b20–21) as a description of how one refocuses a distracted mind during meditation.

16. 念想成時. When used as *verbs*, I translate *nian* 念 as "bring to mind" and *xiang* 想 as "imagine." Here, however, they are nouns. This fixed phrase (and its common variant 此想成時) recurs throughout the *Chan Essentials* and *Method for Curing*. I translate it as "when *this meditation* is complete," meaning the moment when the previously described set of practices has been successfully accomplished. The phrase occurs with reference to patently visionary meditation exercises as well as meditations of a more abstract or discursive nature.

17. Literally, "below the heart" (心下). In anatomical contexts, this means the belly region (*Zhong yi da ci dian*, 335; *Han yu da ci dian*, 7:870).

18. The unusual expression *liang xiang* 兩向 (split wide open) also occurs in *Methods for Curing* 1.8.3. The similar *liang pi* 兩披 and *liang xiang pi* 兩向披 occur in *Chan Essentials* 3.21.2.

19. In other fifth-century meditation texts, *ke* 珂 often describes the color of pure white bones (*ZCSM*, T.614:15.272a20). *YQJYY* explains *ke* as meaning either a kind of shell or a white jade-like stone (T.2128:54.329c3; 501b23–24). Because jade-like bones (denoting longevity or immortality) are a common trope in Chinese literature, I have tried to preserve this resonance by translating *ke* as "*ke*-jade." In 1.12.1 and 1.13.3, the meditator's skeleton is compared explicitly to "white jade."

20. *Huai* 踝, according to *YQJYY* (T.2128:54.314a11), means the protruding bones on the ankles (the lateral and medial malleolus).

the forearm, the wrist, the hand, then all the way to the tips of the fingers. Across this whole area make the flesh split open so that you see half your body as a skeleton.[21]

[1.1.4] [The Skin, Membranes, and Organs]

Having seen half your body as a skeleton, next contemplate your scalp. Seeing your scalp, next contemplate your skin. Seeing your skin, next contemplate the membrane.[22] Contemplating the membrane, next contemplate the brain. Contemplating the brain, next contemplate its channels.[23] Contemplating the [brain] channels, next contemplate the throat. Contemplating the throat, next contemplate the lung-point.[24] Contemplating the lung-point, you will see the heart, lungs, liver, large intestine, small intestine, spleen, kidneys, receptacle of undigested food, and receptacle of digested food.[25]

[1.1.5] [The Eighty Families of Worms]

Within the receptacle of undigested food there are forty families[26] of worms, and for each family there are eighty million small worms. Each worm is born within the channels, where it grows to maturity and then gives birth [to more worms].[27] Roughly three million of them clasp the receptacle of undigested food with their mouths. Each worm has forty-nine heads. Their heads and tails are as thin as the tip of a needle. Of these worms, twenty families are fire worms born from the essence (精) of fire and twenty families are wind worms that arise from the *qi* (氣) of wind.[28] These various worms go in and out of the channels playing freely. The fire worms stir up the wind element, while the wind worms stir up the fire element. Blowing upon each other in this way they cook the undigested food. Each worm

21. Having begun with the *left* toe, it seems that all the previously mentioned body segments refer only to those on the left side of the body.

22. On the "membrane," see 1.5.1, n. 77.

23. 肪[>脈], following the similar *Methods for Curing* 1.5.1 (334b11–14). The "channels" mentioned here are presumably the 404 channels discussed in *Methods for Curing* 1.5.3.

24. On the "lung-point" (*feishu* 肺腧), see "Medical Theories and Terminology" in chap. 3.

25. The "receptacle of undigested food" (生藏) and "receptacle of digested food" (熟藏) are common Chinese Buddhist calques of the Indian anatomical terms *āmāśaya* and *pakvāśaya*, respectively.

26. *Hu* 戶, meaning "household" or "family," is used throughout as a measure word for types or classes of worms (probably from Skt. *kula* 'flock' but also 'household'). This passage speaks of eighty (two sets of forty) such groups, a number that agrees with the classification of bodily worms in the *Yogācārabhūmi* of Saṅgharakṣa (*Xiu xing dao di jing*, T.606:15.188a28–29), the most comprehensive Buddhist meditation treatise available in China before the fifth century. Later passages in the *Chan Essentials* speak of "eighty thousand" (八萬) families of bodily worms. Based on the present passage, I have generally emended 萬 (always written 万 in the manuscripts and woodblock editions) to 十, keeping "eighty" throughout.

27. 一一蟲從諸脈生孚乳產生. Translation tentative.

28. On the use here of the concepts of "qi" (氣) and "essence" (精), see 1.15.2.1, n. 189.

bends back and forth seven times,[29] and each has seven, fire-shooting eyes and seven ears.[30] [244a] Exhaling fire and wiggling their bodies they cook the undigested food. When the undigested food is cooked, the worms return to the channels.

[Within the receptacle of digested food] there are another forty families of worms, each comprising three million small worms whose bodies are as red as fire. Each has twelve heads and each head has four mouths that clasp the receptacle of digested food and make blood flow within the channels. Contemplate them all and make them visible.

[1.1.6] [Vomiting Out the Internal Organs]

Seeing these things, you will further see the various worms go up through the throat. Then further contemplate your small intestine, liver, lungs, spleen, and kidneys. Make them all liquefy and flow into your large intestine, then out your throat and onto the ground.[31]

When this meditation is complete, you will see on the ground [a heap of] shit, urine, and bodily worms[32] crawling all over each other. Pus and blood flow from their impurity-filled mouths.

[1.1.7] [Repentance and Confirmation]

When this meditation is complete, you will see yourself as a complete, snow-white skeleton. If you [instead] see a yellow or black skeleton, you must further repent your transgressions.

Having repented your transgressions you will see the remaining skin fall from your bones,[33] forming a pile on the ground that grows gradually to the size of a begging bowl (*pātra*). It grows larger still, becoming as big as a large urn, until it is as big as a tower of the *gandharvas*.[34] Just as you wish,

29. 上下往復凡有七反. Translation tentative.

30. 身[>耳, P, S, Q, Y, Sgz].

31. Though I retain the expected translations "stomach" (胃) and "large intestine" (大腸), vomiting is here described as food flowing *from* the former *to* the latter and then up the throat; see also *Methods for Curing* 1.3.3. "Large intestine" thus denotes our "stomach." This is, in fact, typical of medieval Chinese Buddhist texts (if not other Chinese sources as well). See, e.g., *Zhong ahan jing*, T.26:1.505c4–9, where the order of digestion is clearly 大腸 → 小腸 → 胃, corresponding to *udaram, antam, antaguṇam* in the corresponding Pāli (*Majjhima-nikāya*, 3.186). See also *Xiu xing dao di jing*, T.606:15.187a20–22.

32. The "bodily worms" (蚘蟲) are the worms that live in the gut, according to *YQJYY*, T.2128:54.595a13.

33. 自見己身，骨上生皮，皮悉褫落. "Remaining skin" is literally the "living skin" (生皮) that, I have understood, remains clinging to the bones, coloring them yellow or black. This skin then falls off in the wake of successful repentance. The meaning might instead be that the meditator here has a vision of skin that newly *grows* (生) on the bones before falling off.

34. A city (城) of the *gandharvas*, a kind of heavenly musician, is usually taken as a magical, spun-from-the-air creation and is a standard Buddhist metaphor for emptiness; see, e.g., 1.17.5 below. To speak of a *tower* (樓) of the *gandharvas*, for the purpose of denoting something's *size*, is extremely peculiar, and is perhaps a sign of a Chinese author's unfamiliarity with the normal use of this metaphor.

it becomes big or small, gradually expanding again to the size of a great mountain.[35] Various worms chew at this heap, pus and blood flowing. Innumerable worms squirm about within the pus. You will further see this mountain of skin gradually decay until only a small amount remains and the worms vie with each other to eat it.

Four *yakṣa*-demons[36] suddenly spring out of the ground, their eyes flaming and their tongues like poisonous snakes. Each *yakṣa* has six heads and each head is different—one like a mountain, the others like the heads of a cat, a tiger, a wolf, a dog, and a rat. Their hands are like those of an ape. The tips of each of their ten fingers are poisonous snakes with four heads, one spraying water, one spraying dirt, one spraying wind,[37] and one spraying fire. Their left legs resemble those of *kumbhāṇḍa*-demons, and their right legs those of *piśāca*-demons. Their horrid appearance is truly frightful. These four *yakṣa*s then stand in a line before the practitioner, each bearing on its back the nine kinds of corpses.[38]

[1.1.8] [Conclusion]

The Buddha said to Kauṣṭhilananda: "This is the initial confirmatory vision of the meditation on impurity" (不淨想最初境界).

The Buddha said to Ānanda: "Preserve these words. Be sure not to forget them. This method of ambrosia, a seed [leading to] the sanctity of the three vehicles, is to be thoroughly expounded for sentient beings in the future age."

[1.1.9] [Kauṣṭhilananda's Attainment]

Having heard the Buddha speak these words, Kauṣṭhilananda carefully contemplated each of these things, and for ninety days thought of nothing else. When the fifteenth day of the seventh month arrived and the community of monks had ended their summer retreat, all the monks made reverence to the World-honored One and then went off where they wished. In the later part of the day Kauṣṭhilananda cultivated and attained, one after the other, the four holy fruits,[39] thereby fully acquiring the three knowledges and six supernatural powers.

35. K[1], P, S, Y, Sgz, and Kg read "as large as Mount Tai (太山)."

36. A *yakṣa* is usually a kind of tree spirit that isn't necessarily threatening or aggressive. In the *Chan Essentials*, they are indistinguishable from the many other demon-like creatures.

37. 石[>風]. Emendation tentative; the heads appear to correspond to the four elements.

38. "Nine kinds of corpses" presumably means one of the canonical lists of the nine (sometimes ten) stages of the decaying corpse that can serve as objects for the contemplation of impurity.

39. Literally, "the four fruits of a *śramaṇa*" (四沙門果), meaning stream-enterer, once-returner, non-returner, and arhat.

[244b] Overjoyed, he bowed his head at the Buddha's feet and said: "World-honored One, today, by means of reflection (思惟), absorption (正受), and *samādhi*, I have brought my life allotment to an end, and I will not be reborn again. I truly know[40] that I have definitely accomplished the pure and holy practice. World-honored One, this teaching is like a vessel of ambrosia. One who uses it will experience the taste of ambrosia. May you, honored one among the gods, thoroughly expound it once again!"

The World-honored One then said to Kauṣṭhilananda: "If you have really obtained these things you should be able to easily perform the eighteen displays of supernatural power."

Kauṣṭhilananda immediately flew into the air and effortlessly performed the eighteen displays of supernatural power. All the other monks then saw that even the conceited and arrogant Kauṣṭhilananda had been tamed, and that following the Buddha's instructions he had become an arhat by fixing his mind on a single spot without becoming distracted by sensory perceptions.

At this time there were fifteen hundred monks with unruly minds in the assembly. Having seen [Kauṣṭhilananda become an arhat], they all rejoiced and immediately went before the Buddha. One after the other they received this method.

[1.1.10] [The Buddha's First Teaching of Meditation]

It was on that occasion that the World-honored One, because of the haughty monk Kauṣṭhilananda, instituted for the first time the rules concerning mental concentration, saying to the fourfold assembly:[41] "From now on, monks, nuns, and laymen or laywomen who strive for the unconditioned path [of nirvana] must fix their thoughts and focus their minds on a single spot. If they shamelessly allow their minds to run wild like monkeys among the six senses, then know that such people are untouchables (*caṇḍalas*) who do not belong to the lineage of the worthies and sages (賢聖). Their minds untamed, they will become the slaves of the guardians of Avīci hell. Evil people such as this will be unable to attain liberation for many eons. These wicked unruly people belong to the lineage of those destined for birth in the triple world, where because of their [unruly] minds they will fall onto the three evil paths of rebirth."

When the monks heard the Buddha's words, they joyfully undertook to carry them out. The Buddha said to Ānanda: "Do you see this monk Kauṣṭhilananda, who has obtained liberation through the contemplation of impurity? You must preserve this teaching and preach it for the assembly." Ānanda said to the Buddha: "It will be thus."

---

40. 知如道真. Translation tentative.

41. The claim here is that this was the first time the Buddha taught meditation.

[1.2] [Second Contemplation: The Skeleton]

[1.2.1] [The First White Bone Contemplation]

[1.2.1.1] [Contemplating the Skeleton]

The Buddha said to Ānanda: Listen carefully, listen carefully, and ponder it well. In the second contemplation [a practitioner] should fix his thoughts on his forehead, and without shifting his thoughts to anything else, carefully contemplate an area in the center of his forehead the size of a fingernail. In this manner he should make his mind still through the contemplation of his forehead. He must think only about his forehead without producing other thoughts. Following this he must contemplate his skull, seeing it to be as white as crystal. In this manner he gradually sees his entire body as white bones, brilliantly white and pure, the [bones of] the body fully complete and mutually connected. He further sees a heap of impurities on the ground, as was explained previously.[42]

[1.2.1.2] [Inverse Contemplation]

When the meditation on impurity is complete, he should be taught an "inverse contemplation"[43] to prevent him from attempting to end his life. [244c] The method for the inverse contemplation is to imagine white light radiating from between his bones, blazing brightly like snow-covered mountains. When he has seen this, the *yakṣas*[44] suck up the pile of impurities before him.

[1.2.1.3] [Skeletons Raising Their Right Hand]

Next he should imagine a skeleton ahead of himself, making it extremely white. When this meditation is complete, he should imagine a second skeleton. After seeing two skeletons, he sees three skeletons. After seeing three skeletons, he sees four skeletons. After seeing four skeletons, he sees five skeletons. He should continue in this manner until he sees ten skeletons. After seeing ten skeletons, he sees twenty skeletons. After seeing twenty skeletons, he sees thirty skeletons. After seeing thirty skeletons, he sees forty skeletons. After seeing forty skeletons, he sees an entire room filled with skeletons, in front, behind, to the left and to the right, row upon row all facing him. Each raises its right hand and points it at the practitioner.

At that moment the practitioner gradually expands his meditation until he sees the inside of the entire building filled with skeletons, row upon row all facing him, white as *ke*-jade or snow, each raising its right hand and pointing it at him. Next, he should expand his mind further until he sees

42. This appears to refer to 1.1.6 above.

43. The "inverse contemplation" (易觀), here to prevent suicide but elsewhere used for other purposes, is discussed under "Treating Meditation Gone Awry" in chap. 2.

44. I presume this points to the *yakṣas* from 1.1.7.

an acre[45] of land filled with skeletons[46] ... a *yojana*[47] ... a hundred *yojanas* ... all of [the four continents of] Jambudvīpa ... Pūrvavideha ... Godānīya ... and Uttarakuru.

Upon seeing the entire world beneath the heavens filled with skeletons, the practitioner's body and mind feel at ease, and he is without any thought of terror at all.

[1.2.1.4] [Skeletons Raising Both Hands]

He should then gradually expand his mind until he sees an area the size of a hundred continents of Jambudvīpa filled with skeletons, row upon row all facing him, each raising its right hand and pointing it at him. Having seen a hundred continents of Jambudvīpa, he should see a hundred Pūrvavidehas ... a hundred Godānīyas ... a hundred Uttarakurus.

When he has seen these things [245a], his body and mind will become calm and joyful, without any thought of terror. With his imagination now sharpened,[48] he will see the entire universe[49] filled with skeletons. Each lowers its two hands and extends its ten fingers. Standing in straight lines, they face the practitioner.

When the practitioner sees these things, he will always see these skeletons whether or not he is in trance. Mountains, rivers, rocks, walls, and all things in the world transform into skeletons.

[1.2.1.5] [Repentance]

When the practitioner sees this, he will see four great fast-flowing rivers, milk-white in color, in each of the four directions. He will see the skeletons swept away by the current.

When this meditation is complete, he should repent further until he sees pure water surging upward[50] into the air. He should then imagine that the water becomes calm and still.

---

45. Literally, one *qing* (頃), a unit of area that was quite a bit larger than an acre.

46. I elide the identically repeating pattern here.

47. In Indian Buddhist literature, a *yojana* (*youxun* 由旬) is invariably a unit of *length*—usually on the order of several miles—though the precise distance varied (Skilling 1998). However, the *Chan Essentials* (and *Methods for Curing*) clearly uses the word to denote a measurement of *area*, both here and throughout. The sense is perhaps "out to a distance of a *yojana*." It could also represent a slight misunderstanding of the meaning of this Indic term (hardly ever defined in Buddhist sources themselves) on the part of a Chinese author.

48. The unusual expression "his imagination now sharpened" (心想利) occurs several other times in the *Chan Essentials* (1.8.1, 3.21.5), always in reference to the moment when a meditator becomes able to expand his vision. The same expression is used similarly in the Contemplation Scriptures (*GFSMH*, T.643:15.691a19–21; *Guan Puxian pusa xing fa jing*, T.277:9.390c6).

49. "Entire universe," here and in other passages, is literally "the Sahā world" (娑婆世界).

50. 住[>注, P, S,Q, Y].

[1.2.1.6] [Conclusion and Naming]

The Buddha said to Ānanda: This is called the "*samādhi* of the surging white radiance of the white bones [associated with] the meditations of as yet unenlightened being."[51] It is also called the "confirmatory vision of birth and death [produced by] the mind-ocean of unenlightened beings."[52]

Because of Kauṣṭhilananda, I have today set forth for you and all sentient beings of the future this method of the *samādhi* of the surging white radiance of the white bones, so that you may restrain your unruly minds and traverse the ocean of birth and death. You, [Ānanda,] must preserve it and must be careful not to forget it.

After the World-honored One spoke these words, he manifested all the signs and features of this *samādhi* of white radiance and showed them to Ānanda.[53] When Ānanda heard what the Buddha said, he joyfully undertook to carry it out.

This is called the first confirmatory vision of the [second contemplation], the white bone contemplation.[54]

[1.2.2] [The Second White Bone Contemplation]

[1.2.2.1] [Broken and Scattered Skeletons]

The Buddha said to Ānanda: When this meditation is complete, the practitioner must be taught another meditation. One who is instructed in this meditation must contemplate his body and make it into a skeleton, making it extremely white and pure, and then make his skull fall down into his pelvis. Settling the mind in one place, he should make this extremely clear.

When this meditation is complete, he should contemplate all four sides of his body. On each side there are skeletons.

When this meditation is complete, in front of himself he [must imaginatively] create a skeleton resembling his own, its head fallen into its pelvis. Imagining one such skeleton, he next imagines two. Imagining two, he next imagines three . . . four . . . five. Imagining five, he continues until he has imagined ten, and similarly until he sees the entire room full of skeletons, each with its head fallen into its pelvis. When he has seen one roomful of these skeletons, he should continue until he sees a hundred roomfuls . . . a *yojana* . . . until he sees innumerable skeletons, their heads fallen into their pelvises.

When this meditation is complete, he see all these skeletons arrayed on the ground before him, some with broken skulls, some with broken necks

51. 凡夫心想白骨白光涌出三昧. The point, I take it, is that this is still a worldly (*laukika*) rather than trans-worldly (*lokottara*) attainment.

52. 凡夫心海生死境界相.

53. This mysterious sentence seems to mean that the Buddha not only explained the visions described above but also caused Ānanda to see them.

54. 白骨觀最初境界. That the meaning is as translated is confirmed by the subsequent discussion of a *second* stage of the white bone contemplation.

[245b], some fallen over, some twisted upon themselves, some with broken waists, some with legs extended, some with legs curled up, some with feet broken in half, some with their skulls fallen into their rib cages, some with their skulls scattered about on the ground, face up or face down, twisted and bent.[55] Above, below, and all around, they fill his room. When this meditation is complete, he continues until he sees limitless, innumerable skeletons scattered about, some large and some small, some broken and some whole. He must still his mind and carefully contemplate these various things, making them extremely clear.

[1.2.2.2] [Emptiness and Non-self of the Scattered Skeletons]

The Buddha said to Ānanda: When the practitioner has seen these things he must reflect:[56] "Formerly the bones were complete, but now they are broken and scattered about in innumerable pieces. Even these skeletons have no fixed existence, and so too this body of mine lacks a self."

Having carefully contemplated this, he must reflect: "There are only bones, scattered about in disorder, where could there be my own or others' bodies?"

When the practitioner has reflected on non-self in this manner, his body and mind will feel at ease and he will be peaceful and joyful.

[1.2.2.3] [The Fires]

The Buddha said to Ānanda: When this meditation has been completed, the practitioner must again be instructed to expand his mind so that he sees scattered bones filling the continent of Jambudvīpa. He then sees that out beyond all the bones great fires arise in all directions, their flames continuing one after the other, burning the scattered bones, fire appearing between the bones of all the skeletons. As for what these fires look like, some are like blazing, flowing water running between the bones, and some are like great mountains closing in from all sides.

When this meditation has been completed, the practitioner will feel extremely afraid. When he emerges from meditation his body will be hot and sweaty. But still he must restrain his mind and contemplate the bones as before, contemplating a single white skeleton and making it very clear.

This time, when the practitioner enters trance he will be unable to

---

55. 縮揧. I translate this unusual expression based on its gloss at *YQJYY*, T.2128:54.674b2–3.

56. Here and throughout, "reflect" translates *siwei* 思惟. In the *Chan Essentials* and *Methods for Curing* this word consistently refers to discursive meditation on Buddhist doctrinal truths. In medieval China, *siwei* was a frequent gloss on the meaning of the word *chan* (*DZDL*, T.1509:25.185b16), and *chansi* 禪思 was a common dual transcription-translation rendering of *dhyāna* (*CSZJJ*, T.2145:55.16a2). In the title of the fifth-century *Si wei lüe yao fa* (T.617), the word seems to be a synonym of *chan*. Chinese Buddhist texts and later Chinese literature also sometimes speak of the "*siwei* tree" (思惟樹) as the name of the tree beneath which the Buddha meditated to achieve awakening (*Han yu da ci dian*, 7:448; *GSZ*, T.2059:50.388b10).

emerge on his own. He will only be able to emerge when someone[57] snaps his fingers.[58]

[1.2.2.4] [The Emptiness of the Fires]

When this meditation is complete, he must arouse his thoughts and think as follows: "During countless eons in the past I did many things productive of burning anguish. Pulled by the force of that karma (業緣所牽), I now see this fire."

He must further think: "This fire comes into existence from the four great elements. My body itself is empty and its four great elements have no master.[59] This raging fire arises adventitiously from emptiness (橫從空起). My own body and the bodies of others are all also empty. This fire is produced by false imagination. What could it burn? Both my body and the fire are impermanent."

The Buddha said to Ānanda: The practitioner must exert himself and carefully contemplate these various things. Contemplating emptiness, there is no fire, and also no bones. One who performs this contemplation will be free of fear, and his body and mind will feel even more at ease than before.

When Ānanda heard what the Buddha said, he joyfully undertook to carry it out.

[1.2.2.5] [Conclusion]

When this meditation is complete, [245c] it is called the accomplishment of the second contemplation, the contemplation of the white bones.[60]

57. 當[>人, Sgz].

58. Here, to be "stuck" in trance seems to be a bad thing. A more favorable depiction of meditators who can be summoned back from trance only at a finger-snap occurs in an anecdote from the *Gao seng zhuan:* "[When the general Wang Kai visited the hermitage of the monk Zhiyan,] he saw Zhiyan and his two companions sitting on meditation chairs, meditating deeply. [Wang] Kai waited for a long while, but they did not awaken. When he snapped his fingers, the three monks open their eyes for a moment but then closed them again." 見其同止三僧，各坐繩床，禪思湛然。恢至良久不覺，於是彈指，三人開眼，俄而還閉。 (*GSZ*, T.2059:50.339b13–18).

59. 我身空寂四大無主. Very similar statements, sometimes speaking of six rather than four elements, occur several times in both the *Chan Essentials* (1.5.3, 3.25.1, 3.26.13) and the *Methods for Curing* (1.14.12). They are all close, in some cases even identical, to a line from Kumārajīva's translation of the *Vimalakīrti-nirdeśa:* "the four elements have no owner, and the body too is without self" (四大無主身亦無我; *Weimojie suo shuo jing*, T.475:14.544c29–545a1). This expresses the notion that both persons and *dharma*s lack self, a stance explicitly endorsed elsewhere by the *Chan Essentials* (1.18.15).

60. 此想成者名第二觀白骨竟. Most of the numbered sections of the *Chan Essentials* conclude with a phrase like this, and the grammar and parsing are, as here, often unclear. The concluding character *jing* 竟 is particularly obscure. I translate it as part of the assigned title, indicating the "accomplishment" or completion of the given practice. It could, however, also be a para-textual marker indicating the end of a given section, a usage seen in the *Five Gates* (*WMCJ*, T.619:15.329a7), which, however, also sometimes uses it in titles (*WMCJ*, T.619:15.328c5).

[1.3] [Third Contemplation: The Oozing Corpse]

[1.3.1] [The World Filled with Oozing Corpses]

The Buddha said to Ānanda: After finishing the second contemplation, the contemplation of the white bones, the practitioner should be further instructed in the method for fixing his thoughts. To fix his thoughts he must first fix his mind on the big toe of his left foot. He should single-mindedly contemplate his big toe and then cause the flesh to darken and ooze like fatty meat scorched by the rays of the sun, continuing gradually until reaching his knee and then his pelvis. Contemplating his left leg, he contemplates his right leg in the same manner.

Contemplating his right leg, he must next contemplate from the pelvis up to the back, the lower neck, the upper neck,[61] the head, the face, and then down to the chest,[62] so that all his limbs, joints, and other body parts become dark and oozing, like fatty meat scorched by the rays of the sun, overflowing with impurity, like a heap of piss and shit. He carefully contemplates his body [like this], making it very clear.

Successfully imagining one oozing corpse, he then imagines two . . . three . . . four . . . five . . . ten. Successfully imagining ten, he sees the whole room filled with dark oozing corpses, like fatty meat scorched by the rays of the sun, overflowing with impurity, like heaps of piss and shit. Row upon row of these impure bodies fill the room. Seeing one roomful, he next sees two roomfuls. Seeing two roomfuls, he continues until he sees innumerable multitudes of impure bodies filling this entire world above, below, and all around.

[1.3.2] [Loathing and Shame]

When this meditation has been completed, the practitioner should think to himself: "In former lives I was greedy and foolish, without any self-awareness. For many years I was heedless, shamelessly craving sensory pleasures and delighting in the objects of the six senses. Today I have contemplated my body. It is overflowing with impurity, and so too the bodies of others. How then could I delight in these things?"

Seeing these things, he develops deep loathing for his body, and full of shame he reproaches himself (慚愧自責). When he exits from trance he sees food and drink to be as deeply repulsive as shit and piss.

[1.3.3] [The Inverse Contemplation]

Next, the practitioner should be instructed in an inverse contemplation. The method for the inverse contemplation is to rouse his imagination.[63]

---

61. Based on the context, I take 頸 and 項 as the "lower" and "upper" neck, respectively. See also 1.5.1.

62. The progression here seems to go up the *back* side of the body to the crown of the head, then down the front until it reaches the chest.

63. 易觀法者，當更起想念. It is peculiar that *what* is to be imagined is not mentioned. There may be missing text.

When this [inverse] meditation is complete, he sees fire suddenly arise amid the impurity surrounding his body. Like vapors in the heat, pure white in color, like a running herd of wild horses,[64] it illuminates all the impurities.

When the practitioner has seen these things, he will feel great happiness, and feeling such happiness his body and mind will be at ease, his mind will be clear, and he will experience extraordinary joy.

[1.3.4] [Conclusion]

The Buddha said to Ānanda: "This is called number three, the contemplation of shame and self-reproach." When Ānanda heard the Buddha's words, he joyfully undertook to carry them out.

When this meditation is complete, it is known as the accomplishment of contemplation number three, the contemplation of shame and the dark oozing corpse.[65]

[1.4] [Fourth Contemplation: The Bloated Corpse]

[1.4.1] [The World Filled with Bloated Corpses]

The Buddha said to Ānanda: When this meditation is complete, the practitioner must further be taught to fix his thoughts and concentrate his mind on his left[66] big toe. He is to carefully contemplate the entire toe and imagine a bloated swelling. Seeing it as bloated and swelling [246a], he imagines it as festering. Seeing it as festering, he imagines it as full of all kinds of pus and blood, blue, black, red, and white. He makes all this pus and blood become extremely foul and hard to bear. He continues gradually, in this manner reaching his knees and then his pelvis, causing everything to become bloated and then burst open,[67] leaking impurity.

Contemplating his left leg, he contemplates his right leg in the same manner. In this way he gradually continues to the hips, the back, the lower neck, the upper neck, the head, the face, and his chest. All parts of his body become bloated, [then] festering, [then] leaking blue, black, red, and white pus, unbearably foul and filthy.

Successfully imagining one, he then imagines two... three... four... five... ten such corpses. Successfully imagining ten, he sees a roomful of

64. "Wild horses" (野馬), an image drawn from the Zhuangzi (Zhu Q. 1990), is normally used in Chinese Buddhist texts to mean a mirage or illusion, similar to "vapors in the heat" (熱時焰), also seen here. In this passage, however, it seems to be a concrete image seen by the meditator. This kind of recasting of abstract images for emptiness (such as the "trunk of a plantain tree") into concrete visionary objects occurs often in the *Chan Essentials* and *Methods for Curing.*

65. 第三津膩慚愧觀.

66. Though the Taishō prints 左, K itself reads 在, as do K[1], P, S, Q, Y, and Kg. Nevertheless, 左 (attested only in Sgz) appears correct.

67. "Burst open" (爛潰) is sometimes the name of one of the nine stages of the decaying corpse (*GFSMH*, T.643:15.686a4–5; *DMDL*, T.618:15.316a18–20).

bloated corpses, above, below, and all around, which all begin to fester until blue, black, red, and white pus flows out, unbearably foul and filthy. He further imagines a *yojana* full of them. Imagining a *yojana*, he continues until he imagines a hundred *yojana*s worth. Imagining a hundred *yojana*s, he continues until he sees the entire universe, above, below, and all around, from the earth to the sky, entirely filled with corpses that are bloated, festering, oozing blue, black, red, and white pus, filled with filth and difficult to bear.

[1.4.2] [Revulsion toward the Body and Rebirth]

The Buddha said to Ānanda: When the practitioner has seen these things, he contemplates his own body as filled with impurities, and he contemplates the bodies of others as also being like this. He then thinks: "This body of mine is extremely loathsome, entirely filled with many impurities."

Having carefully contemplated this, he begins to fear the misfortune that is birth and death. His will becomes firm and he deeply believes in the principles of karma. Whether in trance or not, he constantly sees impurity.

[1.4.3] [Excessive Loathing]

He then wishes to escape [impurity] by abandoning his body [and committing suicide].[68] When he has this thought, he sees the skin and flesh of his whole body fall away like autumn leaves. When he sees his flesh fallen on the ground before him, he is deeply shaken. He becomes afraid, and his body and mind quake and tremble uncontrollably. He feels hot and agitated, like someone sick with fever and oppressed by thirst. When he emerges from trance, his body feels exhausted as if he had been traveling in the desert during the summer with no water to quench his thirst.

When this meditation has been completed, he sees his food, even at mealtimes, as a bloated corpse, and his drink as pus and blood.

When this meditation has been completed, he feels extreme loathing for his body. Contemplating it inside and out, he is unable to find anything pure at all.

[1.4.4] [Inverse Contemplation: The Pure Ground]

The Buddha said to Ānanda: The practitioner must then be further instructed to invert his imagination so that he does not commit suicide and thereby fail to achieve any fruit.

The method for the inverse contemplation is as follows. In the distance, beyond the foul filth, he should make a pure object. Instruct him to fix his mind and imagine [246b] this pure object. When it is clear in his mind's eye, he will want to go toward it and take hold of it. In this manner he gradually expands what he sees, such that out beyond all the impurities there are various pure expanses of beryl-like ground. When he sees these pure places

68. 捨棄此身. See also 1.2.1.2 above.

he wishes to go there. But they become ever farther away and seem impossible to reach.

[1.4.5] [Pure and Impure Both Empty]

The Buddha said to Ānanda: At that moment, you must instruct the practitioner with the following words: "These things you see are just your imagination of the impure. Know that all the assorted filthy things [connected with] your imagination of the impure[69] arise from erroneous thinking, because it is your actions in past lives based on erroneous thinking that have produced your present body. This body of yours is fundamentally impure.[70] Do you now really see this impurity or not? Though you see impurity, out beyond it you see purity.[71] Know that neither purity nor impurity lasts forever. They are merely seen through your imagination in accordance with your sensory faculties.[72] Your impure body itself depends on causes and conditions. It exists when conditions come together, and it will disappear when the conditions go away. The things you see now also depend on, and are conditioned by, your imagining. When you imagine them fully, they exist. When your imagining ceases, they are no more. These images emerge from the five sense organs, whence they enter your mind.[73] All these imaginings come into existence conditioned by your various desires.[74] But such impure imaginings arrive without arriving from somewhere, and depart without going anywhere. You must carefully contemplate each bit of impurity. Neither self nor other can be found within it. The World-honored One has said that both self and other are all entirely empty and quiescent. How much more so what is impure!"

In this manner, the practitioner must be rebuked in various ways, on account of what he has been thinking, and instructed to contemplate emptiness.

He will then see that his hair, body hair, nails, and teeth are all entirely nonexistent. He will suddenly turn away from these impure things, and will concentrate his mind as before and return to the contemplation of the skeleton.

[1.4.6] [Conclusion]

The Buddha said to Ānanda: "Preserve these words. Do not forget this contemplation of impurity and the method for the inverse meditation."

---

69. 此不淨想而雜穢物. Translation tentative.

70. 種子根本皆為不淨. This line might be invoking the technical concept "impure by way of origins" (種子不淨), meaning that one views the body as impure in having originated in impure blood and semen (*DZDL*, T.1509:25.199a2–5; Lamotte 1944–1981, 1151). This idea is discussed explicitly in 3.21.4.

71. This refers to the vision described above in 1.4.4.

72. 隨逐諸根. Translation tentative.

73. 從五情出還入汝心. Translation tentative.

74. The term *yu* 欲 here could also mean "objects of desire."

When Ānanda heard what the Buddha had said, he joyfully undertook to carry it out.

When this meditation has been completed, it is called the accomplishment of contemplation number four, the contemplation of the bloated, bloody, and pus-filled [corpses] together with its inverse meditation.

[1.5] [Fifth Contemplation: The Sack of Skin]

[1.5.1] [The Body Filled with Worms]

The Buddha said to Ānanda: When this meditation is complete, instruct the practitioner to fix his thoughts in a single place and, sitting upright in absorption, to carefully contemplate the big toe of his right[75] foot, making the skin of the toe slowly stretch to the verge of tearing, such that the outer and inner layers of skin become transparent.[76] Beneath the outer layer of skin there is a thin membrane which one must also contemplate.[77] In this manner the practitioner gradually continues until he reaches the knees and then the pelvis, then the left leg in the same way, then the hips, the back, the lower neck, the upper neck, the head, the face, and the chest, until over his entire body the inner and outer layers of skin have in this same manner become transparent, stretched to the verge of tearing, as if they had been inflated from within. His skin becomes incredibly bloated. From the uncountable hundreds of thousands of pores on his body droplets of various kinds of pus and other assorted fluids pour forth faster than a torrential[78] rain, a profusion of pus and blood flowing inside and outside his body. The impurity [246c] is so extreme that it is difficult to bear, as if there were an entire pool of pus or an entire pool of blood filled with various bugs.

When this meditation is complete, he must contemplate within his chest.

---

75. Earlier, the directions were to begin with the *left* foot.

76. The "outer" and "inner" layers of skin, mentioned throughout the *Chan Essentials* and *Methods for Curing*, are, literally, the "thin skin" (*bopi* 薄皮) and "thick skin" (*houpi* 厚皮), respectively. These are common items in the lists of body parts in canonical Chinese Buddhist literature. Although most attested Indic lists of body parts, in the context of the contemplation of impurity, give only one term for skin (usually Skt. *tvac;* P. *taco*), in some Gāndhārī fragments of the *Saṃyuktāgama* (Glass 2007, 52) we find two terms: *tvaya* (Skt. *tvac;* P. *taco*) and *chaḍi* (Skt. *chavī;* P. *chavi*), the second of which does occur in Pāli sources, in other contexts, meaning an "outer" layer of skin in contrast to an inner layer (either *taco* or *camma;* see *Suttanipāta*, 196; *Majjhima-nikāya*, 3.184).

77. The *Chan Essentials* and *Methods for Curing* frequently mention a "membrane" (*mo* 膜) that, as indicated here, is said to lie between the outer (thin) and inner (thick) layers of skin. This is, evidently, not the same "membrane" that often appears in the lists of body parts in Chinese translations of Indian Buddhist texts, where it renders Skt. *mastakaluṅgaṃ*, the "brain membrane." Huilin, in his *YQJYY* (T.2128:54.318b2–3), glosses "membrane" (*mo*), in a list of body parts, by citing the lost Chinese dictionary *Zi tong* 字通 (ca. 500), which says "what lies below the skin and above the flesh is called the 'membrane'" (在皮內肉外曰膜). This definition aligns closely with the usage in the *Chan Essentials* and *Methods for Curing.*

78. 震[>暴]. S, Q, Y, and Sgz read 雹, while Kg reads 電. A very similar line occurs in some of the Contemplation Scriptures (*GFSMH*, T.643:15.669a27; *Guan Puxian pusa xing fa jing*, T.277:9.394a22), and I emend following the reading given there.

[He sees] his entire body as a giant swarm of worms. Then he should again contemplate the big toe of his left foot as it swells up and leaks pus. Blue pus, yellow pus, red pus, and black pus fester and leak out, mixing with one another and intermingling with piss and shit while various worms squirm about therein. The awful filth and horrid stench is unbearable. Filled with revulsion for his body, the meditator no longer craves sensual pleasures and has no wish to continue living.[79]

[1.5.2] [The *Yakṣa* with Fangs and Iron Club]

When this meditation is complete, the practitioner sees a giant *yakṣa*, as big as a mountain, its hair wild and disheveled like a forest of brambles. Its sixty eyes flash like lightning. Its forty mouths each have two fangs, like flaming pillars pointing upward, and tongues like sword trees that reach to its knees. It attacks the practitioner with an iron club that is like a blade mountain.[80] [The practitioner sees] many other things like this. When he sees these things, he becomes terrified, and his body and mind begin to tremble.

These appearances (相貌) are the evil roots of his past-life violations of the precepts.[81] Supposing what is not the self to be the self, what is impermanent to be permanent, and what is impure to be pure, he gave himself over to indulgence and became stained with attachment, craving all kinds of sensual pleasures. He wrongly imagined what is nothing but suffering to be pleasurable, took what is in fact empty to be not empty,[82] and imagined the impure body to be pure. Sustaining himself by means of an evil livelihood, he failed to consider impermanence.[83]

[1.5.3] [Emptiness and Non-self of the *Yakṣa*]

When this meditation is complete, the practitioner must be instructed as follows: "Do not be afraid. This *yakṣa* is merely a wicked vision of your evil mind.[84] It arises from the six elements and is formed of the six elements. You must now carefully contemplate these six elements. The six elements are earth, water, fire, wind, consciousness, and space.[85] In this manner you

79. 不樂受生. Alternatively, "has no wish for [future] rebirth." However, since this thought is about to be *countered* with a meditation on impermanence, I take its meaning to be similar to that in 1.2.1.2 and 1.4.3, where the meditation on impurity prompts thoughts of suicide.

80. "Sword trees" (劍樹) and "blade mountains" (刀山) are standard instruments of torture in Buddhist hells; see also 1.12.7, 1.14.7, and *Methods for Curing* 1.8.2, 1.14.2, 1.14.3, 1.14.4. Their appearance as part of this vision is presumably to be taken as a sign of sin; on this kind of imagery in these texts, see *Chan Before Chan*, chap. 3.

81. 前身毀犯禁戒諸惡根本.

82. Literally, "gave rise to inverted thinking about things that are empty" (於空法中起顛倒想).

83. "Evil livelihood" may be a euphemism for violation of the precepts; see *Methods for Curing* 2.4, n. 230.

84. 是汝惡心猛毒境界.

85. Here the text switches to the system of six primary elements rather than four. Both are used, without a clear pattern, throughout the *Chan Essentials*.

must carefully consider each one of them. Is your body the earth element? The water element? The wind element? The consciousness element? The space element? In this way, one by one, consider from which element your body arises, and from which element it passes away.[86] The six elements have no owner, and the body too is without a self.[87] Why then do you now fear this *yakṣa?* Just as your imagination itself arrives but does not arrive from somewhere and departs without going anywhere, so too this *yakṣa* which you have seen through your imagination. Even if this *yakṣa* comes forward and strikes, simply accept it joyfully and carefully contemplate non-self. For in regard to what is lacking in self, there can be no fear or terror.[88] You must simply have this right understanding as you sit in meditation, carefully contemplating impurity and this *yakṣa*."

[1.5.4] [Multiplication of the Corpses]

Having imagined one [such corpse],[89] he should imagine two, and so on up to countless multitudes of them. He carefully contemplates each one until they are clear.

[1.5.5] [Conclusion]

The Buddha said to Ānanda: "You must preserve well this method for the contemplation of the impurity of the outer layer of skin. Do not forget it." When Ānanda heard what the Buddha said, he joyfully undertook [247a] to carry it out.

When this meditation is complete, it is to be known as the completion of contemplation number five, the contemplation of the outer skin.

[1.6] [Sixth Contemplation: The Mass of Worms]

[1.6.1] [The Inflated Skin Sack]

The Buddha said to Ānanda: When this meditation is complete, [the practitioner] must again be instructed to fix his thoughts on the big toe of his right foot. He must carefully contemplate the toe and make it swell. From toe to head his body swells and darkens, becoming horribly bruised, an inflated skin sack. Inside it is filled with white worms, like kernels of hulled rice. Each worm has four heads.[90] They squirm in circles, biting and eating each other. Worms appear within his flesh, muscles, bones, and marrow, and all his internal organs are consumed by them, leaving only the inner layer of skin atop his bones. This skin is about as thick as silk, and the worms go through it as if tunneling through bamboo leaves. The skin stretches inwardly and outwardly until about to burst. Countless worms squirm excitedly

86. 從何大起，從何大散. Translation tentative.

87. 六大無主，身亦無我. See 1.2.2.4, n. 59.

88. That is, if one knows the *yakṣa* lacks substantial existence one will not be afraid of it.

89. I take this as referring back to the imagination of the corpse described in 1.5.1.

90. A very similar image occurs at *GFSMH*, T.643:15.652c26–27.

within his eye. They tunnel through the eye, filling the eye socket. Each of his body's nine openings become similarly [filled with worms]. Then all the worms come out through the inner layer of skin into the outer layer. When the skin is entirely bored through, the worms all fall to the ground. There are uncountable multitudes forming a big pile in front of the practitioner, like a mountain of worms. They twist around and eat each other.

[1.6.2] [The Giant Worm]

When the practitioner has seen these multitudes of worms, he must further fix his thoughts and carefully contemplate one of the worms, making it devour all the other worms. Only this single worm remains after it has eaten all the other worms.

His mind gradually expanding, he sees this one worm facing him, as big as a dog, its body like a big lump,[91] its nose bent like a horn, sniffing the ground before the practitioner. Its eyes are pure red, like hot iron balls. Seeing these things, he becomes extremely afraid.

[1.6.3] [Contemplation of Non-self]

He must then consider: "How is it that my body suddenly appears in such a state? At first, I saw these worms devour each other, and now I see but one ugly, horrid, and thoroughly frightening worm."

When this meditation is complete, he must contemplate his body [as follows]: "These worms within my body at first did not exist but now they exist, and having come into existence, they will return to nonexistence.[92] These impure things are produced by my imagination (從心想生). They arrive without arriving from somewhere and depart without going anywhere. They are not me, nor are they someone else. My body is formed through the coming together of the six elements. When the six elements disperse, this body will be no more. So too the many worms in front of me arrive without arriving from somewhere and depart without going anywhere. What substance is there, then, to this worm-heap body of mine? These worms have no master and I too am without self."

When he has reflected in this way, the eyes of the worm become gradually smaller. When he has seen this, to an even greater extent than before his body and mind become happy and at ease, calm and joyous.

---

91. *Kundun* 困頓; this must be a phonetic error for, or nonstandard form of, *hundun* 混沌 (lump).

92. 本無今有，已有還無. Similar language is used at *ZCSM*, T.614:15.279a1–3 and *DZDL*, T.1509:25.78c8–10, in reference to mental states. That things are "originally nonexistent but come to exist in the present" is a typical criticism of the Sarvāstivāda-Vaibhāṣika thesis that *dharmas* exist in the three times. See *Apitan piposha lun*, T.1546:28.295b19–20, where this claim is presented as the opinion of non-Vaibhāṣikas and then refuted.

[1.6.4] [Conclusion]

The Buddha said to Ānanda: "You must remember this method for the contemplation of the inner layer of skin and the mass of worms. Do not forget it." When Ānanda heard what the Buddha said, he joyfully undertook to carry it out.

When this meditation is complete, it is called the accomplishment of contemplation number six, the contemplation of the inner skin and the mass of worms [247b].

[1.7] [Seventh Contemplation: The Red and Muddy Bones]

[1.7.1] [The Muddy Skeleton]

The Buddha[93] said to Ānanda: The practitioner next must concentrate his mind and fix his thoughts to a single thing, carefully contemplating the big toe of his right foot. He carefully contemplates his body from head to foot, making the skin and flesh disappear, and all his internal organs, the intestines, stomach, belly,[94] liver, lungs, heart, spleen, and kidneys, fall onto the ground. All that remains are the bones, with tendons still attached, each linked to the other. A thin membrane remains attached to the bones, deep red in color like dark mud or dirty water. He then imagines washing his skin from head to toe with dirty water. He contemplates his body and makes this very clear.

[1.7.2] [Multiplication of the Corpses]

Having contemplated his own body, he imaginatively creates another body, identical to his own, standing on the ground before him. Successfully imagining one, he must imagine two . . . three . . . four . . . five. Imagining five, he continues until he imagines ten. Imagining ten, he then sees the entire room—above, below, and all around—entirely filled with red skeletons, some the color of dark mud, others the color of dirty water, their skin bathed in dirty water. This multitude becomes gradually larger, filling a *yojana*. Imagining one *yojana* filled with skeletons, he imagines two *yojana*s. Imagining two *yojana*s, he gradually increases until he imagines a hundred *yojana*s.

---

93. *Tempyō Chan Essentials 2* (Sgz) begins here. *Tempyō Chan Essentials 1* continues until 1.14.1.

94. Earlier (1.1.4), a "large intestine" (大腸), "small intestine" (小腸), "receptacle of undigested food" (生藏), and "receptacle of digested food" (熟藏) were mentioned. Added here are a "stomach" (胃) and "belly" (腹), making six stomach-like items. Pāli lists of the 32 body parts give only three such items: *antam, antaguṇam,* and *udaram.* Chinese and Sanskrit sources, which usually give 36 or 37 total body parts, often include two more (*āmāśaya* and *pakvāśaya*) for a total of five. We do find, however, six stomach-like organs within the body parts listed for meditation in the *Saddharma-smṛtyupasthāna-sūtra,* which gives *āmāśaya, pakvāśaya, antrāṇi, antraguṇā, udaram,* and *udīryakam,* translated here by Stuart (2015, 328) as "stomach, intestines, colon, mesentery, the belly, and the contents of the belly."

Imagining a hundred *yojanas*, he continues until he sees the entire universe—above, below, and all around—filled in every direction with red skeletons, some the color of dark mud, others the color of dirty water, their skin bathed in dirty water.

[1.7.3] [Conclusion]

The Buddha said to Ānanda: "You must now carefully contemplate[95] this meditation[96] on the red bones. Do not forget it." When Ānanda heard what the Buddha said, he joyfully undertook to carry it out.

When this meditation has been completed, it is known as the accomplishment of meditation number seven, the miscellaneous meditations[97] on the bones deep red like dark mud with skin bathed in dirty water.

[1.8] [Eighth Contemplation: The Fresh Corpse]

[1.8.1] [The Fresh Corpse]

The Buddha said to Ānanda: The practitioner must then be further instructed to fix his mind, concentrate his thoughts, and contemplate the big toe of his left[98] foot. From toe to head he contemplates his own body as a fresh corpse, the flesh slightly jaundiced. Having seen this jaundiced corpse, he must then make the yellow color change to a bluish red.

When this meditation is complete, he sees a fresh corpse on the ground before him, yellow-red in color. Seeing one, he sees two... three... four... five. Seeing five, because his imagination is now sharpened, he perpetually sees his own body as a fresh corpse.

When this meditation has been completed, he sees all the people of the continent of Jambudvīpa as fresh corpses. When this meditation has been completed, he continues to expand it until he sees the entire universe filled with fresh corpses. He sees his own body and the bodies of others in exactly this same way.

When this meditation has been completed, his mind feels happy[99] and his cravings are diminished.

---

95. 汝今諦觀. The Buddha usually tells Ānanda to "preserve" (持) the teaching. However, compare 1.8.2, 1.9.2, 1.10.3, and 1.11.4, which also say "contemplate." These instances where the Buddha appears to direct Ānanda to carry out the previously described meditation, which are not in keeping with the normal format in the *Chan Essentials* or the normal conventions of Buddhist sutra literature, may be further traces of the original master-disciple, meditation-manual format, here insufficiently edited when it was transformed into a sutra; see chap. 4.

96. 相[>想, Sgz, Kg].

97. The obscure name "miscellaneous meditations" (雜想) recalls the "miscellaneous contemplation" (雜想觀) of the *Guan Wuliangshou fo jing* (T.365:12.344c6–7).

98. Sgz and Kg here read "right" (右).

99. 慑[>快], based on the parallel line in 2.19.2.1 (256b2).

[1.8.2] [Conclusion]

The Buddha said to Ānanda: "Carefully [247c] contemplate this meditation on the fresh corpse. Do not forget it." When Ānanda heard what the Buddha said, he joyfully undertook to carry it out.

When this meditation is complete, it is called the accomplishment of meditation number eight, the meditation on the fresh corpse.

[1.9] [Ninth Contemplation: The Intact Skeleton]

[1.9.1] [The White Skeletons]

The Buddha said to Ānanda: The practitioner must then be further instructed to fix his mind, concentrate his thoughts, and carefully contemplate the big toe of his left foot. From toe to head, making his mind free of distraction, he sees the bones of his body, each clearly distinct. They support one another and are mutually connected. None is damaged in any way. They are brilliantly white, with the body hair, head hair, nails, and teeth all complete. Having seen his own body in this way, he reviews it over and over and imagines it to be white and pure.

Imagining a single body, he next imagines two bodies . . . three . . . four . . . five . . . up to ten. Imagining ten bodies, he sees the entire room—above, below, and all around—full of skeletons, their body hair, head hair, nails, and teeth all complete, the purest white in color, like *ke*-jade or snow. Seeing one roomful, he next sees a hundred roomfuls. Seeing a hundred roomfuls, he sees the entire continent of Jambudvīpa. Seeing the entire continent of Jambudvīpa, he continues until he sees the entire universe filled with skeletons, their body hair, head hair, nails, and teeth all complete, extremely white in color, white like *ke*-jade or snow.

When this meditation is complete, his mind becomes peaceful, and he feels extraordinarily happy.

[1.9.2] [Conclusion]

The Buddha said to Ānanda: "Carefully contemplate this meditation on the complete skeleton. Do not forget it." When Ānanda heard what the Buddha said, he joyfully undertook to carry it out.

When this meditation is complete, it is called the accomplishment of meditation number nine, the meditation on the complete body.

[1.10] [Tenth Contemplation: The Detached Skeleton]

[1.10.1] [The Detached Skeletons]

The Buddha said to Ānanda: Next the practitioner must be instructed to fix his mind, concentrate his thoughts, and carefully contemplate the space between the two bones of the big toe of his right foot. He makes his mind focused and still, completely free of distraction. He contemplates the two bones and makes them separate from one another until only their tips are touching. Contemplating these two bones, in this same manner he makes all the bones of his entire body from toe to head separate such that only their tips are touching. From the toe to the head there are three hundred sixty-three bones,[100] and he carefully contemplates each one, making each bone separate. If they are not sufficiently separated, he must with calm mind contemplate carefully until each bone separates until only their tips are touching.

Having contemplated his own body, he must contemplate the body of another. When he has contemplated and seen one body, he must contemplate and see two bodies . . . three . . . four . . . five bodies. Contemplating five, he continues until he has contemplated and seen innumerable white skeletons, their bones each separated with only their tips touching. Seeing these things, in this same manner he further sees a multitude of skeletons in all directions.

[1.10.2] [Vision of the Pure Ocean]

When he has obtained (得) this contemplation, he will spontaneously see (自然見), out beyond all the skeletons, something that resembles a great ocean, calm and pure. His mind being clear and sharp, he sees various multicolored lights [248a] in all directions. Seeing these things, his mind becomes spontaneously peaceful and happy. His body and mind become pure, free of distress, and full of happy thoughts.

[1.10.3] [Conclusion]

The Buddha said to Ānanda: "Carefully contemplate this meditation on the detached bones. Do not forget it." When Ānanda heard what the Buddha said, he joyfully undertook to carry it out.

When this contemplation has been attained, it is called the accomplishment of contemplation number ten, the contemplation of the detached bones.

[1.11] [Eleventh Contemplation: The Light of the White Bones]

[1.11.1] [Sunlight and Moonlight Between the Bones]

The Buddha said to Ānanda: When this meditation is complete, the practitioner should next be instructed to fix his thoughts, concentrate his mind, and carefully contemplate the space between the two bones of the big toe of his right foot, making the bones separate about three finger-widths apart. He then imagines a white light and uses it to support [the now separated bones]. If he is meditating during the night, he should imagine the light of the moon. But if he is meditating during the day, he should imagine the light of the sun. The light links together and supports the bones so they do

100. 解[>節]. The *Yogācārabhūmi* of Saṅgharakṣa also speaks of 363 bones (*Xiu xing dao di jing*, T.606:15.187 b16–17). The *Methods for Curing*, however, speaks of 336 bones (1.3.3 and throughout).

not fall apart. From his toe to his head he makes all three hundred sixty-three bones[101] separate about three finger-widths apart, held together with white light so they do not fall apart, either with the light of the sun if he is meditating during the day, or with the light of the moon if he is meditating at night. He contemplates the space between the bones and makes them radiate white light.

[1.11.2] [The Buddha within the Light]

When he attains this contemplation, he will suddenly see a sixteen-foot buddha[102] within the sunlight. Its halo measures eight feet[103] horizontally and eight feet vertically.[104] Its body is golden, radiating white light all over, brilliant[105] and majestic. Its thirty-two major marks and eighty minor marks are each distinctly apparent. Each major and minor mark is clearly visible, exactly as if the Buddha were present in the world.

[1.11.3] [Emptiness of the Vision]

When he sees this, he must not pay reverence. He must merely carefully contemplate all *dharma*s with a calm mind, bringing to mind the following thoughts: "The Buddha has said that all *dharma*s neither come nor go, their nature being empty and quiescent. All buddhas and tathāgatas are [in truth] the body of liberation, the body of liberation is nothing other than true thusness (真如), and within true thusness there are no *dharma*s that can be seen or grasped."

When he carries out this meditation, he will suddenly see all the buddhas (一切諸佛). Because of having seen the buddhas, his mind will become settled, calm, and happy.

[1.11.4] [Conclusion]

The Buddha said to Ānanda: "Carefully contemplate this radiant light of the white bones.[106] Do not forget it." When Ānanda heard what the Buddha said, he joyfully undertook to carry it out.

---

101. 解[>節].

102. The Buddha was supposedly "sixteen feet" (一丈六) tall, twice the height of a normal person. In Chinese Buddhist texts, a "sixteen-foot image" (一丈六像) often means a *life-sized* statue of the Buddha (*Bukkyō daijiten*, 3731). At the same time, the concept of the "sixteen-foot" Buddha often pointed, for fifth-century Chinese authors at least, to concrete icons, statues, or paintings of the Buddha in general, in contrast to the Buddha's cosmic or other forms (Funayama 1995, 96–98). Here the *Chan Essentials* seems to use the word to mean an image of the Buddha similar to his appearance in icons and paintings.

103. Literally, "one *xun*" (一尋), a *xun* being eight *chi* 尺 (each measuring 24–30 cm). The Buddha is said to have a "one-fathom halo" (*vyāmaprabhā;* Xing 2005, 148). *Vyāma* (an arm's width) was in this case sometimes translated as *zhang* 丈 (*DZDL*, T.1509:25.114c19–26), equal to ten *chi*, but also as *xun* (see, e.g., *Da banniepan jing*, T.374:12.397b3).

104. 圓光一尋左右，上下亦各一尋. See the very similar *GFSMH*, T.643:15.659c2–5.

105. 赤[>赫, Sgz].

106. 汝今諦觀是流光白骨. See 1.7.3 above, n. 95.

When this contemplation has been obtained, it shall be known as the accomplishment of contemplation number eleven, the contemplation of the radiant light of the white bones.

[1.12] [Twelfth Contemplation: The Four Elements and the Ninety-Eight Defilements]

[1.12.1] [The White-Jade Person atop Sumeru]

The Buddha said to Ānanda: Having obtained this contemplation, the practitioner must be further instructed to fix his mind, concentrate his thoughts, and carefully contemplate his spine. In between his vertebrae, using the power of his concentrated mind, he imagines a high platform. He then contemplates his body as a white-jade person (白玉人) sitting there in meditation posture, illuminating everything with the light of his white bones. When performing this contemplation, he makes it extremely clear. Sitting upon this platform, he is like one endowed with the supernatural powers dwelling on Mount Sumeru[107] who can view the four directions without obstacle. [Internally,] he sees his own[108] body clearly. [Externally,] he sees skeletons filling the universe, white like *ke*-jade or snow, row upon row [248b] all facing him, their bodies complete without missing bones.

This is called the completion of the meditation on the white light.[109]

[1.12.2] [The Innumerable Skeletons]

Next he sees the vertical bones, which similarly fill the entire universe. He further sees the horizontal bones, which similarly fill the entire universe.[110] He sees row upon row of blue skeletons... row upon row of black skeletons... row upon row of bloated corpses, without any space between them, filling the entire universe. He further sees corpses leaking pus.[111] He further sees corpses smeared with pus and blood, filling the entire universe... rotting worm-ridden corpses... bodies covered [only] with the outer and inner layers of skin... reddish bloodied corpses... corpses the color of dirty water... mud-colored corpses... skeletons with bones still held together, with head hair, body hair, nails, and teeth... [partially decayed] skeletons in which the three hundred sixty-three bones simply rest against each other... skeletons in which the joints have come apart about three finger-widths held together

107. The ability to ascend Mount Sumeru is often attributed to those who have mastered the six *abhijñā* (*DZDL*, T.1509:25.67b29).

108. 故[>己].

109. 此名白光想成. This is an unusual case where a subsection of one of the numbered contemplations is given its own name.

110. "Vertical" (縱) and "horizontal" (横) are here, apparently, two different types of bones or skeletons. This is peculiar. Within accounts of the contemplation of the corpse in Chinese Buddhist literature, we more normally find, as a formal, named stage listed immediately after that of the complete skeleton, a single moment described as the perception of "scattered" (縱横) bones (*GFSMH*, T.643:15.652c11; *Majjhima-nikāya*, 3.91).

111. 膿癩[>潰]; P's 病癩 is probably a hyper-correction. The expression "leaking pus" (膿潰), to which I have emended, occurs earlier in the text (1.5.1 [246c3]).

with light[112]...skeletons that have been completely scattered so that only white light remains,[113] filling the entire universe.[114]

There are uncountably many skeletons such as this that he should see.

[1.12.3] [The Wind Element]

When he has attained this contemplation, he must think as follows: "This body of mine arises from the four elements, and from seed to branch to leaves[115] it is very impure, exceedingly loathsome. These visions (境界) arise from my mind. When my mind imagines, they are formed (心想則成). When I cease imagining, I do not see them. These appearances[116] are thus seen only in dependence on my contemplation.[117] They appear falsely,[118] dependent on causes and conditions. I must now contemplate the conditionality of all *dharma*s. What is meant by the conditionality of all *dharma*s? The conditionality of all *dharma*s is their arising from the four elements of earth, water, fire, and wind."

The practitioner must then contemplate the wind element. It arises in each of the four directions, each instance of it like a giant snake. Each snake has four heads, two going upward, two going downward.[119] Wind emerges from each of their many ears.

[1.12.4] [The Fire Element]

When this contemplation is complete, the wind transforms into fire. Each of the poisonous snakes breathes out great mountains of fire. Towering

---

112. 節節兩向解離相去三指許間有白光<共相連持>人. I relocate 共相連持 from one manuscript column (17 characters) later. The entire long compound seems to modify the final character "person" (人). Grammatically this is very awkward Chinese, but it could derive from a mechanical translation of a long Indic compound.

113. 唯有白光{共相連持}. See previous note.

114. The final sequence here replicates the progression in the tenth and eleventh contemplations above, which move from the skeleton that is complete, to one in which the bones are slightly separated, to one in which they are further separated with white light holding them together.

115. These images may anticipate the tree of the defilements from later (1.12.7).

116. 想[>相].

117. 是假觀見. Alternatively: "they are seen on the basis of false contemplation."

118. 從虛妄見. Alternatively: "they are seen on the basis of delusion."

119. 二上二下. This inscrutable line is clarified by reference to Dharmakṣema's translation of the *Suvarṇa-bhāsottama-sūtra*, which describes the dispersal of the "snakelike" elements of the body (an old canonical simile) at the time of death, using these precise words. In that context, the meaning is "two going up and two going down," referring to the way the fire and wind elements disperse upward when freed of the body, while the water and earth elements proceed downward (*Jin guang ming jing*, T.663:16.340b1–6). The *Chan Essentials* here and elsewhere (1.12.7; 4.31.8; also, *Methods for Curing* 1.9.5) uses this four-character refrain to depict the "snake" elements in visionary form. That Dharmakṣema's Chinese translation was the source of this language is confirmed by *Chan Essentials* 4.31.8 (265a13), where "two going up and two going down" is immediately followed by the next line in Dharmakṣema's translation, "and so too, twofold in all the directions" (諸方亦二; *dvayādvayaṃ diśavidiśāsu sarvā* [Nobel 1937, 58], "by twos they go in the directions and subdirections" [Emmerick 1970, 21]).

above, they are very frightening. Dwelling within the mountains of fire are various *yakṣa*s, who roam about inhaling the fire and spewing wind from their pores.

This frightful scene[120] fills a single room. Filling one room [248c], it fills two rooms. Filling two rooms, it gradually grows until it fills one *yojana*. Filling one *yojana*, it fills two *yojana*s. Filling two *yojana*s, it grows yet further, filling the continent of Jambudvīpa.

The practitioner then sees the various *yakṣa*s within the mountains of fire inhaling the mountains of burning[121] flames, spewing wind from their pores. They rush about frantically[122] throughout Jambudvīpa. They further grab hold of burning pitchforks,[123] with which they threaten the practitioner.

[1.12.5] [Inverse Contemplation: A Buddha in the Flames]

When he sees these things, he becomes frightened and should seek a method of inverse contemplation. The method for the inverse contemplation is as follows. He first contemplates an image of the Buddha. Then, within each[124] tip of flame he imagines a sixteen-foot buddha-image.[125]

When this meditation is complete, the flames gradually diminish and transform into lotus flowers, the mountains of fire become heaps of transparent gold, and the *yakṣa*s white-jade men. Only the wind element remains, blowing gently back and forth against the lotus flowers. Innumerable transformation buddhas[126] stand in the air like adamantine mountains shining brightly. The winds settle, and all is still.

[1.12.6] [The Water Element]

Then the four poisonous snakes spew water of five colors from their mouths, which fills an area the size of one meditation cot . . . two cots . . . three cots. It continues in this manner until it fills one room . . . two rooms . . . three rooms. It continues in this manner until it has filled ten rooms. When the water has filled ten rooms, the practitioner sees a white light within each stream of

---

120. "Frightful scene" translates *bianzhuang* 變狀, literally, "transformed appearance." The word "transformation" (*bian*) was used from an early date in Chinese Buddhist literature to mean a *vision*, often of something unpleasant (*Zheng fa hua jing*, T.263:9.76c8). The word *bianzhuang* is used similarly in *Methods for Curing* 1.14.4 (339b8); see also the similar *bianhua* 變化 in *Chan Essentials* 4.32.8 (264b16).

121. 吸火負[>焰]山.

122. 周憧; I take this as a phonetic equivalent to 惆悵 (see *YQJYY*, T.2128:54.487b1).

123. 復驚[>擎]夜[>火]叉, tentatively following Sgz and Kg. Possibly 夜 should instead be emended to 鐵, as later the *yakṣa*s carry iron pitchforks.

124. 各<各, P, S, Q, Y, Sgz, Kg>.

125. The meaning here may be that the meditator should first contemplate a physical image (the usual meaning of "sixteen-foot Buddha"; see 1.11.2 above, n. 102) and then "imagine" this image within the flames.

126. On the "transformation buddhas" (*hua fo* 化佛), which frequently appear in the subsequent visionary scenes, see "The Bodies of the Buddha" in chap. 3.

the five-colored water. It is like a crystal pillar with fourteen levels,[127] between each of which there is an empty space from which white water gushes forth into the air, where it then stops and remains still.

[1.12.7] [The Poisonous Dragon and the Tree of the Defilements]

When this meditation is complete, the practitioner will see that within his heart there is a poisonous dragon. The dragon has six heads, and it wraps itself around his heart seven times. Two of its heads breathe out water, two breathe out fire, and two breathe out rock, while wind blows from its ears.[128] From the pores of its body ninety-nine poisonous snakes emerge, going up and down in pairs.[129] The water spewed forth by the poisonous dragon[130] emerges from the practitioner's feet and flows into the white water. [The water] gradually expands in this manner until he sees a full *yojana* of water. After filling one *yojana*, two *yojana*s are filled. After two *yojana*s, it continues like this until the entire continent of Jambudvīpa is filled. When all of Jambudvīpa has been filled, the poisonous dragon emerges from his navel, slowly crawls upward, and enters his eye. Emerging from his eye, it perches atop the crown of his head.

Then, within the waters, a great tree appears whose canopy spreads in all directions. Without leaving the practitioner's body, the poisonous dragon touches the tree with its tongue. On the tip of its tongue appear eight hundred demons (鬼), some of them holding boulders above their heads [ready to throw],[131] with snakes for hands and legs like dogs. There are other demons with the head of a dragon [249a], each of their pores a flame-shooting eye, hundreds of thousands of which cover their bodies. Their teeth are like blade mountains, and they swarm on the ground. There are other demons, each with ninety-nine heads and ninety-nine hands. Their heads are hideous, like those of dogs, jackals, raccoons, cats, foxes, and rats. Around the neck of each of these demons hangs a monkey. These evil demons play in the waters, some climbing up the tree and leaping about and launching themselves into the air frantically.[132]

There are also *yakṣa*-demons, their heads aflame. The monkeys try to extinguish these flames with water, but they are unable to control them and instead make[133] them increase. The raging fires approach the crystal pillar within the waters and suddenly flare up, burning the crystal pillar until it is like molten gold. The flames spread, wrapping around the practitioner's

127. Fourteen appears to be a meaningful number. Later, there is mention of the "fourteen stages" of advanced attainment (4.31.3). See also 1.14.8, 4.31.26, and *Methods for Curing* 1.5.3.

128. Taking "rock" as implying *earth*, we have all four elements here.

129. 如是諸蛇二上二下. See 1.12.3, n. 119.

130. 諸龍, "the various dragons," but only one dragon was mentioned previously.

131. On the image of demons carrying boulders, see 1.14.4, n. 161.

132. 騰躍透擲. Reading 透 as *shu*, meaning "startled" (see *YQJYY*, T.2128:54.668b11).

133. Sgz and Kg read 使[>更], yielding "the flames then grow."

body ten times and then rising above him like a golden canopy, like nets spread out across the top of the tree, forming three layers in all.

Suddenly an evil demon of the four elements[134] appears on the ground, with hundreds of thousands of ears out of which pour water and fire. From the pores of its body small particles of earth rain forth, and it spews a wind that fills the universe. Eighty-four thousand *rākṣasa*-demons also appear, lightning shooting from their pores, each with fangs one *yojana* long. All these creatures romp and play within the waters. From the mountains of fire tigers, wolves, lions, leopards, and other beasts emerge, and they too play within the waters.

When the practitioner sees these things, each of the skeletons, filling the entire universe, raises its right hand.[135] Then the *rākṣasa*s stab the skeletons with iron pitchforks and collect them into a pile. At that moment skeletons of nine different colors, in tightly packed rows, come before the practitioner.[136]

There[137] are many other hundreds of thousands of confirmatory visions [of the four elements and the ninety-eight defilements]. They cannot be described in full.

[1.12.8] [Conclusion]

The Buddha said to Ānanda: "When this meditation is complete, it is called the contemplation of the four elements. You must preserve it. Do not forget it." When Ānanda heard what the Buddha said, he joyfully undertook to carry it out.

When this meditation is complete, it is called contemplation number twelve, the contemplation of the earth, fire, wind, and water elements.[138] It is also called the confirmatory vision of the ninety-eight defilements (九十八使境界).

[1.13] [Thirteenth Contemplation: The Roots of the Defilements]

[1.13.1] [The Opening of the Ground]

The Buddha said to Ānanda: When this meditation is complete, the practitioner must be further instructed to fix his thoughts, concentrate his mind, and carefully contemplate his spine. He imagines all the bones of the spine are white like *ke*-jade or snow. When he has seen the bones of the spine, he then sees all the bones of his body, each resting against the other, become increasingly bright and pure, white like crystal. He sees each and

134. 四大惡鬼. From the context, *not* "four large evil demons."

135. This presumably refers to the skeletons in 1.12.2.

136. This seemingly out of place sentence can be explained as a long belated conclusion to 1.12.2, in whose wake this entire long visionary sequence occurred.

137. Kg here has mixed up the order of several columns of text.

138. Unusually, the conclusion of this numbered section does not speak of the "completion" (竟) of this practice, perhaps because a "second" four-element contemplation comes later.

every bone, both big and small. Each one is bright, like a crystal mirror. The confirmatory visions of the fire, wind, water, and earth elements[139] appear within each bone.[140]

When this meditation is complete, the practitioner sees the ground beneath his meditation cot gradually open up [249b] ... beneath two meditation cots ... three meditation cots ... the [ground of] an entire room ... two rooms ... three rooms. Seeing three rooms, he sees the ground in the area of an entire building gradually opening up.

[1.13.2] [The Wind-Circle]

When he sees these things, he must carefully contemplate in the downward direction, where there is [now] no obstruction.[141]

Various winds arise in the wind-circle below.[142] They head toward the various *yakṣa*s who inhale them. When they have inhaled these winds, from the pores of their bodies emerge *kumbhāṇḍa*-demons. Each *kumbhāṇḍa* spews forth mountains of fire that fill the universe. Within these mountains there suddenly appear innumerable nymphs (妙女) playing music and singing. They come before the practitioner, and are devoured by a horde of fighting *rākṣasa*s.

When the practitioner has seen this, he becomes extremely alarmed and afraid, such that he is unable to control himself. When he emerges from trance, he is perpetually afflicted by pain in his heart and his skull feels as if it is about to burst.

[1.13.3] [The White-Jade Man Shoots Fire]

He must then restrain his mind and enter trance once again. As before, he will see the confirmatory visions of the four elements. When he has seen these confirmatory visions, by the power of the trance of the four elements (四大定力), he sees his body is as white as a person made of jade. From each of his bones fire shoots upward and water flows downward. Wind emerges from his ears, and rocks rain from his eyes.[143]

When he has seen these things, ten giant millipedes appear on the

---

139. This presumably refers to the visions described in 1.12.

140. Invoked here is the trope, common from Indian visionary literature of all traditions, that jewel-like objects—here, the bones—can reflect and display other things (Granoff 1998).

141. The point seems to be that the practitioner is now able to see into the bowels of the earth.

142. The "wind-circle" (風輪; *vāyumaṇḍala*), according to some Indian cosmological schemes, lies at the bottom of the universe, along with the circles of earth and water (Schlingloff 1964, 32n1). The "water nadir" (水際) mentioned in 2.19.2.5 refers to this same scheme. The *Chan Essentials* also mentions an "adamantine nadir" (1.18.17, 4.31.12) that is seemingly the lowest point of all.

143. Emission of fire (upward) and water (downward) is a standard image of advanced meditative power. The Buddha is reported to have performed this miracle on several occasions. Paintings of meditating monks with fire and water emerging from their bodies can be seen throughout Central Asia (Waldschmidt 1930; Tanabe 1981; Greene 2013, 290–291).

ground before him,[144] each five hundred *yojanas* long, with twelve hundred feet resembling poisonous dragons. Water and fire stream from their bodies as they squirm on the ground.

When this meditation is complete, he must devote himself to repenting his past sins. Emerging from trance, he must not speak too much, and except while eating he should stay in a solitary, quiet place where he is to single-mindedly fix his thoughts. He must repent and take butter medicines (酥藥).[145] Only after doing this is he to invert this contemplation method.[146]

[1.13.4] [Conclusion]

The Buddha said to Ānanda: "This contemplation is called the second four-element contemplation.[147] You must preserve it. Do not forget it." When Ānanda heard what the Buddha said, he joyfully undertook to carry it out.

When this meditation is complete, it is called the accomplishment of contemplation number thirteen, the contemplation of the roots[148] of the defilements.[149]

[1.14] [Fourteenth Contemplation: The Earth Element]

[1.14.1] [Inverse Contemplation]

The Buddha said to Ānanda: When this meditation is complete, the practitioner must invert his contemplation. The procedure for the inverse contemplation is as follows. When the fire element begins to move about, he should imagine various mountains. He should imagine the various mountains as ice or frost that is melted by the fire, which, when it blazes high, merely steams his body warm [and does not burn it].

He further imagines a dragon and makes it spew forth rocks that smother the fire. He must then imagine the rocks broken into dust. The dragon further spews forth wind, which gathers up all the tiny particles of dust and piles them up until they form a mountain, upon which innumerable trees and thorny brambles grow spontaneously. Then, pure water of five colors

---

144. *Wanshe* 蚖蛇. In Chinese Buddhist literature, this often translates Indic words meaning "snake" (Karashima 2001, 275). However, the creature depicted here plainly has *legs*. Glossing the term elsewhere, *YQJYY* cites the early medieval Chinese legendarium the *Xuan zhongji* 玄中記 (of uncertain date) to explain *wanshe* as a snakelike creature with legs and poisonous spines (T.2128:54.531c3; 575c13; 618c22). This may be what the authors of the *Chan Essentials* had in mind.

145. Based on 1.14.2 below, "butter medicine" seems to mean butter *as* medicine. On the frequent recommendations in the *Chan Essentials* to consume medicine, see chap. 3.

146. This probably refers to 1.14, the next section.

147. 第二四大觀. P, S, Q, Y, and Sgz (scroll 1 only) read 第十三四大觀. This is probably an overcorrection; section 1.12 was the first four-element contemplation, this is now the second.

148. The expression "roots of the defilements" (結使根本) occurs at *ZCSM*, T.614:15.273b4–7, explaining the standard idea that while *dhyāna* alone merely suppresses the defilements, the attainment of the path removes their roots.

149. *Tempyō Chan Essentials 1* ends here.

flows through the brambles. These waters collect at the summit of the mountain, [249c] frozen still like a mass of ice.

When this meditation is complete, it is called the inverse contemplation of contemplation number fourteen.[150]

[1.14.2] [Butter and Meat Medicines]

The Buddha said to Ānanda: "You must teach this method for the inverse contemplation to monks, nuns, laymen, and laywomen who practice absorption in *samādhi*. Do not forget it!

"I allow those who attain this contemplation of the four elements to eat the medicines of butter and meat.[151] When they eat meat, however, they must rinse it so that it becomes flavorless,[152] and they must eat it as in a time of famine they would eat the flesh of their own children,[153] thinking: 'If I do not eat this meat, I will be driven mad and will die.' For this reason, in Śrāvasti I ordained that monks, in order to cultivate meditation, may eat the three kinds of pure meat."[154]

When Ānanda heard what the Buddha said, he joyfully undertook to carry it out.

[1.14.3] [Rows of Colored Skeletons]

The Buddha said to Ānanda: Having been instructed in the inverse contemplation, he must be instructed to fix his thoughts as before, concentrate his mind, and carefully contemplate his spine, again making it white and pure—hundreds of times more so than before. Because of their clarity and purity, between each[155] vertebra he is able to see all manners of horrible impure things.

When this meditation is complete, he must contemplate his body,

150. The end of contemplation fourteen occurs only at 1.14.8 below.

151. That meat is here *permitted* for certain meditators implies that, when the *Chan Essentials* was composed in the fifth century, it normally was not (see Greene 2016a).

152. 其食肉時洗令無味. This passage may be a rewriting of a line from the Faxian / Buddhabhadra translation of the Mahāyāna *Mahāparinirvāṇa sūtra* (completed ca. 418), one of the key scriptural proof texts for Buddhist vegetarianism in East Asia. In a line notably absent from the more famous Dharmakṣema translation of this text, it is said that if food has meat mixed with it one may eat the food after first putting the food into water so as to separate and remove the meat or, if the meat cannot be fully separated, "removing [the obvious pieces of] meat and getting rid of any broth, thereby *removing its taste*." 却肉去汁壞其本味 (*Da bannihuan jing*, T.376:12.869b15). The *Chan Essentials* seems to take the point here—contrary, I think, to the sense of Faxian's text—to be that one *can* eat meat itself if it is first rinsed of flavor.

153. 如飢世食子肉想. That *all* food should be consumed with such thoughts is an old canonical trope (*Saṃyutta-nikāya*, 2.97–100; *Za ahan jing*, T.99:2.102b18–29). The precise Chinese wording used here occurs in the Dharmakṣema *Mahāparinirvāṇa-sūtra* translation (*Da banniepan jing*, T.374:12.406a13–14).

154. The *vinaya* permits eating "thrice-pure" meat: if it is neither seen, heard, nor suspected that the animal in question was killed expressly for one's own benefit (Ruegg 1980, 234–236). This, however, is not normally linked to the needs of meditators specifically.

155. 二[>一一, Kg]. K[1], P, S, Q, and Y read 三.

transforming it into a skeleton, each bone white, pure, and radiant, like a crystal mirror. Skeletons filling the continent of Jambudvīpa[156] and the confirmatory visions of the contemplation of the four elements appear within each one of the bones.

When he has seen these things, he sees many skeletons arriving from the east. Row upon row of them face the practitioner, as numerous as particles of dust. In this manner the entire universe to the east becomes filled with skeletons, arranged in rows, coming toward the practitioner. It is also like this to the south, west, north, the four intermediate directions, and above and below. Next, row upon row of blue skeletons come toward the practitioner, filling Jambudvīpa, and then gradually increasing until filling the entire universe to the east. It is also like this to the south, west, north, the four intermediate directions, and above and below. Next, row upon row of muddy skeletons . . . row upon row of skeletons the color of muddy water . . . row upon row of red skeletons . . . row upon row of pink skeletons [250a] . . . row upon row of skeletons smeared with pus and blood . . . row upon row of yellow skeletons . . . row upon row of green skeletons . . . row upon row of purple skeletons . . . row upon row of skeletons that are like infected sores,[157] leaking noxious, multicolored pus from between each[158] of their bones, come toward the practitioner, filling Jambudvīpa and then gradually increasing until filling the entire universe to the east. And it is also like this to the south, west, north, the four intermediate directions, and above and below.

[1.14.4] [Fear]

When this meditation is complete, the practitioner feels frightened and sees various *yakṣa*s coming to eat him. He further sees fires appearing on the bones of the skeletons. Flames following one after the other fill the entire universe. He further sees jets of water like crystal pillars emerge from the crowns of the skeletons' skulls. He further sees the fires on the skulls transform into mountains of rock. Then, winds emerge from the ears of the dragon,[159] blowing the fires and shaking the mountains. The mountains spin in the air like potter's wheels, with no gap[160] between them.

When he has seen these things, he becomes extremely frightened, and

156. 閻浮提中一切骨人. Or perhaps: "all the skeletons of [all the people of] Jambudvīpa."

157. 那利(梨 in Kg)瘡(創 in K[1], P, Sgz, and Kg). *Fan fan yu* (T.2130:54.989c8), commenting on *GFSMH*, explains *nali* 那利 as an Indian word meaning "leaking" (漏; C. Chen 2004, no. 563, offers no Indic reconstruction). Zhizhou, citing a passage from the *Methods for Curing* (see Appendix 1, no. 6) where this word appears, glosses it as "infected sore" (毒惡瘡; *Fan wang jing pusa jie ben shu*, Z.687:38.452b18). The original source of the word in Chinese Buddhist literature may be Kumārajīva's *Meditation Scripture*, which says the body is impure "like a *nali* sore beyond the power of medicine to cure" (亦如那利瘡，絕治於醫藥; *ZCSM*, T.614:15.270a17; Yamabe and Sueki 2009, 3, translate it as "boil").

158. 二[>一一, Kg].

159. I presume this refers to the dragon mentioned in 1.14.1.

160. 無分閡[>閡].

because of his fear ten million demons, each different in appearance, carrying boulders and spewing fire,[161] appear and draw near.

[1.14.5] [Non-self of *Dharma*s and the Black Elephant]

The Buddha said to Ānanda: Monks who dwell peacefully with correct mindfulness and are heedful in practice[162] should, if they see these things, be taught the contemplation of the emptiness and absence of self of all *dharma*s.

[To do this,] when he emerges from trance, the practitioner should be taken to a wise person[163] to inquire about the profound truth of emptiness. Having heard this teaching, he should contemplate: "This body of mine was created through the joining together of the impurities of mother and father, is bound together by tendons and painted over with blood, is filled with the thirty-six dirty, oozing, impure things, is dependent on past actions and arises from ignorance. [250b] Contemplating my body, no part of it is worthy of attachment, for it is a rotting, decaying thing."

When he reflects in this way, the skeletons press near. He must then extend his right hand and tap the skeletons with his finger, thinking: "These skeletons come from false imagination and appear only because of incorrect discrimination. My own body is also thus. It arises from the four elements and is but an [empty] village where the six sense gates cohabitate.[164] [My own body being empty], how much more so these bones, which have been produced by empty false [imagination]!"

When he has produced these thoughts (念), the white skeletons shatter into dust, forming a pile on the ground like a snow-covered mountain. As for the other skeletons of various colors, they are suddenly eaten up by a giant snake. On top of the mound of white snow there is a white-jade person, his body straight and imposing, thirty-six *yojana*s tall, with a neck as red as fire and white light glowing in his eyes. The various white waters and crystal pillars all suddenly enter the crown of the white-jade man's head. The many

161. The phrase "carrying boulders and belching fire" (擔山吐火), also found in some of the Contemplation Scriptures (*GFSMH*, T.643:15.651b14), occurs in a number of influential Chinese Buddhist scriptures and later Chinese writings describing the attack of Māra on the eve of the Buddha's awakening (*DZDL*, T.1509:25.242c19–24; *Xiu xing ben qi jing*, T.184:3.471a11; *HMJ*, T.2102:52.94b1–2). Some visual depictions of Māra's attack from Gandhāra and Central Asia similarly show one or more assailants holding large rocks above their heads (Kurita 2003, pl. 226, 230, 231; Grünwedel 1920, pl. 3–4). I presume this is the intended image.

162. 修不放逸. This probably connotes those who do not violate the precepts. The implication here might be that emptiness may only be taught to those who are morally pure, which would fit with the common trope that some people wrongly apprehend emptiness as the negation of karma.

163. "Wise person" (智者), or "wise teacher" as I sometimes translate it, is used elsewhere in the *Chan Essentials* to mean someone who instructs the practitioner in various ways; see 1.18.3, 1.18.11. In *Chan Essentials* 3.23.1, and also *Methods for Curing* 1.9.3, it is the person to whom the meditator must confess violations of the precepts. See also 4.32.12.

164. The six internal sense bases (*āyatana; ru* 入) are often likened to an empty village in that no self can be found among them (see, e.g., *Zeng yi ahan jing*, T.125:2.670a8).

dragons, demons, vipers, snakes, monkeys, lions, and cats all run in fright. Fearing the great fire, they scurry up and down the tree. The ninety-nine snakes [that had emerged from the] pores of [the dragon in the practitioner's heart][165] all gather atop the tree. The poisonous dragon twists and turns, coiling around the tree. The practitioner further sees a black elephant standing beneath the tree.

[1.14.6] [Emptiness of the *Skandha*s and Links]

When he has seen these things, he must with a reverential mind repent during the six daily times. He must avoid excessive talking, remain in a solitary secluded place, and reflect on the emptiness of all *dharma*s [as follows]: "All *dharma*s are empty, and within the emptiness of *dharma*s there is neither earth nor water nor wind nor fire. Material form[166] is a delusion arising from illusory *dharma*s. Sensation is conditioned by causes[167] and arises from past actions. Perception is a delusion, a nonpermanent *dharma*. Consciousness cannot be seen. It belongs to the realm of karma and gives rise to the seeds of craving. In such a manner should I contemplate this body. The earth element appears from emptiness. But a manifestation from emptiness is itself empty.[168] How then could I imagine the earth element to be something solid?[169] Analyzed in this manner, what then is earth?"

When he has performed this contemplation, it is called the contemplation of the external earth element. Carefully contemplating it in every detail, [he sees] the earth element to be lacking in substance.

[1.14.7] [Attacking the Black Elephant]

When he performs this meditation, he sees the mountain of white bones shatter even further, becoming tiny specks of dust. Only [his own] skeleton remains amid the dust, white light linking it together.

Within the white light numerous four-colored lights further appear. From within these lights raging flames then arise, burning the *yakṣa*s. As the fire closes in on the *yakṣa*s, they flee toward the top of the tree, but before

165. The tree (of the defilements) and the dragon within the meditator's heart were first described in 1.12.7.

166. This passage enumerates the five *skandha*s, but, mysteriously, the fourth *skandha* (*saṃskāra;* usually *xing* 行) is missing. We see the same thing at *Chan Essentials* 1.18.4. Speculatively, this might be connected to the tendency in the *Chan Essentials* to subsume the mental defilements, the usual referent of *saṃskāra*, within the four material elements; see "Somatic Soteriology and the Physiology of Desire" in chap. 3.

167. 受是因緣. Translation tentative.

168. 空見亦空. Satō (1931, 203) construes this as "the earth element arises from empty [i.e. false] views, and yet empty views are themselves empty." Grammatically possible, this strikes me as importing a *prajñāpāramitā*-style logic that we do not find elsewhere in the text (but see 3.25.1).

169. 云何{為堅}想地<為堅>. Emendation tentative. "Solidity" (*jian* 堅) is the usual defining mark of the *dharma* of earth. In rejecting this, the passage accords with the "emptiness of *dharma*s" position articulated elsewhere in the *Chan Essentials*.

they can reach it they are trampled by the black elephant. The *yakṣas* then shoot flames that scorch the legs of the black elephant. With a voice like a lion's roar, the black elephant trumpets loudly, proclaiming the teachings of suffering,[170] emptiness, impermanence, and non-self, and also that the body is subject to decay and not long enduring.

After the black elephant's declaration, he battles with the *yakṣas*. The *yakṣas* stab at the black elephant's heart with iron pitchforks. Again the black elephant roars, shaking the ground under an area the size of a house, whereupon the trunk, branches, and leaves of the great tree all begin [250c] to shake. The dragon too spits out fire to scorch the tree,[171] and the snakes, aroused and frightened, reach out their ninety-nine heads[172] to save the tree.

The *yakṣas* then become even more agitated. Grabbing giant boulders, they heave them at the black elephant. But the black elephant advances to catch the boulders with his trunk and flings them at the top of the tree. Like blade mountains, the boulders strike the treetop, and the *yakṣas* then[173] rise up, four-headed poisonous dragons emerging from their pores to spew smoke and flames. It is terrifying.

[1.14.8] [The *Maṇi* Jewel and the Fourteen Threads]

When this meditation is complete, the practitioner sees his heart[174] within his body as a deep pit or well. Within the well is a snake, spewing poison all around. Above the well a *maṇi* jewel appears, held in the air by fourteen silk threads. The poisonous snake extends its head to swallow the jewel. But try as it may, it cannot reach it. Losing its grip, it falls to the ground and is stunned, the fire[175] going back into its heads.

If the practitioner sees this, he must repent and then beg for pleasing food so as to harmonize his four elements.[176] To keep himself calm and stable,[177] he should sit in a sealed chamber (密屋) away from the noise of birds.[178]

[1.14.9] [Conclusion]

The Buddha said to Ānanda: If monks, nuns, laymen or laywomen attain this contemplation, it is known as the attainment of the earth-element

170. 若[>苦, K[1], K, P, Q, Sgz, Kg]. The Taishō is presumably a misprint.

171. The dragon, which earlier seemed to work against the practitioner, now helps the black elephants destroy the tree.

172. 各申九十九頭. There were earlier said to be ninety-nine snakes, so this must mean that each snake extends its (one) head.

173. 是<時, Kg>.

174. 心處. The meaning seems to be the physical site of the heart within the chest.

175. It is unclear to which of the many previously mentioned fires this refers.

176. To "harmonize the four elements" here connotes maintaining bodily health. "Pleasing food" is unclear, but could refer back to 1.14.2 and the need for meditators to eat meat.

177. Alternatively, "calm and stable" could be an effect of eating pleasing food.

178. On the danger of hearing noise while meditating, see also *Methods for Curing* 1.2.1–5.

contemplation. They must diligently fix their thoughts and avoid heedlessness. If they cultivate heedfulness, they will attain the "summit" stage[179] faster than a stream of flowing water. Though they may yet again backslide, they have already escaped from rebirth in the three evil realms. After death, they will be born in Tuṣita heaven in their next life, where they will meet Maitreya, who will teach them about suffering, emptiness, impermanence, and so forth. They will understand immediately and attain the fruit of the non-returner.[180]

The Buddha said to Ānanda: "You must now carefully retain this method for the contemplation of the earth element. Do not forget it. Preach it widely for all sentient beings of the future." When Ānanda heard what the Buddha said, he joyfully undertook to carry it out.

When this contemplation is obtained, it is called the accomplishment of contemplation number fourteen,[181] the earth-element contemplation. It is also called the discernment of the signs (相貌) of the four elements. It is further called seeing the gross signs (麁相) of the five *skandhas*. Those with wisdom will also, [in this moment,] know for themselves the extent of their defilements. Within the four bases of mindfulness, [this contemplation] is called the body as a base of mindfulness, in which one only sees things external to one's own body. This is the first of the four confirmatory visions associated with mindfulness of the body.[182]

One who attains this contemplation will feel physically and mentally happy and will not be argumentative.

[1.15] [Fifteenth Contemplation: The Remaining Four Elements]

[1.15.1] [The Remaining Elements, Externally]

[1.15.1.1] [Fire]

The Buddha said to Ānanda: When this meditation is complete, the practitioner must next contemplate the external fire element [as follows]: "It comes into being from causes and conditions. It arises when conditions are present, and it disappears when they pass away. All this fire arrives without arriving from somewhere and goes away without going anywhere. Quickly flashing before the eyes, it transforms and passes away without stopping for an instant."

When he reflects in this way, the external fire suddenly dies down and does not appear again.

---

179. "Summit" is the second of the four "aids to penetration" (*nirvedha-bhāgīya*), the higher stages of attainment reached in the third sutra. See "The Path to Liberation" in chap. 2.

180. Though rebirth in the Tuṣita heaven is not normally associated with any of the four fruits, the idea expressed here is similar to the traditional notion of the "non-returner," who after death is reborn only once more, in a heavenly realm.

181. Kg here reads *fifteen*, relegating contemplation number fourteen to the brief passage in 1.14.1. Kg remains one number ahead in all subsequent sections up through 3.29.

182. The remaining four are presumably the contemplations of fire, water, and wind in the next section (1.15.1). In 1.15.2 are given the meditations on all four elements "internally." The entirety of 1.14 is thus to be construed as the "external" contemplation of the earth element.

[1.15.1.2] [Water]

He must further reflect: "External waters, such as rivers, streams, ponds, and brooks, are all created through the power of dragons. How then can I now [251a] truly see water?[183] These waters arrive without arriving from somewhere and go away without going anywhere."

When he reflects in this way, the external waters disappear.

[1.15.1.3] [Wind]

He must further give rise to the following thought: "This wind merges with space. The cries and roars of the dragons [I hear] are completely dependent on causes and conditions. What I imagine in this manner does not exist inside, outside, or in between. Only because of my confused mind do I see, wrongly, these things."

When he reflects in this way, the external wind dies down.

[1.15.1.4] [Visions of Impurity]

He must then again fix his thoughts and reflect on his spine within his body. He sees his bones as white like *ke*-jade or snow, and within each bone appear the thirty-six filthy impurities. Or else he sees the skin of his body as a skin bag filled with impurities, innumerable tumors and hundreds of thousands of pustules among them, all leaking a steady stream of pus from the top of the skull in a most disgusting manner. Or else he sees the five organs within his body sucked into his large intestine,[184] which swells and bursts open horribly.

At that moment, because of his meditative power (定力), whether or not he is in trance, he equally sees his own body and the bodies of everyone else to be masses of impurity. He sees the bodies of women as wormy dogs, filthy and impure. He will then naturally be free of lust.[185]

[1.15.1.5] [Conclusion to the Four External Elements]

The Buddha said to Ānanda: When this meditation is complete, it is called the contemplation of the external four elements [associated with] contemplation number fifteen.[186] It is also called the gradual realization and contemplation of emptiness.[187]

The Buddha said to Ānanda: "You must remember my words. Do not

183. The point is perhaps that water, inasmuch as it arises in dependence on something else (the dragons), has no substantial existence.

184. "Large intestine," as discussed above, points to the stomach; see 1.1.6, n. 31.

185. 想[>相].

186. 十四[>五, Kg]. Though I do not follow Kg's alternate numberings in general, here I think it is right to group this section forward with number fifteen rather than backward with contemplation fourteen. Contemplation fifteen is named again below; but contemplation fourteen was also named twice (1.14.1 and 1.14.8).

187. 漸解學觀空. Translation tentative.

forget them." When Ānanda heard what the Buddha said, he joyfully undertook to carry it out.

[1.15.2] [The Four Internal Elements]

[1.15.2.1] [Internal Earth]

The Buddha said to Ānanda: When this meditation is complete, the practitioner must again be instructed to fix his thoughts and carefully contemplate the earth element within his body.

The earth element within his body consists of the bones, teeth, nails, head hair,[188] intestines, stomach, belly, liver, heart, lungs, and everything solid. These are all made of the essential *qi* of the earth element.[189] The external earth element is impermanent. How does one know? For example, when two suns appear, the earth itself becomes dry and scorched. When three suns appear, the rivers, streams, ponds, and swamps all dry up. When four suns appear, the great ocean is reduced by two-thirds. When five suns appear, the great ocean dries up. When six suns appear, the earth begins to burn. When seven suns appear, the earth itself is incinerated.[190] If even the earth element external to the body does not long endure, how much less solid and secure is the earth element within the body.

Then the practitioner should reflect as follows: "Within this body of mine, am I the head hair? Am I the nails? Am I the bones? Am I the five internal organs? As I carefully contemplate each part of the body in this manner, nowhere can I find myself."

He carefully contemplates the bones one by one: "Whence do these bones arise?[191] Where were they at the moment [of conception,] when the blood and semen of mother and father were joined? When [the embryo] was like milk curds?[192] [251b] When it was like a foamy bubble? When it was a *kalala?* When it was an *arbuda?*[193] At those moments, where were the bones? Thus do I know that while these bones exist now, they did not exist originally. Having come into existence, they will return to nonexistence. These bones have the same character as space. And just as the external earth element is impermanent, so too is the internal earth element."

---

188. Buddhist lists of the body parts for the purpose of meditation invariably begin with the *hair*. That the bones are first here is noteworthy.

189. "Essential *qi*" (*jingqi* 精氣), with its overtones of traditional Chinese metaphysics, is a term not usually found in Chinese translations of Indian Buddhist texts. This is not the only passage in the *Chan Essentials* and *Methods for Curing* where "qi" and "essence" (精) describe the Indian Buddhist primary material elements (*mahābhūta*). See, e.g., 1.1.5, 4.31.22, 4.32.13.2, and *Methods for Curing* 1.9.6. These examples may reflect the texts' Chinese authorship, or they might be creative translations of Indian Buddhist notions such as *svabhāva*.

190. This description of the appearance of multiple suns and the destruction of the earth strongly recalls canonical accounts of the fate of the world at the end of each *kalpa* (*Zhong ahan jing*, T.26:1.428c8–429c27).

191. The meditator here contemplates non-self by considering the absence of a given body part during the process of gestation. See, similarly, *Xiu xing dao di jing*, T.606:15.206b7–10.

192. 如乳<肥, K^1, P, S, Q, Y, Kg>.

193. On the terms here for the stages of the gestating fetus, see Appendix 2.

Having reflected in this way, he then carefully contemplates his body and [sees] all its bones suddenly shatter into dust. When he enters trance and contemplates the bones, he sees only the space where the bones once were, not the bones themselves. But when not in trance he sees his body just as it was before.

[1.15.2.2] [Internal Fire]

Additionally, the practitioner must then contemplate the fire element within his body: "Internal fire comes into existence from external fire,[194] and external fire is impermanent, never remaining still even for a moment. For what reason, then, do the fires in my body burn for such a long time?"

After contemplating the fire element in this way, when he contemplates his bones their fires die down and disappear.

[1.15.2.3] [Internal Water]

Additionally, the practitioner must then contemplate the various instances of the water element within his body: "The water within me is dependent on external water, and just as external water is impermanent and transient, so too does the water within me exist only provisionally, dependent upon conditions. Where could these various waters or this mass of impurity [really] exist?"

[1.15.2.4] [Internal Wind]

[Additionally, he then contemplates the wind element within his body]:[195] "The wind outside my body is impermanent and transient, coming into being based on causes and conditions and passing away when the conditions cease. The various winds within my body are also merely provisional accumulations, a mere contrivance [that moves] as does a mechanical contraption.[196] Where, in fact, is there any wind? It arises only because of false imagination, and is seen only through misperception."

When he reflects in this way, he no longer sees the various winds emerging from the ears of the dragons within his body, and they vanish without a trace.

[1.15.2.5] [Internal Elements Collectively]

In these ways he should carefully reflect on where it is that a person could be said to exist, let alone earth, water, fire, or wind. He should contemplate the earth element as subject to decay, the fire element as an illusion, the wind element as arising from misperception, and the water element as appearing because of false imagination.

---

194. 從外火有<内 K[1], P, Q, Sgz>.

195. Text appears to be missing. We would expect an introduction to the contemplation of the internal wind element, and a conclusion to the contemplation of water in the previous section.

196. *Xiu xing dao di jing* (T.606:15.207b15) also uses the image of a mechanical contraption (*jiguan* 機關; *yantra*) to explain how there can be bodily movement (produced by the internal wind element) without a self.

When he performs this contemplation, he sees his body as the trunk of a plantain tree, without anything solid inside. Or else he sees his heart-organ as foam on the water. He hears sounds from outside as echoes.[197]

When he performs this contemplation, he sees the fires on his bones, the radiant white water, and the winds [that emerged from] the dragons all in a single place. He contemplates the body calmly and tranquilly, not seeing the body to have any distinguishing marks. His body and mind are calm and stable, relaxed and joyous.

[1.15.3] [Conclusion to Contemplation Fifteen]

These confirmatory visions are called the accomplishment of contemplation number fifteen, the contemplation of the four elements.[198]

[251c] The Buddha said to Ānanda: "You must now, with all your might, receive and remember this method for the contemplation of the four elements. Do not forget it. It is to be widely preached for all sentient beings of the future." When Ānanda heard what the Buddha said, he joyfully undertook to carry it out.

[1.16] [Sixteenth Contemplation: The Four Elements and the Restorative Meditation]

[1.16.1] [Heavenly Medicines]

Because he is training in the contemplation of emptiness, his mind and body will become weak and exhausted when performing this contemplation. He should therefore consume butter and other restorative medicines.

In deep meditative trance[199] he must perform the restorative meditation (補想觀).[200] To perform this meditation, he first contemplates his own body, making its layers of skin wrap around each other like the leaves that form the trunk of a plantain tree. Then he should settle his mind and imagine opening the crown of his head. Next he should invite Śakra, Brahmā, and the World Protectors and have them hold in their hands golden vases filled with heavenly medicine. Indra, lord of the gods, is on the left, while the World Protectors are on the right. They pour the heavenly medicine into the crown of his head, and his entire body is filled with it. During all hours of the day and night he must constantly imagine this.

When he emerges from trance, he should seek out restorative medicines and consume good food and drink [enabling him to] meditate comfortably, feeling great joy. After cultivating this restoration of his body for three months, he may again bring to mind other objects of meditation (境界).

Because of the power of his meditative trance, the gods will rejoice. Indra,

197. The trunk of a plantain tree, foam, and echoes are standard similes for emptiness. Here, however, they seem to be concrete visionary images; see also n. 64 in 1.3.3.

198. *Chan Essentials 1* and *Tempyō Chan Essentials 2* both end here.

199. <深, K^1, P, S, Q, Y, Kg>禪定.

200. This section is very similar to parts of *Methods for Curing* 1.5.

lord of the gods, will preach for him the profound teachings of emptiness and non-self. He will praise the practitioner and bow his head before him.

Because he has consumed heavenly medicines, his face will appear peaceful and happy when he emerges from trance, and his skin will be rich and glossy, as if smeared with oil.

[1.16.2] [Conclusion]

When he has seen these things, it is called the accomplishment of contemplation number sixteen, the contemplation of the four elements.[201]

[1.17] [Mindfulness of the Body]

[1.17.1] [Material Form]

The Buddha said to Ānanda: When this meditation is complete, the practitioner must be further instructed to fix his thoughts and concentrate his mind. He should contemplate external material forms [as follows]: "Whence do these material forms arise?"

When he performs this contemplation, he sees the five kinds of external matter[202] as five colored lights encircling his body.

When these signs[203] have appeared, he contemplates his own chest. His sternum gradually becomes pure and clear like a crystal mirror, lovely and radiant. He further sees that the myriad external material forms are as bright as sunlight.

[1.17.2] [The Four Black Elephants]

When he attains this contemplation, a black elephant suddenly appears in each of the four directions. The black elephants roar and trample the myriad material forms into nothingness. The matter of the earth is destroyed, while that in the sky becomes even more resplendent.[204] Then the black elephants wrap their trunks around the tree. The four elephants try[205] to uproot the

201. Unusually, here there is no closing formula of the Buddha entrusting the teaching to Ānanda.

202. This probably means the fivefold classification of matter (*rūpa*) as the objects of the five bodily sense organs.

203. 想[>相].

204. 於虛空中玄黃可愛倍復過常. Here I take *xuanhuang* 玄黃 to mean "colorful" or "adorned." If the elephants represent the *dhyāna*s (see p. 41), we might understand their destruction of the material forms of the earth while making resplendent those of the sky as indicating that *dhyāna* is something that transcends the *kāmadhātu* (of ordinary matter) and gives access to the *rūpadhātu*, the realm of refined matter.

205. 樂[>欲, K¹, K, P, Q, Sgz, Kg]. The Taishō is presumably a misprint. The Taishō records 欲 as a variant, in P only. This reflects the compilation process of the Taishō edition, whose editors had direct access only to P and Sgz and copied the base text (K) and other variants from the Tokyo edition. Here the Tokyo edition must have erroneously printed 樂 and marked no variants. This information was duly copied by the Taishō editors, who then noticed what seemed to be a variant in P. That they failed to record this same variant in Sgz was merely another error.

tree from four sides, but they are unable to budge it. Then four more elephants appear who also wrap their trunks around the tree. They too are unable to move it.

[1.17.3] [Medicine and Repentance]

When [252a] the practitioner has seen these things, he should cover his body upon emerging from trance and seclude himself[206] in a quiet place such as a graveyard, or beneath a tree, or in a hermitage.[207] He must remain tranquil and seek wholesome medicines to restore his body.[208] For a further three months he should cultivate the bodily restoration method described above[209] and pursue it with single-minded ardor, as if extinguishing a fire blazing on his head. He must not be heedless and must not even think of violating any of the precepts he has undertaken. At the six times of the day he must repent his sins.

[1.17.4] [Non-self and Emptiness: The Elephants and the Lion]

Next he must further reflect on non-self and emptiness. The previous confirmatory visions are to be contemplated in detail and made extremely clear.

When this meditation is complete, his sternum becomes gradually brighter, like a transparent divine pearl. The poisonous snakes within his heart again leap up and fly into the air, their mouths breathing fire. They try [again] to suck up the *maṇi* jewel[210] but cannot get hold of it and they fall and crash into the ground as before. Disoriented, they look off into the distance.

The elephants then charge toward the tree again. The various *yakṣa*s, *rākṣasa*s, evil beasts, dragons, and snakes all simultaneously spew poison and battle with the elephants. Then the black elephants wrap their trunks around the tree and pull, screaming loudly. When the elephants pull at the tree, the dragons and *yakṣa*s spew poison and continue their battle, unwilling to desist.

Then, on the ground beneath the tree, there is a lion, eyes shining brightly like adamant, which suddenly leaps up and battles with the dragons. The dragons leap up into the air. Once again, the elephants pull at the tree without stopping, until the earth gradually begins to shake.

---

206. 覆身令密. Translation tentative. This image brings to mind the many medieval Chinese paintings and sculptures in which the meditating monk sits with a robe pulled over his head.

207. "Hermitage" is *alanruo* 阿練若 (Skt. *araṇya*), literally a "forest" or "wilderness" but, in practice, any "tranquil place" (*Fan fan yu*, T.2130:54.1041c24) and hence, concretely, a monastery or temple, even a large one (Zhanru 2003, 61–69; Harrison 2003, 132).

208. This presumably refers to the butter and / or meat mentioned in 1.14.2 and 1.16.1 above.

209. This presumably refers to 1.16.1.

210. This seems to refer to the jewel suspended by fourteen threads in 1.14.8.

[1.17.5] [Earth Is Insubstantial]

When the earth begins to shake, the practitioner should contemplate: "This earth comes into being out of emptiness. It is not a real, substantial *dharma* (非堅實法). It is like a city of the *gandharvas*, like a mirage. It appears because of false [thinking]. Why then does it move?"

When he reflects in this way, he sees[211] his body, between his sternum and the bones of his face, gradually become bright and pure. He clearly sees everything in the world.

When he attains this contemplation, as if beholding his own reflection in a clean mirror, the practitioner sees all the myriad forms and all the impurities external to his body, and he also sees all the impurities within his own body.

[1.17.7] [Conclusion]

When this meditation is complete, it is known as contemplation number seventeen, mindfulness of the body.

<u>The Buddha[212] said to Ānanda: "Carefully preserve these words of consecration[213] concerning bodily mindfulness. Be sure not to forget them. They are to be preached for all sentient beings in the future age, thereby opening up the gate of ambrosia."</u>

<u>When Ānanda heard what the Buddha said, he joyfully undertook to carry it out.</u>

[1.18] [Eighteenth Contemplation: Attainment of the Contemplation of Impurity]

[1.18.1] [The Bones of the Face]

The Buddha said to Ānanda: When this meditation is complete, the practitioner must be further instructed to concentrate his thoughts and ponder deeply, carefully contemplating the bones of his face.

He sees the bones of his face as a white jade mirror, pure inside and out, like a clear mirror. Gradually expanding, he sees the bones of his entire body as a white crystal mirror, pure inside [252b] and out, with myriad forms appearing therein. Soon after, he sees his body as a white jade person, and further sees that it is as pure and clear as beryl, empty inside and out, with

211. 分[>見, K[1], K, P, Q, Sgz, Kg]. The Taishō is presumably a misprint.

212. The underlined text beginning here indicates those passages included in the Wofoyuan inscription (W).

213. The unusual expression "words of consecration" (灌頂章句) seems to occur in only a single Chinese Buddhist text translated from an Indic original: Dharmakṣema's *Jin guang ming jing* (T.663:16.345b14), corresponding, in the extant Sanskrit version, to *mūrdhābhiṣeka-dharmatā-mantrapadāḥ* (Nobel 1937, 117), "magic words for lawful consecration of the head" (Emmerick 1970, 50). This suggests a *dhāraṇī* or other spell used during a ritual of consecration (*abhiṣeka*). The *Chan Essentials* suggests in this way that the words of its instruction have a kind of magical power.

myriad forms appearing therein. He then sees his body as a person made of white silver with only the outer layer of skin remaining. This skin is extremely thin, thinner than heavenly cotton (*karpāsa*), and completely transparent. He next sees his own body as a person made of *jambūdāna*[214] gold, empty inside and out, and finally as a person made of adamant.

[1.18.2] [The Elephants Blocked by Adamantine Mountains]

When he has seen these things,[215] the black elephants double in number, and they again wrap their trunks around the tree. Though they use all their strength they are still unable to move it. The elephants let out a piercing scream, which shakes the earth below, and as it shakes an adamantine mountain emerges out of the earth and comes to rest before the practitioner.

The practitioner now sees adamantine mountains on all four sides around him. He sees the ground in front of him as adamant. He sees the dragons going up and down the tree spewing adamantine pellets, which secures the tree against the elephants' efforts to move it. Now there is only a water of five colors flowing through the branches of the tree up to the top, where it returns down through all the leaves and branches to spill out among the adamantine mountains, filling the earth from the adamant ground below up to the adamantine mountains.

From the five-colored water emerge lights of five colors shining in different directions, some up and some down, their movements unfixed. Black elephants come out from the adamantine mountains and try to drink up the waters, but the dragons spew poison and battle them. Snakes now enter the dragons' ears and join forces with them to fight off the black elephants. The elephants charge with undiminished fury, but it is futile.

[1.18.3] [Heavenly Maidens]

When the practitioner sees this, the waters become luminous and begin to resound with music. Or else they transform into heavenly maidens, who sing while playing the most delightful music. They are truly lovely, unmatched in heaven or on earth, and their music is sublime, with nothing to equal it even in the Trāyastriṃśa heaven.[216] So many are the arts and allurements displayed by these magical maidens that they cannot all be described.

When the practitioner sees these things, he must take care not to become

---

214. 閻浮檀那. As noted by Tsukinowa (1971, 59–60), this word, which also appears in many of the Contemplation Scriptures, is problematic. The similar *yan-fu-tan* 閻浮檀 (or *yan-fu-na-tan* 閻浮那檀) commonly transcribes *Jambūnāda*, the River Jambū, known for harboring gold. But the *yan-fu-tan-na* 閻浮檀那 given here yields the nonsensical *jambūdāna* (which I preserve). Tsukinowa suggested that this strange word reveals the hand of a Chinese author or compiler who may have confused *tan* 檀 with the common *ṭan-na* 檀那 (Skt. *dāna* 'charity').

215. 地[>事]. These characters are very similar in manuscript handwriting.

216. In Buddhist cosmology, the Trāyastriṃśa heaven is the second heaven of the *kāmadhātu* (the sphere of desire) and is ruled by Indra.

attached and follow after them. He must fix his thoughts and bring to mind the impurity of everything that is before him. When he emerges from trance, he must go to see a wise person to ask about the profound principle of emptiness.[217] The wise person should then clarify the meaning of non-self and emptiness for the practitioner.

[1.18.4] [Non-self of All Dharmas]

Then the practitioner must again fix his thoughts as before and contemplate the bones of his body. He sees the bones in his chest, pure, bright, and exquisite, with every impurity appearing within them.

When he has seen this, he must reflect: "As for me, is my hair my self? My bones? Nails? Teeth? Are form, feelings, perceptions,[218] or consciousness the self? [I must] carefully contemplate this. [252c] Is ignorance the self? Or volitional formations,[219] consciousness, name-and-form, the six sense-doors, contact, feeling, attachment,[220] grasping, becoming, birth, old age and death?

"Is the self within the corpse?[221] It is eaten by worms, so how could it be the self? Nor can the living person be the self, since thoughts do not stand still, and in this life no mental state endures permanently.

"Perhaps my head is the self? But there are eight distinct bones[222] in the skull, and within the brain live various worms. When we look inside the head, no self is there at all. Perhaps the eye is the self? But inside the eye there is nothing substantial. Formed of water and earth, it depends on fire for its perspicacity and wind for its movement.[223] When it separates from the body, it is eaten by crows and hawks and nibbled on by worms and maggots. Thus, upon careful contemplation, [one realizes that] the eye too has no owner.[224]

"Perhaps the heart (心) is the self? But the heart only moves by the power

---

217. The sequence here is very similar to what occurs in 1.14.5.

218. Kg adds 行是我耶, thereby "fixing" the incomplete list of the *skandhas* by including a reference to *saṃskāra* (*xing* 行). This is probably a correction by a later editor. Earlier, in 1.14.6, was another, similarly incomplete list of the *skandhas*.

219. Here are listed the remaining twelve links of "dependent origination" (*pratītyasamutpāda*).

220. P, S, Q, Y, and Sgz omit attachment, grasping, and becoming. Kg reads only "and so on up to" (乃至), which would not normally abbreviate only three items in a long list and is probably a later editor's attempt to correct a copy that was missing the three terms.

221. Literally, "death" (死), following from "old age and death" in the previous sentence; the meaning is plainly "corpse."

222. 解[>節]解[>節]各異.

223. 假風動轉. Sgz and Kg read 假風種轉動. This is probably an editorial correction of the reading 假風動轉動 of P, S, Q, and Y, though Sgz and Kg's reading could be correct if we take *fengzhong* 風種 in its early (pre-Kumārajīva) meaning, equivalent to the "wind element" (風大).

224. <亦復無主, Kg>. The sentence would be incomplete without this addition, though Kg may well represent the intervention of a later editor to fix this problem.

of the wind element, never resting for even a moment.[225] Further, six dragons live[226] in the heart, and their limitless poisons are based on the heart.[227] When we analyze these poisons and the other dispositions of the heart, [we realize that] they come into being from emptiness and are only falsely imagined to be the self. When we carefully analyze the *dharma*s of earth, water, fire, and wind, visible objects, smells, tastes, objects of touch, and the twelve links of conditionality, none of them turn out to be the self. Contemplating that the body is without self in this way, how could [we think that it] belongs to the self?[228]

"Is blue the self? Is yellow the self? Is red the self? Is white the self? Is black the self? These five colors exist because of delighting, are born based on attachment, are the stains of the river of desire, are born from the stream of old age and death, are produced by the bandits of affection and love, and are seen because of delusion.[229] The many colors are in truth not the self, but deluded beings (惑著眾生) falsely think they compose the self, while beings with false views (虛見眾生) claim that they belong to the self. If everything is an illusion, where could there be a self? Among illusory *dharma*s, what could belong to it?"

Reflecting in this way, the practitioner suddenly sees the bones of his body becoming pure, bright, and exquisite, with all kinds of rarely seen things appearing within them. He further sees his body becoming as completely transparent as beryl. Just as a person carrying a beryl parasol can look up at the sky and see everything clearly, at this moment, because the practitioner has contemplated emptiness and learned the teaching of non-self with respect to both himself and others, he sees his two legs as tubes of beryl, and looking down he sees [through them] all kinds of marvelous things.

[1.18.5] [The Beryl Ground]

When this meditation is complete, the ground before the practitioner becomes pure, bright, and exquisite, as completely transparent as beryl.

Those who have maintained the precepts fully will see the ground become as pure as it is in the palace of Brahmā. Those who have not fully kept the minor precepts[230] will still see the pure ground, but it will only be crystal [rather than beryl].

225. The phrase "moves merely by the power of the wind element" (風力所轉) occurs verbatim in Kumārajīva's translation of the *Vimalakīrti-nirdeśa*, where it is also used, with reference to the body rather than the mind, as part of an analysis of non-self (*Weimojie suo shuo jing*, T.475:14.539b24).

226. 舉[>居, Kg].

227. "Poison" (*du* 毒) is also the usual word for the three fundamental defilements (*doṣa*) of craving, aversion, and ignorance. The six dragons here surely represent the six senses.

228. 我所{我所}.

229. Here the topic appears to be the meditator's visions, whose reality is being negated.

230. *Weiyi* 威儀, literally "dignified manners" (the term stems from Confucian texts on

[1.18.6] [Smashing the Adamantine Mountains]

When this [253a] meditation is complete, innumerable hundreds of thousands of *yakṣas* and *rākṣasas* spring out of the ground using white-sheep horns, tortoise shells, and white stones to smash the adamantine mountains.[231] Various other demons smash the adamantine mountains with iron hammers. Atop the mountains, five hundred demon spirits with a thousand heads and a thousand hands holding a thousand swords fight the *rākṣasas*. The poisonous snakes and poisonous dragons encircle the mountain and spew forth poison.[232] Additionally, various maidens defend and protect the mountain, playing music, singing songs, and transforming in various ways.

[1.18.7] [Impurity and Non-self of the Maidens]

If the practitioner sees this, he must single-mindedly contemplate. When the maidens appear, he must contemplate them [as follows]:[233] "These women are like painted jars [beautiful on the outside but inside] filled with foulness. They are impure vessels. They are produced from emptiness, come without cause, and do not go anywhere. These appearances (相貌) result from the sins of my evil karma from past lives.[234] This is why I see these women, who are nothing but my own false imagining, an illusion witnessed because of my greed and attachment throughout countless lifetimes."

Then he must intently contemplate the truth of non-self: "My own body is without self, and so too the bodies of others. Everything I see now is dependent on a multitude of causes and conditions. It should not be yearned for. Contemplating these bodies, I see they are impermanent, decaying, and utterly lacking in anything pertaining to a self. Is there a [real] person or living being anywhere to be seen?"

[1.18.8] [Destruction of the Adamantine Mountains]

When he has reflected in this way, he must then single-mindedly contemplate the truth of emptiness and non-self.

When he contemplates non-self, four great demons suddenly approach

ritual), usually means, in a Buddhist context, the minor rules of monastic deportment whose violation entails no serious consequence.

231. "Tortoise shell" (龜甲) and "white-sheep horns" (白羊角) are mentioned in various sources of Indian lore available in China in the fifth century as the only two substances capable of damaging adamant (*vajra*). See *Da banniepan jing*, T.374:12.418b9–13; *DZDL*, T.1509:25.290b6–8 (Lamotte 1944–1981, 4.2091).

232. The adamantine mountain, in that it blocks the elephants from attacking and destroying the tree of the defilements, seems here to be a bad thing. That the *yakṣas* and *rākṣasas* attack (and at 1.18.8, destroy) it suggests they have joined sides with the meditator (just as the initially hostile dragon within the meditator's heart did in 1.14.7).

233. I take the first-person language, explicit below, to begin here, though this could also be an abstract description of what the meditator is to do.

234. 是我宿世惡業罪緣.

from the horizon of the beryl ground in the lower[235] direction and lift up the adamantine mountains. The *yakṣa*s and *rākṣasa*s help the demons attack the adamantine mountains, which gradually crumble and eventually disappear entirely, leaving only the adamantine ground. Then the elephants and evil demons join forces and pull at the tree, but the tree stands firm and will not be moved.

When he has seen these things, he must again joyfully repent his sins.

[1.18.9] [The Transformation Buddhas]

After repenting his sins, he should fix his thoughts as before and contemplate the beryl man [that is his own body].[236] On the beryl ground in the four directions appear four[237] lotus flowers. The flowers are golden in color, each with one thousand leaves and an adamantine dais.[238] On the eastern dais sits a golden image in the posture of meditation, fully endowed with the bodily marks of a buddha, shining and without blemish.[239] A similar figure sits on the daises in the south, west, and north.

The practitioner then sees his own beryl body becoming still more pure, clear, and transparent. Transformation buddhas fill it both within and without, each radiating a miraculous light like a billion suns. Gleaming and resplendent, the light pervades all the worlds of the entire universe, which are filled with transformation buddhas, each showing the thirty-two marks and eighty secondary characteristics. Each mark radiates a thousand rays of light, as brilliant[240] as a hundred thousand suns and moons. Within each ray of light are innumerable buddhas, [253b] which proliferate in this manner beyond reckoning. Within the light [of each of these buddhas] are uncountably more transformation buddhas. All these buddhas then revolve and enter [the practitioner's] beryl body.

He now sees his own body, already a tall and stately mountain made of the seven precious substances, become even more majestic, like Mount Sumeru with its multitude of jewels. The reflection of this mountain appears on the adamantine ground, which becomes even brighter, like the purple *maṇi* jewel[241] of the god Yama. The practitioner's body becomes ever brighter and more pure, like the radiance of innumerable buddhas. [It][242] transforms into a jeweled platform, which also enters the crown of the head of the beryl body.

235. 上[>下, K[1], K, P, Q, Sgz, Kg]. The Taishō is presumably a misprint.

236. See 1.18.1.

237. In place of "four" (四), K[1], P, S, Q, and Y read *hua* 化, yielding "magically created lotus flowers," which is also possible.

238. Literally, a "platform" (臺), meaning the prominent, platform-like carpellary receptacle of a lotus flower.

239. 無缺; or perhaps, "not lacking [any of the marks]."

240. 其光明[>大, Sgz, Kg]盛. This four-character phrase occurs elsewhere in the text.

241. The unusual expression "purple *maṇi* jewel" also occurs in some of the Contemplation Scriptures (*Guan Mile pusa shang sheng doushuai tian jing*, T.452:14.419a12).

242. The subject of "transforms" (化) is not clear; the text may be corrupt.

He sees the ground before him, within the Encircling Iron Mountains,[243] filled with buddhas sitting cross-legged on lotus-flower pedestals on the ground and in the air, with no gap between them. Each transformation buddha fills the entire world with its body, yet they do not obstruct one another. The practitioner further sees that the Encircling Iron Mountains are free of all opacity, like pure beryl. He sees myriad wondrous transformation buddhas [within] all the mountains, rivers, stones, walls, trees, and thickets of Jambudvīpa. He then allows his mind to expand gradually until he sees, in every speck of the earth and sky in all the worlds of the universe, sublime and wondrous buddha images.[244]

[1.18.10] [The Unreality of the Transformation Buddhas]

At that moment the practitioner must contemplate [the truth of] non-self without allowing his mind to focus on the buddha images.

He must then also reflect: "I have heard the Buddha say that the buddhas and *tathāgatas* have two bodies: a body of birth and a Dharma body.[245] What I now see is not the Dharma body, nor is it the body of birth. It is a sight that is dependent on my imagination (假想見), something that arises from emptiness. These buddhas do not come [to me], nor do I go [to them]. How, then, is it possible that these buddha images have suddenly appeared?"

As the practitioner thinks these words, he must do nothing but contemplate his own body as lacking in self and take care not to follow after the transformation buddha images.

He must further[246] carefully contemplate: "This body of mine has ever been impure. Pus flows from its nine openings. Bound by tendons and smeared with blood, [within it] lie the receptacles of undigested and digested food, urine, feces, and eighty[247] families of worms, each accompanied by eighty million smaller worms. What purity could there be in such a body?"

When he reflects in this manner, he then sees his own body as a sack of skin. And when he emerges from trance, he still sees the inside of his body as devoid of bones and his body as a sack of skin. When he contemplates the bodies of others, they too are sacks of skin.

[1.18.11] [Suffering]

When he sees these things, he must go to a wise person to inquire into the teaching of the truth of suffering.

Hearing the teaching of the truth of suffering, he carefully contemplates

243. According to typical Buddhist cosmology, Mount Sumeru (which the practitioner now seems to embody) sits at the center of the world, with the Encircling Iron Mountains (*tiewei shan* 鐵圍山; *cakra-vāḍa-parvata*) forming an outer boundary.

244. "Buddha images" (佛像) here seems to mean the transformation buddhas.

245. On the Buddha's "body of birth" (*shengshen* 生身), see pp. 53–54.

246. W, which recommences here with a new excerpt, adds the words "The Buddha said to Ānanda: O good child" (佛告阿難善男子), thereby smoothing over the discontinuity.

247. 萬[>十, Kg]. See 1.1.5, n. 26.

his body [as follows]: "Dependent on various causes and conditions, one suffers birth—and after being born come sorrow and grief, separation from loved ones, and proximity to those one hates. Such are the various forms of suffering within this world. This body of mine will soon decay. Ensnared by suffering, it is pursued by the evil bandits of the knife-winds[248] and utterly belongs to birth and death. Then I will be burned in the raging fires of the Avīci hell, only to experience rebirth in every type of hideous body, as every kind of beast or animal such as a camel, donkey, [253c] pig, or dog. This manner of suffering is called external suffering.

"[As for internal suffering], within my body are the poisonous dragons and innumerable poisonous snakes of the four elements. Each snake has ninety-nine heads. Evil *rākṣasa*s and evil *kumbhāṇḍa*s gather within my heart. This body-mind is impure to the extreme, an accumulation of evil, vile things with seeds and sprouts [of rebirth in] the three realms that are not yet eliminated. How could I imagine what is so impure as pure? This false, empty thing as made of adamant? Images of buddhas where there are no buddhas? The nature of all worldly formations (一切世間諸行性相) is that they are impermanent, quickly worn away, and destroyed. So too will this body of mine decay, as quickly as one might snap one's fingers. Only through empty imagining do I falsely see this impure thing as pure."

[1.18.12] [The Shaking of the Tree]

When he reflects in this way, the different appearances that he saw his body take on, whether pure like beryl or a sack of skin, suddenly disappear. When he contemplates his body or self, he does not apprehend them at all.

All he sees are the black elephants on all sides trampling the adamantine ground before him and smashing it to pieces. He sees the roots of the tree[249] extending downward with innumerable branchings.[250] Then the black elephants, as before, wrap their trunks around the tree, and innumerable dragons and *rākṣasa*s battle with them. The wild black elephants trample these demons, who fall to the ground in a daze. But still in the air are a great many other demons, wielding wheel-shaped blades, who help the black elephants in their effort to uproot the tree.

Then the tree shakes. When the tree shakes, the practitioner sees the ground beneath his meditation cot shake of its own accord.

[1.18.13] [Restoration, Utter Emptiness, Madness]

[He should do this meditation] every day for ninety days. Then he should beg for fine food and restorative medicines to heal his body, enabling him to sit comfortably, just as in the procedure given before.[251]

---

248. The "knife-winds" (風刀; usually 刀風 in other sources) are winds that arise in the body at the time of death. For a detailed survey of the usage of this term in Indian and Chinese Buddhist literature, see Zacchetti 2004, 203n32.

249. 見地[>此]樹荄. Emendation tentative.

250. 荄[>條, K^1].

251. This presumably refers back to passages such as 1.14.7 or 1.16.1.

Beginning with the first confirmatory vision, he should carefully contemplate everything he has seen in full detail, repeating this sixty times, making it extremely clear and pure. When it is clear and pure, he should again fix his thoughts and contemplate the suffering, emptiness, impermanence, and non-self of the body and the emptiness of everything.

Having reflected in this way, he no longer sees a body when he contemplates his body, no longer sees a self when he contemplates his self, no longer sees a mind when he contemplates his mind. Then, he suddenly sees the great earth, with its mountains, rivers, rocks, and cliffs, disappear completely. When he emerges from trance, he appears drunk or mad.

[1.18.14] [The Emanations]

He must then, with a mind of utmost devotion, carry out a ritual of repentance, make prostrations, and clean the ground [of the sanctuary],[252] setting aside his practice of contemplation.

While making prostrations, even before he has raised his head, he will suddenly see the Tathāgata's true emanation (如來真影), who touches his head and commends him: "O Dharma child (法子), well done, well done! Today you have properly contemplated the buddhas' teaching of emptiness."[253]

Seeing the Buddha's emanation, the practitioner will feel great joy and will [254a] awaken (醒悟) [from his madness].

Then the venerable Mahāpiṇḍola,[254] together with five hundred arhats, flies before the practitioner and exhaustively expounds the profound teaching of emptiness. Seeing the five hundred voice-hearers, he will feel great joy, and bowing his head, he will repent. He then sees the emanations of the venerable Mahāmaudgalyāyana[255] and one thousand two hundred fifty other voice-hearers.

He further sees the emanation of Śākyamuni Buddha.[256] And after seeing the emanation of Śākyamuni Buddha, he then also sees the emanations of the six buddhas of the past. The emanations of these buddhas, like crystal mirrors that shine brightly and are exquisite to behold, extend their right hand, and each one touches the practitioner upon the crown of his head. Then each of the buddhas announces his name.

The first buddha says: "I am Vipaśyin." The second buddha says: "I am

252. This likely refers to something similar to the rituals outlined in *Methods for Curing* 1.9.

253. On the Buddha's so-called emanation, see "Modalities of Encountering the Buddha(s)" and "The Emanations of the Buddhas" in chap. 3.

254. 摩訶賓頭盧. The name "Mahāpiṇḍola" is not, to my knowledge, attested apart from this example, though the famous monk Piṇḍola, surely the referent here, is often called by the more elaborate name Piṇḍolabhāradvāja. "Mahāpiṇḍola" is perhaps the result of an overly enthusiastic use of the honorific prefix "mahā" by our Chinese author. Piṇḍola appears in *Methods for Curing* 1.6.3 as the leader of the five hundred arhats.

255. Mahāmaudgalyāyana's name is here transcribed *Mu-qian-luo-ye-na* 目揵羅夜那 in most editions, but as *Mu-qian-lian* 目揵連 in Sgz and Kg and the peculiar *Mu-qian-luo-lian-ye-na* 目揵羅連夜那 in K[1] (perhaps an attempt to combine the two different transcriptions). In 1.0.1, all versions read *Mu-qian-lian* 目揵連.

256. I take this to be the "Tathāgata's true emanation" from the previous paragraph.

Śikhin." The third buddha says: "I am Viśva."[257] The fourth buddha says: "I am Krakucchanda." The fifth buddha says: "I am Kanakamuni." The sixth buddha says: "I am Kāśyapa."[258] The seventh buddha says: "I am Śākyamuni Buddha, your preceptor.[259] I have come to certify (證) your contemplation of emptiness. Here, in the presence of the six other world-honored buddhas, I certify your knowledge and vision."

[1.18.15] [The Preaching of the Buddha]

When [Śākyamuni] Buddha has spoken these words, the practitioner sees [this] buddha's material body (色身) clearly and distinctly, and also those of the six buddhas.[260] Then each of the seven buddhas radiates light from the white tuft of hair between his eyebrows, one of the marks of a great man. The light shines brightly, illuminating the entire world as well as the beryl body [of the practitioner], making everything clearly visible. When the buddhas have manifested this sign, innumerable radiant transformation buddhas radiate from their pores, filling the earth and sky of all worlds of the universe with their deeply golden bodies. Some of these world-honored

257. The name *Viśva (*pishe* 毘舍) requires some explanation. The third buddha of the past is Skt. Viśvabhū, usually transcribed in Chinese texts as *Pishefu* 毘舍浮. However, the same anomalous two-character transcription seen here in the *Chan Essentials* is found in one of the Contemplation Scriptures (*GFSMH*, T.643:15.660c13), and also at *Methods for Curing* 1.14.10. Taken as a sign of these texts' Chinese authorship by Tsukinowa (1971, 74), Yamabe has noted that the two-character form *can* be found in some authentic Chinese Buddhist translations, but only in verses, presumably used for metrical reasons (1999c, 207–209). Yamabe cogently proposes that the Chinese authors / compilers of these texts thus borrowed the name from such a source without realizing that the shortened form was exceptional.

258. The name of the buddha Kāśyapa is invariably transcribed in Chinese Buddhist texts as *jia-ye* 迦葉. The form here—*jia-ye-pi* 迦葉毘—is problematic and clearly implies an –i stem ending (this Chinese transcription is attested elsewhere, but only as a rendering of *kāśyapīya*, the name of an early Buddhist sect; see *CSZJJ*, T.2145:55.21b3–7; *GSZ*, T.2059:50.403b9). Our Chinese author / compiler has perhaps misremembered the name. More speculatively, it might render an authentic if otherwise unknown *Kāśyapi, reflecting the same kind of –i/–a stem confusion seen in the anomalous transcription of the name "Panthaka," the protagonist of the second sutra of the *Chan Essentials* (see Appendix 4), a confusion that perhaps stems from the influence of Central Asian pronunciations (see Mair 1993, 9–11, who notes several similar examples in the *Xian yu jing* 賢愚經, supposedly based on lectures delivered in Khotan).

259. The Buddha here (and also in 4.31.14) declares himself to be the practitioner's *preceptor* (*heshang* 和上; *upādhyāya*). This recalls ideas most commonly associated with rituals for the transmission of the so-called bodhisattva precepts, first introduced to China in the early fifth century. According to these rituals, the bodhisattva precepts are, formally, transmitted not by a human preceptor but by the Buddha or buddhas (Funayama 2004, 106), and within those rites these buddhas are assigned the titles normally held by human officials during a monastic ordination, including the title *upādhyāya*. The Contemplation Scriptures contain some of the earliest known allusions to such rites and include examples where the practitioner must ask Śākyamuni to be his "preceptor" (*Guan Puxian pusa xingfa jing*, T.277:9.393c11–25). Though the *Chan Essentials* does not explicitly mention the bodhisattva precepts, it was, seemingly, composed in an environment in which bodhisattva-precept rituals were known.

260. The "material body" seems to be taken here as something different from the "emanations."

ones[261] fly, some display the eighteen miraculous transformations, some are engaged in walking meditation, some have entered deep trance, some quietly stand still, and some radiate bright light.

The great preceptor Śākyamuni Buddha, alone, then preaches for the practitioner the four noble truths and elucidates the principles of suffering, emptiness, impermanence, non-self, and the emptiness of all *dharmas*.[262] The six buddhas of the past then explain the twelve causal conditions and expound the thirty-seven elements of the path[263] and also praise the holy practice [of Buddhism]. When the practitioner has seen the buddhas and heard their teachings, he experiences great joy.

[1.18.16] [Illusory Nature of the Buddhas' Material Bodies]

He must then reflect:[264] "All buddhas, the world-honored ones, have two kinds of bodies. What I have seen today are their material bodies (色身), but I have not yet seen their five-part Dharma bodies consisting of [the five pure *skandhas* up to] the knowledge and vision of liberation."[265]

Having reflected in this way, he must be diligent and unslacking in repenting further. At the six times of the day, he must constantly cultivate *samādhi*.

He must think (念) as follows: "These [buddhas'] material bodies are illusions, like dreams, or flames, or firewheels, or cities of the *gandharvas*, or echoes. Thus does the Buddha preach that all constructed *dharmas* are like [254b] dreams, illusions, bubbles, shadows, dew, or lightning. I must now with utmost clarity carefully contemplate all *dharmas* in this manner."

As he contemplates in this manner, the transformation buddhas disappear. If some remain, he should continue to contemplate emptiness. Then, as a result of contemplating emptiness, the transformation buddhas will disappear [entirely], and only the seven buddhas will remain.[266] Then the seven buddhas, together with the assembly of attending voice-hearers, extensively preach to the practitioner the thirty-seven factors that assist in the holy path.[267] Hearing these teachings, he experiences joy in body and mind.

---

261. Here "world-honored ones" seem to denote the transformation buddhas.

262. The "emptiness of all dharmas" (諸法空義) has been added here to the standard list of suffering, emptiness, impermanence, and non-self.

263. The thirty-seven *bodhipakṣika-dharmas*; see 2.19.2.3, n. 332.

264. 應時自思惟. The grammar is slightly peculiar. Sgz and Kg remove the 時.

265. The "five-part Dharma body" (五分法身) usually means the five pure (*anāsrava*) *skandhas* of a buddha: morality, *samādhi*, wisdom, liberation, and the knowledge and vision of liberation. These are the pure counterparts to the ordinary five *skandhas*. In some accounts from Sarvāstivāda doctrinal sources, these together constitute the Buddha's "Dharma body" (Radich 2007, 744–745).

266. I presume this refers to the emanations (影) of the seven buddhas spoken of earlier. The "assembly of attending voice-hearers" would then presumably refer to the emanations of Mahāmaudgalyāyana and the 1,250 voice-hearers mentioned in 1.18.14.

267. 三十七助聖道法. This must refer, again, to the 37 *bodhipakṣika-dharmas*, introduced in 1.18.15 using the more usual Chinese term (三十七道品).

[1.18.17] [Death of the Elephants and Adamantine Beings]

Next, the practitioner again contemplates the teachings of suffering, emptiness, impermanence, and non-self. As he performs this contemplation, the crazed elephants scream loudly and pull at the tree, making it shake. As the tree begins to shake, he sees the ground beneath his room shake in the six different ways.

Then the *yakṣa*s stab the black elephants to death.[268] The myriad black elephants lie dead on the ground. They quickly begin to rot, and white, black, blue, yellow, green, purple, and red pus, as well as red blood, flow out from them, staining the ground. Beetles swarm. Then other bugs with flaming eyes burn the beetles, killing them.

Below, at the adamantine nadir,[269] five adamantine wheels[270] appear, between which are five adamantine beings who hold adamantine swords in their right hand and adamantine clubs in their left hand. They beat the earth with their clubs and hack the tree with their swords.

[1.18.18] [Destruction of the Roots and Branches]

When the practitioner has seen these things, the earth gradually begins to move, and he sees an area the size of a city shake in the six ways. Seeing one city shaking, he sees two cities, and as his sight expands, he sees a *yojana*.[271] Seeing one *yojana*, it continues to expand until he sees the earth in all the worlds of the universe shaking. It shakes [in the six ways], heaving up in the east and sinking in the west, heaving up in the west and sinking in the east, heaving up in the south and sinking in the north, heaving up in the north and sinking in the south, heaving up in the center and sinking on the periphery, and heaving up on the periphery and sinking in the center.

As the earth shakes, the practitioner sees the roots of the great tree extending down to the adamantine nadir. Adamantine beings hack at the roots with swords, severing them. When the roots are severed, the dragons and snakes spew fire and proceed to climb up the tree, where numerous *rākṣasa*s appear, who gather in clumps atop the tree.[272] The adamantine

268. 刺黑象殺. Here *sha* 殺 appears to be a verbal complement to *ci* 刺, with the direct object—the black elephants—positioned between ("stab them dead"). This same, highly vernacular grammatical pattern occurs just below—"burn the beetles, killing them" (燒蜣蜋殺)—and in 4.31.27. Very similar expressions appear in some of the Contemplation Scriptures, where, however, they are put into a more properly literary Chinese locution (*GFSMH*, T.643:15.670a5; c26–27).

269. The "adamantine nadir" (金剛地際; later, 金剛際) is mentioned frequently in the fourth sutra of the *Chan Essentials* and is implied to be the lowest point in the universe (4.31.12–21). See also *Chan Essentials* 2.19.2.5. Indian Buddhist texts also speak of a similar location (*Hua yan jing*, T.278:9.440b16; Schlingloff 1964, 31n9).

270. "Adamantine wheels," arising from the "adamantine nadir," appear again in 4.31.26, where there are fourteen of them. See also *Methods for Curing* 1.14.11, where there are five adamantine wheels as here. Perhaps they denote the five pure *skandha*s.

271. Here *yojana* is transcribed *yu-she-na* 踰闍那 in most editions; Y, Sgz, and Kg read *you-xun* 由旬, the transcription used in most other passages of the text in all editions.

272. 積薪樹上. Translation tentative.

beings take up adamantine clubs and strike at the branches of the tree until they break even though it requires eighty-four thousand strikes before the branches finally break. Then fire shoots from the tips of the clubs, incinerating the tree. Only the heartwood remains, like an immovable adamantine spike (金剛錐) reaching from the summit of the triple-world down to the adamantine nadir.

[1.18.19] [The Three *Samādhi*s]

Having attained this contemplation, the practitioner feels at ease and replete with joy when he emerges from trance. Now, whether in trance or not, his mind is always calm, free of worry as well as delight. But he must continue to be diligent, without resting day or night. And because of his diligence, the world-honored Śākyamuni, together with the six buddhas of the past, appears before him and preaches the profound *samādhi*s of emptiness, non-wishing, [254c] and non-doing.[273] Hearing them, he feels joy, and by carefully contemplating the truth of emptiness in accord with the buddhas' teaching, as surely as does flow a great current of water, he will soon become an arhat.[274]

[1.18.20 Conclusion]

[1.18.20.1] [Fruits of Meditation][275]

The Buddha said to Ānanda: This contemplation of impurity[276] is the great ambrosia that destroys craving, lust, and desire. It can remove the defilements, which for sentient beings are an illness of the mind. Carefully preserve it. Do not forget it. After the Buddha has passed into extinction, monks, nuns, laymen, and laywomen who hear this holy method of ambrosial consecration (甘露灌頂聖法) and are able to restrain their sense faculties, resolutely fix their thoughts, and carefully contemplate the constituents of their bodies will, if their minds are undivided and focused in concentration for even a short period of time, be reborn in heaven when their life has ended.

Furthermore, know that anyone who follows the buddhas' teaching, fixes his thoughts, carefully contemplates a single nail or a single toe bone, and successfully concentrates his mind thereon, will never fall into the three evil rebirths.

Furthermore, one who fixes his thoughts and carefully contemplates, and then comes to see all the white bones of his body, will at the end of his life be reborn in the Tuṣita heaven, where he will meet the bodhisattva named Maitreya, who is to be born [as a buddha] in his next life. Being reborn in this heaven, [the practitioner] will experience great joy. When Maitreya becomes a buddha, he will be the first to hear the Dharma, and he will attain the fruit of arhatship, the three knowledges, the six powers, and all of the eight deliverances.

---

273. On this anomalous list of the three *vimokṣa-mukha*s, see Appendix 2.

274. This passage implies that the practitioner is now certain of becoming an arhat. Doctrinally this would differ from the mainstream position that such certainty occurs only at the time of stream-entry (3.26.16 in the *Chan Essentials*).

275. This section is very similar to 4.32.4 at the end of the fourth sutra.

276. "Contemplation of impurity" here seems to denote the totality of the first sutra.

Furthermore, one who in the contemplation of impurity attains it completely will in this very life see the true emanation of the Buddha, hear the Buddha preach the Dharma, and bring an end to all suffering.

[1.18.20.2] [Entrustment]

At that moment, Ānanda got up from his seat, arranged his robes, bowed to the Buddha, and knelt with his hands folded. He said to the Buddha: "World-honored One, how should I remember this teaching? What is it to be called?"

The Buddha said to Ānanda: "It is called the contemplation [in which] the body is imagined as impure and foul.[277] It is also called the method for destroying [false conceptions of] the self and contemplating non-self and emptiness. You must carefully preserve it and explain it at length to the sentient beings of later ages who are stained by suffering and afflicted by lust."

When the Buddha spoke these words, Indra, the World Protectors, and innumerable other gods scattered *mandāra* flowers, *mahāmandāra* flowers, *mañjūṣaka* flowers, and *mahāmañjūṣaka* flowers above the Buddha and the assembly. Bowing their heads to the Buddha's feet, they praised the Buddha: "The appearance of a Tathāgata in the world is most rare, and he has been able to bring to submission the arrogant, deluded Kauṣṭhilananda. Even more, he has imparted this sweet-dew medicine for the sake of lustful sentient beings in the future, thereby increasing the ranks of those who will be reborn as gods and ensuring that the three jewels will not be cut off. Most excellent, O World-honored One, has been your delightful preaching of this teaching!"

The dragons, *yakṣa*s, *gandharva*s, and all the others then praised the Buddha just as the gods had done. When the venerables Ānanda and Kauṣṭhilananda, the remainder of the one thousand monks, the innumerable gods, and the host of divine beings had heard the Buddha's preaching, they joyfully undertook to carry it out. Making obeisance to the Buddha, they then retired.

[1.18.20.3] [Final Naming of First Sutra]

When this contemplation has been attained, it is called "the ten forms of impurity."[278] It is also called "the confirmatory vision of the discernment of the worms [255a]."[279]

This is the first [meditation], the gate of impurity.[280] It has these eighteen methods. The precise nature of all the various confirmatory visions cannot be explained in full. Upon entering *samādhi*, understanding of them will come of its own accord.

This is the accomplishment of contemplation number eighteen and the first gate [of meditation, the contemplation of impurity].

---

277. 觀身不淨雜穢想. Translation tentative.

278. 十色不淨. I presume this refers to the ten stages of the decaying corpse.

279. 分別諸蟲境界.

280. 是最初不淨門. I take the meaning here to be that the contemplation of impurity is the first gate of meditation (its usual place when the "five gates of *chan*" are listed).

[2] [NANDI THE MEDITATOR]

[2.0] [Introduction]

[2.0.1] [Nandi Requests the Method for Removing Sins]

Thus have I heard. Once, the Buddha was dwelling in the country of Śrāvasti in Anāthapiṇḍada's park in the grove of Prince Jeta[281] accompanied by one thousand two hundred fifty monks. At that time there was a monk in the assembly named Nandi the Meditator who had attained realization while in deep trance some time before and had become an arhat, endowed with the three wisdoms, the six supernatural powers, and fully possessed of the eight deliverances.[282]

Arising from his seat, Nandi arranged his robes and knelt on both knees. Clasping his hands, he said to the Buddha: "Today the Tathāgatha appears in the world, bringing peace and benefit to all. But once the Buddha has passed into extinction and is no longer present, those among the four groups of followers who have[283] karmic obstructions will not see the confirmatory visions even though they have fixed their thoughts.[284] How should they who in this way have defilements and sins ranging from the violation of the minor transgressions (*duṣkṛta*)[285] up to the gravest of sins, repent?[286] How can they extinguish the signs of their sins?[287]

"Again, how should those who wish to cultivate right mindfulness (正念) [but have committed the ten evil deeds, all the way from] killing living beings to holding false views, proceed so as to extinguish the obstructions of their defilements (煩惱障) and evil deeds?"

---

281. *Qi shu* 祇樹. The famous Grove of Jeta (Jetavana), a location also given below as *Qituo lin* 祇陀林 (2.0.2). This inconsistency reappears in the fourth sutra: *Qi shu* in the sutra opening (4.0.1 and 4.0.2) and *Qituo lin* in the body of the narrative. In the *Methods for Curing*, we find *Qihuan* 祇洹 (a full transcription) in the first paragraph (1.1.1), followed by *Qi shu* (1.1.2). Similar variation in the transcriptions of Indic names between the framing narratives and main body of the text has been observed in the *Amitāyus Contemplation Scripture* (as pertains to different words) and has been taken as evidence of that text's status as a compilation of originally distinct sources already written in Chinese (Yamada 1976).

282. In 2.19.2.8, Nandi becomes an arhat only after hearing the Buddha's preaching. This contradiction is unresolved.

283. Jt here adds "many" (多).

284. Jt replaces "fix their thoughts" (繫念) with "have correct mindfulness" (正念), a term seemingly borrowed from later in this paragraph.

285. *Duṣkṛta* (*tuji* 突吉) transgressions are the most minor class of monastic rules.

286. Jt here reads "ranging from minor sins up to grave sins such as killing living beings and having false views" (於小罪乃至重罪殺生邪見之罪), which removes the reference to specifically monastic precepts.

287. For "signs of these sins" (罪相), Jt reads "sins" (罪). "Signs of their sins" might mean the state of impurity of one who has sinned (as at *GFSMH*, T.643:15.655b15–20), but could also denote the visions that appear to those who have sinned (see, e.g., *Fa hua sanmei chan yi*, T.1941:46.954c23–27).

[2.0.2] [The Buddha Consents]

After saying these words, Nandi fell to the ground like a great mountain collapsing. Touching his head to the Buddha's feet, he continued: "May the World-honored One explain it to me, so that sentient beings of the future might always attain right mindfulness and might never part from the sages and worthies."

Then, as a loving father would console his child, the World-honored One said: "Excellent, excellent! O child of good family, you indeed have cultivated a loving mind, and are replete with love.[288] Today, possessed of great compassion and having fully attained the pure faculties, powers, and paths of awakening,[289] you have asked about the method for removing sins for the sake of all sentient beings of the future! Listen carefully, listen carefully,[290] and reflect on it well."

Then a light radiated from the crown of the World-honored One's head. Within this golden light were five hundred transformation buddhas who circled the Buddha seven times and bathed the grove of Prince Jeta in a golden light. When these appearances had been manifested, they reentered the Buddha through the bone in the back of his head.[291]

[2.19] [Bringing to Mind the Buddha]

[2.19.1] [Contemplating the Image]

[2.19.1.1] [Introduction]

Then the World-honored One spoke to Nandi the Meditator and commanded Ānanda:[292] "You two must teach future sentient beings burdened with sinful deeds to bring to mind the Buddha (*nianfo* 念佛) so as to eliminate their sins. Bringing to mind the Buddha[293] will remove the obstructions of deeds, retribution, and defilements."[294]

288. 與慈俱生. Translation tentative.

289. 無漏根力覺道. This precise phrase occurs at *Miao fa lian hua jing*, T.262:9.13b6, where it appears to translate *indriya-bala-bodhyaṅga* (*Saddharmapuṇḍarīkasūtra*, 54). At *Da zhi du lun*, T.1509:25.82a5–6, this same expression characterizes the arhat. These three categories are subgroups within the thirty-seven factors of awakening (*bodhipakṣika-dharmas*), enumerated below (2.19.2.3).

290. Jt here adds "I will preach it to you" (當為汝說).

291. Literally, the "pillow bone" (*zhengu* 枕骨; P, S, Q, Y, and Sgz read *dinggu* 頂骨), the occipital bone of the skull.

292. The statement here that the Buddha addresses these words to Nandi and *also* uses them to "command" Ānanda is rather peculiar; the same pattern is repeated in 2.19.1.13 and 3.21.9.3.

293. Here Jt continues with "First he sees one buddha, then up to ten buddhas. Seeing these buddhas, his mind becomes increasingly perspicacious, and the thirty-two marks are all made clear" (初見一佛，乃至十佛，見佛已，心轉明利，三十二相，皆使分明). This is a summary of 2.19.1.8. Jt resumes a more direct citation at 2.19.1.13.

294. These are the so-called three obstructions (*āvaraṇa*). The "obstruction of deeds" (業障; *karmāvaraṇa*) normally means the five sins of immediate retribution (killing one's mother, father, an arhat, splitting the Sangha, or spilling the blood of a Buddha), which assure rebirth in hell in one's next life and thus impede any advanced soteriological attainment in

To bring to mind the Buddha, the practitioner must first sit up straight, clasp his hands together, close his eyes, and press his tongue against the roof of his mouth. He should concentrate his mind and fix his thoughts, remaining continuously focused. When his mind is fixed, he should then contemplate an image [of the Buddha].[295]

[2.19.1.2] [The Pure Ground][296]

To contemplate the image, he must arouse his imagination (起想念) and contemplate the ground in front of him, making it extremely white and pure. Over an area twenty feet by twenty feet, he must make it even more clear and pure, as if it were a clear mirror.

When he sees the ground in front of him, he should also see the ground to his left, making it clear and [255b] pure as well. He should then see the ground to his right, also making it clear and pure, before finally seeing the ground behind him, making it clear and pure in the same way. He should make all the ground around him as flat as the palm of his hand, and in every direction he should imagine a patch of ground twenty feet square, making all of it clear and pure.

[2.19.1.3] [The Hairs of the *Uṣṇīṣa*][297]

When all the ground has been made clear, he must take hold of his mind firmly again and contemplate the ground in front of him, imagining a lotus flower with a thousand petals, adorned with the seven precious substances. He should further imagine a golden buddha image and then make this golden image sit with legs crossed on the lotus flower. Seeing this image, he should carefully contemplate the mound on the crown of its head,[298] on which he sees hairs, violet in color, each strand thirteen feet long and rolled in a clockwise fashion,[299] leaving a beryl glow around the crown of the head.

---

the present lifetime. The "obstruction of retribution" (報障; *vipākāvaraṇa*) usually means the places of rebirth from which one cannot attain the path (the lower realms, the continent of Uttarakuru, or the *asaṃjñā* heaven). The "obstruction of the defilements" (煩惱障; *kleśāvaraṇa*) refers simply to the presence of defiled mental tendencies (*DZDL*, T.1509:25.100a10–11).

295. "Contemplating the image" (觀像) is a method discussed in other fifth-century Chinese meditation texts, particularly the Contemplation Scriptures (*GSFMH*, T.643:15.690–693; see Ōminami 2001). Usually, the use of an external, physical image is clearly specified. This is not mentioned here explicitly, but it is implied below (2.19.1.13).

296. The progression here, in which the meditator first imagines a pure expanse of ground upon which he then imagines an image of the Buddha, is reminiscent of the *Amitāyus Contemplation Scripture* (*Guan Wuliangshou fo jing*, T.365:12.342a9–20).

297. The ensuing discussion of the physical features of the Buddha's body includes many unusual elements otherwise unknown except in the *Ocean-Samādhi Contemplation Scripture* (see Yamabe 1999c, 234–247 for a detailed comparison).

298. Literally, the "fleshy topknot on the crown of the head" (頂上肉髻). This rare translation of the term *uṣṇīṣa* is also found in several of the Contemplation Scriptures (*Guan Wuliangshou fo jing*, T.365:12.344a9; a15; a28; *Guan Mile pusa shang sheng doushuai tian jing*, T.452:14.419c24; *GFSMH*, T.643:15.696c11).

299. *GFSMH*, T.643:15.649a26–27 similarly describes the Buddha's hair as being twelve and a half "feet" (一丈二尺五寸) long when extended.

From each pore grows a single, curling hair.[300] The practitioner should contemplate all eighty-four thousand hairs,[301] making each of them clear.

[2.19.1.4] [The Face]

When he has seen these things, he should next contemplate the image's face. It is round and full as the moon on the fifteenth day of the month, its magnificent light ever so bright, [its features] clear and distinct.[302] Next he should contemplate the forehead, which is broad, flat, and straight, with the tuft of hair between the eyebrows as white as jade or snow, curled in a clockwise fashion, like a crystal pearl. Next he should contemplate the image's nose, like a cast-gold spike, like the beak of an eagle king,[303] square within the middle of the face. Next he should contemplate the image's mouth, its lips red and beautiful, like a *bimbara* fruit.[304] Next he should contemplate the image's teeth, [seeing that] within the mouth are forty teeth, square, white, and even, and on the teeth are markings that radiate light.[305] Like white pearls, they shine brilliantly [in the center of] the golden face,[306] a distinct red glowing from between them. Next he should contemplate the image's neck, resembling a beryl tube,[307] and then he should contemplate the auspicious swastika on the image's chest.[308] He should make all the marks very clear, with each mark radiating light in five colors.

[2.19.1.5] [The Arms]

Next he should contemplate the image's[309] arms, which are soft and lovely like an elephant king's trunk.[310] Then he should contemplate the image's hands, with ten fingers of different lengths, each one clearly distinct, and double-

---

300. "Hair" in this line is *mao* 毛, not *fa* 髮 as in the previous sentence. *Mao* more properly means body hair, but from the context this seems to still be describing the head hair. That but a single body hair grows from each of his pores is one of the traditional marks of a buddha.

301. Sgz, K[1], P, S, Q, Y add 孔, making the meaning the eighty-four thousand *pores*.

302. Some of these passages, describing the Buddha's appearance, are very closely worded to passages in Dharmakṣema's *Jin guang ming jing* (T.663:16.339a14–25).

303. See, similarly, *GFSMH*, T.643:15.656c20–22.

304. See, similarly, *GFSMH*, T.643:15.648a13–15.

305. 齒上有印印中出光. See, similarly, *GFSMH*, T.643:15.648a16–17.

306. 如白真珠<顯發金顏>. I relocate the words "appear brilliantly [in the center of] the golden face" from sixteen characters (one manuscript column) ahead, where they do not make sense. In the passage from the *Jin guang ming jing* that seems to have inspired many of these lines (T.663:16.339a14–25), these words indeed describe the Buddha's teeth.

307. 琉璃筒. See, similarly, *GFSMH*, T.643:15.648a21–22.

308. The symbol 卍. The auspicious swastika on the chest is frequently described as one of the Buddha's unusual bodily features. In early Chinese Buddhist literature, we sometimes find it in the list of the thirty-two marks (*Tai zi rui ying ben qi jing*, T.185:3.474a15), and sometimes—as is more usual within Indian Buddhist texts—among the eighty secondary marks (*ZCSM*, T.614:15.276c24–25).

309. {佛, P, S, Q, Y, Sgz, Kg}.

310. See, similarly, *GFSMH*, T.643:15.648b8–9.

jointed wrists.[311] The hairs on the back of the hands are like beryl light beams, each pointing outward. The fingernails are like red copper, the tips gold and the center red, or red copper mountains with streaks of purple gold. Next he should contemplate the webbed fingers, like those of a goose king.[312] They are nets of pearls when the hands are open, and invisible when closed.

[2.19.1.6] [The Body and Legs]

Having contemplated the image's hands, he should contemplate its body next. It sits squarely and secure, like a mountain of pure gold, leaning neither forward nor backward, upright in its place. Then he should contemplate the image's legs, with the thighs of a deer king,[313] straight and full.[314] He should contemplate the soles of its feet, which are flat and supple. On the bottom of the feet are markings of lotus flowers and a thousand-spoked wheel. On the tops of the feet are hairs like purple beryl, pointing upward. The toes are even and regularly staggered. The toenails are the color of red copper, and on the tips of the toes are markings of thousand-spoked wheels. The webbing of the toes is like loose woven silk, like the feet of a goose king.

[2.19.1.7] [The Halo]

[He contemplates] all these things, as well as the light from the image's mandorla [255c] and round halo and the light radiating from the crown[315] of its head.[316] Within the field of these lights are transformation buddhas, great assemblies of monks, and transformation bodhisattvas, all circling in orbit, like spinning wheels of fire.[317]

---

311. Literally, "can grasp objects inwardly and outwardly" (手內外握). See, similarly, *GSFMH*, T.643:15.648b24. Like the swastika on the chest, the earliest Chinese translations sometimes present this as one of the thirty-two marks (*Tai zi rui ying ben qi jing*, T.185:3.474a12), while later texts place it among the eighty secondary marks (*ZCSM*, T.614:15.276b28, noting that "grasping inwardly and outwardly" is the "old" translation).

312. Webbed toes and feet "like those of a goose king" is one of the traditional thirty-two bodily marks (*Zhong ahan jing*, T.26:1.493c27). On the meaning of this mark and its possible origins in artistic depictions of the Buddha, see Anālayo 2017, 51–54.

313. "Thighs of a deer king" is one of the thirty-two bodily marks (*Zhong ahan jing*, T.26:1.494a4).

314. 腨直圓滿. Translation tentative.

315. 項[>頂, K[1], K, P, S, Q, Y, Kg, Sgz]. The Taishō is presumably a misprint.

316. I take this passage to refer to the three ways that paintings often depict the light of the Buddha's body: as a large circle of light surrounding the entire body (the mandorla), as a smaller circle of light around just the head or upper part of the body (the halo), and as a set of short, straight beams emerging from the head. All three of these are often present in the same image.

317. The image of smaller buddhas circling the central figure "like spinning wheels of fire" recalls the depictions of the so-called Śrāvasti miracle in Central Asian art, which show the miracle of the Buddha's multiplication of his body as several concentric circles of smaller buddha images forming the mandorla of the central image. For some examples, see Howard and Vignato 2015, 139–148, and T. Zhu 2019.

[2.19.1.8] [Expanded Contemplation]

For the reverse contemplation, he must contemplate in reverse, starting with the feet and proceeding up to the cranial protuberance. For the forward contemplation, he must start from the crown of the head and go down to the feet. He should contemplate the image in this manner. Making his mind clear, he sees only this single image.

Having seen one image, he must continue contemplating until he sees two images. When he sees two images, he makes their bodies appear as beryl, radiating assorted lights, the flames of their halos following one after the other like flaming golden mountains of innumerable transformation buddhas.

Seeing two images, he next sees three images . . . four images . . . five images . . . up to ten images. Seeing ten images, his mind having become increasingly clear and sharp, he sees the entire continent of Jambudvīpa within the four oceans [filled with buddha images].

Ordinary beings with narrow minds (凡夫心狹) will be unable to enlarge [their vision]. [On the other hand,] if it becomes [too] large,[318] the practitioner should restrain his mind and return it to the area within the four oceans, bounded by the Encircling Iron Mountains. He sees buddha images everywhere within the oceans. He sees clearly their thirty-two major and eighty minor marks, each mark radiating innumerable lights.

[2.19.1.9] [Repentance for Impure Visions]

If among these lights he sees any divergent[319] confirmatory visions that are disordered or impure, this is something that occurs as retribution for sin. He must get up from meditation, sweep the sanctuary clean, wash its floors, make fresh [toilet] sticks, and humbly carry out repentance rituals.[320]

Then, he must again settle his mind, steady his thoughts in a single place, and contemplate the image as before. Not taking anything else as his

---

318. 若廣大者. Translation tentative. A similar passage below (3.21.3) also prescribes what to do if the vision becomes excessively large.

319. Reading 一 as 二, following Sgz, Kg, and K[1].

320. See, similarly, 2.20.7 and 4.32.3 below and *Methods for Curing* 1.9 (especially 1.9.4). As discussed in *Chan Before Chan*, chap. 4, the tasks listed here are inspired by the penance of "probation" (*parivāsa*) outlined in the *vinaya*, in which serious breaches of monastic rules are atoned for by temporarily assuming a reduced status and acting as a servant to the other monks and nuns. As Indian *vinaya* texts say of probationers (Schopen 1998, 158), in *Methods for Curing* 1.9.4 the penitent must "clean and empty the toilets." The "fresh sticks" (淨籌) mentioned here (and in 4.32.3) are thus likely the sticks used in China for toilet hygiene (the *vinayas* prescribe various forms of toilet paper, but the "stick" [*chou* 籌] was most common in China; see Heirman and Torck 2012, 92). The *Shami wei yi* (T.1472:24.935a19–26), a handbook for novice monks composed in China in the fifth or sixth century (Ōno 1954, 390–393), describes the making of new toilet sticks (and "willow twigs" for teeth cleaning; these too are mentioned in 4.32.3) as a key duty of the novitiate, whose position at the bottom rung of the monastic hierarchy is the model for the duties mandated during "probation."

object, he must carefully contemplate the space between the eyebrows of the image. Having carefully contemplated the space between the eyebrows of the image, he must then contemplate the other marks, making all of them clear.

If they are not clear, he must repent again and perform various menial services.[321] Then he should restrain his mind and contemplate the image as before. He will now see buddha images seated on lotus flowers everywhere within the four oceans, their august bodies fully endowed with the thirty-two marks.

[2.19.1.10] [Repentance and the Walking Image]

When the practitioner has seen the seated images, he must go on to think (念) as follows: "When the World-honored One was in the world, he carried his bowl and staff, entered villages to beg for food, and traveled everywhere to teach so as to bring blessings and salvation to living beings. Owing to what sin from a past life do I see today only the seated image and not the walking image?"[322]

After this thought, he must repent further. Then, having repented, he must restrain his mind as before, fix his thoughts, and contemplate the image. When he contemplates the image, he sees all the seated images stand up, their large bodies, sixteen feet tall, standing straight up without leaning to one side or the other, fully endowed with the bodily marks and radiance of a buddha.

When he has seen the images stand up, he will further see the images walking. They hold begging bowls and staffs and carry themselves with the noble bearing of a monk. They are surrounded by many assemblies of gods and humans. More buddha images fly through the air radiating golden light. They fill the sky, appearing like golden clouds or mountains of gold, beautiful beyond [256a] compare.

In the sky he sees other buddha images performing the eighteen miraculous bodily transformations[323]—emitting water from their upper bodies

321. See 2.20.7, n. 359.

322. *Xingxiang* 行像 here evidently means "an image of a walking buddha" (as at *GFSMH*, T.643:19.692a23–b5), not "to walk an image" in a procession, as this word often does elsewhere (Tsukamoto 1975, 306–308). In China, the "walking Buddha" was a recognized iconographic form during the fourth and fifth centuries (*Fa yuan zhu lin*, T.2122:53.406b17–18; *CSZJJ*, T.2145:55.92b29–c1). Modern scholars, however, do not, to my knowledge, identify any extant East Asian Buddhist images as belonging to the "walking Buddha" genre (but see Gutman 2002 for examples from Southeast Asia, and Kim 2019 on some possible Indian precedents). In any event, the description here in the *Chan Essentials*—a standing figure holding a staff and bowl—strongly recalls the Chinese paintings and sculptures usually identified as the Medicine Buddha (藥師佛; Baiṣajyaguru), who is often in a standing pose, often carries a staff, always carries a bowl, and is sometimes clearly shown walking (*Dunhuang shi ku quan ji*, 2:68, fig. 56, showing Tang-era wall paintings; Drège 2014, 322, showing illustrated manuscript Pelliot no. 2013; Härtel 1982, fig. 100, gives a rare sculptural example).

323. A similar list of "transformations" (miraculous powers) is given in 4.31.12.

and fire from their lower bodies; expanding their bodies to fill the sky and then contracting them as small as mustard seeds; walking on the earth as if it were water and on water as if it were the earth; rising up in the eastern sky and descending in the west, or up in the west and down in the east, or up in the south and down in the north, or up in the north and down in the south, or up in the center and down in the outer regions, or up in the outer regions and down in the center, or up above and down below, or else surging forth below and returning back above. They walk, stand, sit, and lie down unhindered, just as they so desire.

[2.19.1.11] [The Reclining Image]

When he has seen these things, the practitioner must further think: "When the World-honored One was present in the world and instructing the monks, he would sleep on his right side. Therefore I must now contemplate the images as they recline too."

He sees the many images fold their outer monastic robes (*saṅghāṭi*) and place their heads on their right forearms, lying down on their right side. Beneath their right side, golden beds of radiant golden sandalwood spontaneously appear, with wondrous multicolored lotus flowers for bedding. Above the beds are jeweled canopies with dangling garlands, each illuminated by the radiant light of a buddha, like a golden flower, a moon, or a bright star. In the sky, countless jewel-like lights appear, bright masses of clouds filled with transformation buddhas.

[2.19.1.12] [The Falsity of the Many Images]

Seeing the reclining images, the practitioner must then think: "In the past there was a buddha named Śākyamuni, who instructed sentient beings his entire life. After forty-nine years in this world, he disappeared into final nirvana[324] like a fire going out when the fuel is spent, extinguished without remainder. Today I use my mind to imagine, and by imagining I see many images. In arriving these images do not arrive from somewhere, and in going do not go anywhere. I see them falsely, by way of imagination (從我心想妄見此耳)."

With this thought, the images gradually disappear, leaving only a single image sitting with legs crossed atop a lotus flower. The practitioner carefully contemplates this image, making its thirty-two major and eighty minor marks very clear.

When he has seen this image, it is called [the attainment of] the contemplation of the image.

---

324. Literally, "he *parinirvāṇa*-ized by entering great nirvana" (入大涅槃而般涅槃). Tsukinowa (1971, 107) cites this "bizarre" phrase as proof that the *Chan Essentials* could not be the translation of an Indian text. In fact, this precise expression can be found in authentic Chinese Buddhist translations where it serves as a relatively literal rendering of the formula *nirvāṇadhātau parinirvānti* (*Mohe bore boluomi jing*, T.223:8.393c14–15; *Pañcaviṃśatisāhasrikā-Prajñāpāramitā*, 6–8:51).

[2.19.1.13] [Conclusion]

The[325] Buddha said to Nandi the Meditator and commanded Ānanda: After I have passed into extinction, even though the Buddha is no longer present in the world, monks, nuns, laymen, or laywomen who wish to repent and destroy their sins can quickly purify all evil, sinful karma by fixing their thoughts and carefully contemplating a physical image (形像) [of the Buddha].

[2.19.2] [The Appearance of the Buddha]

[2.19.2.1] [The Emanation]

Having contemplated the image once, he must contemplate it again. The navel of the image will then emit a ray of light.[326] Golden in color, it splits into five beams, one of them shining to the left, one to the right, one to the front, one behind, and one upward. In each light beam are transformation buddhas, one following upon the next until they fill the sky. He must see their appearance clearly and distinctly.

Next, he sees the transformation buddhas ascend to the Brahmā-world and then fill all the worlds of the entire universe.[256b] Like mountains of purple gold, they emit a golden light within each world that shines everywhere unobstructed.

When he sees these things, his mind becomes happy and he sees the seated image before him as if it were the true emanation of the Buddha (如佛真影).

[2.19.2.2] [Consecration by the True Buddha]

Seeing this emanation of the Buddha, he must think: "This is merely an emanation, manifested by the august power, wisdom, and mastery of the World-honored One. What I must now carefully contemplate is the true Buddha (真佛)."[327]

He then immediately sees the [true] body of the Buddha, which is as marvelous as pure beryl encasing adamant, its various adornments formed of the lustrous reflections of a purple-gold light within the adamant, its thirty-two major and eighty minor marks blazing brightly, like graven characters,[328] sublime and pure beyond all description. Holding a pitcher of water in his hands, the Buddha stands in the air. The pitcher is filled with ambrosia-like water. The water is of five colors, each with its own pure light [like that of] a pearl of beryl. The water is soft and smooth, and the Buddha pours it on the practitioner's head. It fills the interior of his body, and he

325. Jt resumes here.

326. For "will then emit a ray of light" (便放一光), P, S, Q, Y, Sgz, and Kg read "make it emit light" (使放一光), and Jt reads "request it to emit light" (請放一光). These differences suggest somewhat different understandings of the nature and mechanisms of the visions.

327. End of *Tempyō Chan Essentials 3* (Sgz) and start of *Tempyō Chan Essentials 4*.

328. The description of the bodily marks as "like graven characters" (猶如印文) is curious, perhaps suggesting that the auspicious swastika on the chest (see 2.19.1.5) has been taken as a model for the other marks.

sees the eighty families of worms gradually shrivel up wherever the water flows within his body. Once the worms have shriveled, he feels relaxed in body and happy in mind.[329]

[2.19.2.3] [The Preaching of the Dharma]

He must then think (念言): "The Tathāgatha, the compassionate father, has consecrated my head with this water of the Dharma, which is ambrosia of the most excellent flavor. This consecration is surely not without meaning."

He must now be instructed[330] to bring forth the following thought (想念): "May the World-honored One preach for me the Dharma!"

Those whose sinful karma has been removed will now hear the Buddha preach the Dharma. When the Buddha preaches the Dharma, he preaches the four bases of mindfulness, the four right efforts, the four bases of magic power, the five faculties, the five powers, the seven factors of awakening,[331] and the eightfold holy path.[332] He analyzes each of these thirty-seven things and explains them to the practitioner. When he has explained them, he further teaches the contemplations of suffering, emptiness, impermanence, and non-self. Having been taught these things, because he has seen the Buddha and heard the marvelous Dharma the practitioner's mind will be liberated and he will soon become an arhat as surely as water follows its course.[333]

[2.19.2.4] [Repentance of Karmic Obstructions]

One with heavy karmic obstructions, on the other hand, will see the Buddha's mouth move without hearing the preaching of the Dharma. Like a deaf person he will hear nothing. At that moment, he must again carry out a ritual of repentance.

Having repented, he must then throw his body to the floor and face the Buddha while sobbing and crying. After persisting in this for a long time, and cultivating all kinds of merit,[334] he will then be able to hear the Buddha's preaching. However, even though he will hear the preaching of the Dharma, he will not understand its meaning.

[2.19.2.5] [Second Consecration and the Water Nadir]

The practitioner will again see the World-honored One pour a pitcher of water over his head. The color of the water, like pure adamant, is extraor-

329. The "contemplating the image" (觀像) section of the *Ocean-Samādhi Contemplation Scripture* (*GFSMH*, T.643:15692a18–21) similarly leads to a visionary encounter with the Buddha in which the meditator's previously impure physical body is purified.

330. 復當更<教, K^{1}>.

331. 七覺<分, W>. This may, however, be a later editorial intervention.

332. This list comprises the so-called thirty-seven "factors that aid in awakening" (*bodhipakṣika-dharmas*), a standard classification of the virtues cultivated along the path to awakening (Gethin 1992) also mentioned in 1.18.15 and 4.32.13.

333. This line is similar to 1.18.19, stating that the meditator will become an arhat "as surely as a great current of water in flow" (如水大流).

334. "Cultivating all kinds of merit" (修諸功德) presumably means carrying out Buddhist rituals.

dinary. Entering through the crown of his head, its colors become distinct—green, yellow, red, and white—as it collects various impurities.[335] After entering through the head, the water moves downward into the middle of his body before coming out through his feet and flowing onto the ground, where, in a spot around ten feet square,[336] it transforms into a light that enters the earth and proceeds gradually deeper until it reaches the water nadir.[337] As the light reaches the water nadir, the practitioner must apply his mind to following [256c] the light as it departs.

He must contemplate the water further. Beneath the water is pure emptiness. He must contemplate it further. Beneath the emptiness is a ground of purple beryl. Beneath that ground is one of gold. Beneath the golden ground is one of adamant. Beneath the adamantine ground he sees empty space. He sees the empty space, a vast emptiness devoid of anything.

When he has seen this, he must again restrain his mind and contemplate the single image of the Buddha as before.[338] The Buddha now shines with a brightness beyond description, and again he consecrates the practitioner's head with water from a pitcher. The water appears as radiant as before, and this happens seven times.[339]

[2.19.3] [Conclusions]

[2.19.3.1] [Conclusion A][340]

The Buddha said to Nandi the Meditator:[341] "This is called the *samādhi* of the contemplation of the image.[342] It is also called the trance of bringing to mind the Buddha. It is also called [the procedure for] removing sinful karma,

---

335. The consecration water, entering the body, cleanses it of impurities, just as earlier (2.19.2.2) it destroyed the bodily worms.

336. For 丈, K[1], P, S, Q, Y, Sgz, and Kg all read 杖, suggesting a thin line rather than a square area.

337. "Water nadir" (*shuiji* 水際) speaks to the same cosmology invoked earlier (1.13.2), in which at the bottom of the universe, along with those of earth and wind, there is a "water wheel" (*apmaṇḍala*) or "water region" (*apskandha*; see *Vimalakītrinirdeśa*, 454, translated as *shuiji* 水際 in *Weimojie suo shuo jing*, T.475:14.555b27). In the present passage, beneath the "water nadir" are gold and adamantine layers, recalling the "adamantine nadir" discussed earlier (1.18.17).

338. This presumably refers to the "true Buddha" mentioned above.

339. The number seven might have some connection to the seven buddhas of the past, whose "true emanations" appeared to the meditator at the end of the first sutra.

340. Within what I label here as the conclusions A–D there are problems of narrative continuity. First, between B and C there is some kind of gap (at the end of B, the interlocutors ask the Buddha to give a further teaching, but this does not occur). Perhaps section B should be placed after section D, thereby serving as an introduction to contemplation twenty. Alternatively, perhaps C and D were later additions. Section C, where Nandi becomes an arhat, presents another problem, as this contradicts the introduction, where Nandi is already an arhat (2.0.1). All of this points to the less-than-fully-edited nature of the narrative portions of the *Chan Essentials.*

341. Jt omits "the Meditator."

342. For "contemplation of the image" (觀像), Jt reads "contemplation of the buddha" (觀佛).

or for rescuing precept breakers. It allows those who have violated the precepts to avoid losing their meditative trance."[343]

The Buddha said to Ānanda: "You must preserve this method of consecration by the *samādhi* of the contemplation of the Buddha (觀佛三昧灌頂之法), and you must extensively expound it for all sentient beings of the future."

[2.19.3.2] [Conclusion B]

When the Buddha spoke these words, the venerable Nandi the Meditator, as well as the many assemblies of gods and the one thousand two hundred fifty monks, all together said: "The World-honored Tathāgata has today, for the sake of sentient beings with much distracted minds, preached this method of removing sins. May the World-honored One now further reveal the ambrosial teachings that will make it possible for sentient beings in the time after the Buddha's extinction to attain the path of nirvana!"

[2.19.3.3] [Conclusion C]

When the monk Nandi the Meditator heard the Buddha explain this *samādhi* of the contemplation of the Buddha, he felt joy in body and mind and immediately entered innumerable *samādhi*s. His mind was suddenly liberated, and he became an arhat, fully endowed with the three wisdoms and the six powers.

[2.19.3.4] [Conclusion D]

The Buddha said to Ānanda: "When this meditation is complete, it is called contemplation number nineteen, the *samādhi* of the contemplation of the Buddha. It is also called the method of consecration. You must carefully preserve it. Do not forget it. Explain it in detail for all sentient beings of the future."

When the Buddha spoke these words, the assembly of monks, hearing what the Buddha said, joyfully undertook to carry it out.

[2.20] [Twentieth Contemplation: Breath Contemplation]

[2.20.1] [Counting and Following the Breath]

The Buddha said to Ānanda: One with much lust, even after obtaining this *samādhi* of the contemplation of the Buddha, will gain no benefit. He still will not attain any of the fruits of the holy path.[344] So he must be taught to contemplate his own body in the manner given previously and again create a skeleton, making it brilliantly white like a snow-covered mountain.[345]

He should then fix his thoughts and concentrate his mind on his navel,

343. 不失禪定. On the idea that transgressions block meditative attainment, see *Chan Before Chan*, chap. 3.

344. "Holy path" is literally "path of the sages and worthies" (賢聖道), a standard rendering of *āryamārga* in pre-Kumārajīva translations. This word is rarely used in Chinese Buddhist literature after the early fifth century.

345. "Previously" presumably means in the first sutra, where the "white bone contemplation" method was taught.

or within his pelvis, and follow the breath as it goes in and out. He counts from one to two, to three, to four, to five, to six, to seven, to eight, to nine, to ten.[346] When he is finished, he should begin again, following the breath as it goes in and out until reaching ten.

Then he should put aside this practice of counting the breath and stop his mind.[347] His mind then becomes calm and [257a] still. He sees his body's skin as a white silk bag. When he has seen this, he no longer sees his bones or knows where the organ of his heart lies.[348]

[2.20.2] [The Coccyx and the Orb of Light]

He must then be instructed to arouse his imagination further, turning his own body—his heart and mind, and trunk and limbs—into white jade. When he has seen this, he must again fix his thoughts on his coccyx within his pelvis[349] and prevent his mind from wandering.

He will then suddenly see above his body a light roughly the size of a coin, which gradually grows larger until it is the size of the eye[350] of a giant *makara* fish. The light encircles him like a gathering cloud. It is like a white cloud within which there is a white light, like that of a crystal mirror. The brightness keeps increasing until his entire body is radiant.

Then a further white light appears, perfectly round like a cartwheel, bright both within and without, brighter than the sun.

[2.20.3] [Counting and Following the Breath]

When the practitioner has seen these things, he must count the breath, as before, from one to two, to three, to four, to five, to six, to seven, to eight, to nine, to ten. Either singly or doubly,[351] long (修) or short, just as he wishes. In this manner, dwelling in a secluded place he should fix his thoughts and not allow his mind to scatter.

Then he must fix his thoughts and again contemplate his coccyx. As he contemplates it, his mind settles and ceases to stir.

---

346. 一數二隨或二數三隨, etc. My translation of this repeating pattern—which occurs again in 2.20.3—is tentative. "Counting" (數) and "following" (隨) recall the first two of the six stages of breath meditation (*ānāpāna*) discussed in many early Chinese meditation texts (Deleanu 1992).

347. 捨數而止. "Stop" (*zhi*) perhaps invokes the third of the six stages of breath meditation (see previous note), when a meditator ceases counting or following the breath and enters a state of focused concentration.

348. 不知心處. I take the point to be that the meditator, having brought the activity of his mind / heart to a standstill, now has a vision of his own body in which the organ of the heart is no longer apparent.

349. "Coccyx" is literally the "great bone of the spine" (脊骨大節). The "great bone within the pelvis" (腰中大節) mentioned later (2.20.3; see also 2.20.12) seems to denote this same location.

350. 耳[>目].

351. This perhaps means that either the meditator counts both inhalations and exhalations or only one or the other.

[2.20.4] [The Brightening of the Orb of Light]

He now sees his body again, and it becomes even brighter than before, [the light above it now][352] roughly the size of a large coin. Redoubling his efforts, he again sees his body, and the light is even brighter, grown to the size of the mouth of a water pitcher.[353] It is brighter than every bright thing in the world. When he has seen this light, he redoubles his striving and does not allow his mind to slacken. Now he sees the light before his chest, roughly the size of a mirror. When he has seen this light, he must strive vigorously as if extinguishing a fire on his head, exerting himself without cease. He sees the light become even more intense, brighter than a heavenly jewel. It is very pure, devoid of imperfection. Seven kinds of light, which shine like the seven precious substances, emerge from his chest and enter the light.

When these signs (相) have appeared, the practitioner becomes extremely happy and spontaneously joyful. His mind feels incomparably peaceful.

[2.20.5] [The Signs of the Twelve Links]

He must now make further effort and not allow his mind to slacken. He will see a cloud-like light encircling his body seven times. Each circle of light transforms into a wheel of light, within which will spontaneously appear the fundamental signs of the twelve links of the chain of conditions.[354]

[2.20.6] [The Signs of Transgression]

If, however, he is not zealous in his practice, and if, giving way to indulgence, he has violated any of the minor precepts, even [merely] a *duṣkṛta* sin, this light will appear black, like a wall or like charcoal. Or else he will see the light as similar to an old torn monk's robe.[355] Having given free rein to his mind and taken the minor sins lightly,[356] the light of undefiled sanctity is thereby obscured.[357]

352. This must refer to the round circle of light mentioned earlier (2.20.2).

353. *Zaoguan* 澡罐. The second character of this word is given variously as 瓶 (Sgz, Kg), 湓 (K[1]), or 灌 (P, S, Q, and Y). This same word appears in several other passages in the *Chan Essentials* and *Methods for Curing*, and the form of the second character varies, even within the same edition across different instances. The meaning, in all cases, seems to be a pitcher or vase of water.

354. What is meant by "fundamental signs" (根本相貌) is not entirely clear, but the idea seems to be that the meditator will perceive the twelve links of *pratītyasamutpāda* in the form of concrete, symbolic images, similar to what we find in the Central Asian meditation text known as the *Yogalehrbuch*, in reference to other doctrinal categories (Ruegg 1967, 165).

355. The torn robe is presumably a symbol of the violation of the monastic precepts.

356. This line is reminiscent of a famous passage from the Mahāyāna *Mahāparinirvāṇa-sūtra*: "Do not take minor sins lightly, imagining them to be blameless. However small the drops of water, they eventually fill the bowl." 莫輕小罪，以為無殃，水渧雖微，漸盈大器 (*Da ban-niepan jing*, T.374:12.451c24–25).

357. "Undefiled sanctity" (賢聖無漏) presumably means transcendent (*lokottara*) stages of the path.

The Buddha said to Ānanda: This method of consecration by means of the contemplation of impurity (不淨觀灌頂法門) [257b] belongs to the lineage of all the sages and worthies. If there is a monk, nun, layman, or laywoman who wishes to cultivate the teachings of the sages and worthies, then I command them to contemplate that all *dharma*s are suffering, empty, impermanent, non-self, and formed through causes and conditions.[358]

As when practicing breath counting, he should focus his mind. He must diligently maintain the precepts, upholding them single-mindedly. He must take even minor transgressions very seriously, repenting them with remorse and taking care not to conceal even tiny violations. If he conceals any violation, he will see the many radiant lights as rotten wood. When he sees this, it will be known that he has violated the precepts.

[2.20.7] [Repentance for Transgressions]

[In such a case,] he must again arouse a sense of shame and remorse (慚愧), repent and rebuke himself, sweep the sanctuary, clean the floors, and perform many kinds of menial service (苦役).[359] He must then make offerings and pay reverence to his teachers and parents. He must look upon his teachers and parents as if they were the Buddha, giving rise to deep reverence. Obeying his teachers and parents, he should seek to make the following vow: "Today I serve my teachers and parents. By this merit may I obtain liberation in every lifetime."

After cultivating merit in this manner, with full remorse, he should count his breaths as before. He will again see the light, radiant and exquisite, just as it was before [he violated the precepts].

[2.20.8] [The Light of Seven Colors]

He must now again fix his thoughts and carefully contemplate his coccyx, making[360] the mind settle on it without wandering even slightly. If his mind should become distracted, he must rebuke himself again[361] and remorsefully repent.

Upon repenting, he will see lights in his navel in all seven colors, like the seven precious substances. He must cause these lights to merge into a single light, brilliantly white and lovely.

358. 因緣<合成, W>.

359. "Menial service" (*kuyi* 苦役) seems to mean the humbling, impure tasks of cleaning, though the word also carries connotations of asceticism (see *Chan Before Chan*, chap. 4, p. 201). The same word is used in. 2.19.1.9 and *Methods for Curing* 1.9.4, also in the context of repentance.

360. 念[>令, P, S, Q, Y].

361. 復當自責，慚愧懺悔. K[1] reads 汝 for 復, yielding: "*you* must again rebuke yourself." This may just be an error. But it could also reflect the hypothesized earlier form of the text; see "The *Five Gates* and the *Chan Essentials*" in chap. 4.

[2.20.9] [The Spear of Light and the Five Points]

When he sees this, he must again be taught to fix his thoughts and meditate as before, contemplating his own white skeleton, which is as white as *ke*-jade or snow. When he sees the white skeleton, he must be instructed to fix his thoughts and concentrate his mind on the crown of his skull.

Now he sees a great bright light shining from the crown of his skull. It looks like a flame the size of a spear[362] in length and thickness. It emerges from the crown of the skull and then reverses itself so that it points downward and reenters through the crown of the skull. Passing through the crown of the skull, it enters his neck bone. Emerging from his neck bone, it enters his chest bone. Emerging from his chest bone, it enters his navel. Emerging from his navel, it enters his coccyx. After entering his coccyx, it disappears.[363]

[2.20.10] [Śākyamuni Appears within the Cloud of Light]

With its disappearance, there immediately appears a spontaneously arising great cloud of light.[364] It is adorned with jewels and pure jewel-flowers more exquisite than all other material forms.[365] Within the cloud is a buddha named Śākyamuni, replete in radiance, endowed with the thirty-two major and eighty minor marks, each one radiating a thousand lights. These lights are extremely bright, blazing forth like a hundred thousand million suns. This buddha preaches the teaching of the four truths. His light dazzling, he stands before the practitioner and lays his hand upon his head.

[2.20.11] [The Worms Burned by Fire]

This buddha[366] then instructs the practitioner: "In a former life, owing to lust, hatred, and confusion, you committed many evil deeds. The obstruction of ignorance [257c] has caused you to receive a mortal body[367] for lifetime upon lifetime. You must now contemplate [all the impure things] within your body shriveling up and being burned into oblivion by external fires."

When this buddha has said this, the practitioner must be instructed in the method of the contemplation of impurity as before. He contemplates

---

362. 似如火色，長短麄細，正共[>與]稍等. This would be an easy graphic mistake using the written form 与. My emendation is in light of 2.20.12, where this same imagery appears.

363. This passage clearly alludes to a version of the Indian systems of vital bodily energy points usually referred to as the *cakras*; see chap. 3, pp. 63–64.

364. 應時即有一自然大光明雲. The word *ziran* 自然 appears to be an adjective, "spontaneously arising." The word is used similarly in 2.20.12 below.

365. The unusual expression "more exquisite than all other material forms" (色中上者), as well as the very similar "most exquisite form among material forms" (色中上色), also occurs in several of the Contemplation Scriptures (*Guan Puxian pusa xing fa jing*, T.277:9.390c12; *Guan Wuliangshou fo jing*, T.365:12.342b12; *GFSMH*, T.643:15.647a9–10).

366. 化[>此]. This buddha is never declared to be merely an empty, imagination-produced vision (as the "transformation buddhas" invariably are), suggesting that the transmitted reading is an error.

367. Literally, a "body of birth and death" (生死身).

all the worms within his body shriveling up, and when he has seen this, he must [imaginatively] generate fires to burn them to death.

[2.20.12] [The Heap of Bones]

If the worms do not die, he must again see his body as like white crystal that gleams white spontaneously. When he sees [these] white bones, a light emerges from his head the size and thickness of a spear, which he must extend to fifteen feet in length.

He must now again apply his mind (作念) and drive the head [of his skeleton] backwards. Applying his thoughts (作意) further, he must continue to drive the head backwards until the entire body collapses and his skull rests against his coccyx.[368]

When he sees this, he must continue to contemplate carefully and make the white skeletons[369] become the same color as the light.[370] Then he will see that there are assorted fruits at the edges of the light. When he sees the fruits, he then sees lights emerging from the tops of the fruits. A white light, shining very brightly, appears like a cloud of white jewels. The gleaming white skeletons are exactly the same color as the light. He sees the skeletons fall apart and collapse, their heads on the ground, or else they fragment into individual bones, or else whole skeletons are blown to bits, driven like rain and snow in a strong wind, flickering here and there like lightning.

Collapsed in a heap on the ground, the skeletons form a small mound, like shavings of rotten wood collected in a pile. The practitioner contemplates this heap and sees a stream of spontaneously arising vapor (自然氣) stretching from it into the sky. Like a cloud of gleaming white smoke, it curls clockwise and fills the entire sky before coalescing again in one place.

[2.20.13] [The Nine-Colored Skeleton]

When he has seen this, he must again be instructed to imagine a skeleton. He sees a skeleton with nine different colors in nine clearly divided areas on its surface.[371] In each area there is [another] nine-colored skeleton, vividly colored. This cannot be fully described. Each skeleton must be made fully intact, and each one must be seen reflected without obstruction in the skeleton in front of it. When he has finished this contemplation, he must contemplate further within each color. Like beryl, they are totally transparent, and within each color [are] ninety-nine colors, each of which has many

368. 使頭却向，令身皆倒，以頭拄脊骨，對臍[>腰]大節. The word 腰中大節 appears in 2.20.3 above, seemingly meaning the coccyx.

369. In the ensuing paragraph, multiple skeletons are clearly mentioned; presumably the meditator will have repeated the kinds of methods described in the first sutra, in which the contemplation of one's own skeleton leads to seeing multiple skeletons externally.

370. 使白骨人與光同色. Kg reads 先 in place of 光, yielding "make the bones the same [pure white] color as before."

371. 身有九色九畫分明. Translation tentative. The nine "colors" (色) or perhaps nine "forms" might point to the canonical list of nine stages of the decaying corpse (see also 1.1.7).

nine-colored skeletons within it. These skeletons appear in myriad ways, each distinct in nature while not obstructing one another.

When he has seen these things, he must strive diligently to eliminate all evil.[372]

[2.20.14] [The Body Restored]

When he has seen these things, the cloud of condensed light before him, shaped like a goblet, enters his body. Upon entering through his navel, it enters his spine. Once it has entered his spine, the practitioner sees his body restored to its original state exactly as it was before.

Whether he is in trance or not, because of [his successful practice of] counting the breath [258a], he sees the things previously described constantly.

Seeing these things, he must again be instructed to fix his thoughts and concentrate his mind on the light within his[373] navel, not allowing himself to become distracted. Then his mind enters an extremely peaceful state, and once it is peaceful, he must apply himself to careful investigation and discernment of the liberation of the sages.[374]

[2.20.15] [The Teaching of the Seven Buddhas]

At this juncture, he will again see the seven buddhas of the past, who preach for him the Dharma—that is to say, they preach the four truths, and they preach that the five *skandha*s to which one clings are empty and devoid of self. These buddhas, together with many sages and worthies, come before the practitioner constantly, giving him manifold teachings and instructing him to contemplate the *samādhi*s of emptiness, non-self, non-doing, and non-wishing.[375]

They[376] say: "O Dharma child, you must now carefully contemplate [as follows]: 'Visible things, sounds, smells, tastes, and objects of touch are all impermanent. Not destined to endure, they flash in and out of existence like a bolt of lightning, passing away instantaneously, like an illusion, like wild horses,[377] like shimmering air when it is hot, like a city of the *gandharvas*, like things seen in a dream that are nowhere to be found upon waking,[378]

372. "Strive to eliminate all evil" (滅一切惡) could be an oblique reference to a ritual of repentance.

373. 本[>其]. Emendation tentative.

374. 自學審諦分別諸聖解脫. Translation tentative.

375. On this anomalous list, see Appendix 2.

376. Here W adds "the Buddha" (佛), linking this passage to the preceding excerpt that W includes (2.20.7) even as it changes the visionary encounter into a mere continuation of the Buddha's teaching to Ānanda. On the significance of this change, see "Rewriting the Scriptures at the Wofoyuan" in *Chan Before Chan*, chap. 5.

377. On "wild horses," see 1.3.3, n. 64.

378. 如夢所見覺不知處. Translation tentative. This exact phrase is found in several translations attributed to Zhu Fonian 竺佛念 (fl. ca. 400). See e.g., *Dang lai bian jing*, T.395:12.1118b27; *Da fang deng ding wang jing*, T.477:14.592a8–9.

like the sparks seen when chiseling rock, which vanish as soon as they appear, like birds flying in the sky leaving no trace, like an echo that sounds without a person there who responds.' You must now contemplate further: 'The triple world is like an illusion, like a magical creation.' "[379]

[2.20.16] [The Emptiness of the World]

At that, [the practitioner] sees everything within himself and outside as empty and devoid of anything (空無所有). Like a bird flying in the sky without touching down anywhere, his mind goes beyond the triple world (心超三界). He contemplates how nothing in the world will long endure, not even Mount Sumeru or the vast ocean, and that everything is like a magically created illusion. Contemplating his own body, he sees no sign of a body.[380]

[2.20.17] [The Falsity of the Female Form]

He must then reflect as follows: "The world is impermanent. Nowhere in the triple world is secure. Everything is empty, so where can a body endure? The visible objects of desire and the many women I see before my eyes arise from confusion. They are wrongly seen to be lovely. In truth their nature is to quickly rot and decay.[381] Furthermore, the female form is a cangue that oppresses a man's spirit. Fools delight therein, insatiable, and are unable to extricate themselves from this cangue and shackles.

"But a practitioner[382] realizes the [true] nature of phenomena. He knows they are empty and quiescent, and that objects of desire are like robbers, not to be pined for. Even more, they are like a prison, well secured and hard to escape. Today I contemplate emptiness and turn away from the triple world. I contemplate the world as like foam on the water that quickly fades away. With a mind devoid of imagination (心無眾想), one knows that the things of the world are only bondage and sickness. Ordinary beings, entranced by them, live their entire lives without realizing this. Not knowing [that these things are] suffering, they are unable to free themselves of yearning and attachment. Giving free reign to their passions, maddened and deluded, there is nothing they will not do.

"Today I contemplate these deceptive female forms. They are like echoes or reflected images. Trying to find them, nothing can be grasped. Contemplating these female forms, where are they really? They are only false

379. I take this to be the end of the direct speech of the seven buddhas.

380. Here "body" (身) also construes as "himself." The point is that the meditator contemplates the emptiness of both the external world and his own person.

381. To "quickly rot" (速朽) is an old Chinese term used by those who advocated avoiding sumptuous burial trappings so that the body would "quickly rot" underground (Riegel 1995). These associations may have inspired its use, here and in other fifth-century Chinese Buddhist texts, to denote bodily impermanence (*Weimojie suo shuo jing*, T.475:14.539b13–14; *DMDL*, T.618:15.321a26).

382. Here, notably, the word "practitioner" (行者) is used in the first-person speech of the meditator.

appearances (妄見) that vitiate and afflict me. They cheat ordinary beings, causing vast harm. Today I contemplate these forms as mad flowers[383] that fall when blown by the wind, appearing from nowhere [258b] and disappearing into nothing. Illusory and lacking any substance, still they are clung to by foolish people who delight in them. Like a once paralyzed invalid cured by a skillful physician, I now contemplate them as wholly impermanent. I now contemplate suffering, emptiness, and impermanence, and I see these forms as devoid of any substantial reality. How dismal it is to think of the ordinary beings who hanker after them and never tire of adoring them; sunk in stupidity, they mistakenly cling to them and enjoy them to no end, becoming slaves to the objects of their affection. Pierced by the spear of desire, the pain reaches deep, all the way to their hearts and marrow, and the cangue of affection binds them."

Having reflected in this way, the practitioner then contemplates that everything is entirely empty and quiescent: "These objects of sexual desire and all material things[384] arise from the five *skandha*s and four great elements. Yet the five *skandha*s too have no master in control, and the four great elements lack any nature of their own. Empty of both nature and characteristics (性相俱空), how can they [truly] arise?"

[2.20.18] [Freedom from Lust]

When he contemplates in this fashion, his wisdom becomes clear, and he sees his body as very bright, like a *maṇi* jewel free of obscuration, or like the essence of adamant, pure[385] white and shining. Like a deer who having been suddenly surrounded nonetheless manages to escape from the clutches of the hunters, he contemplates the five *skandha*s and sees they are entirely pure. When he contemplates the six great elements, he is [as unattached] as a bird soaring high with no need to perch.

Having [previously] swallowed the hook of lust,[386] he longs [now] for liberation. Turning away from the female form, he no longer gives rise to passion (情) and naturally crosses over the sea of sexual desire, all defilements driven away, like a school of fish chased into the depths. Ignorance,

383. "Mad flowers" (狂華) seems to mean a false perception. Indian Buddhist texts often compare misperceptions to the "flowers" seen by someone with defective eyes. In Chinese Buddhist literature, however, the term "mad flowers" usually points to a different idea: a flower that fails to bear fruit, symbolizing a practice that outwardly seems correct but does not lead to true benefit (*Xiu xing dao di jing*, T.606:15.195c26–29; *Zhu jing yao ji*, T.2123:54.90c25–26 [citing a passage from the *Da zhi du lun* seemingly not found in its extant versions]; *Chu yao jing*, T.212:4.613c26–27). However, "mad flowers" *does* mean a deluded perception in some of the Contemplation Scriptures (*GFSMH*, T.643:15.674c23–27), another example of the close connection between those texts and the *Chan Essentials*.

384. 此諸婬欲諸色情態. I take *qingtai* 情態 as "thing," but this word can also mean the emotions of affection and love, in which case the two clauses would be synonymous.

385. 青[>清].

386. "Hook of lust" (色鉤) could also be construed as "hook of material form," as *se* 色 can mean both matter (*rūpa*) in general and objects of sexual desire in particular.

aging, and death are burned away by the fire of wisdom. He contemplates material forms as being dirty, vile, and impure, like illusions that never cease.[387] Forever parting from the stain of lust, he is no longer ensnared by material forms.

[2.20.19] [Conclusion]

The Buddha said to Ānanda: "Monks, nuns, laymen, or laywomen in whom lust is prominent must first be instructed to contemplate the Buddha so as to eliminate sin. Only after this should they be further instructed to fix their thoughts and focus the mind. Focusing the mind means counting the breath. This method of counting the breath is the antidote for lust. It is the practice carried out by the [buddhas], the supreme kings of the Dharma. You must carefully preserve it. Do not forget it."

When this meditation is complete, it is called the accomplishment of contemplation number twenty, the breath-counting contemplation.

When Ānanda, Nandi the Meditator, and all the other monks heard what the Buddha said, they joyfully undertook to carry it out.

[3] [PANTHAKA]

[3.0] [Introduction]

[3.0.1] [Panthaka]

Thus have I heard. Once, the Buddha was dwelling in Śrāvasti. On a preaching round, he arrived at the village of Tāla[388] and, together with one thousand two hundred fifty monks, entered it to beg for alms. On his way back from the alms round, he stopped beneath a tree. He washed his feet, gathered up his robes and bowl, spread out his sitting cloth, and sat with legs crossed.

At that time there was a monk named Kātyāyana in the assembly. He had a disciple named Panthaka, who had been a monk for a long time. Panthaka had been reciting a single verse for [258c] eight hundred days but had been unable to do so smoothly.[389] Throughout the day and night he chanted: "Cease evil, practice good, and cultivate heedfulness."[390] All he chanted was

387. 猶如幻惑無有暫停. Translation tentative. P, Sgz, and Kg read 如色幻幻惑無有暫停.

388. *Tāla* (*duoluo* 多羅), in Chinese translations of Indian Buddhist literature, is usually the name of a kind of tree.

389. In the traditional narratives concerning him (see Appendix 4), Panthaka is unable to memorize a verse given to him by his elder brother. This seems also to be the problem here, as he (tries to) recite the verse but cannot do so "smoothly" (通利).

390. 止惡行善修不放逸. Or: "cease evil, practice good, and be diligent in your cultivation." These lines are obviously modeled on the well-known stanzas (sometimes said to encapsulate the teachings of the Buddha): "the avoidance of all evil; the undertaking of good; the cleansing of one's mind; this is the teaching of the buddhas" (Norman 1997, 28, with slight modifications).

these words, but he had not been able to fully grasp them. The venerable Kātyāyana exerted all his skill to instruct his disciple but was unable to get him to fully grasp this verse.

Kātyāyana went to the Buddha and made reverence, circled him three times, and addressed him as follows: "The Tathāgata's appearance in the world has benefited many beings. You have brought benefit and peace to gods and humans, and have universally liberated everyone. Only my disciple has yet to receive your blessings. May you, honored by the gods, enlighten (開悟) him for me and cause him to attain liberation."

[3.0.2] [Panthaka's Past Life]

The Buddha said to Kātyāyana: "Listen carefully, listen carefully. Ponder this well. I, the Tathāgata, will now tell you of what happened long ago in the past." Kātyāyana said: "World-honored One, I do so wish to hear."

The Buddha said to Kātyāyana: "Ninety-one eons ago there was a buddha, a World-honored One, named Vipaśyin, a Thus-come One, Worthy of Offerings, Of Right and Universal Knowledge, Perfect in Conduct and Wisdom, Well-gone, Knower of the World, Unsurpassed One, Tamer of Men, Teacher of Gods and Humans, Buddha, World-honored One.

"This buddha appeared in the world, and when he had finished teaching living beings and liberating people he passed into the extinction of *parinirvāṇa*.[391] After he had passed into extinction, there was a certain monk who was intelligent, knowledgeable, and able to recite the entire Buddhist canon. But he was proud and haughty, indulgent and heedless. He had students, but he was unwilling to teach them. He was stubbornly arrogant and failed to practice correct mindfulness (不修正念).

"After death, this monk fell into a dark, black hell. For ninety eons he remained perpetually in that dark place, ignorant and without knowledge. But because of the merit of having been a monk in the past, he was eventually able to escape from hell and be reborn in heaven. Though he was born in heaven, the light of the heavenly palaces and objects was darkened and obscured, inferior to all other heavens. [Because of the merit of] reciting the Buddhist canon [in a past life], when his life in heaven ended he was reborn here on Jambudvīpa during the age of a buddha. But because of having been arrogant in the past, though he has met the Buddha he is unable to understand the Dharma. I will now preach for him a skillful method for fixing his thoughts [in meditation]."

[3.0.3] [Kātyāyana Entreats the Buddha]

Then Kātyāyana said to the Buddha: "World-honored One, for the sake of this foolish monk Panthaka, as well as all sentient beings of the future who

391. 於般涅槃而取滅度. See 2.19.1.12, where this same formula is worded slightly differently.

are foolishly ignorant and agitated in mind (愚癡亂想眾生), please teach the method of correct contemplation (正觀法)."

[3.21] [Contemplation Twenty-One: Heat]

[3.21.1] [The Buddha Teaches Panthaka]

The Buddha said to Panthaka: "From today onward you must always dwell in a quiet place, concentrate your mind, sit upright, fold your hands and close your eyes, and keep control over your body, speech, and mind. Do not be heedless. It was because of your heedlessness that you suffered bitter torment for many eons. Follow my words and carefully contemplate all *dharmas*."

Panthaka did what the Buddha said, sitting upright and fixing his mind.

[3.21.2] [The Bloated Corpse]

The Buddha said to Panthaka: Without shifting your mind to anything else, you should[392] now carefully contemplate the bone in the large toe of your [right] foot. Make a swelling gradually appear on top of the bone. Then cause it to swell up further [259a]. Next use your mind to make the swelling gradually bigger until it is the size of a bean. Next[393] use your mind to make the swelling rot away and the flesh split open[394] with yellow pus flowing out. Within the yellow pus, blood flows profusely. When the flesh has entirely rotted away from that single bone, you will see only the bone of the right toe, white like *ke*-jade or snow.

When you see this one bone in this manner, gradually expand from the right foot until half the body swells up and rots away, with yellow pus leaking and blood flowing profusely. Make the skin and flesh of half the body split apart, with only the pure, shining white bones remaining. Seeing half the body in this way, now see the entire body swell up and rot away while discharging horrible pus and an outflow of blood mixed[395] with worms crawling and disporting in it. The various things of this sort are as has been described earlier.[396]

[3.21.3] [Multiple Corpses and the Shifting Meditation]

Having contemplated and then seen one [such bloated corpse and skeleton], next see two. Seeing two, go on to see three . . . four . . . five. Seeing five, continue until you see ten. Seeing ten, gradually expand your mind until you see a roomful. And seeing a roomful, continue until you see the entire world full of them.

When you see the entire world full of skeletons, collect [your mind] if

392. 應當. W and K¹ both read 當應.
393. 彼[>復, K¹, K, P, S, Q, Y, Sgz, Kg, W]. The Taishō is presumably a misprint.
394. 兩披. For a similar expression, see 1.1.3.
395. 雄[>雜, P, Q, Sgz, Kg].
396. I presume this refers to the first sutra (1.1.3 and passim).

it becomes too expansive[397] and return it to the contemplation of a single bone as before. After this, shift your meditation (移想) by fixing your thoughts and carefully contemplating the tip of your nose. When you contemplate the tip of your nose, your mind will cease being distracted. When it is no longer distracted, contemplate the bones as before.

[3.21.4] [Impure by Way of Origins]

Next you must imagine that the flesh and skin of your body were created by the conjoining of impure essential *qi* (不淨精氣) when your father and mother coupled. A body such as this is "impure by way of its origins."[398]

[3.21.5] [The Giant Tooth]

Next you must be instructed[399] to fix your thoughts and contemplate your teeth [as follows]: "In the human body, only the teeth are white. My bones are white like these teeth."

When your power of imagination is sharpened, you will see your teeth grow as large as your body.[400]

[3.21.6] [The Forehead and the Nine Meditations]

Then you must shift your meditation and again contemplate your forehead, making the bone in your forehead white like *ke*-jade or snow.

If it does not become white, you must further change your contemplation (易觀) and perform the nine meditations [on the decaying corpse]. This is explained in detail [in the instructions for] the contemplation method of the nine meditations.[401]

When performing this contemplation, those of dull faculties will require between one and three months of careful contemplation before they are able to see [the bone in the forehead]. Those of sharp faculties will see it as soon as they have brought it to mind (一念即見).

[3.21.7] [The Coccyx and the Meditation on Love]

When you have seen these things, you must be further instructed to contemplate the coccyx. Once you see this, then you must contemplate the multicolored skeletons as before.[402]

If this is unsuccessful, you must be further instructed in the contempla-

397. See, similarly, 2.19.1.8.

398. For discussion of this concept, see 1.4.5, n. 70.

399. 復當次教. On the problem of voicing here (the Buddha *is* instructing Panthaka, making the word "instruct" redundant), see "The *Chan Essentials* and the *Five Gates*" in chap. 4.

400. 身體. Kg reads 我體 (my body); if this is not an error, it is perhaps a trace of the hypothesized original, meditation-manual format. See "The *Chan Essentials* and the *Five Gates*" in chap. 4.

401. This seems to refer the reader to another text or source. A similar reference occurs in 3.21.7 below.

402. This may refer back to 2.20.13, or perhaps to the first sutra (e.g., 1.12.2).

tion of love (慈心觀). The contemplation of love is explained in detail [in the section concerning] the *samādhi* of love.

[3.21.8] [Elimination of Other Visions]

When you have learned the contemplation of love, you must be instructed to contemplate the white bones again. If you see other things [apart from the bones], under no circumstances should you follow after them. Merely make the mind clear, so that you see your white skeleton, [white] as a snow-covered mountain.

If you see other things, rouse your mind and eliminate them with this thought: "The Buddha has instructed me to contemplate the bones. Why do these other meditative visions (餘想境界) appear? I must now single-mindedly contemplate the bones."

When you [259b] see the white bones, make the mind calm and clear, free of thoughts of external things. You will see the entire universe filled with skeletons. After you have seen these skeletons, they disappear one by one. Then contemplate your skeleton[403] as before.

[3.21.9] [Narrative Interlude]

[3.21.9.1] [Panthaka Becomes an Arhat]

When Panthaka heard what the Buddha said, he carefully contemplated [as instructed]. His mind clear and free of distraction, he immediately became an arhat, possessed of the three knowledges and six powers and fully endowed with the eight deliverances. He was able to perfectly recollect, without any mistakes, the scriptures he had memorized in his past life.[404]

Thus it was that at this time, because of the foolish, puffed-up monk Panthaka, the World-honored One instituted this pure method for the contemplation of the white bones.[405]

[3.21.9.2] [Verses by the Buddha in Praise of Meditation]

The Buddha then said to Kātyāyana: "Even this foolish monk Panthaka has, by fixing his thoughts, become an arhat. How much more so should a wise person cultivate Buddhist meditation!"

The World-honored One, having seen [Panthaka's attainment of arhatship], then spoke the following verse:

Trance is the ambrosial method,
the concentrated mind destroys all evil.
When wisdom exterminates foolish ignorance,
one is never reborn again.

403. 苦[>骨]. Emendation tentative, but the original reading does not fit the context. The error would have been graphic, not phonetic (Schuessler 2009, 1–1 and 31–1).

404. This sudden recollection of previously memorized texts recalls the original Panthaka narratives (see Appendix 4), where his faulty memory was more explicitly at issue.

405. The implication seems to be that this was the first occasion when the Buddha taught this particular method of meditation; see, similarly, 1.1.10.

Even the foolishly ignorant Panthaka
by concentrating his mind reached attainment.
All the more should the wise
diligently fix their thoughts!

[3.21.9.3] [Conclusion of Panthaka's Story]

The World-honored One then said to Kātyāyana and commanded Ānanda: You must now preserve these words of mine, and use this wondrous teaching to universally save the host of living beings. If in future ages there are foolish, ignorant, haughty, arrogant, evil (邪惡) sentient beings who wish to practice seated meditation (坐禪), they must begin with the contemplation method of Kauṣṭhilananda, then proceed to the method of contemplating the image taught to Nandi the Meditator, and finally they must learn this contemplation method used by the monk Panthaka.

[3.21.10] [The Stage of Heat]

Next, [the practitioner][406] should contemplate his body and see the white bones, white like *ke*-jade or snow. The skeletons[407] then reenter his body, and the glowing light of the white bones entirely disappears.

Seeing this, the practitioner suddenly feels joyous and serene in mind. When he emerges from trance, the crown of his head feels warm, and the pores of his body constantly emit a pleasant scent. Whether in trance or not he constantly hears the wondrous Dharma.

Continuing [his meditation], he further perceives (見) his body becoming warm, and he feels joyful and happy. His countenance appears serene. He needs but little sleep, and his body is free of all pain or trouble.

Having attained this stage of "heat," he constantly feels warmth in his belly and he is perpetually joyful.

People in later ages who wish to learn Buddhist meditation [should] begin with the contemplation of impurity and then proceed to this method. When this contemplation has been obtained, it is called the "stage of heat" (和暖法).[408]

[3.21.11] [Conclusion][409]

[3.21.11.1] [Naming and Entrustment]

The Buddha said to Ānanda: "After I have passed into extinction, monks, nuns, laymen, or laywomen who, during the defiled age [259c], wish to learn absorption and reflection (正受思惟) should begin by fixing their thoughts

---

406. From this point forward the Buddha no longer addresses Panthaka.

407. 時<諸, K[1], K, P, Q, Sgz, Kg>. The Taishō is presumably a misprint.

408. "Heat," first of the four *nirvedha-bhāgīyas*; see p. 23.

409. Section 3.21.11 seems to restate 3.21.10 while framing it more explicitly as words spoken by the Buddha. Possibly this is another trace of the compilation process; see "The *Chan Essentials* and the *Five Gates*" in chap. 4.

and contemplating impurity, and then proceed to this method. This is called the stage of heat."

When one obtains this stage, it is called the completion of contemplation number twenty-one, the contemplation leading to the stage of heat.

The Buddha said to Ānanda: "You must preserve this [teaching concerning] the stage of heat that Kātyāyana has inquired about. Do not forget it."

[3.21.11.2] [Further Signs of the Stage of Heat]

Ānanda then said to the Buddha: "World-honored One, for those sentient beings who uphold this *samādhi* in the future and become firmly established in mental concentration, how can they know with assurance that they have attained the stage of heat?"

The Buddha said to Ānanda: If one who has carefully contemplated all the signs of the defilements,[410] [and has proceeded] from the initial meditation on impurity to this method here, senses warmth throughout his body and mind, with each thought following upon the next without any mental vexation and with a countenance always peaceful and happy, then this is known as the stage of heat.

[3.22] [Contemplation Twenty-Two: Summit]

[3.22.1] [The Flame Emerging from the Brain]

Again, Ānanda, when the practitioner has attained the stage of heat he must be taught to fix his thoughts on his bones, where white light appears. When he sees this white light, the bones themselves scatter and disappear. If other visions appear before him, he must restrain his mind and return it to the contemplation of the white light. He then sees many white lights growing gradually larger, filling the world. When he contemplates his own body, the light becomes still brighter and intensely pure, more brilliant than a snow-covered mountain or even crystal, while his skeleton falls apart in disarray.

When he performs this contemplation, he must keep his mind concentrated for a long time. When his concentration persists, he will see a bright light on the top of his head, like a flame emerging from the brain.

[3.22.2] [The Stage Called Summit]

The Buddha said to Ānanda: If he sees this, he must be further instructed to review his body from head to foot and back fourteen times.

When he has finished this contemplation, he will always see fire emerging from the crown of his head, whether in trance or not, like the light of pure gold. The pores of his body will also emit a golden light, like a shower of gold dust, and his body and mind will feel peaceful and happy. The purple-gold light will then reenter his body through the crown of his head.

---

410. "Signs of the defilements" (結使相) recalls the name of the twelfth contemplation (1.12.8), the "confirmatory vision of the ninety-eight defilements" (九十八使境界).

This stage is called summit. A practitioner who attains this contemplation has attained the summit contemplation.

[3.22.3] [Conclusion]

The Buddha said to Ānanda: "You must preserve this contemplation leading to the stage named summit[411] and preach it extensively for all sentient beings in the future." When Ānanda heard what the Buddha said, he joyfully undertook to carry it out.

When one attains this contemplation, it is called the completion of the stage named summit, contemplation number twenty-two.[412]

[3.23] [Contemplation Twenty-Three: Accessory to the Stage Called Summit]

[3.23.1] [The Pile of Windblown Snow]

The Buddha said to Ānanda: When this meditation is complete, the practitioner must be further instructed to fix his thoughts and contemplate the white bones. He must make the scattered bones[413] collect in one place, in a pile like windblown snow, white like a snow-covered mountain. If he sees this, [it means] he will be able to easily attain the path.

However, if he has violated the precepts, either in this life or a past life, the pile of bones will appear like ash or dirt instead, or he will see various strange creatures[414] on the surface of the pile. In that case he must again repent by [260a] confessing his transgressions (說己過) to a wise person.[415]

After repenting, he will see an intense white light surrounding the pile of bones and reaching up into the formless realms. Whether in trance or not, he will feel constant ease and happiness, his former desires gradually diminishing.[416]

[3.23.2] [Fire Burns Away Impurities]

Next he must again contemplate, and review[417] as before the pus discharging from his nine orifices as well as the impure things [within his body]. He must make all this very clear, with no hesitation or regret in his mind.

---

411. 頂觀[>法]法[>觀], following P, S, Q, Y, Sgz, Kg.

412. I punctuate: 第二十二觀，頂法.

413. The "scattered bones" seems to refer back to 3.22.1.

414. 黑[>異, P, S, Q, Y, Sgz, Kg]物, supported by the *Five Gates* parallel (*WMCJ*, T.619:15.328a7).

415. On the "wise person" (智者), see 1.14.5, n. 163.

416. As discussed in chap. 4, the parallel passages here in the *Five Gates* are usually much shorter. In this line, however, they are more detailed: the meditator is instructed to imagine having sexual intercourse with a former lover and the transformation of this imagined scene into one of impure pus and blood is a sign that the meditator's defilements have been weakened (*WMCJ*, T.619:15.328a6–10). A trace of this scene may remain in 3.23.2, which says that the meditator must review the impure body (his own?) without "hesitation or regret" (疑悔). This sentiment is somewhat out of place in the *Chan Essentials* as it stands. But it would fit well if the "impure body" in question was that of the meditator's former lover, as in the *Five Gates*.

417. "Review" (覆尋), meaning repeat the previous meditation exercise, is similarly used in 3.29.4.

Then as before flames will arise from between his bones, burning away all the impurities. When the impurities are gone, a golden radiance streams from his body and reenters it through the crown of the head. When the light enters his head, he feels an incomparable rapture.

[3.23.3] [Conclusion]

When this contemplation has been obtained, it is called the accomplishment of contemplation number twenty-three, the method that is "accessory to the stage called summit."[418]

[3.24] [Contemplation Twenty-Four: Fire and Non-self]

[3.24.1] [Layered Skin]

Next the practitioner must again be instructed to fix his thoughts, steady his mind, and then contemplate his own body as a bundle of brush.[419] Even when he emerges from trance, he sees his body as the trunk of a plantain tree, as [nothing but] layer upon layer of skin. He must now contemplate this body, which is like plantain leaves [wrapped about each other with no core]. Without bones, it is like a sack of skin filled with air. Whether in trance or not, he constantly sees this.

[3.24.2] [Restorative Medicine]

If his body should become weak, he must then be instructed to contemplate his body gathered back together like a bundle of dry brush. He now sees his body as firm and strong. Seeing it firm and strong, he must consume butter and eat and drink sufficiently.

After this, when he contemplates his body, it again resembles an empty sack. A flame appears inside and burns it up entirely. When his body has been completely consumed, he will constantly see the light of this fire whenever he enters trance.

[3.24.3] [The Fire Meditation]

Having contemplated and then come to see this fire, he will see many fires all around. Whether in trance or not, his body feels hot, like fire. He sees fire emerging from his joints, and also from his pores.

When he emerges from trance, he sees his own body as a great mass of fire, and it becomes unbearably hot. Great mountains of fire come from the four directions and fuse together in front of the practitioner. He sees his own body merging with this fire. This is called the meditation on fire.

---

418. The translation "accessory to the stage called summit" (助頂法) is little more than a guess. I know of no traditional stage of the path to which this would correspond. The Vaibhāṣikas, however, did posit many sublevels for each of the four *nirvedha-bhāgīyas* (Buswell 1997, 594); perhaps something similar is being referenced here.

419. "Brush" (草) is, more precisely, nonwoody plant matter. This recalls the traditional image "like the [pithless] trunk of a plantain tree," meaning emptiness or non-self.

[3.24.4] [Non-self]

Next he must make the fire incinerate his body entirely. While the fire is incinerating his body, he contemplates his body in trance but [sees] no body (觀身無身)—he only sees its incineration by the fire. When it has been entirely incinerated, he suddenly knows that he has no self and that the defilements have likewise been incinerated.[420] [The many different visions possible at this moment] cannot all be described.[421]

[3.24.5] [Conclusion]

This is the meditation on fire, the meditation on the true fire element, and the accomplishment of contemplation number twenty-four, the contemplation of the fire element.

The Buddha said to Ānanda: "You must preserve this contemplation of the fire element and non-self. This contemplation of the fire element is called the fire of wisdom that burns up the afflictions. You must preserve it well and preach it widely for all sentient beings of the future."

When Ānanda heard what the Buddha said, he joyfully undertook to carry it out.

[3.25] [Contemplation Twenty-Five: Fire]

[3.25.1] [The Non-Self of the Fire Element]

The Buddha said to Ānanda: When the practitioner has attained the contemplation of the fire element, he must [260b] again be instructed to fix his thoughts and reflect. Fixing his thoughts on the tip of his nose, he again contemplates the fire [and reflects]: "From where does it arise?"

In contemplating the fire, he contemplates that his own body is entirely without self. When he sees there is no self,[422] the fire spontaneously goes out.

He must think further: "My body is without self, and the four elements have no master. The defilements, as well as the roots of the defilements, arise because of error, and error itself is empty (顛倒亦空). How, then, amid empty *dharma*s could I brazenly see the fire of my body?"

Contemplating in this way, he is unable to find either the fire or the self. This is called the contemplation of the non-self of the fire element.

[3.25.2] [Conclusion]

The Buddha said to Ānanda: "You must preserve this contemplation of the fire element, explaining and preaching it widely for all sentient beings of the future." When Ānanda heard what the Buddha said, he joyfully undertook to carry it out.

---

420. 一切結使皆悉同然. I take *ran* 然 as a full verb ("burn"), in accord with the next paragraph which describes this exercise as one that "burns up the afflictions" (燒諸煩惱).

421. See, similarly, 1.12.7, 1.18.20.3, 3.27.5, and 3.30.6.

422. 既無[>見]有[>無]我, following P, S, Q, Y, Sgz, Kg.

This is called the accomplishment of contemplation number twenty-five.[423]

[3.26] [Contemplation Twenty-Six: The Stream-Enterer]

[3.26.1] [Extinction of the Fire]

The Buddha said to Ānanda: I[424] see that when the fire goes out, it goes out beginning at the tip of the nose and then goes out all at once in the rest of the body. Internally, the heart-fire and the eighty-eight defilements[425] are all extinguished as well, and [the practitioner's] body feels pure, cool, balanced, and harmonized within. He deeply realizes and sees with perfect clarity that there definitely is no self. Whether in trance or not, he always knows that within the body there is no self.

This is called the accomplishment of the contemplation of the extinction [of the view of] non-self.[426]

[3.26.2] [Consecration]

The Buddha said to Ānanda: The practitioner must now again be instructed in the method of meditative consecration.[427] To be consecrated in meditation, he must see his own body as a beam of beryl light that transcends the triple world. He then sees a true buddha (真佛)[428] appear, who pours a pitcher of water onto his head, filling his body from the torso to his limbs. The water flows out through his navel onto the ground as the buddha continues to pour. When the buddha is finished pouring, he disappears. The water that has emerged from his navel is like beryl, its color resembling the glow of purple beryl. The cloud of its light fills the entire universe.

When all the water is out, the practitioner should be instructed to fix his thoughts, [thinking]: "May the World-honored Buddha again anoint my head!"

Suddenly he sees his own body becoming ethereal (身如氣), expanding until it passes beyond the limits of the triple world. He sees water entering

---

423. Unusually, contemplation twenty-five is not given a name.

424. On the problematic voicing here, see chap. 4, p. 9.

425. According to Sarvāstivāda doctrine, stream-entry destroys eighty-eight of the ninety-eight defilements (*Apitan ba jiandu lun*, T.1543:26.811a2–3; *DZDL*, T.1509:25.300c25–27). This takes symbolic form below with the vision of the eighty-eight-headed snake (3.26.16).

426. 滅無我觀. Translation tentative. In 3.24.4, fire engulfed the meditator's body and he knew there was no self. In 3.25.1, the analysis of non-self extends to the fire (i.e., to the level of *dharmas*), now also seen as having no "self." In the present passage, the fire too goes out. Perhaps this means that even the view of non-self is now abandoned. I tentatively adopt this reading in the translation, though it may impute an excessively Madhyamaka perspective. More speculatively, "contemplation of the extinction [of the view of] non-self" (滅無我觀) might be a corruption of two originally distinct titles similar to those given in 3.27.5 (for the water element), where both the "meditation on the extinction of the water element" (滅水大想) and the "true contemplation of non-self" (真無我觀) are discussed.

427. Literally, the "method of contemplating [undergoing a] consecration" (觀灌頂法).

428. See 2.19.2.2 and "The Bodies of the Buddha" in chap. 3.

through the crown of his head and his body solidifying until it is equal to the water and pervades it completely.

He then sees his navel as a lotus flower, from which a live spring bubbles forth, the water overflowing from his body and encircling it like a pond with multiple lotus flowers, each shining with a seven-colored light.[429] With a pleasing voice like that of Brahmā himself, each light preaches the teachings of suffering, emptiness, impermanence, and non-self.

[3.26.3] [The Beryl Vase]

When these signs have appeared, [the meditator] must again be instructed to fold his hands, close his eyes, and sit upright with a concentrated mind. Beginning from the top of his head, he should contemplate the inside of his body. He sees no trace of any bones.[430] Whether in trance or not, he sees his own body as a beryl vase.

[3.26.4] [The Poisonous Dragons]

Now he must arouse his thoughts and imagine[431] [260c] the poisonous dragons of the four elements of his heart. As if looking through an expanded pore of his body, he peers within his heart, where there are six dragons.[432] Each dragon has six heads, and each head spews a fiery torrent of poison that fills the pond [around the practitioner]. The light from each lotus flower flows into the crown of the dragons' heads, and as it enters their heads, the dragons' poison dissipates and their bodies fill with water.

When this meditation is complete, it is called the contemplation of the seven flowers of awakening.[433] Although he sees these signs,[434] he has not yet fully reached the deep levels of trance.

[3.26.5] [Equilibrium of the Four Elements]

He must again be instructed to count his breaths as described before, making his mind balanced, serene, and free of thought.

When this meditation is complete, it is called the contemplation of the equilibrium of the four elements.

---

429. Here the text reads as if each lotus flower has a seven-colored light; below, there are clearly just seven lotus flowers (3.26.7).

430. 想[>相].

431. 使[>作]. The pattern 作 X 想 is common throughout the text.

432. There is some confusion here as to whether there are four or six dragons (corresponding perhaps to the four-element versus six-element systems).

433. This must denote the so-called seven limbs of awakening (*sapta-bodhyaṅga*), which are mentioned explicitly below (3.26.6) and often compared to flowers (*Da bannihuan jing*, T.376:12.870b7–10). See also *Methods for Curing* 1.4.3.

434. 想[>相].

[3.26.6] [Entrustment of the Contemplation of the Seven Thoughts]

The Buddha said to Ānanda: "You must preserve these contemplations of the seven thoughts of awakening[435] and the equilibrium of the four great elements. Do not forget them. Explain them extensively for all sentient beings of the future. Widely expound them to the four groups of Buddhist followers."

When Ānanda heard what the Buddha said, he joyfully undertook to carry it out.

[3.26.7] [Beheading the Dragons]

The practitioner should again be instructed to fix his thoughts, concentrate his mind, and carefully contemplate the water element, which appears within his pores and flows out from his body. Whether in trance or not, he sees his body as a pond of green water, [pure] as a spring on a mountain peak that emerges from the peak and then flows back within it.[436] He sees seven flowers, their colors those of pure adamant, and they radiate a golden light, within which is an adamantine man holding a sharp sword who beheads the six dragons.

The practitioner sees fire emerging from the mouths of the dragons. The fire burns throughout his body, drying up all the water and then going out. When both fire and water have disappeared, he sees his own body becoming gradually whiter until it is adamantine. Whether in trance or not, his mind feels happy and joyful, as one does when anointed with butter. His body and mind feel joyously peaceful, as one would eating pure ghee.

[3.26.8] [External Bodies: Feeding the Hungry Spirits]

Again he must be instructed to fix his thoughts and contemplate [the bodies] of others. Contemplating external objects, because he has directed his imagination outward he suddenly sees a tree on which rare sweet fruit is growing. There are four fruits, shining with four kinds of light,[437] and this fruit tree, like a tree of beryl, spreads over everything.

Seeing this tree, he sees sentient beings of various kinds[438] come before him begging for food, oppressed by the fires of hunger.

Seeing them, he rejoices and takes pity on them, generating the mind

435. "Seven thoughts of awakening" (七覺意) was the standard pre-Kumārajīva translation of *sapta-bodhyaṅga*. It was largely abandoned in post-fourth-century translations.

436. This image recalls the canonical pericope that likens the bliss that pervades the body during the second *dhyāna* to a cool fount of water welling up within a lake with no inflows (Ñāṇamoli and Bodhi 1995, 368). In some early Chinese sources, the image, as here, is of a pool or spring on a mountaintop (see, e.g., *Liu du ji jing*, T.152:39b1–5).

437. Below (3.26.12) it becomes clear that these correspond to the "fruits" of the path up to arhatship.

438. Literally, "born in the four manners" (from egg, womb, moisture, or transformation).

of love. He looks upon these beings who beg from him as he would his own parents undergoing great torment, thinking: "How can I save them?"

With this thought, he contemplates his own body, and as before it turns into pus and blood. Going further, he turns it into chunks of meat, which he gives to the hungry beings. These hungry ghosts (餓鬼) rush forward madly to eat it. Once they have eaten, they are satisfied and disperse.[439]

[3.26.9] [Self and Other Together: More Feeding]

[261a] Then the practitioner must contemplate both his own body and the bodies of others[440] [with this thought]: "My own body and the bodies of others arise from error. In truth they are not the abode of a self or of selves. If either had a self, how would it be possible for me to suddenly see these hungry ghosts coming before me?"[441]

He then sees innumerable hungry ghosts with extremely large bodies. Uncountably many, they have heads as large as giant boulders, and throats as thin as strands of silk hair.[442] Oppressed by the fires of hunger, they cry out, begging for food.

Seeing this, the practitioner must give rise to a loving mind and feed his body to these ghosts. They consume it and become satisfied. When he has seen this, he should again be instructed to contemplate the many hungry ghosts. He sees them surrounding his body on all sides. As before, he feeds his body to the hungry ghosts.

When he has seen this, he should again be instructed to settle his body and concentrate his mind. He must contemplate his own body as a heap of impurities. When he undertakes this contemplation, he immediately sees the bloody, pus-filled flesh of his body rot away piece by piece, forming a pile on the ground before him. He sees the many beings[443] rush forward and eat it.

When he has seen this, he must again contemplate that his own body is born of suffering, exists from suffering, and is by nature perishable, soon to decompose and be eaten by hungry ghosts.

---

439. End of scroll 2 (in the three-scroll editions) and *Tempyō Chan Essentials 4*.

440. The order here follows the format of the canonical *smṛtyupasthāna* sutras, with the meditator first contemplating his own body, then the bodies of others, then both together.

441. The logic of this statement is elusive.

442. "Hungry ghosts" (*preta*) are often depicted with large bellies but thin necks and thus perpetually insatiable. That their *heads* are especially large is a less common, but not unheard of image in Indian Buddhist literature (see, e.g., Stuart 2015, 408–409). The image of hungry ghosts with heads "as large as boulders" would become widely used in later Chinese Buddhism and appears in many apocryphal scriptures (*Da fang deng hua yan shi e pin jing*, T.2875:85.1360b28–c1; *Zhai fa qing jing*, T.2900:85.1431c9–10; this latter text was much cited by Chinese authors for its depiction of hungry ghosts—see *Yulanben jing shu*, T.1792:39.509a3–4).

443. I presume these "beings" (眾生) are the aforementioned hungry ghosts. The corresponding passages in the *Five Gates* similarly speak first of hungry ghosts, then "beings," leaving unclear the relationship between the two (*WMCJ*, T.619:15.328a27–b2).

When he has imagined[444] this, he sees a blazing fire appear within his heart. Igniting the surface of the pond, it completely incinerates the lotus flowers, the hungry ghosts in their multitude of horrible forms, and the water of the pond itself.

[3.26.10] [The Pond of Milk]

When he has seen this, he must again be instructed to carefully contemplate his own body. [He sees it] now restored to its former state.[445] Again contemplating his body, he sees within each of his pores, because of his loving mind, the blood transforming into milk and flowing out onto the ground to form a pond of milk. He sees the hungry ghosts come to the edge of the pond, but because of their sins from previous lives, they are unable to drink the milk. His mind full of love, he looks upon the ghosts as his children and wishes that they might drink. But because of their sins, the milk instantly transforms into pus.[446]

Again he must give rise to a loving mind, and by its power milk gushes forth from his pores, several magnitudes more than before. He thinks: "These hungry ghosts are oppressed by the pain of hunger. Why won't they come forward and drink?"

The hungry ghosts, with enormous bodies dozens of *yojana*s tall and footsteps resounding like five hundred chariots, come before the practitioner moaning "Hungry! Hungry!"

The practitioner, his [261b] mind full of love, gives them milk to drink. When the hungry ghosts drink, the milk becomes pus as soon as it touches their lips. But even though it is pus, owing to the power of the practitioner's loving mind, the hungry ghosts are immediately satisfied.[447]

[3.26.11] [The Beryl Pool]

When he has seen the ghosts satisfied, he contemplates his own body and immediately sees fire shooting out from the soles of his feet, completely incinerating the beings[448] and the various trees.

---

444. 相[>想, Kg].

445. 如前完具身體平復. Compare this with the corresponding passage in the *Five Gates:* "I see that the sentient beings, the water of the pool, and my own body are all restored to their former state." 我見眾生及池中水己身悉平復如故。(*WMCJ*, T.619:15.328b6).

446. 以鬼罪故，乳變成膿，斯須之間. My translation is influenced by the corresponding passage in the *Five Gates:* "Instruct [the practitioner] in the cultivation of love. He says: '*Instantly* my milk transforms into pus, and the beings, oppressed by hunger, consume it.' " 教以慈心觀。若言：我須臾之間，乳化為膿，眾生飢急便食之。(*WMCJ*, T.619:15.328b8–10).

447. Normally, food touched by hungry ghosts (*preta*) becomes inedible, such that they can eat only by way of the power of the Buddha, through the intermediary of the Sangha. Here the meditator appears to take on this role himself. This recalls the story of Maudgalyāyana, who used his meditation-derived power to save his mother, who had been reborn among the hungry ghosts; the story became the origin myth for Buddhist hungry ghost feeding rituals (Teiser 1988, 140–167).

448. These "beings," as above, are presumably the hungry ghosts.

If he sees any strange things at that moment, he must again fix his thoughts and contemplate his body, making his mind unmoving, tranquil, and free of thoughts (無念). When he is free of thoughts, he should make the following vow (誓願): "May I not be reborn again![449] May I not undergo any future existence! May I take no pleasure in the world!"

After making this vow, he sees the ground before him turn to beryl. He sees golden water beneath the beryl ground and his own body as beryl-like as the ground and the same color as the water.[450] The water is warm, and a tree is growing in it, a tree of seven treasures. Its branches and leaves give cooling shade, and on it are four fruits chiming sermons on suffering, emptiness, impermanence, and non-self.

When the practitioner hears these sounds, he suddenly sees himself sinking into the water and moving toward the tree. Carefully contemplating his body, he sees water emerging from the crown of his head and filling the beryl pool.

[3.26.12] [The Fruits on the Tree]

Suddenly fire appears again, and within it is a beryl-like wind. The practitioner sees that the crown of his head is hard and strong. From the crown of his head down to his feet [his body is hard] like adamant.[451] The fire appears again, burning up the adamant and vaporizing the water.

Again he contemplates his body [as follows]: "In the pool that I previously saw in my body,[452] a tree suddenly appeared with branches, leaves, and fruit chiming the pure teachings of suffering, emptiness, impermanence, and non-self. The wondrous fruits have a beautiful sound and are replete with fragrance and taste. I should eat them now."

After he has performed this meditation, he climbs the tree to take the fruit and eat it. He first takes but a single fruit and finds its flavor incomparably sweet and delicious. When he has eaten the fruit, he sees the tree wither but the other three fruits still shine brightly. When he has eaten the fruit, his body and mind become tranquil, and he becomes free of both grief and joy.

[3.26.13] [Impermanence]

He now contemplates that his own consciousness is impermanent, that suffering arises from it, and that consciousness is indeed the fundamental cause of suffering. He contemplates consciousness as being like foam on water, never fixed even for an instant. The four elements have no master, the body is without a self, consciousness has no fixed abode, and all *dharma*s are like

449. 願後世[>不, P, S, Q, Y, Sgz, Kg]生.

450. The unusual grammatical pattern 與 X 正等, seemingly meaning "exactly equal to," occurs frequently in the Contemplation Scriptures (*Guan Puxian pusa guan jing*, T.277:9.390a3–4; *GFSMH*, T.643:15.657c5–6; 663a27).

451. 復見頂上{從頂}堅強<從頂>至乎脚足猶如金剛. Emendation tentative.

452. This presumably refers to the pool seen in 3.26.11.

this. Seven times seven, that is to say, forty-nine times he must carefully contemplate the impermanence of consciousness.

The practitioner then sees his own body as white like *ke*-jade or snow, all the bones connected together. Again he must be instructed to take his right hand and rub his body. His body becomes dirt, and the bones crumble[453] into powder on the ground.[454] Next he must be instructed to contemplate his body as being like air, coming into existence from a sequence of breaths, like a sack of air [filling and emptying] without cease.

[3.26.14] [Destruction of the Eighty-Eight-Headed Snakes]

Again he must be [261c] instructed to contemplate his own body further, and transform it into a white skeleton as before. Seeing the white skeleton, he contemplates his body falling apart into tiny specks of dirt as before, like powder sprinkled onto the ground. He now sees blue skeletons on the ground, and he contemplates crumbling the blue skeletons and sprinkling them on the ground as before. Again he contemplates his body as being made of blue dirt. The dirt becomes a skeleton, entirely black in color. He must crumble this skeleton as before and sprinkle it upon the ground.

Now he contemplates his body as being made of black dirt. He sees that within the black earth are four black snakes, their eyes a fiery red. The snakes draw near to the practitioner, spewing deadly poison at him. But the poison is unable to harm him, turning instead into a fire that starts to burn up the snakes themselves. Then a voice suddenly comes out of the sky, bellowing the teachings of suffering, emptiness, impermanence, and non-self.

When he sees this, each of the poisonous, eighty-eight-headed snakes is consumed by the fire.[455] Seeing this, he further sees water appearing in the sky and raining down on the poisonous snakes' bodies, extinguishing the fire. Their eighty-eight heads then vanish. When he emerges from trance, he feels peaceful, happy, tranquil, and serene.

[3.26.15] [Purification of the Heart]

Now the practitioner must be instructed again to contemplate his body and imagine[456] it as very large. He sees his body suddenly become very large and shine brightly, as impressive as a mountain made of the seven treasures, and he sees his own heart as a *maṇi* jewel. Now he must contemplate emptiness as before. Contemplating emptiness, he suddenly feels a joyful ease within his body, an incomparable bliss. The seven-treasure light of the previously [seen] lotus flowers[457] flows into his heart. It fills his *maṇi*-jewel heart ten times, which thereby fills with the seven colors of the seven limbs of

453. 末[>抹].

454. Translation tentative. The corresponding passage from the *Five Gates* is similar, but also not clear (*WMCJ*, T.619:15.328b20–22).

455. See 3.26.1, n. 425.

456. 無[>起]高大想. The usual manuscript form 无 is easily mistaken for 起.

457. See 3.26.2.

awakening. He contemplates that his body is empty and free of any distinguishing marks.[458]

At that moment, a light suddenly appears above his head like a golden cloud or a jeweled canopy, or like silver. It enters his body through the crown of the head and shields the light of his *maṇi*-jewel heart. Whether in trance or not, he always sees this. Seeing these things, he will naturally refrain from killing, stealing, fornication, wrong speech, or drinking liquor.[459]

[3.26.16] [Conclusion]

The Buddha said to Ānanda: After I have passed into extinction, when the four groups of disciples, that is to say, monks, nuns, laymen, or laywomen, perform this contemplation, it is to be known as the twenty-sixth correct contemplation.[460] It is also called attaining the path of the stream-enterer.

If someone attains this contemplation, its veracity must still be investigated. If one naturally keeps apart from the five evils,[461] accords with the sutras, does not go against the *vinaya*, and conforms with the *abhidharma*, then these are the signs of the fruit of the stream-enterer.

When Ānanda heard what the Buddha said, he joyfully undertook to carry it out.

[3.27] [Contemplation Twenty–Seven: Candidate to Once-Returner]

[3.27.1] [Keeping It Secret]

The Buddha said to Ānanda: Practitioners who obtain this contemplation[462] must keep it a secret. They must not wantonly tell others about it.[463] They must simply continue their own diligent practice single-mindedly.

[3.27.2] [The Insubstantial Four Elements][464]

Having practiced diligently, [the practitioner] must again [262a] be instructed to contemplate the earth element. The method of contemplating the earth element has been explained previously. Having contemplated the earth element, he must then be instructed to contemplate the water element. To contemplate the water element, he must contemplate his body. He sees[465]

458. 想[>相, Sgz].

459. These are the five precepts, which stream-enterers are incapable of violating (Bodhi 2000, 1954n320).

460. 名第二十六正觀. Alternatively, "contemplation number twenty-six, correct contemplation," though this title seems too generic to have been the intention.

461. That is, the violation of the five precepts mentioned above.

462. It is unclear if this refers to the previous contemplation (3.26, leading to the attainment of stream-entry) or the ensuing one.

463. "Wantonly tell others about it" (妄宣傳) suggests not only revealing the fact of one's attainment but also spreading information about the meditation practice and (perhaps especially) the resulting visions.

464. The next three sections (3.27.2–4) are particularly close to the corresponding passages in the *Five Gates* (*WMCJ*, T.619:15.328c6–21).

465. 身[>見]. Emendation tentative.

the various waters within it while the body itself remains as hard and indestructible as beryl.

If [on the other hand] he sees his body entirely as water, he must be taught an inverse contemplation. If he sees his body entirely as beryl, he must also be taught an inverse contemplation, one in which he contemplates the earth element and turns the beryl body into insubstantial vapor (微氣). He will also see water appearing within his eyes.[466]

If he sees this, it is called the contemplation in which the four elements are made insubstantial (細微四大觀).

[3.27.3] [The Water-Radiance Samādhi]

He must further be instructed to [meditatively] fill his head with water. He will see water emerging from his eyes without falling to the ground. He sees that his eyes have become bubbles filled with water.

When he sees this, the water within his head will be neither warm nor cool, but perfectly balanced between. If the water is warm, then his contemplation is false, for the material substance of the water element is clear and pure, neither warm nor cool.[467]

He must then be instructed to contemplate [his body] from the waist upward. The water therein is neither warm nor cool. Next he should contemplate his throat as a beryl tube. The water in it enters his chest, continues down into his stomach, and then reaches his thighs and knees. He should not allow the water to go into his arms. He makes the water clear and pure, like crystal in appearance. Only if he senses the water as warm is this contemplation true.

When this meditation has been completed, he should be instructed to make the water entirely fill all four limbs,[468] so that he becomes a beryl vessel filled with water. The water then expands gradually until he sees it fill an area the size of his meditation cot. Other people will see this as well. Only if he sees this water as clear and cool is it truly the water element. If he sees it any other way, then he has not truly entered the water-radiance *samādhi*.

[3.27.4] [Non-self of the Water Element]

[His vision] then expands gradually until the entire room is filled with pure, clear water, like beryl vapor. It continues to expand until it fills the entire

466. To make the body like "insubstantial vapor" is, it seems, the remedy when the meditator sees his entire body as (excessively hard?) beryl.

467. The idea seems to be that temperature, a property of heat, does not belong to the *dharma* of water, and therefore should not figure in the meditative perception of water. On the other hand, just below it seems that seeing warm and then cool water is desirable, so the intention here remains somewhat unclear.

468. 通徹四支諸節，水皆滿中. The arms and legs, excluded in the previous section, now also fill with water. The corresponding passage in the *Five Gates* expresses this idea somewhat more clearly (*WMCJ*, T.619:15.328c15).

universe. When he has seen this, he must focus his mind and sit peacefully in a quiet place. His fellow practitioners must be instructed to keep everything pure and not allow him to be disturbed.[469]

Now he will see a purple flame appear on top of the water, and he must consider (憶想): "From where does this water arise? When will it perish?[470] Perhaps the water is the self? But within my body there is no self. Previously, I already contemplated non-self. How, then, does this water now arise out of nothing?"

When he brings to mind these thoughts, the water turns into vapor and gradually evaporates through the top of his head. As the water gradually disappears, leaving only skin, he sees his body is incomparably thin and delicate, like tiny particles of dust or a bundle of grass. Then he sees a fire suddenly appear within his body. After the fire has incinerated his body entirely, upon contemplating his body [he sees] nothing. [He knows that] there is and never has been a self and that both he and other beings are entirely nonexistent.

At that moment, the practitioner's mind becomes peaceful and incomparably refined.[471]

[3.27.5] [Conclusion]

When this meditation is complete it is called contemplation number twenty-seven, the true contemplation of non-self (真無我觀). It is also called the meditation on the extinction of the water element (滅水大想). It is further called candidacy for the fruit of the once-returner.[472]

As for the remaining[473] refined visions of this stage of sainthood,[474] [262b] they are marvelously subtle beyond compare and cannot be fully described. If the practitioner sits in meditation cultivating the various *samādhi*s and attains the *samādhi* of non-self, he will see them naturally.

The Buddha[475] said to Ānanda: "You must preserve [this exposition of] the subtle and marvelous confirmatory visions of the true water element

469. On the danger of noise to meditators, see, similarly, 1.14.7 and *Methods for Curing* 1.1.2.

470. The sequence here is close to that given earlier for fire (3.25.1 and 3.26.1).

471. "Refined" (*weixi* 微細), here in reference to the mind, is the same word used earlier (3.27.2) to describe how the solid beryl body becomes increasingly insubstantial.

472. 向斯陀含. Sarvāstivāda doctrine posits, in addition to the four fruits, the stages of "candidate" for each fruit (*pratipannaka;* often *xiang* 向, as here, and as in *DZDL*, T.1509:25.224a13–15).

473. Since higher attainments are described below, the point must be that there are other visions associated with *this* attainment, or other unmentioned gradations within the attainment. See, similarly, 3.30.6.

474. 微細賢聖法界. I construe the grammar as 賢聖法之界, taking 界 as equivalent in meaning to *jingjie* 境界. Alternatively, emend 賢聖法[>境]界, producing roughly the same sense.

475. 佛{佛, P, S, Q, Y, Sgz, Kg}.

and broadly expound it for all sentient beings of the future." When Ānanda heard what the Buddha said, he joyfully undertook to carry it out.

[3.29] [Contemplation Twenty-Nine:[476] *The Once-Returner]*

[3.29.1] [Water and Fire Merging]

The Buddha said to Ānanda: When the practitioner has attained this contemplation, he must be instructed further in the method for contemplating the water element. This contemplation of the water element is extremely refined. Making the water element merge with the fire element, he sees his body as vapor, like a ray (影) of beryl.

He then contemplates the area around his navel and flames arise there. Looking at them directly is like gazing into the light of the sun. He may see flames arising from his navel or emerging from his nose, or from his mouth. [The flames] go in and out of his ears and eyes as he wishes.[477]

If he sees this, he will then see fire emerging from all his pores. Once the fire has emerged, clear[478] water will follow after it. In his body he sees water rising and fire descending, or fire rising and water descending.[479]

When this meditation is complete,[480] he sees the water and fire within his body as neither warm nor cool. His body and mind are serene. When he contemplates his body [he sees] no body.[481] He abides at ease, free of obstruction. This is called the fruit of the once-returner. It is also called the true confirmatory vision [of that attainment].[482]

After he has seen these things, he will never see his body [as truly existing] whether in trance or not. When he enters trance, other people too will see fire and water going in and out of his pores.

---

476. Among all the editions, only Kg, which has been one ahead since 1.14 (see 1.14.9, n. 181), includes a contemplation number twenty-eight.

477. The passage is considerably clearer in the *Five Gates:* "Next he must contemplate the fire element. Instruct him to contemplate the four sides of his navel. [Ask him] where there is fire. If he says: 'I see fire emerging from my navel,' or 'emerging from my nose,' or 'emerging from my mouth,' or 'emerging from my eyes,' then instruct him to contemplate further." 次觀火大。教令觀齊四邊，何處有火。若言我見齊上火起，或言從鼻中出，或言從口中出，或言眼耳中出者。教令更觀。(*WMCJ*, T.619:15.328c22–24).

478. 淥. Or "green" (綠), following Kg.

479. The expression "water rising and fire descending, fire rising and water descending" (水上火下火上水下) commonly describes the "twin miracle" (*yamaka-pratihārya*) by which arhats or buddhas emit fire and water from their bodies; see also n. 143 in 1.13.3. Since it is stated below that other people too will see this fire and water, I presume the intention here is indeed to describe this process.

480. {觀身無身}此想成時. See next note.

481. <觀身無身>. I relocate these four characters from one manuscript column (sixteen characters) earlier, where they are, it seems to me, hopelessly out of place. This same expression occurs in 3.24.4.

482. 境界實相. Translation tentative.

[3.29.2] [Countermeasure for Lust]

[However] one with excessive lust will [instead] see fire entering through the crown of his head and going out through his penis,[483] and then filling his body.[484] So too with water.

Such a person must further contemplate the fire above his head, like a cloud canopy of *jambūdāna* gold. He may then see underneath his body what looks like a flower made of the seven treasures. He becomes serene in mind, peaceful and happy, a state beyond comparison with any worldly pleasures. Even when he exits from trance, he still feels bodily delight, such that even others can observe his meditative bliss and golden complexion. Śakra and the gods pay reverence to him, saying in unison: "O great worthy one! Now your suffering has ended, you will definitely accomplish the fruit of the once-returner."

Hearing this he rejoices. His body cultivated in trance,[485] his mind free of obstacles, peaceful and joyous he roams freely in the *samādhi* of non-self and gradually enters the gate of the *samādhi* of emptiness while the *samādhi*s of non-wishing and non-doing all appear before him.

[3.29.3] [One of Dull Faculties]

When the practitioner sits, he will naturally discern in his meditation all of the subtle, marvelous, and wonderful confirmatory visions.[486] But for one of dull faculties, the Great Teacher, the World-honored One, will appear and explain them. Through seeing the Buddha and rejoicing upon hearing the Dharma, [the one of dull faculties] will then instantly attain the path of the once-returner.

[3.29.4] [Instructions to Repeat]

Next, the practitioner must apply his mind and review the above contemplation twenty-five times so that he becomes extremely [262c] proficient in it.

---

483. *Shen'gen* 身根 (probably from Skt. *narāṅga* 'male member') means penis at *GFSMH*, T.643:15.683b11–28 (see Yamabe 2014). In *Methods for Curing* 1.14.2, male and female genitalia are contrasted as *shen'gen* and *nügen* 女根, making clear that *shen'gen* is marked as "penis" specifically.

484. The corresponding passage in the *Five Gates* here reads: "[The meditator says:] I see fire emerge from my head. Or else he says: it emerges from my *anus*" (我見火從頂上出。或言從下道出; *WMCJ*, T.619:15.328c26–27). *Xiadao* 下道, the "lower path," means "anus" at *Mohesengqi lü*, T.1425:22.514c15–16; perhaps from Skt. *cyuti* (fall, but also the lower realms of rebirth), or *adhodvāra* (lower doorway). I thank Phyllis Granoff for these suggestions.

485. 修身禪定. The contrast with "mind" (心) suggests that *shen* 身 here refers specifically to the body.

486. Presumably this means the attainment of the *samādhi*s listed at the end of the previous section.

[3.29.5] [Conclusion]

The Buddha said to Ānanda: You must preserve this contemplation of the water element, contemplation number twenty-nine.[487] Do not forget it. One who attains this contemplation is called a once-returner, and also a "well returner" (善往來).[488] Because of deeds in a previous life that produced good roots, you[489] have now encountered a good teacher, made pure [your] practice of the teachings, and attained this path of the once-returner.

When Ānanda heard what the Buddha said, he joyfully undertook to carry it out.

[3.30] [Contemplation Thirty: The Non-returner]

[3.30.1] [The Fire Element]

The Buddha said to Ānanda: Monks, nuns, laymen, or laywomen who attain this subtle and marvelous contemplation of the water element must then be instructed in the method for the peaceful, marvelous, sublime, and extraordinary contemplation of the fire element.

Performing this contemplation, one sees within one's navel a marvelous fire, shaped[490] like a shining lotus flower, like a fiery mass of hundreds of thousands of millions of pieces of *jambūdāna* gold.

[3.30.2] [The Bright Fire Jewel]

When [the practitioner] has seen this, he must again be instructed to contemplate the fire within his body. When he contemplates the internal fire, he sees the fire of his heart, which glows perpetually with a purity and radiance surpassing that of a hundred thousand million billion magic moon jewels.

Whether in trance or not, it is as if he were carrying a bright fire jewel [so bright] he is concerned that others might see it. But this brightness is only within his own heart. Others do not see it. It gradually becomes even brighter. He sees his body now as a bright crystal mirror and his heart as a magic moon jewel. [They are so bright] he worries[491] that others might see them, but they are not actually able to see these things.

---

487. Unusually, the numbering of the contemplation is here made part of the Buddha's direct speech.

488. This term is unattested elsewhere. However, *wanglai* 往來 (returner) by itself is an attested archaic translation of *sakṛdāgāmin* (once-returner); see Karashima 1998, 454. Given the context, this must be the meaning here.

489. The problematic intrusion here of the second-person pronoun "you" (汝) when nominally referring to the abstract "practitioner" may be a remnant of the original, master-disciple dialog format of this material; see "The *Chan Essentials* and the *Five Gates*" in chap. 4.

490. 床[>狀, K^1, K, P, Q, Sgz, Kg]. This error in the Taishō presumably occurred when the character 狀 was misread as 牀, then printed using the interchangeable form 床.

491. 慮<恐, K^1, K, P, Q, Sgz>. Kg reads 恐慮. The Taishō is presumably a misprint.

[3.30.3] [The *Maṇi* Jewel within the Ocean]

When he enters trance, his heart is so illumining that he sees the rough forms (麁相) of all the worlds in the universe. He clearly sees the continent of Jambudvīpa, Mount Sumeru, and the waters of the great ocean, within which he sees a royal *maṇi* jewel burning brightly.[492]

[3.30.4] [The Nine Successive Absorptions]

When he has seen these things . . . at that moment he sees the Buddha,[493] who explains to him in detail the nine sequential absorptions ("nine sequential absorptions" means the nine moments of the immediately successive path)[494] and the eight deliverances. These contemplations do not need to be studied ahead of time (不須豫受). When the Buddha appears, he will explain them himself.

Those of sharp faculties will, upon hearing the Buddha preach, immediately attain arhatship from within the ninth moment of the immediately successive path, thereby skipping the stage of the non-returner, just as easily as a pure white cloth takes dye.[495]

---

492. The unusual term "royal *maṇi* jewel" (摩尼珠王) also appears in some of the Contemplation Scriptures (*Guan Wuliangshou fo jing*, T.365:12.342c28).

493. 見此事已爾時見佛. The text appears corrupt. Based on the way these expressions are used throughout the *Chan Essentials*, it would be very peculiar for "having seen these things" (見此事已) to be followed immediately by "at that time" (爾時), as the latter expression usually begins a new section. There may be text missing after "having seen these things."

494. Though not marked, I take this sentence as an interlinear comment. Without it, we would want to take "nine sequential absorptions" (九次第定) and "eight deliverances" (八解脫) as denoting two well-known sets of advanced meditative attainments often mentioned in tandem: the ninefold sequence of the four *dhyānas*, four formless *samāpattis*, and the trance of cessation (collectively the *navānupūrva-samāpattayaḥ*) and the eight "deliverances" (*vimokṣa*), a set of attainments that overlap with the *dhyānas* to some extent (Hurvitz 1979). These categories were widely known in early medieval China as advanced states of meditation (see, e.g., *Meisōden shō*, Z.1523:77.355a20). The interlinear gloss, however, asks us to read these labels in reference to Sarvāstivāda path theory: the "nine sequential absorptions" are thus explained as the "nine [moments of the] immediately successive path" (九無閡; *ānantarya-mārga*), a reading that makes the eight "deliverances" construe as the first eight of the "nine moments [of the path of] liberation" (九解脫; *vimukti-mārga*). In Sarvāstivāda doctrine these are the eighteen mental moments through which a meditator becomes liberated from a given sphere of existence (Cox 1992, 89). The concept of the *ānantarya-mārga* was never, to my knowledge, translated into Chinese as "nine sequential absorptions" (九次第定). The commentator—who may well have been the same person as the author—was perhaps influenced by the next paragraph, where the meditator attains arhatship "from within the ninth moment of the immediately successive path." We are, then, asked to understand that the Buddha preaches *almost* all the final states before arhatship, with the very last one (the ninth moment of the *ānantarya-mārga*) taking place moments later. See also *Methods for Curing* 1.14.14.

495. This common image from Buddhist literature describes the attainment of arhatship in some Contemplation Scriptures (*GFSMH*, T.643:15.674a1–3). In early Buddhist scriptures, it more commonly describes stream-entry (see, e.g., *Majjhima-nikāya*, 2.145).

[3.30.5] [The Wind Element]

Those of dull faculties, however, must be further instructed in the contemplation of the wind element.

In the contemplation of the wind element, the practitioner sees all instances of the wind element, [including the] extremely subtle and minute. Subtle beyond subtle, this can be seen with the mind's eye but cannot be described [in words].

Then the wind mixes with fire, and the fire mixes with wind. Water enters the fire, wind enters the water, and fire enters the wind. Wind, fire, and water [go in and out] through his pores just as he so wills it.

There is also another wind, of ten colors like the light of ten jewels [263a]. It emerges from his bodily pores, reenters through the crown of his head, exits through his navel, and then enters again through his feet. It then exits through every part of his body all at once and reenters between his eyebrows, exiting again from between his eyebrows and then reentering through all parts of his body.

[3.30.6] [Other Visions]

Innumerable confirmatory visions such as these, which are the lights of sanctity,[496] the seeds of sanctity, and the attainment of sanctity (諸賢聖法), all appear from the wind element and then return into the wind element. Only arhats can fully discern the complete features of the subtle and marvelous confirmatory visions of this contemplation of the wind element.[497] It is not something that can be fully described in words. When the practitioner sits in meditation, he will naturally see them.

[3.30.7] [Conclusion]

If the practitioner sees these things, he has purified all his defilements (練諸煩惱) and become a non-returner.

This contemplation of the wind element is called contemplation number thirty, the appearance of the confirmatory visions corresponding to the stage of the non-returner.

The Buddha said to Ānanda: "You must preserve this method for the contemplation of the wind element, which has these exalted confirmatory visions and corresponds to [one who is a] non-returner.[498] Do not forget it."

When Ānanda heard what the Buddha said, he joyfully undertook to carry it out.

---

496. "Light of sanctity" (賢聖光明) was used in 2.20.6 to describe the vision of an orb of light that disappears when the meditator commits a transgression.

497. 此風大觀具足相貌微妙境界. The point would seem to be that the previous description of the various forms of the wind element are but a small sample of what will be seen by arhats.

498. 阿那含相應最勝境界風大觀法.

[4] [AGNIDATTA]

[4.0] [The Story of Agnidatta]

[4.0.1] [Agnidatta Inquires with Mahākāśyapa]

Thus have I heard. Once, the Buddha was dwelling in Śrāvasti together with one thousand two hundred fifty monks in Anāthapiṇḍada's park in the grove of Prince Jeta.

At that time the venerable Mahākāśyapa had a disciple named Agnidatta, an ascetic[499] from the city of Rājagṛha, who had ordained as a Buddhist monk and was pursuing the path under the venerable Mahākāśyapa by cultivating ascetic practices and following the twelve *dhūta*s.[500] After five years, he had become a non-returner but was unable to advance further to become an arhat.

Agnidatta arose from his seat and went to [Mahā]kāśyapa. Arranging his robes, he placed his hands together and bowed to Mahākāśyapa, saying: "Preceptor (和上)! I have followed you, O preceptor, cultivating diligently for five years as if putting out a fire on my head, and I have become a non-returner. But now my body and mind are exhausted (身心疲懈), and I am unable to advance further to unsurpassed liberation. Please, O preceptor, quickly instruct me!"

[4.0.2] [Mahākāśyapa Enters *Samādhi*]

Mahākāśyapa entered *samādhi* and contemplated Agnidatta's mind. He discerned that this monk [Agnidatta][501] had not yet eliminated his impurities, and that at the end of his life he would be reborn in the heaven of the non-returners.[502]

Mahākāśyapa emerged from *samādhi* and said: "O disciple, with my perfect mastery of body and mind I have just entered the *samādhi* of mastery to examine the fate that awaits you owing to your deeds in past lives. It will be impossible for you to become an arhat in your present life."

When Agnidatta heard these words, sorrowful tears rained down his face, and he said: "O preceptor, I do not desire birth in heaven. My aversion to rebirth is the same as that of a terminally ill person who seeks the knife of impermanence [i.e., death]."[503]

---

499. 苦得尼揵子兒. This curious description of Agnidatta and its possible meanings are discussed in Appendix 4, n. 8.

500. Mahākāśyapa is remembered as the foremost disciple of the Buddha in the practice of austerities (*dhūta*).

501. Here and elsewhere, Agnidatta is called "this monk" (比丘). Given that he was introduced with a specific name, this reversion seems odd and is possibly a trace of an earlier version of the story in which the protagonist was a generic monk.

502. Non-returners are reborn just once more, in a pure, heavenly realm in which they will become arhats.

503. 無常力[>刀]. The meaning of the exceedingly rare term "knife of impermanence"

Mahākāśyapa replied: "Well said, well said, O disciple. For indeed rebirth is dreadful, like a raging fire that burns everything in its path. It is truly [263b] detestable. I have inspected your faculties today, but I have not been able to see them entirely clearly. The World-honored One is now in Jeta's Grove, together with his monks. We should go to him."

[4.0.3] [Mahākāśyapa Asks about Agnidatta]

So this monk [Agnidatta] put on his robe, took his bowl, and followed behind Mahākāśyapa to Jeta's Grove, where the Buddha was staying. There they saw the World-honored Buddha, his figure in the midst of the assembly like a mountain of gold, endowed with majestic virtue and carriage and fully possessing the thirty-two major and eighty minor marks. They paid reverence to the Buddha, circled him seven times, and stood to one side.

Then Mahākāśyapa knelt, placing his hands together, and said: "O World-honored One, this disciple of mine who follows behind me, Agnidatta, cultivates the twelve *dhūta*s, dwells in profound trance, and has become a non-returner. But he is unable to advance further to completely dry up the ocean of defilements. May the World-honored One preach for him the practice of pure liberation, the profound ambrosial consecration!"[504]

[4.0.4] [Agnidatta's Past Life]

[4.0.4.1] [The Age of the Buddha Great Radiance]

The World-honored One addressed Agnidatta: It is good, Agnidatta, that you have asked about this matter. I will now explain[505] it for you. Listen well and reflect carefully!

Innumerable generations in the past, there was a buddha named Great Radiance, a Thus-come One, Worthy of Offerings, Of Right and Universal Knowledge, Perfect in Conduct and Wisdom, Well-gone, Knower of the World, Unsurpassed One, Tamer of Men, Teacher of Gods and Humans, Buddha, World-honored One. When this buddha appeared in the world, he taught living beings using the three modes of instruction.[506]

After his work of liberating beings was finished [and he departed], during the age of the semblance teachings[507] a king named Brahmadatta ruled the country named Vārāṇasī. This king had a son named Armor of Forbearance, who had resolutely aroused the aspiration for unsurpassed awakening and omniscience. He had made a vow to refrain from killing,

is made clear in a passage from the *Ocean-Samādhi Contemplation Scripture* (*GFSMH*, T.643:15.660c5).

504. 甚深灌頂甘露淨解脱行.

505. 脱[>説, K^1, K, P, Q, Sgz, Kg]. The Taishō is presumably a misprint.

506. The "three modes of instruction" (三種示現; *trīni prātihāryāṇi*) refer to the buddhas' instruction by way of body (miraculous display), speech, and mind (reading a disciple's mind).

507. The "age of the semblance teachings" (像法) usually refers to the era, beginning some centuries after the death of a given buddha, when only a distorted or imperfect form of Buddhism remains (Nattier 1991).

cultivated the ten wholesome actions, and tirelessly practiced the six perfections (*pāramitās*).

[4.0.4.2] [The Sick Child]

In that country there was a prominent man named Moon Sound, who enjoyed a life of great leisure. One day his only son was suddenly beset by a fever. The wind element entered his son's heart, driving him mad, and he went into the streets of the city killing people with a sharp sword. Because this prominent man loved and cared for his son, he took a portable incense burner out beyond each of the four gates of the city, burned incense, scattered flowers, and made a sacred oath: "I will give all that I possess to any sage, doctor, or master of spells who can cure my son of his madness!"

Just then the prince Armor of Forbearance was strolling outside the city, and he saw this prominent man who out of love for his son was praying for help. Delighted, the prince declared: "This prominent man diligently cultivates a mind of love for everyone's sake.[508] His son has contracted a serious illness. May all the holy sages (神仙) arouse their compassion and come to this spot to save this man's son!"

[4.0.4.3] [The Prescription of Blood]

No sooner had he said these words than a great sage named Savor of Radiance [263c] flew through the air from the Snowy Mountains to present himself before the prominent man, to whom he said: "Your son's misfortune is a result of his fever. Because of it, he gave rise to anger, and this opened his heart channel, allowing wind to enter his heart and drive him mad.[509] It is said in the scriptures of the sages that one stricken ill because of a stirring of the wind element needs blood from the heart of a son of good family free of all anger. A cure can be had by smearing one's body with this blood and then eating a bean-sized piece of that son of good family's bone marrow.

[4.0.4.4] [The Prince Considers a Solution]

Hearing what this sage said, the man bowed before the prince right there in the middle of the street and said: "O Earth Ruler,[510] this sage has said that my son's illness can only be cured with the blood and marrow of someone whose mind is free of anger and full of love. I will stab myself to draw blood for my son to drink, and I will break my bones to extract marrow to feed him. Please, O prince, grant me permission to do this!"

The prince said: "Good sir, I have heard that the Buddha has said that

---

508. Why the prince says that the man cultivates love "for the sake of everyone" (普為一切) remains unclear when, according to the story, he was praying only for the recovery of his son.

509. *Methods for Curing* 1.3.1 similarly describes madness resulting from wind entering the "heart channel" (心脈).

510. This Chinese term (*ditian* 地天) often translates *pṛthivī*, meaning the "earth god," but also used, as here, as a term of address for rulers (see, e.g., *DZDL*, T.1509:25.90a25).

children who give trouble to their parents will be reborn in a deep hell, never to escape. How could you wish to damage your own body to heal your son? Wait a moment and I will devise a solution to this problem."

Hearing the prince's command, the prominent man was pleased. He bowed to the prince's feet and returned home to put his son on an elephant and send him to the prince. When the prince saw the son, he poured pure ghee over his head [in an attempt to cure him].

The sage Savor of Radiance said to the prince: "You could pour this medicine over his head for ninety days and he would still not be cured. What he requires is the blood of a person whose heart is free of all anger and full of love."

[4.0.4.5] [The Prince Sacrifices Himself]

Now the prince thought to himself: "Any other living being would give rise to anger [when making this sacrifice]. So I will rescue him from the suffering of this illness and save his life. I now make this vow to seek the path to buddhahood. When I become a buddha in a future life, then too I will give away my immortal Dharma body (施此法身常命) [by bestowing teachings]."[511]

After making this vow, the prince cut open his body and smeared the prominent man's son with his blood. He smashed his bones, extracted the marrow, and fed it to him. When the prominent man's son ate it, his illness was cured.

[4.0.4.6] [The Prince Is Restored]

The prince, his bones broken, fainted and collapsed to the ground. Heaven and earth shook in the six ways, and Śakra, Brahmā, the World Protectors, and innumerable gods all alighted beside the prince.

They said to the prince: "What do you seek in using your own body to cure another person's illness? Do you seek to become Lord Śakra, or Lord Māra, or Brahmā, or a wheel-turning monarch? What rebirth within the three realms do you seek?"

The prince said to Lord Śakra: "I do not seek for any noble position within the three worlds. What I seek is unsurpassed, [264a] perfect awakening."

When Lord Śakra heard these words, he said to the prince: "You have pierced your body and broken your bones to extract the marrow. Your body now trembles and shakes with pain. Do you feel any regret?"

The prince then made an oath: "If it is truly the case that I have not had even an atom of regret at any point from when I first pierced my body up to now, then may my body be restored to its former state!" As soon as he uttered this oath, his body was restored exactly as it was before.

---

511. On the Indian Buddhist trope of renouncing the body to generate the merit needed to pursue the bodhisattva path, see Ohnuma 2007.

[4.0.4.7] [The Prince's Verses]

When Lord Śakra saw this, he said to the prince: "O prince, your awesome virtue is truly beyond compare! Your will is strong, and you will definitely become a buddha. When you do, I pray that you will liberate me first."

When [Śakra] uttered this prayer, the prince expressed assent in silence and then spoke the following verse:

May it be that when I become a buddha,
I universally liberate gods and humans,
my body and mind unobstructed,
universally bestowing love on all,
and may I also liberate you.
I will make all classes of living beings,
dwell happily forever
in great nirvana.

When the prince completed this verse, all the gods rained flowers upon him as an offering and further rained innumerable hundreds of thousands of precious jewels, filling his palace, which the prince then used to practice almsgiving. By giving ceaselessly[512] he fully cultivated all the *pāramitā*s and eventually became a buddha.

[4.0.4.8] [Agnidatta's Past Life: Conclusion]

The Buddha said to Mahākāśyapa: That king of Vārāṇasī is now my father, King Śuddhodana. The prominent man, Moon Sound, is now you, Mahākāśyapa. The son of the prominent man is now Agnidatta. Prince Armor of Forbearance is now Śākyamuni Buddha, myself. And Lord Śakra is now Śāriputra.

[4.0.5] [The Instruction to Agnidatta]

The Buddha said to Mahākāśyapa: In that past life this monk Agnidatta went mad owing to a disturbance of the wind element, and for this reason when he now enters the trance of the four elements, he hesitates and does not proceed into the trance of the wind element.[513] Indeed were he to enter the trance of the wind element, his head would split into seven pieces when contemplating the four elements, his heart would tear open, and he would die. [Accordingly] he must [instead] be taught to cultivate love (慈心).

The World-honored One then said to Agnidatta: You must now contem-

512. "Giving ceaselessly" (布施不止) might also be understood as "not stopping at giving," meaning also cultivating the remaining *pāramitā*s; this fits the context but does some violence to the grammar.

513. The normal way to become an arhat, evidently; see, similarly, 3.30.6, where it is said that only arhats know the full extent of the meditation on the wind element.

plate all sentient beings, who are oppressed by the five kinds of suffering. You should arouse great love for them and wish that they escape from suffering [and that they] contemplate the impermanence, suffering, emptiness, and non-self of [the five *skandha*s of] material form, sensations, perceptions, formations, and consciousness.

[4.0.6] [Agnidatta's Attainment]

When Agnidatta heard what the Buddha said, his mind was suddenly liberated, and he immediately became an arhat, possessed of the three knowledges and six powers and endowed with the eight deliverances. He leapt into the air right in front of the Buddha and performed [264b] the eighteen displays of magic power [that only arhats can perform].

Alighting on the ground, he bowed his head to the Buddha's feet and said: "World-honored One! The Tathāgata has now explained the details of my past lives, has explained [the cultivation of] love, and has thoroughly expounded the four noble truths. By the Buddha's power I have immediately shattered the karma that had entangled me[514] in the triple world and have become an arhat.

O you who are honored by the gods, [please explain] for the sake of the evil, impure sentient beings of future ages who are reborn in the age of the five corruptions[515] because of the sins of their evil karma: if, like me, they have cultivated the ascetic practices, practiced the trances, attained the stage of the non-returner, and yet are overcome with hesitation and do not progress further, what method should they cultivate so as to leave behind all suffering?"

[4.31] [The Final Contemplation]

[4.31.1] [Contemplation of the Buddha]

The Buddha said to Agnidatta: Listen carefully, listen carefully, and reflect on it well. Inspired by you, Agnidatta, for the sake of all future living beings I will now thoroughly explain how a non-returner can become an arhat and will make clear all the subtle confirmatory visions [associated with this path].

For one in whom there is an abundance of wind element sickness (風病多者), entering the trance of the wind element is likely to cause madness born of the wind element.[516] Such a person must be taught to contemplate the Buddha. As for how he should be instructed to contemplate the Buddha,

514. *Jieye* 結業, which I translate loosely as "karma that has entangled me," is usually understood to mean "karma created on the basis of the mental defilements" (*Kōsetsu Bukkyōgo daijiten*, 318). It also sometimes refers to the rebirth voluntarily undergone by bodhisattvas (*DZDL*, T.1509:25.106b21–22; 146a28–29).

515. The age of the "five corruptions" (五濁) was variously interpreted in Buddhist literature (Chappell 1980, 139–143); most relevant here is its usage in accounts of the decline of Dharma, where it describes the eras after the Buddha's death.

516. The curious expression "likely to cause madness" (喜發狂病) also occurs in *Methods for Curing* 1.14.4 and in certain Contemplation Scriptures (*GFSMH*, T.643:15.691c24–25).

he must be instructed to contemplate the Buddha's ten powers, four fearlessnesses, eighteen unique qualities, great compassion, great love, and three bases of mindfulness.[517]

[4.31.2] [Vision of Innumerable Buddhas]

When the practitioner contemplates these things, he will suddenly see the material bodies of innumerable buddhas, each adorned with the subtle and marvelous marks. Some fly through the air performing the eighteen displays of miraculous power. Some, within each of their bodily marks, display innumerable hundreds of thousands of miraculous scenes (變化). When he has seen these things, he must, with a mind of reverence and devotion, imagine scattering fragrant flowers onto these buddhas.

Then he must reflect as follows: "The five *skandhas* and four great elements within my body are all impermanent, perishing, and not enduring. Both the branches and the roots of the defilements are also impermanent. I am now bringing to mind the Buddha's ten powers, four fearlessnesses, eighteen unique qualities, great compassion, and great love. A material body ornamented with virtues such as these may be compared to a precious vase filled with magic gems that by their power splendidly illuminate the vase. But the gems have no self, and the vase too is without an owner. [Appearing otherwise] only for the sake of living beings, the Buddha too is thus. He lacks the nature of materiality (色性) and has no material image (色像), his liberation being completely pure. Contemplating the Buddha's ten powers from the power to know what is proper and improper up to the power consisting in the knowledge of the destruction of the defilements, the eighteen unique Buddha-qualities, his great compassion and his great love, why then do I now see these innumerable material images?"

When he has performed this meditation, he sees pure gold images filling the entire universe. In the four noble postures of walking, standing, sitting, and lying down, they preach of suffering, emptiness, impermanence, and non-self.

---

517. This list of the Buddha's attributes is repeated in 4.31.3, and nearly identical lists are given in 4.31.2 and 4.31.14. Insofar as the "eighteen unique qualities" (*āveṇikadharmas*)—what distinguishes a buddha from a mere arhat or *pratyekabuddha*—are here equated with the Buddha's "Dharma body" (4.31.14), these lists appear similar to definitions of the Dharma body found in Sarvāstivāda sources (Radich 2010, 134–137). Those sources, however, usually define the eighteen unique qualities as, precisely, the ten powers, four fearlessnesses, great compassion, and three bases of mindfulness (three ways a buddha maintains mindfulness under all circumstances). Other definitions of the eighteen qualities can be found in Mahāyāna sources (see *Kōsetsu Bukkyōgo daijiten*, 659–660), where they are often named immediately after the ten powers and four fearlessnesses, just as here in the *Chan Essentials* (see, e.g., *Da zhi du lun*, T.1509:25.76a5). Still, this list—with compassion and the three bases of mindfulness following the eighteen qualities—is extremely unusual. In Chinese Buddhist literature, it seems to occur only in the *Ocean-Samādhi Contemplation Scripture* (*GFSMH*, T.643:15.667a28–29; 687c7)—yet another example of otherwise anomalous language or ideas shared between these two texts alone.

[4.31.3] [The Fourteen Stages of Sainthood]

Though he sees these things, he must further reflect as follows: "These various buddhas are [in actuality] formed through the coming together of virtues—namely, precepts, concentration, wisdom, liberation, knowledge and vision of liberation, [264c] the ten powers, four fearlessnesses, the eighteen unique qualities, great compassion, great love, and the three bases of mindfulness.[518] How could they have material form?"

When performing this meditation, he must carefully contemplate each buddha and imagine them all as unobstructed in body and mind and free of any materiality.[519] He further sees his own body as [immaterial], a cloud in the sky. He contemplates the *skandha*s to which he clings[520] as lacking any innate nature.

He suddenly feels a great happiness. He sees his body as a mass of lotus flowers filling the universe in all directions. He sees seated buddhas sitting atop lotus flowers, preaching the profound teachings of emptiness, non-self, non-wishing, and non-doing, and the entrances to the fourteen stages of sainthood.[521]

[4.31.4] [The Hells]

The Buddha said to Agnidatta: A practitioner who sees these things must then be instructed in the [meditative cultivation of] love. One so instructed should be taught[522] to contemplate the hells.

The practitioner will then immediately see the eighteen hells with their chariots of fire, burning coals, blade mountains, and sword trees.[523] The beings suffering there are his parents, extended family, associates, teachers, and

518. Here the so-called five pure *skandha*s of a buddha (see 1.18.16, n. 276) are combined with the unusual list of attributes given in the previous section.

519. 令一切佛身心無礙亦無色想. I take the pattern 令X想 as equivalent to 作X想, meaning imagine X. Alternatively, we might emend 令[>念]. The unusual expression "unobstructed in body and mind" appears in the Mahāyāna *Mahāparinirvāṇa-sūtra* as part of a description of the Buddha (*Da banniepan jing*, T.374:12.545c27).

520. "*Skandha*s to which he clings" translates *shouyin* 受陰, a technical term that usually translates *upādānaskandha*, meaning the five *skandha*s of the unenlightened person, who still clings to them as a self.

521. The number fourteen was mentioned in several earlier visions, perhaps alluding to these "fourteen stages of sainthood" (聖賢十四境界); see 1.12.6, 1.14.8, and *Methods for Curing* 1.5.3. What these fourteen stages are is unclear, although several different groupings of fourteen higher attainments are mentioned in the writings of sixth-century Chinese Buddhist exegetes (*Fa hua yi shu*, T.1721:34.461b19–20; *Da sheng yi zhang*, T.1851:44.656c29; *Mohe zhi guan*, T.1911:46.30c28–29). See, additionally, *Chan Before Chan*, chap. 2, n. 110.

522. 敬[>教, K[1], K, P, Q, Sgz, Kg]. The Taishō is presumably a misprint.

523. Many Buddhist sources available in Chinese translation by the early fifth century mention these stereotypical features of hell (see, e.g., *Zeng yi ahan jing*, T.125:2.767a11–12). A very similar set of passages on contemplating the beings of hell in the context of the meditative cultivation of love can be found in some of the Contemplation Scriptures (*GFSMH*, T.643:15.674c7–12).

disciples from past lives. He sees each of them, their bodies burned by the raging fires of the Avīci hell. Some are burning over their entire bodies. Some are made to climb sword trees. Some are made to walk up blade mountains. Some are thrown into cauldrons of boiling liquid. Some are made to enter rivers of ash. Some are made to drink boiling shit. Some are made to swallow red-hot iron balls. Some are made to drink molten copper. Some are made to lie on beds of nails. Some are tied to copper pillars. Some are made to enter forests of swords, their bodies sliced into innumerable pieces. Some have their eyes repeatedly ripped out and hot iron balls pressed into their eye sockets.

[4.31.5] [The Remaining Realms]

Or else he sees hungry ghosts,[524] their bodies tens of *yojana*s tall, eating fire and burning coals. Some drink pus and blood, which as they drink transform into molten copper. Their bodies ignite in flames, and molten copper flows from the soles of their feet.[525] Or he sees the dark places among the Encircling Iron Mountains, filled with many living beings who resemble *rākṣasas* feeding upon each other. He also sees many *yakṣa*s, their naked bodies black and thin. Each has two upward-pointing fangs and flaming bull-like heads with horns dripping in blood. He further sees all the evil beasts of the world—tigers, wolves, lions, and so forth. They too devour each other. He further sees all the suffering of the domestic animals.[526] Or else he sees the *asura*s, who with severed ears and noses experience much suffering.[527]

He sees all beings in the three worlds. They are driven by desire, only to experience painful suffering. He contemplates that even existence among the mindless gods[528] is as brief as a flash of lightning, an illusion, and that they too will be reborn in hell before long. In short, all beings, wherever they may be in the twenty-five states of existence[529] of the three worlds, have

524. The vision now moves from hell into the other bad realms of rebirth.

525. 足跟銅流. Translation tentative.

526. The word I translate as "domestic animals" (*chusheng* 畜生) commonly denotes the entire animal realm of Buddhist cosmology. But in this passage, it is evidently contrasted to the wild beasts mentioned in the previous sentence, suggesting that our author(s) take its meaning more specifically as *domesticated* animals, what *chusheng* usually means in literary Chinese outside a Buddhist context. See, similarly, 4.31.28, 4.32.7, 4.32.9, and 4.32.11 below. This usage of *chusheng* may be another sign of the text's Chinese authorship.

527. This peculiar image of *asuras*—the "fighting gods" or "titans" of Buddhist cosmology—with severed noses and ears recalls a passage from the *Ocean-Samādhi Contemplation Scripture* in which the Indra severs the ears, noses, hands, and feet of the attacking *asuras* (*GFSMH*, T.643:15.647b7–9).

528. The "mindless gods" (無想天; *asaṃjñi-sattva*) are reborn as such by cultivating the "absorption of mindlessness" (*asaṃjñi-samāpatti*), a nominally non-Buddhist meditative practice distinguished from the better known "trance of cessation" (*nirodha-samāpatti*) only with great scholastic ingenuity (Sharf 2014, 140–147). Here the point is simply that such beings have particularly long life spans.

529. The "twenty-five states of existence" (二十五有) is a classification of the realms of rebirth often associated with the Mahāyāna *Mahāparinirvāṇa-sūtra* (*Kōsetsu Bukkyōgo daijiten*, 1045; *Bukkyō daijiten*, 4032).

karma that leads them to suffering the three bad realms of rebirth [in hell, the realm of the hungry ghosts, and the animal realm].

[4.31.6] [These Beings Cannot Be Helped]

When the practitioner sees the beings in the three worlds experiencing suffering, he sees them as clearly as something he gazes at in the palm of his hand. He then gives rise to deep love and compassion and produces a mind of pity and concern. He sees that these beings are now experiencing this terrible retribution as a result of their evil actions in previous lives. When he sees this, he brings forth tears of compassion and wishes to [265a] save them. But though he exerts his mind to the utmost, they cannot be saved.

Then, his mind full of pity, he is filled with revulsion toward rebirth and does not wish to remain long within it. He becomes afraid, as if someone were attacking him with a knife. When he has seen this, he again arouses love and compassion. But though he desires to save those who are suffering, they cannot be helped.

[4.31.7] [Ignorance Is the Cause of Suffering]

Then the practitioner should reflect: "These beings [suffer] because of ignorance, because[530] ignorance is the cause of the formations, formations are the cause of consciousness, consciousness is the cause of mentality and materiality, mentality and materiality are the cause of the six sense spheres, the six sense spheres are the cause of sense contact, sense contact is the cause of sensation, sensation is the cause of attachment, attachment is the cause of grasping, grasping is the cause of coming into being, coming into being is the cause of birth, and birth is the cause of old age, death, sorrow, grief, suffering, and despair."

[4.31.8] [How Ignorance Operates][531]

The practitioner further reflects: "From where does ignorance come? How does it grow and develop (孚乳產生) such that it fills the triple world? Contemplating ignorance, [I see that] it grows depending on the earth element,[532] moves relying on the wind element, gets its solidity from the earth element, is nurtured by the fire element, and is given multifariousness by the water element.[533]

"As for how it moves, the nature of the wind element is constant motion, the nature of the water element is to flow, the nature of the fire element is to blaze [upward], and the nature of the earth element is solidity. Of the four elements, two naturally go upward [wind and fire], two naturally go

530. The text now proceeds through the twelve links of dependent origination (*pratītyasamutpāda*).

531. This section presents a seemingly alternate version of *pratītyasamutpāda*.

532. On the unusually strong linkage here between ignorance and the material elements, see "Somatic Soteriology and the Physiology of Desire" in chap. 4.

533. 水成眾性. Translation tentative.

downward [earth and water], and by twos they also go in each of the directions.[534] In the east [the elements (?)] become the *skandha* of material form,[535] in the south the *skandha* of sensations, in the west the *skandha* of conceptions, in the north the *skandha* of volitional formations, and above, in the upward direction, the *skandha* of consciousness.

"These five *skandhas* [to which beings] cling depend on ignorance for their existence and are born from the occurrence of sensory contact. With pleasant sensory contact as the cause, various kinds of sensation arise. And with sensation as the condition, attachment, clinging, and coming into being arise.[536] With coming into being as the condition, one is born somewhere within the triple world. The ninety-eight defilements and the various kinds of entangling karma bind living beings without hope of escape. All such karma arises from ignorance and depends on deluded attachment[537] for its existence.

[4.31.9] [The Emptiness of Ignorance]

"Yet when we consider the origin of ignorance, from where does it arise such that it spreads throughout the triple world, becoming a great snare for living beings? I must contemplate the true character[538] of ignorance. From where does it arise? Is ignorance the earth element? Is it something other than the earth element? Is it contained within the earth element? Does it arise from the earth element? Is it destroyed by the earth element? Yet the nature of the earth element is that it is originally empty. Upon investigation, earth has no owner.[539] How much more so ignorance!

"As for the arising of deluded attachment, this comes about through dependence on volitional formations. Yet these volitional formations, as well

534. 二上二下諸方亦二. See 1.12.3, n. 128.

535. 東方者成色陰性. Translation tentative. Correlating the five *skandhas* with the directions is most unusual.

536. Here follows the usual progression of dependent origination (*pratītyasamutpāda*): sense contact (觸; *sparśa*) → sensation (受; *vedanā*) → attachment (愛; *tṛṣṇā*) → clinging (取; *upādāna*) → coming into being (有; *bhava*).

537. "Deluded attachment" (*chiai* 癡愛), a word that appears frequently in the ensuing sections, is defined in some modern dictionaries of Buddhist terminology as "ignorance and attachment" (*Kōsetsu Bukkyōgo daijiten*, 952), two of the three primary defilements. However, medieval Chinese Buddhist authors often used this word as a single concept against which the defilement of "ignorance" was then contrasted (see, e.g., Zhiyi's *Miao fa lian hua jing xuan yi*, T.1716:33.757c29–758a1). In Buddhist translations *chi* 癡 does regularly render "ignorance" (from the triad craving, aversion, and ignorance). But the Chinese word *chi* also connotes "infatuation" (Kroll 2015, 50), and thereby potentially includes the idea of lustful desire as well.

538. 識[>實]相. "Consciousness" (識) here seems out of place. The expression "true character of ignorance" (無明實相) appears in Kumārajīva's *Chi shi jing* (T.482:14.656a1), supposedly the source for the meditations on *pratītyasamutpāda* in his *Zuo chan sanmei jing* (as reported at *CSZJJ*, T.2145:55.65b5–6). In the *Chi shi jing*, the context for the expression "true character of ignorance" is the contemplation of the ultimate emptiness of ignorance, precisely the same as here in the *Chan Essentials*.

539. 推地無主. Translation tentative. Kg is missing 推.

as attachment, clinging, and coming into being, are stirred into motion by the wind element, are born from the water element, and are nurtured by the fire element.[540]

"Carefully contemplating each of these four elements, they in truth have no inherent characteristics and are equal to [emptiness,] the ultimate limit of reality.[541] How then could they [truly] lead living beings about, binding them to the triple world and causing them to be burned by the afflictions?"

[4.31.10] [Recoiling from Rebirth]

Having reflected in this way, the practitioner becomes afraid of birth and death and recoils from rebirth in the blissful heavens. He contemplates the heavenly palaces as dreams, illusions, dew, lightning, or echoes. He sees the living beings of the triple world [265b] undergoing limitless suffering on the spinning wheel of rebirth.

When he has seen these things, he becomes despondent and takes no delight in the world. He seeks to obtain nirvana as quickly as the flow of a rapid current, and he strives for liberation in each moment.

[4.31.11] [Contemplation of the Breath]

Now he must again be instructed to count his breath: He counts from one to two, to three, to four, to five, to six, to seven, to eight, to nine, and to ten. He counts from ten to one hundred, from one hundred to one thousand.[542] Following however many breaths, he restrains the air firmly.[543]

He then sees his own body as a hundred thousand million withered lotus flowers. A wind blows from all directions, scattering the withered flowers. He then becomes beryl, a beryl vessel, within which he sees his heart as a giant flowering tree stretching from the adamantine nadir below up to the summit of the triple world, with four marvelous fruits, like magic jewels, each glowing with six kinds of light that illuminate the entire universe.

540. Mentioned here are precisely those members of the *pratītyasamutpāda* list normally classified as actions (*karma*) or mental defilements (*kleśa*), as opposed to those (the sense organs, sensation itself) that are the *fruits* of past karma (Dhammajoti 2009a, 418–423). The *Chan Essentials*, in other words, may be making a carefully articulated doctrinal point that the nominally mental realm of desire is in fact entirely dependent on the four material elements. See "Somatic Soteriology and the Physiology of Desire" in chap. 4.

541. "Limit of reality" (實際) is a common rendering of *bhūtakoṭi*, which usually implies emptiness. In very early Mahāyāna texts, the word sometimes had the less favorable meaning of the (inferior) nirvana of the arhats (Sharf 2002a, 229–230).

542. Here we find the same (less than fully clear) pattern describing breath counting that was given in 2.20.1 and 2.20.2.

543. "Restrain the air firmly" (攝氣令住) seems to mean hold the breath. This recalls non-Buddhist Chinese breathing practices (see, e.g., *Baopuzi nei pian jiao shi*, 149–150). Early Indian descriptions of Buddhist meditation usually say that holding the breath is a misguided practice (Bronkhorst 1986). Still, it is sometimes recommended in later Buddhist literature (Kragh 2015, 345).

[4.31.12] [The Many Buddhas]

When the practitioner sees these things, he then sees many buddhas, each surrounded by a retinue of great disciples, filling the universe from the adamantine nadir up to the summit of the triple world. Some of these buddhas fly through the air emitting water from their upper body and fire from their lower body; some ascend in the eastern sky and descend in the west, or ascend in the west and descend in the east, or ascend in the south and descend in the north, or ascend in the north and descend in the south, or ascend in the center and descend in the outer regions, or ascend in the outer regions and descend in the center; some make their bodies large enough to fill the sky and then become as small as mustard seeds. Just as they desire, without any hindrance, they freely manifest these powers.

Or the practitioner sees voice-hearers immersed in the trance of the four great elements (入四大定). Their bodies are like masses of brightly burning fire, like golden vessels filled with water of many colors. The practitioner then sees himself immersed in these trances, just like the voice-hearers.

[4.31.13] [The Dharma Body and the Flowering Tree of the Heart]

Then the practitioner must be instructed as follows: "Though you now see many buddhas and voice-hearers, you must contemplate [the real body of] these World-honored Ones, the formless body of great liberation, the fruit of the one beyond study. You must now carefully restrain your mind and count the breath as before." (The method of breath counting has sixteen parts.[544] These will not be explained here.)[545]

Then, having counted his breath, the practitioner's mind becomes calm and tranquil and he does not see any [of the buddhas].

Next, he must again be instructed to contemplate his lotus flower heart, a flowering tree with four fruits[546] like *maṇi* jewels, radiating six kinds of light. This light is very bright, illuminating all places from the summit of the triple world down to the adamantine nadir.

He then sees the trunk of the flowering tree of his heart bending, as if about to break. Yet it is unfathomably thick [and so does not].

[4.31.14] [The Dharma Body]

At that moment, he should contemplate the Dharma body of the buddhas as follows: "The buddhas' Dharma body relies on the material body for its existence (因色身有). The material body is like a golden vase. The Dharma body is the *maṇi* jewel [within the vase]. I must [265c] carefully contemplate that within the material body lies [the Dharma body, comprising] the ten

544. The sixteen modes (*ṣoḍaśākāra*) of breath contemplation; see Demiéville 1954, 415n1.

545. End of Sgz scroll 5 (*Tempyō Chan Essentials 5*).

546. 上有四菓, following Kg. K reads 樹上有菓, while K[1], P, Q, S, and Y read 上有菓.

powers, four fearlessnesses, eighteen unique qualities, great compassion, great love, and unobstructed liberation.[547]

"[The Dharma body's] spiritual knowledge is limitless; it is a supremely marvelous sphere[548] that cannot be seen with the eyes or known by the mind. All things neither come nor go, do not abide and do not decay, and are equal to the ultimate limit of reality. Foolish common people are hounded by the bandits of old age and death, have false and perverted views, and because of these perverted views are reborn in the three unhappy realms of rebirth. Swept about by the fast moving waters of the river of attachment and desire, they are drowning in the triple world. How could I [be so foolish as to] be like those common people and see these buddhas through false imagining?

"Long ago my great preceptor[549] Śākyamuni Buddha gave away his head, eyes, marrow, brain, kingdom, and family and undertook hundreds of thousands of austerities in his pursuit of liberation. He has now transcended birth and death and abides in great nirvana, which is ultimately tranquil, and from which there is no further rebirth. Just as do the buddhas of the past, he abides in that place of eternal happiness. He is without any awareness of past, present, or future.[550] His body and mind unmoving, he is peaceful and without activity. How could one imagine in any way a body such as this, formed of wisdom as it is? How could it transform or move in any way? What I now see appears because of false imagining and is based on causes and conditions, and is therefore something misperceived, something with material form."

When he has reflected in this way, all the buddhas and all the holy saints vanish, appearing no more. Only the single buddha [Śākyamuni] remains, attended by his four great disciples.

[4.31.15] [The Purification of the Four Elements: Wind]

Śākyamuni, the World-honored One, then preaches for the practitioner the contemplation method for purifying the four great elements (四大清淨觀法). He says: "O Dharma child! All saints and sages of the past, present, or future,[551] when they cultivate this practice,[552] naturally [begin by] cultivating the contemplation of the wind element.[553]

---

547. On this list, see 4.31.1, n. 517.

548. *Jingjie* 境界, which I here translate loosely as "sphere" (rather than "confirmatory vision"), since in this case it is used pointedly in reference to an "object" of contemplation said to be beyond all concrete forms.

549. On the Buddha as the meditator's "preceptor" (和上), see 1.18.14, n. 259.

550. 亦無去來現在諸智. Translation tentative.

551. 過去三世諸賢聖. This line is peculiar because "three times" (三世) usually means past, present, and future, making the word *guoqu* 過去 (past) redundant.

552. 觀此行時. Here and in the next sentence, *guan* 觀 needs to be construed as meaning meditative "cultivation" in a broad sense (as if translating *bhāvayati*).

553. In this section, the meditation proceeds through the four elements in reverse order (from wind to fire, to water, to earth).

"To contemplate the wind element, first contemplate within your body.[554] From the flowering tree of your heart arises a small amount of wind, which gradually grows larger until it fills your entire body. Filling your body, it exits through your pores and fills the room. You will see this slight wind, after filling one room, fill the entire building. Filling the building, it will gradually fill an entire acre. Filling an acre, it continues to increase until it fills one *yojana*. Then two...three...four...five *yojana*s. Filling five *yojana*s, it expands until it fills ten *yojana*s. Beginning from just a faint stirring, the wind gradually expands until it fills the entire universe from its summit down to the adamantine nadir. Having pervaded all these places, it returns and reenters through the crown of your head, making the flowers of your heart tree gradually [266a] wither and fall.[555] You now see your body as completely transparent, like a crystal mirror."

[4.31.16] [Water]

At this juncture, [the practitioner] must be further instructed to contemplate the water element. To contemplate the water element, he first contemplates the interior of his body. From the tips of the flowering heart tree emerges a slight stream of water, like gaseous beryl (琉璃氣). It gradually grows until it is a white cloud filling the interior of his body. Filling his body, it emerges through the six organs[556] and surges out through the crown of his head. It then circles his body seven times, like a line of white clouds raining soft drops of water.

The water fills his meditation cot, and after filling this one meditation cot, it gradually becomes larger until it fills the room. Filling the room, it then fills the building...the city...ten acres...one hundred acres...one *yojana*. The water is pure white, like the glow of white beryl, faint and ethereal. This vision cannot be seen by those possessing the eyes of ordinary beings.

The water gradually grows larger until it fills two *yojana*s. Filling two *yojana*s, it fills three...four...five...ten...a hundred *yojana*s...all of Jambudvīpa...the entire universe from the summit of the triple world down to the adamantine nadir. The water, ethereal as a cloud, then returns and reenters through the crown of the practitioner's head.

[4.31.17] [Fire]

When he has seen these things, he must be further instructed to contemplate the fire element. To contemplate the fire element, he first contemplates

554. It is unclear where the speech of the (visionary) buddha ends.

555. The sequence here mirrors that in 4.31.11.

556. The "six organs" (六根) are usually the six *sense* organs (including the mind). This can hardly be the meaning here. Dictionaries do record this term as a generic reference to the body and limbs in non-Buddhist sources, but only from a much later era (*Han yu da ci dian*, 2:39). Some of the Contemplation Scriptures, however, provide comparable examples of this usage of the word (*GFSMH*, T.643:15.652c28; 672c22–23).

the interior of his body. At the tip of his flowering heart tree, among the leaves, there is a faint fire, like the gleam of gold. It emerges from the tip of his heart and fills his body. It then exits through his pores, gradually expanding until it fills his meditation cot...the room...the building...a city...ten acres...a hundred acres...one *yojana*. The fire becomes white, brighter than a pearl, and whiter than even crystal or a snow-covered mountain. Infused with red light, it forms a multitude of patterns, gradually expanding until it fills two *yojanas*. Filling two *yojanas*, it fills three...four...five *yojanas*, and filling five *yojanas*, it keeps growing until it fills a hundred *yojanas*...all of Jambudvīpa... [266b] the entire universe from the summit of the triple world down to the adamantine nadir. It then returns and reenters through the crown of his head.

[4.31.18] [Earth]

When he has seen these things, he must next be further instructed to contemplate the earth element. Contemplating the earth element, he sees the flowering heart tree within his body become gradually larger until it is a cloud of adamant filling his body. Filling his body, it then fills his meditation cot...the room...the building...a city...an acre...a hundred acres ...one *yojana*. After filling one *yojana*, it changes color, becoming blue. It gradually expands until it fills the entirety of two *yojanas*. Filling two *yojanas*, it fills three...four...five *yojanas*. Then, having filled five *yojanas*, it keeps growing until it fills a hundred *yojanas*...all of Jambudvīpa...the entire universe from the summit of the triple world down to the adamantine nadir. It then returns and reenters through the crown of his head.

[4.31.19] [The Cessation of Earth]

When he has seen these things, he must be instructed to contemplate the earth element again. When he contemplates the earth element, he sees it as an adamantine cloud, so difficult to shatter it seems impossible that it would ever cease.

When he performs this contemplation, he sees the world-honored buddha Śākyamuni sitting upon an adamantine throne, accompanied by a retinue of five hundred disciples. They sit before the practitioner, and in unison they praise the noble truth of cessation.

When he hears these words, he must contemplate that the earth element is produced through causes and conditions, and that it is supported by ignorance.[557] [Yet] ignorance itself has no essential nature, and deluded attachment too has no controlling power. What is empty, false, and conditioned is only provisionally named ignorance, and this is also true for attachment, grasping, and coming into being.

557. The ensuing discussion of *pratītyasamutpāda* is similar to that in 4.31.9, where, however, ignorance was said to depend on the earth element (here the relation is reversed).

[4.31.20] [Earth and Fire]

When he reflects in this way, he sees that from the tip of the flowering tree within his heart a fire gradually appears, igniting the adamantine cloud [of the earth element]. Every bit of this cloud within the folds of the leaves [of his heart tree] merges with the fire and fills the interior of his body. Filling his body, the earth and fire, moving together, fill his meditation cot. Filling his meditation cot, it fills the room... the building... the city. Filling the city, it gradually expands until it fills ten acres... a hundred acres... one *yojana*... two... three... four... five *yojana*s... a hundred *yojana*s... [266c] all of Jambudvīpa. Owing to their different natures,[558] earth and fire mutually stimulate each other, filling the entire universe from the summit of the triple world down to the adamantine nadir. Then they return and reenter through the crown of his head.

[4.31.21] [Wind and Water]

When he has seen these things, the practitioner must be instructed to contemplate the wind element again. To contemplate the wind element, he contemplates the interior of his body. A purple colored wind appears within his flowering heart tree. Then water enters the tree and washes away the wind's color, making it the same color as the water. When the wind moves the water gushes, filling the interior of his body. Gradually growing larger, [the wind-water mixture] fills his meditation cot. Filling his meditation cot, it fills the room... the building... the city... one *yojana*. After filling one *yojana*, the wind blows upon the water, and because the essential natures of water and wind differ, the water becomes blazing beryl foam. Mutually stimulating each other even more, [the wind and water] fill two *yojana*s, then three... four... five *yojana*s... a hundred *yojana*s... all of Jambudvīpa... the universe from the summit of the triple world down to the adamantine nadir.

[4.31.22] [The Pure Four Elements Fill the Universe]

When the practitioner has seen these things, he then sees fire emerge from all his pores. The fire blazes brightly, filling the triple world. Then it passes beyond the triple world, becoming a flower of pure gold. Within the flower are fruits interspersed among the petals, and in their radiance is a voice preaching the salvific teachings of the four noble truths and the twelvefold chain of conditioned arising.

The practitioner now sees water of all kinds appearing within his body. Warm and slippery, the water flows out of his pores and spreads everywhere throughout the triple world. The water emits light, shining up to the summit of the triple world, where it enters the fruits found in the glow of the fire.[559]

558. Fire moves up, and water down, as mentioned in 4.31.8.

559. 入火光菓中. Presumably this means the light enters the previously mentioned fruits located in the flower made of transformed fire.

He further sees winds of all kinds appearing within his body. Filling the interior of his body, they emerge from his pores and gradually expand until they blow in all directions, filling the triple world. Then they transform into golden clouds, which enter the fruits found in the glow of the fire. An extremely fine and subtle earth *qi* pervades the four elements.[560]

[4.31.23] [The Emptiness of the Four Elements]

When the practitioner has seen these things, then he must be instructed to contemplate the five *skandhas*. He contemplates the *skandha* of matter as follows: The *skandha* of matter depends on the earth element for its existence, and yet the earth element itself is not fixed. It is born from ignorance, for [as it is said in the formula for *pratītyasamutpāda*] with ignorance as a condition there is the illusory appearance of mentality and materiality.[561] Contemplating the character of matter, it is therefore empty, constructed, and not ultimately real (虛偽不真). Furthermore, it lacks any place of origin (亦無生處), appearing only provisionally through causes and conditions (假因緣現). Yet that which is dependently originated is empty of essential nature (因緣性空), and thus is the *skandha* of matter. The natures of [the remaining *skandhas* of] sensation, perception, formations, and consciousness are also empty, and they lack any solid core of existence. Contemplating these five *skandhas*, they lack any true causes and conditions (實無因緣), and they do not [really] come into [267a] existence. How then could the four elements [truly] expand and fill the triple world [as I have seen]?"

[4.31.24] [The Four Elements Fill the World Again]

When the practitioner reflects in this way, he sees fire emerge through his pores, fill the triple world, and then reenter his body through his pores. He further sees the earth element emerging through his pores like an adamantine cloud, filling the triple world, and then returning into his body through the pores. He further sees the water element emerging through his pores like a fine dust, filling the triple world, and then returning into his body through the pores. He further sees the wind element, its force now very weak, emerging through his pores, filling the triple world, and then returning into his body through the pores. Eight hundred times do the four elements emerge from and reenter through the pores in this manner.

[4.31.25] [The Elements Become Insubstantial]

When he has seen these things, he must count his breath as before. He must seal the breath (閉氣) within his body for a period of seven days.[562]

560. 復有地氣，極為微薄，彌滿四大. In *Methods for Curing* 1.9.6, the "earth *qi*" (地氣) is something beyond (or inclusive of) the four elements themselves. This may also be the implication here, but the earth element itself is not mentioned in 4.31.22, so this "earth *qi*" could simply mean the earth element. See also 1.15.2.1.

561. *Ming se* 名色 (*nāma-rūpa*), the fourth item in the *pratītyasamutpāda* formula.

562. As in 4.31.11, this seems to mean holding the breath in some fashion.

He will then suddenly see the earth element become gradually more insubstantial. The ground beneath his meditation cot becomes gradually insubstantial (漸漸空). He sees the ground beneath the room becoming gradually insubstantial... the building... the city... ten acres... a hundred acres... one *yojana*... two... three... four... five... ten... a hundred *yojanas*... the eight thousand *yojanas* of the continent of Jambudvīpa... the ten thousand *yojanas* of the continent of Pūrvavideha... the thirty thousand *yojanas* of the continent of Godānīya... the forty thousand *yojanas* of the continent of Uttarakuru. Seeing Uttarakuru, he sees Mount Sumeru, the waters of the four oceans, the mountains, rivers, rocks, walls, and every solid thing beneath the four heavens all gradually become insubstantial. Seeing everything beneath the four heavens,[563] his mind continues to expand until every solid thing throughout the entire universe—the great earth, mountains, rivers, rocks, and walls—becomes entirely insubstantial, such that there is nowhere for his mind to alight (心無所寄).

[4.31.26] [The Adamantine Wheels]

At this moment, the practitioner suddenly sees the adamantine nadir, where there are fourteen adamantine wheels. Surging upward from the adamantine nadir and knocking against one another, they arrive [267b] all at once before the practitioner.[564] Then fire suddenly flares on the tips of the marvelous flowers of his heart tree, burning up the leaves of the tree. The four fruits fall onto the practitioner's head, enter his body, and come to rest in his heart. His mind becomes clear and lucid, and he will be able to see through walls.[565]

[4.31.27] [The Six Elephants and the Adamantine Warrior]

Six elephants then appear, pitch black in color.[566] They trample the earth to pieces and suck up all the water. Winds blow bitterly upon the elephants,[567] and fire emerges from their ears, burning them into nothing. The poisonous snakes of the four elements climb to the top of the tree [to safety].

The practitioner then sees a man who looks like a mighty warrior. He pulls on the great tree as if to uproot it, and from the adamantine nadir up to the summit of the triple world the tree begins to shake. The four bright jewel-like fruits in the practitioner's heart unleash a great fire, which burns the tree until it shrivels and is blown away like a cloud of dust.

---

563. Kg here skips 17 characters.

564. *Methods for Curing* 1.14.14 describes the attainment of arhatship in a very similar manner.

565. The power to "see through walls" (見障外事) is described similarly at *DZDL*, T.1509:25.348a2–3 and *Guan puxian pusa xing fa jing*, T.277:9.389c7–9.

566. 正[>色] 色[>正], following K[1], K, P, Q, Kg. The Taishō is presumably a misprint.

567. 風吹象殺. See 1.18.17, n. 268.

[4.31.28] [Emptiness of the Internal Four Elements]

When the practitioner has seen these things, [he must think]: "The external elements of fire, wind, earth, and water that I now contemplate[568] are impermanent and quickly perishing. I must now contemplate that the four elements within my body—fire, earth, water, and wind, all arising continuously—are just the same. Ignorance is empty and devoid of being.[569] It is provisional, false, a misperception, [nonexistent] like fire and ice [at the same time].[570]

"For all those belonging to the triple world, owing to deluded attachment the coarse attributes of the thirty-three million thought-born *dharma*s are successively brought to mind in each of the nine hundred and ninety turnings [of the mind each second].[571] The seeds and branches of the ninety-eight defilements fill the triple world, and because of these defilements, one undergoes limitless rebirths either in hell, where raging fires scorch one's body, or as a hungry ghost drinking molten copper and swallowing hot iron balls,[572] never hearing of "food" or "water" for hundreds of thousands of years, or as a domestic animal, such as a camel, donkey, pig, or dog, all of whom undergo much hardship and suffering at the hands of men.[573] All of this results from deluded attachment. Today, however, I contemplate this deluded attachment as having no essential nature."

[4.31.29] [The Three *Samādhi*s]

When the practitioner has reflected in this way, Śākyamuni Buddha emits a golden light.[574] Surrounded by his retinue of disciples, he says to the

568. 我今觀於水[>外, Kg]火風等[>地]及與水大. My emendations here are tentative.

569. As in 4.31.9, 4.31.19, and 4.31.23, a link is made here between ignorance and the material elements.

570. "Fire and ice" expresses logical impossibility and hence nonexistence (like the "horns of a rabbit" or the "child of a barren woman"). See, similarly, *Da banniepan jing ji jie*, T.1763:37.419c27–28.

571. 緣於癡愛，三十三億念生法，九百九十轉次第念麁相. My translation of this line is highly tentative. However, the basic idea here and in the ensuing sentences is clearly the relatively standard one that in each second the mind turns to a new object many times, with each such "turning" producing new defilements and karma. A strikingly similar description of such things occurs in one of the most important early Chinese writings on the topic of Buddhist meditation, the preface to the *Anban shou yi jing* (of An Shigao) by Kang Senghui 康僧會 (d. 280), which describes the unruly mind as follows: "In a finger snap the mind turns nine hundred and sixty times; in each full day there arise thirteen million thoughts" 彈指之間，心九百六十轉，一日一夕十三億意。 (*CSZJJ*, T.2145:55.43a11–12; on this preface, see Link 1976).

572. Swallowing molten copper and hot iron balls is a punishment usually associated with hell, not the realm of the hungry ghosts. However, as Costantino Moretti has pointed out (2017), the *Saddharma-smṛtyupasthāna-sūtra* tells of certain kinds of hungry ghosts that undergo tortures similar to those of the hells. The *Chan Essentials* gives other unusual depictions of hungry ghosts that find parallels in this same source (see 3.26.9, n. 442).

573. On "domestic animals," see 4.31.5, n. 526.

574. This is presumably the same Śākyamuni seen in 4.31.15.

practitioner: "Do you now understand? The nature of matter is vacant and quiescent. And this is also true of sensation, perception, formations, and consciousness, the remaining *skandha*s. You must now carefully cultivate the *samādhi*s of empty signlessness, non-doing, and non-wishing.[575]

"In the *samādhi* of emptiness, one contemplates material forms [and realizes that] material form and all *dharma*s have utter emptiness as their nature. [Realizing] this multifarious emptiness is called the *samādhi* of emptiness.

"In the *samādhi* of non-wishing, one contemplates that nirvana has the nature of formless quiescence. One contemplates that birth and death are the same as ultimate truth. When one contemplates them in this way, one does not wish for birth and death and does not long for nirvana. One contemplates that the ultimate point of genesis[576] of birth and death is empty tranquility, and that the nature of nirvana too is subsumed within emptiness and yet can still be distinguished from it. This is called the *samādhi* of non-wishing.

"In the *samādhi* of non-doing, one sees neither mind nor body, nor any bodily activity carried out in any posture. One does not see nirvana as something that arises. One sees only the noble truth of cessation, which is the profound realization of utter [267c] emptiness."

[4.31.30] [The Final Destruction of the Defilements]

When the practitioner hears the World-honored Buddha explain the *samādhi*s of emptiness, signlessness, and non-wishing,[577] his body and mind become calm and tranquil. As soon as he hears of them he understands, and roaming freely through the three gates of emptiness, [signlessness, and non-wishing][578] as easily as a strong man might bend and stretch his arm, he transcends the raging defilements of ninety million rebirths[579] and

575. On this anomalous list of the three *samādhi*s, see Appendix 2.

576. The term "ultimate point of genesis" (*benji* 本際) is, in translated Chinese Buddhist literature, sometimes a rendering of the technical term *bhūtakoṭi*, another common translation of which (*shiji* 實際) appeared just above; see 4.31.9, n. 541.

577. Here the three *samādhi*s are given in their proper form, unlike in 4.31.29.

578. 三空門. I take this to mean "the three gates [beginning with] emptiness," that is to say, the three *samādhi*s previously enumerated.

579. The expression "raging defilements of ninety million rebirths" (九十億生死洞然之結) requires some explanation. Though here it pertains to arhatship, elsewhere the elimination of huge numbers of "raging defilements" (洞然之結) is associated with stream-entry. We see this in 4.31.31, in *Methods for Curing* 1.3.5 and 1.14.13, in the Contemplation Scriptures (*GFSMH*, T.643:15.652a18; 662c6), as well as in a passage from a late fourth-century translation of the *Saṃyuktāgama* (*Bie yi za ahan jing*, T.100:2.441a15–17; absent from *Za ahan jing*, T.99:2.157b18 and *Saṃyutta-nikāya*, 1.210). A possible Indic counterpart to this idea comes into focus from the *Xian yu jing* (T.202:4.384c17–18; 396c6–7), which dates to the fifth century. The *Xian yu jing*, in this same context, uses the same terms and can be aligned with a parallel in the *Divyāvadāna*, which describes stream-entry as involving the destruction of: "the mountain of the false view of self that has twenty rising peaks" (*viṃśatiśikharasamudgataṃ satkāyadṛṣṭiśailaṃ;* cited in Yamabe 1999c, 192–193). A similar image, also featuring the key word "peak" (*śikhara*), occurs in the *Saddharma-smṛtyupasthāna-sūtra*, which states that at the moment of highest meditative attainment: "the peaks of many hundreds of thousands of births

becomes an arhat, free of future rebirth, his purity fully established, possessing true knowledge, his mind completely and wholly liberated, free of any residue of the defilements. He naturally obtains the [sixth] supernormal power, the knowledge of the destruction of the outflows [that is gained only by arhats]. As for the other five supernormal powers, he must use other methods of cultivation to obtain them.[580] The full explanation of these six powers is given in more detail in the Abhidharma.

[4.31.31] [Conclusion]

After the World-honored One explained to Agnidatta the visions of sanctity [experienced when] the mind accords with emptiness,[581] and also the characteristics of the eleven universal entrances,[582] he became silent, composed himself, and entered the "*samādhi* of non-dispute" (無諍三昧), emitting colored lights that illuminated the entire world.[583] At that moment, the minds of two hundred fifty monks in the assembly were liberated and they became arhats. Fifty laymen shattered the raging defilements of twenty million rebirths and became stream-enterers. And the host of gods, having heard the Buddha's teaching, was greatly delighted.

[4.32] [Entrustment and Injunctions]

[4.32.1] [Naming the Sutra]

Then the venerable Ānanda arose from his seat and said to the Buddha: "World-honored One, first you preached the method of contemplating impurity for Kauṣṭhilananda. Then you preached the method of breath counting for Nandi the Meditator. Finally, you have preached the contemplation

are cut down from the mountain of the cycle of rebirth" (*anekāni janmaśatasahasrāṇi śikharāṇi saṃsāraparvatād viśīryante;* Stuart 2015, 536–537, slight modifications). All these passages explain a moment when a definitive limit has been made to the otherwise endless cycle of rebirths (as occurs at stream-entry, for example). The Chinese word *dongran* 洞然 (raging fire) in the seemingly equivalent passages is, admittedly, slightly mysterious. To judge from the few possible Indic parallels above, it may be an attempt to render *śikhara*, meaning "peak" but also perhaps construable as "pointed flame" (as the related *śikhā* can mean). In the Contemplation Scriptures, arguably this same concept is reformulated as the countless "sins of birth and death" (生死之罪) that the practices are claimed to eliminate, a phrase that has long puzzled scholars (see Unebe 1981).

580. Here it is claimed that one can obtain liberation (the sixth *abhijñā*) without needing to first gain the other five magical powers that are usually held to be the fruits of *dhyāna*.

581. 賢聖空相應心境界. Translation tentative.

582. The "universal entrances" (一切入; *kṛtsnāyatana*) are a series of meditations best known from Pāli sources as the *kasiṇas*, where they figure prominently in the *Visuddhimagga*. Not specifically mentioned earlier in the *Chan Essentials*, the first four *kṛtsnāyatana* meditations are in fact the contemplations of the four elements of earth, water, fire, and wind, precisely what has been of such importance here in the fourth sutra. In 4.32.1 below, the teachings delivered to Agnidatta are given the collective name "contemplation of the four elements." These titles contrast with the opening narrative, which stressed the practice of the cultivation of love (慈心; *maitrī*). This is not the only example in the *Chan Essentials* of this kind of inconsistency (see "Outline and Structure of the *Chan Essentials* and *Methods for Curing*" in chap. 2).

583. 普照世尊 [>界, K^1, K, P, Q, Kg]. The Taishō is presumably a misprint.

of the four elements for Agnidatta.[584] Under what designation should I preserve these many subtle and wondrous teachings? Under what name should they be preached to later generations?"

The Buddha said to Ānanda: "This scripture is to be named the *Secret Essential Methods of Chan* (禪法祕要).[585] It should also be known as the method of the white bone contemplation, the nine successive meditations, the miscellany of contemplation methods, the procedure for breath meditation, the meditation [leading to] the successive attainment of the four fruits, and the elucidation of the confirmatory visions (分別境界). Using these names you must preserve it. Do not forget it!"

[4.32.2] [Praise for the Sutra]

The Buddha said to Ānanda: After my death, these contemplations should be studied by monks, nuns, nuns in training, novice monks, novice nuns, laymen, or laywomen who wish to learn the teaching of the buddhas of the three times, who wish to cut off the seeds of birth and death, to cross over the river of the afflictions, to dry out the ocean of rebirth, to dispose of the seeds of attachment, to cut off the flow of the defilements, and to turn away from delight in the five objects of sensory desire and take delight in nirvana. These contemplations are so meritorious that whoever practices them will attain the four fruits [of stream-enterer, once-returner, non-returner, and arhat] and like Mount Sumeru be a radiant light for the entire world.

[4.32.3] [Four Rules for Practitioners]

The Buddha said to Ānanda: After my death, monks, nuns, laymen, or laywomen who wish to study the teachings [of this sutra] must separate themselves from four evil things. What are the four?[586]

First, they must perfectly keep the precepts and prohibitions and must also never violate any of the minor rules. If they have violated any of the five categories of the monastic precepts,[587] they must wholeheartedly carry out a ritual of repentance to purify themselves. When one is pure with respect to the precepts, one is said to be [268a] adorned by the practice of purity (莊嚴梵行).

Second, they must stay far away from noisy commotion, dwell alone in peaceful tranquility, fix their thoughts to a single thing [by meditating], delight in the practice of silence, and tirelessly cultivate the profound twelve austerities as if extinguishing a fire on their heads.

Third,[588] to remove their obstructing sins they must sweep the sanctuary, wash its floors, distribute willow twigs and fresh [toilet hygiene] sticks, and perform menial services.

---

584. Panthaka, protagonist of the third sutra, is not mentioned here.

585. This title differs slightly from those usually assigned to the *Chan Essentials* (see Appendix 3).

586. This entire section closely resembles portions of the *Guan Yaowang Yaoshang er pusa jing* (T.1161:20.663a10–18), one of the Contemplation Scriptures.

587. For *wuzhong jie* 五眾戒 in this meaning, see *DZDL*, T.1509:25.226a2–3.

588. The tasks listed here are similar to those outlined in 2.19.1.8.

Fourth,[589] throughout the night and day they must sit upright without lying down, and must not doze off or allow their bodies to lean to the side. They always happily dwell in graveyards, beneath trees, or in a forest hermitage, sustaining themselves as the deer do, and dying like them as well.[590]

Anyone among the four classes of disciples who practices these four things is to be known as a practitioner of asceticism (苦行人). One who practices asceticism in this manner will, in a short time, definitely attain the four holy fruits.

[4.32.4] [The Merit of Seeing the Bones][591]

The Buddha said to Ānanda: Among the four classes of disciples who cultivate this method for fixing the mind, there may be those who contemplate and then see, with utmost clarity, the image of the white bones in a single small portion of their bodies, such as the tip of the toe or the tip of the finger. Know that such people, if they see a single finger, a single nail, or the entire skeleton, will definitely be reborn in the Tuṣita heaven because of the sharpness of their minds. [Such people] have put an end to all their suffering in the three unhappy realms of rebirth. Though they are not yet liberated, they will never again be reborn in the unhappy realms. Know that such people possess merit that will not decay, and that they have escaped forever the miseries of the three lower paths of rebirth.

How much greater, then, to see all the skeletons [described in this scripture]! Those who see these skeletons, though not yet liberated and not possessing any undefiled merit,[592] have nonetheless escaped from the painful torments of the three lower rebirths and the eight difficult situations. Know that these people will always be reborn where they can see the buddhas. In a future lifetime they will meet Maitreya at the first dragon flower[593] assembly and will be first to hear the Dharma and attain liberation.

---

589. I follow K, Q, S, and Y, which place the words "fourth" here. K[1] and Kg place them seventeen characters (one manuscript column) later, before the injunction to dwell in graveyards. P includes both readings.

590. The forest-dwelling ascetic, in Indian literature, is often described as "deer-like." To "sustain themselves as the deer" suggests foraging for food, a frequent mark of the Chinese hermit.

591. The paraphrase of this section in a sixth-century monastic code known from a single Dunhuang manuscript is the earliest surviving direct citation of the *Chan Essentials* in later literature (see Appendix 1).

592. "Undefiled merit" (無漏功德; perhaps from *anāsrava-puṇya*) probably means a *lokottara* (transcendent) attainment along the path rather than "merit" that is merely good karma.

593. "Dragon flower" (龍華) is the name of the tree beneath which the future buddha Maitreya will achieve awakening. In fifth- and sixth-century China, it was understood that Maitreya will hold three different "assemblies" beneath this tree. Epigraphic evidence shows that attendance at these assemblies was a common postmortem aspiration during this era (Hou 1998, 196–204). Interestingly, as Hou shows, in the earlier part of this period the typical prayer is merely to meet Maitreya at the time of the three assemblies. Beginning in the early sixth century, the inscriptions change, and the wish to be present at the "first assembly" (初會) becomes common. It is this latter goal that is stated here in the *Chan Essentials*.

[4.32.5] [Monks Who Falsely Claim to Meditate]

The Buddha said to Ānanda: There may be monks, nuns, laymen, or laywomen who, while within the Buddhist fold, ceaselessly covet personal gain. Out of desire for fame they dissemble and perform evil. Not actually practicing seated meditation, heedless in their conduct of body and speech, they only claim to practice seated meditation out of greed for personal gain.

A monk such as this violates a *sthūlātyaya* transgression.[594] If he does not confess within the required time, and does not then repent, after a short time he will have violated a *saṅghāvaśeṣa* transgression.[595] Should an entire day go by, when the second day is reached know that this monk becomes a thief among humans and gods, a murderous *rākṣasa*-demon, someone destined to fall into the evil realms, a violator of the grave sins.[596]

[4.32.6] [Nuns Who Falsely Claim to Meditate]

There may be nuns who put on wily charms (妖冶邪媚) because they desire personal gain, and are insatiably greedy like a cat stalking a mouse, covetous without respite. In truth never practicing meditation, they still claim to practice meditation. Heedless in their conduct of body and speech, they claim to practice meditation out of greed for offerings.

A nun such as this violates a *sthūlātyaya* transgression. If she does not immediately confess and then repent, after but a short time she will have violated a *saṅghāvaśeṣa* transgression. Should [268b] an entire day go by, when the second day is reached know that this nun becomes a thief among humans and gods, a murderous *rākṣasa*,[597] someone destined to fall into the evil realms, a violator of the grave sins.

[4.32.7] [Monks and Nuns Who Falsely Claim Attainment]

If a monk or nun who has not in fact seen the white bones claims to have seen them, or similarly [falsely claims to see the confirmatory visions of]

594. *Sthūlātyaya* (偷蘭遮; P. *thullaccaya*), literally "serious," is a categorization used in some *vinaya* traditions for the mere *attempt* to carry out a grave (*pārājika* or *saṅghāvaśeṣa*) transgression (Durt 1979). The point here would seem to be that to say one meditates when one does not is an attempt to falsely claim meditative attainment (which is a *pārājika*). See also the next note.

595. Expressed here, and in the next sentence, is the idea that transgression can increase in severity if not promptly confessed. This is a standard principle of *vinaya* law pertaining to *saṅghāvaśeṣa* (*sengcan* 僧殘) transgressions (also invoked here), where one extra day of probation (*parivāsa*) is added to the required expiation for each day the offense was concealed (Nolot 1996, 116–136). Here and in the application of the *sthūlātyaya* category, we see that the author(s) of the *Chan Essentials* were drawing from a reasonably sophisticated understanding of *vinaya* law.

596. "Grave sins" (重罪) must mean the *pārājika*. Indeed, the language used here seems to borrow from the *vinaya* accounts of the fourth *pārājika*, where those who falsely claim meditative attainment are called "thieves" (賊; Hirakawa 1993–1994, 1:305–306).

597. A *nun* should probably be a *rākṣasī*, but the Chinese does not make this distinction.

breath meditation,[598] then this monk or nun deceives the gods, dragons, demons, and spirits, and cheats the people of the world.[599] Such evil people are the children of demons. Speaking falsely, they say that they have attained the contemplation of impurity and the other contemplations up to the stage named summit.[600]

At the end of their lives, these liars will definitely fall into the Avīci hell faster than a torrential downpour,[601] where they will live for an entire eon. Exiting hell, for eight thousand years they will be reborn among the hungry ghosts, where they will swallow hot iron balls.[602] Exiting from the realm of the hungry ghosts, they will be reborn among the domestic animals, where for their entire lives they will carry heavy burdens and after death will be skinned. After five hundred such lifetimes, they will again be reborn as human beings, where they will suffer the fate[603] of being deaf, blind, mute, dumb, lame, or afflicted with many illnesses. The suffering like this that such a person will undergo cannot be fully described.

[4.32.8] [Laymen Who Falsely Claim to Meditate]

A layman incurs a sin of inattention if he claims to practice meditation when in fact he does not practice meditation, or claims to be pure[604] when in fact he is not pure. He is a doer of an impure thing, fallen and unable to arise, a foul untouchable (*caṇḍala*), a companion of the wicked, a rotten seed that will not produce sprouts of goodness.[605]

If, because he covets personal gain without respite, he allows five days to pass [without confessing], then he will have committed the great sin of

598. Compare with *Methods for Curing* 1.9.2.

599. Notice that unlike the false claim merely to meditate, no possibility of atonement is allowed in the case of a false claim of actual attainment.

600. See 3.22.1–3.

601. 雹[>暴]雨. 電光 (W); 電雨 (Kg). See 1.5.1, n. 78.

602. See 4.31.28, n. 572.

603. Literally, "wear the clothing of" (以為衣服). This expression may derive from Kumārajīva's translation of the *Lotus Sutra* (*Miao fa lian hua jing*, T.262:9.16a2–5). See also *GFSMH*, T.643:15.671c12–13.

604. 梵行. This could also mean celibacy (*brahmacarya*), something a Buddhist layman might well boast about.

605. The terminology in this passage seems to draw from Dharmakṣema's early fifth-century translation of the *Youposai jie jing*, which contains an expanded set of lay precepts that was influential in the formation of the Chinese systems of the bodhisattva precepts. In this text, laymen who violate the "minor" (輕) lay precepts are declared "guilty of a sin of inattention, fallen and unable to rise, doers of an impure thing." 失意罪，不起墮落，不淨有作。(*Youposai jie jing*, T.1488:24.1049c1–3; cf. *Pusa shan jie jing*, T.1583:30.1016a25). These are the same terms, in the same order, listed here. A layman who violates the "grave" lay precepts, meanwhile, will be "unable to obtain even the stage of the heat (*ūṣmagata*), let alone become a stream-enterer or attain the other fruits up to non-returner. He is known as a layman who has broken the precepts, a stinking *caṇḍala* of a layman who is tied up with impurity." 是人即失優婆塞戒，是人尚不能得煖法，況須陀洹至阿那含。是名破戒優婆塞，臭旃陀羅垢結優婆塞。(*Youposai jie jing*, T.1488:24.1049b5–8; cf. *Pusa shan jie jing*, T.1583:30.1015a18–21). This language is also echoed here, though less exactly.

false speech. Such a greatly evil person is a slave to demons, on par with *caṇḍalas*, butchers, and *rākṣasas*. It is certain that he will be reborn in the three evil realms. When such a layman is about to die, he will be greeted by an inauspicious vision of the eighteen hells with their chariots of fire and ovens of ash;[606] he is certain beyond doubt to fall into the three evil realms.

[4.32.9] [Laymen Who Falsely Claim Meditative Attainment]

There may be a layman who has not in fact obtained the contemplation of impurity or other attainments up to the stage of heat[607] and yet who, out of overweening pride[608] proclaims to the great assembly:[609] "I have attained the contemplation of impurity" or the like up to the stage of heat.

Know[610] that a layman who does this is a thief among gods and men, one who cheats humans, gods, dragons, and the remainder of the eight groups of nonhuman beings. Such a layman, upon death, will fall straight into the Avīci hell faster than a torrential downpour. After an entire long eon, when his life in hell is finished, he will be reborn among the hungry ghosts, where for eight thousand years he will swallow hot iron balls. Exiting from the realm of the hungry ghosts, he will be reborn among the domestic animals, where for his entire life he will carry heavy burdens and after death will be skinned.[611] After five hundred such lifetimes he will again be reborn as a human being, where he will suffer the fate of being deaf, blind, mute, dumb, lame, or afflicted with many illnesses. The suffering like this that he will undergo cannot be fully described.

[4.32.10] [Laywomen Who Falsely Claim to Meditate]

If a laywoman, claiming magical power so as to delude the masses,[612] says that she practices meditation when in fact she does not, then this laywoman incurs a sin of inattention. She is impure and bound up with filth, a doer of an impure thing, fallen and unable to arise, a foul *caṇḍala* [268c]. Such a

606. This seems to describe an inauspicious deathbed vision. On *bianhua* 變化 meaning "inauspicious vision," see 1.12.4, n. 120.

607. Note that the highest listed attainment for monks and nuns in 4.32.7 was "summit." Was "heat" considered the highest possible attainment for a layperson? Normally the highest attainment available to a layperson is the stage of non-returner (see, e.g., *Youposai jie jing*, T.1488:24.1049b8–9, where a layman's false claims list attainments up to non-returner).

608. "Pride" is specifically *excluded* as an excuse for false declarations of attainment, making for a stricter understanding than even the *vinaya*, which always makes an exception, in the fourth *pārājika*, for false claims to sanctity made out of pride, that is to say, false but *sincere* claims (*Vinayapiṭaka*, 3.90; Prebish 1975, 52–53; Hirakawa 1993–1994, 1:298–323).

609. "Great assembly" (大眾) usually means a *monastic* community. The scenario here seems to envision a case where a layperson was declaring his meditative attainment to members of the clergy.

610. This passage is nearly, but not exactly, the same as that in 4.32.7 above.

611. Here again *chusheng* 畜生 seems to mean specifically *domestic* animals (see 4.31.5, n. 526).

612. Interestingly, the otherwise nearly identical passage on false claims by lay*men* (4.32.8) does not include this line about "claiming magical power so as to delude the masses" (顯異惑眾).

laywoman is a companion of the wicked, a follower of Māra, and is certain to fall into the three evil realms of rebirth.

If she does not immediately confess and repent, then after a short time, when five days have passed,[613] this laywoman, who covets without respite, who claims to be pure when not actually pure, who claims to practice meditation when not actually doing so, will be a great evil-doer, certain to fall into the three evil realms where she will undergo rebirth according to her karma.

[4.32.11] [Laywomen Who Falsely Claim Attainment]

If a laywoman has in truth not obtained the contemplation of impurity or other attainments up to the stage of heat and yet, out of overestimating pride, declares to the assembly, "I have attained the contemplation of impurity" or the like up to the stage of heat, then such a laywoman is a thief among gods and men. When her life is over, she will fall straight into the Avīci hell faster than a torrential downpour, where she will stay for an entire long eon. When her life in hell is over, for eight thousand years she will be born among the hungry ghosts, where she will swallow hot iron balls. Exiting from the realm of the hungry ghosts, she will be reborn among the domestic animals, where for her entire life she will carry heavy burdens and after death will be skinned. After five hundred such lifetimes, she will again be reborn as a human being, where she will suffer the fate of being deaf, blind, mute, dumb, lame, or afflicted with many illnesses. The suffering like this that she will undergo cannot be fully described.

[4.32.12] [Those Who Do not Obtain Visions]

The Buddha said to Ānanda: There may be monks, nuns, laymen, or laywomen who fix their thoughts and concentrate their minds, who keep their minds free of distraction, sit upright in absorption, concentrate their minds in a single place, and block off their sense faculties (閉塞諸根). Even though they do not obtain any confirmatory visions (雖無境界), such people, their minds calm, will by the power of their concentrated minds (念定力故) be reborn in Tuṣita heaven, where they will meet Maitreya. They will then be reborn on earth together with him when he becomes a buddha. Present at the first dragon flower assembly, they will be among the first to hear the Dharma and realize the path of liberation.[614]

[4.32.13] [Keeping One's Attainment Secret]

[4.32.13.1] [Introduction]

Further, O Ānanda, in the impure, evil age after the Buddha has passed away, there may be monks, nuns, laymen, or laywomen who do in fact culti-

613. The wording of this line is slightly different, and less clear, than in 4.32.8 above, but I have taken the meaning to be the same.

614. W continues for approximately fifty more unreadable characters before the concluding colophon.

vate purity (修梵行), who practice the twelve *dhūta*s, who adorn their bodies and minds,[615] who practice mental concentration, who cultivate the white bone contemplation, who contemplate impurity, and who, entering into profound confirmatory visions (入深境界), their mind's eye perspicacious, reach meditative attainment (通達禪法). People such as this from among the four groups of Buddhist followers, must keep secret their actions of body, speech, and mind for the sake of the prosperity of Buddhism and to prevent the extinction of the teaching.[616]

[4.32.13.2] [Like a Medicine Consumed in Secret]

For example, suppose that after becoming sick in body and mind a person is told by a skillful doctor to take pure ghee as medicine. At that, the sick person goes to the king of the country and begs for pure ghee. Out of pity, the king bestows this gift but commands the sick person to drink the ghee within a sealed room where there is no wind or dust, and after drinking it, to close his mouth and regulate the *qi* of the four elements (調四大氣) so they remain in balance.

So too if a monk or nun has consumed the medicine of ambrosial consecration [of meditation], this must not be wantonly spoken of to anyone apart from his or her wise guiding teacher. If others are told, their attainments (境界) will be lost. [269a] This will also constitute a *saṅghāvaśeṣa* violation.[617]

Even laypersons, eager to cultivate trance and attain the five powers, must not say to others: "I have gotten a sacred technique of supernatural power."[618] They should rather keep everything secret. How much more so, then, must fully ordained monks and nuns not proclaim to others their attainment of the contemplation of impurity or other attainments

615. This recalls 4.32.3, where those who maintain the precepts are described as "adorned by the practice of purity" (莊嚴梵行).

616. "Keep secret their actions of body speech and mind" (當密身口意) seems to mean that they must not speak to others about their attainments, but also, as suggested by the parable in 4.32.13.2, that they not let others know they are practicing meditation at all. This entire section closely resembles the final chapter of the *Ocean-Samādhi Contemplation Scripture*, "on the secret practice of the contemplation of the Buddha" (觀佛密行品), whose opening passage states: "Beings of the future who attain this *samādhi* of the recollection of the Buddha... *must be instructed to keep secret their actions of body, speech and mind.*" 未來眾生其有得是念佛三昧者...<u>當教是人密身口意</u> (*GFSMH*, T.643:15.695b9–11). Further analogies about the need for secrecy then follow, similar to those given in the remainder of 4.32.13.

617. According to all known *vinaya*s, knowingly false claims to meditative attainment constitute a *pārājika* (the most serious of transgressions), but a *true* claim is only a transgression when made to a layperson, and even this is a relatively minor offense (see, e.g., *Shi song biqiu boluotimuzha jie ben*, T.1436:23.474a25–27). The *Chan Essentials*, in saying that even true claims may be made only to one's teacher lest it be a comparatively serious *saṅghāvaśeṣa* transgression, is thus considerably more restrictive than the *vinaya* itself. See, similarly, n. 608 in 4.32.9.

618. 神通仙呪術. The wording here suggests some kind of spoken incantation, but given the context perhaps refers to some kind of oral instructions in meditation.

up to the stage of heat. If they speak of such matters to others, their attainments will vanish, and this will cause people to become suspicious of Buddhism.[619]

[4.32.13.3] [The Buddha Makes a New Rule]

For this reason, before this assembly, I now lay down the following rule: monks and nuns who have attained the contemplation of impurity or the other attainments up to the stage of heat[620] must conceal their practice. When they have made their minds clear and sharp, they may speak of this only to their guiding teacher possessed of wisdom. They must not spread this information widely or speak about it to others. If they speak of it to others out of desire for personal benefit, they right away commit a *saṅghāvaśeṣa* violation. If time passes and, feeling no remorse in their mind, they do not repent, then it becomes a grave sin as explained previously.

[4.32.13.4] [The Poor Man and the Wicked Ruler]

Again, Ānanda, after the Buddha has passed into extinction, in the time when there is no buddha present in the world, seekers of liberation from among the four groups of disciples who attain the contemplation of impurity must keep it secret.[621] They must not let others know.

For example, suppose there is a poor man, without parents, living in an evil age governed by a wicked ruler. If while digging a well this poor man, because of his good karma from previous lives, were to unexpectedly find buried treasure and thereby gain rare and precious things, he would hide the treasure and tell no one since he is afraid of the evil ruler. Instead, he would keep it hidden, drawing from it to support his family and secretly enjoying happiness. So too after the Buddha has passed into extinction, if a disciple from among the four groups of followers attains the bliss of meditation, he must keep it secret and not speak of it widely. If he speaks of it, he commits a grave sin.

[4.32.13.5] [The Sick Son and the Secret Medicine]

Further, Ānanda, it is similar to the case of a prominent man whose only son contracts a grave illness that causes his hair and eyebrows to fall out. The prominent man thinks to himself: "I am old, and I have only this one, gravely ill son. Where can I find a skillful doctor?" With this thought, he spends a great sum of money to recruit a skillful doctor, and owing to merit generated in previous lives, this prominent man unexpectedly finds a doctor extremely learned in medical techniques.

619. The idea seems to be that speaking of one's attainment causes it to disappear, leaving the person in the situation of having claimed an attainment that he or she no longer possesses. This passage is paraphrased in Zhishou's *vinaya* commentary (see Appendix 1, 4a).

620. Above (4.32.7), for monks and nuns the rule spoke of attainments up to "summit," not "heat." We should perhaps then here emend 暖[>頂].

621. 當密藏祕[>之]; see *GFSMH*, T.643:15.695c4, which is very similar.

The prominent man then says: "Master, please show your compassion. I have but this one son, who has long suffered from this malady. I beg you to treat him! If you can cure him, then with the exception of my person I will without fail give you all my wealth, which is as great as that of Vaiśravaṇa, protector god of the northern direction."

The skillful doctor then says to the prominent man: "You must first construct an extremely well-sealed dark chamber with walls seven layers thick. Then have your son take this medicine [and sit there]. After he has taken it, he will be cured, but only if he neither looks at nor speaks to anyone for a period[622] of four hundred days."

The Buddha said to Ānanda: After the Buddha [269b] has passed into extinction, a disciple from among the four groups of Buddhists who practices meditation and seeks liberation must, like that gravely sick person, follow the teachings of the skillful doctor and stay in a secluded place, such as a graveyard, beneath a tree in the forest, or in a forest hermitage, and must cultivate the profound path of the worthies and sages. He must conceal his actions and remain silent while within his mind he cultivates the four Brahma practices,[623] the four bases of mindfulness,[624] the four right efforts, the four bases of magic power, the five roots, the five powers, the seven factors of awakening, the eightfold sagely path, the four trances, and the four unlimited minds, and finally roams through the innumerable gates of the profound *samādhi* of emptiness until he attains the six powers[625] [and becomes an arhat].

Single-mindedly he must secretly practice all these amazing, meritorious activities, being extremely careful not to vainly declare in front of others that he has attained any superhuman states.[626] If he declares that he has attained any superhuman states, then he will assuredly fall into the Avīci hell as explained previously.

[4.32.14] [The Fate of the Teachings: The First Fifteen Hundred Years]

The Buddha[627] said to Ānanda: In the first one hundred years after my death, the contemplation of impurity [taught in this text] will circulate in

622. 輕[>經, K¹, K, P, Q, Kg]. The Taishō is presumably a misprint.

623. The "four Brahma practices" (四梵行) are the four *brahma-vihāras*, the meditative cultivation of love, compassion, sympathy, and equanimity. Mentioned below are the "four unlimited minds" (四無量心; *apramāṇa*), which in Indian Buddhist literature are normally synonymous with the *brahma-vihāras*. That the *Chan Essentials* includes both of these terms as clearly separate items may be another indication of its Chinese authorship. Q, S, Y, and P remove "four" (四), perhaps an attempt to resolve the contradiction by making this a generic statement about cultivating "purity" (梵行).

624. Here follow the thirty-seven *bodhipakṣika-dharmas*, often discussed earlier (see e.g., 1.18.15 and 2.19.2.3).

625. 神道[>通, K¹, K, P, Q, Kg]. The Taishō is presumably a misprint.

626. False claims to "superhuman states" (過人法; *uttarimanuṣyadharma*) are what the fourth *pārājika* prohibits.

627. 為[>佛, K¹, K, P, Q, Kg]. The Taishō is presumably a misprint.

Jambudvīpa, where it will restrain those who are heedless and allow them to contemplate the four truths. Those who then cultivate this contemplation of impermanence[628] for but a single day will attain liberation just as easily as when I was still present in the world.

In the second hundred years, only half my disciples will cultivate the contemplation of impermanence and attain liberation. In the third hundred years...only one in four...in the fourth hundred years...only one in five ...in the fifth hundred years...only one in ten...in the sixth hundred years...only one in a hundred...in the seventh hundred years...only one in a thousand...in the eighth hundred years...only one in ten thousand...in the ninth hundred years...only one in ten million...after one thousand years...only a few dozen among billions and billions will do so. Beyond a thousand years, though this contemplation of impermanence will still circulate in Jambudvīpa, only one or two disciples out of hundreds of millions of billions will cultivate it and attain liberation thereby.

[4.32.15] [The Fate of the Teachings after Fifteen Hundred Years][629]

After fifteen hundred years, if monks [269c], nuns, laymen, or laywomen praise or proclaim the contemplations of impermanence, suffering, emptiness, or non-self, there will be many who, their minds consumed with jealousy, attack them with knives, axes, rocks, or shards of pottery and curse them as follows: "Fools! When has there ever been in this world things such as impermanence,[630] suffering, emptiness, or non-self? The flesh of the human body is pure beyond measure. How could one perversely say that it is impure? Evil people! You must all be expelled!"

[4.32.16] [Signs of the Disappearance of the Dharma]

When signs such as this have appeared, not even one person among hundreds of thousands will cultivate the contemplation of impermanence. When these signs have appeared, the banner of the Dharma will have fallen, the sun of wisdom will have set, and sentient beings will be as if blind. Though there may be disciples of the buddha Śākyamuni, the monastic (*kāṣāya*) robes they wear will be like flags hung on trees, which spontaneously become

628. "Contemplation of impurity" and "contemplation of impermanence" seem to mean the teachings of the *Chan Essentials* as a whole.

629. This section deploys a common trope from Mahāyāna sutra literature: a prophecy that the teachings of the sutra will, after the Buddha's death, be ignored, forgotten, or reviled. Such claims attest to the real or imagined opprobrium that the genuinely novel (relative to early Buddhist literature) Mahāyāna texts met when they first appeared. For the *Chan Essentials* to tell such a prophecy about the doctrines of impermanence, suffering, emptiness, and non-self—fundamental and entirely noncontroversial Buddhist teachings—is thus extremely curious. We may hypothesize that it reflects the specifically *Chinese* context in which the *Chan Essentials* was composed, where it was Mahāyāna literature and doctrines that were the dominant Buddhist discourse.

630. {觀}.

white [like the clothes of the laity].[631] Any remaining nuns will be like harlots making their living selling their flesh on the streets. Laymen will act like *caṇḍala*s, butchering animals without limit. Laywomen will be lustful, impious, and deceitful beyond measure. When these signs appear, it means that the unsurpassed true Dharma of Śākyamuni will have disappeared forever.

[4.32.17] [Final Entrustment and Conclusion]

The Buddha said to Ānanda: You must preserve the Buddha's words, and in the future widely expound their meaning for the four classes of disciples. Do not forget[632] them! Further, Ānanda, to the beings of the future you must proclaim the following words: "The great teaching of the Tathāgata will soon perish.[633] You must now make diligent effort in your practice of Buddhism. You must contemplate suffering, emptiness, impermanence, and non-self."

When the Buddha spoke these words, eight thousand young gods realized the truth of impermanence, parted from stain and defilement, and attained the purity of the Dharma eye.[634] Five hundred monks right then and there ceased to cling to anything and with their defilements eliminated and minds liberated, became arhats.[635]

Then the venerable[636] Agnidatta, together with one thousand two hundred fifty other monks, as well as various gods and dragons, upon hearing the Buddha preach this teaching on the contemplation of impermanence, became liberated in mind, each of them thoroughly comprehending suffering, emptiness, and impermanence. Bowing their heads to the Buddha's feet, they joyfully undertook to uphold the teaching.

---

631. The spontaneous transformation of monastic robes into white (lay) clothing as a sign of the decay of Buddhism is mentioned in the *Fa mie jin jing* (T.396:12.1119b2–4), which existed by no later than the late fifth century (*CSZJJ*, T.2145:55.28c18) and was widely cited to this effect by Chinese authors (*Fa yuan zhu lin*, T.2122:53.1012a2–3). The image of robes "like flags draped on trees" may derive from the Mahāyāna *Mahāparinirvāṇa-sūtra*, which says that after the Buddha's death lazy monks will happily cast aside their robes like flags draped over trees (*Da banniepan jing*, T.374:12.399a12–18).

632. 妄[>忘, K, P, Q, Kg]. The Taishō is presumably a misprint.

633. 不久心[>必, K^1, K, P, Q, Kg]沒. The Taishō is presumably a misprint.

634. To attain the "Dharma eye" usually means to become a stream-enterer.

635. This is a standard description of arhatship, identically worded in several of Kumārajīva's translations (see, e.g, *Weimojie suo shuo jing*, T.475:14.538c29–539a6).

636. 長[>尊]者. For Agnidatta, a monk, to be called *zhangzhe* 長者—a term that usually means "householder" (Skt. *gṛhapati*) in Buddhist texts—would be odd.

Secret Essential Methods for Curing Meditation Sickness

(*Methods for Curing*)

Zhi chan bing mi yao fa 治禪病祕要法

(T.620:15.333a7–337c18)

[1] Methods for Curing the Seventy-Two Sicknesses That Disturb the Minds of Forest-Dwelling [Meditators][1]

Questions of the Venerable Śāriputra from the Forest-Dwelling Section of the *Saṃyuktāgama*[2]

[1.1] [Introduction]

[1.1.1] [The Five Hundred Monks]

Thus have I heard. Once, the Buddha was dwelling in Śrāvasti, in Sudatta's park in the grove of Prince Jeta, together with one thousand two hundred fifty monks. It was summer, the fifteenth day of the fifth month. Five hundred monks of the Śākya clan were dwelling in the bamboo grove cultivating the forest dwellers' practice. Cultivating their minds through meditation on the twelve [links of *pratītyasamutpāda*], while performing breath meditation they entered the beryl *samādhi*.[3]

1. 治阿練若亂心病七十二種法. This is apparently the title of the whole first sutra of the *Methods for Curing*. That there are seventy-two sicknesses in total is mentioned again at the conclusion (1.15.3). To what this number refers is unclear, as there are far fewer methods in the text as we have it.

2. Though there is no evidence that the *Methods for Curing* was ever part of a "Saṃyuktāgama" (one of the key collections of early Buddhist sutras), later Chinese authors took this claim at face value (see Appendix 1).

3. One later citation of this passage (Appendix 1, 10b) implies that "twelve" here means the twelve *dhūtas*. While this is possible, the *Damoduoluo chan jing* (T.618:15.320c5–6; 324a16) mentions a "beryl *samādhi*," a quite unusual term, in connection with the contemplation of the twelve links of *pratītyasamutpāda*, suggesting that this is the meaning of the number twelve here. The idea of the "beryl *samādhi*" is presumably modeled on the "adamantine *samādhi*" (*vajropama-samādhi*), the state of meditation immediately preceding liberation.

[1.1.2] [Virūḍhaka's Elephants]

Just then Virūḍhaka, son of King Prasenajit, was riding on a great fragrant elephant accompanied by five hundred other sons of prominent men. Near the edge of Jeta's grove, they put on a Naluo performance,[4] got their elephants drunk, and staged an elephant fight in which a troupe of black lotus elephants[5] made horrid roars, like thunderclaps interspersed with the faint screeching of a cat.

The Śākya monks, including Nandi the Meditator and Upanandi, were startled, their hair standing on end, and being immersed in the contemplation of the wind element, were driven mad. Emerging from trance, they were unrestrained, like drunken elephants.[6]

The venerable Ānanda ordered the other monks: "Lock the doors! These Śākyas have gone mad and might cause harm."

[1.1.3] [The Five Kinds of Madness]

The other monks went to Śāriputra and said: "O venerable one, your wisdom is unobstructed, and fear vanishes in your wake as from the victory banner of lord Indra. Please have compassion and rescue these Śākyas from the suffering of their madness!"

At that, Śāriputra got up from his seat and led Ānanda by the hand[7] to the Buddha. He circled the Buddha three times, and after making prostrations, knelt down before the Buddha with joined palms and addressed him: "O World-honored One, may you, honored by the gods, bestow your compassion on all. In forest-dwelling monks of the future, madness may arise in five different ways: one, because of loud sounds; two, because of bad reputation;[8] three, because of desire for personal gain; [333b] four, because of external winds; five, because of internal winds. May you, honored by the gods, please explain to me, for the sake of people such as this, how these five illnesses may be cured!"

[1.1.4] [The Buddha Consents]

The World-honored One smiled and a five-colored light emerged from his mouth, circled him seven times, and reentered his body through the crown of the head. Then he said to Śāriputra: "Listen carefully, listen carefully, and reflect on it well. I will now explain this to you."

---

4. *Naluo xi* 那羅戲. *Naluo* is attested elsewhere as a transcription of a Middle Indic form of Skt. *naṭa* (actor / dancer); see Karashima 2001, 187.

5. 蓮華黑象. Translation tentative. Perhaps a kind or breed of elephant.

6. In the story of Agnidatta (*Chan Essentials* 4.0.4.2), "wind" madness led to the transgression of killing. That the monks here become "unrestrained" (不可禁制) suggests a similar mishap, and below, in 1.2.1, madness is said to initially produce "evil speech," again suggesting a close connection between madness and transgression.

7. 牽阿難手. A rather unusual image.

8. "Bad reputation" (惡名) could be a euphemism for violation of the precepts.

[1.2] [The Method for Curing a Perturbed Mind][9]

[1.2.1] [The Heart Channels Become Agitated]

When a practitioner is practicing the forest dwellers' way [of meditation] and cultivating his mind by [contemplation of] the twelve [links], if his mind organ is touched within by an unpleasant external noise, the four hundred and four channels[10] will at once become agitated owing to excess tension in his heart. Because wind is the strongest [of the four elements], it is the first to produce madness, shaking the heart channels and causing the five kinds of wind to enter the throat, where they initially produce evil speech.

[1.2.2] [The Mirror of Evil Deeds]

In this case the practitioner must be instructed to consume milk, honey, and *harītakī* fruit[11] and to fix his mind on a single thing. He must first imagine a crystal mirror and contemplate himself within the mirror performing various deeds of madness, [i.e., transgressions]. When he sees this, he should be further instructed[12] with the following words: "You now see yourself within the clear mirror performing deeds of madness and delusion. Your parents and kinsmen also see you doing these wicked things. I will now teach you how to separate yourself from madness and delusion. You must remember this."

[1.2.3] [Ghee within the Eardrums]

The practitioner must first be taught to remove the sound.[13] The method for removing the sound is as follows. He must press his tongue upward against his palate. Then he should imagine a *maṇi* pearl within each of his ears. From the tips of these wish-fulfilling pearls, which are like droplets of milk, ghee flows out and coats the eardrums[14] so that they no longer register

9. The title of this section is the actual name of the method, given in the Chinese, in interlinear-comment sized text at the end.

10. No other independent account of this idea is known in Chinese Buddhist literature, but the 404 channels are clearly linked to the concept of 404 possible illnesses (101 for each of the four elements). See chap. 3, pp. 67–68. Zhanran, when summarizing this passage (see Appendix 1, 3c), even calls them the "four hundred four illness-channels" (四百四病脈; *Zhi guan fu xing chuan hong jue*, T.1912:46.400a17–18).

11. 阿[>訶]梨勒. Not "fake" Sanskrit, as Tsukinowa argued (1971, 105), as correcting for a simple graphic error yields the usual transcription of Skt. *harītakī*, the Indian myrobolan plum that was held to be a powerful medicine (*Zengyi ahan jing*, T.125:2.650c25–27; *Jin guang ming jing*, T.663:16.352a18–19; cf. Nobel 1937, 180). Dried myrobolan was available for sale in China by the Tang dynasty. A small sample is even preserved among the personal effects of the Japanese emperor Shōmu 聖武 (d. 756), now in the Shōsōin treasury of Tōdaiji (Trombert 2010, 766).

12. 復當更觀[>教, P, S, Y]. The ensuing line seems clearly to be the speech by which someone else, presumably the teacher, instructs the meditator, recalling the format of the *Five Gates*; see "The *Chan Essentials* and the *Five Gates*" in chap. 4.

13. This may be a play on the word *sheng* 聲, "sound" but also "reputation."

14. 耳根. Literally, the "ear organ," the minute bit of sensitive matter that registers sound.

sound. Even if there is a loud noise, they will remain unmoving, as if coated in thick oil.

[1.2.4] [The Adamantine Canopy]

When this meditation is complete, the practitioner should next imagine a nine-layered adamantine canopy emerging from the royal wish-fulfilling pearls and covering his body. An adamantine flower appears below, upon which he sits. Adamantine mountains with no gap between them surround him on all four sides, so that external sounds are completely blocked. Within each of the mountains are seven seated buddhas, who instruct him in the four bases of mindfulness. There is now total silence. He hears no external sounds. He follows only the teachings of these buddhas.

[1.2.5] [Conclusion]

This is called the method for removing disturbance, the meditation that removes evil sounds. [The Buddha] said to Śāriputra: You practitioners[15] must cultivate this and not forget it. This is called the method for curing a perturbed mind.

[1.3] [The Method for Softening and Curing the Internal Wind Element]

[1.3.1] [Internal Wind Sickness]

Next, Śāriputra, having removed external sounds, one must remove internal sounds. Internal sounds occur when the six sensory organs, having been shaken by external sounds, perturb the heart channel and cause five kinds of evil wind to enter and stir the heart, causing singing, dancing, and all sorts of strange behavior.

[1.3.2] [The Fire Jewel Heart]

You must teach this person the heart-cleansing contemplation (洗心觀). For the heart-cleansing contemplation, the practitioner first contemplates his heart, making it gradually brighter until it is a fire jewel, its four hundred and four channels, like the leaves of the trunk of a beryl-gold plantain tree, reaching to the tip.[16] The fire jewel heart emits a vapor (氣), neither cold nor hot, neither thick [333c] nor thin, that wafts into the channels. The practitioner now imagines Lord Brahmā[17] holding a *maṇi* jewel mirror, reflecting the practitioner's chest. He sees his own chest [in the mirror] as a royal *maṇi* jewel, beautiful and pure, with a fire jewel as the heart.

15. 汝等行者. Or perhaps "*your* practitioners," meaning Nandi, Upanandi, and the others whose madness prompted this teaching.

16. 四百四脈如毘琉璃黃金芭蕉直至心邊. Translation tentative.

17. "Lord Brahmā" (*fanwang* 梵王) is the classical Indian god Brahmā, who in Buddhist cosmology is the ruler of only one set of heavens. The other gods who live in these heavens (mentioned in 1.5.5 below) are usually called "brahma gods" (*fantian* 梵天).

[1.3.3] [The Divine Boy Irrigates the Channels]

Lord Brahmā holds an imperial seal,[18] within which is a white lotus flower. Atop the white lotus flower is a divine boy (天童子). Holding up fresh milk in his hands, he emerges from the royal *maṇi* jewel and pours the milk into the channels [of the practitioner's heart]. The milk drips downward to the tip of the heart. The divine boy then holds two needles, one golden and one blue. He places two gold flowers against the sides of the heart and runs the needles through them seven times.[19] When he has finished, the heart returns to its former state of relaxation. He further rinses the heart with the milk. The milk drips into the large intestine, and when the large intestine is full it flows into the small intestine.[20] When the small intestine is full, the milk drips from it, drop by drop, into the mouths of the eighty[21] families of worms. When the worms are full, the milk circulates throughout the body, irrigating the three hundred thirty-six bones.

[1.3.4] [The Pond of Milk]

Next, the practitioner must imagine a pond of milk with a white lotus flower growing in it, upon which he sits, bathing himself with milk. He imagines a cotton cloth, white like a lotus flower, wrapping around his body seven times. Lord Brahmā takes milk from his own body and rinses out the practitioner's mouth. Having done this, Lord Brahmā takes a parasol and holds it above the practitioner's head. Seeing many amazing confirmatory visions in Lord Brahmā's parasol, the practitioner regains his sanity[22] and is no longer disturbed.

[1.3.5] [The Five Hundred Monks Become Arhats]

When the Buddha had spoken these words, the five hundred Śākya monks followed the Buddha's instructions exactly. Their minds became clear, and they contemplated [the five *skandhas*] of matter, sensations, perceptions, volitional formations, and consciousness as impermanent, suffering, empty, and non-self. No longer clinging to the world, they understood the truth of emptiness and regained their sanity in a flash, smashing the raging

---

18. Literally, "the seal of a wheel-turning monarch" (轉輪印). Seal-wielding deities appear in many apocryphal Chinese Buddhist texts from the late fifth century, and the therapeutic use of seals has a long and broad history in Chinese religion (Strickmann 2002, 123–193; Copp 2018).

19. This presumably means he sews the flowers onto the heart.

20. As in *Chan Essentials* 1.1.6, the large intestine precedes the small intestine in the order of digestion.

21. 萬[>十, Kg]. See *Chan Essentials* 1.1.5, n. 26.

22. Literally, regains his "original mind" (本心). This idea is mentioned at the conclusion to the first sutra as well (1.15.5). In this passage, the contextual meaning is as translated, but the notion of recovering one's original mind may also invoke the idea of awakening and liberation.

defilements of eighty million [rebirths][23] and becoming stream-enterers [certain to] continue their cultivation and become arhats endowed with the three wisdoms, six powers, and eight deliverances.[24]

At that time the monks, hearing what the Buddha had said, joyfully undertook to carry it out. This is called the method for softening and curing the internal wind element.[25]

[1.4] [Curing Imbalances in the Four Elements]

[1.4.1] [The Fire Element]

Further, Śāriputra, one who wishes to practice meditation should skillfully contemplate the four great elements and adjust according to the season.

In spring he should enter the fire *samādhi*, thereby warming his body.[26] If the fire becomes too strong, his body will overheat, and he must correct this by imagining the flames of the fire as wish-fulfilling jewels. They emerge from his pores, and in the midst of the flames he imagines golden lotus flowers, upon which sit transformation buddhas who preach the curing of illness with three different jewels: a "moon essence" *maṇi* jewel, a "starlight" *maṇi* that is blue in color with a white glow, like a star, and a crystal *maṇi*. He imagines the three jewels, one shining on top of his head, one shining on his left [333a1] shoulder, and one shining on his right shoulder. When he has seen the three jewels, he then imagines the light of the jewels emerging from the pores of his body, extremely cool and refreshing. With his body and mind relaxed, he can enter the fire *samādhi* without incurring harm.

This is called the method for curing [imbalances resulting from] the *samādhi* of the fire element.

[1.4.2] [The Earth Element]

Further, Śāriputra, in autumn one should enter the earth *samādhi*. Immersed in the earth *samādhi*, the practitioner will see the many forms of earth: a hundred thousand stone mountains, iron mountains, encircling iron mountains, and adamantine mountains. Each of the three hundred thirty-six bones of his body becomes hundreds of thousands of mountains, steep and jagged in appearance.[27]

To cure this, he must imagine and carefully contemplate these mountains as being as insubstantial as the trunk of a plantain tree. He must contemplate them one by one in this manner, using the ten similes for emptiness from the sutras.[28] He then sees the great earth, in all directions, becoming

---

23. On the "raging defilements," see *Chan Essentials* 4.31.30, n. 579.

24. A stream-enterer is certain to attain arhatship within seven rebirths. In 1.15.5 below, the five hundred Śākya monks indeed "complete" (具) their attainment of the six powers.

25. 柔軟治四大內風法.

26. On the correlations between the seasons and meditations on the primary elements, see chap. 3, pp. 65–66.

27. 山神[>貌]巖崿. Emendation tentative.

28. The allusion here is probably to Kumārajīva's translation of the *Vimalakīrti-nirdeśa*

white beryl and white jewel flowers. He sees Śāriputra, Maudgalyāyana, Kāśyapa, and Kātyāyana sitting within caves of white adamant, sunk within the earth as if it were water.[29] They preach for the practitioner the "separation and coming together of the five"[30] and the impermanence of the earth element. When the practitioner sees these things, his body and mind become relaxed and he regains his sanity.

This is called the method for curing [imbalance of] the earth element.

[1.4.3] [The Water Element]

Further, Śāriputra, if the practitioner enters the water *samādhi* and sees his body as a giant surging fountain of water, his three hundred thirty-six bones all washed away, and if he sees the world in all directions filled with blue, white, or red water, then he must quickly be cured.

The method for curing [this imbalance in the] water element is as follows. First, he must contemplate his body and make it an auspicious *maṇi* jewel vase (摩尼珠吉祥之瓶), with golden flowers covering the top. He must then make the waters of the ten directions flow into the vase. Seven flowers emerge from the auspicious vase, their seven stalks each clearly apparent. Within each stalk are seven jets of water. Within each jet of water are seven golden flowers, and upon each flower sits a buddha preaching the seven limbs of awakening.[31]

This is called the method for curing [imbalance in the] water element.

[1.4.4] [The Wind Element]

Further, Śāriputra, if a practitioner who enters the wind *samādhi* sees his body as a nine-headed snake, each head with nine hundred ears and innumerable mouths, its pores, ears, and mouths like deep gorges emitting violent winds, then he must quickly be cured.

The method for curing is as follows. The practitioner must be taught to

(*Weimojie suo shuo jing*, T.475:14.539b15–21)."Ten similes" (十譬) for emptiness, with the trunk of a plantain tree appearing first, are mentioned in the Contemplation Scriptures (*GFSMH*, T.643:15.674c23–28). A poem on the "ten similes" by Xie Lingyun 謝靈運 (385–433) is preserved (*Guang hong ming ji*, T.2103:52.200a28), and the short "poem on the ten similes" (十喻詩) attributed to Kumārajīva himself may also be based on this list (*Yi wen lei ju*, 76.3b).

29. 履地如水. This formulaic phrase normally describes the magic power of moving through solid objects as freely as if they were water (see, e.g., *Chan Essentials* 2.19.1.10). The idea may be to suggest that these famous arhats have been able to enter the impenetrable caves by virtue of their magical power (recalling, perhaps, the legend in which Mahākāśyapa, after the Buddha's death, entered the solid rock of a mountain and remains there, in *samādhi*, until the appearance of Maitreya).

30. 五破五合. Unclear. Speculatively, this could be an error for 五根五力 (the five faculties and five powers). This would fit with the evident progression, in 1.4.3 and 1.4.4, through the final elements of the thirty-seven *bodhipakṣika-dharmas* (the seven limbs and the eightfold path).

31. On seven flowers as a symbol of the seven limbs of awakening, see *Chan Essentials* 3.26.4, n. 433.

contemplate his body, making for it an adamantine seat.[32] On each side he imagines an adamantine wheel to block the wind. Seven adamantine flowers emerge from the adamantine wheels,[33] upon which are transformation buddhas holding pitchers[34] of water. Within each pitcher is a six-headed dragon that moves about inhaling the winds of the ten directions and making[35] them still. The practitioner then sees the seven buddhas and the four great voice-hearers,[36] who again explain for him the seven limbs of awakening and then gradually reveal the eightfold holy path.

This is called the method for curing [imbalance in] the internal wind element.

[1.5] [The Enveloping Butter[37] Contemplation to Soften the Four Elements and Allow the Gradual Attainment of the Confirmatory Visions of Sanctity][38]

[1.5.1] [Illnesses]

Further, [334b] Śāriputra, if the four elements of the practitioner's body become imbalanced,[39] he may become alternately angry and happy, or sad and joyful. Or he may begin to crawl about on his stomach, or else may pass gas (放下風). He must be taught to immediately cure such sicknesses.

---

32. The "adamantine seat" (金剛座; *vajrāsana*) is where the Buddha sat at the moment of his awakening.

33. 金<剛>. The mention of "adamantine wheels" elsewhere (*Chan Essentials* 1.18.17, 4.31.26; *Methods for Curing* 1.14.11), suggests this is correct. Alternatively, emend {金}剛 in the previous sentence.

34. 澡灌 (K, K^1, J, Q, and Kg; 澡罐 in P, S and Y). See *Chan Essentials* 2.20.4, n. 353.

35. 今[>令, K, K^1, J, P, Q, Kg]. The Taishō is presumably a misprint.

36. Presumably Śāriputra, Maudgalyāyana, Kāśyapa, and Kātyāyana, mentioned in 1.4.2.

37. 擁酥. In the *Mohe zhi guan*, Zhiyi discusses this method and calls it the "*warm* butter method for curing exhaustion" (煖蘇治勞損法; T.1911:46.109a22–23; cf. Swanson 2017, 2.1345), suggesting that his sources read 煖 in place of 擁. I tentatively retain 擁. Following 1.5.7 below, I interpret it as meaning "enveloping."

38. Here "confirmatory vision" is *eryan jingjie* 爾焰境界. *Eryan* is relatively well attested as a transcription of Skt. *jñeya* (*Fan fan yu*, T.2130:54.989c18). Literally "what is to be known," *jñeya* was used in the context of meditation to mean the ideal object of which the meditator should gain perception—in the *Yogalehrbuch*, the extant Indic source bearing the closest similarity to the *Chan Essentials* and *Methods for Curing*, it is the most general term for the visionary scenes the meditator comes to perceive (Schlingloff 1964, 80, 103, 105, 107, 109). Along with similar terms such as *ālambana* and *viṣaya*, the word *jñeya* was often translated into Chinese as *jingjie* 境界 (medieval Chinese commentators often gloss *eryan* as *jingjie;* see *Sheng man bao ku*, T.1744:37.16b4–5), which I have generally translated as "confirmatory vision." *Eryan jingjie* is, therefore, a combination transcription-translation. Why the *Methods for Curing* here uses this word rather than just *jingjie* is not clear. It may be relevant, however, that the only other known example of the word *eryan jingjie* is in Buddhabhadra's famous meditation text the *Damoduoluo chan jing* (T.618:15.324b16–17), describing the objects seen by the buddhas in their meditation. This occurs in the same section of that text that also mentions the unusual concept of the "beryl *samādhi*" that figures in the opening story of the *Methods for Curing* (see 1.1.1). It thus seems likely that the *Damoduoluo chan jing* was one of the sources that the author(s) of *Methods for Curing* was inspired by.

39. Literally, "coarse" (*cuse* 麁澁). This probably derives from Skt. *karkaśa* (hard, coarse, rough), often the word that denotes the problematic state of the four elements that create bodily illness (Salguero 2014, 72).

[1.5.2] [Contemplation of the Skin][40]

The method for curing this is as follows. First, he must, beginning from the tip of his toe, contemplate the outer layer of his skin.[41] He sees this outer layer of skin, itself ninety-nine layers thick, swelling up as if filled with air. Next he must contemplate the inner layer of skin, also ninety-nine layers thick, like the [layered leaves of the trunk of] a plantain tree. Next he must contemplate the thin membrane [between the inner and outer layers of skin].[42] As thin as a cataract on the eye, composed of ninety-nine layers, it bulges outward to the verge of tearing.

[1.5.3] [The Channels]

Next he must contemplate his muscles, which also have ninety-nine layers, like the leaves [of the trunk of] a plantain tree. Within the muscles are worms, as tiny as autumn goose down. Each worm has four heads, four mouths, and ninety-nine tails. Next he must contemplate his bones, shining white like white beryl, ninety-eight layers thick, like the leaves of [the trunk of] a plantain tree. The four hundred four channels reach into the bones transmitting fluids up and down. Next he must contemplate the bone marrow, ninety-eight layers thick and like a cobweb in appearance.

When he has contemplated all of his bones, he must next contemplate his skull. Beneath each strand of hair there are four hundred four channels that go straight into the brain. Everything else—such as the outer layer of skin, the inner layer of skin, the bones—is here just as it is elsewhere in the body. The only difference is that the brain membrane has only fourteen layers. The brain itself has four sections, ninety-eight layers, and four hundred four channels that flow directly into the heart.

[1.5.4] [The Organs]

The meditator must carefully contemplate his stomach, intestines, spleen, kidneys, liver, lungs, heart, gallbladder, throat, lung-point,[43] the receptacles of undigested and digested food and the eighty[44] families of worms, causing everything to become transparent, glimmering white, and pure, bright and pure like white beryl encased within layers of the skin.

[1.5.5] [The Adamantine Sword]

In this manner he must contemplate each bone of his body, making all three hundred thirty-six bones clear and apparent and concentrating his mind upon them. He should repeat this one thousand nine hundred ninety-nine

40. Sections 1.5.2–4 resemble portions of *Chan Essentials* 1.1.4 and 1.5.1.

41. On the outer (thin) and inner (thick) layers of skin, see *Chan Essentials* 1.5.1, n. 76.

42. Following *Chan Essentials* 1.5.1, the "membrane" lies between the thin (outer) and thick (inner) layers of skin.

43. On the "lung-point," see *Chan Essentials* 1.1.4 and chap. 3, p. 65.

44. 萬[>十, Kg]. See *Chan Essentials* 1.1.5, n. 26.

times. Then he should gather his breath and smoothly count his inhalations and exhalations. He should then imagine Lord Brahmā holding a divine water pitcher. Together with a host of brahma gods, Lord Brahmā approaches and gives the practitioner an adamantine sword. Taking the sword, he should slice a piece off the top of his own skull the size of a piece of agate and then place it on his left knee.[45]

[1.5.6] [Medicine from Lord Brahmā's Topknot]

Within the water pitcher grow nine white lotus flowers.[46] A boy emerges from the first flower and falls in line behind Lord Brahmā. This boy is white in color, like a white-jade man. He holds a white pitcher full of ghee. The magic jewel in Lord Brahmā's topknot then exudes medicinal herbs that mix into the ghee, and the boy pours the ghee into the practitioner's skull. It enters the channels within the brain and flows downward, reaching all the way to the tip of his left big toe. His body becomes entirely filled, saturated out to the outer layer of skin. Bit by bit, half his body is filled. When half has been filled, it continues until his entire body is filled. When his entire body is filled, the medicines flow through the four hundred four channels, [334c] irrigating[47] and filling his three hundred thirty-six bones.

[1.5.7] [The Himalayan Butter]

He should then pick up the piece of his skull and put it back on his head. The boy then takes a blue medicine and spreads it on the practitioner's head. The medicine seeps into his pores. Fearing that external winds might enter the practitioner, Lord Brahmā then prepares some Himalayan butter (雪山酥), fresh and pure, dripping with ghee. Like a barrier of crystal, [the butter] envelops the practitioner's body forty-nine times. It then grows larger, becoming a lake of pure ghee. The practitioner sits on a lotus flower made of white butter under a canopy of butter within a cave of butter. Lord Brahmā's medicine of compassion (慈藥) is mixed throughout the butter.

He must carefully contemplate this nine hundred ninety-nine times.

[1.5.8] [The Red Medicine]

He must next imagine that within the second lotus flower there is a red boy. This boy spreads a red medicine through the practitioner's hair and all over the pores of his body. The red medicine is absorbed through the outer layer of his skin, eventually reaching the marrow of his bones. His belly[48] becomes bright (明), and his entire body gradually becomes soft and supple.

---

45. This passage seemingly alludes to trepanation (surgical opening of the skull), which was practiced in ancient India.

46. 生白蓮花九節九莖九重. Translation tentative. I take *jie* 節 'node,' *jing* 莖 'stem,' and *zhong* 重 [>臺? 'dais'] as somehow indicating the different parts of the flowers.

47. 觀[>灌]. Emendation tentative.

48. See *Chan Essentials* 1.1.2, n. 17.

[1.5.9] [The Yellow Medicine]

From the third lotus flower a golden boy emerges, who spreads a yellow medicine through the practitioner's hair and over all the pores of his body. The yellow medicine is absorbed through his outer skin, eventually reaching the marrow of his bones. His belly becomes blue, and his entire body gradually becomes more and more supple.[49]

[1.5.10] [The Blue Medicine]

In the fourth lotus flower, there is a beryl-colored boy who spreads blue medicine with his right hand through the practitioner's hair and over all the pores of his body. The blue medicine is absorbed through his outer skin, eventually reaching the marrow of his bones. His belly becomes red.

Into each of his pores the boy inserts a needle pointing downward, and through the soles of his feet he inserts two needles pointing upward.[50] Three lotus flowers, containing three fire jewels radiating red light, appear above the practitioner's heart. The light shines upon his heart, gently warming the belly area beneath it.

The boy then inserts three needles into each of the joints of the practitioner's two palms, upward or downward depending on the channel in question.[51] This balances (調和) the various *qi*, makes[52] the four hundred four channels free of turmoil, and strengthens the large intestine and kidney channels. Taking five needles, the boy then stimulates the left intestine channel, manipulating the needles with inconceivable skill and refinement. He then removes them and hides them beneath his fingernails. With his hands he massages the practitioner's body all over.

[1.5.11] [The Green Medicine]

In the fifth lotus flower, there is a green boy who pours a jade pitcher of green medicine into the practitioner's anus. It fills his large and small intestines, his five viscera, and all the channels of his body. Then it flows back out through his anus, carrying with it various worms and impurities while not diminishing the [previously applied] ghee. When the worms are entirely removed, the liquid stops flowing. The boy then spreads a dry green medicine through the practitioner's hair and over all the pores of his body. The dry green medicine is absorbed through the outer skin, eventually reaching the marrow of his bones. His belly becomes white, [335a] and his entire body gradually becomes even more soft and supple.

---

49. 遍體漸漸增長復更增長[>柔, K^1, P, S, Y, Q]軟. Translation tentative.

50. As noted by Salguero (2014, 85–86), this is a clear reference to acupuncture.

51. 各下三針，隨脈上下. What "upward" and "downward" mean here is not entirely clear. I assume it has something to do with regulating the competing energies of the four elements, with fire and wind tending upward while earth and water tend downward (as discussed in *Chan Essentials* 4.31.8, and elsewhere).

52. 生[>令]四百四脈不觸. Emendation tentative. Keeping the original reading, perhaps: "vivifies the 404 channels but does not disturb them."

[1.5.12] [The Rose Medicine]

In the sixth lotus flower, there is a purple boy who cleans the channels with rosewater from a rose-jewel pitcher. Then the rose-colored water is made to exit the practitioner's body through the pores, carrying with it all the worms living beneath his body hair. The boy spreads a dry rose-colored medicine through his hair and over all the pores of his body. The dry rose-colored medicine is absorbed through his outer skin, eventually reaching the marrow of his bones. His belly becomes even brighter, like gleaming white snow, and his entire body gradually becomes even more soft and supple.

[1.5.13] [The Adamantine Nail]

In the seventh flower, there is a yellow boy who pierces the practitioner's hands, feet, and the two sides of his heart with adamantine nails. Then he rubs the practitioner's six organs with a royal wish-fulfilling jewel, making the organs experience the bliss of the highest level of trance.[53] [The practitioner's body] becomes thoroughly soft and supple, as if all his wrinkles were smeared with pure fat.

[1.5.14] [The Adamantine Medicine]

In the eighth flower, there is an adamant-colored boy who pours adamant-colored medicine from two pitchers into the practitioner's ears and pores. Just as when being massaged each of the body's joints are adjusted in turn, so too does this medicine travel through each joint of his chain-like body.

[1.5.15] [The Five-Colored Medicine]

In the ninth flower, there is a boy the color of a *maṇi* jewel. He emerges from the mouth of [Lord Brahmā's] pitcher and comes before the practitioner. He places the five fingers of his right[54] hand inside the practitioner's mouth, and a five-colored medicine flows from the tips of his five fingers. When the practitioner contemplates his body after consuming this medicine, his heart and its channels are as pure as a clear mirror, surpassing even crystal or *maṇi* jewels. Then the boy feeds the practitioner the flower stalks. They are crunchy like lotus root, and their juices are ambrosia.

[1.5.16] [The Throne of Lord Brahmā]

When he has eaten the stalks, only the nine flowers remain. Within each flower there is a Lord Brahmā. They give the practitioner a Brahmā throne to sit upon. When he sits on it, a great canopy made of the seven precious substances extends above him, and the Lords Brahmā each instruct the practitioner in the method for cultivating love. By the power of these lords, the buddhas of the ten directions arrive before the practitioner and preach

53. "Six organs" (六根) seems to point here to the entirety of the physical body, not the "six sense organs" in the usual Buddhist sense; see *Chan Essentials* 4.31.16.

54. 内[>右].

for him [the method for cultivating] love, compassion, mutual joy, and equanimity.[55] In accordance with his capacity they give him medicine that makes the four elements of his body soft and supple.

[1.5.17] [Conclusion]

[The Buddha] said to Śāriputra: "You must preserve and preach for the four groups of Buddhists this method for contemplating Lord Brahmā's consecration of the crown of the head with enveloping butter, which makes the four elements of the body soft and supple and tames the ninety-eight defilements and all illness, both internal and external."[56]

When Śāriputra and the venerable Ānanda heard what the Buddha had said, they joyfully undertook to carry it out.

[1.6] [The Method for Curing Blockage][57]

[1.6.1] [The Arising of Blockage]

Further, Śāriputra, if a forest-dwelling monk employs his mind [in meditation] with too much tension, is too rough with his breathing, or sleeps in too Spartan conditions, he will, owing to external winds, become afflicted by cold. As a result, his stomach tube[58] and spleen and kidney channels will become agitated, and wind will stir within his tendons. A reverse *qi* (逆氣) will stagnate in his chest. All his joints will leak water, which will accumulate in his chest [335b]. His blood will roil (激血), his *qi* will erupt (氣發), his head will ache, his back will swell (背滿), and all his tendons will seize up. This must be treated quickly.

[1.6.2] [The Waters of Anavatapta]

The method for curing it is as follows. First, the practitioner must take excellent, nourishing worldly medicine.[59] He should then lie down on his back, count his breaths, and settle himself.

He should then imagine Lake Anavatapta,[60] its waters filling a full

55. The four *brahma-vihāras* (*apramāṇas*), associated with rebirth in the brahma heavens.

56. 柔軟四大伏九十八使身內身外一切諸病梵王灌頂擁酥灌[>觀]法. This entire long phrase seems to modify the final 灌[>觀]法, in the manner of a long Indic compound mechanically translated into Chinese.

57. 治噎法. On "blockage" (噎), see chap. 3, p. 64.

58. 脾[>胃, K, K[1], J, P, Kg]管.

59. 肥膩世間美藥. Alternatively, he must consume: "fat, which is an excellent worldly medicine."

60. Lake Anavatapta is the source of the four great rivers in Indian Buddhist cosmography. Its description here includes numerous elements—the four animal heads, the ground of golden sand, and the "chariot-wheel" flowers—found in canonical accounts (*DZDL*, T.1509:25.114a15–28; *Chang ahan jing*, T.1:1.116c16–117a1). Normally, however, the animal heads lie at the edges of the lake in the cardinal directions, the water flowing from them becoming the four great rivers—rather different from the situation here. For a detailed study of the legends of Lake Anavatapta in medieval Chinese translations of Indian Buddhist literature, see Zhu L. 2016, 89–96.

yojana.[61] The bottom of the lake is golden sand, and there is a golden wheel as big as a chariot's made of four precious substances. From it grows a golden flower, within which are four jeweled animal heads: an elephant's, whose trunk spouts water, as well as those of a lion, a horse, and a bull, all of whose mouths spout water. These waters circle the lake seven times. In the middle of the four animal heads is the dragon king of Lake Anavatapta in a palace made of the seven precious substances.

[1.6.3] [The Arhats of Anavatapta and Jīvaka]

By his power, fifteen hundred lotus flowers of various colors grow from the wish-fulfilling jewel on the crown of the dragon king's head. Five hundred are blue lotus flowers, upon which are seated Piṇḍola and the remainder of the five hundred arhats. The flowers close at sunset and open again at dawn. The canopies above the monks' heads are made of the seven precious substances, as are their seats on the lotus flowers below.

Upon five hundred golden lotus flowers sit Cundrava[62] and the remainder of the five hundred novices. The flowers close at sunset and open again at dawn. The canopies above the novices' heads are made of the seven precious substances, as are their seats on the lotus flowers below.

Upon five hundred red lotus flowers sit Upananda, Vasumitra,[63] and the other great arhats. Some say this is the five-hundred-person retinue of the great bodhisattva [the dragon king].[64] The flowers close at sunset and open again at dawn. The canopies above the monks' heads are made of the seven precious substances, as are their seats on the lotus flowers below.

There is further a tall dais made of the seven precious substances, eight thousand feet wide, extending upward directly in front of the palace of the dragon king of Anavatapta. Upon this dais are five hundred boys, their bodies the color of pure gold. The first is named Jīvaka,[65] the second is named Good Fortune,[66] and the last is named Empowered by Consecration (灌頂力).

[1.6.4] [The Abaddha Medicine]

One who wishes to cure the illness of blockage should first bring to mind the venerable Piṇḍola and the fifteen hundred people mentioned previously. When he sees them all clearly, the venerable Piṇḍola will bring forward

61. On *yojana* as a unit of area rather than length, see *Chan Essentials* 1.2.1.3, n. 57.

62. *Chun-tuo-po* 淳陀婆, mentioned again in *Methods for Curing* 2.11. This name is unknown in other sources. *Chun-tuo* 淳陀, however, is a common transcription of the famous Cundra, the Buddha's final disciple, ordained on the eve of his *parinirvāṇa*.

63. *He-xu-mi-duo* 和須蜜多 (see *Fan fan yu*, T.2130:54.998c1).

64. The dragon king of Lake Anavatapta is sometimes said to be a seventh-stage bodhisattva (*DZDL*, T.1509:25.114a16–17), so I presume this is the referent here.

65. Jīvaka is a famous physician mentioned in many Buddhist scriptures (Salguero 2009); his appearance here as a "boy" is somewhat odd.

66. 善財; *Sudhana*.

the boy Jīvaka, who holds out the white medicinal herb named *abaddha*[67] used by the dragon king of Anavatapta. (The *abaddha* herb tastes like sugarcane and is shaped like a lotus root. Its flavor is also like rock sugar.) When the practitioner has consumed this medicine, his blockage will be cured, his four [bodily] elements will be balanced, and his vision will become clear.

[1.6.5] [Attainment]

For one who aspires to the Great Vehicle, Jīvaka, Good Fortune, and the remainder of the five hundred boys will preach the teachings of the Great Vehicle. As a result, the practitioner will be able to see the sixteen noble ones led by Bhadrapāla,[68] as well as Maitreya and the remainder of the one thousand bodhisattvas [who will become buddhas during] this auspicious eon.[69] By means of this, the practitioner will produce the aspiration for the complete, perfect awakening of a buddha (*anuttarasaṃyaksambodhi*), and he will become fully endowed with the six *pāramitās*.

For one who aspires to become a voice-hearer, the venerable Piṇḍola will preach the four bases of mindfulness and the other [*bodhipakṣika-dharmas*] up to the eightfold holy [335c] path. After ninety days, the practitioner will become an arhat.

[1.6.6] [Conclusion]

[The Buddha] said to Śāriputra: "You must preserve this method for curing blockage. Do not forget it." When Śāriputra and Ānanda heard what the Buddha said, they joyfully undertook to carry it out.

[1.7] [The Method for Curing Practitioners Injured by Lust][70]

[1.7.1] [Blocked Sense Organs Lead to Madness]

Further, Śāriputra, if in a practitioner who has entered trance a perception of something desirable produces lust,[71] the wind of lust will stir the four hundred four channels connecting his eyes and sexual organs, which will

---

67. *A-po-tuo* 菴婆陀. Though this word is not attested elsewhere, *po-tuo*, in another context, is explained in the *Da zhi du lun* as a transcription of *baddha* 'bound' (*DZDL*, T.1509:25.408b25–26). *A-po-tuo* thus could be *abaddha*, "unbound," an apt name for the medicine that both cures "blockage" and leads to liberation!

68. This must refer to the *Pratyutpanna-samādhi* (*Banzhou sanmei jing* 般舟三昧經), in which the main interlocutor is the lay bodhisattva Bhadrapāla 跋陀婆羅 and his cohort of sixteen bodhisattvas (Harrison 1990). This company is also mentioned at *GFSMH*, T.643:15.645c15–16.

69. *Xianjie* 賢劫 (*bhadra-kalpa*). This is the name of the present eon of the universe, so called because of the large number of buddhas who will appear during it.

70. 治行者貪婬患法.

71. 欲覺起貪婬. I take 欲覺 as the subject and 貪婬 as the object of 起. This is awkward. But see *WMCJ*, T.619:15.326c5 and 328a1 for examples where *jue* 覺 is similarly modified by an adjective. The basic idea—that sensory perception can cause great harm for someone immersed in trance—is similar to the frame story (1.1.2).

begin to move all at once.[72] [Because] the sense organs are blocked off, the heart wind will be stirred, leading to the disturbance of the heart and then, by consequence, to madness.[73] Possessed by *guimei* demons, he will think, day and night, only of the objects of his desire.

This must quickly be cured, as urgently as extinguishing a fire on one's head.

[1.7.2] [The Womb]

The method for curing this is as follows. The practitioner must be instructed to contemplate the womb.[74]

The womb is located below the receptacle of undigested food and above the receptacle of digested food. Its membrane is ninety-nine layers thick, like the placenta of a stillborn pig.[75] From it emerge four hundred four channels like the spreading roots of a tree. It is like a bag filled with shit. Its nineteen hundred folds are like the leaves of the trunk of a plantain tree, and the eighty[76] families of worms swarm around it. The four hundred four channels and the receptacle of the child are like the intestines of a horse. They extend down to the vaginal opening (產門), which is the size and shape of a round bracelet. Round on top and pointed on the bottom, it is shaped like a tooth.[77] Between each of its ninety-nine layers there are four hundred four worms, each with twelve heads and twelve mouths.

[1.7.3] [The Female Reproductive Fluids]

When [a woman] drinks water, the essence of water (水精) enters the channels and is distributed to the worms. The water enters the heads of the *piluo* worms,[78] which go to the vaginal opening at the midpoint of each month, from whence leaks an impure liquid, like fetid pus, that is the vomit of these worms. After entering the mouths of nine or ten worms, [the water] emerges from the six openings of the worms' twelve [heads][79] as the fetid red sludge

72. 風動四百四脈，從眼至身根，一時動搖. On *shen'gen* 身根 meaning penis, see *Chan Essentials* 3.29.2, n. 483. See also 1.7.4 below.

73. 諸情閉塞，動於心風，使心顛狂，因是發狂. See similarly 1.8.1. There too the meditator, immersed in trance, cannot act out his desires through the normal means, leading the winds to rebound on his heart / mind, causing madness.

74. *Zizang* 子藏. This Chinese term for "womb" rarely if ever occurs in Chinese translations of Indic Buddhist literature. But its stated location—between the receptacles for undigested and digested food—accords with Indian Buddhist accounts of fetal gestation (see, e.g., *Apidamo da piposha lun*, T.1545:27.507a21–22; *Xiu xing dao di jing*, T.606:15.187c22).

75. 死猪胞. Translation tentative.

76. 萬[>十, Kg]; agreeing with *Fa yuan zhu lin*, T.2122:53.793b21.

77. 具[>貝, K, K¹, J, Kg, P, Q]齒. The Taishō is presumably a misprint.

78. 毘羅蟲. Unknown. Buddhist accounts of the bodily worms frequently name numerous varieties (see, e.g., *Xiu xing dao di jing*, T.606:15.188a28–c2).

79. 入九十蟲口中從十二蟲六竅中出. Or, possibly, the water "enters the mouths of ninety worms and emerges from the six openings of twelve worms." The six openings are presumably the two eyes, two ears, mouth, and nose. I take this sentence to be an elaboration of the previous one, explaining more fully how the water is vomited out by the worms as menstrual blood.

[of menstrual blood], within which squirm yet more worms, as tiny as autumn down.

[1.7.4] [Male Anatomy]

In a man's body, because of sins from past lives, the four hundred four channels spread from the eyes throughout the four limbs, reaching then to the entrails and finally to the place below the receptacle of raw food and above the receptacle of digested food,[80] bounded on its two sides by the lung-point and kidney channels.[81] Each channel contains sixty-four twelve-headed twelve-mouthed worms that squirm against each other. Shaped like little rings, they are full of blue pus as unbearably smelly and foul as the ejaculate of a wild boar.[82]

As they extend to the "hidden organ" [of the penis],[83] they divide into three branches, two branches on the top side [of the penis (?)]. Like the leaves of the trunk of a plantain tree, there are twelve hundred channels [wrapped around each other] here. Within each channel live wind worms, as tiny as autumn down, shaped like the beaks of *pilanduo* birds.[84] Within the mouths of these worms live the tendon worms (筋色蟲). (These worms look like tendons. They latch onto the womb and stir its channels, sucking up essence as they move in and out. The male worms are blueish white, and the female ones deep red.) Seventy-eight thousand in number, they connect like linked rings and have ninety-eight eyes like *jushiluo* birds.[85] Going upward, the channels connect to the heart and then all the way to the crown of the head.[86]

[1.7.5] [Male Sexual Fluid]

When a man's [336a] eye encounters a visible form, wind stirs his heart. The four hundred four channels fall sway to the wind, moving without cease. The eighty thousand[87] families of worms open their mouths in unison. A

---

80. The production of male sexual fluid occurs in the location corresponding to the site of the womb in the female body.

81. 肺腴腎脈於其兩邊. The citations of this passage in the *Fa yuan zhu lin* (T.2122:53.793c2) and *Zhu jing yao ji* (T.2123:54.186c4) read 肺脾, implying "the *lung*, *spleen*, and kidney channels." I retain "lung-point" (肺腴). The "lung-point," as we have seen, is located near the throat (*Chan Essentials* 1.1.4). So the meaning here, if this reading is correct, must be some kind of channel associated with it.

82. 野猪精. Above, the womb was also compared to porcine anatomy.

83. *Yinzang* 陰藏. This word commonly denotes the penis in Chinese Buddhist texts but usually refers specifically to the Buddha's penis, owing to its being "hidden" within its sheath (one of the thirty-two marks). The *Methods for Curing* seems to have taken it as a generic word—possibly a further sign of Chinese authorship.

84. 毘蘭多. Unknown.

85. 瞿師羅. Unknown. The word is however attested in Chinese Buddhist texts as a transcription of the (human) name Ghosila (*Zhong ahan jing*, T.26:1.532c10).

86. See, similarly, 1.5.3.

87. Kg, along with *Fa yuan zhu lin* (T.2122:53.793c14) and *Zhu jing yao ji* (T.2123:54.186c13) read *eighty* (八十). Though I have in other passages followed the readings "eighty" for the worms of the stomach, these worms appear to be a different set, so I tentatively retain "eighty thousand."

pus-like substance flows from their eyes and through the channels until it reaches the top of the [tendon] worms' heads. These worms shake wildly, lose control, and charge toward the woman's sexual organs.[88]

Male essence, which is blueish white, comprises the tears of these worms. Female essence, which is brownish red, comprises the pus of the worms. [Both are] created through the perfume-like conditioning of the ninety-eight defilements,[89] the eighty thousand families of worms, and the movements of the earth, water, fire, and wind elements.

[1.7.6] [Purifying the Organs with Impure Sexual Fluids]

[The Buddha] said to Śāriputra: If a follower of the Buddha wears the clothing of shame,[90] takes the medicine of shame, and wishes to seek liberation and traverse the suffering of the world, then he must learn this method, which is like the drinking of ambrosia.

One learning this method should imagine the aforementioned womb, female sexual organs (女根), male sexual organs,[91] and worms large and small that open their mouths, tense their bodies,[92] open wide their eyes, and vomit up the pus [of the sexual fluids].

He should then turn it over with his hand and place [the sexual fluid] on his left knee.[93] He should count his breath and settle it, contemplating these things one thousand nine hundred ninety-nine times. When this meditation is complete, he should place it on his right knee, and contemplate these things as before. He should then turn it over with his hand again and cover the top of his head with it. He should make this worm-ridden impurity go first into his eyes, then into his ears, nose, and mouth, such that there is no place it does not go.

[1.7.7] [Seeing All Beings as Impure]

After he has seen these things, viewing attractive women or men, even gods or goddesses, will be like looking at worms in the infected sores[94] of a leper, at the ghoulish figure of a hellish *Jianbanduoluo* demon,[95] or the raging fires

88. This appears to describe the moment of ejaculation.

89. 九十八使所熏修法.

90. In some of the Contemplation Scriptures, this expression "wear the clothing of shame" (著慚愧衣) seems to mean to purify oneself through repentance (*GFSMH*, T.643:15.682a20–25; *Guan Xukongzang pusa jing*, T.409:13.677b24). *Methods for Curing* 1.9.11 also speaks of the "medicine of shame" and the "clothes of humility" in connection with repentance.

91. 男子身分. This term denotes the penis at *GFSMH*, T.643:15.685a12–15.

92. 竪耳[>身, Kg].

93. 以手反之置左膝端. We might instead understand that the practitioner should "turn over his hand and place it on his left knee." But, given how things develop, I think the meditator is here manipulating the imagined ejaculate, which he eventually then places into his eyes to complete the cycle by bringing the impure sexual fluid back into contact with the eyes whose stimulation produced it.

94. *Nali chuang* 那利瘡; see *Chan Essentials* 1.14.3, n. 157.

95. 箭半多羅. Unknown.

of the Avīci hell. The practitioner must carefully contemplate his own body and the bodies of others. The bodies of all living beings in the sphere of desire are impure in this way.

[The Buddha] said to Śāriputra: Do you now understand? The sexual organs of living beings are fundamentally and in every way entirely, indescribably impure. One must merely count the breath and single-mindedly contemplate this.

[1.7.8] [Conclusion]

One who takes the medicine [of this practice] is a great man, a teacher of humans and gods, a master of men to be trained.[96] He has escaped from the mud of desire, no longer to be drowned by the waters of the defilements or the great river of attachment, nor will he be seduced by baneful, deceptive succubi.[97] Know that such a person, though he has not yet escaped from birth and death, has a body as fragrant as an *utpala* flower. He will be a fragrant elephant king among men, unequaled even by the mighty Maheśvara, a mighty man venerated by gods and men.

[The Buddha] said to Śāriputra: "You must preserve this teaching and preach it for the four groups of Buddhists. Do not forget it."

When Śāriputra and Ānanda heard what the Buddha said, they joyfully undertook to carry it out.

[1.8] [The Method for Curing the Wound of Personal Benefits][98]

[1.8.1] [Madness Caused by Craving for Personal Gain]

Further, Śāriputra, a practitioner whose heart is burned by the fires of greed, into which an evil wind shoots the poisonous arrows of [desire for] personal gain, will because of his greed become disoriented. Day [336b] and night he will ponder ways to exercise his greed,[99] like a cat stalking a mouse, his mind never knowing satisfaction.[100] As if poisoned by the "seven-steps-to-death" snake,[101] this evil person accumulates within himself[102] the five hundred poisonous snakes of [desire for] personal benefit and sensuous objects.[103] From moment to moment the searing fires in his heart burn

---

96. These are two of the traditional epithets of the Buddha.

97. 婬泆不祥幻色妖鬼.

98. 治利養瘡法. The curious expression "wound of personal benefits" (利養瘡) appears at *DZDL*, T.1509:25.164b26–c1; Lamotte (1944–1981, 867) sees this as a reference to the *Vālurajja-sutta* of the *Saṃyutta-nikāya* (2.238), describing how gain, honor, and fame are like a rope that cuts through one's flesh when tightened.

99. 思念貪方便.

100. The language here is very similar to *Chan Essentials* 4.32.6.

101. 七步蛇 (Skt. *saptapadāśi;* Hirakawa 1997, 18). This snake is mentioned in some sources as having a poison so potent that victims die after seven steps (*Apitan piposha lun*, T.1546:28.186a19–21).

102. 集在身上[>中, K, K¹, J, P, Q, Kg]. The Taishō is presumably a misprint.

103. *Huaxi* 滑細 (smooth and fine), the standard pre-Kumārajīva translation of *spraṣṭavya*, the objects of the bodily sense organ (later translated into Chinese as *chu* 觸).

without respite. Throughout all hours of the day and night the vicious wind of the defilements fans the fuel of [craving for] personal gain that burns ceaselessly within his heart as the snakes vie with one another to incinerate the sprouts of his wholesome roots.

For this reason he becomes a wild demon of darkness (狂亂黑鬼), enraged by fierce poison. When he sees someone else acquire something of benefit, it is like an arrow piercing his heart, a needle poked in his eye, a nail hammered into his ear. When his sense organs are blocked off [in trance],[104] the five hundred evil snakes,[105] the poisonous dragons of the four elements, the five blade-wielding thieves, and the six village-[raiding] demons spring up all at once.[106] He goes mad as a result and must be quickly treated.

[1.8.2] [Monastic Robes Like Swords]

The method for curing this is as follows. First, he must count his breath and concentrate his mind, and then imagine an image of the sixteen-foot Buddha, its body the color of purple gold, endowed with the thirty-two marks, sitting on a bejeweled lion's seat within a cave made of the seven precious substances on Mount Gṛdrakūṭa, and accompanied by the four groups of followers.

[This Buddha] then preaches the method for destroying desire: "O Dharma child, you must now contemplate the things to which in your greed you cling—monastic robes, the six requisites,[107] and the various other implements—as a forest of brambles. Within the seams[108] [of your robes] appear sword trees, hundreds of thousands of iron nails, and worms with iron beaks that devour you. Cauldrons of molten copper, iron saws, and iron beds are your sitting cloths.[109] Boiling shit, poisonous snakes, iron balls, cauldrons of boiling liquid, forests of knives and swords, millions of brambles,

---

104. See, similarly, 1.7.1 above.

105. 五百五[>惡]蚢. Emendation tentative.

106. The imagery here draws from several famous canonical similes that liken the four elements to poisonous snakes, the five *skandha*s to sword-wielding men, the six internal sense bases (*āyatana*) to an empty village, and the six external sense bases to six village-raiding bandits (*Saṃyutta-nikāya*, 4.173–174; Bodhi 2000, 1237–1238; *Zengyi ahan jing*, T.125:2.670a3–9; *Za ahan jing*, T.99:2.313c11–18).

107. The "six requisites" (*liu wu* 六物), an early list of the personal possessions permitted for monks and nuns, normally are the three monastic robes, begging bowl, sitting cloth, and water strainer (*Kōsetsu Bukkyōgo daijiten*, 1460).

108. 針[>縫, J, Kg]縫之中.

109. Compare with *DZDL*, T.1509:25.154b24–29: "When one who breaks the precepts puts on monastic robes, it will be like hot copper or an iron saw being pressed against the body; holding a begging bowl it will be like holding a bowl filled with molten copper; eating will be like swallowing a hot iron ball, or like drinking molten copper; receiving offerings will be as if being attacked by the demons of hell; entering the monastery will be as if entering hell; sitting on a seat it will be like sitting on a bed of hot iron."

rivers of fire, molten copper, liquid ash, and pus and blood are your food and drink."

[1.8.3] [Vision of Hell]

When [this visionary] World-honored One has spoken these words, he becomes silent. He then causes the practitioner to see himself lying within a city ringed by seven iron walls.[110] He sees five hundred *rākṣasas* who stretch his mouth open wide and with eighteen iron tongs pull out his tongue. With innumerable iron plows shaped like sword trees, they plow his tongue. Molten copper flows from the hooves of the iron plow oxen.[111] Within the bodies of the iron oxen[112] there are hundreds of thousands of kinds of worm-infested pus.

[1.8.4] [Fear]

Contemplating and seeing these things, the practitioner becomes alarmed and his hair stands on end. Whether in trance or not, he sees his clothing as blood-specked pus and shit [upon his body] with iron-beaked worms and forests of razor blades for ornaments. He sees his food as the pus, shit, piss, and blood that ooze from the ears of hundreds of thousands of tiny parasitic worms. He sees his begging bowl filled with the pus and poisonous vomit of all kinds of worms—worms with eighty mouths, wind worms, fire worms, water worms, earth worms, and hell worms. He sees any fruit [he eats] as iron balls or razor blades.

[1.8.5] [Verses on Impurity by the Buddha][113]

The World-honored One[114] then spoke the following verses:

It is because of craving and fondness for delicious flavors
that birth and death are not yet severed.
With bitter regret will such a one
vainly undergo hardship and suffering [336c].
The body is foul, like a corpse,
leaking impurity from its nine openings.
Fools who crave the body are thus no different
from worms in a dung heap delighting in excrement.
A wise one must rather contemplate the body [as it is],
not craving for the polluted things of this world.

---

110. This probably denotes the Avīci hell, which the *Ocean-Samādhi Contemplation Scripture* describes as: "square, eight thousand *yojanas* [on a side], surrounded by seven rings of iron walls and covered in seven layers of iron nets." 縱廣正等八千由旬，七重鐵城，七層鐵網。(*GFSMH*, T.643:15.668c4–5).

111. The "hell of thorns" (刺林地獄) is described similarly at *GFSMH*, T.643:15.672b18–c5.

112. 鐵卒[>牛].

113. On these verses, see Appendix 1, 3d.

114. It is impossible to say if this verse is spoken by the visionary buddha encountered by the meditator, or by the Buddha preaching the *Methods for Curing* to Śāriputra.

Unattached and free of craving,
this is what is called true nirvana.
To practice single-mindedly
as the buddhas have taught,
counting the breath while dwelling in a quiet place—
this is called [truly] practicing the austerities (頭陀).

[1.8.6] [Conclusion]

[The Buddha] then said to Śāriputra: "It is simply indescribable the extent to which [desire for] personal benefits causes harm and destroys roots of good. One must simply count the breath, concentrate the mind, and contemplate.

"One[115] who takes this medicine is a great man, a teacher of humans and gods, a master of men to be trained. He has escaped from the mud of desire, no longer drowned by the waters of the defilements or the great river of affection, nor burned by the bane of personal benefits. Know that such a person, though he has not yet escaped from birth and death, will have a fragrant body, like an *utpala* flower. He will be a fragrant elephant king among men, unequaled even by the mighty Maheśvara, a mighty man, venerated by gods and men."

[The Buddha] said to Śāriputra: "You must preserve [this teaching] and preach it for the four groups of Buddhists. Do not forget it."

When Śāriputra and Ānanda heard what the Buddha said, they joyfully undertook to carry it out.

[1.9] [The Method for Curing Violations of the Precepts][116]

[1.9.1] [The Precept Breaker]

Further, Śāriputra, monks, nuns, probationary nuns, novice monks, novice nuns, laymen, or laywomen who have received the Buddha's precepts may go mad in body and mind.[117] Just as wild monkeys might destroy crops root and branch before they have come to fruition, so too these practitioners, before the precept matter[118] has sprouted [in attainment], violate precepts ranging from the [minor] *duṣkṛta* to the [most serious] *pārājika* offenses.

Like drunken elephants who pay no attention to the good or evil of what they do and trample and destroy all manner of good things, being unaware of where they are going, so too do the seven groups of Buddhist practitio-

115. The conclusion here is nearly identical to 1.7.8 above.

116. 汝[>治, K, K[1], J, P, Q, Kg]犯戒法. The Taishō is presumably a misprint. I discuss this section of the *Methods for Curing* at length in *Chan Before Chan*, chap. 4.

117. 身心狂亂. As in the opening narrative (1.1.2) and first section (1.2.2), madness here is specifically linked to violation of the precepts.

118. "Precept matter" (*jiese* 戒色) is equivalent to what later Chinese Buddhist texts call the "precept essence" (*jieti* 戒體), a subtle form of matter implanted within one's body at the time of ordination that serves as the precondition for future soteriological attainment. The term "precept matter" is attested only in a few early fifth-century texts; it may have originally been a translation of *saṃvara*-[*avijñapti*]-*rūpa* (Hirakawa 1964, 165–222; Greene 2016b).

ners[119] trample and destroy the blue lotus pond of the pure precepts, becoming most abject precept breakers. Like crazed dogs that chase and bite whatever they see, be it a person, a stick, or a beast, so too whenever these evil people meet auspicious fields of merit such as buddhas, arhats, or pure monks, they curse, vilify, slander, and abuse them.

Having drunk this poison [of transgression], their entire bodies will become flush with blood, they will feel burning fire in all their joints, and they will become deranged. The raging wind of defilements stirs the mountain of the afflictions, and with eyes of lust, hands and feet of hatred, and bodies of stupidity they blunder through the world sowing the seeds of evil. Having planted such seeds for themselves, they further instruct others to do so. They seek out the *rākṣasa* jailers of hell, the bull-headed hell guardians,[120] evil demons of the eon-ending fires, the spirits of sword trees [337a], and the eighteen lords of hell beginning with King Yama, and constantly treat them as their kinsmen, friends, and teachers, associating with these hell-beings day and night.

[1.9.2] [The Madness and Evil Visions of the Precept Breaker]

These precept breakers, the fires of evil having entered their hearts, for the sake of personal benefit and fame, claim to be good and fully endowed with the awesome virtue of a monk or nun. When going to a wise teacher of meditation,[121] they are like a magician who fools and deludes the eyes. Though these deceitful people claim to be practitioners of the austerities,[122] the evil wind of their precept breaking blows upon the flowers of evil karma, which are constantly scattered over them. With their vicious speech they slander others, and the perfume of their evil thoughts imbues their bodies and minds, which become like the foul-smelling *eraṇḍa* flower,[123] or like a worm-infested dog.

---

119. 四[>七]眾亦爾; seven groups were listed above.

120. The "bull-headed hell guardians" (牛頭阿傍) are well-known figures in Chinese depictions of Buddhist hell, both textual and visual. The word *epang* 阿傍 (or *ebang* or *apang*), long thought by modern scholars to be a transcription of an unknown Indic term (Demiéville 1929, 7–8), must derive from an earlier *ni li pang* 泥犁[var. 犂 / 黎]傍[var. 旁], attested in several very early translations and directly corresponding, in parallel passages, to the Pāli *niraya-pāla* 'hell guardian' (*Bimo shi Mulian jing*, T.67:1.868a20; *Majjhima-nikāya*, 1.337; *Tie cheng nili jing*, T.42:1.827a24; *Majjhima-nikāya*, 3.179). Phonetically, this is a close but not exact match: *pang* 傍[旁] may be a semantic translation (in the sense of follower or attendant), or perhaps a word chosen for being simultaneously a semantic translation and a close but not exact phonetic one. (I would like to thank Alan [Yi] Ding, Diego Loukota, Dan Lusthaus, and the late Karashima Seishi for their help piecing together this information.) Within later Chinese apocryphal literature, the *apang*/ *epang*s are often described as the rulers of the subdivisions of hell (Moretti 2016, 160).

121. Literally, "one wise in the forest methods" (練若知法者).

122. The verses in 1.8.5 explain that practicing the "austerities" (頭陀) means being a true practitioner of meditation; I take the meaning here to be similar.

123. The *Da zhi du lun* compares the precept-breaking monk to a foul-smelling *eraṇḍa* (*yilan* 伊蘭) flower within a grove of sandalwood (*DZDL*, T.1509:25.154b21–22).

Though they do practice meditation (行禪定), they falsely claim that the confirmatory visions of breath counting appear to them. But from the very beginning, they see a blackened buddha like the leg of a black elephant, or like a person covered in ash; they see monks with smashed heads and broken legs, and nuns adorned in flower garlands; they see divine elephants transforming into monkeys with flaming hair that approach and cause disturbance; or else they see wild foxes or wild jackals with a hundred thousand tails, within which are innumerable insects and other assorted vile things; or else they see starving camels, pigs, or dogs; or they see a monk attacked by *kumbhāṇḍa*-demons, evil *yakṣa* spirits, and murderous *rākṣasa*s, each wielding an assortment of weapons and vicious fires.

As a result, they go mad. They dance and sing, lie on the ground in filth, and perform various evil actions. They must quickly be cured.

[1.9.3] [Repentance and Initial Visions of Purification]

The method for curing is as follows. [The precept breaker] must address his various teachers and, speaking himself with utmost sincerity,[124] repent all the evil actions he has committed. The wise ones must then instruct this monk to bring Śākyamuni Buddha to mind and then the remainder of the seven buddhas. After bringing the seven buddhas to mind, he must bring the thirty-five buddhas[125] to mind and, further, must bring to mind the numerous bodhisattvas, arouse aspiration for the Great Vehicle, and contemplate the emptiness of *dharma*s. Feeling deep shame, he must imagine that each of these buddhas pours a pitcher of water over his head. He must further imagine being reborn in the Avīci hell or the other eighteen hells, where he undergoes much torment, and that within these hells he cultivates the six recollections,[126] chanting "Homage to the Buddha! Homage to the Dharma! Homage to the Sangha of monks!"

[When he has done this,] in his dreams the buddhas will, from the white tuft of hair between their eyebrows, emit a light that relieves his hellish suffering.

[1.9.4] [Toilet-Cleaning Penance]

Having seen these things, he will be like a debtor whose mind is full of shame and who seeks to repay what he owes. His intention resolute, he must remove his outer robe (*saṅghāti*) and wear only his under robe (*antarvāsa*). Going before the pure monks, he must cast his body to the ground like a great mountain collapsing. His heart filled with shame, he must repent all his sins, and for eight hundred days perform menial services for the other monks

124. 至誠至[>自, K, K[1], J, P, Q, Kg]說. The Taishō is presumably a misprint.

125. On the thirty-five buddhas, a common object of worship in Mahāyāna repentance rituals, see Python 1973, 99.

126. The recollections (*anusmṛti*) of the Buddha, the Dharma, the Sangha, the precepts, giving, and the happiness of heaven (*Kōsetsu Bukkyōgo daijiten*, 1459).

[such as] cleaning and emptying the toilets. At the conclusion of the eight hundred days he should bathe, put on his *saṅghāti*, enter the sanctuary, concentrate his mind, place his palms together, and carefully contemplate, [337b] for between one and seven days, the light of the white tuft of hair between the Buddha's eyebrows, one of the marks of the great man.

[1.9.5] [Meditation on the Body: The Snakes and the Giant Tree][127]

Then [the penitent] must go back to see the wise teacher and [again] seek to repent. The wise teacher must say to him: "O monk, you must now contemplate your body as a golden vase filled with four poisonous snakes, two of which go up while two go down, each spewing poison most dreadfully. Next contemplate a dragon with six heads that encircles the vase and spews poison that drips into the mouths of the snakes. A great tree [covering] the four directions[128] emerges from the golden vase and fills the triple world. The black elephants approach and try to uproot the tree. On all four sides fire springs forth."

[1.9.6] [Explanation of the Symbols]

When he sees these things [the wise teacher] must say to him: "O monk, you should know, the golden vase is the earth *qi*.[129] The blue snake is born of the wind element; it is the poison that is the wind element. The green snake is born of the water element; it is the poison that is the water element. The white snake is born of the earth element; it is the poison that is the earth element. The yellow snake is born of the fire element; it is the poison that is the fire element. The six-headed dragon is the five *skandha*s of your person plus space [as the sixth].[130] Such a body is vile and impure. How could you give way to evil, violating the precepts without restraint?"

[1.9.7] [Further Meditation and Atonement]

Having spoken these words, [the wise teacher] must then further instruct [the practitioner] to clean the sanctuary, wash the floors, and perform menial services. He is to be further instructed to contemplate the Buddha until he sees the Buddha emit a golden light and stroke his head with his hand. Only after this should he be instructed in the contemplation of impurity. After he

127. The imagery here is familiar from the *Chan Essentials;* see sections 1.14, 1.17, 1.18, and 4.31.27.

128. 四方大樹. Translation tentative. Possibly emend 方[>大], "a great tree *of the four elements*," making the tree symbolize the external material world, which would fit the context.

129. 金瓶者是地氣也. (For 地氣, "earth *qi*," P, S, Y, and Q read 蛇器, "the vessel of the snakes"). Here the "earth *qi*" (see also *Chan Essentials* 4.31.22) is clearly described as a container that holds the other four elements rather than just the earth element itself, and would seem to refer to "materiality" in general.

130. I know of no traditional grouping that combines the five *skandha*s with space (空; *ākāśa*). This would, however, cover the same territory as the scheme of the six primary elements (the four material elements, consciousness, and space).

has fully traversed the gate of impurity and is without further obstacles, he may then recite the precepts together with the Sangha [and, hence, will again be counted as a full member of the monastic community].

[1.9.8] [The Ritual of Readmittance]

One who wishes to recite the precepts [and thereby formally rejoin the Sangha as a pure monk or nun] must make the following formal announcement: "I, the monk so-and-so (or, the nun so-and-so), have finished eight hundred days of menial service, have performed the contemplation of the poisonous snakes, have completed the meditation on hell, have further contemplated a single buddha, recited the repentance text,[131] and in the contemplation of impurity, I have again[132] reached the stage of the nonexistence of self and other,[133] where I have had a confirmatory vision of the Buddha pouring a pitcher of water over my head. And in my dreams a god appeared and told me I was pure.[134] That I am now fully humble is something I know for certain. Please permit me [to rejoin the Sangha]."

A *vinaya* master must then question the practitioner regarding [his adherence to] the rules of the *vinaya*, and he must be instructed to recite the precepts eight hundred times. Only after this will he have regained the state of being no different than a pure monk.[135]

[1.9.10] [Consequences of Transgression][136]

[The Buddha] said to Śāriputra: If Buddhists from the seven groups of followers violate a minor precept and allow two nights to pass without repenting, then these people, though they practice meditation, will never obtain the path in their present lifetimes. If they violate a grave precept, they will fall into hell, and when they emerge from hell they will be reborn as animals for three entire eons. After this they will be reborn in the human realm, but even though born in a human body they will be poor and crippled. For seventy-seven lifetimes they will neither see the Buddha nor hear the Dharma, and their physical faculties will be impaired.

For this reason, when they violate even minor *duṣkṛta* precepts the wise should be as afraid as if they had been stabbed with a knife. They should be greatly ashamed. How much more so the grave precepts!

One who is able to take this medicine [that restores one's status as a] holder of the precepts[137] is known as [337c] a supreme penitent (最上慚愧) and a hero of humility (忍辱丈夫).

131. Literally "repentance method" (懺悔法), this seems to point to a text of some kind.

132. The word "again" (還復) here seems to imply that the practitioner's meditative attainment, lost when he violated the precepts, has now been restored.

133. 無我人鏡[>境, P, S, Q, Y].

134. 說已[>己]清淨.

135. 然後方與如淨比丘得無有異.

136. Compare with *Chan Essentials* 4.32.5–11.

137. Literally, the "medicine for / of the maintenance of the precepts" (持戒藥); I take

[1.9.11] [Verses in Praise of Repentance]

The World-honored One then spoke the following verses:

Breaking the precepts makes the mind impure.
Much as a vile, dog-like thief
who seeks personal benefits everywhere,
this one is destroyed by his own greedy mind.
He must take the medicine of shame,
wear the clothes of humility
and the flower garland of repentance,
and perfume himself with the incense of a virtuous mind.
Wholeheartedly contemplating the marks of the Buddha,
he eliminates suffering and despair.
He must further meditate upon the emptiness of *dharmas*,
cultivating the mind and contemplating impurity.
This is called the Tathāgata's medicine of ambrosial consecration.
The minds of those who consume it become free of worry
and can reach the other shore of nirvana.
That which accords with the Dharma should be cultivated,
and that which is not the Dharma should not be done.
In this age, just as in past ages,
those who practice the teachings will attain salvation.
Following the teachings of the Buddha,
maintaining the precepts and practicing the austerities [of true meditation],
free of evil bodily or mental conduct,
one quickly arrives at liberation.

[1.9.12] [Conclusion]

The World-honored One then said to Śāriputra: "You must remember this medicine for curing violations of the precepts. Do not forget it."

When Śāriputra and Ānanda heard what the Buddha said, they joyfully undertook to carry it out.[138]

[1.10] [The Method for Curing Those Who Relish Pleasing Sounds][139]

[1.10.1] [The Cause of Sickness]

Further, Śāriputra, there may be those among the four groups of Buddhist followers who relish music and take part in musical performances. As a

---

this to mean the ritual itself, which allows transgressors to again be counted as upholders of the precepts.

138. The first scroll of the 2-scroll recensions ends here (*Methods for Curing 1*). *Kongō-ji Methods for Curing*, the sole surviving exemplar of the one-scroll format, continues uninterrupted.

139. 治樂音樂法.

result, their winds will stir. Like unbridled horses, rutting dogs,[140] or royal stags,[141] they sink into deluded attachment. Their minds become like glue, sticking to everything they encounter, unable to be restrained. They must quickly be cured.

[1.10.2] [The Goddess]

The method for curing this is as follows. [The practitioner must] first imagine a goddess of unparalleled beauty. Various musical instruments that produce thousands of kinds of music appear spontaneously in her hands. The practitioner [338a], seeing this goddess who is hundreds of thousands of times more beautiful than any other material form, and hearing this heavenly music that surpasses any in the world, becomes bewitched as he beholds these forms and hears these sounds.

[1.10.3] [The Impure Body of the Goddess]

He must then be taught to contemplate the six sense organs of this goddess.[142] Because of the power of his breath counting [while meditating thus], the following confirmatory visions arise. He sees six poisonous snakes appear in her lovely eyes. They go out from her eye organ and into her ear organ. He further sees two creatures that look like rapacious griffins.[143] Letting out a harsh cry they split open her head, pull out her brains, and fight with one another to eat them. He sees a cat, a rat, a dog, and a jackal, who vie with one another to eat her other four organs.

[1.10.4] [Revulsion from Female Beauty]

As a result of this, [the practitioner] will see the bodies of all women as nothing but the thirty-six foul impure things. Their garlands are like the parasitic worms of the womb. Their musical instruments are like a teeming

---

140. Literally, "a dog in autumn" (秋狗); according to some Indian Buddhist texts, autumn is the mating season for dogs (*Apidamo da piposha lun*, T.1545:27.361a19–22).

141. 伊尼利鹿王. This is apparently a translation-transcription (featuring a transcription unattested elsewhere) of Skt. *aiṇeya* (also attested as *eṇi;* see Gnoli 1977, 1:50.19), a "black antelope" or "royal stag." This word, in Buddhist literature, is used exclusively in the compound *aiṇeyajaṅgha*, "thighs like a royal stag," one of the Buddha's thirty-two physical marks. Its appearance here in a totally different context may be a sign of our text's Chinese authorship. (See 1.7.4 above, for another case, the "hidden organ" of the Buddha's penis, where an item specific to the list of the Buddha's marks was taken by the authors of the *Methods for Curing* as a generic word.)

142. 觀此女人六情諸根. Or, place a full stop after "goddess," with "six sense organs" describing where, within the goddess, the ensuing visions appear. Either way, that the vision begins with the eyes and ears suggests that "six sense organs" here has the normal Buddhist meaning. Yet this passage also seems to want this category to mean the entire physical body of the goddess. This recalls earlier passages that also oddly used "six sense organs" to mean the body as a whole (*Chan Essentials* 4.31.16; *Methods for Curing* 1.5.13).

143. A "griffin" (*chixiu* 鵄鵂) is described in Chinese sources as a nocturnal bird of prey with the head of a cat (*Han yu da ci dian*, 12.1083).

mass of dung beetles, like groaning wild jackals. He finds their bewitching words utterly repellent, like the cries of demons.

He therefore feels revulsion. He should then go to his wise teacher and confess his past evil actions, repenting with utmost sincerity. The wise teacher must then instruct the practitioner in the contemplation of impermanence.

[1.10.5] [Conclusion]

[The Buddha] said to Śāriputra: "You must remember this method for curing those who delight in music. Do not forget it."

When Śāriputra and Ānanda heard what the Buddha said, they joyfully undertook to carry it out.

[1.11] [The Method for Curing Those Enamored of Melodic Chanting and Composing Religious Poetry][144]

[1.11.1] [The Arising of Sickness]

Further, Śāriputra, a practitioner may be fond of composing or performing religious verse. When he sings verses of praise with his beautiful voice, it is like wind rustling the leaves of a Śāla tree. When he produces refined and elegant tones, his voice is like that of the gods, pleasing to the ears of others. He composes pleasing lyrics that bring joy to others. But as a result of his fame, he becomes haughty and proud, and his mind resembles unkempt grass blown about by the wind of the defilements. Everywhere and at all times he holds up the banner of pride, beats the drum of arrogance, and rings the bells of false views.[145] As a result, he goes mad, and he is unable to count his breath, like a foolish ape whose mind is never still as he gathers fruits and flowers here and there. This must quickly be cured.

[1.11.2] [The *Gandharva*]

The method for curing this is as follows. [The practitioner] should first imagine a tall pillar made of the seven precious substances. On the top of the pillar is a divine musician (*gandharva*) with a body like white jade. Swaying his body, he chants verses, and a large lotus flower, upon which stand a hundred thousand monks, emerges from his pores. The *gandharva*'s voice has tens of thousands of tones, surpassing the practitioner's by a millionfold. In this way, the practitioner's pride gradually diminishes.

---

144. 治好歌唄偈讚法. I take *jizan* 偈讚 to mean the *composing* of religious poems. This activity is specifically mentioned below. *Gebai* 歌唄 I take as the various kinds of melodic recitation that Buddhist monastic regulations permit but also deem close to (prohibited) forms of secular singing. For a survey of the terminology of singing and chanting in the *vinaya*, where the dangers of infatuation with one's own voice are a common theme, see C. Liu 2018; and Demiéville 1929, 96–113.

145. The final clause presents some textual difficulties: 弄諸脈零 (K, K^1); 弄諸見鈴 (P, S, Y, Q); 上下諸脈零 (J, Kg). I follow P, S, Y, and Q, making a parallelism with the previous clauses. The reading of J and Kg is surely an error based on 弄 written in its variant form 卡 (as it appears in K^1).

[1.11.3] [The Prideful Monks Receive Their Punishment]

The wise teacher should then further instruct the practitioner to carefully contemplate the top of the pillar. He sees the top of the pillar as a crystal mirror. The monks [standing on the large lotus flower], their minds sullied by pride for their own voices, transform into *rākṣasa*s who scream horribly and shoot flame from their mouths. Various *yakṣa*s approach from all sides and pull out the monks' tongues, rip out their still-beating hearts, and place them on top of the pillar. Their[146] howling and crying is like the bray of a drunken elephant [338b], or like the screeching of wailing *piśāca*s.

[1.11.4] [Revulsion from Beautiful Music]

Because of [seeing] these things, when he next encounters beautiful singing or a beautiful voice, it sounds to him [as harsh as the sound of] someone vilifying his parents as scoundrels. Accordingly, he will feel revulsion rather than delight in listening to these sounds and will wish to escape from them. The wise teacher must then instruct him to contemplate the eight kinds of suffering, as explained in [the section on the] the contemplation of the eight kinds of suffering.[147]

[1.11.5] [Conclusion]

[The Buddha] then said to Śāriputra: "You must remember this method for curing [those enamored of] hymns. Do not forget it."

When Śāriputra and Ānanda heard what the Buddha said, they joyfully undertook to carry it out.

[1.12] [Curing Diarrhea Resulting from Excess of the Water Element][148]

[1.12.1] [Sickness Arising from the Water Samādhi]

Further, Śāriputra, there may be a Buddhist practitioner who enters the *samādhi* of the water element such that water emerges from all over his body and he can no longer see his body or mind, which become like giant oceans. Emerging from trance, he feels no desire to eat or drink and suffers from a burning sensation in the stomach region. His water channels become increasingly agitated, and he suffers from continual diarrhea. This must quickly be cured.

146. This could refer either to the tortured monks or the demons.

147. This passage seems to refer the reader to some other text or source. (See, similarly, *Chan Essentials* 3.21.6 and 3.21.7). The "eight kinds of suffering" is a standard canonical classification of all possible types of suffering.

148. 治水大猛盛因是得下. "Down-going" (*xia* 下) commonly means diarrhea in early Chinese medical texts (Tessenow and Unschuld 2008, 463–464).

[1.12.2] [The *Garuḍa*]

The method for curing this is as follows. [The practitioner] must imagine a golden-winged bird[149] upon which rides a monk. They fly at ease over the great ocean, the various dragons and *rākṣasa*s fleeing in terror. The bird catches a dragon, and the frightened dragon, about to be eaten, drinks up all the water [of the ocean] and turns into four snakes. This royal golden-winged bird grasps the four snakes in his beak. The monk sits on it, unable to find any water. The royal golden-winged bird shoots fire from his eyes to burn the snakes. The snakes are afraid, and like the magical creations of a conjurer they suddenly disappear and enter the monk's body.

[1.12.3] [The God Uttaraga]

The practitioner should then emerge from trance and consume worldly medicines for curing diarrhea. He should imagine two fire jewels, like hot rocks, one in his stomach tube, where it warms the channels, and one at the anus. He should imagine the god of the Himalayas, Uttaraga,[150] who is six feet tall and as white as shell or snow. He bestows upon the practitioner a fragrant medicine named Sahanaka.[151]

Before taking this medicine the practitioner must first produce the aspiration for unsurpassed awakening. After taking it, he will be free not only from diarrhea, but from all four hundred four illnesses for the rest of his life.

[1.12.3] [Procedure for Invoking Uttaraga and the Other Gods]

One who wishes to make this god come with all due haste[152] must first purify himself through bathing and refrain from eating the five pungent foods (五辛), drinking alcohol, or consuming meat. Dwelling in a quiet place, he should concentrate his mind by counting his breaths, and for seven days he should chant this god's name (稱彼神名) and bring to mind his image (念彼神像).

This great god of the Himalayas, [Uttaraga,] will then come before the practitioner together with [the remainder of] the twelve radiant gods

---

149. "Golden winged bird" is the usual Chinese translation of *garuḍa*, the roc-like bird of Indian mythology known for feasting on the *nāga*s.

150. *Yuduojia* 鬱多伽 (below written *yuduoluojia* 鬱多羅伽), probably Uttara-ga, "Upward-Goer," who, it seems, cures the "down-going" (下) of diarrhea.

151. *Suohe'najia* 娑呵那伽. This name is unattested elsewhere. Perhaps from Skt. **sahanaka* 'maker of endurance'? The Mahāyāna *Mahāparinirvāṇa-sūtra* also mentions a medicine from the Himalayas named *suohe* 娑呵 (**saha*), the mere sight of which will cure all sickness (*Da banniepan jing*, T.374:12.511c1–4).

152. 疾疾來者. This language recalls the traditional Chinese closing formula for prayers to the gods: "quickly, quickly, in accord with the statutes" (疾疾如令).

(白光神).[153] These gods first preach the Dharma, after which they will bestow medicine and also teach the twelve gates of trance.[154]

These gods are all great fifth-stage bodhisattvas. One who is sick should first bring to mind the god Uttaraga, and next bring to mind the remainder of the twelve radiant gods: Vigor (*śūra*), Strength (*dṛḍha*), Might (*nārāyaṇabala*), Wisdom (*cāritamati*), Power (*prabhu*), Strong-arms (*subāhu*), Kumāra (鳩摩羅), Unconquerable (*durdharṣa*), Radiance, Radiance King, and Medicine King [338c].[155]

[1.12.4] [The Teachings of the Twelve Gods]

When [the practitioner] sees these gods, he inquires about a different teaching with each of them. They first cause the practitioner to see the bodhisattva Maitreya, and in Maitreya's abode he sees Mañjuśrī and all the other bodhisattvas, as well as the buddhas of the ten directions.

If the practitioner has not violated the four grave prohibitions,[156] either in this life or past lives, then when he sees these gods, he will immediately realize the path.[157]

If, however, he has violated the precepts, then after the gods have instructed him, he must perform repentance rituals for one thousand days. Only after this will he be able to see Maitreya bodhisattva, Mañjuśrī, and the other great saints, and then finally attain the path.

[1.12.5] [Conclusion]

[The Buddha] said to Śāriputra: "As a result [of excess] water, diarrhea may arise for a practitioner and the four hundred four illnesses may then stir. If he wishes to cure this, he must promptly take this medicine of Saha[naka] and do the other things [mentioned previously]. When his sickness is completely removed and he has eliminated the ocean of karmic obstructions, he will quickly realize the path. Therefore, you all must diligently remember this method. Do not forget it."

When Śāriputra and Ānanda heard what the Buddha said, they joyfully undertook to carry it out.

---

153. Only eleven other names are given, so Uttaraga must be one of the twelve.

154. The "twelve gates of trance" (十二門禪), a common topic of discussion in many early Chinese Buddhist meditation texts (including the eponymous *Shi er men jing* 十二門經 of An Shigao; see Zacchetti 2003), are the four *dhyāna*s, the four *apramāṇa*s, and the four formless meditations.

155. The first eight of these names have been drawn from the early fifth-century Chinese translation of the *Anantamukha-nirhāra-dhāraṇī-sūtra;* see Appendix 2. I give the Sanskrit names following Inagaki's reconstructions (1987, 68).

156. "Four grave prohibitions" (四重禁) presumably means the *pārājika* transgressions.

157. "Path" is here *daoji* 道跡 (literally, "traces of the path"), an early translation of the attainment of stream-entry (*Kōsetsu Bukkyōgo daijiten*, 1014), though sometimes a generic reference to advanced attainment (see Lamotte 1944–1981, 3.1665n3). Here either meaning would fit.

[1.13] [The Method for Curing Pain in the Head and Eyes and Deafness in the Ears Resulting from the Fire Element][158]

[1.13.1] [The Arising of Sickness]

Further, Śāriputra, if flames emerge from a practitioner's joints when he enters the fire *samādhi*, and fire arises simultaneously in his large and small intestines, thereby heating and stimulating his fire channels (火脈), when he emerges from trance his head will ache slightly, all his channels will tense and contract, his eyes will become red,[159] and he will have difficulty hearing. One who becomes sick in this manner must quickly be cured.

[1.13.2] [The Beryl Vase]

The method for curing this is as follows. He should first imagine a beryl vase filled with multicolored water, within which grow flowers made of various kinds of jewels. Atop the flowers are hundreds of thousands of transformation buddhas and numerous transformation bodhisattvas. They each radiate light from the white tuft of hair between their eyebrows, and the light illuminates the fires, turning them into golden dragons. Seeing this, the practitioner becomes happy.

[1.13.3] [Extinguishing the Fires]

He should then imagine placing the vase beneath the fires, with the stigmas of the flowers reaching up toward the buddhas. When he touches the vase, his hands feel cool and refreshed. Throwing his entire body down before the vase, he prostrates to the buddhas and immediately sees the transformation buddhas emit light from between their eyebrows. It falls gently upon each part of his body as a shower of ambrosia. Each place it touches transforms into beryl, and the ambrosia flows into his large intestine.[160] When it is filled with ambrosia, the fires gradually go out and are replaced with jeweled flowers glowing red and white.

[1.13.4] [Maheśvara]

He should then imagine the god Maheśvara, who approaches the practitioner riding a golden bull and carrying a jeweled water pitcher. Within the water is a medicine named "poison destroyer" (破毒), which he gives to the practitioner. Maheśvara then places a pearl named Candramaṇi (which in the language of Song [China] means "moon essence")[161] on the crown of the

158. 治因火大頭痛眼痛耳聾法.

159. According to the *Fo yi jing*, an early Chinese scriptural account of Buddhist medicine based on the four-element theory of disease, fire-illnesses are linked to problems with the eyes (T.793:17.737a28).

160. 因灌大腸{大腸小腸, K[1]}. J reads 因灌大腸大腸, while P, S, Q, and Y read 因灌大腸小腸.

161. 宋言月精. This interlinear comment has been wrongly incorporated into the text in K[1], J, and Kg.

practitioner's head. Medicines drip from the pearl into his ears, eyes, and nose. As soon as the practitioner sees these things, he will be cured.

Maheśvara, a great bodhisattva who constantly disports himself in the *śūraṅgama-samādhi*,[162] then emits a bright light from between his eyebrows [339a] that becomes an image of the Buddha surrounded by five hundred transcendent beings (仙人). [This Buddha] then preaches for the practitioner an ambrosial healing method.[163]

[1.13.5] [Conclusion]

[The Buddha] said to Śāriputra: "You must remember this teaching. Do not forget it."

When Śāriputra and Ānanda heard what the Buddha said, they joyfully undertook to carry it out.

[1.14] [The Method for Curing Insanity Caused by the Terror of Seeing Inauspicious Things upon Entering the Earth-Element Samādhi*]*[164]

[1.14.1] [The Dark Mountains]

Further, Śāriputra, upon entering the earth-element *samādhi* a practitioner may see dark mountains in all directions, within whose crags are innumerable *kumbhāṇḍa*s, squatting on piles of dirt, with forked penises (身根分端) and extremely ugly. Numerous *yakṣa*s charge forward to seize control of five of the mountains, causing the *kumbhāṇḍa*s to become dreadfully afraid. Crying out horribly they approach the practitioner. He now sees demons with disheveled hair wielding great iron clubs tipped with boulders. They too approach. He further sees *yakṣa*s dancing about with boulders lifted high above their heads. [Female] *rākṣasas*[165] wielding trees [as weapons] approach the *yakṣa*s and fight with them angrily. [There are also] *piśāca*s who carry black boulders above their heads and hold dead tigers in their mouths.

[1.14.2] [The Fighting Demons]

Seeing these things, the practitioner becomes alarmed and gets goose bumps. Because of his fear, the *rākṣasa*s become more aggressive in their battle with the *yakṣa*s. When the *rākṣasa*s gain the advantage, they decapitate the *yakṣa*s, slice off the hands and feet of the *piśāca*s, wearing them as garlands, and the penises of the *kumbhāṇḍa*s, which they use as decorative head ornaments. Dancing wildly before the practitioner, their fangs point upward like the branches of sword trees. Hail rains from their eyes and lightning flashes.

Then the *yakṣa*s gain the upper hand. They capture the *rākṣasa*s, tear the skin from their faces, and gouge out their vulvas. They cut off the penises of the *kumbhāṇḍa*s and the hands and feet of the *piśāca*s, turning them into

162. The *śūraṅgama-samādhi* (*samādhi* of the heroic stride) is both a meditative state mentioned in various Mahāyāna scriptures and itself the title of a famous Mahāyāna scripture.

163. Or, he preaches "the gate of ambrosia, which is a method for healing." The term "gate of ambrosia" (甘露門; *amṛta-dvāra*) sometimes means Buddhist meditation itself.

164. 治入地三昧見不祥事驚怖失心法.

165. It becomes clear below that these demons are female.

decorative head ornaments, earrings, or neck-piercings. Dancing wildly before the practitioner, they shake their bodies, shout loudly, and produce a medley of horrible, frightening sounds.

[1.14.3] [The Goddess Vimalatī]

The practitioner then sees the goddess Vimalatī,[166] mother of the gods of the four great oceans, lying on her back upon the ocean. She has one thousand heads and two thousand hands and feet.[167] She stretches her body across the four directions, exposing her vulva, which stands tall and foreboding like a blood-smeared mountain with many terrible sword-tree hairs. Within it grows a tree resembling a thicket of blade mountains, and from it stream innumerable demons with donkey ears, bull heads, lion mouths, horse hooves, wolf tails, and *kumbhāṇḍa* penises.

He also sees a great dragon emerging from it several tens of *yojana*s long, with hundreds of thousands of heads. He sees a bestial demon emerging with the body of lion and ten thousand feet, within the claws of which are hundreds of thousands of poisonous snakes. He further sees emerge hungry ghosts, their bodies tens of millions of *yojana*s tall, vomiting forth poison and fire and carrying [339b] boulders above their shoulders. He further sees emerge a thousand wolves sharing a single tail but with separate bodies, whose teeth are like stone spikes.[168] He further sees emerge a thousand tigers whose tails bear heads. Their bodies pressed together closely, they walk with heads bowed down. He further sees emerge a dragon-woman adorned with garlands and extremely beautiful[169] who is then eaten by the *yakṣa*s. He further sees emerge from it all manners of evil, wild beasts such as cats, rats, apes, jackals, and evil fox spirits, [as well as] the spirits of the Whirlpool-Burner mountain of the Avīci hell,[170] the spirits of the eighteen hells, nine

166. *Pi-mou-lou-zhi* 毘牟樓至. This name is unattested elsewhere and my reconstruction is speculative.

167. 有千頭各二千手足. Or perhaps, "a thousand heads *each with* two thousand hands and feet."

168. "Stone spike" recalls the "hell of stone spikes" (尖石地獄) mentioned at *GFSMH*, T.643:15.673c13. Imagery characteristic of Buddhist hellscapes frequently describes aspects of the visionary scenes in the *Chan Essentials* and *Methods for Curing*.

169. 甚脱[>悦, K[1], K, J, P, Q, Kg]人目. The Taishō is presumably a misprint.

170. 阿鼻地獄沃焦山神. This is a curious element of Buddhist cosmography that eventually figured in many apocryphal Chinese Buddhist texts and other Chinese compositions (see, e.g., *Ci bei dao chang chan fa*, T.1909:45.939c6). According to pre-Buddhist Chinese legends, Whirlpool Burner (沃焦) is a large rock far in the eastern ocean around which the seawaters swirl and then evaporate, thereby preventing the ocean from overflowing (*Zhuangzi ji shi*, 565–566, citing the lost commentary of Sima Biao 司馬彪 [ca. 237–306]; see also *YQJYI* [Huilin], T.2128:54.432a11, citing Guo Pu's 郭璞 [276–324] autocommentary to his *Jiang fu* 江賦, which describes it more like a cliff). The *Ocean-Samādhi Contemplation Scripture* (*GFSMH*, T.643:15.668c27–29), whose account of hell was influential in later Chinese Buddhism, explains that the "Whirlpool Burner mountain" is the tip of a large mountain that reaches down into the Avīci hell, whence comes its heat. It is to this object, which aligns Indian Buddhist and pre-Buddhist Chinese cosmographies and which had evidently taken shape in the Chinese imagination by the early fifth century, that the *Methods for Curing* here refers, if only in passing.

million bull-headed hell guardians, eighty million hungry ghosts, a thousand million dung beetles, and five hundred million parasitic worms.

[1.14.4] [The Angry Demons]

Some of these many horrible demons in this frightening scene hold blade-mountains, some hold sword-trees, some shake Mt. Sumeru, some shake the Yugaṃdhara or Encircling Iron Mountains.[171] The practitioner then sees his own body filling the earth, his three hundred thirty-six bones as tall as mountains, reaching up to the formless realms. Water emerges from his navel, with the poisonous snakes of the four elements sporting within it. Fire emerges from his mouth with ten evil *rākṣasa*s scurrying within it. Wind emerges from his ears and anus, blowing upon the mountains. All these demons and gods approach him, glaring hatefully with bulging eyes. At this, the practitioner becomes afraid and is likely to go mad.

If the practitioner sees such things, he must quickly be cured.

[1.14.5] [The Sun God and the Moon God]

The method for curing this is as follows. He must first imagine a sun together with a sun god (日天子) who rides in his palace[172] made of the four precious substances and plays hundreds of thousands of kinds of beautiful music. The sun shines down from above the dark mountains,[173] making them gradually brighter. Having imagined one sun, the practitioner should next imagine two suns. Imagining two suns, he must next contemplate the three hundred thirty-six white bones of his body, as white as the snow-covered mountains upon which the suns shine. Then, above his head, he imagines the moon god accompanied by hundreds of thousands of attendants in his palace made of the four precious substances. The moon god places a moon pearl on the practitioner's head.

When this meditation is complete, he imagines a third sun above the mountains,[174] exactly the same as those described above. When he has seen this sun, he next imagines the bone at the crown of his head, and rising over the snow white mountain [of his bones] appears another moon. Seeing this moon, he must imagine a fourth sun above the mountains, which shines upon the dark mountains. Seeing this sun, he must imagine the mountain of the three hundred thirty-six white bones of his own body, each corner facing another (the four corners [of each bone] positioned directly across from one

171. The Yugaṃdhara mountains are those that immediately ring Mount Sumeru. On the Encircling Iron Mountains, see *Chan Essentials* 1.18.9, n. 243.

172. The Indic word for "palace" (Skt. *vimāna*) also means "chariot," and the palaces of the gods are often envisaged as flying structures that the gods ride across the heavens.

173. This must refer to the dark mountains mentioned in 1.14.1.

174. 想第三山上復有一日. The grammar is peculiar. Given the context, "third" must refer to the *sun*, not the mountain; this word was perhaps a marginal comment that got incorporated into the text (see also the next note).

another),[175] and in the space between each corner there are moon gods radiating moonlight[176] who grasp the two pearls [of the facing bone corners] and hold them together.[177] In this manner, at each joint the practitioner should fix his mind on the space between the corners of each of the bones for ten inhalations and exhalations, carefully contemplating and making it very clear. He sees the twenty-eight asterisms on each bone. [The bones] are bright and lovely, like pearls made of the seven precious substances.

[1.14.6] [The *Garuḍa* Scatters the Dragons]

When this meditation is complete, the practitioner next imagines a royal golden-winged bird that wears a *maṇi* pearl atop its head. It chases after the four panicked snakes and six dragons [339c], while the demons and spirits of the mountains run about frantically.

[1.14.7] [Divination of *Śīla*]

If [the sun and moon] appear dark in color, this is retribution for the violation of the precepts in a past life. The practitioner must then diligently repent in order to purify his *śīla* (尸羅). When his *śīla* has been purified, the light of the sun and moon will become ever brighter.

If he thinks evil thoughts, speaks evil words, or commits [even] a minor *duṣkṛta* offense, then black dirt will rain upon the *maṇi* pearl [on the head of the golden-winged bird]. The sun and moon will become obscured with dust, and Jupiter will no longer follow its course. The king of the *asura*s will suddenly appear, with his nine hundred ninety-nine hands and one thousand heads, shading the sun and moon and obscuring Jupiter.

This is called backsliding. The bandits of transgression have robbed the practitioner with the sword of evil thoughts and the fire of evil speech. If he wishes to take the excellent, ambrosial medicine, he must first maintain the precepts and be pure in all minor matters of conduct (持戒淨諸威儀), repenting his karmic obstructions and evil sins.

[1.14.8] [Moonlight Holding the Bones Together]

Then he must concentrate his mind, sit upright without moving, count his inhalations and exhalations, seal his breath within,[178] and contemplate his three hundred thirty-six bones as before. He must make the corners of the bones face one another, and [see therein] all those things associated with the asterisms and the moon explained previously.

175. The words "the four corners positioned directly across from one another" (四角皆相對也) appear in full-sized characters, but they seem clearly to be a gloss on the previous words "each corner facing each other" (皆角相向), which in the Chinese is indeed somewhat unclear. I take "corner" here to mean the bump-like protrusions at the end of a bone (the condyles).

176. 月光<月, K[1], J, P, S, Q, Y, Kg>天子.

177. 手捉兩珠兩向持. Or, perhaps the "pearls" are different objects held by the gods.

178. That one must "seal the breath" (閉氣) is also mentioned at *Chan Essentials* 4.31.25.

His mind then becomes increasingly perspicacious, and within each joint he sees moonlight, like a piece of cloth, and starlight, like thread, stitching [the bones] together.

[1.14.9] [The Seven Suns]

He then sees a fourth sun appear, [and by its heat] the waters of the four oceans are reduced by two-thirds.[179] He sees a fifth sun appear, which melts away Mount Sumeru itself and dries up the oceans. He sees a sixth sun appear, and he imagines all the mountains gradually melting away. He sees a seventh sun appear, which incinerates the entire earth. All the demons and *rākṣasa*s fly into the air, but the pillars of flame follow behind them all the way to the [heavens of] the realm of desire, and then further to the [heavens of the] realm of form. They try to keep going to the formless realm, but they are engulfed by the mass of fire, their hands and feet twisting and burning and their dreadful shrieking shaking the earth. (When one enters this *samādhi*, the earth shakes slightly, like a spinning carriage wheel.)[180]

With all due haste the practitioner must hold his mind (持心) firm and imagine his three hundred thirty-six bones as an adamantine mountain, beautiful in form, surpassing even Mount Sumeru [in firmness], unmoved by earth, water, fire, or wind.[181] He sees only the four snakes [of the four elements], holding *maṇi* jewels in their mouths and dwelling within the mountain of his skeleton.[182]

[1.14.10] [The Emanations of the Seven Buddhas]

He must then imagine the emanations of the buddhas.[183] He sees, at the adamantine nadir, an adamantine pillar topped with a *maṇi*-jewel mirror within which appear the emanations of the seven buddhas of the past. He must carefully contemplate the white tuft of hair between the eyebrows of these buddhas Vipaśyin, Śikhin, Viśva,[184] Krakucchanda, Kanakamuni, Kāśyapa, and Śākyamuni. When he sees the white tuft of hair between their eyebrows, it is as if pure crystalline water were cleansing his bones. Bathed by this water from the white tufts of hair, his three hundred thirty-six bones become brilliantly white, pure and sparkling as a mirror, beyond all compare.

---

179. The ensuing description of the seven suns and the incineration of the earth is clearly modeled on canonical presentations of the destruction of the world (though not the formless realms) at the end of each *kalpa* (see, e.g., *Zhong ahan jing*, T.26:1.428c8–429c27).

180. These characters appear as an interlinear note in all versions of the text.

181. See, similarly, *GFSMH*, T.643:15.696b4–10, which says that the body of one who practices *nianfo* will be like the "adamantine mountain" that survives the *kalpa*-ending holocaust.

182. This image suggests that the four bodily elements have now been brought into a state of balance, curing the excess of earth with which this section began.

183. See "Modalities of Encountering the Buddha(s)" and "The Emanations of the Buddhas" in chap. 3.

184. See *Chan Essentials* 1.18.14, n. 257.

[1.14.11] [Consecration by the Buddhas]

Because of this, he now sees five adamantine wheels[185] mounted atop pillars made from the seven precious substances. They emerge from below, spinning in the air [340a] and preaching the teaching of the four truths. Though he sees and hears all this, he keeps his mind fixed in its contemplation of his mountain-like skeleton. He will then see the buddha Śākyamuni pour a pitcher of water over his head, and so too the other six buddhas.

[1.14.12] [Preaching of the Buddhas]

The buddha Śākyamuni then addresses him: "O Dharma child, you must carefully contemplate that matter, sensations, perceptions, volitional formations, and consciousness are painful, empty, impermanent, and devoid of self."

[Śākyamuni] then further explains the teachings of emptiness, signlessness, non-doing, and non-wishing.[186] He explains that the body is empty and quiescent, that the four elements have no master, that in the five *skandha*s there is nowhere to make one's home, that they are ultimately quiescent and extinguished, the same as empty space.

As a result [of hearing these teachings], the practitioner immediately awakens to the impermanence and fragility of the world.

[1.14.13] [Attainment of the First Three Fruits]

He now contemplates the four truths. During the space of five breaths, he smashes through the raging defilements of twenty million [rebirths] and becomes a stream-enterer.[187] In the space of the next ten breaths, he escapes from the flood of desire and becomes a once-returner. In the space of the next ten breaths, he cuts off the gross defilements,[188] the defilements of the sphere of desire,[189] and the roots of all these defilements, and becomes a non-returner, one who will never again return to the realm of desire.[190]

---

185. *Chan Essentials* 1.18.17 also mentions five adamantine wheels, which participate in the near destruction of the tree of the defilements.

186. See Appendix 2.

187. On the term "raging defilements" (洞然之結), see *Chan Essentials* 4.31.30, n. 579.

188. The term "gross defilements" (鈍使), if it is not equivalent to the "defilements of the sphere of desire" mentioned next, is of uncertain meaning. Interestingly, this may be the earliest known example of this word, which became an important technical concept in sixth- and seventh-century Chinese Buddhist scholasticism, where the ten principal defilements were divided into five "gross" and five "acute" (利) defilements (*Fa hua jingyi ji*, T.1715:33.604c4–6; *Fa jie ci di chu men*, T.1925:46.667c3–10; *Da sheng yi zhang*, T.1851:44.584b5–12). This follows a division, but not the name, found in the *Abhidharmakośa-bhāṣya* (279), which contrasts the five *anuśaya* that "have the nature of being a view" (*dṛṣṭisvabhāva*) from the five that do not.

189. "Defilements of the sphere of desire" are probably what are usually called the five "lower" (*avarabhāgīyā*) defilements that bind one to the *kāma-dhātu* and whose destruction is the characteristic of the non-returner.

190. "To never again return to the realm of desire" (不還欲界) is a standard characterization of the non-returner in Chinese translations of the Āgamas (see, e.g., *Bie yi za ahan jing*, T.100:2.446b17–18).

[1.14.14] [Arhatship]

In the space of the next ten breaths, he disports himself in emptiness and, his mind free of any entanglement, dwells in the thirty-fourth mental moment[191] where he attains a non-diminishing, indestructible deliverance from the ten root-[defilements],[192] thereby smashing the mountain of the ninety-eight defilements.

The Dharma banners of the light of wisdom of the valiant general[193] then arrive from the four directions. Precious adamantine seats emerge from below and in knocking against each other expound the teachings of emptiness.[194] The five adamantine wheels come to rest beside the practitioner's left knee, where they spontaneously expound the teachings of the nine moments of the immediately successive path and the eight moments of the path of liberation.[195] Voice-hearers from the past, immersed in the beryl *samādhi*, appear before the practitioner. Then the buddha Śākyamuni ex-

---

191. 住三十四心相應. This passage references the complex theories about the moment of awakening found in Sarvāstivāda-Vaibhāṣika scholasticism. According to certain of these theories, the realization of each of the four fruits occurs across thirty-four mental moments comprising the so-called *darśana-* and *bhāvanā-mārgas* (the "path of seeing" and the "path of meditation"). In the sixteen moments of the *darśana-mārga*, one contemplates the four noble truths (four moments for each), after which one becomes a stream-enterer up to a non-returner. The *bhāvanā-mārga* that then follows is comprised of a further eighteen moments (*Piposha lun*, T.1547:28.446c4–12). By this reckoning, the "thirty-fourth mental moment" spoken of here in the *Methods for Curing* would be the final moment of the awakening process (arhatship).

192. 解脫十根本不滅不壞. Translation tentative. The words "non-diminishing" and "indestructible" may be significant. Sarvāstivāda-Vaibhāṣika literature distinguishes various kinds of "deliverance" (*vimukti*) depending on whether they can suffer degradation or not (*Abhidharmakośabhāṣyam*, 372–374). This is why some arhats, even though liberated, can regress from that state. The deliverance of a buddha is distinguished from that of an arhat by being necessarily immune to such degradation (*nāsti vimuktiparihāṇiḥ*); this is the eleventh of a buddha's eighteen "unshared qualities" (*aveṇikadharma*). The *Da zhi du lun* describes this quality of a buddha as his "suffering no diminishment of deliverance" (解脫無減; T.1509:25.247b14–15). It also contrasts deliverances that are "destructible" (壞解脫) from those that are not (T.1509:25.250c21). The *Methods for Curing* seems to draw from this terminology in order to categorize what is here achieved by the arhat as similar to something normally reserved for buddhas.

193. 大勇猛將慧光法幢. Translation tentative. "Valiant general" presumably means the Buddha or buddhas, perhaps in reference to the defeat of Māra's armies. Since it is a well-known image, I take *fachuang* 法幢 here as "Dharma *banner*" rather than *pillar* (as I have usually translated *chuang*).

194. *Chan Essentials* 4.31.26 gives a similar description of the attainment of arhatship. The image of the adamantine seats knocking against each other is very close to a passage in one of the Contemplation Scriptures that describes the moment of the Buddha's awakening: "At the adamantine nadir there suddenly and miraculously appear two adamantine seats *that knock against each other*, their sound shaking the entire universe and causing the earth to quake in the six different ways" (金剛際自然化生二金剛座，互相振觸，聲振三千大千世界，令此大地六種振動; *GFSMH*, T.643:15.654a10–12).

195. 九無礙八解脫. See *Chan Essentials* 3.30.4, n. 107.

pounds for him the meaning and character of the confirmatory visions of the adamantine *samādhi*.[196]

With this, the practitioner becomes tranquil. No longer aware of his own body or mind, he enters the adamantine *samādhi*. He emerges from the adamantine *samādhi* as a great arhat, having obliterated the mountain of the defilements, having severed the roots of affliction, having dried up the river of ignorance, having eradicated death, old age, and despair,[197] having brought to a definitive end his allotted time within the cycle of rebirth, having fully established his holy practice, having become like purified gold, having put an end to all desire, and having accomplished what is to be accomplished.

[1.14.15] [The Buddhas of the Ten Directions]

Those who aspire to the awakening of a buddha, when first seeing the light from the white tuft of hair of the seven buddhas, [instead of the above] will see that light split into ten[198] separate rays that turn into jeweled flowers, ten jeweled trees, and ten jeweled terraces, all arrayed in the air. The buddhas of the ten directions too will then emit glowing water that cleanses all the practitioner's bones, as described previously. And from within the buddhas' white tuft of hair emerges the growing sound of the preaching of the eighteen practices of love, the eighteen practices of great compassion, the eighteen practices of great joy, and the eighteen practices of great equanimity.[199]

[1.14.16] [The Practices of the Bodhisattva]

Having received these instructions, [the practitioner] cultivates the four measureless minds [of love, compassion, joy, and equanimity]. Becoming fully possessed of the four measureless minds, he is then taught the ten kinds of clear mind.[200] Coming to possess these, he is then taught that "form itself is emptiness; it is not that emptiness occurs with the destruction of form."[201] Contemplating emptiness in this way, he is then taught the six

196. "Adamantine *samādhi*" (金剛譬定), literally, the "adamant-like *samādhi*," is a calque of *vajropama-samādhi*, the meditative state in which, according to mainstream Buddhist doctrine, arhatship is achieved (see, e.g., *ZCSM*, T.614:15.280c5). (Chinese Buddhist texts more usually give simply *jin'gang ding* 金剛定 or *jin'gang sanmei* 金剛三昧.) In Mahāyāna literature, the adamantine *samādhi* assumes an analogous role. Its nature was a topic of much analysis among Chinese Buddhists in the fifth, sixth, and seventh centuries (Buswell 1989, 104–115).

197. 老死奴[>怨, S, Y, Kg]滅.

198. The number ten presumably has a symbolic valence in reference either to the "buddhas of the ten directions" as the source of the bodhisattva teachings (as opposed the seven historical buddhas who instruct the one questing for arhatship) or to the ten bodhisattva stages.

199. Love, compassion, joy, and equanimity are the objects of the four *apramāṇa* meditations. I am unaware of any formal division of these into eighteen steps or methods (though we might recall that the contemplation of impurity, in the first sutra of the *Chan Essentials*, was also divided into eighteen levels; see *Chan Essentials* 1.18.20.3).

200. 十種明心. This seems to be a technical term; it is otherwise unattested.

201. 色即是空，非色滅空. This may be a direction citation of Kumārajīva's translation of the *Vimalakīrti-nirdeśa* (*Weimojie suo shuo jing*, T.475:14.551a19–20).

methods of the bodhisattva.[202] Practicing the six methods, he then cultivates [340b] the six remembrances and brings to mind the Dharma body of the buddhas. Bringing to mind the Dharma body of the buddhas, he then arouses the mind of dedicating [merit] (迴向心). After dedicating merit, he takes the four universal vows[203] in order not to forsake living beings. With the four vows established, he acquires the bodhisattva precepts. With the bodhisattva precepts completely acquired, he begins practice of the approximate *dāna-pāramitā*.[204] When the [first] approximate *pāramitā* is obtained, he begins cultivation of the remainder of the ten approximate *pāramitā*s.

[1.14.17] [The First Bodhisattva Stage]

When this meditation is complete, he contemplates emptiness both inwardly and outwardly. He sees before him hundreds of thousands of innumerable buddhas who anoint his head with water, tie pieces of silk cloth around his neck,[205] and preach for him the teaching of emptiness. He now understands emptiness and enters the ranks of the bodhisattvas.

This is called the first confirmatory vision of the bodhisattva path, that of the stage of nature.[206] In this method [of the bodhisattva], many give rise to pride. One must be aware of this. These are the features of the first confirmatory vision for those who have given rise to the aspiration for the awakening of a buddha.

[1.14.18] [Conclusion]

[The Buddha] then said to Śāriputra: "This is called [the method] for curing [problems arising from] the earth *samādhi*,[207] and for destroying the frightful signs of ignorance, mother of the three poisons. You must remember it. Do not forget it."

When Śāriputra and Ānanda heard what the Buddha said, they joyfully undertook to carry it out.

---

202. 菩薩六法. Unclear. Perhaps the six *pāramitās*, but those are mentioned separately below.

203. 四弘誓. This is one of the earliest attested examples of the term "four universal vows," which in later Chinese Buddhism becomes the standard formulation of the bodhisattva's intention to bring all living beings to awakening.

204. The "approximate *pāramitās*" (相似波羅蜜) are preparatory steps to be fulfilled before the practice of the pure *pāramitās* (*DZDL*, T.1509:25.139b1–6). In the *Ocean-Samādhi Contemplation Scripture* (*GFSMH*, T.643:15.694c4–7), as here, they are associated with the first bodhisattva stage.

205. 以繒繫頭[>頸]. Emendation tentative. The meditator of the *Yogalehrbuch* also has visions of a silk cloth being tied around the neck (Schlingloff 1964, 81, 83, and 142).

206. 性地菩薩最初境界. The "stage of [first acquiring the bodhisattva] nature" (性地) is often the *second* bodhisattva stage (*DZDL*, T.1509:25.421c8–12). However, in a passage from one of the Contemplation Scriptures (that resembles the present passage in other ways as well), the first bodhisattva stage is given this name (*GFSMH*, T.643:15.694a16–18). On fifth- and sixth-century Chinese theories about the bodhisattva stages, see Funayama 2011.

207. 此名治地三昧{增上慢}. The word "pride" here has likely been miscopied from one manuscript column (17 characters) earlier, where it also appeared.

[1.15] [The Method for Curing the Wind Element]

[1.15.1] [The Arising of Sickness]

Further, Śāriputra, while in the wind *samādhi* a practitioner may see five kinds of wind emerge from the nine openings of his body, as if they were deep gorges. He may also see, from each of the three hundred thirty-six bones of his body white as a snow-covered mountain, a wind that blows forth various *kṛtya*-demons.[208] (A *kṛtya* is a zombie.) The *kṛtya*s hold iron clubs and wear garlands made from a thousand skulls. They come before the practitioner together with ninety-eight species of dragons and demons. When he sees these creatures, the practitioner becomes alarmed and his hairs stand on end. He goes mad as a result or else contracts eczema.[209] This must quickly be cured.

[1.15.2] [The Four Transcendents of Incense Mountain]

The method for curing this is as follows. He should first contemplate the four transcendents of Incense Mountain[210] in the Himalayas, who are great bodhisattvas. He must imagine them and their sixteen-foot golden bodies. In one hand they hold flowers, in the other hand golden wheels, and in their mouth they hold fragrant medicines. They shield the practitioner with their bodies to prevent any winds from arising. Using flowers, they cast a spell over a vessel of water, from which a dragon appears and sucks up all the wind. The dragon's body swells to an enormous size and then lies down on

---

208. "Various *kṛtya*-[demons]" (諸藹吉支) poses some difficulties. Kumārajīva's *Lotus Sutra* mentions a demon called *ji-zhe* 吉遮, a transcription of a middle Indic form of *kṛtya* (Karashima 2001, 519), usually a magician-created spirit. Zhiyi's commentary to the *Lotus Sutra*, however, glosses *ji-zhe* as "zombie" (起尸鬼; *Miao fa lian hua jing wen ju*, T.1718:34.147a5), the same gloss the *Methods for Curing* gives for *ai-ji-zhi* 藹吉支. These terms were evidently seen, by Chinese commentators, as the same thing. In *Methods for Curing* 2.2 below, however, we find either *tou-la-ji-zhi* 偷臘吉支 (K) or *tou-ai-ji-zhi* 偷藹吉支 (others). K's reading is supported by Zhiyi's citation (Appendix 1, 3i–k), and Zhanran, commenting on Zhiyi, even explains *tou-la* 偷臘 semantically as "stealing seniority," that is, falsely inflating one's monastic age (*Zhi guan fu xing chuan hong jue*, T.1912:46.409b7–8). Perhaps, then, 諸藹吉支 in *Methods for Curing* 1.15.1 is an error for 偷臘吉支. This would require assuming the interlinear commentary was written *after* the error occurred. Lacking a satisfying solution, I read 偷藹吉支 at *Methods for Curing* 2.2, translate *tou* 偷 there as "thieving," and here in 1.15.1 leave *ai* 藹 as an unexplained phonetic component of (some form of) *kṛtya*. Medieval pronunciations of *zhi* 支 (LH *tśe*; MC *tśje*) imply here a (plausible) middle Indic **kicce* (cf. the Pāli *kicca*); I owe this suggestion to Jan Nattier.

209. "Eczema" (白癩病)—the translation is not intended as medically accurate—is described in medieval Chinese medical texts as a disease of the skin that produces white patches and a fiery painful feeling (*Zhong yi da ci dian*, 433, citing the early seventh-century *Zhu bing yuan hou lun* 諸病源侯論). This condition is mentioned in many Chinese translations of Indian Buddhist texts. Kumārajīva's *Lotus Sutra* seemingly uses the word to translate the phrase "the body becomes spotted" (*kāyaś citro bavişyati*; Karashima 2001, 9–10). Other texts describe it as a condition involving pus- and blood-filled boils (*Pini mu jing*, T.1463:24.821a12–13).

210. On the mythical location of Incense Mountain (香山; *gandha-mādana*), see *Bukkyō daijiten*, 1063.

the ground in a deep sleep. The practitioner must contemplate this dragon. It is wrapped in layer upon layer of skin like the leaves of the trunk of a plantain tree, unable to breathe out any air.

[1.15.3] [The Spell]

The World-honored One then spoke a spell:[211]

> *Namofotuo Namodamo Namosengjia Namomohelishi Pisheluoshe Aiduotuodatuo Suomanda Basheluochi Tuoluojuetushitu Shulishuli Moheshulihumolihumolechi Xidanpiyanpi Ayanpili Jiujujuchi* [340c] *Pusatuoluonichi Ashantimojumojuli Yingyixumixumixumoxu Mosaguohe.*

When the World-honored One had spoken this spell, he said to Śāriputra: This magic spell that I have now spoken was previously spoken by innumerable past buddhas. In the future, Maitreya and the other bodhisattvas of this fortunate eon will also preach it. This magic spell has as much power as the god Maheśvara. It can purify the minds of evil monks living during the five hundred years of the later age and harmonize excesses and deficiencies in the four elements of their bodies. It can also cure the four hundred four illnesses of the heart, the [inauspicious] visions produced by [disturbance of] the four hundred four channels,[212] the ninety-eight defilements, and the seeds of sexual desire. It can also cure the evils of both karmic obstructions and transgressions of the precepts, permanently eliminating them without remainder. It is known as the *dhāraṇī* that cures the sorrow of the seventy-two sicknesses. It is also known as the *dhāraṇī* that extirpates the roots of the five kinds of ignorance.[213] It is also called the [the spell that causes one] to presently see all the buddhas and voice-hearers who preach the true teaching that destroys all defilements.

[1.15.4] [Verses in Praise of the Spell]

The World-honored One then spoke the following verse:

> The nature of all things is without ultimate ground,
> and in this way emptiness should be contemplated.
> If you can contemplate the four elements [as empty],
> you will not be harmed by the defilements.
> If you take medicine, practice meditation,

---

211. I group the "words" of this *dhāraṇī* following the spacing presented in K (the various editions group the words somewhat differently). I have omitted the *fanqie* 反切 pronunciation guides given in the text to some of the more obscure characters. I also refrain from attempting to reconstruct the (putatively) Indic words or sounds.

212. 四百四脈所起境界.

213. 拔五種陰無明根本陀羅尼. I have read 陰無明 as "ignorance." Alternatively, 五種陰 might point to the five *skandhas*, the "dark elements" (*yin* 陰) as they were often translated in early texts.

recite this *dhāraṇī*,
and single-mindedly bring all buddhas to mind,
then the defilements will never again arise.
The ocean of affliction will be drained forever
and the river of attachment will run dry.
With nothing left to cause desire,
you can declare yourself liberated.
Free of trouble, the mind at peace,
you playfully wield the six magic powers
and also teach this
dhāraṇī to others.

When the World-honored One finished speaking this verse, he said to Śāriputra: "Know that after I have passed into nirvana, a monk, nun, layman, or laywoman who manages to hear this profound secret method for the purification of *śīla* and this *dhāraṇī* of the victory banner of the king of radiant light, which is a medicine for the illnesses that arise while practicing meditation, can be known to have planted good roots under not merely one, two, three, four, or five buddhas, but to have cultivated the aspiration for one of the three kinds of awakening[214] in the presence of innumerable hundreds of thousands of buddhas. Know that all such persons, upon hearing this profound secret method and cultivating it properly, are in their last rebirth[215] and will soon attain, like a quickly flowing stream, the four holy fruits or the bodhisattva practices.

[1.15.5] [Attainments of the Assembly]

When the Buddha had spoken, the five hundred Śākya monks progressed even further and completed their attainment of all six supernormal powers [and became arhats] [341a].[216] Upon hearing the Buddha's teachings, one thousand laborers (*śūdras*) from Śrāvasti, who in their past lives had gone mad while practicing trance, immediately experienced great happiness and became stream-enterers. Eighty million gods were able to cure their bodily illnesses and with their bodies and minds free of trouble, they immediately gave rise to the aspiration for the supreme path [of buddhahood] and rained heavenly flowers upon the Buddha and the great assembly. When the eight groups of nonhumans consisting of the gods, dragons, and others heard what the Buddha had said, they proclaimed in unison:"The Tathāgata

214. "Aspiration for [one of the] three kinds of awakening" (三種菩提之心) presumably refers to the aspiration to become an arhat, a *pratyekabuddha*, or a buddha. This expression also appears in some of the Contemplation Scriptures (*GFSMH*, T.643:15.662c17–19; *Guan Xukongzang pusa jing*, T.409:13.677c23).

215. 最後邊身. See *DZDL*, T.1509:25.64a21–22 citing a parallel to *Saṃyutta-nikāya*, 1.14, "one who possesses his final body" (*antimadehadhārī*).

216. This seems to complete the promise made in 1.3.5, where the five hundred Śākya monks, having attained stream-entry, were said to be assured of future arhatship.

appears in the world to cure maddened, demonic practitioners who hold heretical views (狂惡邪見羅刹行人), making them regain their original minds and become beautiful flower pillars.[217] How extremely pleasing and delightful. Excellent, O World-honored One! You are as precious as the *udumbara* flower which appears but once in each age."

[1.15.6] [Verses in Praise of the Buddha]

Then the great assembly spoke the following verse of praise:

O prince of the solar lineage,
descendant of the Sugarcane King,
maternal nephew of Starlight Moon,
son of Lady Maya.[218]
At birth you took seven steps,
each step shaking the cosmos,
and the gods of the ten directions came in greeting
to you, who have auspicious marks thirty-two in number.
Casting aside your throne as if it were spittle,
you sat beneath the *pippala* tree.
There, at the auspicious adamantine seat of awakening,
you defeated innumerable demons,
attained the path of *bodhi*,
your face pure like the full moon,
mental stains eliminated forever.
We now bow down to you with all our hearts,
O most excellent of the Śākyas,
who, possessed of supreme compassion,
helps all living beings
to escape forever from the suffering of birth and death.

[1.15.7] [Conclusion]

When the World-honored One heard the fourfold assembly speak these verses, to encourage them yet further he extended his golden hands and touched the heads of Śāriputra and Ānanda to entrust them with this teaching.

When Śāriputra, Ānanda, and the rest of the assembly heard what the Buddha said, they joyfully undertook to carry it out.

---

217. 花幢; or perhaps, "flower banners." The intended image is obscure. This rare term appears in some of the Contemplation Scriptures (*Guan Wuliangshou fo jing*, T.365:12.342a17). In the *Ocean-Samādhi Contemplation Scripture*, the enormous penis of the Buddha is described as "like a lotus flower pillar" (*GFSMH*, T.643:15.685a24).

218. The Buddha is often said to descend from the "solar lineage" (*sūryavaṃśa*) of King Ikṣvāku ("sugarcane"), a standard genealogy for Indian sages (*Fo suo xing zan*, T.192:4.1a8). "Starlight Moon" (星光月) must somehow point to Mahāprajāpatī, the Buddha's foster mother and maternal aunt.

[2] THE METHOD FOR CURING BEGINNING MEDITATORS ATTACKED BY GHOULS AND DISTURBED IN VARIOUS WAYS SO THEY ARE UNABLE TO ATTAIN CONCENTRATION[219]
AS ASKED BY THE VENERABLE ĀNANDA

[2.1] [Lekuñcika]

Thus have I heard. Once, the Buddha was dwelling in Śrāvasti, in Sudatta's park in the grove of Prince Jeta, in a place near the debate hall built by Lady Mallikā,[220] where *nalilou*-demons[221] reside.

At that time, Lekuñcika and nine hundred ninety-nine other sons of prominent men had just been ordained as monks, with Ānanda, Mahākāśyapa, and Śāriputra as their preceptors. Mahākāśyapa instructed these one thousand monks, but while they were in seclusion practicing breath meditation they were attacked by ghoulish demons.

They saw one demon whose head [341b] was [large and bulbous with a thin neck], like a lute (*pipa* 琵琶). It had four eyes and two mouths, and its entire face glowed. It tickled[222] the monks beneath their armpits and all over their bodies, murmuring "*buti buti*."[223] Like a spinning fire wheel or flash of lightning, it appeared and disappeared, preventing the practitioners' minds from becoming concentrated.

[2.2] [Dispelling Buti]

One who sees this must quickly be cured.[224] The method for curing is as follows. The practitioner must be instructed to close his eyes and silently curse the demon Buti: "I know you! You are a thieving *kṛtya*-demon[225] who feeds on the fire and filthy odors of this world. You delight in [causing] those

---

219. 初學坐者鬼魅所著種種不安不能得定治之法.

220. On Lady Mallikā, a wife of King Prasenajit (father of Virūḍhaka, who appeared in *Methods for Curing* 1.1.2), see Malalasekera 1937, 2:455–457. The debate hall she established in one of her pleasure parks is well known, but no other source, to my knowledge, puts it in the Jetavana as the *Methods for Curing* does here.

221. 那利樓. Unknown.

222. The *Fan fan yu*, citing this passage, explains "tickle" (擊攊) as the action that occurs when "a demon pokes a person, causing their mind to become unbalanced" (T.2128:54.669b15). It appears to be a semi-technical term from *vinaya* literature for an action forbidden to monks and nuns, corresponding to *aṅgulipratodana* 'finger poking' (Tatia 1975, *pāyantika* no. 67; *Mishasai wu fen jie ben*, T.1422a:22.198a2; *Shi song lü*, T.1435:23.112a28–b10). Given what follows (in 2.5 below), "tickle" may be a euphemism for sexual stimulation.

223. *Buti* (埠惕) might perhaps derive from **bhūtika* (from *bhūta* 'ghost'). Zhiyi (Appendix 1, 3i–j) cites the word in a different form, as either *zhui-ti* 槌惕 (*Mohe zhi guan*, T.1911:46.116a12) or *dui-ti* 堆剔 (*Xiao zhi guan*, T.1915:46.470b22; Sekiguchi 1961, 219). *Zhui* 槌 and *dui* 堆 could be phonetic variants of each other, but only graphic variants of *bu* 埠 (Schuessler 2009, nos. 28–11 and 28–12).

224. Unusually, the instructions are not explicitly framed as the words of the Buddha.

225. 偷臘[>藹]吉支, following K[1], J, P, S, Q, Y, and Kg. See 1.15.1, n. 208.

with false views to break the precepts.[226] But I uphold the precepts and am not afraid of you."

A monk or nun should then recite the opening passage of the monastic rules.[227] A layperson should recite the three refuges, the five precepts, or the eight precepts. This demon will then crawl away.

[2.3] [Countering Demons in the Future Age]

When Ānanda heard this, he said to the Buddha: "World-honored One, having learned from you this method for staving off the demon Buti, these monks, sons of prominent men, have escaped from evil and will no longer be harassed by ghoulish demons. But in later ages, a thousand years after the Buddha's *parinirvāṇa*, there will be monks who wish to teach monks, nuns, laymen, or laywomen how to dwell in a quiet place, count the breath, and fix the mind in breath meditation.

"There may then be demons who in order to disrupt the teachings of Buddhism transform into rodents, black or red, and claw at the practitioner's heart or scratch his feet, hands, ears, or elsewhere. Or else they caw like crows, moan like ghosts, or make whispering sounds. There may be fox spirits that take the form of young women, making themselves beautiful and coming to the practitioner to massage his body and speak of improper things. Or [demons] that appear in the form of dogs, howling without cease. Or else as a flock of carnivorous birds making every kind of sound from whispering quietly to harsh cries. They may come to the practitioner as small children making assorted sounds, a hundred thousand of them in rows of ten.[228] Or the practitioner might see cobras, worms, bugs, crickets, snakes, or vipers entering his ears, buzzing like a hornet king. Or entering his eyes, like blowing sand.[229] Or they might strike his heart (觸心), causing severe disturbance and driving him mad, such that he goes away from his quiet place [of meditation] and does heedless things. How can this be cured?"

[2.4] [Past Life of Buti]

The Buddha said to Ānanda: Listen carefully and ponder well what I now tell you. If a practitioner is afflicted by such demons, you must explain for him the method of curing demonic interference.

The demon Buti has sixty-three names. During the age of the past buddha Kanakamuni, there was a monk who was about to become a stream-

226. 汝為邪見喜破戒種. Translation tentative.

227. In the Chinese translations of the *vinaya*, "the opening passage of the precepts" (*jiexu* 戒序) means the first section of the *prātimokṣa*, containing the ritual invocations spoken prior to the recitation of the rules themselves. To recite this section alone is classified as the most basic form of the recitation of the precepts (*Wu fen lü*, T.1421:22.122a23–27; *Shi song lü*, T.1435:23.421c10–15; *Si fen lü*, T.1428:22.823b1–4) and is sometimes said to be equivalent to reciting all the precepts (*Sapoduo pini piposha*, T.1440:23.543a21–22).

228. 百千為行十十五五若一二三. Translation tentative. Kg reads 百千為行十五若一.

229. 如迸酪[>落]沙, following *YQJYY*, T.2128:54.669b21.

enterer. But because of his evil livelihood,[230] he was expelled by the other monks. When his life ended, he was filled with hatred, and he vowed to become a ghost. Even now he still harasses Buddhist practitioners. He will live [as a ghost] for one eon, after which he will die and fall into the Avīci hell [341c]. You must remember his names [and call them to ward him off], so that you may keep your mind concentrated and not be disturbed by him.

[2.5] [Repentance for Nocturnal Emissions]

The World-honored One then said: Buti is an evil *yakṣa*[231] also known as the "dream demon." Seeing it in one's dreams, one will have a nocturnal emission.[232] One must then get up and repent: "Buti has come! Because of my past evil deeds, I have met this baleful demon who destroys the precepts. I will now spur on my mind, restrain my sense organs, and not allow myself to be heedless."

[2.6] [The Other Names of Buti]

When [Buti] flies through the air, it is named "air demon" (空鬼); between the sheets it is named "belly crawler" (腹行鬼). It has three more names [not listed here] and another ten[233] names: *shensuo, jiafu, qiuna, qiuni, zhili, fuchou, fuchoua, mole, jiasha,* and *guohe.* [It is also named] road demon, *chimei* (魑魅), *wangliang* (魍魎), pus drinker, spit eater, water spirit, fire spirit, mountain spirit, forest spirit, wife demon, man demon, boy demon, girl demon, *kṣatriya* demon, Brahmin demon, *vaiśya* demon, *śūdra* demon,[234] walker, crawler, rider, donkey ears, tiger head, cat meow, hawk demon, owl demon, vulture demon, crow demon. It can also take the form of one of the demons and spirits of the eight groups [of nonhumans],[235] [and is otherwise called]

---

230. "Evil livelihood" (邪命), for monks or nuns, usually means supporting oneself illicitly, through activities such as fortune-telling or commerce rather than alms. This does not fit the present context. We might instead consider a passage in the *Ocean-Samādhi Contemplation Scripture* where "evil livelihood" means boasting or lying about one's meditative attainments (*GFSMH*, T.643:15.695b10–13; note other resemblances to *Chan Essentials* 4.32.1–12 as well). That the monk who became the Buti demon was "expelled" (擯) might similarly connote a *pārājika* violation, such as making intentionally false claims to meditative attainment.

231. 埠惕{埠惕}是惡夜叉. Alternatively, the line "Buti is an evil *yakṣa*" (埠惕是惡夜叉) could be an interlinear note wrongly incorporated into the text. Or, the creature could here be intentionally named "Buti-buti."

232. *Shijing* 失精 regularly means a nocturnal or other seminal emission in the Chinese translations of *vinaya* literature (see, e.g., *Shi song lü*, T.1435:23.443a4–26).

233. 一[>十]名. Arbitrarily dividing the ensuing syllables into ten names, taking the "three names" as pointing to additional (unlisted or lost) names, and then further counting "dream demon" from the previous paragraph, we arrive at sixty-three names, the number given below. This calculation is, needless to say, speculative.

234. The names of the four classical Indian social classes are here given in transcription.

235. Often listed among the audiences for Buddhist sutras, the "eight groups" (八部) of nonhumans are *devas*, *nāgas*, *yakṣas*, *gandharvas*, *asuras*, *garuḍas*, *kiṃnaras*, and *mahoragas*.

exhauster, eight horned, white rat, lotus colored, fox demon, *guimei*-demon, insect-spirit demon, the four evil *piśāca*-demons, and *kumbhāṇḍa*-demon.

These are this demon's sixty-three horrific forms and names.

[2.7] [The Seven Buddhas and the Spell to Remove Demons]

If they cause disturbance, the practitioner must count his breath and make himself very calm. He should focus his mind and bring to mind the seven buddhas of the past, chanting their names: "Homage to the buddhas Vipaśyin, Śikhin, Viśva,[236] Krakucchanda, Kanakamuni, Kāśyapa, and Śākyamuni." After chanting these names, he should hold firm in his mind the all-sound *dhāraṇī*[237] [by] speaking the following spell: *A mi a mi jia li she suan di li fu qi nou chi tou ti ta tou ti ta mo he jia lou ni jia mi duo luo pu ti sa duo.*

Those whose minds are disturbed and who are harassed by the Buti demon may see hallucinations (諸幻境界). They must chant this *dhāraṇī*, the names of the seven buddhas, and that of Maitreya bodhisattva. They must focus their minds, count their breaths, and then chant the *prātimokṣa* one hundred times. The evil demons will then be quelled, and monks, nuns, laymen, and laywomen who practice the path will never again be disturbed by them.

[2.8] [Entrustment to Ānanda]

The Buddha said to [342a] Ānanda: "To help Buddhist practitioners make progress, avoid distracted thoughts, and enter *samādhi*, you must remember this method, which banishes evil demons, instills proper conduct, and purifies body, speech, and mind.[238] Remember it well. Do not forget it."

When Ānanda heard what the Buddha said, he joyfully undertook to carry it out.

[2.9] [The Demons of Itchy Palms]

Further, Ānanda, while sitting in meditation a practitioner may suffer from pain in his ears, aching joints, itchy palms, pain on the soles of his feet, fluttering in his belly, twitching in his neck, blurry vision, a numb bottom,[239] or demons who come near and whisper, scatter incense and flowers, or perform mischief. This must quickly be cured.

[2.10] [The Medicine Bodhisattvas]

The method to cure this is as follows. First, the practitioner must contemplate the two bodhisattvas Medicine King and Medicine Lord,[240] who pour

236. See *Chan Essentials* 1.18.14, n. 257.

237. 一切音聲陀羅尼. Translation tentative.

238. 淨身口意調伏威儀擯惡鬼法.

239. 坐處朏. Commenting on this passage, *YQJYY* explains the rare word 朏 as equivalent to *bi* 痺 [var. 痹] 'numbness' (T.2128:54.669c4).

240. Medicine King 藥王 and Medicine Lord 藥上 are mentioned together in Kumārajīva's translation of the *Lotus Sutra* (*Miao fa lian hua jing*, T.262:9.60c27–28) and are the cultic focus of one of the Contemplation Scriptures (*Guan Yaowang Yaoshang er pusa jing*).

water from golden vases over his head. Next he must contemplate the divine lord (神王) of the Himalayas,[241] who approaches the practitioner and places a white flower over his head. It radiates white light that infuses his pores, immediately relaxing his body and eliminating all unusual symptoms. He then sees the boy Jīvaka, who scatters divine flowers (仙人花) over his head. Magic medicine rains down from each flower, infusing his pores and completely eliminating all his discomfort and numbness and also driving away forever the many whispering demons.

[2.11] [Preaching of the Dharma]

The bodhisattvas Medicine King and Medicine Lord then preach the Mahāyāna teachings of the equality of all things (平等摩訶衍法). So too, the divine lords of Fragrance Mountain in the Himalayas, and the boy Jīvaka, will teach him the twelve gates of trance in accordance with his capacities.[242] To cure his illnesses they will also bestow on him medicines,[243] treatments, and spells. As a result, he will see the venerable Piṇḍola and the other arhats, as well as the five hundred novices [led by] Cundrava. All at once they will approach the practitioner, and each arhat will preach methods for curing illness.[244]

Following the Buddha's teachings, some of the arhats will instruct the practitioner[245] to [imagine] boring a hole in the top of his skull and gradually emptying out the inside. When his entire body is empty, [the arhats] will anoint him with oil while the god Brahmā pours golden medicine into his body until it is full.[246] The bodhisattva Medicine King will then preach the teachings.

If he has aroused the intention of becoming a voice-hearer, then following the teachings given by Piṇḍola he will become a stream-enterer. If he has put forth the aspiration for the Great Vehicle, then following the teachings given by the bodhisattvas Medicine King and Medicine Lord he will attain the *samādhi* in which all the buddhas appear before him.[247]

---

241. 雪山神王. This may refer to Uttaraga, who appeared in 1.12.3.

242. Many of the figures here—Jīvaka, Piṇḍola, Cundrava, the five hundred arhats and five hundred novices—are also mentioned in 1.6.3–5. That passage too states that different teachings are given according to level of aspiration.

243. 隨病湯[>賜]藥.

244. 所[>即]說種種治病之法.

245. Literally, "this monk" (此比丘). This is one of the few passages that explicitly marks the "practitioner" as a monk.

246. This recalls 1.5.5–6.

247. 諸佛現前三昧. This *samādhi* is mentioned in several of the Contemplation Scriptures (*Guan Puxian pusa xing fa jing*, T.277:9.390c23; *Guan Wuliangshou fo jing*, T.365:12.346b3; *GFSMH*, T.643:15.693c7). It presumably derives from the *samādhi* that lends its name to the famous *Pratyutpanna-buddha-saṃmukhāvasthita-samādhi-sūtra* (Harrison 1990).

[2.12] [Final Instructions]

The Buddha said to Ānanda: After I have passed away, those among my four groups of disciples who wish to sit in meditation should first sit quietly for seven days. Then they should cultivate their minds through breath counting for seven days and should further take the medicines [already presented] for removing sickness so as to eliminate noises and do away with numbness in the legs. They should concentrate their minds and restrain their thoughts, cultivate their bodies and minds, and harmonize the material elements of their bodies so that they waste no time in bringing their minds to perfect concentration. They must not violate even the minor precepts or the basic rules of deportment. They should protect the precepts they have received as they would their very eyes, as a gravely ill person would [diligently] follow the teachings of a skilled [342b] doctor. They should count [their breaths] in order, not getting behind or losing their place. They should follow the words of the sages as diligently as one would extinguish a fire on one's own head. This is called curing one's sickness and taking the medicine that warms the body (是名治病服煖身藥).

[2.13] [Final Entrustment]

The Buddha said to Ānanda: "You must remember this teaching. Do not forget it." When the venerable Ānanda heard what the Buddha said, he joyfully undertook to carry it out.

APPENDIX 1

Citations of the *Chan Essentials* and *Methods for Curing*

This appendix lists the most important citations and references to the *Chan Essentials* and *Methods for Curing* in sources dating from before the Tang dynasty. (Excluded from the list are some late-Tang subcommentaries to works listed here, in which the same passages are re-cited.) The titles by which these citations refer to the material in question are discussed in more detail in Appendix 3 (table 9).

1. A sixth-century monastic code

Chan Essentials 4.32.4 is paraphrased, as the teachings of a / the "*chan* scripture," in a short monastic rule book believed to date from the early sixth century that is known from a single Dunhuang manuscript seen by Tsukamoto Zenryū in the 1920s.[1]

2. Essential selections from the canon (*Zhong jing yao lan* 眾經要攬)

This collection of over two hundred scriptural excerpts, arranged according to ten categories, is known from several Dunhuang manuscripts and dates to the sixth century.[2] It includes:

a. A relatively precise citation of *Chan Essentials* 4.32.12.[3]
b. A loose citation of *Methods for Curing* 1.8.1–6.[4]

1. Tsukamoto 1975, 295. For a study and edition of this text based on Tsukamoto's copy, see Moroto 1990, 68–96. The present whereabouts of the original manuscript are unknown.

2. Zhang 2015. Six Dunhuang manuscripts are known to contain portions of the text.

3. See Stein no. 514 (*Dunhuang bao zang*, 4:216b) and *Guo jia tu shu guan cang Dunhuang yi shu*, 43.180 (BD no. 3159).

4. This passage is only extant on manuscript Haneda no. 727 (*Tonkō hikyū*, 9:190).

3. Zhiyi's meditation manuals and their commentaries

Zhiyi (writing in the late sixth century) often cites both the *Chan Essentials* and *Methods for Curing* under the name "the Āgamas" (*Ahan* 阿含) or "the Saṃyuktāgama" (*Za ahan* 雜阿含).[5]

a. *Shi chan boluomi ci di fa men*, T.1916:46.506a20–21, briefly alludes to the methods for "meditative imagination" (*jiaxiang* 假想) in the *Methods for Curing*, calling them the "secret methods for curing chan illness" (治禪病祕法).
b. *Mohe zhi guan*, T.1911:46.109a22–23, discusses *Methods for Curing* 1.5 (calling it the "Saṃyuktāgama").
c. *Zhi guan fu xing chuan hong jue*, T.1912:46.400a3–b4. Zhanran's 湛然 (711–782) commentary to 3b, summarizes and cites the first sutra of the *Methods for Curing*.
d. *Shi chan boluomi ci di fa men*, T.1916:46.488a3–10, cites as "a / the chan scripture" verses from *Methods for Curing* 1.8.5.
e. *Xiao zhi guan*, T.1915:46.464a6–13. Same as 3d.
f. *Mohe zhi guan*, T.1911:46.111c27–28, cites the "Āgamas" as saying that a vision of the death of an eighty-eight-headed snake is a sign that one is about to attain stream-entry. This is a reference to *Chan Essentials* 3.26.14–16.[6]
g. *Mohe zhi guan*, T.1911:46.117c15–18, alludes without attribution to the story of Mahākauṣṭhilananda in *Chan Essentials* 1.0.1–1.1.10 as proof that the contemplation of impurity can lead to arhatship.
h. *Zhi guan fu xing chuan hong jue*, T.1912:46.412a2–12. Zhanran's commentary to 3g, cites *Chan Essentials* 1.0.3 and summarizes 1.1.1–10.
i. *Shi chan boluomi ci di fa men*, T.1916:46.507a15–24, as the "*chan* scripture" summarizes *Methods for Curing* 2.2–7 on the "demon Buti" (埠惕鬼).
j. *Xiao zhi guan*, T.1915:46.470b22–470c2. Same as 3i. Many other medieval meditation manuals that draw from the *Xiao zhi guan* end up including this material.[7]
k. *Mohe zhi guan*, T.1911:46.116a11–23 and *Zhi guan fu xing chuan hong jue*, T.1912:46.409b7–17. Same as 3i and 3j.

---

5. On Zhiyi's citations of these texts, see also Sengoku 1980. The opening lines of the *Methods for Curing* attribute it to the "Saṃyuktāgama" (*ZCB*, T.620:15.333a11).

6. Other medieval Chinese authors refer to this same idea, without attribution. See, in particular, Jizang's 吉藏 (549–623) *Jin gang bore shu*, T.1699:33.110a9–10 and Guanding's 灌頂 (561–632) *Da banniepan jing shu*, T.1767:38.208c10–11, where it is said to be a matter of a dream.

7. See, in particular, *Qi xin lun shu* (Wŏnhyo), T.1844:44.223b25–c24 and *Da sheng qi xin lun yi ji* (Fazang), T.1846:44.284a16–b18. These commentaries touch on the content of the *Methods for Curing* only by way of Zhiyi's text (see Sekiguchi 1961, 29–39).

4. Early Tang-dynasty *vinaya* commentaries

a. *Si fen lü shu*, Z.734:42.323b16–19. The sole surviving scroll of the vinaya commentary of Zhishou 智首 (567–635) summarizes and quotes *Chan Essentials* 4.32.13.2–3.
b. *Si fen lü shan fan bu que xing shi chao*, T.1804:40.97a5–7 and 107c1–3. Daoxuan's 道宣 (596–667) primary vinaya commentary, cites *Methods for Curing* 1.9 as proof that one can atone for *pārājika* violations.
c. *Si fen biqiuni chao*, Z.724:40.762a4–9. Daoxuan's commentary to the nuns' rules. Same as 4b.

5. Tang-dynasty Buddhist encyclopedias (mid-seventh century)

a. *Fa yuan zhu lin*, T.2122:53.793b14–794a6 (*Zhu jing yao ji*, T.2123:53.186b16–187a8), cites *Methods for Curing* 1.7 on the bodily worms.
b. *Fa yuan zhu lin*, T.2122:52.853a14–29 (*Zhu jing yao ji*, T.2123:53.135b20–c5), cites *Chan Essentials* 4.32.5 and 4.32.7 on those falsely claiming meditative attainment.
c. *Fa yuan zhu lin*, T.2122:52.904c19–905a9, cites *Methods for Curing* 1.2.1 and 1.15.3 on a spell for destroying obstacles to meditation.
d. *Fa yuan zhu lin*, T.2122:52.981b6, attributes to the "Saṃyuktāgama" the statement "one should not eat the five pungent foods" (不應食五辛). No such statement occurs in any surviving Chinese version of the *Saṃyuktāgama*, but a nearly identical line appears at *Methods for Curing* 1.12.3, and this must be the source.

6. Zhizhou's 智周 (668–723) commentary to the *Brahma-net Sutra*

(*Fan wang jing pusa jie ben shu*, Z.687:38.452a8–c3), cites *Methods for Curing* 1.7 in full.

7. Cave 59 of the Wofoyuan 臥佛院

Carved excerpts of the *Chan Essentials*, drawn from throughout the text, dated by colophon to 735 (Greene 2018).

8. An eighth-century Chan lineage text

Li dai fa bao ji, T.2075:51.183a13–16 (Yanagida 1971, 107–108; Adamek 2007, 326), summarizes the first sutra of the *Methods for Curing*. This text survives only among the Dunhuang manuscripts.

9. Writings of Fazhao 法照 (fl. late eighth century)

Jing tu wu hui nian fo song jing guan xing yi, T.2827:85.1255a4–27 (Pelliot no. 2066).

Fazhao's ritual manual for worshiping the Buddha, cites and paraphrases passages from *Chan Essentials* 2.0.1–2.19.3.

10. Chengguan's 澄觀 (738–d. after 806)[8] commentaries to the *Hua yan jing* 華嚴經

a. *Da fang guang fo hua yan jing shu*, T.1735:35.666a9–12, briefly cites *Methods for Curing* 1.3.1.
b. *Da fang guang fo hua yan jing sui shu yan yi chao*, T.1736:36.334a25, cites *Methods for Curing* 1.1.3–1.3.2 nearly in full.

8. On the date of Chengguan's death, see Hamar 2002, 62–67.

APPENDIX 2

Internal Evidence of Chinese Authorship and Dating

In Chapter 4, I discuss the external evidence suggesting that the *Chan Essentials* and *Methods for Curing* were assembled in China on the basis of preexisting meditation manuals written in Chinese. This appendix takes up the purely internal evidence of their Chinese authorship.

Tsukinowa Kenryū, who showed their close connection to the Contemplation Scriptures, was the first to argue that the *Chan Essentials* and *Methods for Curing* cannot have been the mere translations of Indic originals (1971, 102–109). Though this claim is ultimately correct, his argument that these texts are *obvious* forgeries is overblown. In fact, upon closer examination few of Tsukinowa's examples prove certain at all.[1] There are, however, many other, less easily disputed traces within the texts suggesting that the authors or final compilers were indeed drawing their knowledge of Buddhism not from a direct familiarity with Indic Buddhist literature, but from Chinese Buddhist sources. This appendix assembles four of the most persuasive such examples.

1. Tsukinowa relies largely on *ex silentio* observations: "unusual" expressions that he asserts, without proof, could not occur in a genuinely translated text. Many of these claims are easily problematized, as Yamabe has shown in the case of the Contemplation Scriptures (1999c, 186–195). Tsukinowa's arguments about the *Chan Essentials* and *Methods for Curing* are much the same. To take but a few examples: he labels as "fake" Sanskrit words easily explainable as graphic variants or textual errors (see n. 11 in *Methods for Curing* 1.2.2); he objects to the dual presence in the same text of the transcription *anban* 安般 (*ānāpāna*) and its usual Chinese translation "breath counting" (*shu xi* 數息), even though this occurs in some unquestionably genuine Chinese Buddhist translations (see, e.g., *Zeng yi ahan jing*, T.125:2.556a28–b9); and similarly for the two distinct epithets *tianzun* 天尊 and *shizun* 世尊, both usually translations of *bhagavan* (see, e.g., *Zheng fa hua jing*, T.263:9.125a9–18).

I relegate many others, some only suggestive, to the notes to the translations, where they may be consulted by those interested in these details.[2]

Evidence of Chinese Authorship

1. Terminological confusion (a): *wuyuan* 無願 and *wuzuo* 無作

The *Chan Essentials* and *Methods for Curing* frequently discuss the canonical Buddhist category of the three "gates to deliverance" (*vimokṣa-mukha*), that is, the three advanced meditative attainments involving the realization of "emptiness" (*śūnyatā*) "signlessness" (*animitta*), and "desirelessness" (*apraṇihita*). Medieval Chinese Buddhist texts consistently translated the first two of these as *kong* 空 and *wuxiang* 無相, respectively. The third term, *apraṇihita*, had two distinct translations reflecting two different interpretations of its meaning: *wuyuan* 無願 (non-wishing) and *wuzuo* 無作 (non-doing).[3] However, the *Chan Essentials* and *Methods for Curing* often give all four of these Chinese terms as part of a single list.[4] Further, even when it was seemingly realized that there should only be three terms, there is confusion as to which they are. In one passage, they are parsed incorrectly: *kong* (emptiness) and *wuxiang* (signlessness) are taken together, as a single concept (a reasonable enough interpretation from the Chinese terms alone), while *wuyuan* (non-wishing) and *wuzuo* (non-doing) are treated individually.[5] In another passage, *wuxiang* (signlessness) is omitted even as both translations of *apraṇihita* are included (*Chan Essentials* 1.18.19). Given that this list is, in Indian Buddhist literature, a fixed formula, we must conclude that these passages reflect the work of an author whose knowledge of these terms came from Buddhist literature in Chinese translation, where the forms used had been inconsistent and where even a learned reader might well make these mistakes.[6]

2. See the notes to *Chan Essentials* 1.0.4, 1.1.1, 1.2.1.3, 1.12.3, 1.18.14, 1.2.2.4, 1.12.2, 1.12.3, 1.15.2.1, 1.18.14, 2.0.2, 2.19.1.4, 4.31.28, 4.32.3, 4.32.8, 4.32.13.5; *Methods for Curing* 1.7.4, 1.14.3; and 1.14.16. See also, in Appendix 4, the discussion of the name of the protagonist of the first sutra of the *Chan Essentials*.

3. See Deleanu (2000, 93–95n24) for a detailed treatment of the meaning of the term *apraṇihita* in this context. Modern scholars have different opinions about the precise meaning of this word and, like medieval Chinese translators, have adopted a number of distinct renderings.

4. See *Chan Essentials* 2.20.15, 3.29.2, 4.31.3, 4.31.29, and *Methods for Curing* 1.14.12.

5. *Chan Essentials* 4.31.29. In 4.31.30, a correct list is given.

6. Chen Zhiyuan, commenting on my earlier work on this topic, has noted that we do find a few Chinese Buddhist texts unquestionably translated from Indian sources in which the four terms *kong*, *wuxiang*, *wuyuan*, and *wuzuo* appear sequentially (Chen Z. 2019, 81n7). However the context of the passages he notes is never the *vimokṣa-mukha*, as it is in the *Chan Essentials* and *Methods for Curing*. Moreover, these examples cannot explain the cases from the *Chan Essentials* in which only three terms appear even as *wuyuan* and *wuzuo* are treated as two distinct items.

2. Terminological confusion (b): the stages of the embryo

In *Chan Essentials* 1.15.2.1, the meditator is directed to contemplate the impermanence of his body by considering that its bones were not present in the earliest stages of life:

> Where were they at the moment [of conception,] when the blood and semen of mother and father were joined? When [the embryo] was like milk curds? When it was like a foamy bubble? When it was a *kalala?* When it was an *arbuda?* (*Chan Essentials* 1.15.2.1)

This passage draws from lists of the stages of embryo growth in Indian Buddhist (and non-Buddhist) literature (Kritzer 2009). The authors of the *Chan Essentials* obviously knew of these theories, but they were also, it seems, confused about the relationship between the Indic names of the stages and the Chinese translations of these names, both of which had appeared in earlier Chinese Buddhist texts. "Foamy bubble" (*pao* 泡), for example, was the typical Chinese translation of the stage named *arbuda*,[7] yet the *Chan Essentials* clearly presents these two as separate moments. So too for the *kalala* stage, given both in transcription (*geluoluo* 歌羅邏) and in its typical semantic translation, as the moment when the male and female essences of semen and blood first join.[8] Here again, redundancy was created because the authors evidently drew, directly or indirectly, on Buddhist technical vocabulary as it appeared in Chinese Buddhist literature.

3. Verses on craving and impurity

Methods for Curing 1.8.5 presents eight five-character couplets on the perils of craving, the impurity of the body, and the necessity of meditation.[9] The first half of these verses appears to have been taken from a translation by Kumārajīva.[10] Though we cannot completely rule out the possibility that a purported "translator" of the *Methods for Curing* merely borrowed Kumārajīva's translation of what were known to be the same verses, this is more likely a

7. *DMDL*, T.618:15.315c23–24. The similar *bao* 胞 is used at *DZDL*, T.1509:25.90a10 and *Bie yi za ahan jing*, T.100:2.476b18–19 (*Saṃyutta-nikāya*, 1.205). The transcription of *arbuda* in the *Chan Essentials—anfutuo* 安浮陀—can be found in various sources extant by the early fifth century, including the *Da banniepan jing* (T.374:2.446a27).

8. The *Da zhi du lun*, for example, defines *geluoluo* 歌羅羅 (*kalala*) as "the moment when the red and white essences have joined" (赤白精和合時; T.1509:25.90a9–10).

9. These are the same verses cited by Zhiyi; see Appendix 1, no. 3, d–e.

10. *Da bao ji jing*, T.310:11.446c11–14. This section, the *Pūrṇa-paripṛcchā* (*Fulouna hui* 富樓那會), is attributed to Kumārajīva at *Chu san zang ji ji*, T.2145:55.11a2.

case where a pre-existing Chinese text was one of the sources for the composition of the *Methods for Curing*.[11]

4. THE EIGHT GODS OF THE HIMALAYAS

Methods for Curing 1.12.2–3 discusses the "twelve radiant gods" (十二白光神) of the Himalayas, who bestow medicine and instructions in meditation. Though the first and last three of these gods are unknown from other sources, the remaining eight names exactly match the names of the eight "gods of the Himalayas" (雪山之神) found in Buddhabhadra's early fifth-century translation of the *Anantamukha-nirhāra-dhāraṇī-sūtra*.[12] This correspondence is unlikely to have occurred by chance, as Buddhabhadra's rendition of these names is distinctive (relative to the seven other Chinese versions of this text) in having semantically translated all of the names except one, left inexplicably in transcription, Kumāra (鳩摩羅). Moreover, Buddhabhadra's translation of this text was widely used in south China in the fifth century.[13] The authors of the *Methods for Curing* must have borrowed the names from it or from an active cult to those gods inspired by it.

Dating

Among the pieces of evidence presented above are cases of borrowing from previously translated Chinese Buddhist texts. These examples, along with other considerations, help establish an earliest possible date for the final compilation of the *Chan Essentials* and *Methods for Curing*. Specifically, the *Methods for Curing* draws from a translation by Kumārajīva (no. 3 above) that was done between the years 410 and 420 (*CSZJJ*, T.2145:55.11c22–24). The *Chan Essentials* has no borrowings quite this clear, but does seem to rely in a few passages on Dharmakṣema's translation of the *Survarṇabhāsottama-sūtra*, completed no earlier than 420.[14] In the second sutra, the form of the protagonist's name (Nandi *the Meditator*) is otherwise attested only in the Chinese translation of the *Mahāsāṅghika-vinaya*, produced in south China in 420 (see Appendix 4). We may thus conclude that the texts cannot have reached their final form before roughly the beginning of the Song dynasty in 420. A Song-dynasty date is also suggested by an interlinear gloss in *Methods for Curing* 1.13.4.

Meanwhile, the colophon indicating the activities of Juqu Jingsheng (see Chapter 4) records the date of 455. The texts presumably existed by no

11. Interestingly, we find a different translation of these same verses in the *Chan yao jing* (T.609:15.238c24–27), a short, incomplete meditation treatise attributed to Kumārajīva that may be an alternate translation of the *Chan fa yao jie* (T.616).

12. *Chu sheng wu liang men chi jing*, T.1012:19.684c11–16. On the *Anantamukha-nirhāra-dhāraṇī-sūtra* (and its many Chinese translations), see Inagaki 1987.

13. It is listed, for example, among the texts personally copied by the imperial prince and Buddhist devotee Xiao Ziliang 蕭子良 (460–495) and kept in his library (*CSZJJ*, T.2145:55.86b16).

14. See n. 119 in *Chan Essentials* 1.12.3, and n. 302 in 2.19.1.4.

later than this time. This interval 420–455, essentially the Yuanjia 元嘉 era of Song emperor Wendi 文帝, also seems to align with a prophecy given by the Buddha at *Chan Essentials* 4.32.15 concerning the fate of the texts during an era 1,500 years after the Buddha's death. The prophesied era must have coincided with the time, in the minds of the author(s), when the texts were first put into circulation. If we imagine that the authors had in mind or were influenced by the chronology reported by Faxian 法顯 (d. ca. 420) in the records of his travels to India, where he claims that the Buddha had died exactly 1,500 years prior, this would again point to the first circulation of the texts around the beginning of the Song dynasty.[15]

15. *Gao seng Faxian zhuan*, T.2085:51.865a26–27. Faxian here tells of a ritual performed at the annual unveiling of the Buddha's tooth relic at the Abhayagiri monastery in Sri Lanka. At this time, he says, an announcement is made declaring how long it has been since the Buddha's death. Faxian gives 1,497 years, presumably the number he heard while he was there several years earlier. This dating of the Buddha's death to ca. 1100 BCE is unattested from any other Indian sources (Palumbo, n.d.). It must, however, have been at least reasonably well known in south China during the fifth century because similar 1,500year prophecies can be found in some other Buddhist scriptures translated during this era (see, e.g., *Mohe maye jing*, T.383:12.1013c19). Later Chinese-authored sources also occasionally refer to it (*Li dai san bao ji*, T.2034:49.23a16). On the various early Chinese theories concerning the date of the Buddha's death, see Zürcher 1972, 271–274.

APPENDIX 3

Circulation of the Texts in the Manuscript Era

This appendix considers the different formats and titles under which the *Chan Essentials* and *Methods for Curing* circulated during the manuscript era (Tang and pre-Tang). Information on the specific editions of the texts used in the translations, some of which are discussed here, is found in the introduction to the translations in Part II.

Extant Formats

A few fragments aside, complete or nearly complete copies of the *Chan Essentials* and *Methods for Curing* survive in (1) editions derived from the woodblock printed Chinese Buddhist canons (the basis of modern editions such as the Taishō edition), and (2) manuscript editions from Japan, which are sometimes arranged and titled rather differently. I use the following names to refer to the extant *formats* of the two texts (each of which is represented by more than one edition or copy).

Chan Essentials 1, 2, 3

The three scrolls of the three-scroll recension of the *Chan Essentials.* This is the format of the text in the printed canons (under the name *Chan mi yao fa jing* 禪祕要法經), as well as in the three-scroll Kongō-ji manuscript and other three-scroll Japanese manuscript editions (some of which bear a slightly different title, *Chan fa mi yao jing* 禪法祕要經).[1]

Tempyō Chan Essentials 1

The format represented by scroll 1 of the five-scroll Shōsōin manuscript (*Kunaichō shōsōin jimusho shozō shōgozō kyōkan* no. 268), with dedicatory prayer

1. Three-scroll Japanese manuscripts of the *Chan Essentials* to which I have not had direct access are found in the collections of Saihō-ji 西方寺, Matsuosha 松尾社, and Ishiyamadera 石山寺 (*Nihon genson hasshu issaikyō mokuroku*, 241). From the length of these copies, in sheets of paper (Nakao 1997, nos. 2382–2384), they are of the complete text, not merely the first three scrolls of a 4- or 5-scroll recension.

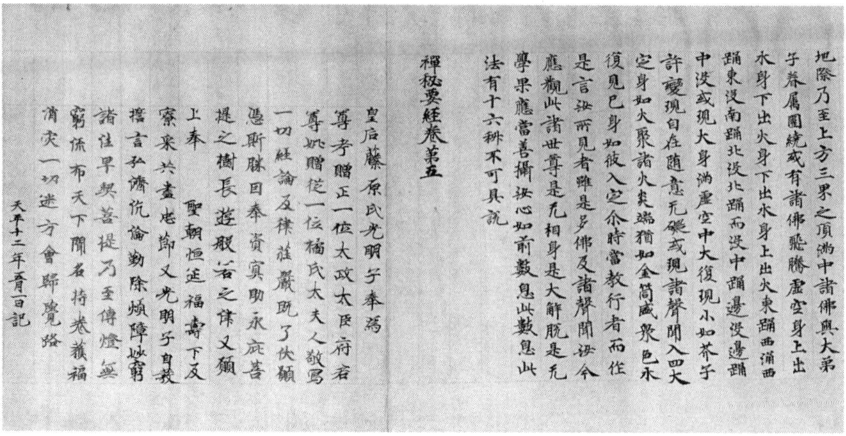

Figure 1. Final page of the fifth scroll of the Shōsōin manuscript of the *Chan Essentials*. The dedicatory inscription identifies the text as part of the complete Buddhist canon copied between 737 and 756 under the patronage of Fujiwara no Asukabehime 藤原安宿媛 (Kōmyōshi 光明子). The Shōsōin Treasures, courtesy of the Imperial Household Agency.

dated to Tempyō 12 (740 CE),[2] titled *Chan fa mi yao jing* 禪法祕要經.[3] As discussed below, the length of this scroll suggests it derives from a four-scroll recension of the complete *Chan Essentials*.

Tempyō Chan Essentials 2, 3, 4, 5

The format of scrolls 2–5 of the Shōsōin manuscript (*Kunaichō shōsōin jimusho shozō shōgozō kyōkan* nos. 269–272), all titled *Chan mi yao jing* 禪祕要經. There are several other extant Japanese manuscripts in the format of *Tempyō Chan Essentials 1–5*.[4]

2. The dedicatory inscription, which is not a record of the exact date the text was copied, shows that the Shōsōin manuscript was part of the so-called 5 / 1 (after the date of the dedication) Buddhist canon sponsored by Fujiwara no Asukabehime 藤原安宿 between 737 and 756 (Lowe 2017, 125–129).

3. This title is found at the end of the scroll. The outer wrapper, obviously redone, gives the same title found on scrolls 2–5.

4. I have examined photographs of two different 4-scroll manuscripts of the *Chan Essentials* from Nanatsudera, each matching *Tempyō Chan Essentials 1–4*. Nattorishingūji 名取新宮寺 holds manuscripts of scrolls 1, 2, 3, and 5 of what seems to be this same recension (*Nattori shingūji issaikyō chōsa hōkokusho*, 184–185). As does the Shōsōin manuscript, the first scroll (only) of all these examples bears the slightly different title *Chan fa mi yao jing*. A nearly complete Japanese manuscript of the fourth scroll of this same recension of the *Chan Essentials*, bearing a colophon dating it to the year 1123, is currently held in the Hubei provincial museum (Hubei sheng bo wu guan 2006, 37). This manuscript was acquired from Kōzan-ji 高山寺 in the late nineteenth century. It shares unique textual variants with the Shōsōin manuscript and is presumably in a copying lineage from it.

Methods for Curing 1, 2

The two-scroll recension of the *Methods for Curing* transmitted in the printed editions of the Chinese canon, under the name *Zhi chan bing mi yao fa* 治禪病祕要法.

Kongō-ji Methods for Curing

A one-scroll recension of the *Methods for Curing*, known from Kongō-ji and other Japanese manuscript collections.[5]

Relationship between the Extant Formats

The extant recensions of the *Chan Essentials* and *Methods for Curing* cover most of the same material, but they are arranged differently, as seen in figure 2. The relative lengths are to scale: *Methods for Curing 1* and *2* are each almost precisely the same size (roughly 15 Tang-dynasty-sized manuscript sheets) as *Tempyō Chan Essentials 2, 3, 4,* and *5,* each of which are in turn precisely half the length of *Chan Essentials 1, 2,* and *3.*

A striking feature of the Shōsōin manuscript of the *Chan Essentials* is that its scrolls 1 and 2 partially overlap (fig. 2). Scroll 1 (*Tempyō Chan Essentials 1*) must have originally stemmed from a quite differently formatted text. Its title also differs slightly from the other scrolls. To judge by its length, it probably belonged to a four-scroll recension of the *Chan Essentials.* (Though no such four-scroll recensions have survived, their existence is noted in some Tang-dynasty catalogs; more on this below.)

How did these differently arranged scrolls come to be grouped as a single text? We can deduce the answer from a note included in the *Kaiyuan shi jiao lu* catalog of 730, a catalog that greatly influenced the subsequent shape of the Chinese Buddhist canon and was also taken as authoritative by the sutra copyists of eighth-century Japan who were responsible for the Shōsōin manuscript (Lowe 2017, 128). In this note, the compiler Zhisheng 智昇 describes the existence of another text, no longer extant, that combined material from both the *Chan Essentials* and *Methods for Curing.*[6]

Zhisheng says he originally had access to two different texts titled *Chan Essentials*: a three-scroll *Chan mi yao fa* (禪祕要法) attributed to Kumārajīva, which Zhisheng deemed authentic, and a five-scroll *Chan mi yao jing* (禪祕要經), labeled as a translation of Dharmamitra. The Dharmamitra text, Zhisheng decided, was to be discarded:

5. Similar manuscripts, to which I have not had access, are held in the Nanatsudera, Ishiyamadera, and Kōshō-ji collections (*Nihon genson hasshu issaikyō mokuroku*, 236).

6. Zhisheng's comments about the text are noted briefly by Tsukinowa in his original study of the *Chan Essentials* and *Methods for Curing* (1971, 109).

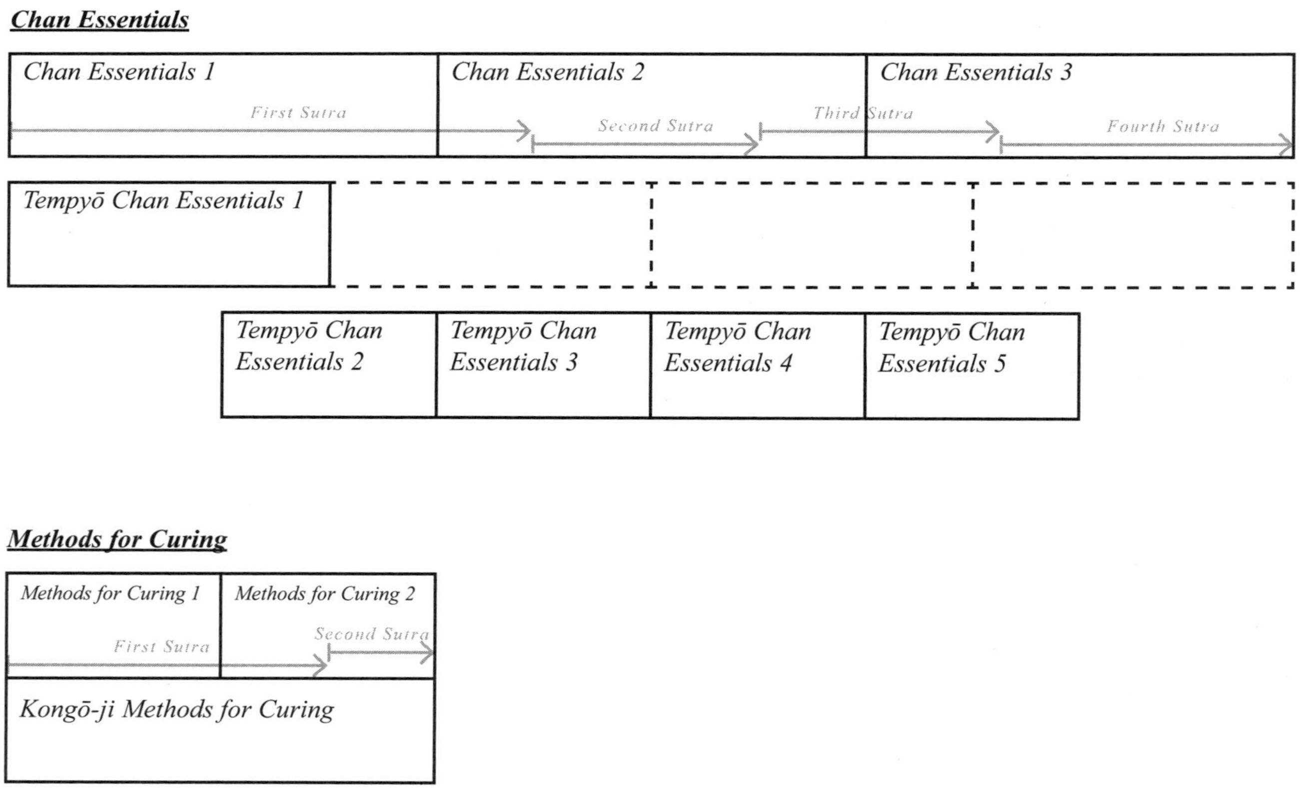

Figure 2. Relationship between the extant formats of the *Chan Essentials* and *Methods for Curing* (left to right).

> This scripture, [the five-scroll *Chan mi yao jing*,] was supposedly translated by Dharmamitra and is supposedly an alternate translation of the [three-scroll] *Chan Essentials* (*Chan mi yao fa*) translated by Kumārajīva. I have carefully examined [both texts.] [The five-scroll *Chan mi yao jing*] is corrupt and clearly not the original [of Dharmamitra]. Its first scroll contains the same text as the *Methods for Curing* (*Zhi chan bing mi yao fa*), though it is incomplete, comprising only half of it. Starting with its second scroll, [the five-scroll *Chan mi yao jing*] matches Kumārajīva's *Chan Essentials* beginning from the middle of that text's first scroll. But it is incomplete at the end of that text's third scroll, missing ten or so pages. [The parts paralleling Kumārajīva's *Chan Essentials*] have been evenly divided into four scrolls and then joined to the first scroll, making up a five-scroll text. As for Dharmamitra's [original] translation, no copy can now be found.[7]

If we assume that the three-scroll *Chan Essentials* (of Kumārajīva) that Zhisheng saw is equivalent to the received *Chan Essentials 1–3*, whose copies continue to bear Kumārajīva's name,[8] then scrolls 2–5 of the "Dharmamitra" *Chan mi yao jing* seen by Zhisheng would be equivalent to *Tempyō Chan Essentials 2–5*. Scroll 1 of Zhisheng's text, however, was clearly not *Tempyō Chan Essentials 1*. Zhisheng says that scroll 1 was equal to "half" the *Methods for Curing* (*Zhi chan bing mi yao fa*), a text that for Zhisheng existed in a one-scroll recension presumably equivalent to what we find as *Kongō-ji Methods for Curing* today.[9] The first "half" of such a text would be equal to *Methods for Curing 1*. Putting everything together, Zhisheng's five-scroll *Chan mi yao jing*, compared with the extant recensions, can be reconstructed as seen in figure 3.

It makes sense that Zhisheng would see this text as problematic, as there would be a clear lack of continuity between the first and second scrolls and the last scroll would cut off abruptly without a conclusion (as does *Tempyō Chan Essentials 5*). But it also allows us to guess how *Tempyō Chan Essentials 1–5* came to exist: a five-scroll text like the one seen by Zhisheng must have been "corrected" by removing the problematic first scroll and replacing it with the first scroll of a different version of the *Chan Essentials*. This created the unusual overlap between *Tempyō Chan Essentials 1* and *2*.

A final puzzle: was the *Tempyō Chan Essentials 1–5* recension created in Japan? Or copied from a Chinese exemplar already arranged in this way?

---

7. 右一經，云是宋代三藏曇摩蜜多譯，云與姚秦三藏鳩摩羅什所譯禪祕要法同本異出。今撿尋上下，文極交錯，非是本經。初之一卷乃是治禪病祕要法，文仍不盡至半而止。第二卷已去，即是羅什所譯禪祕要法，從第一卷過半生起。至第三卷末，文亦不盡，欠十餘紙。均為四卷，通前成五。其曇摩蜜多譯者，時闕其本。(*Kaiyuan shi jiao lu*, T.2154:55.664c16–23)

8. Zhisheng describes the 3-scroll, Kumārajīva *Chan mi yao jing* as 84 sheets in length (*Kaiyuan shi jiao lu*, T.2154:55.693a10). Assuming the usual format of 25 columns per sheet with 16–18 characters per column (Fujieda 1999, 178), this would equal the totality of *Chan Essentials 1–3*.

9. Zhisheng's 1-scroll *Zhi chan bing mi yao fa* was 28 sheets (T.2154:55.692c06), equivalent to the totality of *Methods for Curing 1–2*.

Zhisheng's 5-scroll *Chan mi yao jing*

Methods for Curing 1	*Tempyō Chan Essentials 2*	*Tempyō Chan Essentials 3*	*Tempyō Chan Essentials 4*	*Tempyō Chan Essentials 5*

Figure 3. The five-scroll *Chan mi yao jing* (of Dharmamitra) seen by Zhisheng.

No definite conclusion can be reached. The detailed records from eighth-century Japanese scriptoria first mention a three-scroll *Chan mi yao jing* copied in Tempyō 3 (731), and four- and five-scroll versions beginning in 735. But because these records usually do not tell us the size of the copied texts (in sheets of paper), it is difficult to determine what these recensions looked like exactly.[10]

Sui-Tang Records

Here I give information about the circulation of the *Chan Essentials* and *Methods for Curing* in the Sui and Tang dynasties based on four kinds of sources: (1) transmitted scriptural catalogs, (2) the titles by which the texts were cited in other works (see Appendix 1), (3) Xuanying's 玄應 (fl. 650) *Da tang zhong jing yin yi* 大唐眾經音意, and (4) scriptural catalogs and other records from Dunhuang-area libraries. (The records from pre-Sui sources are discussed in Chapter 4.)

1. Transmitted scripture catalogs

The lists of extant texts[11] seen by the compilers of Buddhist catalogs from the Sui and Tang consistently describe a *Zhi chan bing mi yao fa* 治禪病祕要法 (with very slight variations in the title), attributed to Juqu Jingsheng and one

10. The 3-scroll text copied in Tempyō 3 (731) was 91 sheets (*Dai Nihon komonjo*, 7.16)—presumably the complete *Chan Essentials 1–3*. In Tempyō 8 (736) a 5-scroll text (*Dai Nihon komonjo*, 7.70) was copied. But this could have been either *Tempyō Chan Essentials 1–5* or the 5-scroll text seen by Zhisheng. A 5-scroll *Chan mi yao jing* was brought to Japan by Genbō 玄昉 in 735 (Yamamoto 2007, 180), but again we do not know what it contained. A record from Tempyō 10 (738) indicates the copying of a 4-scroll *Chan mi yao jing* (*Dai Nihon komonjo*, 7:201). This could have been a complete 4-scroll version of the *Chan Essentials*, but could also merely have been equivalent to *Tempyō Chan Essentials 1–4*, like the present 4-scroll Nanatsudera manuscripts. I have examined all references to texts with titles similar to the *Chan Essentials* listed in Kimoto's index (1989) and have found no records of a *Chan mi yao jing* scroll 1 in a length (~15 sheets) plausibly equal to scroll 1 of Zhisheng's excluded version. Provisionally, it seems quite possible that the 5-scroll text brought to Japan by Genbō was already the "corrected" version seen today as *Tempyō Chan Essentials 1–5*.

11. Excluding titles listed in the "translation history" sections. Those sections, because they draw from previous catalogs to list all known (or imagined) works of a given translator, even those no longer extant at the time, are of limited value for understanding the forms in which texts actually circulated at any given time.

scroll in length (with 28 sheets of paper, when this information is listed).[12] These are all surely the extant *Methods for Curing*, in a one-scroll recension as is the *Kongō-ji Methods for Curing*. For texts similar in title to the *Chan Essentials*, the situation is more complicated (table 8). Most Sui-Tang catalogs list two distinct texts whose titles begin *Chan mi yao* (禪祕要): one attributed to Kumārajīva, in three or four scrolls, and another attributed to Dharmamitra, in three, four, or five scrolls. We know that Zhisheng, in 730, saw a five-scroll *Chan mi yao jing* (Dharmamitra) containing material from both the present *Chan Essentials* and *Methods for Curing* (as discussed above). Do earlier catalog entries for a Dharmamitra *Chan mi yao jing* point to a similar text? This remains unclear. Other information to be introduced below will lead to even more uncertainty about the exact content of any text bearing either of these titles during this era.

2. CITATIONS

The early citations of content from the *Chan Essentials* and *Methods for Curing* (listed in Appendix 1) use many different *titles* (table 9). The crucial takeaway from this data is that from as early as the sixth century the title *Chan mi yao jing* (禪祕要經) was used to cite content presently found in *both* the *Chan Essentials* and the *Methods for Curing*. Some of these examples (nos. 2, 4, 7, and 9 in table 9) can be explained as instances of Zhisheng's five-scroll *Chan mi yao jing*. However, one example (no. 6) cannot, as here the title *Chan mi yao jing* cites material from *Methods for Curing 2*, which was not part of Zhisheng's text. This citation cannot be explained on the basis of any known recension of the texts.

3. XUANYING'S *DA TANG ZHONG JING YIN YI* 大唐眾經音義

This twenty-five-scroll glossary of terms from the Buddhist scriptures, compiled in the mid-seventh century, attests to arrangements of the *Chan Essentials* and *Methods for Curing* that are different from any known versions.[13] To judge from where the words that Xuanying glosses appear in extant texts

12. The "canon" (入藏錄) section of the *Kaiyuan shi jiao lu*, under the text called *Zhi chan bing mi yao fa*, includes a note stating: "also in 2 scrolls" (T.2154:55.692c5). This is almost certainly an attempt to reconcile the canon list with the historical catalogs, not a sign that Zhisheng personally saw such a text. Indeed, also listed here is the alternate title *Chan yao mi mi zhi bing jing* 禪要祕密治病經, the name of Juqu Jingsheng's *chan* text in sixth-century sources but not one that any other Sui-Tang source uses for a then-circulating text. There is no clear evidence of a 2-scroll *Methods for Curing* until the tenth century.

13. Xuanying's glossary is transmitted as a 25-scroll independent version, often titled *Yi qie jing yin yi* 一切經音義, and a version partially incorporated into Huilin's 慧琳 ninth-century 100-scroll compendium that is also called *Yi qie jing yin yi* (T.2128). On the versions of Xuanying's text, see Xu 2008, 1:xiv–xvii, whose critical editions I have used (1:420–421). Huilin also glosses a 3-scroll *Chan Essentials* (*YQJYY*, T.2128:54.674a9–c7) and a 1-scroll *Methods for Curing* (*YQJYY*, T.2128:54.668c2–669c4); these seem to be the transmitted recensions.

Table 8. Sui-Tang catalog records pertaining to the *Chan Essentials*

Catalog[a]	*Title*	*Ascribed translator*	*Scrolls / sheets*	*Corresponds to*
T.2146	*Chan mi yao* 禪祕要	Dharmamitra	3 (or 5)	?
	Chan mi yao fa 禪祕要法	Kumārajīva	3	*Chan Essentials 1–3* ?
T.2034	*Chan mi yao jing* 禪祕要經	*Unstated*	3	?
T.2147	*Chan mi yao* 禪祕要	Dharmamitra	4 (or 3)	?
	Chan mi yao fa 禪祕要法	Kumārajīva	3	*Chan Essentials 1–3* ?
T.2148 and 2157	*Chan mi yao jing* 禪祕要經	Dharmamitra	5 / 71	Zhisheng's 5-scroll *Chan mi yao jing*
	Chan mi yao fa 禪祕要法	Kumārajīva	3 / 75	*Chan Essentials 1–3*
T.2153	*Chan mi yao jing* 禪祕要經	Dharmamitra	5 (or 3)[b]	Zhisheng's 5-scroll *Chan mi yao jing* (?)
	Chan mi yao jing 禪祕要經	Kumārajīva	4	*Tempyō Chan Essentials* 1 plus ?
T.2154 and 2157	*Chan mi yao jing* 禪祕要經	Dharmamitra	5	Zhisheng's 5-scroll *Chan mi yao jing*
	Chan mi yao jing 禪祕要經	Kumārajīva	3 / 84	*Chan Essentials 1–3*

[a] T.2146 (594 CE), *Zhong jing mu lu* 眾經目錄 of Fajing 法經; T.2034 (597 CE), *Li dai san bao ji* 歷代三寶紀; T.2147 (602 CE), *Zhong jing mu lu* 眾經目錄 of Yancong 彥悰; T.2148 (664 CE), *Zhong jing mu lu* 眾經目錄 of Jingtai 靜泰; T.2157 (665 CE), *Da tang nei dian lu* 大唐内典錄; T.2153 (695 CE), *Da zhou kan ding zhong jing mu lu* 大周刊定眾經目錄; T.2154 (730 CE), *Kaiyuan shi jiao lu* 開元釋教錄; T.2157 (794 CE), *Zhenyuan xin ding shi jiao lu* 貞元新定釋教錄. The data here is gathered exclusively from the catalog (rather than history) sections of these sources.

[b] 二[>三]. I assume this is an error, as Dharmamitra's chan text is not elsewhere recorded in 2 scrolls.

(table 10), he had a text whose first three scrolls (A, B, and C) were equivalent to Zhisheng's five-scroll *Chan mi yao jing* but whose title was *Zhi chan bing mi yao jing* (i.e., *Methods for Curing*). This leads to the conclusion that not only did texts titled *Chan Essentials* circulate with content from the *Methods for Curing* (e.g., Zhisheng's text and nos. 2, 4, 6, 7, and 9 in table 9), but additionally a text titled *Methods for Curing* circulated with content from the *Chan*

Table 9. Titles used in citations of the *Chan Essentials* and *Methods for Curing*

Source (Appendix 1), listed chronologically	*Title used in citation*	*Content drawn from*
1. *Zhong jing yao lan* (2a)	*Chan mi yao jing* 禪祕要經	*Chan Essentials 3* (but not *Tempyō Chan Essentials 5*)
2. *Zhong jing yao lan* (2b)	*Chan mi yao jing* 禪祕要經	*Methods for Curing 1*
3. *Si fen lü shao fan bu que xing shi chao* (4b)	*Zhi chan bing jing* 治禪病經	*Methods for Curing 1*
4. *Fa yuan zhu lin* (5a)	*Chan mi yao jing* 禪祕要經	*Methods for Curing 1*
5. *Fa yuan zhu lin* (5b)	*Chan mi yao jing* 禪祕要經	*Chan Essentials 3* (but not *Tempyō Chan Essentials 5*)
6. *Fa yuan zhu lin* (5c)	*Chan mi yao jing* 禪祕要經	*Methods for Curing 1* and *2*
7. *Fan wang jing pusa jie ben shu* (6)	*Chan mi yao jing* 禪祕要經 and *Zhi chan bing jing* 治禪病經	*Methods for Curing 1*
8. Wofoyuan cave 59	*Chan mi yao jing* 禪祕要經 and *Chan fa mi yao* 禪法祕要	*Chan Essentials 1, 2,* and *3*
9. *Li dai fa bao ji* (8)	*Chan mi yao jing* 禪祕要經	*Methods for Curing 1*
10. *Jing tu wu hui nian fo song jing guan xing yi* (9)	*Chan mi yao* 禪祕要	*Chan Essentials 2*
11. *Da fang guang fo hua yan jing shu* (10a; 10b)	*Zhi chan bing jing* 治禪病經	*Methods for Curing 1*
12. *Zhi guan fu xing chuan hong jue* (3h)	*Chan fa mi yao jing* 禪法祕要經	*Chan Essentials 1*

Essentials. All of this should induce great skepticism about our ability to discern precisely what lies behind any such titles when we see them listed in earlier catalogs. An attempt to align Xuanying's text with known other recensions is given in figure 4.

4. DUNHUANG CATALOGS

Although the Dunhuang and Turfan manuscripts themselves preserve only a few small fragments of either the *Chan Essentials* or the *Methods for Curing*, records indicate that the libraries of Dunhuang-area monasteries possessed and frequently copied these texts, under a variety of formats and titles, throughout the eighth, ninth, and tenth centuries. Using the transcriptions of all known Dunhuang scripture catalogs and copying records painstakingly compiled by Fang Guangchang (1997), we find the following information.

Table 10. Xuanying's *Da tang zhong jing yin yi* 大唐眾經音義

Title as cited by Xuanying	*Extant versions where glossed words appear*
A. *Zhi chan bing mi yao jing* 治禪病祕要經 scroll 1	*Methods for Curing 1*
B. Ibid., scroll 2	*Chan Essentials 1* (second half only) =? *Tempyō Chan Essentials 2*
C. Ibid., scroll 3	*Chan Essentials 2* (first half only) =? *Tempyō Chan Essentials 3*
D. *Chan mi yao fa* 禪祕要法 scroll 2 (only)	*Chan Essentials 1* (first half only)[a] =?
E. *Zhi chan bing mi yao fa* 治禪病祕要法	*Methods for Curing 2*

[a] For this text, Xuanying only glosses two terms, making identification difficult. It could well have been, however, an otherwise unknown format equaling only the first half of *Chan Essentials 1,* that is, those parts of *Chan Essentials 1* that are *not* included in *Tempyō Chan Essentials 2* (the second half). Something equivalent to *Tempyō Chan Essentials 1* is also possible, or even the whole of *Chan Essentials 1,* if Xuanying intentionally did not gloss terms from the second half because they were already covered in his glosses to text B.

S.2079 A shelf catalog of the Longxing 龍興 temple library (Fang 1997, p. 445). Lists a *Chan mi yao jing* 禪祕要經 in five scrolls, a *Chan mi yao fa* 禪祕要法 in three scrolls, and a *Zhi chan bing mi yao fa* 治禪病祕要法 in one scroll (p. 470).

P.4029 Another catalog of the Longxing temple, dated by Fang to the ninth or tenth century (p. 488). Lists a *Chan mi yao fa* 禪祕要法 in three scrolls.[14]

Φ.179 A short catalog, dated by Fang to the late ninth century (p. 526), lists a *Chan mi yao jing* 禪祕要經 (five scrolls) and a *Chan mi yao fa* 禪祕要法 (three scrolls).

P.3852 A fragment of a list of scriptures verified as present in the library of the Longxing temple in the year 848. Mentions a *Zhi chan bing mi yao fa* 治禪病祕要法 in one scroll (p. 558).

P.3240 A record of scriptures copied and volume of paper used. Lists the "first" (上) scroll of a *Zhi chan bing jing* 治禪病經 (presumably the *Methods for Curing*) in 15 sheets (p. 991). A sexagesmial date of Renyin 壬寅 is given. (This is the only known evidence of a two-scroll *manuscript* copy of the *Methods for Curing,* the format that became standard in the printed canons.)

14. This manuscript includes marks next to certain texts, perhaps a checklist of texts present in the library; there is no marking next to the *Chan mi yao fa.*

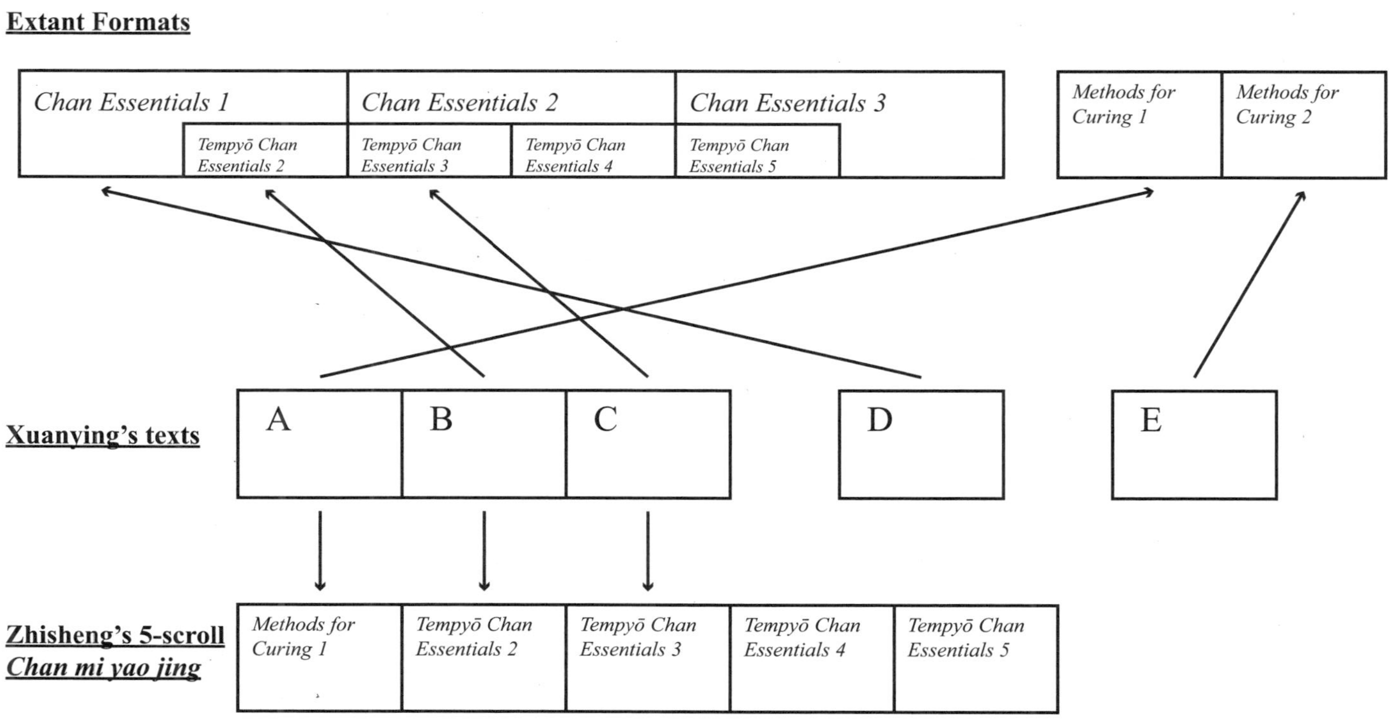

Figure 4. Correspondence between extant and reconstructed formats of the *Chan Essentials* and *Methods for Curing*.

P.3010 A record of newly copied scriptures to be entered into the library of the Longxing temple, written during the Tibetan occupation period (p. 870). Lists a *Chan mi yao jing* 禪祕要經 (five scrolls) and a *Chan mi yao fa* 禪祕要法 (three scrolls).

S.476r; P.3855v; S.2712r Records of texts lent to other temples or individuals (pp. 730, 745, 785). Mention of a *Chan mi yao* 禪祕要 (S.476 and P.3855) or *Chan mi yao jing* 禪祕要經 (S.2712) in ten scrolls. This large size can be explained with reference to P.3855v, whose entry reads "The *Chan mi yao* etc., ten scrolls" 禪祕要等十卷. From the other Dunhuang catalogs, we know that the three texts *Chan mi yao jing* 禪祕要經 (five scrolls), *Chan fa yao jie* 禪法要解 (two scrolls), and *Chan mi yao fa* 禪祕要法 (three scrolls) were often grouped into a single "bundle" (帙). Here, it would seem, the entire bundle was lent and denoted under the name of the first text within it.[15]

15. That these three texts were housed in the same bundle conforms to the specification in the *Da tang nei dian lu* (T.2149:55.312b4–6). Scripture bundles had their own labels (Rong 1999, 251–252).

APPENDIX 4
Sources of the Narratives and Protagonists

Assembled here is information about the protagonists and frame stories in each of the individual sutras of the *Chan Essentials* and *Methods for Curing*. This is not a comprehensive survey of all possible sources for these figures and their associated tales. Its intention is primarily to suggest the kind and range of sources, explicit and implicit, that the author(s) or compiler(s) of these texts drew from, sometimes directly but more often in a somewhat roundabout way, in the process of crafting them into the literary form of a Buddhist sutra.

Mahākauṣṭhilananda

The name Mahākauṣṭhilananda (摩訶迦絺羅難陀) is unknown as such in other sources. Tsukinowa, for this reason, considered it "fake" Sanskrit (1971, 107). Yet as Tsukinowa himself noted, the first half of the name (*Mo-he-jia-xi-luo* 摩訶迦絺羅) closely resembles the normal Chinese transcription of "Mahākauṣṭhila" (*Mo-he-gou-xi-luo* 摩訶拘絺羅), one of the Buddha's ten great disciples. A confusion between *jia* 迦 and *gou* 拘, either graphic or phonetic (Schuessler 2009, 10–1 and 18–4), is thus quite likely, and the first half of this name probably began, or was originally intended, as "Mahākauṣṭhila." The remainder—the usual transcription of the common name "Nanda"—in fact supports this idea and provides a possible source of inspiration. Among the arhats named in the opening passages of Kumārajīva's translation of the *Lotus Sutra* are none other than Mahākauṣṭhila and Nanda, listed in this order.[1] These are supposed to be separate names. Yet a Chinese reader could easily have taken them together, as a single person named "Mahākauṣṭhila-nanda," inspired perhaps by the very next name in this list, Sundarananda.

1. *Miao fa lian hua jing*, T.262:9.1c26

In fact, there is indirect evidence that "Mahākauṣṭhilananda" was sometimes taken, by medieval Chinese readers of the *Lotus Sutra*, as a single name.[2]

Nandi the Meditator

The second sutra of the *Chan Essentials* features Nandi the Meditator (禪難提), who also appears in the *Methods for Curing*. Nandi is a common name in Buddhist literature, but Nandi *the meditator* points specifically to the monk discussed in most *vinaya* traditions as a forest ascetic who broke his vow of celibacy (Clarke 2009). Named Nandi or Nandika in most accounts, he is named "Nandi the Meditator" in the Chinese translation of the *Mahāsāṅghika-vinaya*, completed in 420, which enjoyed a certain prestige in south China in the early fifth century.[3]

Nandi the Meditator in the *Chan Essentials* is connected to his namesake from the *vinaya* in a more substantial way as well. Nandi is introduced (2.0.1) as a meditation master and arhat who asks the Buddha to help those who are unable to reach meditative attainment because of their heavy karmic obstructions (*yezhang* 業障). To this end, the Buddha explains the method of "bringing to mind the Buddha" (*nianfo*), said to destroy sin, as well as meditation on the breath and the contemplation of impurity for those plagued by lust (2.20, 2.20.6). That Nandi inspires teaching on methods for eliminating "sin" and "lust" suggests a clear debt to the *vinaya* tales concerning the monk of this name, who in those sources is also provided with a special method of atonement in order to heal his burden of sin motivated by lust. This canonical backstory, however, goes entirely unmentioned in the *Chan Essentials*, where Nandi pointedly makes his request not for his own sake, but for others. There are some traces that an earlier version of the *Chan Essentials* narrative might have been framed as providing a solution for Nandi's own troubles, for even while Nandi is introduced as already an arhat, this is contradicted by the conclusion where Nandi becomes an arhat after hearing the Buddha's teachings (2.19.3.3). If Nandi was originally the target

2. Sugi 守其 (fl. 1250), editor of the second Koryŏ canon, mentions in his collation notes (Buswell 2004) that in compiling the 30-scroll edition of the *Fo mingjing* he corrected an "error" in which the names "Mahākauṣṭhila" and "Nanda," within a set of invocations of the names of famous arhats, had been wrongly combined into a single name (*Fo mingjing*, T.441:14.191b8–10). In both the second Koryŏ edition of the 30-scroll version (T.441:14.232a24–27), and the 16-scroll Nanatsudera version of the *Fo mingjing* (Makita and Ochiai 1994–2000, 3:474), the names Mahākauṣṭhila and Nanda are listed, in order, but separated and each preceded with the word "homage to" (南無). We cannot know how far back the "error" noted by Sugi went, but its presence shows that even outside the *Chan Essentials*, a figure named "Mahākauṣṭhilananda" was not an entirely unknown personage in medieval China.

3. *Mohesengqie lü*, T.1425:22.232a17. In the 420s and 430s there was much debate when monks of the imperially supported Qihuan 祇洹 (Jetavana) temple wanted to follow this *vinaya*'s rules for eating with the hands while sitting in what was criticized by some as an ungainly squatting posture (Yoshikawa 1984, 152–158; Kamata 1982, 3:97–100).

of the Buddha's instructions, that would also align more closely with the structure of the other narratives of the *Chan Essentials* and *Methods for Curing*.

Panthaka

In the third sutra of the *Chan Essentials*, Panthaka (槃直迦)[4] is described as a student of the Buddha's great disciple Kātyāyana. He is introduced as hopelessly dull, having been unable to grasp a short verse of the teaching even after trying for eight hundred days (3.0.1). The Buddha is then prompted to explain that Panthaka was actually a learned monk in a past life, but his arrogance led him to neglect meditation and, in consequence, to be reborn in hell and eventually to take on his present dull-witted incarnation (3.0.2). To cure this problem, the Buddha provides a special method of meditation that allows Panthaka to quickly become an arhat (3.21.1–9).

Panthaka's name and story clearly link him to the figure usually known as Cūḍapanthaka, "Panthaka the younger." Cūḍapanthaka appears in early Buddhist scriptures as an intellectually dull but meditatively gifted monk. His story was often cited to make the point that textual knowledge is not a prerequisite for advanced attainment.[5] In the usual tales, he was first ordained by his elder brother, also named Panthaka. Proving unable to memorize a short verse even after months of effort, Cūḍapanthaka is judged by his brother to lack the aptitude to be a monk and is sent away. The Buddha later finds Cūḍapanthaka alone and abandoned and gives him a teaching that quickly leads to his becoming an arhat. Some versions of the story also explain Cūḍapanthaka's difficulties with memorization as a result of bad karma from a previous lifetime in which he had mocked another monk's foolishness.[6]

The Panthaka of the *Chan Essentials* shows an undeniable inheritance from the better known tales about him: beyond his name there is the basic plot of a monk who cannot memorize a short verse given by his preceptor, owing to bad karma, but is eventually helped by the Buddha and becomes

---

4. Though Panthaka is clearly the inspiration for this character, this transcription of the name is unattested elsewhere. Indeed, *zhi* 直 clearly implies Panthi̱ka (Schussler 2009, 5–12). Such a spelling is unattested. But it would not be a shocking variation given the frequent interchange between i / a in middle Indic dialects and the Chinese transcriptions of them (see Palumbo 2013, 5n12, for other examples).

5. *Zeng yi ahan jing*, T.125:2.767c6. In this story, a king said he would make offerings to all the Buddha's disciples *except* Cūḍapanthaka because he lost a debate. Cūḍapanthaka later performs a miracle and the king realizes that poor debating skills (i.e., lack of textual or doctrinal learning) do not imply a lack of sanctity. The *Xian yu jing* (T.202:4.381a3–6) says that Cūḍapanthaka's story shows that those who maintain the precepts can become arhats even if they cannot recite more than a single verse of teachings.

6. For the many Pāli sources, see Burlingame 1921, 299n1. Cūḍapanthaka's story is also included in the *Mūlasarvāstivāda-vinaya* and the *Divyāvadāna* (Rotman 2017, 201–240), and in many Indian sources in Chinese translation, including the *Dharmapāda* commentary *Fa ju pi yu jing* (T.211:4.588c28–589b8), the *Mahāvibhāṣā* (*Apidamo da piposha lun*, T.1545:27.902a7–c10), and *DZDL*, T.1509:25.268a.

a famous meditator. But other elements of the *Chan Essentials* story positively contradict the known Indian tales of Panthaka—notably, that he is the disciple of Kātyāyana rather than his own elder brother.

Agnidatta

The fourth sutra of the *Chan Essentials* has its longest and most developed narrative introduction. Yet the source of its protagonist, named Agnidatta (阿祇達多), is also the least clear. The best known Agnidatta in classical Buddhist literature is a Brahmin householder who, in a story told in the *vinaya*, forgot his promise to supply food to the Buddha and his monks during a rainy season, leaving them compelled to eat horse fodder.[7] Any connection between this tale and the narrative in the *Chan Essentials*, wherein Agnidatta is described as an ascetic monk, is difficult to discern.[8] After years of (Buddhist?) practice this Agnidatta had become a "non-returner" (*anāgāmin*) but was still unable to become an arhat. This scenario clearly positions the fourth sutra as a continuation of the third, which ended with the attainment of the stage of the non-returner (3.30.7). Mahākāśyapa, after declaring that Agnidatta's past karma prevents him from becoming an arhat in this lifetime (4.0.2), takes him to the Buddha who, after explaining the past-life causes of Agnidatta's present obstacles (4.0.4.1–8), provides a solution in the form of special meditation instructions.[9] As in the other sutras, after Agnidatta follows the initial instructions and quickly becomes an arhat (4.0.6), the Buddha continues to preach, to Ānanda, what is clearly intended as the continuation of these same instructions.

Nandi the Meditator and Upanandi

The narrative of the first sutra of the *Methods for Curing* begins with "five hundred monks of the Śākya clan" meditating in the woods near the Jetavana monastery, having entered the "beryl *samādhi*" (1.1.1). When piercing

7. *Shi song lü*, T.1435:23.98b28–29; *DZDL*, T.1509:25.121c13.

8. The term used to describe Agnidatta, 苦得尼揵子兒, is peculiar. *Ni-qian-zi* 尼揵子 usually names the figure Pāli sources call Nigaṇṭhanātaputta, "the Nigaṇṭha, son of Nāta," that is, Mahāvīra the founder of Jainism (*Chang ahan jing*, T.1:1.25a22), though in some cases it translates simply Skt. *nigrantha* (P. *nigaṇṭha*), meaning a generic naked (or Jain) ascetic (*Zeng yi ahan jing*, T.125:2.744a28; *Majjhima-nikāya*, 1.92). If we assume that Agnidatta is not himself a Jain monk, perhaps *er* 兒 is to be taken as "son" and Agnidatta is the son of a Jain ascetic? Speculatively, but in keeping with the tendency of these narratives to draw from known but minor personages from other Buddhist sources, a Jain ascetic named "Austere" (Kude 苦得) is mentioned in the Mahāyāna *Mahāparinirvāṇa-sūtra* (*Da banniepan jing*, T.374:12.561b3–4). The claim could be that Agnidatta is his son. A third possibility, which I have followed in the translation, would be to think that the authors of the *Chan Essentials*, being less than fully familiar with the religious world of India, thought that "nigrantha" (尼揵子) was a *generic* word for a practitioner of austerities and hence could reasonably describe a Buddhist monk.

9. Yamabe (1999c, 105n87) sees a vague parallel between Agnidatta's past life and a tale in the *Da fang bian fo bao en jing* (beginning at T.156:3.137c18).

cries from the drunken elephants of Prince Virūḍhaka and his friends disturb their meditations, these monks—the two figures Nandi the Meditator and Upanandi 優波難提 are mentioned by name—are driven mad and become "unrestrained, like drunken elephants," an expression that is probably a euphemism for violating the precepts (1.1.2). The Buddha then provides a number of methods for healing this and other problems that can arise for meditators.

This story is a hodgepodge of famous characters from Buddhist literature. First is Prince Virūḍhaka, usually remembered for his invasion of the Buddha's home city of Kapilavastu and his slaughter of the men of the Śākya clan, in some versions by trampling them with elephants.[10] There is a clear resonance between this well-known plot and the narrative in the *Methods for Curing*, where Virūḍhaka's elephants similarly injure, in a different way, a large group of Śākya monks. We can perhaps detect a particular link to the version of Virūḍhaka's story told in a collection of Buddhist narratives compiled in China in the fifth century where, uniquely as far as I can determine, Virūḍhaka uses *drunken* elephants to attack the Śākya men, who here are (again, uniquely) described as not only the Buddha's kin but also his religious disciples.[11]

As for Nandi the Meditator and Upanandi, the two monks mentioned by name, Nandi the Meditator has already appeared in the second sutra of the *Chan Essentials*. But the presence of an "Upanandi" together with the theme of misbehaving monks strongly recalls the duo Nanda and Upananda, two of the "gang of six" whose antics inspire many episodes of law giving in the *vinaya* (C. Liu 2013). Even more specifically, the story line in the *Methods for Curing*—the curing of madness and the unrestraint it provokes—suggests a connection to the monk named Nandi, who in most *vinaya*s inspires the institution of what is called the "non-insanity procedure," the formal legal act of the Sangha that declares a monk or nun *no longer* insane and hence not guilty of earlier transgressions that, ipso facto, are now deemed to have been committed during a time of insanity.[12] Whether, in any given *vinaya* tradition, the Nandi of the non-insanity procedure is supposed to be the Nanda / Nandi of the "gang of six" is unclear. But the direct inspiration for the *Methods for Curing* may have been the Chinese translation of the

10. *Chu yao jing*, T.212:4.625a1–2; *Zeng yi ahan jing*, T.125:2.691b29–c26. There are many other versions of the story in early Chinese Buddhist literature (Pu 2013).

11. *Da fang bian fo bao en jing*, T.156:3.151c2–25. Another point arguing that this version was the source for the *Methods for Curing* is that in it Virūḍhaka attacks a country named *She-wei-guo* 舍維國. This must be a mistake for *She-yi-guo* 舍夷國, the "kingdom of the Śākyas" (as in *Chu yao jing*, T.212:4.669b14; *Fa ju pi yu jing*, T.211:4.591a5; *Sapoduo pini piposha*, T.1440:23.548b25; *Si fen lü*, T.1428:22.860c2). The anomalous *She-wei-guo* 舍維國 was then perhaps taken by the compilers of the *Methods for Curing* as *She-wei-guo* 舍衛國, that is, Śrāvasti, Virūḍhaka's home city.

12. *Si fen lü*, T.1428:22.914b15–c29. Nandi is also the instigator of the non-insanity procedure in the *Pini mu jing* (T.1463:24.807c14–18) and the *Mahāsāṅghika-vinaya* (see next note). Cf. *Vinayapiṭaka*, 2:80–82.

Mahāsāṅghika-vinaya—whence, as mentioned above, the name "Nandi the Meditator" was seemingly borrowed—which, uniquely, introduces the non-insanity procedure with a story of *two* monks, one named Nandi, and the other whose name was likely Upanandi.[13]

Lekuñcika

The second sutra of the *Methods for Curing* begins with a short story of a group of monks attacked by demons while meditating. Only one monk is named: Lekuñcika (Luoxunyue 羅旬踰), a figure well known in Indian Buddhist lore as a monk who was perpetually unable to obtain alms, owing to his bad karma. All versions of Lekuñcika's tale share this theme of the ineluctable influence of past evil karma and the failure to obtain alms.[14] In some versions, Lekuñcika accepts his fate and, meditating assiduously, becomes an arhat just before starving to death. In others, the Buddha intervenes to delay (but not outright prevent) Lekuñcika's death, giving him enough time to become an arhat. The *Avadānaśataka* tells perhaps the most interesting version: here Lekuñcika discovers that by cleaning a stupa each day he can generate just enough good karma to temporarily override his bad karma and obtain food. (One day he oversleeps, and missing his daily chance to earn good karma, starves to death.) Though the name Lekuñcika is surely taken from these stories, I can discern no clear narrative connection between them and that of the meditators plagued by demons who inspired the second sutra of the *Methods for Curing*.

13. The two figures in the *Mahāsāṅghika-vinaya* are named Nandi and *Bo-zhe* Nandi 鉢遮難提 (*Mohe sengqie lü*, T.1425:22.332a12–c19). This second name is, admittedly, mysterious. Given the ubiquity of the monks of the "gang of six" as the instigators of rule giving in the *vinaya*, I suspect that *bo-zhe* 鉢遮 is an error for *you-bo* 優鉢 (perhaps 優鉢 > 鉢優 > 鉢遮), commonly used in the *Mohe sengqie lü* to render "upa," making the second monk "Upanandi."

14. On the stories of Lekuñcika, see Lin 1949, 278–290 and Karashima and Vorobyova-Desyatovskaya 2015, 197–199. The transcription of Lekuñcika's name given in the *Methods for Curing* matches that of the so-called *Luoxunyue jing* 羅旬踰經, translated sometime between the fourth and fifth century (*CSZJJ*, T.2145:55.23c9). The text is lost, but a long citation is preserved at *Jing lü yi xiang*, T.2121:53.84b22–85a6.

References

Manuscripts and editions of the *Chan Essentials* and *Methods for Curing* are discussed in the introduction to the translations at the beginning of Part II.

Primary Texts, Collections, and Reference Works

Abhidharmakośabhāṣyam. Edited by P. Pradhan. Patna: K. P. Jayaswal Research Center, 1975.

Aṅguttara-nikāya. Edited by R. Morris and E. Hardy. London: Pali Text Society, 1885–1900.

Apidamo da piposha lun 阿毘達磨大毘婆沙論, T.1545, vol. 27.

Apidamo shun zheng li lun 阿毘達磨順正理論, T.1562, vol. 29.

Apitan ba jiandu lun 阿毘曇八犍度論, T.1543, vol. 26.

Apitan piposha lun 阿毘曇毘婆沙論, T.1546, vol. 28.

Baopuzi nei pian jiao shi 抱朴子內篇校釋. Edited by Wang Ming 王明. Beijing: Zhong hua shu ju, 2002.

Bie yi za ahan jing 別譯雜阿含經, T.100, vol. 2.

Bimo shi Mulian jing 弊魔試目連經, T.67, vol. 1.

Bukkyō daijiten 佛教大辭典. Edited by Mochizuki Shinkō 望月信亨. 10 vols. Tokyo: Sekai seiten kankō kyōkai, 1958–1963.

Chan fa yao jie 禪法要解, T.616, vol. 15.

Chan yao jing 禪要經, T.609, vol. 15.

Chang ahan jing 長阿含經, T.1, vol. 1.

Cheng shi lun 成實論, T.1646, vol. 32.

Chi shi jing 持世經, T.482, vol. 14.

Chu san zang ji ji 出三藏記集, T.2145, vol. 55.

Chu sheng wu liang men chi jing 出生無量門持經, T.1012, vol. 19.

Chu yao jing 出曜經, T.212, vol. 4.

Ci bei dao chang chan fa 慈悲道場懺法, T.1909, vol. 45.

Da banniepan jing 大般涅槃經, T.7, vol. 1.

Da banniepan jing 大般涅槃經, T.374, vol. 12.

Da banniepan jing ji jie 大般涅槃經集解, T.1763, vol. 37.

Da banniepan jing shu 大般涅槃經疏, T.1767, vol. 38.

Da bannihuan jing 大般泥洹經, T.376, vol. 12.

Da bao ji jing 大寶積經, T.310, vol. 11.

Da fang bian fo bao en jing 大方便佛報恩經, T.156, vol. 3.
Da fang deng ding wang jing 大方等頂王經, T.477, vol. 14.
Da fang guang fo hua yan jing shu 大方廣佛華嚴經疏, T.1735, vol. 35.
Da fang guang fo hua yan jing sui shu yan yi chao 大方廣佛華嚴經隨疏演義鈔, T.1736, vol. 36.
Da fang guang hua yan shi e pin jing 大方廣華嚴十惡品經, T.2875, vol. 85.
Da sheng qi xin lun 大乘起信論, T.1666, vol. 32.
Da sheng qi xin lun yi ji 大乘起信論義記, T.1846, vol. 44.
Da sheng yi zhang 大乘義章, T.1851, vol. 44.
Da tang da ci'en si san zang fa shi zhuan 大唐大慈恩寺三藏法師傳, T.2053, vol. 50.
Da tang nei dian lu 大唐內典錄, T.2149, vol. 55.
Da zhi du lun 大智度論, T.1509, vol. 25.
Dai nihon komonjo: hennen monjo 大日本古文書: 編年文書. 25 vols. Tokyo: Tokyo teikoku daigaku, 1901–1940.
Damoduoluo chan jing 達摩多羅禪經, T.618, vol. 15.
Dang lai bian jing 當來變經, T.395, vol. 12.
Divyāvadāna. Edited by E. B. Cowell and R. A. Neil. Cambridge: Cambridge University Press, 1886.
Dunhuang bao zang 敦煌寶藏. Edited by Huang Yongwu 黃永武. 140 vols. Taibei: Xin wen feng chu ban gong si, 1981–1986.
Dunhuang shi ku quan ji 敦煌石窟全集. 26 vols. Shanghai: Shanghai ren min chu ban she, 2000–2001.
E cang Dunhuang wen xian 俄藏敦煌文獻. 17 vols. Shanghai: Shanghai gu ji chu ban she, 1992–2001.
Fa hua jing yi ji 法華經義記, T.1715, vol. 33.
Fa hua sanmei chan yi 法華三昧懺儀, T.1941, vol. 46.
Fa hua yi shu 法華義疏, T.1721, vol. 34.
Fa jie ci di chu men 法界次第初門, T.1925, vol. 46.
Fa ju pi yu jing 法句譬喻經, T.211, vol. 4.
Fa mie jin jing 法滅盡經, T.396, vol. 12.
Fa yuan zhu lin 法苑珠林, T.2122, vol. 53.
Fan fan yu 翻梵語, T.2130, vol. 54.
Fan wang jing pusa jie ben shu 梵網經菩薩薩戒本疏, Z.687, vol. 38.
Fo ming jing 佛名經, T.441, vol. 14.
Fo suo xing zan 佛所行讚, T.192, vol. 4.
Fo yi jing 佛醫經, T.793, vol. 17.
Fu fa zang yin yuan zhuan 付法藏因緣傳, T.2058, vol. 50.
Gao seng Faxian zhuan 高僧法顯傳, T.2085, vol. 51.
Gao seng zhuan 高僧傳, T.2059, vol. 50.
Gaoli da zang jing 高麗大藏經. 48 vols. Taibei shi: Xin wen feng chu ban gong si, 1982.
Gaoli da zang jing chu ke ben ji kan 高麗大藏經初刻本輯刊. 81 vols. Chongqing: Xi nan shi fan da xue chu ban she, 2013.
Guan ding jing 灌頂經, T.1331, vol. 21.
Guan fo sanmei hai jing 觀佛三昧海經, T.643, vol. 15.
Guan Mile pusa shang sheng doushuai tian jing 觀彌勒菩薩上生兜率天經, T.452, vol. 14.
Guan Puxian pusa xing fa jing 觀普賢菩薩行法經, T.277, vol. 9.
Guan Wuliangshou fo jing 觀無量壽佛經, T.365, vol. 12.
Guan Yaowang Yaoshang er pusa jing 觀藥王藥上二菩薩經, T.1161, vol. 20.
Guang hong ming ji 廣弘明集, T.2103, vol. 52.

Guo jia tu shu guan cang Dunhuang yi shu 國家圖書館藏敦煌遺書. 146 vols. Beijing: Beijing tu shu guan chu ban she, 2005.
Han yu da ci dian 漢語大詞典. Edited by Luo Zhufeng 罗竹风. Beijing: Zhong hua shu ju, 1986.
Hong ming ji 弘明集, T.2102, vol. 52.
Hua yan jing 華嚴經, T.278, vol. 9.
Jiankang shi lu 建康實錄. Edited by Zhang Chenshi 張忱石. Beijing: Zhong hua shu ju, 2009.
Jin gang bore shu 金剛般若疏, T.1699, vol. 33.
Jin guang ming jing 金光明經, T.663, vol. 16.
Jing lü yi xiang 經律異相, T.2121, vol. 53.
Jing tu wu hui nian fo song jing guan xing yi 淨土五會念佛誦經觀行儀, T.2827, vol. 85.
Jiumoluoshi fa shi da yi 鳩摩羅什法師大義, T.1856, vol. 45.
Kai yuan shi jiao lu 開元釋教錄, T.2154, vol. 55.
Kōsetsu Bukkyōgo daijiten 広說佛教語大辞典. Edited by Nakamura Hajime 中村元. Tokyo: Tōkyō shoseki, 2001.
Kunaichō shōsōin jimusho shozō shōgozō kyōkan 宮内庁正倉院事務所所蔵聖語蔵経巻. Tokyo: Hakkō hatsubai Maruzen, 2000–. CD ROM and DVD.
Li dai fa bao ji 曆代法寶記, T.2075, vol. 51.
Li dai san bao ji 歷代三寶紀, T.2034, vol. 49.
Liu du ji jing 六度集經, T.152, vol. 3.
Lushan ji 廬山記, T.2095, vol. 51.
Majjhima-nikāya. Edited by V. Trenckner and R. Chalmers. London: Pali Text Society, 1979.
Meisōden shō 名僧傳抄, Z.1523, vol. 77.
Miao fa lian hua jing 妙法蓮華經, T.262, vol. 9.
Miao fa lian hua jing wen ju 妙法蓮華經文句, T.1718, vol. 34.
Miao fa lian hua jing xuan yi 妙法蓮華經玄義, T.1716, vol. 33.
Mishasai wu fen jie ben 彌沙塞五分戒本, T.1422a, vol. 22.
Mohe bore boluomi jing 摩訶般若波羅蜜經, T.223, vol. 8.
Mohe maye jing 摩訶摩耶經, T.383, vol. 12.
Mohe zhi guan 摩訶止觀, T.1911, vol. 46.
Mohesengqie lü 摩訶僧祇律, T.1425, vol. 22.
Nattori shingūji issaikyō chōsa hōkokusho 名取新宮寺一切經調查報告書. Tagajō: Tōhoku rekishi shiryōkan shinkōkai, 1980.
Nihon genson hasshu issaikyō mokuroku 日本現存八種一切経目録. Tokyo: Kokusai bukkyōgaku daigakuin daigaku gakujutsu furontia jikkō iinkai, 2006.
Pañcaviṃśatisāhasrikā-Prajñāpāramitā. Edited by Kimura Takayasu 木村高尉. Tokyo: Sankibō busshorin, 1986–2009.
Pi'naiye 鼻奈耶, T.1464, vol. 24.
Pini mu jing 毘尼母經, T.1463, vol. 24.
Piposha lun 鞞婆沙論, T.1547, vol. 28.
Pusa shan jie jing 菩薩善戒經, T.1583, vol. 30.
Qi xin lun shu 起信論疏, T.1844, vol. 44.
Qing Guanyin jing shu 請觀音經疏, T.1800, vol. 39.
Saddharmapuṇḍarīkasūtra. Edited by P. L. Vaidya. Darbhanga: Mithila Institute, 1960.
Saṃyutta-nikāya. Edited by L. Feer. London: Pali Text Society, 1991.
San fa du lun 三法度論, T.1506, vol. 25.
Sapoduo pini piposha 薩婆多毘尼毘婆沙, T.1440, vol. 23.

Shami wei yi 沙彌威儀, T.1472, vol. 24.
Sheng man bao ku 勝鬘寶窟, T.1744, vol. 37.
Shi chan boluomi ci di fa men 釋禪波羅蜜次第法門, T.1916, vol. 46.
Shi song biqiu boluotimuzha jie ben 十誦比丘波羅提木叉戒本, T.1436, vol. 23.
Shi song lü 十誦律, T.1435, vol. 23.
Shinsan Dai Nihon zoku zōkyō 新纂大日本續藏經. Edited by Nishi Yoshio 西義雄 and Tamaki Kōshiro 玉城康四郎. 90 vols. Tokyo: Kokusho Kankōkai, 1975–1989. CD-ROM and DVD. Chinese Buddhist Electronic Text Association (CBETA), 2008–2016.
Si fen biqiuni chao 四分比丘尼鈔, Z.724, vol. 40.
Si fen lü 四分律, T.1428, vol. 22.
Si fen lü shan fan bu que xing shi chao 四分律刪繁補闕行事鈔, T.1804, vol. 40.
Si fen lü shu 四分律疏, Z.734, vol. 42.
Si nian chu 四念處, T.1918, vol. 46.
Si wei lüe yao fa 思惟略要法, T.734, vol. 15.
Song ban Qisha da zang jing 宋版磧砂大藏經. 40 vols. Taibei: Xin wen feng chu ban gong si, 1987.
Śrāvakabhūmi. Edited by Śrāvakabhūmi Study Group. 3 vols. Tokyo: Sankibō, 1998–2017.
Sutta-nipāta. Edited by Dines Andersen and Helmer Smith. London: Pali Text Society, 1984.
Tai zi rui ying ben qi jing 太子瑞應本起經, T.185, vol. 3.
Taishō shinshū daizōkyō 大正新修大藏經. Edited by Takakusu Junjirō 高楠順次朗 and Watanabe Kaigyoku 渡邊海旭. 85 vols. Tokyo: Taishō issaikyō kankōkai, 1924–1932. CD-ROM and DVD. Chinese Buddhist Electronic Text Association (CBETA), 2008–2016.
Tie cheng nili jing 鐵城泥犁經, T.42, vol. 1.
Tonkō hikyū 敦煌秘笈. 10 vols. Osaka: Takeda kagaku shinkō zaidan, 2009–2013.
Vimalakīrtinirdeśa. Tokyo: Taisho University Press, 2004.
Vinayapiṭaka. Edited by H. Oldenberg. London: Pali Text Society, 1997.
Weimojie suo shuo jing 維摩詰所說經, T.475, vol. 14.
Wu fen lü 五分律, T.1421, vol. 22.
Wu men chan jing yao yong fa 五門禪經要用法, T.619, vol. 15.
Xian yu jing 賢愚經, T.202, vol. 4.
Xiao zhi guan 小止觀 (修習止觀坐禪法要), T.1915, vol. 46.
Xiu xing ben qi jing 修行本起經, T.184, vol. 3.
Xiu xing dao di jing 修行道地經, T.606, vol. 15.
Yi qie jing yin yi 一切經音義, T.2128, vol. 54.
Yi wen lei ju 藝文類聚. *Si ku quan shu* 四庫全書 edition.
Youposai jie jing 優婆塞戒經, T.1488, vol. 24.
Yulanben jing shu 盂蘭盆經疏, T.1792, vol. 39.
Yun ji qi qian 雲笈七籤. 5 vols. Beijing: Zhong hua shu ju, 2007.
Za apitan xin lun 雜阿毘曇心論, T.1552, vol. 28.
Zeng yi ahan jing 增一阿含經, T.125, vol. 2.
Zhai fa qing jing 齋法清淨經, T.2900, vol. 85.
Zheng fa hua jing 正法華經, T.263, vol. 9.
Zhi guan fu xing chuan hong jue 止觀輔行傳弘決, T.1912, vol. 46.
Zhong ahan jing 中阿含經, T.26, vol. 1.
Zhong jing mu lu 眾經目錄 (of 594 CE), T.2146, vol. 55.

Zhong yi da ci dian 中医大辞典. Beijing: Ren min wei sheng chu ban she, 1995.
Zhonghua da zang jing 中華大藏經. 106 vols. Beijing: Zhong hua shu ju, 1984–1996.
Zhu jing yao ji 諸經要集, T.2123, vol. 54.
Zhuangzi ji shi 莊子集釋. Edited by Wang Xiaoyu 王孝魚. 3 vols. Beijing: Zhong hua shu ju, 2004.
Zuo chan sanmei jing 坐禪三昧經, T.614, vol. 15.

Secondary Sources

Abe Takako 阿部貴子. 2011. "*Shomonji* no 'yōgāchāra'" 『声聞地』の「ヨーガーチャーラ」. *Chizan gakuhō* 智山學報 60:21–47.
———. 2014. "*Zenhiyōhōkyō* ni okeru hakkotsukan ni tsuite" 『禅秘要法経』における白骨観について. *Bukkyō bunka ronshū* 仏教文化論集 11:332–363.
Adamek, Wendi. 2007. *The Mystique of Transmission: On an Early Chan History and Its Contexts.* New York: Columbia University Press.
Anālayo. 2014. "The Mass Suicide of Monks in Discourse and *Vinaya* Literature." *Journal of the Oxford Centre for Buddhist Studies* 7:11–55.
———. 2015. "Healing in Early Buddhism." *Buddhist Studies Review* 32 (1):19–33.
———. 2017. *Buddhapada and the Bodhisattva Path.* Hamburg Buddhist Studies 8. Freiburg: Projektverlag.
Aoki Takashi 青木隆. 1989. "*Shidai zenmon* ni okeru ichini no mondai" 『次第禅門』における一二の問題. *Indogaku Bukkyōgaku kenkyū* 印度學佛教學研究 38 (1):221–224.
Ashmore, Robert. 2010. *The Transport of Reading: Text and Understanding in the World of Tao Qian (365–427).* Cambridge, MA: Harvard University Press.
Bemmann, Martin, and Sun Hua 孫華, eds. 2018. *Buddhist Stone Sutras in China: Sichuan Province, Volume 4.* Wiesbaden: Harrassowtiz.
Bernon, Olivier de. 2000. "Le manual des maîtres de kammaṭṭhāna." PhD diss., INALCO (Paris).
Beyer, Stephan. 1977. "Notes on the Vision Quest in Early Mahayana." In *Prajnaparamita and Related Systems,* edited by Lewis Lancaster, 329–340. Berkeley: Group in Buddhist Studies.
Bielefeldt, Carl. 1988. *Dōgen's Manuals of Zen Meditation.* Berkeley: University of California Press.
Bingenheimer, Marcus. 2011. *Studies in Āgama Literature: With Special Reference to the Shorter Chinese Saṃyuktāgama.* Taibei: Xin weng feng.
Bizot, F. 1992. *Le chemin de Laṅkā.* Paris: École Française d'Extrême-Orient.
Blum, Mark L. 2013. *The Nirvana Sutra, Volume 1.* Berkeley, CA: Bukkyo Dendo Kyokai.
Bodhi, Bhikkhu. 2000. *The Connected Discourses of the Buddha.* 2 vols. Somerville, MA: Wisdom.
Bokenkamp, Stephen R. 2007. *Ancestors and Anxiety: Daoism and the Birth of Rebirth in China.* Berkeley: University of California Press.
Boucher, Daniel. 2014. "What Is a 'Hīnayāna Zealot' Doing in Fifth-Century China?" In *Buddhism across Asia: Networks of Material, Intellectual and Cultural Exchange,* edited by Tansen Sen, 85–99. Singapore: Institute of Southeast Asian Studies.
Bretfeld, Sven. 2015. "Purifying the Pure: The Visuddhimagga, Forest-Dwellers and the Dynamics of Individual and Collective Prestige in Theravāda Buddhism." In *Discourses of Purity in Transcultural Perspective (300–1600),* edited by Nikolas Jaspert, Stefan Köck, and Matthias Bley, 320–347. Leiden: Brill.

Bronkhorst, Johannes. 1986. *The Two Traditions of Meditation in Ancient India*. Stuttgart: Franz Steiner Verlag.

Burlingame, Eugene Watson. 1921. *Buddhist Legends*. 3 vols. Cambridge, MA: Harvard University Press.

Buswell, Robert E., Jr. 1989. *The Formation of Ch'an Ideology in China and Korea: The Vajrasamādhi-Sūtra, a Buddhist Apocryphon*. Princeton, NJ: Princeton University Press.

———. 1997. "The 'Aids to Penetration' (*Nirvedabhāgīya*) According to the Vaibhāṣika School." *Journal of Indian Philosophy* 25 (6):589–611.

———. 2004. "Sugi's Collation Notes to the Koryŏ Buddhist Canon and Their Significance for Buddhist Textual Criticism." *Journal of Korean Studies* 9 (1):129–184.

Campany, Robert Ford. 1993. "Buddhist Revelation and Taoist Translation in Early Medieval China." *Taoist Resources* 4 (1):1–30.

———. 2012. *Signs from the Unseen Realm: Buddhist Miracle Tales from Early Medieval China*. Honolulu: University of Hawai'i Press.

Cao Ling 曹凌. 2011. *Zhongguo fo jiao yi wei jing zong lu* 中國佛教疑偽經總錄. Shanghai: Shanghai gu ji chu ban she.

Chappell, David. 1980. "Early Forebodings of the Death of Buddhism." *Numen* 27 (1):122–154.

———. 2005. "The *Precious Scroll of the Liang Emperor*: Buddhist and Daoist Repentance to Save the Dead." In *Going Forth: Visions of Buddhist Vinaya*, edited by William M. Bodiford, 40–67. Honolulu: University of Hawai'i Press.

Chen, Chin-chih. 2004. "Fan Fan-yü: Ein Sanskrit-chinesisches Wörterbuch aus dem Taisho-Tripiṭaka." PhD diss., Rheinischen Friedrich-Wilhelms-Universität zu Bonn.

Chen, Jinhua. 2004. "The Indian Buddhist Missionary Dharmakṣema (385–433): A New Dating of his Arrival in Guzang and of his Translations." *T'oung Pao* 90 (1):215–263.

———. 2005. "Some Aspects of the Buddhist Translation Procedure in Early Medieval China." *Journal Asiatique* 293 (2):603–662.

Chen Zhiyuan 陳志遠. 2019. *Fo jiao li shi yi shi de xing qi* 佛教歷史意識的興起. *Wen shi zhe* 文史哲 372 (3):74–86.

Clarke, Shayne. 2009. "Monks Who Have Sex: *Pārājika* Penance in Indian Buddhist Monasticism." *Journal of Indian Philosophy* 37:1–43.

Collins, Steven. 1982. *Selfless Persons*. Cambridge: Cambridge University Press.

Cone, Margaret. 2001. *A Dictionary of Pāli. Part I, a–kh*. Oxford: Pali Text Society.

Copp, Paul. 2018. "Seals as Conceptual and Ritual Tools in Chinese Buddhism, ca. 700–1000, CE." *Medieval History Journal* 4 (2):15–48.

Cox, Collett. 1988. "On the Possibility of a Non-existent Object of Consciousness." *Journal of the International Association of Buddhist Studies* 11 (1):31–87.

———. 1992. "Attainment through Abandonment." In *Paths to Liberation: The Mārga and Its Transformations in Buddhist Thought*, edited by Robert M. Gimello and Robert E. Buswell Jr., 63–106. Honolulu: University of Hawai'i Press.

Crosby, Kate. 2000. "Tantric Theravāda: A Bibliographic Essay on the Writings of François Bizot and Others on the Yogāvacara Tradition." *Contemporary Buddhism* 1 (2):141–193.

———. 2005. "Devotion to the Buddha in Theravada and Its Role in Meditation." In *The Intimate Other: Love Divine in Indic Religions*, edited by Anna S. King and John Brockington, 244–277. Hyderabad: Orient Longman.

———. 2013. *Traditional Theravada Meditation and Its Modern-Era Suppression.* Hong Kong: Buddha-Dharma Centre of Hong Kong.

Davidson, Ronald M. 2017. "Magicians, Sorcerers and Witches: Considering Pre-tantric, Non-sectarian Sources of Tantric Practices." *Religions* 8, no. 188.

Deleanu, Florin. 1992. "Mindfulness of Breathing in the *Dhyana Sutras*." *Transactions of the International Conference of Orientalists in Japan* 37:42–57.

———. 1993. "Sravakayana Yoga Practices and Mahayana Buddhism." *Bulletin of the Graduate Division of Literature, Waseda University* 20 (special):3–12.

———. 2000. "A Preliminary Study on Meditation and the Beginnings of Mahāyāna Buddhism." *Annual Report of the Institute for Research in Advanced Buddhology at Soka University* 3:65–113.

———. 2012. "Far From the Maddening Strife for Hollow Pleasures: Meditation and Liberation in the Śrāvakabhūmi." *Journal of the International College for Postgraduate Buddhist Studies* 16:1–38.

Demiéville, Paul, ed. 1929. *Hôbôgirin: Vol. 1.* Tokyo: Maison franco-japonaise.

———. 1937. "Byō." In *Hôbôgirin: Vol. 3,* 224–270. Tokyo: Maison franco-japonaise.

———. 1954. "La Yogācārabhūmi de Saṅgharakṣa." *Bulletin de l'École Française d'Extrême-Orient* 44 (2):339–436.

Dessein, Bart. 2014. "Contemplation of the Repulsive: Bones and Skulls as Objects of Meditation." In *Hindu, Buddhist, and Daoist Meditation,* edited by Halvor Eifring, 117–148. Oslo: Hermes.

Dhammajoti, Bhikkhu Kuala Lumpur. 2009a. *Sarvāstivāda Abhidharma.* 4th ed. Hong Kong: Centre for Buddhist Studies, University of Hong Kong.

———. 2009b. "The Aśubhā Meditation in the Sarvāstivāda." *Journal of the Centre for Buddhist Studies (Sri Lanka)* 7:248–295.

Donner, Neal. 1977. "The Mahayanization of the Chinese Dhyana Tradition." *Eastern Buddhist,* n.s., 10 (2):49–65.

Drège, Jean-Pierre. 2014. "Les manuscrits illustrés." In *La fabrique du lisible: la mise en texte des manuscrits de la Chine ancienne et médiévale,* edited by Jean-Pierre Drège and Costantino Moretti, 317–322. Paris: Collège de France.

Dumoulin, Heinrich. (1958) 1994. *A History of Zen Buddhism.* New York: Macmillan.

Durt, Hubert. 1979. "Chūranja." In *Hôbôgirin: Vol. 5,* 507–522. Tokyo: Maison franco-japonaise.

Edgerton, Franklin. 1953. *Buddhist Hybrid Sanskrit Grammar and Dictionary.* New Haven, CT: Yale University Press.

Eifring, Halvor. 2016. "What Is Meditation?" In *Asian Traditions of Meditation,* edited by Halvor Eifring, 1–26. Honolulu: University of Hawai'i Press.

Eltschinger, Vincent. 2009. "On the Career and the Cognition of *Yogins.*" In *Yogic Perception, Meditation and Altered States of Consciousness,* edited by Eli Franco, 169–214. Vienna: Verlag der Österreichischen Akademie der Wissenschaften.

Emmerick, R. E. 1970. *The Sūtra of Golden Light.* London: Luzac.

Endō Jirō 遠藤次郎, Nakamura Teruko 中村輝子, Yamaki Hidehiko 八巻英彦, and Miyamoto Hirokazu 宮本浩和. 1993. "Tan no kigen: Kanyaku butten ni mirareru tan no kentō" 痰の起源: 漢訳仏典にみられる痰の検討. *Nihon isshigaku zasshi* 日本医師学雑誌 39 (3–4):333–344.

Fang Guangchang 方廣錩. 1997. *Dunhuang fo jiao jing lu ji jiao* 敦煌佛教經錄輯校. 2 vols. Nanjing: Jiangsu gu ji chu ban she.

Faure, Bernard. 1986. "The Concept of One-Practice Samādhi in Early Ch'an." In *Traditions of Meditation in Chinese Buddhism,* edited by Peter N. Gregory, 99–128. Honolulu: University of Hawai'i Press.

Forte, Erika. 2020. "Images of Patronage in Khotan." In *Buddhism in Central Asia I: Patronage, Legitimation, Sacred Space, and Pilgrimage*, edited by Carmen Meinert and Henrik Sørensen, 40–60. Leiden: Brill.

Freud, Sigmund. (1955) 2010. *The Interpretation of Dreams*. Translated by James Strachey. New York: Basic Books.

Fujieda Akira 藤枝晃. 1999. *Moji no bunkashi* 文字の文化史. Tokyo: Iwanami shoten.

Fujita Kōtatsu 藤田宏達. 1970. *Genshi jōdo shisō no kenkyū* 原始浄土思想の研究. Tokyo: Iwanami shoten.

———. 1990. "The Textual Origins of the *Kuan Wu-liang-shou ching*." In *Chinese Buddhist Apocrypha*, edited by Robert E. Buswell Jr., 149–175. Honolulu: University of Hawai'i Press.

———. 2007. *Jōdo sanbukyō no kenkyū* 浄土三部経の研究. Tokyo: Iwanami shoten.

Fukunaga Katsumi 福永勝美. 1980. *Bukkyō igaku jiten* 仏教医学事典. Tokyo: Yuzankaku shuppan.

Funayama Tōru 船山徹. 1995. "Rikuchō jidai ni okeru bosatsukai no juyō katei: Ryūsō, Nansei ki o chūshin ni" 六朝時代における菩薩戒の受容過程: 劉宋・南斉期を中心に. *Tōhō gakuhō* 東方学報 67:1–135.

———. 1998. "*Mokuren mon kairitsuchū gohyaku keijūji* no genkei to hensen" 『目連問戒律中五百軽重事』の原型と変遷. *Tōhō gakuhō* 東方学報 70:203–290.

———. 2002. " 'Kanyaku' to 'chūgoku senjutsu' no aida: kanbun butten ni tokuyū na keitai o megutte" 「漢訳」と「中国撰述」の間: 漢文仏典に特有な形態をめぐって. *Bukkyō shigaku kenkyū* 仏教史学研究 45 (1):1–28.

———. 2004. "The Acceptance of Buddhist Precepts by the Chinese in the Fifth Century." *Journal of Asian History* 38 (2):97–120.

———. 2005. "Seija kan no ni keitō: rikuchō zuitō bukkyōshi chōkan no ichi shiron" 聖者観の二系統: 六朝隋唐仏教史鳥瞰の一試論. In *Sankyō kōshō ronsō* 三教交渉論叢, edited by Mugitani Kunio 麦谷邦夫, 373–408. Kyoto: Kyōto daigaku jinbun kagaku kenkyūjo.

———. 2006. "Masquerading as Translation: Examples of Chinese Lectures by Indian Scholar-Monks in the Six Dynasties Period." *Asia Major*, 3rd ser., 19 (1–2):39–55.

———. 2007. "Kyōten no gisaku to henshū: *Yuikyōsanmai kyō* to *Sharihotsu mongyō*" 経典の偽作と編輯: 『遺教三昧經』と『舍利弗問經』. In *Chūgoku shūkyō bunken kenkyū* 中国宗教文献研究, 83–108. Kyoto: Rinsen shoten.

———. 2011. "Buddhist Theories of Bodhisattva Practice as Adopted by Daoists." *Cahiers d'Extrême-Asie* 20:15–33.

———. 2013. *Butten wa dō kan'yaku sareta no ka: sūtora ga kyōten ni naru toki* 仏典はどう漢訳されたのか: スートラが経典になるとき. Tokyo: Iwanami shoten.

———. 2015. "Chinese Buddhist Apocrypha." In *Brill's Encyclopedia of Buddhism*, vol. 1, *Literature and Languages*, edited by Jonathan A. Silk, 283–291. Leiden: Brill.

———. 2019. *Bukkyō no seija* 仏教の聖者. Kyoto: Rinsen shoten.

Geaney, Jane. 2002. *On the Epistemology of the Senses in Early Chinese Thought*. Honolulu: University of Hawai'i Press.

Gethin, R. M. L. (Rupert). 1992. *The Buddhist Path to Awakening*. Leiden: Brill.

———. 1998. *The Foundations of Buddhism*. Oxford: Oxford University Press.

———. 2006. "Mythology as Meditation: From the Mahāsudassana Sutta to the Sukhāvativyūha Sūtra." *Journal of the Pali Text Society* 28:63–112.

Gimello, Robert M. 1976. "Chih-yen (602–668) and the Foundations of Hua-yen Buddhism." PhD diss., Columbia University.

Glass, Andrew. 2007. *Four Gāndhārī Saṃyuktāgama Sūtras.* Seattle: University of Washington Press.

Gnoli, Raniero. 1977. *The Gilgit Manuscript of the Saṅghabhedavastu.* Roma: Istituto italiano per il Medio ed Estremo Oriente.

Granoff, Phyllis. 1998. "Maitreya's Jeweled World: Some Remarks on Gems and Visions in Buddhist Texts." *Journal of Indian Philosophy* 26 (4):347–371.

Greene, Eric M. 2012. "Meditation, Repentance, and Visionary Experience in Early Medieval Chinese Buddhism." PhD diss., University of California, Berkeley.

———. 2013. "Death in a Cave: Meditation, Deathbed Ritual, and Skeletal Imagery at Tape Shotor." *Artibus Asiae* 73 (2):265–294.

———. 2016a. "A Reassessment of the Early History of Chinese Buddhist Vegetarianism." *Asia Major,* 3rd ser., 29 (1):1–43.

———. 2016b. "Seeing *Avijñapti-rūpa*: Buddhist Doctrine and Meditative Experience in India and China." In *Buddhist Meditative Traditions: Comparison and Dialog* (*Fo jiao chan xiu chuan tong: bi jiao yu dui hua* 佛教禪修傳統: 比較與對話), edited by Kuo-pin Chuang 莊國彬, 107–170. Taipei: Dharma Drum Publishing Corporation.

———. 2016c. "Visions and Visualizations: In Fifth-Century Chinese Buddhism and Nineteenth-Century Experimental Psychology." *History of Religions* 55 (3):289–328.

———. 2017. "Healing Sicknesses Caused by Meditation." In *The Sourcebook of Buddhism and Medicine,* edited by C. Pierce Salguero, 373–381. New York: Columbia University Press.

———. 2018. "The *Scripture on the Secret Essentials of Meditation*: The Authority of Meditation in the Kaiyuan Era." In *Buddhist Stone Sutras in China: Sichuan Province 4,* edited by Martin Bemmann and Sun Hua, 75–92. Wiesbaden: Harrassowitz.

———. 2021. *Chan Before Chan: Meditation, Repentance, and Visionary Experience in Chinese Buddhism.* Honolulu: University of Hawai'i Press.

Grünwedel, Albert. 1920. *Alt-Kutscha.* Berlin: O. Elsner verlagsgesellschaft.

Guo Fuchun 郭富纯 and Wang Zhenfen 王振芬. 2007. *Lüshun bo wu guan cang xiyu wen shu yan jiu* 旅顺博物馆藏西域文书研究. Shenyang shi: Wan juan chu ban gong si.

Gutman, Pamela. 2002. "A Burma Origin for the Sukhothai Walking Buddha." In *Burma: Art and Archaeology,* edited by Richard Blurton and Alexandra Green, 35–44. London: British Museum Press.

Haberman, David L., and Jan Nattier. 1996. "What Ever Became of Translation?" *Religious Studies News* 11 (4):13.

Hamar, Imre. 2002. *A Religious Leader in the Tang: Chengguan's Biography.* Tokyo: International Institute for Buddhist Studies.

Hansen, Valerie. 2017. *The Silk Road: A New History with Documents.* Oxford: Oxford University Press.

Harrison, Paul. 1982. "Sanskrit Fragments of a Lokottaravādin Tradition." In *Indological and Buddhist Studies,* edited by L. A. Hercus, 211–234. Canberra: National University, Faculty of Asian Studies.

———. 1990. *The Samadhi of Direct Encounter with the Buddhas of the Present.* Tokyo: International Institute for Buddhist Studies.

———. 2003. "Mediums and Messages: Reflections on the Production of Mahayana Sutras." *Eastern Buddhist,* n.s., 35 (1–2):115–152.

———. 2018. "Early Mahāyāna: Laying out the Field." In *Setting Out on the Great Way:*

Essays on Early Mahāyāna Buddhism, edited by Paul Harrison, 7–31. Sheffield, UK: Equinox Publishing.

Härtel, Herbert, ed. 1982. *Along the Ancient Silk Routes: Central Asian Art from the West Berlin State Museums.* New York: Metropolitan Museum of Art.

Hartmann, Jens-Uwe, and Hermann-Josef Röllicke, eds. 2006. *Dieter Schlingloff: Ein buddhistisches Yogalehrbuch.* Munich: Iudicium.

Heiler, Freidrich. 1922. *Die Buddhistische Versenkung.* Munich: Verlag von Ernst Reinhardt.

Heirman, Ann. 2002. *Rules for Nuns according to the Dharmaguptakavinaya.* Delhi: Motilal Banarsidass Publishers.

Heirman, Ann, and Mathieu Torck. 2012. *Pure Mind in a Clean Body: Bodily Care in the Buddhist Monasteries of Ancient India and China.* Gent: Ginkgo Academia Press.

Hirakawa Akira 平川彰. 1964. *Genshi Bukkyō no kenkyū* 原始仏教の研究. Tokyo: Shunjūsha.

———. 1993–1994. *Nihyakugojukkai no kenkyū* 二百五十戒の研究. 4 vols. Tokyo: Shunjūsha.

———. 1997. *Bukkyō Kan-Bon daijiten* 佛教漢梵大辭典. Tokyo: Reiyūkai, Hatsubaimoto Innātorippusha.

Hong, De. 2014. "The Development of Buddhist Repentance in Early Medieval China." PhD diss., University of the West.

Hou Xudong 侯旭东. 1998. *Wu liu shi ji bei fang min zhong fo jiao xin yang: yi zao xiang ji wei zhong xin de kao cha* 五六世纪北方民众佛教信仰: 以造像记为中心的考察. Beijing: Zhongguo she hui ke xue chu ban she.

Howard, Angela F., and Giuseppe Vignato. 2015. *Archaeological and Visual Sources of Meditation in the Ancient Monasteries of Kuča.* Leiden: Brill.

Hubei sheng bo wu guan 湖北省博物館, ed. 2006. *Hubei sheng bo wu guan cang Riben juan zi ben jing ji wen shu* 湖北省博物館藏日本卷子本經籍文書. Shanghai: Shanghai ci shu chu ban she.

Hu-von Hinüber, Haiyan. 1994. *Das Poṣadhavastu: Vorschriften für die buddhistische Beichtfeier im Vinaya der Mūlasarvāstivādins.* Reinbek: Verlag für Orientalistische Fachpublikationen.

Hurvitz, Leon. 1977. "The Abhidharma on the 'Four Aids to Penetration.'" In *Buddhist Thought and Asian Civilization*, edited by Leslie Kawamura, 59–104. Emeryville, CA: Dharma Publishing.

———. 1979. "The Eight Deliverances." In *Studies in Pali and Buddhism*, edited by A. K. Narain, 121–169. Delhi: B. R. Publishing Corporation.

Inagaki, Hisao. 1987. *The Anantamukhanirhāra-dhāraṇī Sūtra and Jñānagarbha's Commentary.* Kyoto: Nagata bunsho.

Inamoto Yasuo 稲本泰生. 2000. "Shōnankai chūkutsu to Sōchū zenji: Hokuchō sekkutsu kenkyū josetsu" 小南海中窟と僧稠禅師: 北朝石窟研究序説. In *Hokuchō Zui-Tō Chūgoku bukkyō shisōshi* 北朝隋唐中国仏教思想史, edited by Aramaki Norotoshi 荒牧典俊, 270–310. Kyoto: Hōzōkan.

Irisawa Takashi 入澤崇. 1999. "Kanmuryōjukyō no haigo ni aru mono" 観無量寿経の背後にあるもの. In *Jōdokyō no sōgōteki kenkyū* 浄土教の総合的研究, edited by Tagawa Takao 香川孝雄, 111–132. Kyoto: Bukkyō daigaku sōgō kenkyūjo.

Ishibashi Nariyasu 石橋成康. 1991. "Shinshutsu nanatsudera zō *Seijō hōgyō kyō* kō" 新出七寺蔵『清浄法行経』攷. *Tōhō shūkyō* 東方宗教 78:69–87.

Iyanaga, Nobumi. 2019. "An Early Example of *Svasthāveśa* Ritual: A Chinese Hagiography of the Early Fifth Century." *Circulaire de la Societé Franco-Japonaise des Études Orientales* 42:1–32.

Ji Yun 纪贇. 2009. *Huijiao* Gao seng zhuan *yan jiu* 慧皎《高僧传》研究. Shanghai: Shanghai gu ji chu ban she.

Ji Zhichang 紀志昌. 2007. *Liang jin fo jiao ju shi yan jiu* 兩晉佛教居士研究. PhD diss., National Taiwan University.

Jones, Charles B. 2008. "Was Lushan Huiyuan a Pure Land Buddhist? Evidence from His Correspondence with Kumārajīva about *Nianfo* Practice." *Chung-Hwa Buddhist Journal* 21:175–191.

Joo, Bong Seok. 2007. "The Arhat Cult in China from the Seventh through Thirteenth Centuries: Narrative, Art, Space and Ritual." PhD diss., Princeton University.

Kagawa Takao 香川孝雄. 1999. "*Kanmuryōjukyō* no seiritsu mondai shikō" 『観無量寿経』の成立問題試考. In *Jōdokyō no sōgōteki kenkyū* 浄土教の総合的研究, edited by Kagawa Takao 香川孝雄, 13–38. Kyoto: Bukkyō daigaku sōgō kenkyūjo.

Kaltenmark, Max. 1969. "Jing yu ba jing" 景與八景." In *Tōyō bunka ronshū* 東洋文化論集, 1147–1154. Tokyo: Waseda daigaku shuppanbu.

Kamata Shigeo 鎌田茂雄. 1982. *Chūgoku Bukkyō shi* 中国仏教史. 6 vols. Tokyo: Tōkyō daigaku shuppankai.

Karashima, Seishi. 1998. *A Glossary of Dharmarakṣa's Translation of the Lotus Sutra*. Tokyo: International Research Institute for Advanced Buddhology, Soka University.

———. 2001. *A Glossary of Kumārajīva's Translation of the Lotus Sutra*. Tokyo: International Research Institute for Advanced Buddhology, Soka University.

———. 2012. *Die Abhisamācārikā Dharmāḥ: Verhaltensregeln für buddhistische Mönche der Mahāsāṃghika-Lokottaravādins*. 3 vols. Tokyo: International Research Institute for Advanced Buddhology, Soka University.

Karashima, Seishi, and Margarita I. Vorobyova-Desyatovskaya. 2015. "The *Avadāna* Anthology from Merv, Turkmenistan." In *The St. Petersburg Sanskrit Fragments 1*, 145–523. Tokyo: International Research Institute for Advanced Buddhology, Soka University.

Kasugai Shin'ya 春日井真也. 1953. "Kanmuryōjubutsukyō ni okeru shomondai" 観無量寿仏経に於ける諸問題. *Bukkyō bunka kenkyū* 仏教文化研究 3:37–50.

Kim, Minku. 2019. "Where the Blessed One Paced Mindfully: The Issue of Caṅkrama on Mathurā's Earliest Freestanding Images of the Buddha." *Archives of Asian Art* 69 (2):181–216.

Kimoto Yoshinobu 木本好信. 1989. *Narachō tenseki shosai bussho kaisetsu sakuin* 奈良朝典籍所載仏書解説索引. Tokyo: Kokusho kankōkai.

Kimura Eiichi 木村英一, ed. 1960. *Eon kenkyū: yibun hen* 慧遠研究: 遺文篇. Tokyo: Sōbunsha.

Kodama Daien 小玉大円, Nakayama Shōkō 中山正晃, and Naomi Gentetsu 直海玄哲. 1992. "Yugashi to zen kyōten no kenkyū (I)" 瑜伽師と禅経典の研究 (I). *Bukkyō bunka kenkyū kiyō* 仏教文化研究所紀要 31:115–134.

———. 1993. "Yugashi to zen kyōten no kenkyū (II)" 瑜伽師と禅経典の研究 (II). *Bukkyō bunka kenkyūjo kiyō* 仏教文化研究所紀要 32:166–179.

Kragh, Ulrich Timme. 2015. *Tibetan Yoga and Mysticism*. Tokyo: International College for Postgraduate Buddhist Studies.

Kritzer, Robert. 2009. "Life in the Womb: Conception and Gestation in Buddhist Scripture and Classical Indian Medical Literature." In *Imagining the Fetus: The Unborn in Myth, Religion, and Culture*, edited by Vanessa Sasson and Jane Marie Law, 73–90. Oxford: Oxford University Press.

———. 2017. "Aśubhabhāvanā in *Vibhāṣā* and *Śrāvakabhūmi*." In *Śrāvakabhūmi and Buddhist Manuscripts*, edited by Jundo Nagashima and Seongcheol Kim, 27–60. Tokyo: Nombre Inc.

Kroll, Paul W. 2015. *A Student's Dictionary of Classical and Medieval Chinese*. Leiden: Brill.

Kumamoto, Hiroshi. 2012. "Textual Sources for Buddhism in Khotan." In *Buddhism across Boundaries*, edited by John R. McRae and Jan Nattier, 142–149. *Sino-Platonic Papers* 222.

Kuo, Li-ying. 1994. *Confession et contrition dans le bouddhisme chinois du Ve au Xe siècle*. Paris: École Française d'Extrême-Orient.

Kurita, Isao. 2003. *Gandhāran Art*. Tokyo: Nigensha.

Kuwayama Shoshin 桑山正進. 1992. *Echō ō go tenjikukoku den kenkyū* 慧超往五天竺國傳研究. Kyoto: Kyōtō daigaku jinbun kagaku kenkyūjo.

Lai Wenying 賴文英. 2001. "Bei chuan zao qi de fa hua sanmei chan fa yu zao xiang" 北傳早期的法華三昧禪法與造像. *Yuan guang fo xue xue bao* 圓光佛學學報 6:75–95.

Lai, Whalen. 1983. "T'an-ch'ien and the Early Ch'an Tradition: Translation and Analysis of the Essay 'Wang-shih-fei-lun.'" In *Early Ch'an in China and Tibet*, edited by Whalen Lai and Lewis R. Lancaster, 65–88. Berkeley: Asian Humanities Press.

Lamotte, Étienne. 1944–1981. *Le traité de la grande vertu de sagesss*. 6 vols. Louvain-la-neuve: Institut Orientaliste, Université de Louvain.

La Vallée Poussin, Louis de. 1937. "Mūsila and Nārada: le chemin du nirvāṇa." *Mélanges chinois et bouddhiques* 5:189–222.

———. 1988. *Abhidharmakośabhāṣyam*. 4 vols. Translated by Leo M. Pruden. Berkeley: Asian Humanities Press.

Lewis, Todd. 2014. *Buddhists: Understanding Buddhism through the Lives of Practitioners*. Chichester: Wiley Blackwell.

Li Fuhua 李富华 and He Mei 何梅. 2003. *Han wen fo jiao da zang jing yan jiu* 汉文佛教大藏经研究. Beijing: Zong jiao wen hua chu ban she.

Lin, Li-ko'uang. 1949. *L'Aide-mémoire de la vraie loi*. Paris: Adrien-Maisonneuve.

Link, Arthur. 1976. "Evidence for Doctrinal Continuity of Han Buddhism from the Second through the Fourth Centuries." In *Papers in Honor of Professor Woodbridge Binham*, edited by James B. Parsons, 55–126. San Francisco: Chinese Materials Center.

Liu, Cuilan. 2013. "Noble or Evil: The *Saḍvārgika* Monks Reconsidered." *Acta Orientalia* 66 (2):179–195.

———. 2018. "Reciting, Chanting, and Singing: The Codification of Vocal Music in Buddhist Canon Law." *Journal of Indian Philosophy* 46:713–752.

Liu Guangtang 劉廣堂. 2006. "Lüshun bo wu guan cang Xinjiang chu tu han wen fo jing xie ben zong shu" 旅順博物館藏新疆出土漢文佛經寫本綜述. In *Lüshun bo wu guan cang Xinjiang chu tu han wen fo jing guo ji xue shu yan jiu hui* 旅順博物館藏新疆出土漢文佛經國際學術研究會, edited by Lüshun bo wu guan and Ryūkoku daigaku, 1–34. Kyoto: Ryūkoku daigaku bungakubu.

Lo, Vivienne. 2005. "Quick and Easy Chinese Medicine: The Dunhuang Moxibustion Charts." In *Medieval Chinese Medicine*, edited by Vivienne Lo and Christopher Cullen, 227–251. London: RoutledgeCurzon.

Lopez, Donald S., Jr., ed. 1995. *Buddhism in Practice*. Princeton, NJ: Princeton University Press.

———. 2015. *The Norton Anthology of World Religions: Buddhism*. New York: W. W. Norton.

Loukota, Diego. 2019. "Made in China? Sourcing the Old Khotanese Bhaiṣajyaguru-vaiḍūryaprabhasūtra." *Journal of the American Oriental Society* 139 (1):67–90.

Lowe, Bryan. 2017. *Ritualized Writing: Buddhist Practice and Scriptural Cultures in Early Japan.* Honolulu: University of Hawai'i Press.

Mai, Cuong T. 2009. "Visualization Apocrypha and the Making of Buddhist Deity Cults in Early Medieval China." PhD diss., Indiana University.

Mair, Victor. 1993. "The Textual and Linguistic Antecedents of the Sutra of the Wise and the Foolish." *Sino-Platonic Papers* 38.

Makita Tairyō 牧田諦亮 and Fukui Fumimasa 福井文雅, eds. 1984. *Tonkō to Chūgoku Bukkyō* 敦煌と中国仏教. Tokyo: Daitō shuppansha.

Makita Tairyō 牧田諦亮 and Ochiai Toshinori 落合俊典, eds. 1994–2000. *Nanatsu-dera koitsu kyōten kenkyū sōsho* 七寺古逸經典研究叢書. 6 vols. Tokyo: Daitō Shuppansha.

Malalasekera, G. P. 1937. *Dictionary of Pāli Proper Names.* London: J. Murray.

Masefield, Peter. 1987. *Divine Revelation in Pali Buddhism.* Colombo: Sri Lanka Institute of Traditional Studies.

Maspero, Henri. 1971. *Le Taoïsme et les religions chinoises.* Paris: Gallimard.

Matsuda Shin'ya 松田慎也. 1989. "Shūgyōdōchikyō no toku anbannen ni tsuite" 修行道地経の説く安般念について. *Indogaku Bukkyōgaku kenkyū* 印度學佛教學研究 74:18–23.

McMahan, David L. 2008. *The Making of Buddhist Modernism.* Oxford: Oxford University Press.

McRae, John R. 1992. "Encounter Dialog and the Transformation of the Spiritual Path in Ch'an." In *Paths to Liberation,* edited by Robert E. Buswell Jr. and Robert Gimello. Honolulu: University of Hawai'i Press.

Mochizuki Shinkō 望月信亨. 1946. *Bukkyō kyōten seiritsu shiron* 佛教經典成立史論. Kyoto: Hōzōkan.

Mollier, Christine. 2008. *Buddhism and Taoism Face to Face.* Honolulu: University of Hawai'i Press.

Moretti, Costantino. 2016. *Genèse d'un apocryphe Bouddhique: le Sūtra de la Pure Délivrance.* Paris: Collége de France, Institut des Hautes Études Chinoises.

———. 2017. "The Thirty-Six Categories of 'Hungry Ghosts' Described in the Sūtra of the Foundations of Mindfulness of the True Law." In *Fantômes dans l'Extrême-Orient d'hier et d'aujourd'hui,* edited by Marie Laureillard and Vincent Durand-Dastès. Paris: Presses Inalco.

Moroto Tatsuo 諸戸立雄. 1990. *Chūgoku bukkyo seidoshi no kenkyū* 中国仏教制度史の研究. Tokyo: Hirakawa shuppansha.

Mukhopadhyaya, Sujitkumar. 1950. "An Outline of Principal Methods of Meditation." *Visva-Bharati Annals* 3:110–150.

Myōjin Hiroshi 明神洋. 1993. "Zenkan kyōten ni okeru nenbutsukan: so no imi to kigen ni tsuite" 禅観経典における念仏観: その意味と起源について. *Bukkyōgaku* 仏教学 35:59–79.

Naitō Tatsuo 内藤竜雄. 1958. "Shutsusanzōkishū no senshū nenji ni tsuite" 出三蔵記集の撰集年次について. *Indogaku Bukkyōgaku kenkyū* 印度學佛教學研究 13:162–163.

Nakao Takashi 中尾堯, ed. 1997. *Kyōto myōrenjizō* Matsuosha issaikyō *chōsa hōkokusho* 京都妙蓮寺蔵「松尾社一切経」調査報告書. Tokyo: Ōtsuka kōgeisha.

Ñāṇamoli, Bhikkhu. 1976. *The Path of Purification: Visuddhimagga.* 2 vols. Berkeley: Shambhala.

Ñāṇamoli, Bhikkhu, and Bhikkhu Bodhi. 1995. *The Middle Length Discourses of the Buddha*. Somerville, MA: Wisdom.
Nattier, Jan. 1991. *Once upon a Future Time: Studies in a Buddhist Prophecy of Decline*. Berkeley: Asian Humanities Press.
Nemec, John. 2009. "Translation and the Study of Indian Religions." *Journal of the American Academy of Religion* 77 (4):757–780.
Nishi Yoshio 西義雄. 1975. *Abidatsuma Bukkyō no kenkyū: sono shinsō to shimei* 阿毘達磨仏教の研究: その真相と使命. Tokyo: Kokusho Kankōkai.
Nobel, Johannes. 1937. *Suvarnabhāsottamasūtra*. Leipzig: Otto Harrassowitz.
Nolot, Édith. 1996. "Studies in Vinaya Technical Terms I–III." *Journal of the Pali Text Society* 22:75–150.
Nōnin Masāki 能仁正顕. 1993. "*Kanmuryōjukyō* no nenbutsu sanmai to sono haikei" 『観無量寿経』の念仏三昧とその背景. *Indogaku Bukkyōgaku kenkyū* 印度學佛教學研究 41 (2):835–839.
Norman, K. R. 1969. *The Elders' Verses I: Theragāthā*. London: Pali Text Society.
———. 1997. *The Word of the Doctrine (Dhammapada)*. Oxford: Pali Text Society.
Nukariya Kaiten 忽滑谷快天. 1925. *Zengaku shisōshi* 禪學思想史. Tokyo: Genkōsha.
Obeyesekere, Gananath. 2012. *The Awakened Ones: Phenomenology of Visionary Experience*. New York: Columbia University Press.
Ōchō Enichi 横超慧日. 1958–1979. *Chūgoku bukkyō no kenkyū* 中国仏教の研究. 3 vols. Kyoto: Hōzōkan.
Odani Nobuchiyo 小谷信千代. 1995. "Gojō shinkan no seiritsu katei" 五停心観の成立過程. *Ōtani daigaku kenkyū nenpō* 大谷大学研究年報 46:47–100.
———. 1996. "Zenkyō ni okeru yugagyōsha: daijō ni kakehashi suru mono" 禅経における瑜伽行者ー大乗に架橋する者. *Bukkyōgaku seminā* 仏教学セミナー 63:22–34.
Ogiwara Unrai 荻原雲來. 1979. *Kan'yaku taishō Bon-Wa daijiten* 漢訳対照梵和大辞典. Tokyo: Suzuki gakujutsu zaidan.
Ohnuma, Reiko. 2007. *Head, Eyes, Flesh, and Blood: Giving Away the Body in Indian Buddhist Literature*. New York: Columbia University Press.
Ōminami Ryūshō 大南竜昇. 1975. "Sanmai kyōten ni okeru kenbutsu to kanbutsu" 三昧経典における見仏と観仏. *Indogaku Bukkyōgaku kenkyū* 印度學佛教學研究 23 (2):235–238.
———. 1977. "Gojō shinkan to gomonzen" 五定心観と五門禅. In *Bukkyō no jissen genri* 仏教の実践原理, edited by Sekiguchi Shindai 関口真大, 71–90. Tokyo: Sankibō busshorin.
———. 2001. "*Kanbutsusanmaikai kyō* kanzōhin no kōsatsu" 『観仏三昧海経』観像品の考察. In *Bukkyō bunka no kichō to tenkai: Ishigami Zen'ō kyōju koki kinen ronbunshū* 仏教文化の基調と展開: 石上善応教授古稀記念論文集, 3–30. Tokyo: Sankibō busshorin.
Ōno Hōdō 大野法道. 1954. *Daijō kaikyō no kenkyū* 大乗戒經の研究. Tokyo: Risōsha.
Ōtani Tetsuo 大谷哲夫. 1970. "Chūgoku shoki zenkan jidai ni okeru 'za' no keitai" 中国初期禅観時代における「坐」の形態. *Shūgaku kenkyū* 宗学研究 12:198–211.
Otokawa Bun'ei 乙川文英. 1995. "*Zenjōtōmyōron* kenkyū (3) indo chūgoku chibetto bunken ni mirareru zenjōhō o megutte" 『禅定灯明論』研究 (3) インド・中国・チベットの文献に見られる禅定法をめぐって. *Bukkyō shigaku kenkyū* 仏教史学研究 38 (2):1–30.
Overmyer, Daniel. 1990. "Buddhism in the Trenches: Attitudes toward Popular Religion in Chinese Scriptures Found at Tun-huang." *Harvard Journal of Asiatic Studies* 50 (1):197–222.

Palumbo, Antonello. 2003. "Dharmarakṣa and Kaṇṭhaka: White Horse Monasteries in Early Medieval China." In *Buddhist Asia*, edited by Giovanni Veradi and Silvio Vita, 167–216. Kyoto: Italian School of East Asian Studies.

———. 2013. *An Early Chinese Commentary on the Ekottarika-āgama*. Taipei: Dharma Drum Publishing.

———. n.d. "What Chinese Sources Really Have to Say about the Dates of the Buddha." Unpublished paper. http://eprints.soas.ac.uk/id/eprint/13044.

Pas, Julian F. 1977. "The *Kuan-wu-liang-shou Fo-ching*: Its Origin and Literary Criticism." In *Buddhist Thought and Asian Civilization*, edited by Leslie S. Kawamura and Keith Scott, 194–218. Emeryville, CA: Dharma Publishing.

Prebish, Charles S. 1975. *Buddhist Monastic Discipline: The Sanskrit Prātimokṣa Sūtras of the Mahāsāṃghikas and Mūlasarvāstivādins*. University Park: Pennsylvania State University Press.

Pu Chengzhong. 2013. "Chinese Versions of Virūḍhaka's Massacre of the Śākyans: A Preliminary Study." *Indian International Journal of Buddhist Studies* 14:29–47.

Pulleyblank, Edwin G. 1991. *Lexicon of Reconstructed Pronunciation in Early Middle Chinese, Late Middle Chinese, and Early Mandarin*. Vancouver: UBC Press.

Python, Pierre. 1973. *Vinaya-viniścaya-upāli-paripṛcchā (Enquête d'Upāli pour une exégèse de la discipline)*. Paris: Adrien-Maisonneuve.

Radich, Michael. 2007. "The Somatics of Liberation: Ideas about Embodiment in Buddhism from Its Origins to the Fifth Century C.E." PhD diss., Harvard University.

———. 2010. "Embodiments of the Buddha in Sarvâstivāda Doctrine: With Special Reference to the **Mahāvibhāṣā*." *Annual Report of the Institute for Research in Advanced Buddhology at Soka University* 13:121–172.

———. 2011. "Immortal Buddhas and Their Indestructible Embodiments: The Advent of the Concept of *Vajrakāya*." *Journal of the International Association of Buddhist Studies* 34:227–290.

———. 2018. "A Triad of Texts from Fifth-Century Southern China: The **Mahāmāyā-sūtra*, the *Guoqu xianzai yinguo jing*, and a *Mahāparinirvāṇa-sūtra* Ascribed to Faxian." *Journal of Chinese Religions* 46 (1):1–41.

———. Forthcoming. "Reading the Writing on the Wall: 'Sengchou's' Cave at Xiaonanhai, Early Chinese Buddhist Meditation, and Unique Portions of Dharmakṣema's **Mahāparinirvāṇa-mahāsūtra*." *Journal of the International Association of Buddhist Studies*.

Rhie, Marylin M. 2002. *Early Buddhist Art of China and Central Asia, Volume 2*. Leiden: Brill.

Riegel, Jeffrey. 1995. "Do Not Serve the Dead as You Serve the Living: The *Lüshi chunqiu* Treatises on Moderation in Burial." *Early China* 20:301–330.

Robinet, Isabelle. 1993. *Taoist Meditation*. Translated by Julian F. Pas and Norman J. Girardot. Albany: State University of New York Press.

Robinson, Richard H. 1967. *Early Madhyamika in India and China*. Madison: University of Wisconsin Press.

Rong, Xinjiang. 1999. "The Nature of Dunhuang Library Cave and the Reasons for Its Sealing." Translated by Valerie Hansen. *Cahiers d'Extrême-Asie* 11:247–275.

Rotman, Andy. 2017. *Divine Stories: Divyāvadāna, Part 2*. Boston: Wisdom Publications.

Ruegg, David Seyfort. 1967. "On a Yoga Treatise in Sanskrit from Qizil." *Journal of the American Oriental Society* 87 (2):157–165.

———. 1980. "Ahiṃsā and Vegetarianism in the History of Buddhism." In *Buddhist Studies in Honour of Walpola Rahula*, 234–241. London: Gordon Fraser.
Sakaino Kōyō 境野黄洋. 1935. *Shina Bukkyō seishi* 支那佛教精史. Tokyo: Sakaino Kōyō hakushi ikō kankōkai.
Sakurabe Hajime 櫻部建. 1975. *Bukkyōgo no kenkyū* 仏教語の研究. Kyoto: Buneidō.
———. 1980. "On the *Wu-T'ing-Hsin-Kuan*." In *Indianisme et bouddhisme: mélanges offerts à Mgr Étienne Lamotte*, 307–312. Louvain: Publications de l'Institut Orientaliste de Louvain.
Salguero, C. Pierce. 2009. "The Buddhist Medicine King in Literary Context: Reconsidering an Early Medieval Example of Indian Influence on Chinese Medicine and Surgery." *History of Religions* 48 (3):183–210.
———. 2010. "Buddhist Medicine in Medieval China: Disease, Healing, and the Body in Cross-cultural Translation (Second to Eighth Centuries C.E.)." PhD diss., Johns Hopkins University.
———. 2014. *Translating Buddhist Medicine in Medieval China*. Philadelphia: University of Pennsylvania Press.
———. 2017. "Understanding the Doṣa: A Summary of the Art of Medicine from the *Sūtra of Golden Light*." In *Buddhism and Healing: An Anthology of Premodern Sources*, edited by C. Pierce Salguero, 30–40. New York: Columbia University Press.
Sasaki Kentoku 佐々木憲徳. (1938) 1978. *Zenkan hattenshiron* 禅観発展史論. Tokyo: Pitaka.
Satō Taishun 佐藤泰舜. 1931. *Kokukyaku issai kyō: kyōshūbu* 國譯一切經：經集部. Vol. 4. Tokyo: Daitō shuppansha.
Schipper, Kristofer. 1995. "The Inner World of the *Lao-Tzu Chung-Ching*." In *Time and Space in Chinese Culture*, edited by Chun-chieh Huang and Erik Zürcher, 114–131. Leiden: Brill.
Schlingloff, Dieter. 1964. *Ein Buddhistisches Yogalehrbuch*. Berlin: Akademie-Verlag.
Schmithausen, Lambert. 1982. "Versenkungspraxis und Erlöende Erfahrung in der *Śrāvakabhūmi*." In *Epiphanie des Heils: Zur Heilsgegenwart in indischer und christlicher Religion*, edited by Gerhard Oberhammer, 59–85. Leiden: Brill.
Schopen, Gregory. 1998. "Marking Time in Buddhist Monasteries: On Calendars, Clocks, and Some Liturgical Practices." In *Sūryacandrāya: Essays in Honour of Akira Yuyama on the Occasion of His 65th Birthday*, edited by Paul Harrison and Gregory Schopen, 157–180. Swisttal-Odendorf: Indica et Tibetica Verlag.
Schuessler, Axel. 2009. *Minimal Old Chinese and Later Han Chinese*. Honolulu: University of Hawai'i Press.
Sekiguchi Shindai 関口真大. 1961. *Tendai shōshikan no kenkyū: shogaku zazen shikan yōmon* 天台小止観の研究: 初学座禅止観要文. Tokyo: Tendaigaku kenkyūjo.
———. 1969. *Tendai shikan no kenkyū* 天台止觀の研究. Tokyo: Iwanami Shoten.
Sengoku Keisho 仙石景章. 1980. "*Shidai zenmon* ni inyōserareru zenkyō ni tsuite" 『次第禪門』に引用せられる禪經について. *Indogaku Bukkyōgaku kenkyū* 印度學佛教學研究 29:134–135.
Sharf, Robert H. 2002a. *Coming to Terms with Chinese Buddhism*. Honolulu: University of Hawai'i Press.
———. 2002b. "On Pure Land Buddhism and Ch'an / Pure Land Syncretism in Medieval China." *T'oung Pao* 88:282–331.
———. 2014. "Is Nirvāṇa the Same as Insentience? Chinese Struggles with an Indian Buddhist Ideal." In *India in the Chinese Imagination*, edited by John Kieschnick and Meir Shahar, 131–160. Philadelphia: University of Pennsylvania Press.

Shaw, Sarah. 2006. *Buddhist Meditation: An Anthology of Texts from the Pāli Canon.* London: Routledge.

Shinohara, Koichi. 2015. "Rethinking the Category of Chinese Buddhist Apocrypha." *Studies in Chinese Religions* 1 (1):70–81.

Shiozaki Yukio 塩崎幸雄. 2006. *Shin kokuyaku daizōkyō: zenjō kyōten bu* 新国訳大蔵経: 禅定経典部. Vol. 2. Tokyo: Daizō shuppan.

Silk, Jonathan A. 1997. "The Composition of the Guan Wuliangshoufo jing." *Journal of Indian Philosophy* 25:181–256.

———. 2000. "The *Yogācāra Bhikṣu.*" In *Wisdom, Compassion, and the Search for Understanding: The Buddhist Studies Legacy of Gadjin M. Nagao*, edited by Jonathan A. Silk, 265–314. Honolulu: University of Hawai'i Press.

———. 2008. "The *Jifayue sheku tuoluoni jing*—Translation, non-translation, both or neither?" *Journal of the International Association of Buddhist Studies* 31 (1–2):369–420.

Silverstein, Michael, and Greg Urban, eds. 1996. *Natural Histories of Discourse.* Chicago: University of Chicago Press.

Skilling, Peter. 1998. "A Note on *Dhammapada* 60 and the Length of the *Yojana.*" *Journal of the Pali Text Society* 24:149–170.

Skjærvø, Prods Oktor. 2012. "Khotan, An Early Center of Buddhism in Chinese Turkestan." In *Buddhism across Boundaries*, edited by John R. McRae and Jan Nattier, 265–344. Sino-Platonic Papers 222.

Smart, Ninian. 1958. *Reasons and Faiths.* London: Routledge & Paul.

Sørensen, Henrick H. 2012. "The History and Practice of Early Chan." In *Readings of the Platform Sutra*, edited by Morten Schlütter and Stephen F. Teiser, 53–76. New York: Columbia University Press.

Stevenson, Daniel B. 1986. "The Four Kinds of Samadhi in Early T'ien T'ai Buddhism." In *Traditions of Meditation in Chinese Buddhism*, edited by Peter N. Gregory, 45–97. Honolulu: University of Hawai'i Press.

———. 1987. "The T'ien-t'ai Four Forms of Samadhi and Late North-South Dynasties, Sui and Early T'ang Buddhist Devotionalism." PhD diss., Columbia University.

Strickmann, Michel. 1996. *Mantras et mandarins: le bouddhisme tantrique en Chine.* Paris: Gallimard.

———. 2002. *Chinese Magical Medicine.* Stanford, CA: Stanford University Press.

Stuart, Daniel M. 2015. *A Less Traveled Path: Saddharmasmṛtyupasthānasūtra Chapter 2.* Vienna: Austrian Academy of Sciences Press.

Sueki Fumihiko 末木文美士. 1986. "*Kanmuryōjukyō* kenkyū" 『観無量寿経』研究. *Tōyō bunka kenkyūjo kiyō* 東洋文化研究所紀要 101:163–225

———. 1992. "Kan muryōju kyō: kanbutsu to ōjō" 観無量壽経: 観佛と往生. In *Jōdo bukkyō no shisō, ni* 浄土仏教の思想, 二, 3–198. Tokyo: Kōdansha.

Swanson, Paul L. 2017. *Clear Serenity, Quiet Insight: T'ien-t'ai Chih-i's Mo-ho chih-kuan.* Honolulu: University of Hawai'i Press.

Swearer, Donald K. 1995. "The Way of Meditation." In *Buddhism in Practice*, edited by Donald S. Lopez Jr., 207–215. Princeton, NJ: Princeton University Press.

Tada Kōshō 多田孝正. 1976. "Shidai zenmon shoshutsu no hokkoku shozenshi no tsūmyōkan" 次第禅門所出の北国諸禅師の通明観. *Shūkyō kenkyū* 宗教研究 50 (1):1–21.

Tai Huili 邰惠莉. 2007. "*E Cang Dunhuang wenxian* di 17 ce bu fen xie jing can pian de ding ming yu zhui he" 《俄藏敦煌文献》第17册部分写经残片的定名与缀合. *Dunhuang yan jiu* 敦煌研究 102:99–103.

Tanabe, Katsumi. 1981. "Iranian Background of the Flaming and Watering Buddha Image in the Kushan Period." *Bulletin of the Ancient Orient Museum* 3:69–81.

Tanaka Fumio 田中文雄. 1997. "Gotai toji nyotaizan hō kō" 五体投地如太山崩考. *Tōhō shūkyō* 東方宗教 89:55–72.

Tatia, N. 1975. *The Prātimokṣasūtra of the Lokottaravādimahāsāṅghika School.* Patna: Kashi Prasad Jayaswal Research Institute.

Teiser, Stephen F. 1988. *The Ghost Festival in Medieval China.* Princeton, NJ: Princeton University Press.

———. 2007. "Social History and the Confrontation of Cultures: Foreword to the Third Edition." In Erik Zürcher, *The Buddhist Conquest of China*, 3rd ed., xiiv–xxviii. Leiden: Brill.

Tessenow, Hermann, and Paul U. Unschuld. 2008. *A Dictionary of the Huang Di nei jing su wen.* Berkeley: University of California Press.

Tian Xiaofei. 2005. "Seeing with the Mind's Eye: The Eastern Jin Discourse of Visualization and Imagination." *Asia Major*, 3rd ser., 18 (2):67–102.

Tōdō Kyōshun 藤堂恭俊. 1960. "Kumarajū yakushutsu to iwareru zenkyōten no setsuji suru nenbutsukan" 鳩摩羅什訳出と言われる禅経典の説示する念仏観. In *Fukui hakushi shōju kinen tōyō shisō ronshu* 福井博士頌壽記念東洋思想論集, 398–411. Tokyo: Fukui hakushi shōju kinen ronbunshū kankōkai.

Tokuno, Kyoko. 1990. "The Evaluation of Indigenous Scriptures in Chinese Buddhist Bibliographic Catalogs." In *Chinese Buddhist Apocrypha*, edited by Robert E. Buswell Jr., 31–74. Honolulu: University of Hawai'i Press.

Trombert, Eric. 2010. "Produits médicaux, aromates et teintures sur le marché de Turfan en 743." In *Médecine, religion et société dans la Chine médiévale*, edited by Catherine Despeux, 711–768. Paris: Collège de France.

Tsukamoto Zenryū 塚本善隆. 1975. *Chūgoku chūsei Bukkyōshi ronkō* 中国中世仏教史論攷. Tokyo: Daitō Shuppansha.

Tsukinowa Kenryū 月輪賢隆. 1971. *Butten no hihanteki kenkyū* 仏典の批判的研究. Kyoto: Hyakkaen.

Tu Yanqiu 涂艷秋. 2006. *Jiumoluoshi bore si xiang zai Zhongguo* 鳩摩羅什般若思想在中國. Taibei: Li ren shu ju.

Unebe Toshihide 畝部俊英. 1981. "*Kanmuryōjukyō* ni okeru shōmyō shisō: sho kankyō rui no 'shōshi no zai' no bun o chūshin to shite" 『觀無量寿経』における称名思想：諸観経類の「生死之罪」の文を中心として. *Dōhō daigaku ronsō* 同朋大学論叢 44/45:146–184.

Unschuld, Paul U. 1985. *Medicine in China: A History of Ideas.* Berkeley: University of California Press.

Vetter, Tilmann. 2000. *The "Khandha Passages" in the Vinayapiṭaka and the Four Main Nikāyas.* Wien: Verlag der Österreichischen Akademie der Wissenschaften.

Waddell, Norman. 2001. "Hakuin's *Yasenkanna.*" *Eastern Buddhist*, n.s., 34 (1):79–119.

Wagner, Rudolf G. 1971. "The Original Structure of the Correspondence between Shi Hui-Yüan and Kumārajīva." *Harvard Journal of Asiatic Studies* 31:28–48.

Waldschmidt, E. 1930. "Wundertätige Mönche in der ostturkistanischen Hinayana Kunst." *Ostasiatische Zeitschrift* 1:1–9.

———. 1950–1951. *Das Mahāparinirvāṇa-sūtra.* Berlin: Akademie Verlag.

Wang, Eugene Y. 2014. "The Shadow Image in the Cave: Discourse on Icons." In *Early Medieval China: A Sourcebook*, edited by Wendy Swartz et al., 405–427. New York: Columbia University Press.

Wang Huei-hsin. 2001. "Zhiyi's Interpretation of the Concept '*Dhyāna*' in his *Shi Chan Boluomi Tsidi* [sic] *Famen*." PhD diss., University of Arizona.

White, David Gordon. 2003. *Kiss of the Yoginī: "Tantric Sex" in its South Asian Contexts.* Chicago: University of Chicago Press.

Willemen, Charles. 2012. *Outlining the Way to Reflect.* Mumbai: Somaiya Publications.

Williams, Bruce. 2002. "Mea Maxima Vikalpa: Repentance, Meditation and the Dynamics of Liberation in Medieval Chinese Buddhism, 500–650 CE." PhD diss., University of California, Berkeley.

Wiltshire, Martin G. 1983. "The 'Suicide' Problem in the Pali Canon." *Journal of the International Association of Buddhist Studies* 6 (2):124–140.

Wright, Arthur F. 1959. *Buddhism in Chinese History.* Stanford, CA: Stanford University Press.

Wu, Jiang, and Lucille Chia, eds. 2016. *Spreading Buddha's Word in East Asia: The Formation and Transformation of the Chinese Buddhist Canon.* New York: Columbia University Press.

Xing, Guang. 2005. *The Concept of the Buddha: Its Evolution from Early Buddhism to the Trikāya Theory.* London: RoutledgeCurzon.

Xu Shiyi 徐時儀. 2008. *Yi qie jing yin yi san zhong jiao ben he kan* 一切經音義三種校本合刊. 3 vols. Shanghai: Shanghai gu ji chu ban she.

Yamabe Nobuyoshi 山部能宜. 1999a. "An Examination of the Mural Paintings of Toyok Cave 20 in Conjunction with the Origin of the *Amitayus Visualization Sutra.*" *Orientations* 4:38–44.

———. 1999b. "The Significance of the Yogalehrbuch for the Investigation into the Origin of Chinese Meditation Texts." *Bukkyō Bunka* 9:1–75.

———. 1999c. "The Sutra on the Ocean-like Samadhi of the Visualization of the Buddha." PhD diss., Yale University.

———. 2010. "Two Chinese Meditation Manuals in Conjunction with Pozdneyev's Mongolian Manual." In *From Turfan to Ajanta: Festchrift for Dieter Schlingloff on the Occasion of his Eightieth Birthday,* edited by Eli Franco and Monika Zin, 1045–1057. Bhairahawa, Rupandehi: Lumbini International Research Institute.

———. 2014. "Indian Myth Transformed in a Chinese Apocryphal Text: Two Stories on the Buddha's Hidden Organ." In *India in the Chinese Imagination: Myth, Religion, and Thought,* edited by John Kieschnick and Meir Shahar, 61–80. Philadelphia: University of Pennsylvania Press.

———. 2016. "Āraya shiki setsu no jissenteki haikei ni tsuite" アーラヤ識説の實踐的背景について. *Tōyō no shisō to shūkyō* 東洋の思想と宗教 33:1–30.

Yamabe, Nobuyoshi, and Fumihiko Sueki. 2009. *The Sutra on the Concentration of Sitting Meditation.* Berkeley, CA: Numata Center for Buddhist Translation and Research.

Yamabe Nobuyoshi 山部能宜, Fujitani Takayuki 藤谷隆之, and Harada Yasunori 原田泰教. 2002. "Memyō no gakuha shozoku ni tsuite: *Saundarananda* to *Shōmonji* no hikaku kenkyū" 馬鳴の学派所属について：Saundarananda と『聲聞地』の比較研究. *Bukkyō bunka* 仏教文化 12:1–65.

Yamada Meiji 山田明爾. 1976. "Kangyōkō: Muryōjubutsu to Amidabutsu" 観経考: 無量寿仏と阿弥陀仏. *Ryūkoku daigaku ronshū* 龍谷大学論集 408:76–95.

Yamamoto Yukio 山本幸男. 2007. "Genbō shōrai kyōten to 'gogatsu tsuitachi kyō' no shosha (ge)" 玄昉将来経典と「五月一日経」の書写（下）. *Sōai daigaku kenkyū ronshū* 相愛大学研究論集 22: 226–177.

Yanagida Seizan 柳田聖山. 1971. *Shoki no zenshi II: Rekidai sanbōki* 初期の禅史 II: 歴代三宝記. Tokyo: Chikuma Shobō.

Yoshikawa Tadao 吉川忠夫. 1984. *Rikuchō seishinshi* 六朝精神史. Kyoto: Dōhōsha.

Yu, Taishan. 2006. "A Study of the History of the Relationship Between the Western and Eastern Han, Wei, Jin, Northern and Southern Dynasties and the Western Regions." *Sino-Platonic Papers* 173.

Zacchetti, Stefano. 2003. "The Rediscovery of Three Early Buddhist Scriptures on Meditation: A Preliminary Analysis of the *Fo shuo shi'er men jing*, the *Fo shuo jie shi'er men jing*. Translated by An Shigao and Their Commentary Preserved in the Newly Found Kongō-ji Manuscript." *Annual Report of the Institute for Research in Advanced Buddhology at Soka University* 6:251–300.

———. 2004. "Teaching Buddhism in Han China: A Study of the *Ahan koujie shi'er yinyuan jing* T1508 Attributed to An Shigao." *Annual Report of the Institute for Research in Advanced Buddhology at Soka University* 7:197–225.

Zhang Xiaoyan 張小艷. 2015. "Dunhuang ben *Zhong jing yao lan* yan jiu" 敦煌本『眾經要覽』研究. *Dunhuang Tulufan yanjiu* 敦煌吐魯番研究 15: 279–320.

Zhanru 湛如. 2003. *Dunhuang fo jiao lü yi zhi du yan jiu* 敦煌佛教律儀制度研究. Beijing: Zhong hua shu ju .

Zhu Lishuang 朱麗雙. 2016. "Cong Yindu dao Yutian: Han, Zang wen xian ji zai de A'napodaduo long wang" 從印度到于闐: 漢藏文獻記載的阿那婆答多龍王. *Dunhuang tulufan yanjiu* 敦煌吐魯番研究 16:89–102.

Zhu Qingzhi 朱慶之. 1990. "Ye ma yi zheng" 野馬義證. *Gu han yu yan jiu* 古漢語研究 7:17–18.

Zhu, Tianshu. 2019. *Emanated Buddhas in the Aureole of Buddhist Images from India, Central Asia, and China.* Amherst, NY: Cambria Press.

Ziporyn, Brook. 2003. *The Penumbra Unbound: The Neo-Taoist Philosophy of Guo Xiang.* Albany: State University of New York Press.

Zürcher, E. 1972. *The Buddhist Conquest of China.* 2nd ed. Leiden: Brill.

———. 1982. "Perspectives on the Study of Chinese Buddhism." *Journal of the Royal Asiatic Society* 2:161–176.

———. 1995. "Obscure Texts on Favourite Topics: Dao'an's *Anonymous Scriptures.*" In *Das andere China: Feschrift für Wolfgang Bauer zum 65. Geburtstag*, edited by Helwig Schmidt-Glintzer, 161–181. Wiesbaden: Harrassowitz Verlag.

Zysk, Kenneth G. 1991. *Asceticism and Healing in Ancient India.* Oxford: Oxford University Press.

———. 1993. *Religious Medicine: The History and Evolution of Indian Medicine.* New Brunswick, NJ: Transaction Publishers.

Index

Page numbers in **bold** refer to tables.

About the Author

Eric M. Greene teaches in the Department of Religious Studies at Yale University. His research focuses on the early history of Buddhism in China and the dynamics of the transmission and translation of Indian Buddhist practices and literature to China between roughly 150 and 800 CE. His articles have appeared in *T'oung Pao*, *Journal of Chinese Religions*, *Artibus Asiae*, *Journal of the International Association of Buddhist Studies*, *Asia Major*, *History of Religions*, and *Journal of the American Oriental Society*, among other places. He is presently working on a project concerning Chinese Buddhism in the second and third centuries and the earliest Chinese translations of Indian Buddhist literature.